Information Sharing and Data Protection in the Area of Freedom, Security and Justice

Franziska Boehm

Information Sharing and Data Protection in the Area of Freedom, Security and Justice

Towards Harmonised Data Protection Principles for Information Exchange at EU-level

Springer

Dr. Franziska Boehm
University of Luxembourg
Interdisciplinary Centre for Security, Reliability and Trust (SnT)
6, rue Richard Coudenhove Kalergi
1359 Luxembourg
Luxembourg
franziskaboehm1@aol.de
or franziska.boehm@uni.lu

Fonds National de la Recherche Luxembourg

Printed with the support of the FNR Luxembourg

ISBN 978-3-642-22391-4 e-ISBN 978-3-642-22392-1
DOI 10.1007/978-3-642-22392-1
Springer Heidelberg Dordrecht London New York

Library of Congress Control Number: 2011941399

Printed on acid-free paper

Springer is part of Springer Science+Business Media (www.springer.com)

Acknowledgements

This thesis is the result of my work as a research assistant from 2007 to 2011 under the guidance of Professor Herwig Hofmann at the University of Luxembourg. It was defended in April 2011.

First and foremost, I wish to express my gratitude to my supervisor, Professor Herwig Hofmann. His support and guidance during the years of my research have made it possible for me to write and finish this thesis. My profound thanks go to him for his confidence in my work. It was also an extraordinary privilege to have been guided by Professor Spiros Simitis who not only took part in my jury, but who was always available for discussions over the last few years when I needed his advice. He and his publications have been a constant inspiration and an important guide during the research. I would like to express my deepest appreciation and I profoundly thank him for his encouragement and his indispensable advice. I would also like to thank Mark Cole, Associate Professor at the University of Luxembourg, for his invaluable comments and his continual academic support over the last years. He always had the time to discuss and was open to my ideas. The thesis would look far less complete without his contributions.

The idea for the research dates back to my years at the University of Gießen where I wrote my master thesis on a data protection related topic under the supervision of Professor Thilo Marauhn, who continuously supported my scientific interest and whom I thank for his support also in the framework of my thesis. Hielke Hijmans from the European Data Protection Supervisor and Professor Stefan Braum, at the University of Luxembourg, took part in my Jury and gave tips and advice along the way. I am likewise indebted to Garth Hall and Lawrence Siry who improved the legibility of the manuscript. Their annotations have been always very helpful.

Very warm thanks go to my colleagues at the University of Luxembourg. I have made good friends in this faculty and I am deeply grateful for the moments I have shared with you, be it for a chat or a scientific discussion. It is difficult to mention names, some are Dr. Florence Giorgi, Sandra Schmitz, Lawrence Siry, Miroslava Borissova, Jenny Metzdorf, Dr. Roger Tafoti, Mariana Ignatescu and Dr. Isabelle

Rueda but there are many more, and I would like to thank all of them for their help, time and encouragement, especially during the final stage of the PhD. Of course, friends from outside the University, especially from Berlin and Gießen deserve a special mention as well. Without their moral, emotional and social support, this thesis would never have been written. Ida Danke, Julia Horländer, Johanna Schmidt, Maike Gappa, Christin Noak, Lars Hoffmann, and Ole Westphal are only a few Berlin friends of so many others. Thorsten Dreimann, Markus Berliner, Ines Heylmann, Dr. Kai Purnhagen and Til Kappen as well as Julia Heieis, Andrea Kristekova, Jan Lizak, Jörg Piper, Anja Pavlenko, Martin Faix and Sonia Kienitz, all of whom I met in Gießen, supported me in every imaginable way. I also would like to thank my family, especially my parents, Evelyne and Clemens, and my sisters, Annina and Nina, for their constant and unconditional support. I owe all of you more than just the mentioning in the thesis.

Most of all, I am particularly thankful to Dr. Tobias Lochen, who stood always by me through the last years and was there when I needed his support. He spent so many hours reading the manuscript and encouraging me in difficult moments. I am more than grateful for his companionship and his belief in me.

Finally, without the indestructible belief in my abilities shown to me by my dear grandparents, Gertrud and Georg Libor, I would have never had the strength to start (and to finish) the PhD project. Their constant support and encouragement has led me to this result. This book is therefore dedicated to them.

Luxembourg Franziska Boehm

Contents

Abbreviations

AFIS	Anti-fraud information system (in context of OLAF)
AFIS	Automated fingerprint information system (in context of Eurodac)
AG	Advocate general
AZR	Ausländerzentralregister
CCTV	Closed-circuit television
CEPOL	European police college
CIS	Customs information system
CMS	Case management system
C-SIS	Central EU section of the Schengen information system
C-VIS	Central EU section of the visa information system
Doc	Document
DPA	Data protection authority
DPO	Data protection officer
EC Treaty	Treaty establishing the European community
ECHR	European convention of human rights
ECRIS	European criminal records information system
ECtHR	European court of human rights
EDPS	European data protection supervisor
EEAS	European external action service
e.g.	*exempli gratia* (for example)
EIS	Europol information system
EJN	European judicial network
EMCDDA	European monitoring centre for drugs and drugs addiction
et seq.	*et sequens* (and the following)
EU	European Union
Eurodac	European dactyloscopy
Eurojust	European Union's judicial cooperation unit
Europol	European police office
FBI	Federal Bureau of Investigation

FDPJ	Framework decision on the protection of personal data in police and judicial cooperation in criminal Matters
FIDE	Fichier d'Identification des Dossiers d'Enquête Douanière (Customs File Identification Database)
FRG	Federal Republic of Germany
FYROM	Former Yugoslav Republic of Macedonia
G-10 Act	German Act to monitor mail and telephone communication (Gesetz zu Artikel 10 des Grundgesetzes vom 13. August 1968, BGBl. I p. 949)
GDR	German Democratic Republic
i.e.	*id est* (that is)
Info-ex	(Former) Information exchange system at Europol
Interpol	International criminal police organisation
IT	Information technology
JIT	Joint investigations team
JSA	Joint supervisory authority (SIS, CIS)
JSB	Joint supervisory body (Europol)
MRS	Mail registration system of OLAF
N-SIS	National section of the Schengen information system
N-VIS	National section of the visa information system
OECD	Organisation for economic cooperation and development
OJ	Official journal of the European Union
OLAF	European Anti-Fraud Office, Office européen de lutte Antifraude
p.; pp.	Page, pages
Para	Paragraph
PNR	Passenger name record
RABITs	Rapid border interventions teams (of Frontex)
SIENA	Secure information exchange network
SIRENE	Supplementary information request at the national entry (additional data exchange possbilitiy in the framework of the SIS)
SIS II	Second generation of the Schengen information system
SIS	Schengen information system
SITCen	Joint situation centre
SSMA	Special surveillance means act
TEU	Treaty on European Union
TFEU	Treaty on the functioning of the European Union
UK	United Kingdom
UNDOC	United Nations Office on drugs and crime
US	United States
v.	Versus
VAT	Value added tax
VIS	Visa information system
Vol.	Volume

Introduction

Information exchange in the European Union (EU) constitutes an essential part of the different policies of the EU. In many policy fields, information sharing is crucial for decision making and does not necessarily include the exchange of personal information.[1] However, in certain fields, information exchange contains personal data and therefore affects the rights of individuals. In areas related to law enforcement and judicial cooperation, such as the Area of Freedom, Security and Justice (AFSJ), horizontal information sharing, including the exchange of personal data, has become an essential tool in the internal security policy of the EU. The process of European integration and communitarisation has considerably supported the establishment of Union bodies, agencies and information systems in this area.[2] Traditional national law enforcement and judicial structures are complemented by horizontal EU arrangements increasingly governed by a network type of governance.[3] Personal data are therefore not only exchanged between Member States and with third states, but also between EU bodies. Analysing the information exchange taking place at EU level between the relevant EU actors is therefore a challenging task.

Post 9/11 policy concepts, such as the Hague programme and the Stockholm programme promote an enhanced cooperation and coordination of law enforcement agencies and other agencies within the AFSJ.[4] Under their influence, formerly not related policy areas, such as the prevention of crime and immigration, are linked

[1] Compare Hofmann et al. (2011). Chap. 12, pp. 411–490.

[2] Mitsilegas (2009), p. 161.

[3] Den Boer et al. (2008).

[4] On this subject: The Hague Programme: strengthening freedom, security and justice in the European Union, Council doc. 16054/04 of 13 December 2004, point 2.5, p. 25, in the following: The Hague Programme, Council doc. 16054/04 of 13 December 2004; The Stockholm Programme – An open and secure Europe serving and protection the citizen, Council doc. 17024/09 of 2 December 2009, adopted by the Council on 10/11 December 2009, point 4.1, pp. 35/36, in the following: The Stockholm Programme, Council doc. 17024/09 of 2 December 2009.

F. Boehm, *Information Sharing and Data Protection in the Area of Freedom, Security and Justice*, DOI 10.1007/978-3-642-22392-1_1,

and lead to an intensive cooperation between AFSJ actors of a completely different legal nature, vested with different powers.[5] In absence of a unified approach to data protection in judicial and criminal matters[6] and without being limited by the former pillar constraints, legally and structurally different bodies, equipped with different tasks, exchange and transfer personal data within and outside the EU. The result is that data collected for one specific purpose may be transferred and used for other purposes completely unrelated to the original collection. This ever increasing cooperation at multiple levels touches upon different data protection regimes. While information and personal data exchange has been identified as a priority in this field, data protection guarantees risk to be undermined by this practice.[7] The central question of this research is therefore "Does the EU internal data exchange comply with its own data protection standards?".

This research examines the inter-agency cooperation between AFSJ actors such as Europol, Eurojust or Frontex as well as the Commission's anti-fraud unit, OLAF, which led to the conclusion of agreements providing for mutual information exchange in recent years.[8] In addition, the access of law enforcement and judicial agencies to data stored in the European information systems, such as the Customs- (CIS), the Schengen- (SIS) or the Visa Information System (VIS) and Eurodac occupies an increasingly important place in the AFSJ. It is therefore analysed in detail.

When considering the increasing cooperation between the mentioned AFSJ actors, tensions between the rights of individuals and security interests[9] are bound to occur. The current development in the AFSJ calls for maximum cooperation in terms of data exchange between the actors involved, the rules regulating such exchanges however vary to a great extent and are far from being harmonised. Questions relating to the coherence and the respect of data protection rules within this cooperation network of the AFSJ actors seem to be pushed into the background. This unbalanced situation can have a profound impact on the rights of individuals.

---

[5] Mitsilegas (2009), p. 223.

[6] Council Framework Decision 2008/977/JHA on the protection of personal data processed in the framework of police and judicial cooperation in criminal matters, OJ 2008, L-350/60, in the following: FDPJ, OJ 2008, L-350/60, represents a first step towards a comprehensive framework in this area; the FDPJ is however very restricted in scope as it is for instance not applicable to the data processing of most of the AFSJ law enforcement agencies, such as Europol and Eurojust, as well as at other AFSJ exchange systems, i.e. the SIS or the CIS; moreover, excluded from the scope is also the internal processing of the Member States in police and criminal matters; the scope and the guarantees of the FDPJ are illustrated in more detail in Chaps. A III 1 c and A III 2.

[7] To the general necessity to establish an effective data protection framework with regard to former third pillar bodies, see Paeffgen (2006), pp. 63–86, in particular pp. 77–79.

[8] Compare note from the General Secretariat to the Standing Committee on operational cooperation on internal security (COSI), final report on the cooperation between JHA agencies, Council doc. 8387/10 of 9 April 2010.

[9] For the understanding and the importance of the term "security" in the EU, see Kotzur (2009); Möstl (2009); Grabenwarter (2009b).

It is worth pointing out that, even though the context in which information is used is changing rapidly, no evaluation or overview of the existing data collection, processing and data-sharing systems, including a thorough assessment of their effectiveness, their possible overlapping effects, proportionality and their respect of data protection rights have thus far been carried out.[10]

In the light of these considerations, the data protection rights of the individuals concerned by the increasing AFSJ cooperation play a decisive role. The establishment of a strategic approach for the exchange of information in the AFSJ is urgently needed to balance the rights of individuals against the multiple and still increasing possibilities that personal data will be exchanged by and between AFSJ actors.[11] Therefore, analysing the different data protection regimes and the existing arrangements providing for personal data exchange in the AFSJ is an essential in order to detect possible shortcomings in this complex cooperation structure.

I. Brief Background on Data Protection in EU Law

Data protection in EU law constitutes a relatively new individual right encompassed in Article 8 Charter of Fundamental Rights as well as in Article 16 TFEU. It protects against the potential misuse of information by governmental and non-governmental actors.[12] The basic concepts of data protection are included in Article 8 Charter of Fundamental Rights stipulating that:

1. Everyone has the right to the protection of personal data concerning him or her.
2. Such data must be processed fairly for specified purposes and on the basis of the consent of the person concerned or some other legitimate basis laid down by law. Everyone has the right of access to data which has been collected concerning him or her, and the right to have it rectified.
3. Compliance with these rules shall be subject to control by an independent authority.

Article 8 (2) Charter of Fundamental Rights includes basic quality standards and individual rights which have to be respected when processing personal data. In addition to the prohibition of data processing for unspecific and undefined purposes, the fairness of the processing and the access to and the rectification of personal data are crucial elements in data protection law. Independent supervision is a further

[10] Communication from the Commission to the European Parliament, the Council, the European Economic and Social Committee and the Committee of the Regions – Delivering and area of freedom, security and justice for European's citizens – Action Plan implementing the Stockholm Programme, COM(2010) 171 final, in particular p. 6.

[11] Ibid.

[12] On the general risks of data processing in databases see Simitis (2006), p. 65, para 10.

important element to make data processing legitimate. These rather broad principles need to be specified in the different contexts of processing.

The current understanding of data protection as a fundamental right under Article 8 Charter of Fundamental Rights is intrinsically linked to the right to private life included in Article 8 European Convention of Human Rights (ECHR).[13] While private life is a broad term which embraces issues concerning the protection of an individual's personal space which go far beyond data protection[14] such as the right to be let alone[15] or the right to develop personal relationships with each other,[16] the protection of personal data is one important aspect of the right to private life.[17] This historical background is the reason why, prior to the adoption of EU data protection instruments, such as the Data Protection Directive 95/46,[18] Article 16 TFEU and Article 8 Charter of Fundamental Rights, public international law instruments of the Council of Europe played the central role in interpreting data protection principles in the EU context. The first instruments specifying the right to data protection at European level were therefore not EU instruments, but instruments of the OECD and the Council of Europe.

The economic orientated OECD Guidelines of 1980 governing the protection of privacy and trans-border flows of personal data (OECD Guidelines)[19] and the Convention of the Council of Europe for the Protection of Individuals with regard to Automatic Processing of Personal Data (Convention No. 108) were the first

[13] Both concepts (data protection and private life) are twins but not identical; compare Siemen (2006); De Hert and Schreuders (2001), p. 42; for the coherency between ECHR and Charter of Fundamental Rights see Schneiders (2010), pp. 145–245; Steiner et al. (2006), pp. 115–144.

[14] Kuner (2009), pp. 307–317, in particular p. 309.

[15] The first description of the right to privacy was made by *Warren* and *Brandeis* in their famous article in the Harvard Law Review in 1890. They described the right as "the right to be let alone", see Warren and Brandeis (1890).

[16] Compare ECtHR case law: *Niemietz v. Germany*, Application no. 13710/88, of 16 September 1992, para 29.

[17] Compare ECtHR case law: *Z. v Finland*, Application no. 22009/93, judgment of 25 February 1997, para 95; *Peck v. United Kingdom*, Application no. 44647/98, judgment of 28 January 2003, para 78; *L.L. v France*, Application no. 7508/02, judgment of 10 October 2006, para 43; *Biriuk v Lithuania*, Application no. 23373/03, judgment of 25 November 2008, para 39; *I v Finland*, Application no. 20511/03, judgment of 17 July 2008, para 38; *S. and Marper v the United Kingdom*, Application nos. 30562/04 and 30566/04, judgment of 4 December 2008, para 103; *C.C. v. Spain*, Application no. 1425/06, judgment of 6 October 2009, para 31; see also: Breitenmoser (1986), p. 245; (Kugelmann 2003) pp. 16–25; Meyer-Ladewig (2006), Article 8, para 11; Moreham (2008).

[18] Directive 95/46/EC of the European Parliment and the Council of 24 October 1995 on the protection of the individuals with regard to the processing of personal data and on the free movement of such data, OJ 1995, L-281/31, in the following: Directive 95/46 OJ 1995, L-281/31.

[19] OECD Recommendation concerning Guidelines governing the protection of privacy and trans-border flows of personal data of 23 September 1980.

international instruments which included data protection rules in Europe.[20] In addition to these first instruments, the interpretation of Article 8 ECHR by the European Court of Human Rights (ECtHR) contributed to the specification of basic data protection principles inherent to the right to private life. The relevant case law of the ECtHR is further detailed in Chap. A.

Due to the former pillar structure, different rules exist in EU law for the protection of personal data. Prior to the adoption of the Lisbon Treaty,[21] Directive 95/46, Regulation 45/2001[22] and Article 286 EC Treaty[23] (now Article 16 TFEU) guaranteed data protection rules in former first pillar matters.[24] Excluded from the scope of these instruments was data processing in former second and third pillar matters.[25] Data processing in these areas was for a long time exclusively governed by the aforementioned public international law instruments of the Council of Europe.[26] In November 2008, the Data Protection Framework Decision 2008/977/JHA on personal data processed for police and judicial cooperation in criminal matters (FDPJ) was finally adopted with the intention of covering data processing in (former) third pillar matters.[27] Its scope is however, very restricted and does not cover data processing of Europol and Eurojust,[28] nor of the data exchange systems,

---

[20] Convention for the Protection of Individuals with regard to Automatic Processing of Personal Data, 28 January 1981, CETS No. 108. In the following: Convention No. 108.

[21] To the general changes in the different policy areas through the Lisbon Treaty, see Fastenrath and Nowak (2009).

[22] European Parliament and Council Regulation (EC) 45/2001 of 18 December 2000 on the protection of individuals with regard to the processing of personal data by the Community institutions and bodies and on the free movement of such data, OJ 2001, L-8/1 (referred to as Regulation 45/2001, OJ 2001, L-8/1 in the following).

[23] Brief comments on the scope and the content of Article 286 EC Treaty can be found in Callies and Ruffert (2007), pp. 2332–2334; Léger (2000), pp. 1849–1851; Lenz and Borchardt (2006), pp. 2495–2504.

[24] For more details see Chap. A III 1.

[25] Article 3 (2) Directive 95/46, OJ 1995, L-281/31 and Chap. A III 1.

[26] Convention No. 108, the ECHR standard and in addition Recommendation R (87) 15 of the committee of ministers to member states regulating the use of personal data in the police sector, adopted on 17 September 1987; The importance of the ECHR for the protection of fundamental rights in Europe is underlined by Breitenmoser et al. (2006), pp. 1–385; for a general overview of the Council of Europe see Wittinger (2005).

[27] Council Framework Decision 2008/977/JHA of 27 November 2008 on the protection of personal data processed in the framework of police and judicial cooperation in criminal matters, OJ 2008, L-350/60 (in the following referred to as FDPJ, OJ 2008, L-350/60), equivalent to Directive 95/46, the processing refers to automatic and non-automatic processing of personal data, Article 2 (a) FDPJ.

[28] Europol considers in recital (12) of Council Decision of 6 April 2009 establishing the European Police Office, OJ 2009, L-121/37: "A Council Framework Decision on the protection of personal data processed in the framework of police and judicial cooperation in criminal matters will be applicable to the transfer of personal data by Member States to Europol. The relevant set of data-protection provisions in this Decision will not be affected by that Framework Decision and this Decision should contain specific provisions on the protection of personal data regulating these

such as the SIS or the CIS.[29] This patchwork of applicable data protection rules in the EU makes it difficult to evaluate the data processing actually taking place in a specific area of the EU, such as the AFSJ. Therefore, in a first step, it is necessary to identify the policies covered by the AFSJ.

II. What is the Area of Freedom, Security and Justice?

As mentioned above, the EU's activity in the field of personal data exchange takes place to a great extent in the AFSJ.

The term AFSJ is a political notion describing several policies brought together under the umbrella of an overarching concept. Introduced by the Treaty of Amsterdam and further developed in the Lisbon Treaty, this policy aims at achieving the facilitation of the free movement of persons while ensuring at the same time "the safety and security of their peoples by establishing an area of freedom, security and justice".[30] Article 3 (2) TEU specifies this objective by emphasising that "The Union shall offer its citizens an area of freedom, security and justice without internal frontiers, in which the free movement of persons is ensured in conjunction with appropriate measures with respect to external border controls, asylum, immigration and the prevention and combating of crime".[31]

The competence in the AFSJ is shared between the EU and the Member States.[32] Title V TFEU specifies the policies of the AFSJ. They are a mix of former first as

matters in greater detail because of the particular nature, functions and competences of Europol"; the equivalent at Eurojust is recital (13) Council Decision 2009/426/JHA of 16 December 2008 on the strengthening of Eurojust and amending Decision 2002/187/JHA setting up Eurojust with a view to reinforcing the fight against serious crime, OJ 2009, L-138/4, stating that: "Council Framework Decision 2008/977/JHA of 27 November 2008 on the protection of personal data processed in the framework of police and judicial cooperation in criminal matters is applicable to the processing by the Member States of the personal data transferred between the Member States and Eurojust. The relevant set of data protection provisions of Decision 2002/187/JHA will not be affected by Framework Decision 2008/977/JHA and contains specific provisions on the protection of personal data regulating these matters in more detail because of the particular nature, functions and competences of Eurojust".

[29] FDPJ, OJ 2008, L-350/60, recital 39.

[30] Consolidated version of the Treaty on European Union, OJ 2010, C-83/13, preamble, in the following: TEU; for an overview and the historical development of the AFSJ and its main policy fields refer to Monar (2009), pp. 749–797; Haratsch et al. (2010), pp. 495–509; Streinz (2005), pp. 377–383; Walker (2004); Craig and De Burca (2008), pp. 229–267; Möstl (2010), pp. 125–127; to the beginnings of police and judicial cooperation, compare Hailbronner (1996).

[31] Article 3 (2) TEU.

[32] Consolidated version of the Treaty on the functioning on the European Union, OJ 2010, C-83/47, Article 4 (2) lit (j), in the following: TFEU.

well as former third pillar policies.[33] Four main areas stand out: policies on border checks, asylum and immigration, judicial cooperation in civil as well as in criminal matters and police cooperation.[34]

To implement these policies, the political goals are realised by the adoption of multi-annual work programmes which establish general priorities and political objectives in this area. Four different strategic work programmes, the Vienna (1998), the Tampere (1999), the Hague (2004) and the Stockholm programme (2009), have been adopted in order to specify the politics covered by the AFSJ. Although multi-annual work programmes are not legally binding instruments,[35] these programmes set different political goals which are subsequently legally implemented by the instruments available to the European legislator, primarily by way of Directives, Regulations and Council Decisions. As a result thereof, these programmes have a substantial effect on the future institutional policy and often directly influence legislative actions in this area.

The Hague programme adopted in 2004 for instance promoted the enforced cooperation of the actors in the AFSJ and introduced the "availability principle" which should govern law enforcement related data exchange from then on.[36] Bilateral agreements between EU bodies and provisions in secondary legislation were foreseen to exchange data and leading, amongst others, to a reinforced inter-agency cooperation.[37] Other measures aimed to allow mutual access to databases or their common use. National databases were intended to become "interoperable"[38] and direct access to central EU databases such as the SIS were to be established

[33] The Provision on police and judicial cooperation in criminal matters (former Title VI EU Treaty) are former third pillar policies whereas the provisions on asylum and immigration were regulated under former first pillar Community law (Title IV EC Treaty).

[34] Title V Chapters 2–5 TFEU; to the beginnings of criminal justice cooperation, see Cullen and Jund (2002).

[35] Opinion of the European Data Protection Supervisor (in the following: EDPS) on the Communication from the Commission to the European Parliament and the Council, an area of freedom, security and justice serving the citizen of 10 July 2009, para 4.

[36] The Hague Programme, Council doc. 16054/04 of 13 December 2004, point 2.1, p. 18: "With effect of 1 January 2008 the exchange of such information should be governed by conditions set out below with regard to the principle of availability, which means that, throughout the Union, a law enforcement officer in one Member State who needs information in order to perform his duties can obtain this from another Member State and that the law enforcement agency in the other Member State which holds this information will make it available for the stated purpose, taking into account the requirement of ongoing investigations in that State". For criticsm with regard to the Hague programme, compare Braum (2007).

[37] Mitsilegas (2009), p. 222; for the emerge of agencies in the integrated administration structure of the EU in recent years, compare Hofmann and Türk (2009), in particular pp. 362–365; Hofmann and Türk (2006).

[38] To the beginnings of the use of the term interoperability in the EU, compare De Hert and Gutwirth (2006); to the term interoperabiility, see the conprehensive analysis of Wallwork and Baptista (2005).

whereby data protection standards would be "strictly observed".[39] As a main consequence of this instrument, which covered the period from 2005 to the end of 2009, more and more data were shared and the actors in the AFSJ worked closer together than before. The period after 2009 is now covered by the Stockholm programme valid from 2010 to 2014 endorsing the availability principle while repeating the data protection pleas.[40]

III. Research Topic: Information Sharing in the AFSJ and Data Protection Rights

One of the most important tools for the achievement of the AFSJ provided for in the Title V TFEU is a reinforced police and judicial cooperation (Articles 82–89 TFEU), which is carried out in no small part by sharing and exchanging personal data. Article 87 TFEU clarifies that the EU shall establish police cooperation involving all the Member States' competent authorities, including police, customs and other specialised law enforcement services. For this purpose, measures relating to the collection, storage, processing, analysis and exchange of relevant information can be laid down by the European Parliament and the Council.[41] Information in this area is therefore characteristically exchanged "to analyse security threats, identify trends in criminal activity or assess risks in related policy areas".[42]

On a practical level, this cooperation is carried out by a network of European agencies, bodies and Member States authorities exchanging information between each other as well as with third parties based on EU initiatives, administrative agreements or international treaties.[43]

Examples for this development and the actors involved can be found on several occasions regularly connected to the broader context of data exchange for law enforcement purposes at European level.[44] In July 2010 the Commission issued "for

[39] The Hague Programme, Council doc. 16054/04 of 13 December 2004, point 2.1, pp. 18–19.

[40] The Stockholm Programme, Council doc. 17024/09 of 2 December 2009, point 4.2.2, pp. 37–38.

[41] Article 87 (2) TFEU.

[42] Communication from the Commission to the European Parliament and the Council, Overview of information management in the area of freedom, security and justice, COM(2010) 385 final, p. 26.

[43] For example on the Treaty of Prüm which was signed in May 2005 by seven Member States (Belgium, Germany, Spain, France, Luxembourg, the Netherlands and Austria) outside of the framework of the EU and contains provisions about enhanced cross-border cooperation, particularly in combating terrorism and cross-border crime relating to the exchange of DNA profiles, fingerprints and vehicle registration data; in the meanwhile the provisions of the treaty have been transposed in EU law by Council Decision 2008/615/JHA of 23 June 2008 on the stepping up of cross-border cooperation, particularly in combating terrorism and cross-border crime, OJ 2008, L-210/1.

[44] Intensified cooperation and information sharing began with the conclusion of the Schengen agreement in 1985 by only five Member States supplemented by the Schengen Convention 5 years

the first time, a full overview of the EU-level measures in place, under implementation or consideration that regulate the collection, storage or crossborder exchange of personal information for the purpose of law enforcement or migration management" in the AFSJ.[45] The Commission considered that:

> The sheer number of new ideas and the growing body of legislation in the field of internal security and migration management make it necessary to define a core set of principles to serve as a benchmark for the initiation and evaluation of policy proposals in the years to come. These principles build upon and seek to complement the general principles laid down in the EU Treaties, the jurisprudence of the European Court of Justice and European Court of Human Rights and the relevant Inter-Institutional Agreements between the European Parliament, the Council and the European Commission.[46]

The respect of data protection and private life concerns is one of the substantive principles the Commission tends to take into consideration when evaluating the existing and future systems.[47]

The overview given of the information management in the AFSJ is limited to brief comments on the common functions of the instruments, presenting a short descriptive overview of EU measures regulating the management of personal data in the AFSJ. It provides citizens with a brief summary of what information is collected, stored and exchanged about them, by whom and for what purpose[48] by referring to

later providing for the abolition of border controls between Schengen states, common rules on visas, and police and judicial cooperation (Germany, France, Belgium, the Netherlands and Luxembourg concluded, outside the EU structures, the Convention implementing the Schengen agreement (signed in June 1990). This Convention was later implemented in EU law with opts outs of the United Kingdom and Ireland, see The Schengen acquis – Convention implementing the Schengen Agreement of 14 June 1985 between the Governments of the States of the Benelux Economic Union, the Federal Republic of Germany and the French Republic on the gradual abolition of checks at their common borders, OJ 2000, L-239/19. In the meantime, cooperation structures covering different policy aspects have emerged; the adoption of the Maastricht Treaty in 1993 created the so called third pillar covering cooperation in Justice and Home Affairs and the Amsterdam Treaty in 1997 incorporated the Schengen Acquis into the EU structures and established the police and judicial cooperation as an intergovernmental cooperation instrument. Policies such as visas, asylum, immigration and other policies related to free movement of persons were integrated in Community law forming part of the so called first pillar (Title IIIa Treaty of Amsterdam, OJ 1997, C-340/1). In the following years, the intensification of police and judicial cooperation occurred in and outside of the EU structures: at EU level, Europol, the European law enforcement organisation, and the judicial cooperation unit, Eurojust, were founded underlying the former intergovernmental third pillar system. For an excellent analysis of the beginnings of European police cooperation, see Bigo (1996).

[45] Communication from the Commission to the European Parliament and the Council, Overview of information management in the area of freedom, security and justice, COM(2010) 385 final, p. 3.

[46] Ibid p. 24.

[47] Ibid p. 25.

[48] Opinion of the EDPS on the Communication from the Commission to the European Parliament and the Council – Overview of information management in the area of freedom, security and justice, para 3.

various instruments currently in operation, under implementation or consideration. Of all the different instruments mentioned in the document, only six (of over 20) are declared as instruments or bodies collecting and processing personal data at EU level.[49] Explicitly mentioned are the information systems SIS (II), VIS, CIS and Eurodac as well as the agencies Europol and Eurojust. In this contribution, all of these bodies are referred to as AFSJ actors. An assessment of the data protection framework and the problems arising out of the cooperation between the addressed actors is not carried out in the document of the Commission.

The other measures illustrated in the communication include decentralised cross-border exchange (e.g. Prüm Treaty[50]), the collection of personal data at national level and then transferred to third countries (e.g. PNR[51] transfer to the US) or measures concerning exclusively the storage at national level (e.g. Data Retention Directive[52]).

In view of the foregoing, it is clear that information exchange in the AFSJ has become the dominant instrument in police and judicial cooperation in Europe.[53] Personal data are not only exchanged between Member States. European actors play an increasingly important role. The dangers to fundamental rights are evident. The inclusion into a law enforcement database usually has negative effects on the status of the individual. Such persons are typically treated with more suspicion than before. The entry of the data of a visa applicant in a law enforcement database will for instance most likely negatively influence his chances of receiving a visa.[54] In any case, the exchange of data with other authorities enlarges the circle of persons having access to personal data.[55] The more authorities have access, the more

---

[49] Communication from the Commission to the European Parliament and the Council, Overview of information management in the area of freedom, security and justice, COM (2010) 385 final, p. 21.

[50] In the meanwhile transposed in EU law by Council Decision 2008/615/JHA of 23 June 2008 on the stepping up of cross-border cooperation, particularly in combating terrorism and cross-border crime, OJ 2008, L-210/1.

[51] Passenger Name Record (PNR) are flight passenger data which are transferred to the US, this problem is further elaborated in Chap. D III 2.

[52] At EU level, the Council and the Parliament adopted the Data Retention Directive in 2006 to harmonise the Member States provisions to retain telecommunication traffic and location data for the purpose of subsequent law enforcement access: Directive 2006/24/EC of the European Parliament and of the Council of 15 March 2006 on the retention of data generated or processed in connection with the provision of publicly available electronic communications services or of public communications networks and amending Directive 2002/58/EC, OJ 2006, L-105/54.

[53] Niemeier (2010), p. 201.

[54] Compare the former practice of Spain to refuse entry into the States party to the Schengen Agreement as well as to issue a visa for the purpose of entry to a national of a third country, on the sole ground that he is a person for whom an alert was entered in the SIS, without examining the circumstances on a case-by-case basis and verifying whether the presence of that person constitutes a genuine, serious threat affecting one of the fundamental interests of society, case of the European Court of Justice C-503/03, *Commission v. Spain* of 31 January 2006.

[55] For the danger of misusing the CIS for instance by public workers spying in personal records of governmental databases, when having access to it, compare http://www.computerweekly.com/

difficult it gets to correct, block or delete wrongfully entered data. The risks of abuse (intended or not) therefore increase with each and every transfer.[56] The transfer and subsequent use may put data in another context, detached from the original information or the transmission of erroneous information may lead to an economic, political or social discrimination of the person concerned.[57] This danger comes in addition to the interferences outlined above and therefore constitute a separate interference with the applicants' rights under Article 8 ECHR.[58]

Against this background, the growing interactions between the AFSJ actors require efficient control mechanisms. One important vehicle to limit the use of police and judicial power is a high data protection standard.[59] It is therefore in the interest of both the individuals and the actors of the police and the judiciary, whose work is much more tolerated when the rights of individuals are respected, to find a balance between police and judicial needs and the rights of the individuals.[60]

Due to these colliding priorities, various questions emerge from the complexity of the AFSJ cooperation. Which data protection rules are in fact applicable to each of the AFSJ actors (Chap. A)? To what extent are those rights respected by the actors carrying out the cooperation and in which way does the protection of personal data differ at the various AFSJ actors (Chap. B)? How is the data exchange between the AFSJ actors organised and which information is allowed to be communicated to other actors (Chap. C)? If there is currently no unified standard in AFSJ information sharing, is it possible to develop one (Chap. D)?

In light of these questions, it follows that the topic of data protection in the current AFSJ cooperation raises interesting and challenging problems. This contribution will therefore focus on the *data protection problems* arising out of the *mutual cooperation between AFSJ actors which collect, process and transfer personal data at EU level*.

Due to their close interaction with the mentioned AFSJ actors, Frontex and the Commission's anti-fraud unit, OLAF are also included in the analysis. Although OLAF is affiliated with the Commission and is consequently not constituted as an agency, it fulfils investigative tasks and exchanges data with Europol and Eurojust.[61] Therefore it is integrated in the research. Considering all actors exchanging data at EU level, the analysis will refer to the data protection problems

Articles/2010/08/25/242514/More-than-200-public-sector-staff-caught-snooping-on-citizen.htm (accessed February 2011).

[56] Compare *Weber and Saravia v. Germany*, Application no. 54934/00, admissibility decision of 29 June 2006, para 79.

[57] To the general risks of data processing in databases see Simitis (2006), p. 65, para 10.

[58] *Weber and Saravia v. Germany*, Application no. 54934/00, admissibility decision of 29 June 2006, para 79.

[59] De Hert and Vandamme (September 2004), in particular p. 433; Bull (2009), in particular pp. 26–27 (Datenschutz als Machtkontrolle).

[60] Niemeier (2010), p. 201.

[61] To the the role of OLAF in the field of law enforcement at the EU level, compare in general Satzger (2009), pp. 157–162.

occurring in the bilateral cooperation between the agencies Europol, Eurojust and Frontex and the Commissions anti-fraud unit OLAF as well as the exchange of information between the law enforcement and judicial agencies Europol and Eurojust and the European information systems SIS, CIS, VIS and Eurodac.

IV. Terminology

It is important to clarify some terminology essential to the understanding of the terms used throughout this contribution.

For the purpose of this analysis, the definition of "personal data" results from the main definitions used in EU as well as in the Council of Europe instruments relating to personal data. The OECD Guidelines[62] and Convention No. 108[63] were the first instruments specifying this notion. Both instruments refer to personal data as "*any information relating to an identified or identifiable individual*".[64] Recommendation R (87) 15 dealing with the use of personal data in the police sector of the Council of Europe as well as the first EU data protection related instrument, Directive 95/46, later adopted this definition.[65] Community instruments such as Directive 97/66 EC,[66] Regulation 45/2001[67] and the FDPJ[68] refer to an identical definition and add

[62] OECD Recommendation concerning Guidelines governing the protection of privacy and trans-border flows of personal data of 23 September 1980.

[63] Convention for the Protection of Individuals with regard to Automatic Processing of Personal Data, 28 January 1981, CETS No. 108; in the following: Convention No. 108.

[64] Article 1 (b) OECD Guidelines and Article 2 (a) Convention No. 108.

[65] Compare scope and definitions of Recommendation R (87) 15 of the committee of ministers to member states regulating the use of personal data in the police sector, adopted on 17 September 1987 and Article 2 (a), replacing *individual* by *natural person*, of Directive 95/46/EC of the European Parliament and the Council of 24 October 1995 on the protection of the individuals with regard to the processing of personal data and on the free movement of such data, OJ 1995, L-281/31, in the following: Directive 95/46 OJ 1995, L-281/31.

[66] Article 2 Directive 97/66/EC of the European Parliament and of the Council of 15 December 1997 concerning the processing of personal data and the protection of privacy in the telecommunications sector, OJ 1998 L-24/1; replaced by Directive 2002/58/EC of the European Parliament and of the Council of 12 July 2002 concerning the processing of personal data and the protection of privacy in the electronic communications sector (Directive on privacy and electronic communications), OJ 2002, L-201/37 and amended by Directive 2006/24/EC of the European Parliament and of the Council of 15 March 2006 on the retention of data generated or processed in connection with the provision of publicly available electronic communications services or of public communications networks and amending Directive 2002/58/EC, OJ 2006, L-105/54.

[67] Article 2 (a) Regulation (EC) No. 45/2001 of the European Parliament and the Council of 18 December 2000 on the protection of individuals with regard to the processing of personal data by the Community institutions and bodies and on the free movements of such data, OJ 2001, L-8/1.

[68] Article 2 (a) FDPJ (Framework Decision on the protection of personal data processed in the framework of police and judicial cooperation in criminal matters), OJ 2008, L-350/60.

that "an identifiable person is one who can be identified, directly or indirectly, in particular by reference to an identification number or to one or more factors specific to his physical, physiological, mental, economic, cultural or social identity".[69] The ECtHR, as well as the Court of Justice of the EU, follow this definition.[70] Due to different interpretations in national law in the beginnings of EU data protection regulation, the definitions and key terms of Directive 95/46 were clarified in the opinion 4/2007 of the Article 29 Data Protection Working Party[71] on the concept of personal data in 2007.[72] It stipulates that either a content,[73] a purpose[74] or a result[75] element of the information should be present when

[69] This definition was already contained in Article 2 (a) Directive 95/46, compare also Article 2 (a) FDPJ, OJ 2008, L-350/60.

[70] ECtHR case-law: *Rotaru v. Romania*, Application no. 28341/954, judgment of 4 May 2000, para 43; *Amann v. Switzerland*, Application no. 27798/95, judgment of 16 February 2000, para 65 and European Union case law: case C-101/01, *Lindqvist*, judgment of 6 November 2003, para 24.

[71] Directive 95/46 created the Article 29 Working Party which examines questions relating to the interpretation of Directive 95/46 with the aim of contributing to a uniform application of the Directive, compare Article 29 and 30 of Directive 95/46 OJ 1995, L-281/31.

[72] Article 29 Data Protection Working Partly, WP 136, Opinion 4/2007 on the concept of personal data, adopted 20 June 2007; according to opinion 4/2007, the first terms "*any information*" signals a broad concept of personal data and a wide interpretation of this notion. The term could be understood under three different perspectives: nature, content and format. The nature of the information includes any sort of statements about a person. For information to be personal data, it is not necessary to be true or proven. It covers objective as well as subjective in formations, opinion and assessments. The content of the information includes data providing *any sort of information* whether it might touch directly upon private life concerns, or whether it constitutes other information regarding the types of activity undertaken by an individual (working relation, economic, social behaviour, criminal convictions, administrative sanctions etc.). From the point of view of the format or the medium on which information is kept, the concept of personal data refers to all information available in whatever form (alphabetical, biometric, numerical, graphical, photographical, acoustic, on paper, information stored in a computer, videotape, the extraction of information from blood samples etc.).

[73] The "content element is present in those cases where – corresponding to the most obvious and common understanding in a society of the word "relate" – information is given about a particular person, regardless of any purpose on the side of the data controller or of a third party, or the impact of that information on the data subject. Information "relates" to a person when it is "about" that person, and this has to be assessed in the light of all circumstances surrounding the case" Article 29 Working Partly, WP 136, Opinion 4/2007 on the concept of personal data, adopted 20 June 2007, p. 10, para III (2).

[74] The "purpose element can be considered to exist when the data are used or are likely to be used, taking into account all the circumstances surrounding the precise case, with the purpose to evaluate, treat in a certain way or influence the status or behaviour of an individual", Article 29 Working Partly, WP 136, Opinion 4/2007 on the concept of personal data, adopted 20 June 2007, p. 11, para III (2).

[75] A result element is present when information relates to an individual because their use is likely to have an impact on the person's rights and interest, taking into account all circumstances surrounding the case (e.g. different treatment of the person as a result of the processing of the data), Article 29 Working Partly, WP 136, Opinion 4/2007 on the concept of personal data, adopted 20 June 2007, p. 11, para III (2).

considering that the data relate to an individual.[76] The understanding of personal data within the meaning of opinion 4/2007 will be consistently addressed in the present contribution.[77] In short, the broad interpretation of personal data chosen in many EU as well as in the Council of Europe instruments is used here.

Some academics make a distinction between the terms "data" and "information". The word "data" is usually used to describe the input of words or signs which have no autonomous significance.[78] Information is often referred to the meaning of knowledge which can be allocated to data.[79] The data collected in the context of police and judicial work however almost exclusively result in real information on a person.[80] Hence this contribution uses both terms interchangeably.

Basic data protection principles will be defined in Chap. A.

The term "AFSJ" refers to the policies referred to in Title V TFEU mentioned above. "AFSJ actors" for the purpose of the present contribution are the European information systems SIS (II), VIS, CIS and Eurodac as well as the agencies Europol, Eurojust and Frontex. Although, according to the Lisbon Treaty, OLAF is not directly involved in the AFSJ, the body nevertheless plays a role in this area and is therefore also referred to as an AFSJ actor.

The terms "person concerned" and "data subject" are used alternatively and refer to the individuals who are subject to data processing, collection and storage.

The term "operational power" is not further defined but might best be described as "capable of being involved in operations" as well as carrying out investigative

---

[76] Article 29 Working Partly, WP 136, Opinion 4/2007 on the concept of personal data, adopted 20 June 2007, p. 10, para III (2).

[77] The notion "*relating to*" refers to all information about a specific person (individual files, medical records, persons filmed on a video). Objects, data about processes or events may indirectly be protected, for instance when they belong to someone, they may be subject to particular influence by or upon individuals or they may maintain some sort of physical or geographical vicinity with individuals. The Working Party gives the example that in the discussion on the data protection issues raised by RFID tags (radio-frequency identification, a technology using communications via electromagnetic waves to exchange data between an object or person for the purpose of identification and tracking) it clarified that "data relates to an individual if it refers to the identity, characteristics or behaviour of an individual or if such information is used to determine or influence the way in which that person is treated or evaluated". The third element "*an identified or identifiable natural person*" relates to a situation in which a person can be distinguished or in which it is possible to distinguish the person concerned from other individuals. The person can be directly or indirectly identifiable (for instance via a telephone number, a social security number, a passport number or by a combination of significant criteria which allow him to be recognised, names, date of birth etc.). The element "natural person" relates to living individuals. Legal persons are generally not covered by this notion, however, under certain circumstances, legal person may profit from the protection of personal data.

[78] Brouwer (2008a), p. 8 with further references.

[79] Brouwer (2008a), p. 8.

[80] Compare with respect to the information stored in the SIS: Brouwer (2008a), p. 8.

and field work activities, including coordinative tasks in terms of law enforcement, criminal prosecution and preventive police work.[81]

In cases of doubt, the definitions and key expressions of Directive 95/46 are applicable.

V. Limitations of the Research

It is further necessary to identify the limits of the scope of this contribution. The research will focus on the compliance with data protection rules of the actors in the AFSJ. Their data processing framework and their connections are studied. When illustrating the data protection framework applicable to the AFSJ actors (in Chap. A), the contribution will not focus on the history of the EU data protection principles. The research is limited to the principles currently applicable in the AFSJ. However, a detailed research in context of the data protection principles developed by the ECtHR is conducted.

The role of general remedies against infringements of data protection has not been identified as the core research question. This aspect has been profoundly developed by other authors.[82] The respect of the rights of individuals in the framework of AFSJ information sharing, including references to remedies, at EU level is given priority.

The research refers to the protection of personal data in security-related information processing at EU level and does neither include an analysis of the history[83] nor the entire area of criminal cooperation in the EU.[84] Therefore the bilateral cooperation between Member States such as the Prüm cooperation is not subject of this research. Also not included is the analysis of the transfer of personal data from Member States to third states which is for instance carried out in the framework of PNR cooperation between the European airlines and the US.[85] However, references to these instruments are made where necessary.

---

[81] Gärditz (2008), in particular pp. 213–214.

[82] With regard to the enforcement of remedies in the Schengen cooperation, the following thesis gives an excellent overview of the existing problems in this area: Brouwer (2008a); with regard to the possibilities to obtain judicial review against actions of Europol, compare Milke (2003), pp. 133–200; Srock (2006), pp. 76–111; Seong (2005), pp. 232–278; Kistner-Bahr (2010), pp. 139–188; with regard to Eurojust, compare Fawzy (2005), pp. 151–235.

[83] Excellent groundwork analysing the origins of police cooperation in the EU was done by: Bigo (1996).

[84] Data protection in the entire area of EU and US criminal cooperation is dealt with in an excellent manner by: De Busser (2009).

[85] Ibid.

It is also important to note that the contribution will only cover substantive law provisions. The EU institutional framework (European Parliament, Commission and Council) is not directly dealt with.

VI. Sources

The research encompasses principally legal acts and policy documents of the EU and the Council of Europe. The analysis of EU secondary legislation such as Directives, Regulations and Council Decisions builds an essential part of the research. Public international law Guidelines, Recommendations as well as Conventions of relevant actors in the data protection field have been used to narrow down the core principles of the applicable data protection law. With the aim of illustrating the most recent developments, the latest drafts of proposed legal instruments are considered as far as possible.

In order to identify the main data protection principles applicable in the AFSJ, the jurisprudence of the European Court of Human Rights (ECtHR) and of the EU Courts are significant sources of the research.

Legal doctrine, opinions, commentaries, studies and reports serve as an important source of information when interpreting the legislative documents. Due to the nature of the research, it is however worth mentioning that although there exists comprehensive literature in general data protection law, specific legal doctrine concerning data protection shortcomings with regard to the AFSJ actors, in particular regarding Frontex, OLAF, the CIS, the VIS and Eurodac is very limited.

VII. Outline of the Research

In the light of the foregoing considerations, the research is conducted by reference to four main chapters.

In order to examine the compliance of the AFSJ actors with European data protection principles, these principles first need to be identified. Hence, the first chapter (Chap. A) aims at establishing the core data protection principles applicable in the AFSJ. In the centre of attention are in a first step the guarantees of Article 8 ECHR and the jurisprudence of the ECtHR with regard to Article 8 ECHR which build the first "constitutional" basis for European data protection rules (A II). In a second step, the principles developed in the realm of EU law deserve special attention (A III).

On the basis of the data protection principles developed in the first chapter, the focus of the research in the second chapter (Chap. B) will be the compliance of the AFSJ actors with these principles. For this purpose, the existing and the envisaged AFSJ legal instruments are critically analysed. Detecting their shortcomings is in the centre of attention and will help improving the existing rules. To facilitate the understanding of the political and legal background of the different AFSJ actors, this point of the analysis is again divided in two steps. In a first section, the data processing framework of the European agencies Europol, Eurojust, Frontex and the Commission's anti-fraud unit OLAF is critically examined (B II). A second section tests the European information exchange systems on their conformity with European data protection principles (B III). This section should serve as important background information which critically assesses the data processing structure of each of the AFSJ actors before the data protection framework applicable in the cooperation of the AFSJ actors is analysed in the following chapter.

Against this background, the third chapter (Chap. C) provides a critical analysis of the cooperation structures in AFSJ information sharing. This section will demonstrate the difficulty of controlling personal data, once entered into one of the systems and then inter-linked and transferred to other authorities. How do the AFSJ actors exchange personal data? Do they respect European data protection principles? To answer these questions, two aspects merit closer examination. On the one hand the inter-agency cooperation (C I) and on the other hand the data exchange between the AFSJ agencies and the European information systems (C II). The first point of the research studies the data protection shortcomings arising out of the mutual cooperation between Europol, Eurojust, Frontex and OLAF. The second point subjects the data exchange between AFSJ agencies and the SIS, CIS, CIS and Eurodac to an analytical examination. In the course of the analysis, critical reflection is given to the data processing framework of the different actors evaluated in the previous chapter.

In view of the foregoing, several questions arise. Which tendencies observed in the analysis of the AFSJ actors and their connections interfere most significantly with data protection rights? Consequently, as the analysis reveals data protection shortcomings in the legal framework as well as in the cooperation structure between the AFSJ actors, how might these shortcomings be eliminated? Which instruments or measures could substantially improve the rights of individuals in this cooperation network in which data protection rights are currently disregarded? Is it possible to apply a common standard in AFSJ information exchanges? Which vehicles can control the increasing data exchange of the AFSJ actors? These questions are addressed in the fourth chapter (Chap. D). The contribution will at this stage of the analysis focus on the perspectives and will venture to propose some suggestions for improvement.

All in all, essential to the understanding of the respect of the right to data protection in AFSJ information sharing is a thorough assessment and evaluation of the existing data collection, processing and transfer in the AFSJ. This contribution should be seen as a first step to open a debate on an improved balance between the data protection rights of the individuals and the law enforcement interests in the AFSJ in this specific area but also in general.

Chapter A
Data Protection Standard in the AFSJ

In order to study the observance of the AFSJ actors with European data protection principles, these principles have to be identified.

The following analysis will therefore show the basic data protection standard which is applicable to all of the AFSJ actors as well as to the information exchange systems in the AFSJ. It is interesting to analyse, which rules are actually applicable to an area in which former first pillar structures mix with former third pillar rules. Additionally, due to the fact that this area was for a long time exclusively governed by public international law instead of Community law, the jurisprudence of the ECtHR is an essential source in the search of rules for security-related data processing at EU level. After having given a brief introduction relating to the fundamentals of data protection law (Sect. I), in a second subsection (Sect. II) the framework for the discussion consists therefore of the data protection instruments of the Council of Europe, in particular of the European Convention of Human Rights. On the basis of these data protection rules, a third section focuses on the data protection principles applicable in the AFSJ included in EU law (Sect. III).

I Brief Historical Review and Reasons for Data Protection

As mentioned in the introduction, data protection in EU law constitutes a relatively new individual right which has its roots in public international law instruments such as the OECD Guidelines of 1980, Convention No. 108 and in Article 8 ECHR and its interpretation by the European Court of Human Rights (ECtHR). The earliest provisions on data protection at national level have been developed in the 1970s in response to the rise of information technology and the beginning of the computer age. New techniques which allowed for the collection, processing and storage of large amounts of data made it possible for governmental and private actors to use, process and combine more information than ever. For the first time in European

F. Boehm, *Information Sharing and Data Protection in the Area of Freedom, Security and Justice*, DOI 10.1007/978-3-642-22392-1_2,

history, databases could store and processes a huge quantity of personal data.[1] One the one hand, the technical changes facilitated the use of the collected data for various purposes and lead to vast data pools in the property of national authorities. On the other hand, the automatic processing of data increased the risk of misuse of these data.[2]

Against this background, legal scholars point to the fact that every data processing duplicates the risk of abuse (intended or not) of the relevant information.[3] *Simitis* for instance refers to the risks of automated processing. The entry of incorrect data in one database may have serious consequences for the individual concerned when the wrongfully entered data are reproduced in another database, used in another context or even transferred to another actor.[4] The author warns against the risk of losing the context of the original information when processing data automatically. Automated processing often curtails the relevant information which may lead to the removal of important facts from the original information. *Simitis* gives the concrete example, that the reasons for an illness, for an entry in a police file or for the delayed payment of debts may get lost during the automatic processing of data. After repeated data processing, the remaining information may include information limited to an illness, the entry in a police file and the delayed payment without knowing the reasons which lead to these entries. Each of these entries may make it difficult for persons concerned to find a workplace or simply to open a bank account. In the worst case, the transmission of wrong information can lead to an economic, political or social discrimination of the person concerned.[5]

In view of these risks, the national legislators were obliged to adopt rules to standardise data processing. The German federal state of Hessen endorsed the first data protection act worldwide in 1970.[6] Three years later the Swedish legislator followed and adopted the first national data protection law.[7] The German federal legislator enacted its national data protection act in 1977. [8] The Swedish and the

---

[1] Johlen (2006) Article 8, para 1; Simitis (2006), p. 64, para 8.

[2] Simitis (2006), p. 65, para 10.

[3] Simitis (2006), p. 65, para 9.

[4] Simitis (2006), pp. 65 and 66, paras 10–13.

[5] Simitis (2006), p. 65, para 10.

[6] Hessisches Datenschutz Gesetz, 7 Oktober 1970 – GVBl. (Gesetz- und Verordnungsblatt) I, 1970, p. 625; for criticism with regard to the use of the term "data protection" see Simitis (1971), in particular p. 679.

[7] Swedish data protection act, Datalag SFS 1973:289. In addition to the technological development, a census obliged the Swedish legislator to develop rules regulating the processing and the treatment of the collected data. To the international development of data protection legislations, compare the excellent overview in Simitis (2006) pp. 108–117, paras 127–150. The (German) literature approach makes a distinction between the different generations of data protection regulations, for details see Di Martino (2005), p. 33 et seq.

[8] Gesetz zum Schutz vor Missbrauch von personenbezogenen Daten bei der Datenverarbeitung, BDSG, 27 January 1977, BGBl. I, 201.

German data protection acts based on different approaches.[9] The most functional aspects of both approaches were later combined by other European countries which benefited from the experiences made by the Swedish and German legislators. The first French data protection act[10] of 1978, for instance, principally based on the Swedish model.[11]

Due to the technological developments and the national legislative activity, the first European instruments highlighting the importance of data protection rules followed soon. The most influential actor with regard to the development of data protection rights at European level was the Council of Europe. The adoption of Convention No. 108 in the year 1981 and the case law of the ECtHR regarding Article 8 ECHR considerably influenced the development and understanding of data protection rules in Europe in the last decades. Under the influence of Convention No. 108, even countries with hesitant approaches to privacy and data protection rules, such as the United Kingdom, followed suit and adopted its first data

---

[9] The Swedish legislator regulated the processing procedure. Control agencies were established and data processors were obliged to disclose their processing modalities and to reveal their methods of collection. Processors had to make a declaration about the procedure of processing and could thereupon receive a processing permit when the procedure was in compliance with the requirements of the control authority. The obligation to obtain a permit from the national control authority made it possible to react in each individual case and facilitated the adaptation to the fast developing technological challenges. However, this procedure implicated enormous administrative efforts and for this reason the Swedish legislator renewed the data protection act already in 1982. Nonetheless, the Swedish data protection act is the basis for the European tradition of the "omnibus approach" which means that general binding rules regulate the legal relations in the public as well as in the private sector. The German legislator followed the so called global approach or self-assessment model. A framework of generally binding rules regulated the processing of personal data, i.e. general rules on data protection built a regulatory framework but details were controlled by the data processors themselves. In consequence each data processor was held responsible for its own area and for the implementation of the general rules within its field of activity. The control authority did not intervene during the data processing procedure as long as no conflict between the data processor and the person concerned emerged. In principle, the German legislator enacted global rules instead of specific regulations formulated by the Swedish legislator. Additionally, the German data protection act was not applicable to private actors; the rules were only applicable to German public authorities. Nevertheless, the Swedish and the German approach represent the basis for following data protection acts in other European countries. For more details compare Burkert (2003), p. 93 et seq.; Ellger (1990), p. 421 et seq.

[10] Loi no. 78–17 du 6 Janvier 1978 relative à l'informatique, aux fichiers et aux libertés. See with regard to the beginnings of French data protection Maisl (1987); Mallet-Poujol (1999); Nugter (1990), pp. 77–106; Weill (1987).

[11] Some differences nevertheless existed, i.e. even though the act was applicable to public as well as private actors (omnibus approach) and established a control agency, the CNIL (Commission Nationale de l'Informatique et des Libertés), only the public sector was obliged to get prior authorisation for the data processing. For data processing by private actors a notification was sufficient. Nowadays, this system, composed of authorisation and notification, still exists (even though it is modified in details). In consequence, the French data protection act is a combination of the German and the Swedish models. The need of prior authorisation is based on the Swedish data protection act and the notification duty on the German data protection rules. Compare Gruber (2007); Mitrou (1993), pp. 185 et seq.

protection act in 1984.[12] The relevance of the Council of Europe instruments for the shaping and interpretation of data protection rights at EU level is further illustrated in the following section.

II. Council of Europe: Art. 8 ECHR, Convention No. 108 and Recommendation R (87) 15

Illustrating the current European data protection standard from the point of view of the ECtHR allows for the derivation of general data protection principles also for EU law. Article 6 TEU thereby guarantees the respect of fundamental rights as guaranteed by the ECHR and provides for the accession of the EU to the ECHR.[13] Article 52 (3) of the Charter of Fundamental Right underlines the close connection of the rights enumerated in the Charter and the rights of the ECHR by stipulating that in so far as the Charter contains rights which correspond to the rights of the ECHR, "the meaning and the scope of those rights shall be the same as those laid down by the Convention [ECHR]".[14]Additionally, with regard to data protection law, important EU data protection instruments are a further development of the ECHR standard and its Conventions and refer to them.[15] The jurisdiction of the Strasbourg Court is crucial to the development of data protection rights in Europe. Over the last years, the ECtHR developed a data protection system by continually emphasising the respect of the core values of European data protection principles.[16]

---

[12] The Data Protection Act 1984. Although in 1976 the United Kingdom already established a committee (the Lindop Committee) in order to prepare a data protection act, it took almost 10 years to eventually adopt binding rules on data protection. This first data protection act of 1984 was heavily criticised and later amended by the second data protection act in 1998, around 16 month later than required under Directive 95/46. The second data protection act extended data protection rules to forms of manual processing and made important changes with regard to the rights of individuals in data protection law in the United Kingdom. For details see Pinegar (1984); Bainbridge (2005); Carey (2004); Lloyd (1998); Hamilton and Jay (2003); Singleton (1998).

[13] With regard to the consequences of the accession, see Lock (2010).

[14] Article 52 (3) of the Charter of Fundamental Rights, OJ 2010, C-83/02 and joined cases C-92/09 and C-93/09, *Volker and Markus Schecke GbR and Hartmut Eifert* v. *Land Hessen*, judgement of 9 November 2010; compare for a deepend understanding of Article 52 (3) of the Charter and of the influence of the ECHR on the Charter of Fundamental Rights, Ziegenhorn (2009); Gebauer (2007), in particular pp. 343–349; Müller Graff (2006).

[15] Recitals (10) and (11) of Directive 95/46/EC of the European Parliament and the Council of 24 October 1995 on the protection of the individuals with regard to the processing of personal data and on the free movement of such data, OJ 1995, L-281/31; Recitals (40) and (41) Council Framework Decision 2008/977/JHA of 27 November 2008 on the protection of personal data processed in the framework of police and judicial cooperation in criminal matters, OJ 2008, L-350/60; for a brief overview, refer to Breitenmoser et al. (2006), pp. 399–410.

[16] For an excellent overview of the development towards a right to data protection in Europe see Siemen (2006).

The ECtHR repeatedly emphasised that the ECHR is a "living instrument" whose interpretation facilitates immediate adaptation to specific situations.[17]

Although it seems to be difficult to derive principles of general application from the case law tailored to a specific situation, the ECtHR succeeds nonetheless in developing a comprehensive data protection framework.[18] Admittedly, it does not cover all difficulties arising in an EU law enforcement context and is the lowest common denominator as the guarantees of the ECHR apply in a public international law context, but the interpretations of the ECtHR have attained a far-reaching significance for the EU over the years and cooperation between the EU and the Council of Europe in fundamental rights matters continually improves.[19] The Memorandum of Understanding between the Council of Europe and the European Union, adopted in May 2007, clarifies that the EU will refer to the Council of Europe standards, in particular to the ECHR, when developing its fundamental rights standards.[20] Decisions, reports, conclusions, recommendations and opinions of the Council of Europe should be systematically taken as the first Europe-wide reference source for human rights.[21] As corroborated by the Memorandum as well as the case law of the European Courts, this proposal merely confirms existing practice.[22] In a Communication from the Commission to the European Parliament and the Council about the AFSJ, the accession to the ECHR is mentioned as priority

[17] See for example: *Tyrer v. the United Kingdom*, Application no. 5856/75, judgment of 25 April 1978, para 31; *Loizidou v. Turkey*, Application no. 15318/89, judgment of 23 March 1995, para 71; *Mamatkulov and Askarov v. Turkey*, Application nos. 46827/99 and 46951/99, judgment of 4 February (2005), para 121.

[18] See Siemen (2006).

[19] De Schutter (2008). See also: joint declaration on cooperation and partnership between the Council of Europe and the European Commission of 3 April 2001, available at: http://www.jp.coe.int/Upload/110_Joint_Declaration_EF.pdf (accessed February 2011); Memorandum of Understanding between the Council of Europe and the European Union of 10 May 2007, CM(2007) 74, available at: https://wcd.coe.int/ViewDoc.jsp?Ref=CM(2007)74&Language=lanEnglish, (accessed February 2011).

[20] Memorandum of Understanding between the Council of Europe and the European Union of 10 May 2007, CM(2007)74, points 16 and 17. This declaration follows a proposal made in the Juncker report on the future relationship between the Council of Europe and the EU which was adopted in April 2006 by the Parliamentary Assembly of the Council of Europe; see De Schutter (2008), p. 511; Juncker Report "A sole ambition for the European continent" of 11 April 2006, available at: http://assembly.coe.int/Sessions/2006/speeches/20060411_report_JCJuncker_EN.pdf (accessed February 2011).

[21] Juncker Report "A sole ambition for the European continent" of 11 April 2006, available at: http://assembly.coe.int/Sessions/2006/speeches/20060411_report_JCJuncker_EN.pdf (accessed February 2011), p. 6.

[22] Memorandum of Understanding between the Council of Europe and the European Union of 10 May 2007, CM(2007)74, point 17; Case C-465/00, *Rechnungshof v. Österreichischer Rundfunk and Others*, judgment of 20 May 2003, paras 10 and 19; details to the relation between the EU Courts and the ECtHR can be found in Häberle (2009), in particular pp. 460–480.

issue.[23] By emphasising that the Union's accession will complete the system of protection in this field, the Commission recognises the close relationship between the fundamental rights system of the ECHR and the EU. The Communication assumes that the accession will encourage the case-law of the European Court of Justice and the ECtHR to develop in step.

Certainly, one important benefit of the close relationship between fundamental rights interpretations of the EU and the Council of Europe is the far reaching scope of the ECtHR's jurisdiction which goes beyond the previously restricted competences of the EU Courts in common foreign and security policy as well as in police and judicial cooperation in criminal matters. The ECtHR's jurisdiction can stipulate overarching principles in fields where the control of European Courts was limited by the treaties.[24] Many EU instruments and national legal orders refer directly or indirectly to the ECHR provisions and their interpretation.[25] The ECHR standard is therefore the broadest and farthest-reaching data protection standard in Europe applicable regardless of (former) EU pillars, national borders or competence obstacles.

The structure of the following section mirrors the method generally used by the ECtHR to examine whether data processing complies with Article 8 ECHR: Does the data processing fall within the scope of Article 8 ECHR, is there an interference with the right to private life and is this interference justified because it is in accordance with the law, pursues a legitimate aim and is necessary in a democratic society.

---

[23] Communication from the Commission to the European Parliament and the Council, an area of freedom, security and justice serving the citizen, COM(2009) 262 final of 10 June 2009, paragraph 2, p. 7, compare also Lock (2010).

[24] The former limitations of the European Courts are summarised in Bieber et al. (2006), pp. 250–252; With regard to the impact of the ECtHR on the interpretation of privacy, compare De Hert and Guthwirth (2006).

[25] See for instance: Article 6 (2) EU Treaty, United Kingdom's Human Right Act 1998 (HRA), schedule 1, paragraph 2 (1) a ("A ECtHR or tribunal determining a question which has arisen in connection with a Convention right must take into account any judgment, decision, declaration or advisory opinion of the European ECtHR of Human Rights") or Administrative Act of Luxembourg 2007/A, Vol. 1 p. 35. See also: Judgment of the Second Senate of the German Constitutional Court of 14 October 2004, 2 BvR 1481/04, *Görgülü*, headnotes: "The principle that the judge is bound by statute and law (Article 20.3 of the Basic Law (Grundgesetz – GG)) includes taking into account the guarantees of the European Convention for the Protection of Human Rights and Fundamental Freedoms and the decisions of the European ECtHR of Human Rights (ECHR) as part of a methodologically justifiable interpretation of the law. Both a failure to consider a decision of the ECHR and the "enforcement" of such a decision in a schematic way, in violation of prior-ranking law, may violate fundamental rights in conjunction with the principle of the rule of law.

In taking into account decisions of the ECtHR, the state bodies must include the effects on the national legal system in their application of the law. This applies in particular when the relevant national law is a balanced partial system of domestic law that is intended to achieve an equilibrium between differing fundamental rights". For the English legal system see as well: Coppel (2007).

1. Data Protection Guarantees of Article 8 ECHR

In the last years, there has been a strong development towards a right to data protection within the framework of Article 8 ECHR.[26] Even though data are not expressly protected by this Article, the ECtHR insists that the protection of personal data is of fundamental importance to a person's enjoyment of his or her right to respect for private and family life.[27] It is commonly acknowledged that data protection guarantees originate from the further development of the right to private life stipulated in Article 8 ECHR, nowadays forming a vital part of this right.[28] The guarantees of Article 8 ECHR therefore represent the basis for an overarching European data protection standard. It reads as follows:

1. Everyone has the right to respect for his private and family life, his home and his correspondence.
2. There shall be no interference by a public authority with the exercise of this right except such as is in accordance with the law and is necessary in a democratic society in the interests of national security, public safety or the economic well-being of the country, for the prevention of disorder or crime, for the protection of health or morals, or for the protection of the rights and freedoms of others.

Understanding and analysing the ECtHR's application of the Convention's right to respect for private life is a crucial element in the search of the right to data protection in the Council of Europe context. At this point, it is worth briefly examining the obligations which Article 8 ECHR states in general, before analysing the details of the scope of the right to data protection entailed in the protection of the right for private life based on Article 8 ECHR.

---

[26] See analysis of Siemen (2006); Marauhn and Meljnik (2006), paras 29 and 39.

[27] *Z. v Finland*, Application no. 22009/93, judgment of 25 February 1997, para 95; *Peck v. United Kingdom*, Application no. 44647/98, judgment of 28 January 2003, para 78; *L.L. v France*, Application no. 7508/02, judgment of 10 October 2006, para 43; *Biriuk v Lithuania*, Application no. 23373/03, judgment of 25 November 2008, para 39; *I v Finland* Application no. 20511/03 of 17 July 2008, para 38; *S. and Marper v the United Kingdom*, Application nos. 30562/04 and 30566/04, judgment of 4 December 2008, para 103; *C.C. v. Spain*, Application no. 1425/06, judgment of 6 October 2009, para 31; see also: Breitenmoser (1986), p. 245; Kugelmann (2003), p. 16 et seq.; Meyer-Ladewig (2006), Article 8, para 11; Moreham (2008), pp. 44–79.

[28] *Z. v Finland*, Application no. 22009/93, judgment of 25 February 1997, para 95; *Peck v. United Kingdom*, Application no. 44647/98, judgment of 28 January 2003, para 78; *L.L. v France*, Application no. 7508/02, judgment of 10 October 2006, para 43; *Biriuk v Lithuania*, Application no. 23373/03, judgment of 25 November 2008, para 39; *I v Finland*, Application no. 20511/03, judgment of 17 July 2008, para 38; *S. and Marper v the United Kingdom*, Application nos. 30562/04 and 30566/04, judgment of 4 December 2008, para 103; *Niemietz v. Germany*, Application no. 13710/88, judgment of 16 September 1992 para 29; *Pretty v. United Kingdom*, Application no. 2346/02, judgment of 29 April 2002, para 61; *P.G. and J.H. v. United Kingdom*, Application no. 44787/98,judgment of 25 September 2001, para 56; see also: Breitenmoser (1986), p. 245; Kugelmann (2003), p. 16 et seq.; Meyer-Ladewig (2006), Article 8, para 11; Moreham (2008); Ovey and White (2006), pp. 286–297; Siemen (2006), pp. 57–132.

a) General Obligations of Article 8 ECHR

Article 8 ECHR as seen by the ECtHR entails two types of obligations, a negative and a positive one.[29] The negative obligation requires the states to assure an exercise free of interference of the rights specified in Article 8 ECHR unless the conditions in Article 8 (2) ECHR are fulfilled, which means that the state should refrain from taking certain actions.[30] The positive obligation entails the adoption of measures designed to protect the individual's rights of Article 8 ECHR, in particular against interference by others.[31]

Generally, with regard to negative obligations, the ECtHR examines firstly if there has been an interference with one of the rights stipulated in Article 8 (1) and if so, whether the interference can be justified by the rights outlined in Article 8 (2) ECHR in a second step. The focus in positive obligations cases is more on the obligation of states to assure the protection of individual's private life through the adoption of protective measures.[32] The ECtHR stipulates that "while the essential object of Article 8 is to protect the individual against arbitrary interference by the public authorities, it does not merely compel the State to abstain from such interference: in addition to this negative undertaking, there may be positive obligations inherent in an effective respect for private or family life. These obligations may involve the adoption of measures designed to secure respect for private life even in the sphere of the relations of individuals between themselves".[33] Further the ECtHR emphasises that the boundaries between the State's positive and

[29] This is widely acknowledged in literature and ECtHR's case law, see Dröge (2003); Gómez-Arostegui (2005); Siemen (2006), p. 179 et seq.; Mowbray (2007), pp. 485–593, especially p. 519 et seq. See also: *Airey v. Ireland*, Application no. 6289/73, judgment of 9 October 1979, para 32 or *Z. and others v. the United Kingdom*, Application no.29392/95, judgment of 10 May 2001, para 74; compare also De Hert and Guthwirth (2006).

[30] Moreham (2008), pp. 44, 46.

[31] Moreham (2008), pp. 44, 46. 42. To the positive obligation in the ECHR, see *Özgür Gündem v. Turkey*, Application no. 23144/93, judgment of 16 March 2000, para 42: "The Court has long held that, although the essential object of many provisions of the Convention is to protect the individual against arbitrary interference by public authorities, there may in addition be positive obligations inherent in an effective respect of the rights concerned. It has found that such obligations may arise under Article 8 (see, amongst others, the *Gaskin v. the United Kingdom* judgment of 7 July 1989, Series A no. 160, pp. 17–20, §§ 42–49) and Article 11 (see the *Plattform "Ärzte für das Leben" v. Austria* judgment of 21 June 1988, Series A no. 139, p. 12, § 32). Obligations to take steps to undertake effective investigations have also been found to accrue in the context of Article 2 (see, for example, the *McCann and Others v. the United Kingdom* judgment of 27 September 1995, Series A no. 324, p. 49, § 161) and Article 3 (see the *Assenov and Others v. Bulgaria* judgment of 28 October 1998, Reports 1998-VIII, p. 3290, § 102), while a positive obligation to take steps to protect life may also exist under Article 2 (see the *Osman v. the United Kingdom* case of 28 October 1998, Reports 1998-VIII, pp. 3159–61, §§ 115–17)".

[32] For the positive obligations of Article 8 in general see Mowbray (2007), pp. 485–593, especially p. 519 et seq.

[33] *Van Kück v. Germany*, Application no. 35968/97, judgment of 12 June 2003, para 70.

negative obligations under Article 8 ECHR are not easy to define, as the applicable principles are rather similar. In clarifying whether or not such an obligation exists, attention must be paid to the fair balance which has to be struck between the general interest and the interests of the individual.[34] In both situations the State enjoys a particular margin of appreciation.[35]

In a data protection context these two obligations may collide as Article 8 ECHR for instance may justify restrictions on the disclosure of information and at the same time may give a right to access information. The following analysis will show to what extent personal data are protected in the framework of the right to respect for private life and which types of positive obligations exist in this context. The ECtHR uses the traditional three-step analysis – scope, interference and justification – to find out whether a Member States has violated Article 8 ECHR in this respect.

b) Scope of Article 8 ECHR with Regard to Data Protection

Article 1 ECHR covers the general scope of the ECHR, implying a territorial, a personal and a material requirement.[36] According to it, every signatory state of the Convention "shall secure to everyone within their jurisdiction the rights and freedoms" of section one of the ECHR, including the rights guaranteed in Articles 2–18 ECHR and the rights contained in the additional protocols.[37]

The state is obliged to respect the rights of the Convention within the borders of its "jurisdiction" (territorial scope).[38] Article 1 ECHR in connection with Article 34 ECHR restricts the liability of states to governmental actions.[39] There may be nevertheless effects on third parties when a state is held responsible for failing its positive obligation to protect the individual against interferences from private actors.[40] The rights of the ECHR generally apply to every person of the contracting state including civil servants, third country nationals or soldiers providing that they are subjected to the jurisdiction of one of the Convention's states (personal scope "ratione personae").[41] The claim of an alleged violation is restricted to the rights

---

[34] *Van Kück v. Germany*, Application no. 35968/97, judgment of 12 June 2003, para 71.

[35] *Van Kück v. Germany*, Application no. 35968/97, judgment of 12 June 2003, para 71; to the "margin of appreciation doctrine", see Gebauer (2007), pp. 248–253.

[36] Meyer-Ladewig (2006), Artikel 1, para 1; there is also a temporal requirement which refers to interferences before the ECHR entred into force, see Article 35 ECHR.

[37] Meyer-Ladewig (2006), Artikel 1, para 1.

[38] To the details see Ovey and White (2006), pp. 24–34 or Clapham (2006), pp. 387–400 and *Ilascu and others v. Moldova and Russia*, Application no. 48787/99, judgment of 8 July 2004.

[39] Ovey and White (2006), pp. 31–32.

[40] The notion of positive obligations and the exact extent to which a State may be liable for private actions will considered later in this chapter. To the liability for acts of international organisations, see Ovey and White (2006), p. 29–30.

[41] To the restrictions, see Meyer-Ladewig (2006), Artikel 1, para 10.

and freedoms set forth in the ECHR and in its additional protocols (material requirement).[42]

Data protection elements could be found in cases concerning the protection of the right to private life as guaranteed in Article 8 ECHR since the beginning of the ECHR's interpretation.[43] Up to the late 1990s, the ECtHR avoided using the term "data protection" in the context of Article 8 ECHR when describing the effects of what today is commonly understood as protection of personal data.[44] That is why analysing data protection effects and implications in the ECtHR's case law is always closely connected to the meaning of private life in the course of Article 8 ECHR. This has to be briefly specified.

The term private life in Article 8 ECHR indicates a range of different interests accumulated under the notion of an overarching principle. The ECtHR has repeatedly stated that it is "a broad term not susceptible to exhaustive definition".[45] Some authors qualify the right with regard to the ECtHR's jurisdiction as "ill-defined and amorphous".[46] This assessment arises out of the ECtHR's "unwillingness" to identify categories permitting a clear classification of the content of the right to respect for private life.[47]

However, over the years, the ECtHR specified the scope of Article 8 ECHR with regard to data protection while logically remaining within the boundaries of the scope of private life. For this reason, *Siemen* concludes that the scope of a right to data protection reaches so far as the scope of the right to respect for private life.[48] Whereas in the past, the right to data protection was very closely attached to the right to private life, in recent years, the ECtHR seems to apply the right to data protection more independently from its private life roots.[49] The analysis in the

---

[42] Meyer-Ladewig (2006), Artikel 1, para 1.

[43] *Klass v. Germany*, Application no. 5029/71, judgment of 6 September 1978; *Malone v. the United Kingdom*, Application no. 8691/79, judgment of 2 August 1984; *Leander v. Sweden*, Application no. 9248/81, judgment of 26 March 1987.

[44] The first time the ECtHR used the term "protection of personal data" was in *Z. v Finland*, Application no. 22009/93, judgment of 25 February 1997, para 95.

[45] *Peck v. United Kingdom*, Application no. 44647/98, judgment of 28 January 2003, para 57; *Niemietz v. Germany*, Application no. 13710/88, judgment of 16 September 1992, para 29; *Pretty v. United Kingdom*Application no. 2346/02, judgment of 29 April 2002, para 61; *P.G. and J.H. v. United Kingdom*Application no. 44787/98, judgment of 25 September 2001, para 56; Ovey and White (2006), p. 246; Siemen (2006), p. 57; Meyer-Ladewig (2006), Artikel 8 para 3.

[46] Moreham (2008), pp. 44, 45.

[47] Moreham (2008), pp. 44, 45; see also: Beck (2008), pp. 214–244, 232–235.

[48] Siemen (2006), p. 57.

[49] Compare case *Reyntjens v. Belgium*, Application no. 16810/90, admissibility decision of 9 September 1992, where the commission stated that passport information did not entail personal information raising private life concerns) to cases giving priority to data protection elements: *Panteleyenko v. Ukraine*, Application no. 11901/02, judgment of 29 June 2006; *S. and Marper v the United Kingdom*, Application nos. 30562/04 and 30566/04, judgment of 4 December 2008; *Z. v. Finland*, Application no. 22009/93, judgment of 25 February 1997; for a exceptionally detailed analysis of this development, see Siemen (2006), pp. 79–132.

following will therefore not describe the comprehensive content of the right to private life, but will focus on the data protection elements resulting from the jurisprudence of the ECtHR on Article 8 ECHR.

In early Court judgments, a distinction was made between private and public life.[50] However, since it is not always possible to distinguish clearly which of an individual's activities form part of his public or professional life and which do not, the ECtHR developed a broader understanding of the content of the right to private life over the course of the following years.[51]

After years of discussing the exact content of the right to private life, in *Niemietz v. Germany* the ECtHR intentionally did not give a clear definition of this right.[52] Following the German "Sphärentheorie",[53] the Court first stated that a fundamental component of the right to private life certainly is the "inner circle" in which the individual may live his own personal life as he chooses and to exclude therefrom entirely the outside world not encompassed within that circle. Additionally, the respect for private life must comprise the right to establish and develop relationships with other human beings.[54] Other cases show however that the ECtHR entrenched questions of private life referring to legitimate expectation of

---

[50] Decision of the European Commission of Human Rights, *X. v. Iceland* (1976).

[51] Moreham (2008), p. 44, 45. See also: *Niemietz v. Germany*, Application no. 13710/88, judgment of 16 September 1992, para 29: "The ECtHR does not consider it possible or necessary to attempt an exhaustive definition of the notion of "private life". However, it would be too restrictive to limit the notion to an "inner circle" in which the individual may live his own personal life as he chooses and to exclude therefrom entirely the outside world not encompassed within that circle. Respect for private life must also comprise to a certain degree the right to establish and develop relationships with other human beings. There appears, furthermore, to be no reason of principle why this understanding of the notion of "private life" should be taken to exclude activities of a professional or business nature since it is, after all, in the course of their working lives that the majority of people have a significant, if not the greatest, opportunity of developing relationships with the outside world. This view is supported by the fact that, as was rightly pointed out by the Commission, it is not always possible to distinguish clearly which of an individual's activities form part of his professional or business life and which do not. [...]To deny the protection of Article 8 (art. 8) on the ground that the measure complained of related only to professional activities - as the Government suggested should be done in the present case - could moreover lead to an inequality of treatment, in that such protection would remain available to a person whose professional and non - professional activities were so intermingled that there was no means of distinguishing between them. In fact, the ECtHR has not heretofore drawn such distinctions: it concluded that there had been an interference with private life even where telephone tapping covered both business and private calls [...]; and, where a search was directed solely against business activities, it did not rely on that fact as a ground for excluding the applicability of Article 8 (art. 8) under the head of "private life"[...]".

[52] *Niemietz v. Germany*, Application no. 13710/88, judgment of 16 September 1992.

[53] For a general overview of the German "Recht auf informationelle Selbstbestimmung", refer to, Gartska (2008).

[54] *Niemietz v. Germany*, Application no. 13710/88, judgment of 16 September 1992, para 29.

protection and respect for private life.[55] This broad interpretation of the scope allows adapting the terms of Article 8 ECHR, which were developed in the 1950, in the light of the current data protection context. The ECtHR constantly stresses that the "convention as a living instrument must be interpreted in the light of present-day conditions".[56]

In general, the ECtHR does not specify the scope of the right to data protection in more detail.[57] The Court restricts its argumentation to the reference to Convention No. 108 by emphasising repeatedly that the broad interpretation of Article 8 with regard to private life corresponds to that of Convention No. 108 "whose purpose is to secure [...] for every individual [...] respect for his rights and fundamental freedoms, and in particular his right to privacy with regard to automatic processing of personal data relating to him",[58] such personal data being defined in Article 2 Convention No. 108 as "any information relating to an identified or identifiable individual".[59]

Limits of the scope are therefore not easy to define, as the covered subject matter generally has to comply with the two requirements mentioned in Convention No. 108: firstly, it must be information and secondly, the information must be of personal nature. Exemptions to this general rule exist, but are difficult to find.[60]

In *Smith v. the United Kingdom*, one of the rare cases concerning the personal nature of information, the ECtHR did not clarify the notion in detail.[61] The applicant sought access to business related documents held by a bank with an eye to possible further legal proceedings. The documents mainly dealt with a loan granted to the applicant in his function as managing director and controlling shareholder of an electronic group. The Court clarified that on one hand it would be artificial to declare that the requested files did not concern the applicant; however, on the other, the information at hand did not concern the applicant's identity or personal history, nor did the information have "formative implications"

---

[55] *Copland v. the United Kingdom*, Application no.62617/00, judgment of 3 April 2007, paras 41–42; *Von Hannover v. Germany*, Application no. 59320/00, judgment of 24 June 2004, para 51; Ovey and White (2006), p. 296; to the term legitimate expectation, see Gómez-Arostegui (2005), pp. 153–200.

[56] See for instance: *Tyrer v. the United Kingdom*, Application no. 5856/75, judgment of 25 April 1978, para 31; *Loizidou v. Turkey*, Application no. 15318/89, judgment of 23 March 1995, para 71; *Mamatkulov and Askarov v. Turkey*, Application nos. 46827/99 and 46951/99, judgment of 4 February 2005, para 121.

[57] Esser (2008), in particular pp. 282–283.

[58] Article 1 Convention No. 108.

[59] *Rotaru v. Romania*, Application no. 28341/954, judgment of 4 May 2000, para 43; see also: *Amann v. Switzerland*, Application no. 27798/95, judgment of 16 February 2000, para 65.

[60] One exemption was *Herbecq and the Association "ligue des droits des l'homme" v. Belgium*, Application no. 32200/96 and 32201/96, admissibility decision of 14 January 1998; see also De Hert and Gutwirth (2009), in particular pp. 24–25.

[61] *Smith v. the United Kingdom*, Application no. 39658/05, admissibility decision of 4 January 2007.

for his personality.[62] Additionally the information was not contained in a database currently in use, nor was it obtained through any invasive means. Under such circumstances, the ECtHR denied a violation of Article 8 ECHR without clarifying whether it based its decision on the non-compliance with the scope or with the interference of Article 8 ECHR.

However, while the ECtHR's interpretation of Article 8 ECHR covers in principle any personal information, one can distinguish the different data categories which have been identified as being protected so far. When looking in more detail at the relevant case law, there are several types of data which can be "extracted" from the ECtHR's jurisdiction. Protected data categories are amongst others: any personal information stored in a public file,[63] telecommunication data,[64] audio or video material containing personal information,[65]

---

[62] *Smith v. the United Kingdom*, Application no. 39658/05, admissibility decision of 4 January 2007.

[63] For instance: *Leander v. Sweden*, Application no. 9248/81, judgment of 26 March 1987; *Amann v. Switzerland*, Application no. 27798/95, judgment of 16 February 2000; *Panteleyenko v. Ukraine*, Application no. 11901/02, judgment of 29 June 2006; *S. and Marper v the United Kingdom*, Application nos. 30562/04 and 30566/04, judgment of 4 December 2008; *Z. v. Finland*, Application no. 22009/93, judgment of 25 February 1997; *Rotaru v. Romania*, Application no. 28341/954, judgment of 4 May 2000; *Cemalettin Canl v. Turkey*, Application no. 22427/04, judgment of 18 November 2008; *Segerstedt-Wiberg and others v. Sweden*, Application no. 62332/00, judgment of 6 June 2006; for cellular samples, fingerprints and DNA, see *Mc Veigh and others v. United Kingdom*, Application no. 8022/77, Commission decision of 18 March 1981; *Kinnunen v. Finland*, Application no. 18291/91, Commission decision of 13 October 1993; *S. and Marper v the United Kingdom*, Application nos. 30562/04 and 30566/04, judgment of 4 December 2008.

[64] For instance: *Liberty and others v. the United Kingdom*, Application no. 58234/00, judgment of 1 July 2008, para 56; *Weber and Saravia v. Germany*, Application no. 54934/00, admissibility decision of 29 June 2006, para 78; *P.G. and J.H. v. the United Kingdom*, Application no. 44787/98, judgment of 25 September 2001; *Allan v. the United Kingdom*, Application no. 48539/99, judgment of 5 November 2002, para 35; *Wood v. the United Kingdom*, Application no. 23414/02, judgment of 16 November 2004 and *Doerga v. Netherlands*, Application no. 50210/99, judgment of 27 April 2004; *Kopp v. Switzerland*, Application no. 23224/94, judgment of 25 March 1998; *Halford v. the United Kingdom*, Application no. 20605/92, judgment of 25 June 1997 and *Amann v. Switzerland*, Application no. 27798/95, judgment of 16 February 2000; *Kruslin v. France*, Application no. 11801/85, judgment of 24 April 1990; *Association for European Integration and Human Rights and Ekimdzhiev v. Bulgaria*, Application no. 62540/00, judgment of 28 June 2007.

[65] For instance: *Klass v. Germany*, Application no. 5029/71, judgment of 6 September 1978; *Weber and Saravia v. Germany*, Application no. 54934/00, admissibility decision of 29 June 2006, para 78; *Chalkley v. the United Kingdom*, Application no. 63831/00, judgment of 12 June 2003, para 24; *Lewis v. the United Kingdom*, Application no. 1303/02, judgment of 25 November 2003, para 18; *Khan v. the United Kingdom*, Application no. 35394/97, judgment of 12 May 2000, paras 25–28, and *Armstrong v. the United Kingdom*, Application no. 48521/99, judgment of 16 July 2002, para 19; *Hewitson v. the United Kingdom*, Application no. 50015/99, judgment of 27 May 2003, para 20; *Huvig v. France*, Application no. 11105/84, judgment of 24 April 1990, para 25; *Malone v. the United Kingdom*, Application no. 8691/79, judgment of 2 August 1984; *Valenzuela Contreras v. Spain*, Application no. 27671/95, judgment of 30 July 1998; *Allan v.*

images,[66] medical data,[67] DNA and fingerprints records[68]; personal information published on the internet[69] etc.

It is worth noting that by examining the scope, the ECtHR does not pay attention to the means by which personal data are collected, registered or released.[70] In cases related to access to personal data, the ECtHR generally admits a wide scope to applicants invoking this right, however, under the condition that the requested information contains personal information.[71] Whereas in the past the ECtHR focused on the private nature of the data at issue by examining whether the content of the data was related to the right to private life, the analysis of the data very closely connected to private life is less common nowadays.[72]

---

the United Kingdom, Application no. 48539/99, judgment of 5 November 2002; *P.G. and J.H. v. the United Kingdom,* Application no. 44787/98, judgment of 25 September 2001; *Peck v. the United Kingdom,* Application no. 44647/98, judgment of 28 January 2003, para 57; *Wisse v. France,* Application no. 71611/01, preliminary objection of 20 December 2005; *Perry v. the United Kingdom,* Application no. 63737/00, judgment of 17 July 2002; *Peck v. the United Kingdom,* Application no. 44647/98, judgment of 28 January 2003; *Bykov v. Russia,* Application no. 4378/02, judgment of 10 March 2009.

[66] For instance: *Von Hannover v. Germany,* Application no. 59320/00, judgment of 24 June 2004; *Sciacca v. Italy,* Application no. 50774/99, judgment of 11 January 2005; *Friedl v. Austria,* Application no. 15225/89, judgment of 31 January 1995; *Schüssel v. Austria,* Application no. 42409/98, judgment of 21 February 2002, para 2;

[67] For instance: *Z. v. Finland,* Application no. 22009/93, judgment of 25 February 1997; *M.S. v. Sweden,* Application no. 20837/92, judgment of 27 August 1997; *Gaskin v. the United Kingdom,* Application no. 10454/83, judgment of 7 July 1989; *Martin v. the United Kingdom,* Application no. 27533/95, admissibility decision of 28 February 1996; *Biriuk v. Lithuania,* Application no. 23373/03, judgment of 25 November 2008; *I. v. Finland,* Application no. 20511/03, judgment of 17 July 2008; *Panteleyenko v. Ukraine,* Application no. 11901/02, judgment of 29 June 2006.

[68] *S. and Marper v. the United Kingdom,* Application nos. 30562/04 and 30566/04, judgment of 4 December 2008.

[69] *K.U. v. Finland,* Application no. 2872/02, judgment of 2 December 2008.

[70] See for instance: *Bykov v. Russia,* Application no. 4378/02, judgment of 10 March 2009, para 79; according to Article 3 (1) Convention No. 108 is restricted to automated processing of personal data whereas Directive 95/46 applies to automatic and not automatic means of data processing (Article 3).

[71] *C.G. and others v. Bulgaria,* Application no. 1365/07, judgment of 24 April 2008; *Amann v. Switzerland,* Application no. 27798/95, judgment of 16 February 2000; *Rotaru v. Romania,* Application no. 28341/95, judgment of 4 May 2000; *Gaskin v. the United Kingdom,* Application no. 10454/83, judgment of 7 July 1989; to the limits of this right, see *Smith v. the United Kingdom,* Application no. 39658/05, admissibility decision of 4 January 2007.

[72] Compare case *Reyntjens v. Belgium,* Application no. 16810/90, admissibility decision of 9 September 1992, where the commission stated that passport information did not entail personal information raising private life concerns, and *S. and Marper v the United Kingdom,* Application nos. 30562/04 and 30566/04, judgment of 4 December 2008; for a detailed analysis of this development, see Siemen (2006), pp. 79–132.

In summary, the scope of Article 8 ECHR covers the following activities: storage, release as well as different forms of collection and processing of and access to personal data.[73]

All in all, the question as to whether the right in fact is covered by the guarantees of Article 8 is usually examined in the assessment of the interference.[74] The following case law therefore demonstrates fundamental principles which were developed over the last years.

c) Interferences

The interference is closely related to the scope and refers to it by "shaping" and defining its substance and limits.[75]

Except for the fact that according to Article 8 (2) ECHR the interference must be attributable to a public authority, the ECtHR neither developed an exhaustive definition of the notion of the interference, nor did it specify its requirements in detail over the last few years. In the majority of cases the Court applied a case-by-case approach.

However, the ECtHR increasingly seeks to support the weight of its judgments by stipulating general principles which are supposed to serve as guidelines for similar questions. Clarifying the existence of an interference is nevertheless important for the distinction between actions (or omissions) which interfere with the Convention and which therefore require justification, and activities which are not legally relevant to the Convention.[76] The recognition of a violation of a Convention right due to a failure to act may have effects on third parties, such as private actors. In this way the ECtHR can affirm an indirect secondary effect ("Drittwirkung") of the right at stake.[77]

The following examples of significant judgments, mainly including general principles, should illustrate the ECtHR's approach of what amounts to an interference in a data protection context.

aa) Surveillance and Unwanted Release of Personal Information

Unwanted surveillance can have an influence on an individual's physical and psychological integrity as protected by Article 8 ECHR. In this category, three types of cases occur in connection with data protection: Unwanted listening to and watching of individuals (surveillance), as well as unwanted publishing of personal

---

[73] See also: Ovey and White (2006), pp. 286–299; Grabenwarter (2009a), p. 201, para 10; Meyer-Ladewig (2006), Article 8, para 11-14a; Marauhn and Meljnik (2006), paras 29 and 39; Peters (2003), pp. 160–162.

[74] Grabenwarter (2009a), p. 210, para 25; Heselhaus and Nowak (2006), p. 623 para 31.

[75] Grabenwarter (2009a), p. 112, para 6; Heselhaus and Nowak (2006), p. 623 para 31.

[76] Grabenwarter (2009a), p. 112, para 6.

[77] Ibid.

information. Even if the first two types do not exclusively concern the right to protect personal data, surveillance measures affect components of it in any case, and have a strong influence on the ECtHR's interpretation of the right to data protection in the framework of Article 8 ECHR.

(1) Unwanted Listening

An early example of the protection offered by Article 8 ECHR against unwanted surveillance measures is the judgment in the case *Klass v. Germany* in 1978.[78] *Klass*, a German lawyer, filed a suit against security legislation enacted by Germany monitoring mail and telephone communication (the G-10 Act) in the aftermath of the terrorist threats of the 1970s.

The ECtHR used this case as an opportunity to stipulate basic principles balancing the state's secret surveillance powers against the rights of targeted individuals, in particular the right to be informed of the surveillance measures and the possibility of having recourse to the courts after termination of such measures.[79]

Before however discussing the guarantees of Article 8 ECHR, the Court had to clarify the applicants' victim status, as neither of the applicants had already been the subject of surveillance measures, and the ECHR does not permit individuals to complain against a law *in abstracto*.[80] Due to the secrecy of the measures in question, and the establishment of a system of surveillance under which all German citizens could potentially have their mail, post and telecommunications unknowingly monitored, the ECtHR found that it was intolerable that the guarantees of Article 8 ECHR could be circumvented by the simple fact that the person concerned was kept uninformed of its violation.[81] Therefore, the applicant could claim to be victim of a violation of Article 8 ECHR without proving that he had in fact been the subject of secret surveillance measures.[82]

The fact that *Klass* was allowed to allege a violation of the Convention's rights without proving the he had been the concrete target of the measure at stake plays an essential role, even today. It is not only important in surveillance cases, but also in the context of collective data processing measures where it seems to be impossible for an individual to demonstrate that precisely his/her personal data had been collected or processed.

Additionally the ECtHR declared that secret telephone surveillance and recording constitutes an interference with Article 8 ECHR. It stated that the *mere existence of the legislation* (G-10 Act) itself creates the danger of surveillance. This menace necessarily attacks freedom of communication between users of the postal and

[78] *Klass v. Germany*, Application no. 5029/71, judgment of 6 September 1978.

[79] *Klass v. Germany*, Application no. 5029/71, judgment of 6 September 1978, para 39.

[80] Ibid, paras 33 and 37.

[81] Ibid, paras 36 and 37.

[82] Ibid, para 38.

telecommunication services, and thereby constitutes an interference by a public authority with the exercise of the applicants' right according to Article 8 ECHR.[83]

More recently, the ECtHR confirmed this jurisdiction. In *Liberty and other organisations v. the United Kingdom*, the Court ruled on the lawfulness of the British Communication Act of 1985 which allowed, in principle, the interception of any telecommunication outside the British Islands between 1990 and 1997.[84] The applicant organisations alleged that during the period in question, their telephone, facsimile, e-mail and data communications (including legally privileged and confidential information) were intercepted by an electronic test facility operated by the British Ministry of Defence. Moreover, under the 1985 Act, the authorities had wide discretion to decide which communications (out of the total volume of those physically captured) were listened to or read. Indeed, section 6 of the 1985 Act obliged the Secretary of the State to make "arrangements" to ensure safeguards against abuse of power in the selection process for the examination, dissemination and storage of intercepted material, but those "arrangements" had not been contained in legislation, or otherwise made available to the public.[85] The ECtHR reiterates its finding in *Klass v. Germany* that the mere existence of secret monitoring legislation constitutes a threat of observation for all people who might be affected by this legislation.[86] This threat strikes at the guarantees of Article 8 ECHR and thereby amounts in itself to an interference, irrespective of any measures in fact taken against them.[87]

It is noteworthy in this context that the use of undercover agents to obtain information does not necessarily constitute an interference with Article 8 ECHR, as individuals engaged in a criminal act must therefore be aware that they are running the risk of encountering an undercover police officer whose task would, in fact, be to expose them.[88]

Yet, in general, the *mere existence of legislation* which allows secret monitoring constitutes an interference by a public authority, within the meaning of Article 8 ECHR. However, where the actual fact that interception has taken place is alleged and contested, the ECtHR requires applicants to demonstrate a "reasonable likelihood" that the measures had been actually applied to them.[89]

[83] Ibid, para 41.

[84] *Liberty and others v. the United Kingdom*, Application no. 58234/00, judgment of 1 July 2008, para 64.

[85] Ibid, para 66.

[86] *Liberty and others v. the United Kingdom*, Application no. 58234/00, judgment of 1 July 2008, para 56; see also: *Weber and Saravia v. Germany*, Application no. 54934/00, admissibility decision of 29 June 2006, para 78.

[87] *Liberty and others v. the United Kingdom*, Application no. 58234/00, judgment of 1 July 2008, para 56.

[88] *Lüdi v. Switzerland*, Application no. 12433/86, judgment of 15 June 1992, para 40.

[89] *Halford v. the United Kingdom*, Application no. 20605/92, judgment of 25 June 1997, para 58, and *Kennedy v. the United Kingdom*, Application no. 26839/05, judgment of 18 May 2010, para 123.

In addition to the existence of monitoring legislation, implementation measures, such as the installation of wiretapping instruments in an individual's house,[90] in a prison, (or prison cell)[91] or at the workplace,[92] or the interception of telephone calls,[93] interferes with the right to respect private life.[94] Legislation permitting public authorities to examine and monitor mail, telegraphic messages,[95] as well as the interception (unwanted listening) or monitoring of pager messages[96] or of workplace telephone or internet usage[97] moreover amounts to an interference with Article 8 ECHR.

(2) *Unwanted Watching and Recording in Public and Private Places*

Unwanted watching and recording in private or public places can also interfere with the right to respect for private life.[98] However, the latter will only interfere with Article 8 ECHR if the movements of the person concerned are recorded.[99] There are several cases in which the ECtHR was faced with the question as to whether monitoring or recording in public places constitutes an interference with Article 8 ECHR.

---

[90] *Chalkley v. the United Kingdom*, Application no. 63831/00, judgment of 12 June 2003, para 24; *Lewis v. the United Kingdom*, Application no. 1303/02, judgment of 25 November 2003, para 18; *Khan v. the United Kingdom*, Application no. 35394/97, judgment of 12 May 2000, paras 25–28, and *Armstrong v. the United Kingdom*, Application no. 48521/99, judgment of 16 July 2002, para 19; *Hewitson v. the United Kingdom*, Application no. 50015/99, judgment of 27 May 2003, para 20; *Huvig v. France*, Application no. 11105/84, judgment of 24 April 1990, para 25; *Klass and others v. Germany*, Application no. 5029/71, judgment of 6 September 1978, para 41; *Malone v. the United Kingdom*, Application no. 8691/79, judgment of 2 August 1984, para 64; *Valenzuela Contreras v. Spain*, Application no. 27671/95, judgment of 30 July 1998, para 46.

[91] *P.G. and J.H. v. the United Kingdom*, Application no. 44787/98, para 60 of 25 September 2001; *Allan v. the United Kingdom*, Application no. 48539/99, para 35 of 5 November 2002; *Wood v. the United Kingdom*, Application no. 23414/02, para 33 of 16 November 2004 and *Doerga v. Netherlands*, Application no. 50210/99, para 43 of 27 April 2004.

[92] *Kopp v. Switzerland*, Application no. 23224/94, judgment of 25 March 1998, para 50; *Halford v. the United Kingdom*, Application no. 20605/92, judgment of 25 June 1997, paras 44 and 45, and *Amann v. Switzerland*, Application no. 27798/95, judgment of 16 February 2000, para 45.

[93] *Kopp v. Switzerland*, Application no. 23224/94, judgment of 25 March 2003, para 53.

[94] Moreham (2008), pp. 44, 53.

[95] *Klass and others v. Germany*, Application no. 5029/71, judgment of 6 September 1978, para 41.

[96] *Taylor-Sabori v. the United Kingdom*, Application no. 47114/99, judgment of 22 October 2002, para 19.

[97] *Copland v. the United Kingdom*, Application no.62617/00, judgment of 3 April 2007, para 42.

[98] *Allan v. the United Kingdom*, Application no. 48539/99, judgment of 5 November 2002, para 35; *Khan v. the United Kingdom*, Application no. 35394/97, judgment of 12 May 2000, paras 26–28.

[99] Moreham (2008), pp. 44, 54. For video surveillance in public places by public authorities, see also: Opinion on video surveillance in public places by public authorities and the protection of human rights, adopted by the Venice Commission at its 70th plenary session (16–17 March 2007), Study no. 404/2006, Council of Europe, Strasbourg, 23 March 2007.

In *Perry v. the United Kingdom*, the court made a distinction between, "...the monitoring of the actions of an individual in a public place by the use of photographic equipment which does not record the visual data [...] and the recording of the data and the systematic or permanent nature of the record."[100] Only the latter constituted an interference with the individual's private life.

In *P.G. and J.H. v. the United Kingdom*, a recording of the applicants' voices was made while they answered questions in a public area of a police station as police officers listened to them.[101] This recording was made for further analysis and therefore it was regarded as the processing of personal data about them amounting to an interference with their right to respect for their private life.[102] The ECtHR emphasised that, "There are a number of elements relevant to a consideration of whether a person's private life is concerned by measures effected outside a person's home or private premises. Since there are occasions when people knowingly or intentionally involve themselves in activities which are or may be recorded or reported in a public manner, a person's reasonable expectations[103] as to privacy may be a significant, although not necessarily conclusive, factor. A person who walks down the street will, inevitably, be visible to any member of the public who is also present. Monitoring by technological means of the same public scene (for example, a security guard viewing through closed-circuit television) is of a similar character."

Private-life concerns may arise, however, if any systematic or permanent record comes into existence of such material from the public domain.[104]

Regardless of the restriction to the recording requirement and the reduced privacy expectation in public places, the ECtHR recognises that there is, "... a zone of interaction of a person with others, even in a public context, which may fall within the scope of "private life."[105]

In *Peck v. the United Kingdom*, the disclosure to the media for broadcast use of video footage of the applicant whose suicide attempt was filmed on CCTV

---

[100] *Perry v. the United Kingdom*, Application no. 63737/00, judgment of 17 July 2002, para 38. See also para 41: "Whether or not he was aware of the security cameras running in the custody suite, there is no indication that the applicant had any expectation that footage was being taken of him within the police station for use in a video identification procedure and, potentially, as evidence prejudicial to his defence at trial. [...] The permanent recording of the footage and its inclusion in a montage for further use may therefore be regarded as the processing or collecting of personal data about the applicant."

[101] *P.G. and J.H. v. the United Kingdom*, Application no. 44787/98, judgment of 25 September 2001.

[102] *P.G. and J.H. v. the United Kingdom*, Application no. 44787/98, judgment of 25 September 2001, para 59.

[103] To the term "reasonable expectations" see Gómez-Arostegui (2005), pp. 153–200.

[104] *P.G. and J.H. v. the United Kingdom*, Application no. 44787/98, judgment of 25 September 2001, para 57.

[105] *P.G. and J.H. v. the United Kingdom*, Application no. 44787/98, judgment of 25 September 2001, para 56. See also: *Peck v. the United Kingdom*, Application no. 44647/98, judgment of 28 January 2003, para 57; *Von Hannover v. Germany*, Application no. 59320/00, judgment of 24 June 2004, para 50, and *Sciacca v. Italy*, Application no. 50774/99, judgment of 11 January 2005, para 29.

cameras,[106] amounted to an interference with the applicant's private life, despite the fact that he was filmed in a public place at the time of the attempt.[107]

To determine to what degree the state has interfered with Article 8 ECHR in cases involving the surveillance of public places, the ECtHR distinguishes between surveillance for security reasons and surveillance for unpredictable other reasons.[108] When deciding whether unwanted watching in public places represents an interference with Article 8 ECHR, the forseeability of the use of the surveillance measure is of fundamental importance. The more the person concerned expects not to be monitored in public, the more seriously the person's rights are abridged.

As regards the use of new techniques for surveillance, the question of whether the use of a Global Positioning System (GPS)[109] to track the movements of suspects in the public sphere constitutes an interference, was recently subject to the case *Uzun v. Germany*.[110] The applicant, Mr. *Uzun*, was suspected of having participated in bomb attacks for which an organisation pursuing the armed combat of the Red Army Fraction had claimed responsibility. For surveillance purposes, a GPS receiver had been built into the car of the applicant's accomplice to observe his and *Uzun's* movement. The data collected via GPS surveillance were later used in trial against both. The ECtHR first noted that the collection of data on the applicant to obtain information on the movements of the applicant and his accomplice interfered with their rights protected by Article 8 (1) ECHR.[111] Surveillance via GPS leads to the systematic collection and storage of data revealing in this case the

---

[106] Close circuit television cameras.

[107] *Peck v. the United Kingdom*, Application no. 44647/98, judgment of 28 January 2003. It is noteworthy that the protection of correspondence within Article 8 ECHR extends to all types of communication, whether or not taking place in a private, public or in professional context. The ECtHR stipulated that Article 8 ECHR does not use, as it does for the word "life", any adjective to qualify the word "correspondence", therefore no such distinction is made. See *Niemietz v. Germany*, Application no. 13710/88, judgment of 16 September 1992, para 32. In this context, opening and censoring prisoner's correspondence constitutes an interference with the right to respect for correspondence according to Article 8 ECHR.

[108] *Wisse v. France*, Application no. 71611/01, preliminary objection of 20 December 2005, para 26; *Perry v. the United Kingdom*, Application no. 63737/00, judgment of 17 July 2002, paras 41–42; *Peck v. the United Kingdom*, Application no. 44647/98, judgment of 28 January 2003, paras 59–62.

[109] GPS is defined as "a radio navigation system working with the help of satellites. It allows the continuous location, without lapse of time, of objects equipped with a GPS receiver anywhere on earth, with a maximum tolerance of 50 metres at the time. It does not comprise any visual or acoustical surveillance. As opposed to transmitters, its use does not necessitate the knowledge of where approximately the person to be located can be found.", compare *Uzun v. Germany*, Application no. 35623/05, judgment of 2 September 2010, para 13.

[110] *Uzun v. Germany*, Application no. 35623/05, judgment of 2 September 2010, paras 41–53.

[111] The GPS receiver was placed into a car belonging to a third person (*Uzun's* accomplice) and not into the applicant's car, however, the use of the GPS receiver to obtain information on both suspects consequently constituted an interference with the rights of both, *Uzun v. Germany*, Application no. 35623/05, judgment of 2 September 2010, paras 49–50.

applicant's whereabouts and movements in public places.[112] The data were further used to establish patterns on the applicant's movements. The Court argued that, although the GPS surveillance "is by its very nature to be distinguished from other methods of visual or acoustical surveillance which are, as a rule, more susceptible of interfering with a person's right to respect for private life, because they disclose more information on a person's conduct, opinions or feelings", the systematic collection and storage of data disclosing the whereabouts and movements, mentioned above, amounted to an interference.[113]

In conclusion, unwanted watching and recording in private or public places can interfere with the right to respect for private life. It has to be clarified that whereas recording of the movements of the individual concerned may represent (under the conditions mentioned above) an interference[114] – the use of security cameras per se, whether in public streets or on premises where they serve a legitimate and foreseeable purpose, does not amount to an interference with Article 8 ECHR.[115]

(3) Unwanted Publishing of Personal Information

The unwanted publishing of information principally concerns two problems: the publication of images and the unwanted release of medical information.

The obligation includes the responsibility of the Member States to abstain from the release of pictures of individuals. The ECtHR developed three criteria to assess if disseminating images interferes with Article 8 ECHR: In the above mentioned cases *Peck v. the United Kingdom* and *Perry v. the United Kingdom* the Court asks firstly if publication of the applicant's photos was foreseeable at the time of recording.[116] Secondly, in the *Peck* case, the ECtHR also takes the mental condition of the applicant into consideration. It emphasised that he, "...was in a public street but he was not there for the purposes of participating in any public event and he was not a public figure. It was late at night, he was deeply perturbed and in a state of distress."[117] Finally the

[112] *Uzun v. Germany*, Application no. 35623/05, judgment of 2 September 2010, para 51.

[113] *Uzun v. Germany*, Application no. 35623/05, judgment of 2 September 2010, para 52.

[114] In *Friedl v. Austria*, Application no. 15225/89, judgment of 31 January 1995, para 48, the Commission stressed three factors when assessing if there was an interference with Article 8 in a case concerning a photograph taken on a demonstration: "*whether the taking of photographs amounted to an intrusion into the individual's privacy, whether it related to privacy matters or public incidents, and whether the material thus obtained was envisaged for a limited use or was likely to be made available to the general public*".

[115] *Perry v. the United Kingdom*, Application no. 63737/00, judgment of 17 July 2002, para 40.

[116] *Peck v. the United Kingdom*, Application no. 44647/98, judgment of 28 January 2003, para 62, and *Perry v. the United Kingdom*, Application no. 63737/00, judgment of 17 July 2002, para 38.

[117] *Peck v. the United Kingdom*, Application no. 44647/98, judgment of 28 January 2003, para 62, further, the ECtHR adds: "While he was walking in public wielding a knife, he was not later charged with any offence. The actual suicide attempt was neither recorded nor therefore disclosed. However, footage of the immediate aftermath was recorded and disclosed by the Council directly to the public in its CCTV News publication. In addition, the footage was disclosed to the media for

ECtHR assesses the way in which the images were taken. All in all, the foreseeability of the recording, the circumstances and the way in which images are recorded must be considered when publishing images of a person in public.

As to the disclosure of medical information, as a general rule, release of such information usually constitutes an interference with Article 8 ECHR due to the high sensitivity of the information at stake.[118] Dissemination of medical records without the consent of the person concerned during court proceedings, for instance, clearly interferes with the right to private life, as the release of such information widens the circle of people acquainted with the details of a disease, making it possible that very private information comes into the public sphere.[119]

With regard to the notion of "publication", the ECHR Commission[120] noted in *Lupker v. Netherlands* that if photographs were kept in police or other official archives, and were used exclusively for the purpose of the identification of the offenders in the criminal proceedings against the applicants, and there was no suggestion that they have been made available to the general public or used for any other purpose, then they were not taken in a way which constitutes an intrusion upon the applicant's privacy.[121]

Generally, if the state decides to publish photos or video material of individuals, it has to pay attention to the circumstances in which the material was taken, the foreseeability of publication at the time of recording and the situation in which the individuals concerned were filmed.

bb) The Right to Be Free from Gathering, Collection, Use and Storing of Personal Information

(1) Gathering, Use and Storing of Personal Information

The first case that is classified as one of the key cases in developing a right to data protection within the framework of Article 8 ECHR while being part of the right to

---

further broadcasting and publication purposes. Those media included the audiovisual media [...] The applicant's identity was not adequately, or in some cases not at all, masked in the photographs and footage so published and broadcast. He was recognised by certain members of his family and by his friends, neighbours and colleagues".

[118] See for instance, medical data published in newspapers or court proceeding: *Panteleyenko v. Ukraine*, Application no. 11901/02, judgment of 29 June 2006, paras 56–58; *Z. v. Finland*, Application no. 22009/93, judgment of 25 February 1997, para 71; *M.S. v. Sweden*, Application no. 20837/92, judgment of 27 August 1997, paras 33–35; *C.C. v. Spain*, Application no. 1425/06, judgment of 6 October 2009, para 26.

[119] *Panteleyenko v. Ukraine*, Application no. 11901/02, judgment of 29 June 2006, paras 56–58.

[120] Before the entry into force of Protocol No. 11 in 1998 which changed, amongst other, the procedural framework of the ECtHR, the ECHR was also overseen by a Commission which decided on the admissibility of complaints by individuals; it is referred to as ECHR Commission in the following.

[121] *Lupker v. Netherlands*, Application no. 18395/91, judgment of 7 December 1992, para 5.

respect for private life, is a case dealing with the storing and usage of personal information.[122] In *Leander v. Sweden*, the applicant started to work as a temporary replacement in a post of museum technician at the naval museum on a Swedish military base. After a few days of working he was told to leave his workplace as the employer obtained secret information from the Swedish secret service. After this termination, the applicant requested to be informed of the exact reasons for his sudden dismissal, but they were withheld.

The ECtHR stated in 1987, "It is uncontested that the secret police-register contained information relating to Mr. Leander's private life. Both the *storing and the release* of such information, which were coupled with a refusal to allow Mr. Leander an opportunity to refute it, amounted to an interference with his right to respect for private life as guaranteed by Article 8 § 1."[123]

In subsequent cases, the ECtHR confirms this interpretation by reiterating that, "...both the storing by a public authority of information relating to an individual's private life and the use of it," amount to interference with Article 8 ECHR, even if the information contained no sensitive information and had possibly never been consulted.[124] In connection with the increasing storing of telecommunications data,[125] the ECtHR regularly refers to the *Amann v. Switzerland* case, and clarified for instance in *Copland v. the United Kingdom* that the collection and storage of telephone data, especially the numbers dialled, as well as information relating to e-mail and internet usage, without the knowledge of the persons concerned, also interferes with Article 8 ECHR.[126]

Even where personal information has not been collected by any intrusive or secret means, these files nevertheless fall within the scope of Article 8 ECHR.[127] In *P.G. and J.H. v. the United Kingdom* the ECtHR takes into consideration the definition of data within Convention No. 108. Article 2 Convention No. 108 classifies personal data as, "any information relating to an identified or identifiable individual."[128] Then the Court refers to the case *Amann v. Switzerland*, where the storing of information about the applicant on a card in a file was found to be an

---

[122] *Leander v. Sweden*, Application no. 9248/81, judgment of 26 March 1987.

[123] *Leander v. Sweden*, Application no. 9248/81, judgment of 26 March 1987, para 48 (emphasis added).

[124] *Amann v. Switzerland*, Application no. 27798/95, judgment of 16 February 2000, para 65, and *Panteleyenko v. Ukraine*, Application no. 11901/02, judgment of 29 June 2006, para 56; *S. and Marper v the United Kingdom*, Application nos. 30562/04 and 30566/04, judgment of 4 December 2008, para 67.

[125] For instance through the Date Retention Directive, compare Chap. D III 1.

[126] *Copland v. the United Kingdom*, Application no. 62617/00, judgment of 3 April 2007, para 44.

[127] *P.G. and J.H. v. the United Kingdom*, Application no. 44787/98, judgment of 25 September 2001, para 57. The Court refers to the case *Rotaru v. Romania*, Application no. 28341, judgment of 4 May 2000, paras 43–44.

[128] *P.G. and J.H. v. the United Kingdom*, Application no. 44787/98, judgment of 25 September 2001, para 57.

interference with Article 8 ECHR, although it contained no sensitive information, and had possibly never been consulted.[129]

In addition to the storing of communication information, the retention of *cellular samples, DNA profiles* and *fingerprints* constitutes an interference with the right to respect for private life. Since *Mc Veigh and others v. the United Kingdom*, the question of whether the retention of fingerprints alone amounts to an interference was highly controversial.[130] At that time, the question was left open by the ECtHR. A subsequent decision did not recognise the retention of fingerprints as an interference with Article 8 ECHR.[131] Recently, in *S. and Marper v. the United Kingdom* the ECtHR clarified that fingerprints contain exclusive information about an individual allowing for precise identification in a wide range of circumstances.[132] Retention of this information without the consent of the individual concerned cannot be regarded as neutral or irrelevant.[133] Accordingly, the ECtHR considered, "...that the retention of fingerprints on the authorities' records in connection with an identified or identifiable individual may in itself give rise, notwithstanding their objective and irrefutable character, to important private-life concerns."[134]

Finally, both the retention of cellular samples and DNA profiles on the one hand, and the retention of fingerprints on the other, constitutes an interference.[135]

The different methods of gathering and collecting personal information may also interfere with the right to private life.[136] Files or data gathered by security services or other authorities of the state,[137] as well as the metering and subsequent transfer of data obtained in this way to public authorities,[138] constitutes an interference with the right to respect for private life.

---

[129] *Amann v. Switzerland*, Application no. 27798/95, judgment of 16 February 2000, paras 65–67.

[130] *Mc Veigh and others v. United Kingdom*, Application no. 8022/77, Commission decision of 18 March 1981.

[131] *Kinnunen v. Finland*, Application no. 18291/91, Commission decision of 13 October 1993.

[132] *S. and Marper v the United Kingdom*, Application nos. 30562/04 and 30566/04, judgment of 4 December 2008, para 84; see also Beattie (2009).

[133] *S. and Marper v the United Kingdom*, Application nos. 30562/04 and 30566/04, judgment of 4 December 2008, para 84.

[134] *S. and Marper v the United Kingdom*, Application nos. 30562/04 and 30566/04, judgment of 4 December 2008, para 85.

[135] *S. and Marper v the United Kingdom*, Application nos. 30562/04 and 30566/04, judgment of 4 December 2008.

[136] *Leander v. Sweden*, Application no. 9248/81, judgment of 26 March 1987, para 48; *S. and Marper v. the United Kingdom*, Application nos. 30562/04 and 30566/04, judgment of 4 December 2008, para 67; Siemen (2006), p. 135 et seq.

[137] *Amann v. Switzerland*, Application no. 27798/95, judgment of 16 February 2000, para 65; *Panteleyenko v. Ukraine*, Application no. 11901/02, judgment of 29 June 2006, para 56; *Z. v Finland*, Application no. 22009/93, judgment of 25 February 1997 and *Rotaru v. Romania*, Application no. 28341/954, judgment of 4 May 2000.

[138] *Malone* v. *the United Kingdom*, Application no. 8691/79, judgment of 2 August 1984, para 84.

Further, the ECtHR deals with (restricted) disclosure of sensitive data and systematic collection and storage of information by public authorities.[139] In this context, even public information can fall within the scope of private life, "...where it is systematically collected and stored in files held by the authorities".[140]

(2) Transfer of Personal Data

Inextricably linked with the storing of personal data is the subsequent use, and in some cases, the transfer of information obtained. In *Malone v. the United Kingdom*, the British post office, and the British Telephone Company, respectively, made use of a "meter check", a device which registers the numbers dialed and the time and duration of the call on a particular telephone, to collect telephone data. These data were released to the British police without the consent of the subscriber. The ECtHR stated that, "...the Court does not accept [...] that the use of data obtained from metering, whatever the circumstances and purposes, cannot give rise to an issue under Article 8. The records of metering contain information, in particular the numbers dialed, which is an integral element in the communications made by telephone." Consequently, release of that information to the police without the consent of the subscriber also amounted to an interference with the right to private life.[141]

Another type of interference is the transfer of medical records containing highly personal and sensitive data to other authorities. The ECtHR refers to the purpose limitation principle in this context. Disclosing medical data to another authority without the patient's consent interferes with Article 8 ECHR even though the information may remain confidential.[142] In *M.S. v. Sweden* a patient's records had been transferred to another office due to the fact that the applicant enacted a compensation claim.[143] The ECtHR held that the transfer of the medical information to the authority responsible for compensation claims did not serve the same purpose as the storing of the information in question to assure medical treatment at the clinic. The fact that the applicant had sought treatment at a clinic did not mean that she would consent to the data being disclosed to another authority, or to a wider circle of public servants.[144] By initiating compensation proceedings against the alleged violation, the applicant does not waive his/her right to confidentiality.[145]

The next decision refers to the transmission of data to other authorities and contains important statements relating to the aforementioned context of the

---

[139] *Z. v. Finland*, Application no. 22009/93, judgment of 25 February 1997 and *Rotaru v. Romania*, Application no. 28341/954, judgment of 4 May 2000.

[140] *Rotaru v. Romania*, Application no. 28341/954, judgment of 4 May 2000, para 43; *Panteleyenko v. Ukraine*, Application no. 11901/02, judgment of 29 June 2006, para 56.

[141] *Malone v. the United Kingdom*, Application no. 8691/79, judgment of 2 August 1984, para 84.

[142] *M.S. v. Sweden*, Application no. 20837/92, judgment of 17 August 1997, para 35.

[143] *M.S. v. Sweden*, Application no. 20837/92, judgment of 17 August 1997.

[144] Ibid, para 35.

[145] Ibid, para 32.

cooperation between the different AFSJ actors. In *Weber and Saravia v. Germany*, the ECtHR was faced with an amendment of the German G 10 act extending the powers of the Federal Intelligence Service with regard to the recording of telecommunications in the course of so-called strategic monitoring, as well as the use of personal data obtained thereby, and their transmission to other authorities.[146] Whereas the same legislation, in its initial version, was already the subject of the case *Klass v. Germany*, the ECtHR goes a step further than in this earlier judgment. While reiterating the acceptance of an interference through the mere existence of monitoring legislation, it additionally holds that the *transmission of data* to other authorities and the *subsequent use by them* enlarges the group of individuals with knowledge of the personal data intercepted and can therefore lead to investigations being instituted against the persons concerned.[147] This danger constitutes a *further separate interference* with the applicants' rights under Article 8 ECHR.[148]

cc) Summary of Interferences Within the Framework of Negative Obligations

Summarising, within the scope of negative obligations, the following activities constitute a separate interference with Article 8 ECHR:

- Measures of secret surveillance and recording (e.g. *Klass v. Germany* and *Liberty and others v. the United Kingdom*);
- The mere existence of monitoring legislation (e.g. *Klass v. Germany*);
- The implementation measures of monitoring legislation, such as the installation of wiretapping instruments in an individual's house, in a prison or prison cell, or at the workplace, or the interception of telephone calls (e.g. *Khan v. the United Kingdom* or *Kopp v. Switzerland*);
- The interception via GPS, (*Uzun v. Germany*);
- The recording of a person's voice for further analysis (e.g. *P.G. and J.H. v. the United Kingdom*);
- The unwanted watching and recording in private or even public places, in the latter case, only if recorded (e.g. *Perry v. the United Kingdom*). General rule: The more the person concerned expects not to be monitored in public, the more serious the interference;
- The dissemination of photos or videos if not foreseeable at the time of shooting (e.g. *Peck v. the United Kingdom*): the circumstances in which the material was taken, the foreseeability of dissemination at the time of recording and the situation in which the persons concerned were photographed/filmed have to be taken into account;

[146] *Weber and Saravia v. Germany*, Application no. 54934/00, admissibility decision of 29 June 2006.

[147] Ibid, para 79.

[148] Ibid, para 79.

- The omission to prevent the dissemination of photos or videos taken in a private context (e.g. *Peck v. the United Kingdom*);
- The dissemination of medical records (e.g. *Z. v. Finland*);
- The collection, retention and storing of personal information (including telephone data or information relating to e-mail and internet usage), as well as its release, whereby even public information can fall within the scope of private life where it is systematically collected and stored in files held by the authorities (e.g. *Rotaru v. Romania*);
- The retention of cellular samples, DNA profiles and fingerprints (e.g. *Marper v. the United Kingdom*);
- The different methods to gather and to collect personal information (e.g. *Weber and Saravia v. Germany*), and
- The transfer of personal data to third parties (e.g. *Malone v. the United Kingdom* or *Weber and Saravia v. Germany*).

dd) Interferences with Regard to Positive Obligations: The Denying of the Right to Access Personal Data

In the context of positive obligation cases, i.e. cases in which the state interferes with Article 8 ECHR by omitting to do something, the denying of the access to personal data plays an important role.

Personal information such as data stored in public files, data about an individual's early development, medical data, information about risks to one's health resulting from environmental pollution, information permitting to asses risks resulting from participation in nuclear tests or tests including toxic chemicals can contain information which might be of vital interest for individuals concerned.

In this context, the most delicate question for states regarding the right of access is surely the question of releasing information stored in secret security files. In this regard, already in *Leander v. Sweden*, the refusal to allow the applicant an opportunity to refute raised allegations which were based on secret service information amounted to an interference with Article 8 ECHR. In this case, the ECtHR had not yet based its decision on the fact that access had been denied, as shown by its subsequent clarification that the right of access to data kept in secret service files as such is not enshrined in the ECHR, but nevertheless considered it to be a potential element of an interference.[149]

In *C.G. and others v. Bulgaria* the ECtHR elucidates that when a state takes a decision to the detriment of an individual on national security grounds basing itself on secret service information, the person concerned must at least be able to challenge the assertion that national security is at stake.[150] An independent

[149] *Leander v. Sweden*, Application no. 9248/81, judgment of 26 March 1987, paras 48, 59 and 67.
[150] *C.G. and others v. Bulgaria*, Application no. 1365/07, judgment of 24 April 2008, para 40.

authority or court must be able to assess whether the invocation of the concept of national security has no reasonable basis in the facts or reveals an interpretation of national security that is unlawful or contrary to common sense and arbitrary.[151]

Twenty years after the *Leander v. Sweden* decision, in the case *Segerstedt-Wilberg and others v. Sweden* the ECtHR clarified this position by emphasising that the Court considers it as established that the refusal to advise the applicants of the full extent to which information was being kept about them on a security police register amounted to an interference with Article 8 ECHR.[152]

The refusal to grant access to information concerning an individual's origin, medical data or information related to other risks to the individual's health may also interfere with the right to private life.

In one of the first cases related to this question, in *Gaskin v. the United Kingdom* dealing with access to childhood social service records, the ECtHR clearly stipulates that such information is undeniably related to private and family life and that the question of access thereto falls within the scope of Article 8 ECHR. However, it concluded that by refusing the applicant complete access to the records, the United Kingdom can not have "interfered" with Article 8 ECHR. Therefore the Court went directly to the justification and analysed whether there had been a positive obligation for the state to grant access.[153]

Consequently, when it is questionable whether a state has to allow access to personal data, the ECtHR directly examines whether or not such a positive obligation exists and if a fair balance had to be struck between the general interest of the community and the interests of the individual.

With regard to medical data and information related to the risks to an individual's health mentioned above, the Court applies the same approach.[154]

d) Justification

According to Article 8 (2) ECHR, the interference with the right to private life must satisfy three conditions to be considered legal: it must be in accordance with the law, it must pursue one or more of the legitimate aims referred to in paragraph 2 and

---

[151] Ibid.

[152] *Segerstedt-Wiberg and others v. Sweden*, Application no. 62332/00, judgment of 6 June 2006, para 99.

[153] *Gaskin v. the United Kingdom*, Application no. 10454/83, judgment of 7 July 1989, paras 41–42; see for a similar case: *M.G. v. the United Kingdom*, Application no. 39393/98, judgment of 24 September 2002, para 27.

[154] *Martin v. the United Kingdom*, Application no. 27533/95, admissibility decision of 28 February 1996; *K.H. and others v. Slovakia*, Application no. 32881/04, judgment of 28 April 2009, paras 44–46; *McGinley and Egan v. the United Kingdom*, Application nos. 21825/93 and 23414/94, judgment of 9 June 1998; *Roche v. the United Kingdom*, Application no. 32555/96, judgment of 19 October 2005; *Guerra and others v. Italy*, Application no. 14967/89, judgment of 19 February 1998.

it must be necessary in a democratic society in order to achieve the aim or aims.[155] These aims can be the interests of national security, public safety or the economic well-being of the country, the prevention of disorder or crime, the protection of health or morals, or the protection of the rights and freedoms of others. Generally, the ECtHR examines very carefully the question of justification carrying out a detailed proportionality assessment in cases related to data protection issues.

aa) In accordance with the Law

To be in accordance with the law, the interference in question must have some basis in domestic law.[156] In addition, this basis must be adequately accessible: the citizen must be able to have an indication as to whether his behaviour is adequate in the circumstances of the legal rules applicable to a given case.[157] A norm cannot be regarded as a law unless it is formulated with sufficient precision to enable the citizen to regulate his/her conduct: the individual must be able to foresee – if need be with appropriate advice –, to a degree that is reasonable in the situation, the consequences which a given action may entail.[158] The use of indefinite legal terms/ concepts does not conflict with Article 8 ECHR as long as they are further defined by "settled case-law" [159] specifying those terms and as long as they are not "deduced from a wide construction of statutory provisions or court decisions".[160] Consequently the impugned measures refer additionally to the quality of law, requiring that the law be accessible to the person concerned, who must moreover be able to foresee its consequences for him.Finally, the measure must be compatible with the rule of law.[161] The notion "in accordance with the law" implies conditions which go well beyond the mere existence of some legal basis in domestic law.[162]

155 *Weber and Saravia v. Germany*, Application no. 54934/00, admissibility decision of 29 June 2006, para 80, *Liberty and others v. the United Kingdom*, Application no. 58234/00, judgment of 1 July 2008, para 58.

156 The wording in Articles 9, 10 and 11 ECHR differs from the wording "in accordance with the law". In these articles the formulation "prescribed by the law" has been chosen. The ECtHR clarified that both formulations have to be interpreted in an identical way, as a different interpretation could lead to different conclusions in respect of the same interference. See *Silver v. the United Kingdom*, Application no. 5947/72 and others, judgment of 25 March 1983, para 85.

157 Ovey and White (2006), p. 224.

158 *Silver v. the United Kingdom*, Application no. 5947/72 and others, judgment of 25 March 1983, paras 85–88.

159 *Huvig v. France*, Application no. 11105/84, judgment of 24 April 1990, para 28, and *Kruslin v. France*, Application no. 11801/85, judgment of 24 April 1990, para 35.

160 *Valenzuela Contreras v. Spain*, Application no. 27671/95, judgment of 30 July 1998, para 57, and *Kopp v. Switzerland*, Application no. 23244/94, judgment of 25 March 1998, paras 60 and 73.

161 *Kopp v. Switzerland*, Application no. 23244/94, judgment of 25 March 1998, para 55.

162 *Amann v. Switzerland*, Application no. 27798/95, judgment of 16 February 2000, para 55.

(1) Basis in Domestic Law

The ECtHR applies a wide margin of interpretation of the term "law".[163] The expression within the meaning of the ECHR refers back to national law, including rules of public international law applicable in the state concerned.[164] It covers not only statute but also unwritten law.[165] "Law" in the expression "in accordance with the law" has always been understood in its "substantive" sense, not in its "formal" one.[166] Moreover, it includes enactments of lower rank than statues.[167]

Additionally, the Court's power to review compliance with domestic law is limited and it is in the first place for the national authorities, particularly the courts, to interpret and apply that law.[168] However, the limits of this power are not always easy to set.[169] While the ECtHR occasionally examines compliance of the legal basis with domestic law in general, the specific examination remains with national courts.[170]

In the data protection context, a special problem regarding the "extraterritoriality" of the basis in domestic law could arise concerning the monitoring of international wireless telecommunications, i.e. telecommunications "which are not effected via fixed telephone lines, but, for example, via satellite or radio relay links".[171] Signals from foreign countries are monitored by interception sites situated in one state which subsequently uses the collected data for its own purposes.

In *Weber and Saravia v. Germany*, the ECtHR was faced with the question whether such a form of monitoring constitutes a valid statutory basis in domestic law because the interception might have interfered illegally with the sovereignty of the foreign states in which the person being monitored resided.[172] The Strasbourg Court briefly comments that signals emitted from foreign countries are monitored

---

[163] Siemen (2006), p. 141.

[164] *Weber and Saravia v. Germany*, Application no. 54934/00, admissibility decision of 29 June 2006, para 87 (with further references).

[165] *Sunday Times v. the United Kingdom*, Application no. 6538/74, judgment of 26 April 1979, para 47.

[166] *Huvig v. France*, Application no. 11105/84, judgment of 24 April 1990, para 28.

[167] *De Wilde, Ooms and Versyp v. Belgium*, Application no. 2832/66 and others, judgment of 18 June 1997, para 93, and *Huvig v. France*, Application no. 11105/84, judgment of 24 April 1990, para 28: "*In a sphere covered by the written law, the "law" is the enactment in force as the competent courts have interpreted it in the light, if necessary, of any new practical developments*".

[168] *Barthold v. Germany*, Application no. 8734/79, judgment of 25 March 1985, para 48, and *Chappell v. the United Kingdom*, Application no. 10461/83, judgment of 30 March 1989, para 54.

[169] Siemen (2006), p. 141.

[170] See for an exhaustive review of the compliance with domestic law: *Chappell v. the United Kingdom*, Application no. 10461/83, judgment of 30 March 1989, paras 52 et seq.; *Kopp v. Switzerland*, Application no. 23244/94, judgment of 25 March 1998, paras 62 et seq.; or *Craxi v. Italy*, Application no. 25337/94, judgment of 17 July 2003, paras 77 et seq.

[171] *Weber and Saravia v. Germany*, Application no. 54934/00, admissibility decision of 29 June 2006, para 88.

[172] *Weber and Saravia v. Germany*, Application no. 54934/00, admissibility decision of 29 June 2006, paras 83–88.

by interception sites situated on German territory and the data collected are used in Germany and therefore the territorial sovereignty of foreign States as protected in public international law is not infringed.[173]

(2) Quality of the Law

To specify the first criterion within the justification's examination, the ECtHR developed further criteria, such as compliance with the rule of law as well as accessibility and foreseeability of the legal basis in domestic law.

Compliance with the rule of law not only means a superficial connection to the roots of the rule of law, moreover, the phrase implies – and that follows from the object and purpose of Article 8 – that "there must be a measure of legal protection in domestic law against arbitrary interferences by public authorities with the rights safeguarded by paragraph 1 Article 8".[174] Two other criteria with which domestic law has to comply are accessibility and foreseeability.

The first principle usually does not meet major problems. However, for instance the non-publication of a domestic act interferes with the accessibility criterion.[175]

In addition, in case a law confers discretion, it must indicate the scope of that discretion, although the ECtHR recognises "the impossibility of attaining absolute certainty in the framing of laws and the risk that the search for certainty may entail excessive rigidity".[176]

(3) Foreseeability

With regard to data protection, situations in which executive power is exercised in secret are commonly occurring. The threat of arbitrariness is apparent. To comply nonetheless with the requirement of the quality of law, the law's foreseeability plays a key role.[177] Precise formulations which enable an individual to regulate his behavior and to foresee the consequences which a given action may entail – to a degree that is reasonable in the circumstances – are most important.[178] Individuals to whom a law applies must be able to predict its application.

Where the contested measure takes place in secret, the criterion of foreseeability must be seen in this context: The ECtHR emphasises that especially in the context of

---

[173] *Weber and Saravia v. Germany*, Application no. 54934/00, admissibility decision of 29 June 2006, para 88.

[174] *Malone v. the United Kingdom*, Application no. 8691/79, judgment of 2 August 1984, para 67.

[175] *Silver v. the United Kingdom*, Application no. 5947/72 and others, judgment of 25 March 1983, para 87.

[176] *Silver v. the United Kingdom*, Application no. 5947/72 and others, judgment of 25 March 1983, para 88.

[177] Siemen (2006), p. 147.

[178] *Sunday Times v. the United Kingdom*, Application no. 6538/74, judgment of 26 April 1979, para 49.

secret measures of surveillance, such as the interception of communications, foreseeability "cannot mean that an individual should be able to foresee when the authorities are likely to intercept his communications so that he can adapt his conduct accordingly".[179] But, although in certain situations the foreseeability needs to be restricted, the risks of arbitrariness, especially where an authority vested in the executive is exercised in secret, needs to be taken into account. It is therefore indispensable to have understandable and detailed rules on the interception of telephone conversations, especially in view of the fast technological progress made in this field.[180] It would be contrary to the rule of law, if the domestic law is not sufficiently clear to give the individual adequate protection against arbitrary interference.

The ECtHR has developed the following minimum safeguards in order to avoid abuses of power related to secret measures of surveillance. To comply with the foreseeability requirement, the following conditions must be laid down in the applicable legal basis[181]:

- The nature of the offences which may give rise to an interception order,[182]
- A definition of the categories of people liable to have their telephones tapped,
- A limit on the duration of telephone tapping,
- The procedure to be followed for examining, using and storing the data obtained,
- The precautions to be taken when communicating the data to other parties and
- The circumstances in which recordings may or must be erased or the tapes destroyed.

On the basis of these detailed conditions, the ECtHR examines the quality of law in similar cases.[183] The Court repeatedly emphasised that tapping of telephone

[179] *Weber and Saravia v. Germany*, Application no. 54934/00 Admissibility Decision, para 93 of 29 June 2006; see also: *Malone v. the United Kingdom*, Application no. 8691/79, judgment of 2 August 1984, para 67.

[180] *Weber and Saravia v. Germany*, Application no. 54934/00, admissibility decision of 29 June 2006, para 93.

[181] *Weber and Saravia v. Germany*, Application no. 54934/00, admissibility decision of 29 June 2006, para 95; these criteria were developed at first in: *Huvig v. France*, Application no. 11105/84, judgment of 24 April 1990, para 34, and *Kruslin v. France*, Application no. 11801/85, judgment of 24 April 1990, para 35.

[182] Whereby the state does not have to set out exhaustively by name the specific offences giving rise to an interception, but "sufficient detail" should be provided of the nature of the offences in question, see *Kennedy v. the United Kingdom*, Application no. 26839/05, judgment of 18 May 2010, para 159.

[183] See *Weber and Saravia v. Germany*, Application no. 54934/00, admissibility decision of 29 June 2006, paras 93 and 94, or *Association for European Integration and Human Rights and Ekimdzhiev v. Bulgaria*, Application no. 62540/00, judgment of 28 June 2007, para 75: "In the context of covert measures of surveillance, the law must be sufficiently clear in its terms to give citizens an adequate indication of the conditions and circumstances in which the authorities are empowered to resort its secret and potentially dangerous interference with the right to respect for private life and correspondence [. . .]. In view of the risk of abuse intrinsic to any system of secret surveillance, such measures must be based on a law that is particularly precise. It is essential to

conversations and other forms of interception constitute a serious interference with private life (and correspondence) and must therefore be based on a "law" that is particularly precise.

In *Valenzuela v. Spain* the ECtHR made clear that even a constitutional basis permitting telephone tapping has to comply with the requirements stipulated above.[184] In that case, the only legal basis allowing telephone interception in Spain stemmed from the Spanish Constitution. It did not provide the guarantees developed by the ECtHR case law and there was no implementing provision concretising the broad constitutional standards. Even though the Spanish judiciary had developed criteria filling the gap, the ECtHR criticised that guarantees derived from a wide construction of statutory provisions or court decisions were not sufficient to satisfy the foreseeability requirement as laid down by the ECtHR.[185]

In *Amann v. Switzerland* the ECtHR returned to the detailed criteria and considered that the Swiss legal bases allowing to record telephone calls did not comply with the Court's requirements as the surveillance measures did not contain any "indication as to the persons concerned by such measures, the circumstances in which they may be ordered, the means to be employed or the procedures to be observed".[186]

In *Bykov v. Russia*, the government tried to circumvent the ECtHR principles by arguing that existing regulations on telephone tapping were not applicable to a radio transmitting device and that therefore no judicial authorisation for the use of such a device was required.[187] The ECtHR clearly points out that by using a radio-transmitting device instead of telephone tapping equipment, the degree and the nature of the intrusion involved remain virtually identical and that as a result, the same procedural principles apply equally to the use of radio-transmitting tools.[188] Legislation permitting in general so-called "operative experiments" without regulating any technical monitoring details of radio-transmitting does not satisfy the requirements of the quality of law as understood by the ECtHR.[189]

In addition to secret measures of surveillance, in context of actions concerning national security, the requirement of foreseeability also plays a special role. In the aforementioned case *C.G. and others v. Bulgaria* the emphasis lays on the fact that

---

have clear, detailed rules on the subject, especially as the technology available for use is continually becoming more sophisticated [. . .]." To the limits of restriction of the foreseeability criterion, see also: *Antunes Rocha v. Portugal*, Application no. 64330/01, judgment of 31 May 2005, paras 69–80.

[184] *Valenzuela Contreras v. Spain*, Application no. 27671/95, judgment of 30 July 1998, para 60.

[185] Ibid, para 57.

[186] *Amann v. Switzerland*, Application no. 27798/95, judgment of 16 February 2000, para 58. See also, Siemen (2006), p. 148.

[187] *Bykov v. Russia*, Application no. 4378/02, judgment of 10 March 2009, para 77.

[188] Ibid, para 79.

[189] Ibid, paras 77–83.

threats to national security may vary in character and may be unexpected or difficult to define in advance.[190] However, even under such circumstances, the concepts of lawfulness and the rule of law in a democratic society require that a decision taken to the detriment of an individual and affecting fundamental rights is subject to a form of adversarial proceedings before an independent authority or court to effectively examine and analyse the reasons and the relevant evidence on which the decision is based. If needed, appropriate procedural restrictions on the use of classified information could be taken. However, the individual must be able in any case to challenge the assertion that national security is a risk.[191]

The case *Kennedy v. the United Kingdom* entails an interesting argument of the applicant which also matters at EU level: *Kennedy* claimed that the term "serious crime", used in a British act to justify restrictive measures, in particular telephone tapping, is not sufficiently clear and therefore blurs the boundaries of what is foreseeable in terms of the ECHR.[192] In view of the Court, the reference to serious crime seems to comply with the foreseeability requirement, although only under the condition that the term is further explained in the interpretative provisions of the contested act as well as in the act itself.[193] It stipulates: "... the reference to serious crime, together with the interpretative clarifications in the Act, gives the citizens an adequate indication as to the circumstances in which and the conditions on which public authorities are empowered to resort to secret surveillance measures".[194]

While the linking of the lawfulness of the term "serious crime" to the presence of additional clarifications provided for within the act, seems to indicate that the term "serious crime" alone would probably not meet the terms of the foreseeability criterion of the ECHR, the question remains regrettably unanswered in the end. However, the wording used by the ECtHR supports the conclusion that supplementary explanations are necessary to be in compliance with the foreseeability standard of the ECHR. Without prejudice to the findings in Chaps. B and C, this ECtHR statement should be kept in mind, in particular when considering that almost all EU instruments later discussed make use of the term "serious crime" to justify measures interfering with the right to data protection.

In conclusion, concerning the foreseeability criterion in secret tapping cases the ECtHR lays down detailed model principles with which the parties of the Convention have to comply, regardless of the device used for the wiretapping. In cases where national security is invoked to justify a decision to the detriment of an individual, the ECtHR assures that an independent authority overlooks the evidence at issue.

190 *C.G. and others v. Bulgaria*, Application no. 1365/07, judgment of 24 April 2008, para 40.

191 Ibid.

192 *Kennedy v. the United Kingdom*, Application no. 26839/05, judgment of 18 May 2010, para 159.

193 Ibid.

194 Ibid.

In contrast to visual or acoustical means of surveillance, the foreseeability requirement in cases in which the authorities made use of a GPS is less strict. In the case *Uzun v. Germany* the surveillance via GPS was found to be less susceptible of interfering with the right to respect for private life than (telephone) tapping.[195] Therefore, the requirement to have the surveillance measure previously ordered by a judge does not apply when using a GPS for surveillance purposes. In this case, the Court agreed that it was sufficient if only the prosecution ordered a suspect's surveillance via GPS.[196] However, other safeguards, such as judicial review, the possibility to exclude evidence obtained from an illegal GPS surveillance and a provision ensuring the respect of the proportionality principle, must have been in place before the surveillance via GPS can be ordered.[197] Moreover, the German Criminal Code provided for the information of the person under surveillance under certain circumstances.[198]

A further restriction applies to the foreseeability criterion where the law confers discretion.[199] According to the ECtHR, a law which confers discretion is not in itself contradictory to the requirement of foreseeability, "provided that the scope of the discretion and the manner of its exercise are indicated with sufficient clarity, having regard to the legitimate aim of the measure in question, to give the individual adequate protection against arbitrary interference [. . .]".[200] In general, the scope of the discretion must be indicated,[201] whereas the definition and interpretation of the scope depend on the issue at stake.[202]

In *Leander v. Sweden*, the ECtHR underlined that, even though the law provided a wide discretion on the national police board as to what information could be entered in the police register, detailed provisions about the "hand out procedure" and about the transfer to other authorities sufficiently assured the applicants rights.[203]

In the case *M.S. v. Sweden* the applicant submitted that the disclosure of her medical records by a clinic had exceeded the request of a public authority,

---

[195] *Uzun v. Germany*, Application no. 35623/05, judgment of 2 September 2010, paras 41–53, compare Sect. II 1 c aa 2.

[196] *Uzun v. Germany*, Application no. 35623/05, judgment of 2 September 2010, para 71.

[197] Ibid, paras 64–74.

[198] Ibid, para 72.

[199] Siemen (2006), p. 146.

[200] *Gillow v. the United Kingdom*, Application no. 9063/80, judgment of 24 November 1986, para 51, and *Amann v. Switzerland*, Application no. 27798/95, judgment of 16 February 2000, para 56.

[201] *Silver and others v. the United Kingdom*, Application no. 5947/72 and others, judgment of 25 March 1983, para 88.

[202] Siemen (2006), p. 146.

[203] "*Furthermore, the Ordinance contains explicit and detailed provisions as to what information may be handed out, the authorities to which information may be communicated, the circumstances in which such communication may take place and the procedure to be followed by the National Police Board when taking decisions to release information*", *Leander v. Sweden*, Application no. 9248/81, judgment of 26 March 1987, para 55.

consequently, too many data concerning the applicant's medical condition had been revealed.[204] Whilst the office had only asked for medical records relating to the time of her injury allegedly sustained at work in 1981, the clinic had produced records covering a period up to 1986. The ECtHR clearly emphasised that the decisive factor in determining the scope of the imparting authority's duty to provide information is the relevance of the information rather than "the precise wording" of the demand.[205] Therefore the interference was found to have a legal basis and to be foreseeable as regards Article 8 paragraph 2 ECHR. While these two cases were decided some time ago, they still express the Court's understanding of a wide discretion conceded to the Member States in discretion cases.

However, as to the limits of discretion, the ECtHR clearly states in *Liberty v. the United Kingdom* that if domestic law confers extensive discretion it has to provide "adequate protection against abuse of power" and "the scope or manner of exercise" of the discretion conferred on the State, e.g. to intercept and examine external communications.[206] In addition, the provisions restricting the discretion have to be accessible to the public.[207] The ECtHR refers to *Weber and Saravia v. Germany* and concludes that it is possible for a State to make public certain details about the operation of a scheme of external surveillance without compromising national security by, amongst others, enacting detailed provisions about the use, storage, communication and destruction of the obtained data.[208] The German legislator provided for rules on storing and destroying of the data involved, such as a 6 month review period whether the data obtained were still necessary to achieve the purpose for which they had been obtained by or transmitted to them.[209] If that was not the case, the relevant data had to be destroyed and deleted from the files or access to them had to be blocked and the destruction had to be recorded in minutes.[210] The legal basis in *Liberty v. the United Kingdom* was not in compliance with these criteria as it did not contain any indication of the procedure to be followed for selecting for examination, sharing, storing and destroying the data obtained and was additionally not set out in a form available to the public.[211]

Summarising, foreseeability can be restricted by the discretion set down in the relevant law. This discretion generally is a wide one. However, two factors have to be taken into account: Firstly, the scope of the discretion, secondly, its limits which have to be clearly defined and which must be accessible to the public.

---

[204] *M.S. v. Sweden*, Application no. 20837/92, judgment of 17 August 1997.

[205] Ibid, para 37.

[206] *Liberty and others v. the United Kingdom*, Application no. 58234/00, judgment of 1 July 2008, para 69.

[207] Ibid, paras 67 and 69.

[208] Ibid, para 68.

[209] Ibid.

[210] Ibid.

[211] Ibid, paras 68 and 69.

Moreover, foreseeability becomes important in context with *collection and storing* of personal data.[212] The ECtHR developed certain minimum requirements with which a domestic legal basis has to comply. In the view of the ECtHR, in *Rotaru v. Romania* the legal basis provided for gathering, recording and archiving of information affecting national security, but it did not lay down any limits on the exercise of those powers.[213] The Court criticised that the Romanian Law did not define the type of information that might be recorded, the categories of people against whom surveillance measures might be taken, the circumstances in which such measures might be taken or the procedure to be followed.[214] In addition it did not contain provisions regulating the age of information held or the length of time for which it might be kept. Further, the contested law did not contain an explicit, detailed provision concerning the persons authorised to consult the files, the nature of the files, the procedure to be followed or the use that might be made of the information thus obtained.[215] Consequently, the ECtHR developed detailed criteria with which domestic law has to comply when regulating the collection and storage of personal information.

As a result, when assessing the quality of law in data protection cases, the foreseeability of the legal basis plays a crucial rule.

For specific cases, the ECtHR developed a catalogue of protective measures. Three different factors have to be basically taken into consideration:

- In the context of *secret measures of surveillance*, for instance in wiretapping cases, the nature of the offences which give rise to an interception order, the categories of people liable to have their telephones tapped, a limit on the duration of the tapping, the procedure to be followed for examining, using and storing the data obtained, rules regulating the transfer of data to other parties and the circumstances in which recordings have to be erased or the tapes destroyed, have to be laid down in the legal basis.
- In case the domestic law provides *discretion*, its scope, its limits as well as the relevance of the information disclosed have to be set out in the national provisions.
- A legal basis regulating *collection and storage* of personal data must include provisions about the type of information that might be recorded, the categories of people against whom surveillance measures might be taken, the circumstances in which such measures might be taken and the procedure to be followed. In addition, it must include provisions regulating the age of information held, the length of time for which this information might be kept, explicit and detailed provisions concerning the *persons authorised to consult the files*, the nature of

---

212 Siemen (2006), p. 149.

213 *Rotaru v. Romania*, Application no. 28341/954, judgment of 4 May 2000, para 57.

214 Ibid.

215 Ibid.

the files, the procedure to be followed and the use that might be made of the information thus obtained.

In consequence, when evaluating the foreseeability criterion in data protection cases, the ECtHR developed specific and detailed requirements which have to be fulfilled by the domestic law to be in accordance with the law. *Siemen* assumes that this "technique" sometimes goes beyond the principle of a limited examination power of the ECtHR as regards the abstract interpretation of domestic law.[216] Principally, the Court has to be careful to rule on whether domestic law conformed to the ECHR *in abstracto* – usually its examination competence is limited to the present case.[217] In *Huvig v. France* the ECtHR recognised this problem and states that "since it [the ECtHR] must ascertain whether the interference complained of was "in accordance with the law", it must inevitably assess the relevant French law in force at the time in relation to the requirements of the fundamental principle of the rule of law. Such a review necessarily entails some degree of abstraction. It is none the less concerned with the "quality" of the national legal rules applicable to Mr. and Mrs. Huvig in the instant case".[218]

The Court added that especially tapping and other forms of interception of telephone conversations represent a serious interference with private life and correspondence and must accordingly be based on provisions that are particularly precise.[219] For this reason it would be essential to have clear, detailed rules on the subject, in particular as the technology available for use is constantly becoming more complicated.[220]

bb) Legitimate Aim

After assessing whether the interference is in accordance with the law, the measure at stake has to pursue the legitimate aims of paragraph 2 Article 8 ECHR. These aims are the interest of national security, public safety and the economic well-being of the country as well as the prevention of disorder or crime, the protection of health, morals or the rights and freedoms of others. No final definition of these aims exist, however, the ECtHR acknowledges a wide margin of appreciation to the Member States.[221] In *Z. v. Finland* the ECtHR emphasised that an *ex post facto*

---

[216] Siemen (2006), p. 150; compare also *Golder v. the United Kingdom*, Application no. 4451/70, judgment of 21 February 1975, para 46.

[217] *Golder v. the United Kingdom*, Application no. 4451/70, judgment of 21 February 1975, paras 39 and 46.

[218] *Huvig v. France*, Application no. 11105/84, judgment of 24 April 1990 para 31; to this problematic, see also: Siemen (2006), p. 150.

[219] *Huvig v. France*, Application no. 11105/84, judgment of 24 April 1990, para 32.

[220] Ibid.

[221] Siemen (2006), p. 151; Meyer-Ladewig (2006), Article 8, p. 180, para 41.

assessment of the legitimate aim does not comply with the Court's requirements by stressing that the legitimate aim has to be evaluated at the time when the contested measures are taken and the relevant authorities sought to achieve a legitimate aim.[222] In the vast majority of the cases, the ECtHR examines the necessity of the interference in much more detail than the legitimate aim, as examining this point permits an exhaustive and sophisticated analysis with regard to the conflicting interests.

cc) Necessary in a Democratic Society

In the following section, it has to be determined whether the means provided under the impugned measure for the achievement of the above mentioned aim remain within the bounds of what is necessary in a democratic society.

At various occasions, the ECtHR has stated its general understanding of the phrase "necessary in a democratic society". In *Silver v. the United Kingdom* clarifies that:

> – the adjective "necessary" is not synonymous with "indispensable", neither has it the flexibility of such expressions as "admissible", "ordinary", "useful", "reasonable" or "desirable" [...];
> – the Contracting States enjoy a certain but not unlimited margin of appreciation in the matter of the imposition of restrictions, but it is for the Court to give the final ruling on whether they are compatible with the Convention [...];
> – the phrase "necessary in a democratic society" means that, to be compatible with the Convention, the interference must, inter alia, correspond to a "pressing social need" and be "proportionate to the legitimate aim pursued" [...].[223]

With regard to Article 8 (2) ECHR, in *Kvasnica v. Slovakia* and *Kennedy v. the United Kingdom* the Court added:

> – The Court has to determine whether the procedures for supervising the ordering and implementation of the restrictive measures are such as to keep the interference to what is necessary in a democratic society;
> – in addition, the values of a democratic society must be followed as faithfully as possible in the supervisory procedures if the bounds of necessity, within the meaning of Article 8 (2), are not to be exceeded.[224]

Summarising, the ECtHR is in search for a balance between the demands of the general interest of the Member States and the requirements of the protection of the individual's fundamental rights.[225] Member States enjoy a wide *margin of*

---

[222] *Z. v Finland*, Application no. 22009/93, judgment of 25 February 1997, para 75.

[223] *Silver v. the United Kingdom*, Application no. 5947/72 and others, judgment of 25 March 1983, para 7.

[224] *Kennedy v. the United Kingdom*, Application no. 26839/05, judgment of 18 May 2010, para 154, and *Kvasnica v. Slovakia*, Application no. 72094/01, judgment of 9 June 2009, para 80.

[225] *Soering v. the United Kingdom*, Application no. 14038/88, judgment of 7 July 1987, para 89.

appreciation which is given both to the domestic legislator and to the judicial bodies that are called upon to interpret and apply the law in force.[226] This margin is an expression of judicial self-restraint and a concession to the Member States regarding the principle of the choice of means.[227] However, it is subject to European supervision[228]; therefore the exceptions provided for in paragraph 2 of Article 8 ECHR have to be interpreted narrowly. The scope of this margin depends on such factors as the nature and seriousness of the interests at stake and the gravity of the interference.[229] That means that it varies depending on the circumstances of the case, the subject-matter and its background.[230] In addition, it is not identical as it regards each of the different aims justifying restrictions on paragraph 1 of Article 8 ECHR.[231]

This flexible and casuistic approach implies that there is neither a definition of the margin of appreciation doctrine, nor is there one common academic consensus explaining the content of this principle.[232]

---

[226] *Handyside v. the United Kingdom*, Application no. 5493/72, judgment of 7 December 1976, para 48.

[227] Siemen (2006), pp. 154–155; see more generally to the doctrine of the margin of appreciation: Mowbray (2007), pp. 629–633; Greer (2006), pp. 222–226; Lavender (1997); Brems (1996), Arai-Takahashi (2002); Callewaert et al. (1998); Hutchinson (1999). Critical to this doctrine: Jones (1995); Brauch (2004–2005).

[228] *Funke v. France*, Application no. 10828/84, judgment of 25 February 1993, para 55, and *Kennedy v. the United Kingdom*, Application no. 26839/05, judgment of 18 May 2010, para 154.

[229] *Z. v Finland*, Application no. 22009/93, judgment of 25 February 1997, para 99, and *Peck v. United Kingdom*, Application no. 44647/98, judgment of 28 January 2003, para 77.

[230] *Rasmussen v. Denmark*, Application no. 8777/79, judgment of 28 November 1984, para 40: "The scope of the margin of appreciation will vary according to the circumstances, the subject-matter and its background; in this respect, one of the relevant factors may be the existence or non-existence of common ground between the laws of the Contracting States".

[231] *Dudgeon v. the United Kingdom*, Application no. 7525/76, judgment of 22 October 1981, para 52, and *Sunday Times v. the United Kingdom*, Application no. 6538/74, judgment of 26 April 1979, para 59.

[232] Greer (2006), pp. 222–223; Ovey and White (2006), p. 233; Sottiaux and van der Schyff (2008), pp. 115–156, 134. Due to the vagueness of this doctrine, some argue for the elimination of it, see Partly dissenting opinion of Judge de Meyer in *Z. v Finland*, point III, Application no. 22009/93, judgment of 25 February 1997: In the present judgment the Court once again relies on the national authorities' "margin of appreciation". I believe that it is high time for the Court to banish that concept from its reasoning. It has already delayed too long in abandoning this hackneyed phrase and recanting the relativism it implies. It is possible to envisage a margin of appreciation in certain domains. It is, for example, entirely natural for a criminal court to determine sentence – within the range of penalties laid down by the legislature – according to its assessment of the seriousness of the case. But where human rights are concerned, there is no room for a margin of appreciation which would enable the States to decide what is acceptable and what is not. On that subject the boundary not to be overstepped must be as clear and precise as possible. It is for the Court, not each State individually, to decide that issue, and the Court's views must apply to everyone within the jurisdiction of each State. The empty phrases concerning the State's margin of appreciation – repeated in the Court's judgments for too long already – are unnecessary circumlocutions, serving only to indicate abstrusely that the States may do anything the Court does not consider

However, by applying the margin of appreciation to private life protection cases there is a broad consent on the relationship between the seriousness of the interference, the nature of the rights at stake and the scope accorded to the margin of appreciation[233]: the more intimate or private areas of private life are affected, the narrower the scope of the margin of appreciation acknowledged to the Member States will be.[234] Where there is no common understanding within the Member States of the Council of Europe as to the importance of the interest at stake or as to how best to protect it, the margin will be wider.[235]

The following analysis will show whether this observation remains valid with regard to data protection cases and whether general conclusions can be drawn by analysing the relevant case law. It has to be clarified in advance that a clear division between the categories stipulated in the following will not be possible. The circles of different actions do intersect and overlap since the case law on hand sometimes fits into more than one category.

(1) Retention of Information Relating to Criminal Offences Including Biometric Data[236]

The ECtHR has held that the retention of information related to criminal offences of the past can be necessary in a modern democratic society for the prevention of disorder and crime.[237] Until recently, Member States enjoyed a wide margin of appreciation, not at least because, in the cases examined by the ECtHR in this context, the information obtained was only kept in a general administrative file recording the events in question. The information was not entered into an automatic

---

incompatible with human rights. Such terminology, as wrong in principle as it is pointless in practice, should be abandoned without delay.

233 Greer (2006), p. 224.

234 Siemen (2006), p. 156; Ovey and White (2006), p. 234. See also: *S. and Marper v the United Kingdom*, Application nos. 30562/04 and 30566/04, judgment of 4 December 2008, para 102; *Z. v Finland*, Application no. 22009/93, judgment of 25 February 1997 and *Dudgeon v the United Kingdom*, Application no. 7525/76, judgment of 22 October 1981; *S. and Marper v the United Kingdom*, Application nos. 30562/04 and 30566/04, judgment of 4 December 2008.

235 *Dickson v. the United Kingdom*, Application no. 44262/04, judgment of 4 December 2007, para 78; *S. and Marper v the United Kingdom*, Application nos. 30562/04 and 30566/04, judgment of 4 December 2008, para 102.

236 Biometric data are defined in the Article 29 Working Partly, WP 136, Opinion 4/2007 on the concept of personal data, adopted 20 June 2007, pp. 8 and 9, para III (1) as "biological properties, physiological characteristics, living traits or repeatable actions where those features and/or actions are both unique to that individual and measurable, even if the patterns used in practice to technically measure them involve a certain degree of probability. Typical examples of such biometric data are provided by fingerprints, retinal patterns, facial structure, voices, but also hand geometry, vein patterns or even some deeply ingrained skill or other behavioural characteristic (such as handwritten signature, keystrokes, particular way to walk or to speak, etc.)" and DNA information.

237 *Friedl v. Austria*, Application no. 15225/89, judgment of 31 January 1995, para 66.

data processing system.[238] The ECHR Commission found a relatively slight interference with the applicant's right to respect for his private life in cases related to the keeping of records relating to criminal offences of the past.[239] They could reasonably be considered as necessary in a democratic society for the prevention of disorder and crime. In *Friedl v. Austria* the ECHR Commission concluded that "even if no criminal proceedings are subsequently brought and there is no reasonable suspicion against the individual concerned in relation to any specific offence, special considerations, such as combating organised terrorism, can justify the retention of the material concerned".[240] However, the keeping (and publishing) of an inaccurate police report obviously violates Article 8 ECHR.[241]

It is noteworthy that in *Friedl v. Austria*, the ECtHR attached special weight to the fact that the photographs concerned had not been entered into a data-processing system and that the authorities had taken no steps to identify the persons photographed by means of data processing.[242] *Siemen* argued that from a present day perspective, this argument could no longer serve as justification of the interference, as nowadays almost every database would operate with an automatic data processing system. In view of the various possibilities of collecting, exchanging as well as interlinking or storing data in vast databases, *Siemen* doubted that the ECtHR would decide in the same way which it did 15 years ago. [243]

In *S. and Marper v. the United Kingdom* this observation proved to be true.[244] The applicants opposed the fact that British authorities retained DNA and fingerprint data of them taken during a previous investigation despite the acquittal of one of them and the discontinuance of the criminal proceedings against the other.[245]

On the one hand, the ECtHR recognised the importance of the use of modern scientific techniques of investigation and identification as regards cellular samples, DNA and fingerprint information, on the other hand it underlined the limits of their storage and use. It referred to the principles specified in Convention No. 108 of the

---

[238] *Friedl v. Austria*, Application no. 15225/89, judgment of 31 January 1995; *X. v. Germany*, Application no. 1307/61, Commission decision of 4 October 1962.

[239] *Friedl v. Austria*, Application no. 15225/89, judgment of 31 January 1995, para 66.

[240] *Friedl v. Austria*, Application no. 15225/89, judgment of 31 January 1995, para 66. The reference to "*special considerations, such as combating organised crime*" is astonishing, in particular under the perspective that the defendant state did not refers to this justification. See Siemen (2006), p. 159.

[241] *Cemalettin Canli v. Turkey*, Application no. 22427/04, judgment of 18. November 2008, paras 42–44.

[242] *Friedl v. Austria*, Application no. 15225/89, judgment of 31 January 1995, paras 49–51.

[243] Siemen (2006), p. 159.

[244] *S. and Marper v. the United Kingdom*, Application nos. 30562/04 and 30566/04, judgment of 4 December 2008.

[245] Compare to this case: De Beer et al. (2010).

Council of Europe and laid emphasis on the need for safeguards when automatic processing is concerned, in particular when such data are used for police purposes.[246] It emphasised that statistics on hits between large databases and crime scenes are not sufficient to justify the establishment of such databases as "the figures do not reveal the extent to which this "link" with crime scenes resulted in convictions of the persons concerned or the number of convictions that were contingent on the retention of the samples of unconvicted persons".[247] Nor do they reveal that the high number of successful matches with crime-scene evidence was only achieved "through indefinite retention of DNA records of all such persons".[248]

It stressed that the retention of data must be proportionate in relation to the purpose of collection and insisted on a limited period of storage.[249] England, Wales and Northern Ireland appeared to be the only jurisdictions within the Council of Europe to allow the indefinite retention of fingerprint and DNA material of any person of any age suspected of any recordable offence.[250] The Court was "struck by the blanket and indiscriminate nature of the power of retention in England and Wales".[251] Data were retained irrespective of the nature or gravity of the offence or the age of the suspect, there existed only limited possibilities to have the data removed from the database, additionally there was no provision for independent review of the justification for the retention according to defined criteria (such as the seriousness of the offence, previous arrests, the strength of the suspicion against the person and any other special circumstances).[252] No time limit was provided.[253] This lack of corrective provisions led to the risk of stigmatisation, stemming from the fact that persons in the position of the applicants, who had not been convicted of any offence and are entitled to the presumption of innocence, have their data stored in a law enforcement database while being treated in the same way as convicted persons.[254]

Against this background, the ECtHR found that the retention of the fingerprints, cellular samples and DNA profiles in a nationwide database failed to strike the balance between the competing interests and that the state had overstepped any tolerable margin of appreciation.[255]

---

[246] *S. and Marper v. the United Kingdom*, Application nos. 30562/04 and 30566/04, judgment of 4 December 2008, para 103.

[247] Ibid, para 116.

[248] Ibid.

[249] Ibid, para 107.

[250] Ibid, para 110.

[251] Ibid, para 119.

[252] Ibid.

[253] Ibid.

[254] Ibid, para 122.

[255] Ibid, para 125.

This decision allows the derivation of important general principles as regards the minimum data protection standard in databases serving crime detection and prevention. States must consider the following rules[256]:

- First, the presumption of innocence demands a different treatment of data of persons who have been convicted of an offence and those who have never been.
- A distinction has to be made between serious and less serious offences.
- The age of the suspected has to be taken into account.
- Possibilities to have the data removed from the database have to be established.
- Provisions for independent review of the justification for the retention according to defined criteria, such as the seriousness of the offence, previous arrests, the strength of the suspicion against the person and any other special circumstances, have to assure the lawfulness of the provided measure.
- Finally, retention has to be limited in time.

All in all, the case *S. and Marper v. the United Kingdom* shows an important development towards an increasing awareness and sensibility of the Court vis-à-vis the fast changing technology and the risks resulting from the collection and retention of personal data in modern databases. The mandatory establishment of corrective provisions and procedural rights such as provisions to have the data removed from the database, keep up with the current state of technological possibilities and correct the constrained approach taken in *Friedl v. Austria* 15 years ago.

(2) Data Collection, Storing and Retention with Regard to Measures Against Terrorism and Transmission of Data to Third Parties

One of the first cases dealing with measures regarding legislation enacted against terrorism established basic criteria still applicable in those cases. In the aforementioned judgment *Klass and others v. Germany* from 1978, the German government referred to the protection of national security and the prevention of crime to justify security legislation (G-10 Act) implementing secret mail, post and telephone surveillance.[257] The applicants, lawyers, public prosecutors and judges, claimed

[256] Ibid, paras 66–125.

[257] *Klass v. Germany*, Application no. 5029/71, judgment of 6 September 1978; for measures such as fingerprinting or photographing during detention and/or the retention of records after release do not constitute a breach of Article 8, see *Mc Veigh and others v. United Kingdom*, Application no. 8022/77, Commission decision of 18 March 1981. As regards the notion of "national security", the ECtHR has not yet found a clear Definition. In *C.G. and others v. Bulgaria*, Application no. 1365/07, judgment of 24 April 2008, it admits that: "It is true that the notion of "national security" is not capable of being comprehensively defined (see Esbester v. the United Kingdom, no. 18601/91, Commission decision of 2 April 1993, unreported; Hewitt and Harman v. the United Kingdom, no. 20317/92, Commission decision of 1 September 1993, unreported; and Christie v. the United Kingdom, no. 21482/93, Commission decision of 27 June 1994, DR 78-A, p. 119, at p. 134). It may, indeed, be a very wide one, with a large margin of appreciation left to the executive to

among others that the G-10 Act empowers the authorities to monitor their correspondence and telephone communication without requiring the authorities to subsequently inform the persons concerned of the measures taken against them.[258] After clarifying the notion of victim, the Court accepts that the mere existence of legislation permitting secret measures could interfere with the right of individuals, even if those measures did not in fact apply to them.[259]

In determining whether the interference is justified, the ECtHR bases itself on two facts: Firstly, it recognises the technological progress made in espionage and surveillance techniques.[260] Secondly, it refers to the development of terrorism in Europe in the years before 1978. The ECtHR held that: "Democratic societies nowadays find themselves threatened by highly sophisticated forms of espionage and by terrorism, with the result that the State must be able, in order effectively to counter such threats, to undertake the secret surveillance of subversive elements operating within its jurisdiction. Therefore, the Court has to accept that the existence of some legislation granting powers of secret surveillance over the mail and telecommunications is, under exceptional conditions, necessary in a democratic society in the interests of national security and/or for the prevention of disorder or crime".[261]

Even though this statement was made in 1978, it exemplarily illustrates the Court's understanding with regard to secret surveillance measures and legislation enacted against terrorism. Member States enjoy a wide margin of appreciation relating to the implementation of counter terrorism measures.

The Court, however, restricts its approach to the effect that it is nevertheless aware "of the danger such a law poses of undermining or even destroying democracy on the ground of defending it".[262] It affirms that the Member States may not, in the name of the struggle against espionage and terrorism, adopt whatever measures they consider appropriate.[263] It demands adequate and effective guarantees against abuse on the one hand which depend on the other hand "on all the circumstances of the case, such as the nature, scope and duration of the possible measures, the grounds required for ordering such measures, the authorities competent to permit, carry out and supervise such measures, and the kind of remedy provided by the respective national law".[264] In this case, in the Court's view, the G-10 Act laid down strict conditions regarding the implementation of surveillance measures and

determine what is in the interests of that security. However, that does not mean that its limits may be stretched beyond its natural meaning."

[258] *Klass v. Germany*, Application no. 5029/71, para 26 of 6 September 1978.

[259] Ibid, para 34.

[260] Ibid, para 48.

[261] Ibid.

[262] Ibid, para 49.

[263] Ibid.

[264] Ibid, para 50.

the processing of the information thereby obtained.[265] Subsequent to a detailed examination of the German legislation, the ECtHR concludes that the G-10 Act is justified in the light of paragraph 2 Article 8 ECHR and does not exceed the limits of what is deemed being necessary in a democratic society in the interests of national security and for the prevention of disorder or crime.[266]

Equally related to anti-terrorism measures in the 1970s is the case *A., B., C. and D. v. Germany*. It concerns the recording and storing of telephone conversations, which the applicants had had with a law firm whose telephone had been tapped, as a lawyer working in this firm was accused of taking active and decisive part in setting up an information centre serving to exchange information between detained persons suspected of terrorist activities as well as disseminating terrorist ideas aimed at violent revolution.[267]

The ECtHR concludes that the storing of telephone records even beyond the actual need and not related to any criminal acts, can be in accordance with Article 8 ECHR since a definite answer with regard to the question of which records would finally be relevant in criminal proceedings could only be given at the end of the process against the suspect.[268] In other words, storing of telephone records during a criminal investigation is justified until the end of the proceedings for which they were originally obtained, whether or not they are related to criminal acts. However, the ECHR Commission took into consideration that the data had been destroyed after the conviction of the suspect and had not been used for any other purpose than remaining available as possible evidence in the proceedings against the suspect.[269]

The wide margin of appreciation of Member States in cases related to the prevention of terrorist crime is also reflected in *Murray v. the United Kingdom*.[270] The ECtHR emphasises that "terrorist crime falls into a special category. Because of the attendant risk of loss of life and human suffering, the police are obliged to act with utmost urgency in following up all information [...]".[271]

In *Murray v. the United Kingdom*, the applicant was arrested and accused of collecting money for the Provisional Irish Republican Army (Provisional IRA).

[265] *Klass v. Germany*, Application no. 5029/71, judgment of 6 September 1978, para 52: "The measures in question remain in force for a maximum of three months and may be renewed only on fresh application; the measures must immediately be discontinued once the required conditions have ceased to exist or the measures themselves are no longer necessary; knowledge and documents thereby obtained may not be used for other ends, and documents must be destroyed as soon as they are no longer needed to achieve the required purpose".

[266] *Klass v. Germany*, Application no. 5029/71, judgment of 6 September 1978, para 60.

[267] *A., B., C. and D. v. Germany*, Application no. 8290/78, judgment of 13 December 1979, para 177.

[268] Ibid, para 180.

[269] Ibid.

[270] *Murray v. the United Kingdom*, Application no. 14310/88, judgment of 28 October 1994.

[271] Ibid, para 51.

Amongst others, he contested the taking of photographs without his knowledge or consent as well as the recording of personal details concerning his family life.[272] In evaluating the necessity of such information gathering in a democratic society, the ECtHR clarifies that "it is not for the Court to substitute for the assessment of the national authorities its own assessment of what might be the best policy in the field of investigation of terrorist crime".[273] In view of the threats posed by organised terrorism, the ECtHR concludes that neither recording nor retaining basic personal details concerning the arrested person or even other persons present at the time and place of the arrest, nor taking and retention of photographs can be regarded as falling outside the legitimate bounds of the process of investigation of terrorist crime.[274]

In June 2006, almost 30 years after the *Klass* judgment, an amendment of the G-10 Act was again subject-matter before the ECtHR. In this case, *Weber and Saravia v. Germany*, the applicants impugned the legality of four amendments which extended the powers of the secret service, referring to extended strategic monitoring, the transmission and use of personal data to the Federal Government including the Offices for the Protection of the Constitution and other authorities, the destruction of personal data as well as the failure to give notice of restrictions on the secrecy of telecommunications.[275] The ECtHR examined in detail the applicant's complaints and established important basic principles of general application with which states have to comply when extending the powers of their secret services.[276] To be in accordance with Article 8 ECHR specific and particular minimum requirements have to be fulfilled.

The Court observes that before enacting strategic monitoring, a series of restrictive conditions have to be satisfied. Detailed safeguards against abuse have to be established. Examples are: restriction of monitoring measures to a short period of time (3 months), immediate interruption of the measures if the conditions set out in the monitoring order were no longer fulfilled or the measures themselves were no longer necessary, as well as the destruction of data as soon as they were no longer needed to achieve the purpose pursued.[277] Additionally, independent supervision (in this case a parliamentary board and a special commission) empowered with

---

[272] Ibid, para 84.

[273] Ibid, para 90.

[274] Ibid, para 93.

[275] *Weber and Saravia v. Germany*, Application no. 54934/00, admissibility decision of 29 June 2006.

[276] The ECtHR uses the principles outlined in *Weber and Saravia v. Germany* in subsequent cases as a standard of reference when it comes to the assessment of safeguards and guarantees against abuse, see for instance *Kennedy v. the United Kingdom*, Application no. 26839/05, judgment of 18 May 2010, para 158, and *Association for European Integration and Human Rights and Ekimdzhiev v. Bulgaria*, Application no. 62540/00, judgment of 28 June 2007, para 86.

[277] *Weber and Saravia v. Germany*, Application no. 54934/00, admissibility decision of 29 June 2006, para 114.

substantial power in relation to all stages of interception and the establishment of reporting duties, at least for the Federal Minister authorising monitoring measures, have to be provided.[278] Detailed provisions must regulate storage and destruction of data.[279]

As to the transmission and use of personal data, the ECtHR refers to the contested judgment of the German Federal Constitutional Court which ruled that the transfer of data between the Federal Intelligence Service and the Federal Government could only be accomplished if the personal data contained in the report to the Federal Government were marked and remained connected to the purposes which had justified their collection.[280] These additional safeguards were considered appropriate by the ECtHR for the purpose of limiting the use of the information obtained to what is necessary to serve the purpose of strategic monitoring.[281] With regard to the transmission of personal data to the Offices for the Protection of the Constitution and other authorities and their use by these authorities, the ECtHR found that the German Federal Constitutional Court again adequately counterbalanced the interference by setting reasonable limitations of the offence (s) on behalf of which data transmission was permitted and by providing supervisory mechanisms against abuse.[282] Precautions to be taken when communicating the data to other parties must be laid down in the legal basis allowing for transfer.[283] The German court ordered that, the G-10 could only be applied and data be transmitted if specific facts – as opposed to mere factual indications – aroused the suspicion that someone had committed one of the limited offences listed in a special Article of the G-10 Act.[284] Moreover, the transmission had to be recorded in minutes. Already in *Leander v. Sweden*, the ECtHR referred to the transfer conditions requiring "explicit and detailed provisions as to what information may be handed out, the authorities to which information may be communicated, the circumstances in which such communication may take place and the procedure to be followed" prior to transferring personal data to other authorities.[285]

The ECtHR also takes the view that the provisions for the destruction of data "as soon as they were no longer needed to achieve their statutory purpose, and for the verification at regular, fairly short intervals of whether the conditions for such destruction were met", constituted an important element in reducing the effects of

---

[278] Ibid, para 115.

[279] Ibid, para 116.

[280] Ibid, para 121.

[281] Ibid, para 122.

[282] Ibid, para 129.

[283] *Weber and Saravia v. Germany*, Application no. 54934/00, admissibility decision of 29 June 2006, para 95, and *Kennedy v. the United Kingdom*, Application no. 26839/05, judgment of 18 May 2010, para 144.

[284] *Weber and Saravia*, Application no. 54934/00, admissibility decision of 29 June 2006, para 127.

[285] *Leander v. Sweden*, Application no. 9248/81, judgment of 26 March 1987, para 55.

the interference with the secrecy of telecommunications to an unavoidable minimum. Moreover, the Federal Constitutional Court ruled that data which were still needed for the purposes of court proceedings could not be destroyed immediately and that the supervisory powers of the independent G-10 Commission covered the whole process of using data, including their destruction".[286]

Concerning the subsequent notification of surveillance measures, the ECtHR emphasises that this question is closely linked to the effectiveness of remedies before the courts and therefore to the existence of effective safeguards against the abuse of monitoring powers.[287] It adds: "As soon as notification can be carried out without jeopardising the purpose of the restriction after the termination of the surveillance measure, [...], information should be provided to the persons concerned".[288]

In conclusion, the ECtHR found that adequate and effective guarantees existed against abuses of the State's strategic monitoring powers in the G-10 Act.[289]

In *Weber and Saravia v. Germany* the ECtHR established detailed principles with which the states have to comply when enacting legislation on combatting terrorism or other serious crime. The decision's essential requirements for compliance with Article 8 ECHR include independent control of the surveillance measures and of the data obtained through it, adequate procedures for preserving the data's integrity and confidentiality as well as procedures for its destruction, adequate remedies in case of misuse, independent control and information of the persons concerned after the termination of such measures. Whereas the ECtHR had already carefully examined the G-10 legislation in *Klass and others v. Germany*, in *Weber and Saravia v. Germany* it clearly summarized the most important principles to be respected when setting up anti-terrorism legislation.[290] Cases such as *Kennedy v. the United Kingdom* and *Kvasnica v. Slovakia* later confirmed the standards outlined in this judgment.[291]

Summarising the relevant case law, relatively serious interferences regarding data collection, storing or retention can be justified on the grounds of the establishment of legislation against terrorism, the prevention of crime and the protection of

---

[286] *Weber and Saravia v. Germany*, Application no. 54934/00, admissibility decision of 29 June 2006, para 132.

[287] "since there is in principle little scope for recourse to the courts by the individual concerned unless the latter is advised of the measures taken without his or her knowledge and thus able to challenge their legality retrospectively", Weber and Saravia v. Germany, Application no. 54934/00, admissibility decision of 29 June 2006, para 135.

[288] *Weber and Saravia v. Germany*, Application no. 54934/00, admissibility decision of 29 June 2006, para 135.

[289] Ibid, para 137.

[290] For a breach of these principles, see *Association for European Integration and Human Rights and Ekimdzhiev v. Bulgaria*, Application no. 62540/00, judgment of 28 June 2007 and *Volokhy v. Ukraine*, Application no. 23543/02, judgment of 2 November 2006.

[291] *Kennedy v. the United Kingdom*, Application no. 26839/05, judgment of 18 May 2010 and *Kvasnica v. Slovakia*, Application no. 72094/01 of 9 June 2009.

national security. On the one hand, the ECtHR acknowledges a wide margin of appreciation to the Member States in this respect, on the other hand it demands adequate and effective guarantees against abuse which are examined in detail and require relatively far reaching protection, including rules on the transmission of personal data.

(3) Surveillance Measures

The ECtHR's assessment in *Klass v. Germany* not only refers to data processing with regard to measures against terrorism, it also sets general principles pertaining to cases related to governmental secret surveillance measures.[292] Both aims are often closely connected and therefore can not be clearly distinguished. The ECtHR clearly points out that powers of secret surveillance "characterising as they do the police state, are tolerable under the Convention only in so far as strictly necessary for safeguarding the democratic institutions".[293] Putting the emphasis on the wording "strictly necessary", this statement suggests a strict interpretation of the reasons for justification.[294] However, it is rather a question of whether the two factors mentioned above (technical advances and threat of terrorism) are sufficiently balanced with regard to effective and adequate safeguards provided by the Member States.[295] This evaluation depends on all the circumstances of the case, for instance the nature, scope and duration of the possible measures, the grounds required for ordering them, the authorities competent to authorise, carry out and supervise them, and the kind of remedy provided by the national law in question.[296] As a basic rule, "exploratory or general surveillance" goes beyond what is necessary in a democratic society.[297]

The ECtHR acknowledges a certain discretion in determining the conditions under which the system of surveillance may be operated.[298] Domestic legislation may be adapted to increasing threats and can therefore justify even serious interferences. The ECtHR refers to the *Golder*, *Handyside* and *De Wilde and others* judgments and reiterates that it is not the task of the Court "to substitute for the

---

[292] Siemen (2006), p. 161; to the notion of "secret surveillance" in the ECtHR's jurisprudence, see Cameron (2000), pp. 74–169.

[293] *Klass v. Germany*, Application no. 5029/71, judgment of 6 September 1978, para 42.

[294] Siemen (2006), p. 161.

[295] Ibid, para 48, and *Rotaru v. Romania*, Application no. 28341/95, judgment of 4 May 2000, para 59; Siemen (2006), p. 161.

[296] *Weber and Saravia v. Germany*, Application no. 54934/00, admissibility decision of 29 June 2006, para 106; *Leander v. Sweden*, Application no. 9248/81, judgment of 26 March 1987, para 59.

[297] *Klass v. Germany*, Application no. 5029/71, judgment of 6 September 1978, para 51, and *Leander v. Sweden*, Application no. 9248/81, judgment of 26 March 1987, para 53.

[298] *Klass v. Germany*, Application no. 5029/71, judgment of 6 September 1978, para 49.

assessment of the national authorities any other assessment of what might be the best policy in this field".[299]

Since the implementation in practice of measures of secret surveillance of communications is not open to scrutiny by the individuals concerned or the public, discretion is nevertheless limited.[300] By emphasising that secret surveillance measures "must follow the values of a democratic society as faithfully as possible, in particular the rule of law [. . .]", the Court restricts the discretion.[301] The ECtHR adds that the rule of law demands effective supervision which should usually be carried out by the judiciary, as "judicial control affords the best guarantees of independence, impartiality and a proper procedure".[302]

This careful approach is also reflected in the case *Association for European Integration and Human Rights and Ekimdzhiev v. Bulgaria.* In 2007 the ECtHR set limits to restrict sprawling powers of governmental secret surveillance. In the present case the ECtHR was faced with the Bulgarian "Special Surveillance Means Act" (SSMA) which granted far reaching surveillance rights to the police and the Bulgarian secret service.[303] It held that Bulgarian law does not provide sufficient guarantees against the risk of abuse which is inherent in any system of secret surveillance.[304]

The ECtHR compared the Bulgarian legislation with the German G-10 Act (subject-matter in *Weber and Saravia v. Germany* as well as in *Klass v. Germany*) and primarily based itself on four main arguments:

Firstly, no external independent control assured compliance with the rules of the SSMA. There was no independent review of the implementation of secret surveillance measures or compliance with warrants authorising the use of such means. Nor was there was any control over whether the secret service faithfully reproduced the original data in the written record or whether the data were destroyed within the legal time limit if surveillance has proved fruitless.[305] Solely the Minister of Internal Affairs – who was directly involved in the commissioning of special means of surveillance and whose competences of control were not set out in the law – was entrusted with a certain overall control.

---

[299] *Klass v. Germany*, Application no. 5029/71, judgment of 6 September 1978, para 49. See also *Mersch and others v. Luxembourg*, Application no. 10439/83, 10440/83, 10441/83, 10452/83 10512/83 and 10513/83, admissibility decision of 10 May 1985 with a detailed debate about the different measures provided by the contested Luxembourgish law.

[300] *Amann v. Switzerland*, Application no. 27798/95, judgment of 16 February 2000, para 56.

[301] *Rotaru v. Romania*, Application no. 28341/95, judgment of 4 May 2000, para 59.

[302] Ibid.

[303] *Association for European Integration and Human Rights and Ekimdzhiev v. Bulgaria*, Application no. 62540/00, judgment of 28 June 2007.

[304] Ibid, para 93.

[305] *Association for European Integration and Human Rights and Ekimdzhiev v. Bulgaria*, Application no. 62540/00, judgment of 28 June 2007, para 85. To the lack of supervision, see also: *Volokhy v. Ukraine*, Application no. 23543/02, judgment of 2 November 2006, paras 42–54.

Moreover, the ECtHR identified an apparent lack of regulations precisely specifying the manner of screening the intelligence obtained through surveillance, the procedures for preserving its integrity and confidentiality and the procedures for its destruction.[306]

In addition, the ECtHR refers to the transmission of data to third parties. It compares the Bulgarian legislation with the German G-10 Act and criticises the SSMA for not providing strict rules regulating the transmission of intelligence to other services, nor independent monitoring of those rules.[307]

Finally, the ECtHR reiterates that after the termination of surveillance, "as soon as notification can be made without jeopardising the purpose of the measure", information should be provided to the persons concerned.[308] The SSMA did not provide for notification of persons subjected to surreptitious monitoring under any circumstances nor at any point in time. It even explicitly prohibited the disclosure of information that a person had been subjected to surveillance, or that warrants had been issued for this purpose.[309]

Summarising the Court's arguments in the *Association for European Integration and Human Rights and Ekimdzhiev v. Bulgaria* case, independent control during and after the exercise of secret surveillance measures as well as information of the persons concerned after the termination of such measures, represent essential requirements which have to be fulfilled when states implement surveillance legislation.

Against the background of the weak legislative Bulgarian framework, the ECtHR clarified in *C.G. and others v. Bulgaria* that even a secret service file, if it is used to justify measures against an individual, must contain information making it possible to verify whether or not the secret surveillance measures taken were lawfully ordered and executed.[310]

It is noteworthy that compared to the above mentioned case *Leander v. Sweden*, this judgment seems to show a certain development towards a right of access to secret service files. However, this right is granted only under the following two conditions: first, the legal basis allowing for secret service measures which lead to a secret service entry is doubtful and second, the entry is subsequently used to justify restrictive measures against persons concerned.

Both Bulgarian cases nevertheless demonstrate that the ECtHR is becoming more sensitive as regards the criteria of independent control of secret surveillance measures and the information of persons concerned in connection with measures taken against them. The Court insists that basic data protection principles also apply within the framework of secret surveillance measures.

---

[306] *Association for European Integration and Human Rights and Ekimdzhiev v. Bulgaria*, Application no. 62540/00, judgment of 28 June 2007, para 86.

[307] Ibid, para 89.

[308] Ibid, para 90.

[309] Ibid.

[310] *C.G. and others v. Bulgaria*, Application no. 1365/07, judgment of 24 April 2008, para 48.

Summarising the ECtHR's case law in respect to the purpose and necessity of secret surveillance measures, in general the ECtHR has consistently accepted that national authorities enjoy a fairly wide margin of appreciation in selecting the means for achieving the aim of protecting national security.[311] However, in view of the risk that systems of secret surveillance for the protection of national security may undermine or even destroy democracy under the cloak of defending it, the ECtHR seems to be satisfied that adequate and effective guarantees against abuse exist.[312] These guarantees entail the respect of basic data protection principles, such as independent control of the measures, deletion of unnecessary information, regulations specifying the screening as well as the destruction of information and procedures preserving its integrity and confidentiality, rules regulating the transmission of data to third parties and the informing of persons concerned after termination of surveillance (as soon as notification can be made without jeopardising the purpose of the measure).[313]

Bearing in mind the previous observations, it also has to be taken into consideration that the judgments examined above – except for *Weber and Saravia v. Germany* and the Bulgarian cases – refer to the threat of terrorism of the 1970s. Since then, investigation and tracing methods as well as the forms of terrorism have changed radically. The development of the internet has led to growing fragmentation and complexity of communication. Police and secret services are employing more and more sophisticated technologies and methods of tracking. In the development of those competences, states have to respect the criteria stipulated by the ECtHR's case law. The principles initially developed in the 1970s are still of general application; they have to be cautiously adapted to new technologies and current security challenges. The main values developed in the *Weber and Saravia v. Germany* judgment provide helpful guidance during this process.

(4) Secret Security Files

In *Leander v. Sweden*, the ECtHR expressly refers to the secret collection and storing of personal information.[314] It recognises the necessity to collect and store personal information in registers not accessible to the public as well as the use afterwards when assessing the suitability of candidates for employment in a post of

---

[311] *Leander v. Sweden*, Application no. 9248/81, judgment of 26 March 1987, para 59; *Weber and Saravia v. Germany*, Application no. 54934/00, admissibility decision of 29 June 2006, para 106.

[312] *Weber and Saravia v. Germany*, Application no. 54934/00, admissibility decision of 29 June 2006, para 106.

[313] *Klass v. Germany*, Application no. 5029/71, judgment of 6 September 1978; *Leander v. Sweden*, Application no. 9248/81, judgment of 26 March 1987 and *Association for European Integration and Human Rights and Ekimdzhiev v. Bulgaria*, Application no. 62540/00, judgment of 28 June 2007.

[314] To the notion of "secret security files" in the ECtHR's jurisprudence, see Cameron (2000), pp. 170–258.

importance for national security.[315] After considering the guarantees against misuse, the ECtHR admits a wide margin of appreciation available to the respondent state, in particular in choosing the means for achieving the legitimate aim of protecting national security.[316]

Against this background, more than 20 years after *Leander v. Sweden*, the ECtHR was confronted with three cases coming from Romania, Sweden and Germany challenging the use and the storage of information obtained by a former security service.

In *Rotaru v. Romania* the Romanian state refused to grant to the applicant damages for suffered injustice during the communistic period on the basis of information obtained by the former communist secret service.[317] Although the complaint referred to the question whether the refusal was in accordance with the law, the ECtHR makes interesting remarks as to the supervision procedure of secret service activities. It notesthat even if it is up to the national authorities to interpret and apply domestic law, the system for gathering and archiving information did not provide sufficient safeguards against abuse, for example a supervision procedure during and after the time secret service activities were in force. Such a supervision procedure must follow democratic values, in particular the rule of law and has to be carried out effectively.[318] The ECtHR considers that this was not the case in *Rotaru v. Romania* and therefore decides that the holding and use of data by the Romanian secret service were not in accordance with the law.[319]

In this case, the concurring opinion of judge *Wildhaber*, who was joined by six other judges, is of great interest.[320] The judges agree with the decision of the ECtHR; however they make further observations in view of a possible time limit of the storage and use of the information obtained by a former secret service.[321]

Firstly they refer to the age of the entries. The file contained personal information dating mostly from the years 1946–1948, whereas one entry was made in 1937 where the applicant was bareley 16 years old. They criticise that even if the latter information was declared false by the Bucharest Court of Appeal, the entry was still recorded in the applicant's secret service file. Further he obtained no damages and no corrective actions were taken by the secret service to update the file. Additionally, the judges seriously doubt whether the interference pursued a legitimate aim and whether it was necessary in a democratic society. *Wildhaber* concludes: "In respect of national security as in respect of other purposes, there has to be at least

[315] *Leander v. Sweden*, Application no. 9248/81, judgment of 26 March 1987, para 59.

[316] Ibid.

[317] *Rotaru v. Romania*, Application no. 28341/95, judgment of 4 May 2000.

[318] Ibid, para 59.

[319] Ibid, para 62.

[320] See also: Siemen (2006), pp. 170–171.

[321] Concurring opinion of judge *Wildhaber* joined by the judges *Makaraczyk*, *Türmen*, *Costa*, *Tulkens*, *Casadevall* and *Weber* in *Rotaru v. Romania*, Application no. 28341/95, judgment of 4 May 2000.

a reasonable and genuine link between the aim invoked and the measures interfering with private life for the aim to be regarded as legitimate. To refer to the more or less indiscriminate storing of information relating to the private lives of individuals in terms of pursuing a legitimate national security concern is, to my mind, evidently problematic". Further they criticise that the data collected under a previous regime in an unlawful and arbitrary way continued to be kept on file without adequate and effective safeguards against abuse. The judges admit on the one hand that it should not be for the court to fix a time limit for the destruction of such data or whether comprehensive rights of access and rectification should be guaranteed, but on the other, they emphasise that they do not see a legitimate concern of national security which could justify the continued storing of such information in these circumstances.[322]

The judges conclude that even if a foreseeable legal basis had existed in the *Rotaru* case, the ECtHR "would have had to find a violation of Article 8 nevertheless, either on the ground that there was no legitimate aim for continuing an abusive system of secret files, or because such continuation was clearly not necessary in a democratic society".[323]

The concurring opinion hence clarifies two points:

Firstly it stipulates that the continuous storing of personal information, even in a secret service file, needs to be justified by a significant concern of national security. If this requirement can not be proven by the state, the retention of personal information does not pursue a legitimate aim, i.e. even if the ECtHR can not prescribe a time limit for destruction, it still has the possibility to examine the legitimate aim in detail.

Secondly, if the state is able to prove the pursuance of a legitimate aim, it does not enjoy unlimited discretion to subject individuals to a system of secret service files. Such a system must be strictly necessary for safeguarding democratic institutions, and adequate and effective safeguards against abuse must be established.[324]

Following this concurring opinion in *Rotaru v. Romania*, in 2006, the ECtHR was confronted with the question whether the continued storage of (true) secret service information was justified even 30 years after the entries were made. In *Segerstedt-Wilberg and others v. Sweden*, the Court went a step further than in *Rotaru v. Romania* and recognised a time limit for the storage of rather trivial information.

The ECtHR based its reasoning on the age and the nature of the records.[325] The gravity of the offences once committed played an important role. The ECtHR made a difference between records concerning, on the one hand, information about

---

[322] Ibid.

[323] Ibid.

[324] Ibid.

[325] *Segerstedt-Wiberg and others v. Sweden,* Application no. 62332/00, judgment of 6 June 2006, paras 88–92.

political commitment or the alleged advocacy of violent resistance to police control and, on the other, information concerning bomb threats against the applicant.[326]

In addition to the seriousness of the secret file's content, the age of the records was also taken into account.

In *Segerstedt-Wilberg and others v. Sweden* the ECtHR clearly opposes indefinite data storage by concluding that the retention of rather old (about 30 years) and fairly harmless entries is not necessary for the protection of national security any longer. However, more recent records concerning rather serious information were in accordance with Article 8 ECHR.[327] By arguing in this way, the ECtHR creates indirectly a right to erasure of information which is no longer relevant for the protection of national security or the prevention of disorder and crime. While this right nevertheless depends on the nature and the age of the entries, it constitutes a very important aspect in the development towards a right of deletion of entries in security files.

Related to the retention of data obtained by a (former) secret service is the use of secret service information.

In *Knauth v. Germany* the applicant worked as a nursery-school teacher in Berlin in the German Democratic Republic (GDR).[328] After the reunification she continued working in this profession until she was dismissed in 1994 for having collaborated with the GDR's Ministry of Security. As a consequence thereof, the ECtHR assessed whether there was an interference with the applicant's rights through the use of the information about her political past. In contrast to *Rotaru v. Romania*, the ECtHR found the German legislation to be foreseeable, precise and accessible to everyone and therefore in accordance with the law. As regards the question of a legitimate aim, the ECtHR considers that the dismissal pursued the aims of preventing disorder and protecting the rights of others: "it appeared legitimate for the FRG [Federal Republic of Germany] to carry out an ex post facto review of the conduct of persons who, after reunification, had been incorporated into the civil service, the members of which are the guarantors of the Constitution and of democracy. It also appeared legitimate for the FRG to dismiss from the civil service, after examining each individual case, members who did not satisfy those criteria, for example because they had collaborated with the GDR Ministry of National Security, and above all because they had lied about their collaboration to their new employer".[329] Moreover, the ECtHR carefully and explicitly balanced the severe consequence that the dismissal had for the applicant against the general interest of German society. It came to the conclusion that the interference was not disproportionate to the legitimate aim pursued, especially in consideration of the

[326] Ibid, paras 89–91.

[327] Ibid, paras 89–92.

[328] *Knauth v. Germany*, Application no. 41111/98, admissibility decision of 22 November 2001.

[329] Ibid.

exceptional historical context and the State's margin of appreciation in such matters.

The *Knauth v. Germany* judgment shows the detail and thoroughness with which the ECtHR assesses the question of the use of data obtained by a former secret service. It carefully examines whether the state pursued a legitimate aim and whether the measure at issue is essentially necessary in a democratic society.

e) The Role of Positive Obligations and Direct Horizontal Effect in Data Protection Cases

While most of the cases referred to above deal with privacy violations by public authorities, dangers to the protection of personal data also originate from the private sector. Article 3 of Convention No. 108 stipulates therefore that the Parties of the Convention "undertake to apply this convention to automated personal data files and automatic processing of personal data in the public and private sectors". This reference indicates that the Council of Europe is well aware of possible negative impacts of private data processing.

In some of the cases examined above, the ECtHR developed the duty of Member States to take legislative steps in order to prevent a breach of the right to data protection through private actors. This obligation results from a state's failure to intervene which can result in a failure to secure respect for the rights protected by Article 8 ECHR. In that case, the failure amounts to a breach of Article 8 ECHR even though the interference is not caused directly by the state.[330] This positive element of Article 8 is described by the term positive obligations.[331] The notion is fluid and not clearly defined by the ECtHR. The Court does not clearly distinguish between positive obligations, indirect or even direct secondary effects ("Drittwirkung").[332] However, there is broad and well acknowledged literature on the concept of positive obligations and its derivation.[333]

As the framework for this study is data protection, two aspects are of importance in this context: *Jacobs* and *White* describe the first case as a situation where the State must take *some action* to ensure respect for the rights included in Article

[330] Ovey and White (2006), p. 243.

[331] Ovey and White (2006), p. 243. See generally to Article 8 ECHR: Clapham (2006), pp. 387–400; Greer (2006), pp. 215–216, Wiesbrock (1999), pp. 120–123; Dröge (2003), pp. 13–23, 90–100, 123–137, 158–165; Heringa (2006).

[332] To a comparative analysis of the German term "Drittwirkung" and its signification, see Youngs (1998), pp. 95–97.

[333] See generally to positive obligation of Article 8 ECHR: Clapham (2006), pp. 387–400; Greer (2006), pp. 215–216, Wiesbrock (1999), pp. 120–123; Dröge (2003), pp. 13–23, 90–100, 123–137, 158–165.

8 ECHR.[334] Examples for this type of case are cases where the State must create an access right to personal information.[335]

Secondly, the state could be obliged to take protective measures to defend an individual from interferences by other individuals to ensure respect for the rights included in Article 8 ECHR.[336] Examples for this type of situation are the cases where individuals must be protected against unwanted release of personal information originating from public or even private actors.

aa) Fair Balance Test

In positive obligation cases, the textual basis for a state's responsibility under Article 8 ECHR is the duty to respect the rights elaborated in paragraph one of that provision.[337] The notion of respect as used in Article 8 ECHR is not yet identified definitively, especially in so far as positive obligations are concerned. The ECtHR emphasises that "having regard to the diversity of practices followed and the situations obtaining in the Contracting States, the notion's requirements will vary considerably from case to case and the margin of appreciation to be accorded to the authorities may be wider than that applied in other areas under the *Convention*".[338] As regards negative as well as positive obligations, States enjoy a certain margin of appreciation in determining the steps to be taken to ensure compliance with the ECHR, but if the State has failed to apply one particular positive obligation provided by domestic law, it may still fulfil its positive duty by other means.[339] For that reason, in those cases the criterion "in accordance with the law" of the justification test cannot be applied in the same way as in cases of direct interference by the State.[340] Thus the State enjoys a wider margin of appreciation as regards the choice of means.[341]

However, the applicable principles are mostly similar to a negative obligation.[342] In determining whether or not a positive obligation exists, the ECtHR

---

[334] Ovey and White (2006), p. 243.

[335] Siemen (2006), p. 178.

[336] Ovey and White (2006), p. 243.

[337] Mowbray (2007), p. 585.

[338] *I. v. the United Kingdom*, Application no. 25680/94, judgment of 11 July 2002, para 51.

[339] *Fadeyeva v. Russia*, Application no. 55723/00, judgment of 9 June 2005, para 96.

[340] Ibid.

[341] See *Fadeyeva v. Russia*, Application no. 55723/00, judgment of 9 June 2005, para 96: "Thus, in cases where an applicant complains about the State's failure to protect his or her Convention rights, domestic legality should be approached not as a separate and conclusive test, but rather as one of many aspects which should be taken into account in assessing whether the State has struck a "fair balance" in accordance with Article 8 § 2".

[342] Mowbray (2007), p. 585; Gómez-Arostegui (2005), pp. 153, 157. See also: *Fadeyeva v. Russia*, Application no. 55723/00, judgment of 9 June 2005, para 94; *Powell and Rayner v. the United Kingdom*, Application no. 9310/81, judgment of 21 February 1990, para 41.

pays particular regard to the fair balance that has to be struck between the competing interests of the individual and of the community as a whole.[343] Additionally, even in relation to the positive obligations coming from the first paragraph of Article 8, the aims mentioned in the second paragraph may be of certain significance.[344] As a consequence thereof, in cases where the parties disagree as to whether the measure at issue constitutes an interference with an existing right (negative obligation) or a failure by the State to grant a right which did not previously exist (positive obligation), the ECtHR applies the fair balance test.[345]

bb) Categories of Positive Obligations

Most of the cases in which the ECtHR developed positive obligations concern access rights to personal information included in medical[346] or secret service files. To stay within the limits of the following analysis of the data protection framework of the EU's AFSJ actors, only the access to secret service files including rectification and erasure rights are discussed hereinafter.

(1) Access to Secret Service Files

The central element of cases concerning the access to secret service files is that of balance between the inherent secrecy of the information and the individual's need to understand measures taken against him. As seen above, the ECtHR cautiously

[343] *Powell and Rayner v. the United Kingdom*, Application no. 9310/81, judgment of 21 February 1990, para 41; *Fadeyeva v. Russia*, Application no. 55723/00, judgment of 9 June 2005, para 94.

[344] *Powell and Rayner v. the United Kingdom*, Application no. 9310/81, judgment of 21 February 1990, para 41.

[345] *Dickson v. the United Kingdom*, Application no. 44262/04, judgment of 4 December 2007, paras 69–71: "The Court recalls that, although the object of Article 8 is essentially that of protecting the individual against arbitrary interference by the public authorities, it does not merely compel the State to abstain from such interference. In addition to this primarily negative undertaking, there may be positive obligations inherent in an effective respect for private and family life. These obligations may involve the adoption of measures designed to secure respect for private and family life even in the sphere of the relations of individuals between themselves. The boundaries between the State's positive and negative obligations under Article 8 do not lend themselves to precise definition. The applicable principles are nonetheless similar. In particular, in both instances regard must be had to the fair balance to be struck between the competing interests [...]".

[346] Compare *Gaskin v. the United Kingdom*, Application no. 10454/83, judgment of 7 July 1989; in this context see also: Pitt-Payne (2003), pp. 108–119, 113; *M.G. v. the United Kingdom*, Application no. 39393/98, judgment of 24 September 2002; *K.H. and others v. Slovakia*, Application no. 32881/04, judgment of 28 April 2009; *McGinley and Egan v. the United Kingdom*, Application nos. 21825/93 and 23414/94, judgment of 9 June 1998; *Roche v. the United Kingdom*, Application no. 32555/96, judgment of 19 October 2005 and *Guerra and others v. Italy*, Application no. 14967/89, judgment of 19 February 1998.

approaches such cases by emphasising the state's wide margin of appreciation as regards national security interests.[347]

Whereas in *Leander v. Sweden* the ECtHR emphasised that the right of access to public service is not as such enshrined in the ECHR and consequently it did not recognise a serious interference with *Leander's* rights,[348] another Swedish case in 2006 re-revealed the question whether persons concerned should generally have a right of access to their secret service data files. In *Segerstedt-Wilberg and others v. Sweden*, five applicants contested the refusal of the Swedish authorities to provide them with information concerning their secret service files entries.[349] The ECtHR dealt briefly with this question referring to the *Leander* case: a refusal of full access to a national secret police register is necessary where the State may legitimately fear that the provision of such information may endanger the efficacy of a secret surveillance system designed to protect national security and to combat terrorism.[350] Nevertheless the ECtHR referred to the quality of the law and made clear that in this case, the legal basis guaranteeing the refusal balanced the interest at stake and provided for a clear description of the discretion conferred to the competent authorities.[351] The Court opposed the applicants' opinion that the storage of information in secret police registers for "special reasons" afforded unfettered powers to the police by basing on the argument that no entry could be made exclusively on the

---

[347] *Leander v. Sweden*, Application no. 9248/81 judgment of 26 March 1987, para 59; *C.G. and others v. Bulgaria*, Application no. 1365/07, judgment of 24 April 2008, para 43.

[348] *Leander v. Sweden*, Application no. 9248/81, judgment of 26 March 1987, paras 59 and 67; nevertheless the risks resulting from an underestimation of the dangers of secret collection, storing and use of personal information was subject to the partially dissenting opinion of judges *Pettiti* and *Russo* in *Leander v. Sweden*; although they do not consider an infringement of Article 8 ECHR in the end, they emphasise, with regard to the right of access to personal information concerning the applicant himself, that: "In the case specifically of registers which, being secret, make it impossible for a citizen to avail himself of the laws and regulations entitling him to have access to administrative documents, it is all the more necessary that there should be an effective remedy before an independent authority, even if that authority is not a judicial body". Already in 1987, in the wake of the electronic era, they add: "Consideration also needs to be given to the dangers of electronic links between the police registers and other States' registers or Interpol's register. The individual must have a right of appeal against an entry resulting from a fundamental mistake, even if the source of the information is kept secret and is known only to the independent authority that has jurisdiction to determine the applicant's appeal". Therefore they conclude that: "[...] it is absolutely essential that an independent authority should be able to determine the merits of an entry in the register and even whether there has been a straightforward clerical error or mistake of identity – in which case the national – security argument would fall to the ground". Partially dissenting opinion of judges *Pettiti* and *Russo*, *Leander v. Sweden*, Application no. 9248/81, judgment of 26 March 1987).

[349] *Segerstedt-Wiberg and others v. Sweden*, Application no. 62332/00, judgment of 6 June 2006.

[350] *Segerstedt-Wiberg and others v. Sweden*, Application no. 62332/00, judgment of 6 June 2006, para 102.

[351] *Segerstedt-Wiberg and others v. Sweden*, Application no. 62332/00, judgment of 6 June 2006, paras 79 and 99–104.

basis of an individual's political opinion without his or her consent.[352] Additionally, judicial review of a decision denying the access was assured by several independent review bodies.[353] Under those conditions, the State enjoys a wide margin of appreciation as regards the regulation of access to its secret service files.[354]

In the above mentioned case *C.G. and others v. Bulgaria*, the ECtHR went a step further and clarified that if a secret service file is used to justify restrictive measures against an individual, it must contain information making it possible to verify whether the secret surveillance measures taken were lawfully ordered and executed or not.[355] Whereas in *Leander v. Sweden* the ECtHR still denied the right to access to information which explains why the applicant presented a security risk, in *C.G. and others v. Bulgaria* the Court demands at least an outline of the specific facts serving as a basis for the assessment that the applicant presented a national security risk.[356] It is noteworthy that compared to *Leander v. Sweden*, this judgment shows a certain development towards a right to be informed about the reasons for a decision which is to the detriment of a person concerned even though this information is contained in a secret service file.

Summarising, states are not under a general positive obligation regarding a right of full access to secret service data files,[357] but, there is nevertheless a right to know whether the content of one's own secret service data file was lawfully created if restrictive measures against a person concerned are based on this secret information.

Moreover, the right of access to a secret file can be included in Article 6 ECHR as part of the right to a fair trial.[358] Most importantly this right occurs in cases

[352] *Segerstedt-Wiberg and others v. Sweden,* Application no. 62332/00, judgment of 6 June 2006, para 79.

[353] *Segerstedt-Wiberg and others v. Sweden,* Application no. 62332/00, judgment of 6 June 2006, paras 62–68.

[354] *Segerstedt-Wiberg and others v. Sweden,* Application no. 62332/00, judgment of 6 June 2006, para 103.

[355] *C.G. and others v. Bulgaria,* Application no. 1365/07, judgment of 24 April 2008, para 48.

[356] *C.G. and others v. Bulgaria,* Application no. 1365/07, judgment of 24 April 2008, paras 46 and 47: [. . .] the Court finds it particularly striking that the decision to expel the first applicant made no mention of the factual grounds on which it was made. It simply cited the applicable legal provisions and stated that he "present[ed] a serious threat to national security"; this conclusion was based on unspecified information contained in a secret internal document [. . .]. Lacking even outline knowledge of the facts which had served as a basis for this assessment, the first applicant was not able to present his case adequately in the ensuing appeal to the Minister of Internal Affairs and in the judicial review proceedings.

[357] See also: *Segerstedt-Wiberg and others v. Sweden,* Application no. 62332/00, judgment of 6 June 2006, para 102: "The Court notes that, according to the Convention case-law, a refusal of full access to a national secret police register is necessary where the State may legitimately fear that the provision of such information may jeopardise the efficacy of a secret surveillance system designed to protect national security and to combat terrorism [. . .]".

[358] *Luboch v. Poland,* Application no. 37469/05, judgment of 15 January 2008, paras 49–73.

dealing with lustration proceedings in former communistic regimes.[359] The ECtHR found that it cannot be assumed that a continuing and real public interest remains in imposing restrictions on access to material classified as confidential under former regimes.[360] This finding is motivated by the very nature of lustration proceedings which serve to disclose facts dating back to the communist era and which are not connected to current activities and functions of the security services.[361] In this special case, access had to be granted to assure compliance with the right to a fair trial guaranteed by Article 6 ECHR.[362]

(2) Rectification and Erasure

In the last years, the ECtHR becomes increasingly aware of rectification and erasure rights. Whereas the Court in the 1990s paid little attention to applicants claiming rectification or erasure of personal data, there has been a move towards recognition of those rights in the last years.[363]

In the above mentioned cases *Segerstedt-Wilberg and others v. Sweden* and *Marper v. the United Kingdom*, the ECtHR developed an obligation to erase or rectify personal information contained in public databases or secret service files by acknowledging that the retention of certain information is limited in time and in some cases not necessary in a democratic society anymore. It refers to the core principles of the relevant instruments of the Council of Europe setting limits on the sprawling powers of public authorities to store data. Thereby the ECtHR recognises the right to erase data if they are wrong or no longer needed to safeguard an "actual relevant national security interest".[364] The participation in a political meeting or the entry about resistance to police control during demonstrations 30 years ago are examples of information no longer relevant to national security.[365]

---

[359] *Turek v. Slovakia*, Application no. 57986/00, judgment of 14 February 2006; *Matyjek v. Poland*, Application no. 38184/03, judgment of 24 April 2007; *Luboch v. Poland*, Application no. 37469/05, judgment of 15 January 2008.

[360] *Luboch v. Poland*, Application no. 37469/05, judgment of 15 January 2008, para 61.

[361] *Luboch v. Poland*, Application no. 37469/05, judgment of 15 January 2008, para 61; *Turek v. Slovakia*, Application no. 57986/00, judgment of 14 February 2006; *Matyjek v. Poland*, Application no. 38184/03, judgment of 24 April 2007.

[362] To the right of access as a procedural right, see Siemen (2006), pp. 191–192 discussing *McMichael v. the United Kingdom*, Application no. 16424/90, judgment of 24 February 1995.

[363] For the restricted approach of the ECtHR in the 1990s, see the cases related to transsexuals: *Yvonne Chave neé Jullien v. France*, Application no. 14461/88, admissibility decision of 9 July 1991; *Rees v. the United Kingdom*, Application no. 9532/81, judgment of 17 October 1986; *Cossey v. the United Kingdom*, Application no. 10843/84, judgment of 27 September 1990; *Sheffield and Horsham v. the United Kingdom*, Application nos. 22985/93 and 23390/94, judgment of 30 July 1998.

[364] *Segerstedt-Wiberg and others v. Sweden*, Application no. 62332/00, judgment of 6 June 2006, para 90.

[365] Ibid.

The Court did not take the direct approach of expressly establishing a positive obligation to erasure, instead it chose the path of proportionality by stating that the retention of data has to be proportionate in relation to the purpose of collection and limited in time.[366] In conclusion, states have to enact appropriate measures against the misuse of personal data, including the establishment of erasure and rectification rights.

f) Conclusion: The ECtHR's Case-Law with Regard to Article 8 ECHR – Valuable Support in Searching for European Data Protection Principles in the AFSJ

Taking into account the above observations, the ECtHR is increasingly aware of the data protection elements inherent to its case-law. Whereas earlier interpretations of Article 8 ECHR data protection guarantees were closely attached to the right to private life, recent cases show the development towards a right to data protection as one independent aspect of Article 8. Similar to other guarantees of the ECHR, the scope of this aspect of Article 8 is a wide one. It does not depend on criteria such as the type of the data or the way they were processed. The scope includes all forms of personal information no matter how the data are used. At the same time, it is open to the right to access personal data which plays an increasing role in the ECtHR's jurisprudence.

While the ECtHR sets almost no limits to the scope, it attempts to restrict the application of Article 8 ECHR when examining the interference.

Several categories can be distilled from the ECtHR's case law. In addition to legislation and measures directly restricting the right to data protection, various other actions can interfere with Article 8 ECHR. It is important to underline that each of the following acts constitutes a separate interference with Article 8 ECHR: the storing, the transmission, the release and the retention of data.

Despite the originally restrictive function of the interference criterion, a great number of actions still interfere with Article 8 ECHR. As a consequence, the essential way to distinguish whether an action is in compliance with Article 8 ECHR is to balance the interest of the Member States and the individual's fundamental rights.

In cases dealing with legislation enacted against terrorism, permitting surveillance or collecting and storing of data and the retention of information on past criminal offences, the ECtHR's case law is characterised by the legal pragmatism of prescribing in great detail the kinds of data protection guarantees states have to enact to fulfill the requirements of Article 8 ECHR. Independent supervision, the ability to delete data, and procedural rights such as the obligation to notify are some

[366] See *S. and Marper v. the United Kingdom*, Application nos. 30562/04 and 30566/04, judgment of 4 December 2008, paras 101–126, and *Segerstedt-Wiberg and others v. Sweden*, Application no. 62332/00, judgment of 6 June 2006, paras 90–92.

of detailed principles which the ECtHR has established to keep up with the increasing legislation enacted in the security sector and with steadily more sophisticated technology.

Moreover, the limitation on the categories of individuals against whom surveillance measures may be taken as well as the clear definition of the circumstances and limits of the storing and the use of the information before processing[367] and time limits for storing are essential guarantees following from the respect of Article 8 ECHR. To avoid indiscriminate storing of personal data in governmental databases, the age of the person concerned must be taken into account.[368] It is essential to determine which kind of data are to be stored and for which purposes the data should be used afterwards (purpose limitation principle).[369] This core principle includes the initial determination of the subsequent use of the data and therefore supports the control of the power of data processors.[370] By separating different purposes and, in this way, different powers, the power remains restricted to a predefined and specified purpose.

The existence of independent review and adequate and effective safeguards against abuse, including effective remedies, are key elements to assure compliance with the rule of law.[371] Accessing actors and the persons authorised to consult the files must be defined before the collection of data in security-related data processing.[372]

Because the power of processors increases with the ability to exchange data,[373] the ECtHR clarified in *Weber and Saravia v. Germany* that the types of offences on behalf of which data transmission is permitted must be limited.[374] Further, in order to transmit data to other authorities, the data must be marked and remain connected

[367] *Segerstedt-Wiberg and others v. Sweden,* Application no. 62332/00, judgment of 6 June 2006, paras 88–92; *Liberty and others v. the United Kingdom,* Application no. 58234/00, judgment of 1 July 2008, para 68; *Rotaru v. Romania,* Application no. 28341/954, judgment of 4 May 2000, para 57; *Weber and Saravia v. Germany,* Application no. 54934/00, admissibility decision of 29 June 2006, paras 116 and 127.

[368] *S. and Marper v. the United Kingdom,* Application nos. 30562/04 and 30566/04, judgment of 4 December 2008, para 119; *Segerstedt-Wiberg and others v. Sweden,* Application no. 62332/00, judgment of 6 June 2006, paras 89–92.

[369] *Weber and Saravia v. Germany,* Application no. 54934/00, admissibility decision of 29 June 2006, para 116; *Rotaru v. Romania,* Application no. 28341/954, judgment of 4 May 2000, para 57; see also: *Association for European Integration and Human Rights and Ekimdzhiev v. Bulgaria,* Application no. 62540/00, judgment of 28 June 2007.

[370] Gutwirth (2002), p. 97.

[371] *Rotaru against Romania,* Application no. 28341/95, judgment of 4 May 2000, paras 55–63; *Segerstedt-Wiberg and others v. Sweden,* Application no. 62332/00, judgment of 6 June 2006, para 121.

[372] *Rotaru v. Romania,* Application no. 28341/954, judgment of 4 May 2000, para 57.

[373] De Hert and Gutwirth (2006), in particular p. 30.

[374] *Weber and Saravia v. Germany,* Application no. 54934/00, admissibility decision of 29 June 2006, para 129.

to the purposes which had justified their collection and the transmission must be recorded in minutes.[375] Since the *Leander v. Sweden*, explicit and detailed provisions relating to the access procedure, including a list of the authorities to which information may be communicated as well as the circumstances in which such communication may take place and the procedure to be followed are essential criteria applied in transfer cases.[376]According to ECtHR case law, the subsequent notification of individuals subject to surveillance measures is directly linked to the effectiveness of remedies before the courts and therefore to the existence of effective safeguards against the abuse of monitoring powers.[377] Therefore, notification of the individual should be carried out as soon as possible.[378]

As illustrated in the foregoing, over the years, in view of both the rapid pace of technological change and the policies of security lawmakers, the ECtHR describes in sometimes astonishing detail the measures which have to be introduced to assure conformity with the ECHR.

All in all, the weighting of interests as presently conducted by the ECtHR concentrates more and more on the protection of the individual in the broad context of the growing ability to rapidly distribute all kinds of information. In view of the dangers inherent in wrong or damaging information, the ECtHR attempts to take countermeasures by creating generic standards which then serve as a model in similar cases and give the states concrete instructions on how to best protect their citizens in comparable circumstances.

In doing so, the ECtHR shows a growing awareness vis-à-vis the state's reasons to justify interference. Weighting the state's argument against the interests of the individual is carried out with greater thoroughness than the early years of the ECtHR and leads more and more to a rather comprehensive protection of the right to data protection covering a wide range of everyday situations.

In addition to negative obligations, positive obligations in data protection play an increasing role and are closely connected with access, rectification as well as erasure rights.

The development since *Leander v. Sweden*, where the ECtHR strictly denied the right to access secret service information, thus preventing the applicant from investigating the reasons of the decision taken to his detriment, illustrates a movement towards the right to be informed about such reasons, even if such information might be contained in a secret service file. Over 20 years later, in

[375] *Weber and Saravia v. Germany*, Application no. 54934/00, admissibility decision of 29 June 2006, paras 121 and 127.

[376] *Leander v. Sweden*, Application no. 9248/81, judgment of 26 March 1987, para 55.

[377] *Weber and Saravia v. Germany*, Application no. 54934/00, admissibility decision of 29 June 2006, para 135: "since there is in principle little scope for recourse to the courts by the individual concerned unless the latter is advised of the measures taken without his or her knowledge and thus able to challenge their legality retrospectively".

[378] *Weber and Saravia v. Germany*, Application no. 54934/00, admissibility decision of 29 June 2006, para 135.

C.G. and others v. Bulgaria, the Court demands to reveal the existence of specific facts which justified the refusal of access and classified the applicant as a national security risk.[379] Possibilities of independent review of the access demand and a law balancing the interest of the state against those of the individual are today essential requirements to deny the access to information contained in secret service files.[380]

The question of rectification and erasure rights in the context of law enforcement databases or secret service files is the most difficult to answer. The ECtHR does not directly mention a positive obligation, although it clarifies that the retention has to be proportionate in relation to the purpose of collection and limited in time.[381] By putting the question under the umbrella of the proportionality criterion, the Court recognises the right to erase wrong data or data which are no longer necessary to safeguard national security.

All in all, in particular the development in recent years illustrates the great awareness of the ECtHR in respect of the data protection right of individuals. Over the years, the standards of the ECtHR have become much more specific, giving detailed instructions regarding the extent to which states have to change their national legislation to comply with the ECHR. The dangers resulting from growing data processing and storing in large databases will be progressively taken into account. Besides the negative obligation to protect an individual from interferences of the state, positive obligations such as the possible development of an access right to personal data play an increasingly important role.

2. *Data Protection Elements and Restrictions with Regard to Articles 5, 6, 10 and 13 ECHR*

In addition to the protection offered by Article 8 ECHR, there are several data protection elements contained in other articles of the ECHR. Those elements cover, on the one hand, "pure" data protection aspects and on the other, access rights as well as restrictions to data protection.

---

379 *C.G. and others v. Bulgaria*, Application no. 1365/07, judgment of 24 April 2008, paras 46 and 47: "[...] the Court finds it particularly striking that the decision to expel the first applicant made no mention of the factual grounds on which it was made. It simply cited the applicable legal provisions and stated that he "present[ed] a serious threat to national security"; this conclusion was based on unspecified information contained in a secret internal document [...]. Lacking even outline knowledge of the facts which had served as a basis for this assessment, the first applicant was not able to present his case adequately in the ensuing appeal to the Minister of Internal Affairs and in the judicial review proceedings."

380 See cases: *Segerstedt-Wiberg and others v. Sweden,* Application no. 62332/00, judgment of 6 June 2006 and *C.G. and others v. Bulgaria*, Application no. 1365/07, judgment of 24 April 2008.

381 See *S. and Marper v. the United Kingdom*, Application nos. 30562/04 and 30566/04, judgment of 4 December 2008, paras 101–126, and *Segerstedt-Wiberg and others v. Sweden,* Application no. 62332/00, judgment of 6 June 2006, paras 90–92.

a) Article 5 ECHR

In connection with the right to personal liberty and security as guaranteed by Article 5 ECHR, the Court assessed that the failure to make documents available to the applicant's lawyer constituted a violation of Article 5 (4) ECHR.[382] The refusal of rapid access precluded the opportunity of effectively challenging the statements or views on which the detention decision was based.[383] With regard to the interpretation of the requirements of a "reasonable suspicion" of Article 5 (1) lit c ECHR, which is necessary to arrest a person, the ECtHR stipulated that the use of confidential information to justify a detention decision is in accordance with Article 5 ECHR.[384]

b) Article 6 ECHR

Other procedural guarantees including data protection elements are incorporated in Article 6 ECHR. Article 6 (1) ECHR establishes among others that "everyone is entitled to a fair and public hearing within a reasonable time by an independent and impartial tribunal established by law". Directly connected to the principle of equality of arms and enshrined in the wider concept of a fair trial, is the right to have an adversarial trial.[385] This means that both parties must be given "the opportunity to have knowledge of and comment on the observations filed and the evidence adduced by the other party".[386] Article 6 (1) ECHR read together with Article 6 (3) lit. d ECHR therefore grants to a certain extent a right to access court files and a right of judicial review exercised by an independent judge.[387]

Limitations to the right to disclosure of all information in the context of a court hearing may arise from interests of national security, the protection of witnesses or secret investigation methods.[388] In those cases, evidence or other information may be withheld to assure protection of other individuals or to safeguard an important

---

[382] *Lamy v. Belgium*, Application no. 10444/83, judgment of 30 March 1989; Article 5 (4) ECHR states: "Everyone who is deprived of his liberty by arrest or detention shall be entitled to take proceedings by which the lawfulness of his detention shall be decided speedily by a court and his release ordered if the detention is not lawful".

[383] *Lamy v. Belgium*, Application no. 10444/83, judgment of 30 March 1989, para 29. See also: Ovey and White (2006), p. 153.

[384] *Murray v. the United Kingdom*, Application no. 14310/88, judgment of 28 October 1994, paras 50–63; Siemen (2006), p. 205.

[385] Ovey and White (2006), p. 176.

[386] *Rowe and Davis v. the United Kingdom*, Application no. 28901/95, judgment of 16 February 2000, para 60; *Ruiz-Mateos v. Spain*, Application no. 12952/87, judgment of 23 June 1993, para 63; *Edwards and Lewis v. the United Kingdom*, Application nos. 39647/98 and 40461/98, judgment of 27 October 2004, paras 46 and 48.

[387] Meyer-Ladewig (2006), Article 6, para 45 a; Siemen (2006), pp. 206–207.

[388] Ovey and White (2006), p. 177; Meyer-Ladewig (2006), Article 6, para 41.

public interest.[389] In some cases, even an intense press campaign can influence the fairness of a trial.[390] Nevertheless information may only be retained if it is strictly necessary.[391]

On several occasions, the Court was further faced with the question whether the admission as evidence of information obtained in breach of Article 8 ECHR (for instance the unlawful use of a covert listening device), conflicts with the requirements of fairness guaranteed by Article 6 (1) ECHR.[392] In only one of the cases, the Court found a violation of Article 6 ECHR: in *Allan v. the United Kingdom*, the applicant was in pre-tail detention and expressed his wish to remain silent during the interrogation.[393] However, the police used the applicant's cellmate to obtain evidence, including taped conversations. Since the ECtHR cannot rule in general on the admissibility of evidence as such, it had to assess whether the proceedings as a whole, including the way in which the evidence was obtained, were fair.[394] In this case, the evidence, obtained in the described way, constituted the principal evidence relied on by the prosecution at the applicant's trail.[395] The Court considered that under such circumstances, besides the violation of Article 8 ECHR, there has also been a breach of Article 6 ECHR.

c) Article 10 ECHR

Article 10 (2) ECHR contains a limitation on the freedom of expression relating to the prevention of the disclosure of information received in confidence. This option, which restricts the freedom of expression, is rarely used. It is invoked in cases where the government wants to control the publication of books or press articles disclosing internal governmental or secret service information or hinder the

---

[389] Ovey and White (2006), p. 177; see *Rowe and Davis v. the United Kingdom*, Application no. 28901/95, judgment of 16 February 2000, para 61; *Ruiz-Mateos v. Spain*, Application no. 12952/87, judgment of 23 June 1993, para 63; *Edwards and Lewis v. the United Kingdom*, Application nos. 39647/98 and 40461/98, judgment of 27 October 2004, paras 46 and 48; *P.G. and J.H. v. the United Kingdom*, Application no. 44787/98, judgment of 25 September 2001, para 68.

[390] *Craxi v. Italy*, Application no. 34896/97, judgment of 5 December 2002, para 104; Meyer-Ladewig (2006), Article 6, para 60 c.

[391] *Rowe and Davis v. the United Kingdom*, Application no. 28901/95, judgment of 16 February 2000, para 61.

[392] *Khan v. the United Kingdom*, Application no. 35394/97, judgment of 12 May 2000, paras 25–28; *P.G. and J.H. v. United Kingdom*, Application no. 44787/98, judgment of 25 September 2001, paras 37–38; *Allan v. the United Kingdom*, Application no. 48539/99, judgment of 5 November 2002 paras 45–53; *Bykov v. Russia*, Application no. 4378/02, judgment of 10 March 2009, paras 94–105.

[393] *Allan v. the United Kingdom*, Application no. 48539/99, judgment of 5 November 2002.

[394] *Allan v. the United Kingdom*, Application no. 48539/99, judgment of 5 November 2002, para 42.

[395] Ibid, para 45.

publication of information about judicial investigation proceedings.[396] Limitations on the exercise of this right start from the date where the confidential information is in the public sphere (e.g. a banned book is available in another country). From that day on, the disclosure of the information can no longer be subject to punishment.[397]

In addition, despite the fact that on several occasions the Court discussed the question whether the right to freedom of expression of Article 10 ECHR guarantees an access right to information held by the authorities, the ECtHR has held for a long time that this right is not included in the Article.[398] While the Court in 2003 still found it "difficult to derive from the Convention a general right of access to administrative data and documents",[399] recently, the Court advanced towards a broader understanding of the concept of freedom to receive information.[400]

In *Társaság a Szabadságjogokért v. Hungary* the ECtHR explicitly declared that there is a development "towards the recognition of a right of access to information" within the framework of Article 10 ECHR.[401] Hungarian courts refused a non-governmental organisation access to a complaint pending before the constitutional court concerning a parliamentarian's request for examination of amendments to the criminal code in relation to drug-related offences. The government argued that access must be denied because the opinion of the parliamentarian, who lodged the

---

[396] See the "Spycatcher" cases, where the ban on a book reprint was found to be an interference with Article 10 ECHR: *Observer and Guardian v. the United Kingdom*, Application no. 13585/88, judgment of 26 November 1991 and *Sunday Times v. the United Kingdom*, Application no. 13166/87, judgment of 26 November 1991; *Editions Plon v. France*, Application no. 58148/00, judgment of 18 May 2004; see also: *Weber v. Switzerland*, Application no. 11034/84, judgment of 22 May 1990, where the fine the applicant had to pay for breaching the confidentiality of a judicial investigation was found to be an interference with Article 10 ECHR; to the latter, see also: *Stoll v. Switzerland*, Application no. 69698/01, judgment of 25 April 2006.

[397] Meyer-Ladewig (2006), Article 10, para 29; *Observer and Guardian v. the United Kingdom*, Application no. 13585/88, judgment of 26 November 1991; *Sunday Times v. the United Kingdom*, Application no. 13166/87, judgment of 26 November 1991; *Editions Plon v. France*, Application no. 58148/00, judgment of 18 May 2004.

[398] For background information on Article 10 ECHR, compare Cole et al. (2008), in particular pp. 161–207; *Leander v. Sweden*, Application no. 9248/81, judgment of 26 March 1987, para 74; *Gaskin v. the United Kingdom*, Application no. 10454/83, judgment of 7 July 1989, paras 51–53; *Roche v. the United Kingdom*, Application no.32555/96, judgment of 19 October 2005, paras 171–173; since *Leander v. Sweden*, the ECtHR continuously reiterates that "the freedom to receive information prohibits a Government from restricting a person from receiving information that others wish or may be willing to impart to him and that that freedom cannot be construed as imposing on a state, in circumstances such as those of the present case, positive obligations to ... disseminate information of its own motion", *Roche v. the United Kingdom*, Application no.32555/96, judgment of 19 October 2005, para 172 and the judgments mentioned above.

[399] *Loiseau v. France*, Application no. 46809/99, admissibility decision of 18 November 2003.

[400] *Társaság a Szabadságjogokért v. Hungary*, Application no. 37374/05, judgment of 14 April 2009, para 35, and *Sdružení Jihočeské Matky v. Czech Republic*, Application no. 19101/03, admissibility decision of 10 July 2006.

[401] *Társaság a Szabadságjogokért v. Hungary*, Application no. 37374/05, judgment of 14 April 2009, para 35.

constitutional complaint, constitutes private data which could not be released without his consent. The ECtHR drew a comparison between the applicant's functions in society and those of the press. Similar to the press, non-governmental organisations would exercise the role of a "social watchdog" by informing the public of political and social matters.[402] To hinder access to information of public interest contradicts this role being essential to the functioning of a democratic society.[403] Therefore, the Court considers that "it would be fatal for the freedom of expression if public figures could censor the press and public debate in the name of their personality rights".[404] Consequently, the refusal breached the applicant's right to have access to information of public interest.[405]

The case *Társaság a Szabadságjogokért v. Hungary* clearly shows the development towards the creation of an access right inherent to Article 10 ECHR to information of public interest granted to the press and other organisations taking part in the shaping of public opinion. This access right refers to the access of documents in the sense of EU Regulation 1049/2001 and should not be confused with the right of access to a file in criminal proceedings and can therefore be distinguished from the individual right to be informed about personal data in the context of Article 8 ECHR.[406]

Another interesting case, further discussed in Chap. B,[407] in the framework of Article 10 ECHR relating to the EU Commission's investigative powers is *Tillack v. Belgium* from 2007[408]: OLAF, the European Anti Fraud Office, being part of the EU Commission, suspected *Tillack*, a German journalist, of having bribed a EU civil servant by paying him 8000 Euros in exchange for confidential information. Thereupon OLAF opened an investigation and lodged a complaint against Mr. *Tillack* with the Belgian judicial authorities which searched his home as well as his workplace seizing his working papers and tools. The applicant later complained to the European Ombudsman who came to the conclusion in his report that OLAF's suspicions based on rumors and that the unit had made incorrect and misleading statements in its submissions to the Ombudsman.[409]

Additionally, the applicant filed a suit under former Article 230 (4) EC Treaty against the EU Commission arguing that the actions of the Belgian police followed from the decision of OLAF to investigate him.[410] The national authorities would

---

402 Ibid, para 36.

403 Ibid, para 38.

404 Ibid, para 37.

405 Ibid, paras 38–39.

406 For the distinction, see White (2009), in particular p. 66.

407 See Chap. B II 3 b.

408 *Tillack v. Belgium*, Application no. 20477/05, judgment of 27 November 2007.

409 Special Report from the European Ombudsman to the European Parliament following the draft recommendation to the European Anti-Fraud Office in complaint 2485/2004/GG.

410 T-193/04, *Tillack v. Commission*, judgment of 4 October 2006 and C-521/04 P (R), *Tillack v. Commission*, judgment of 19 April 2005, see in more detail: White (2010), in particular p. 90 and White (2009), in particular pp. 64–65.

have had no other choice but to comply with OLAF's request to seize evidence. The EU Commission, on the other side, disagreed with this opinion and referred to it as an autonomous decision of the national authorities to start investigations. The crucial question, however, was whether the sending of information from OLAF to the national authorities constitutes a legally binding act allowing a claim under Article 230 EC. The Court of First Instance agreed with the EU Commission's arguments and reached the conclusion that such a transmission does not give rise to any binding legal effects in relation to Mr. *Tillack*. The final decision to institute investigations lies within the sole responsibility of the national authorities.[411] The European Court of Justice later confirmed the judgment.[412] In consequence, OLAF's investigation reports are not legally binding acts and Mr. *Tillack's* complaint was rejected.

The ECtHR case dealt with Mr. *Tillack's* complaint against the searches of his home and workplace by the Belgian authorities.[413] The Court found that the searches in question amounted to an interference with the applicant's right to freedom of expression, specifically the right of a journalist to protect his sources, and were not justified by the exceptions provided for in Article 10 (2) ECHR. The ECtHR proceeded on the assumption that the right not to reveal one's sources is part of the right to information and has to be treated with the greatest caution, in particular in the applicant's case where the suspicions were based on vague, unconfirmed rumors.[414]

It is worth pointing out that even if the cases deal with different subject matters, Mr. *Tillack* succeeded in obtaining damages from Belgium but failed with his complaint before the European Courts. The problems arising in this context are further analysed in Chap. B II 3 b.

d) Article 13 ECHR

Furthermore, the violation of Article 8 ECHR relatively often follows a breach of Article 13 ECHR which assures the availability of an effective remedy within the national legal order to enforce the substance of the Convention's rights.[415]

While Article 13 ECHR is mostly understood as guaranteeing a remedy only under the condition of a prior ECHR violation, in *Klass v. Germany* the ECtHR

---

[411] T-193/04, *Tillack v. Commission*, judgment of 4 October 2006.

[412] C-521/04 P (R), *Tillack v. Commission*, judgment of 19 April 2005, para 28.

[413] *Tillack v. Belgium*, Application no. 20477/05, judgment of 27 November 2007.

[414] *Tillack v. Belgium*, Application no. 20477/05, judgment of 27 November 2007, para 65.

[415] *Peck v. the United Kingdom*, Application no. 44647/98, judgment of 28 January 2003, para 99; *Kirov v. Bulgaria*, Application no. 5182/02, judgment of 22 May 2008; *Association for European Integration and Human Rights and Ekimdzhiev v. Bulgaria*, Application no. 62540/00, judgment of 28 June 2007; *Rotaru v. Romania*, Application no. 28341/954, judgment of 4 May 2000, para 57; Ovey and White (2006), p. 460.

ruled on the applicability of Article 13 ECHR without demanding the violation of another Convention right.[416] In more recent cases, the ECtHR nevertheless examines Article 13 in conjunction with other provisions of the ECHR.[417]

In *Peck v. the United Kingdom* the ECtHR clearly stipulates that if no efficient remedy exists in national law in case of a breach of Article 8 ECHR, this lack of compensation amounts to a further violation of Article 13 ECHR.[418] In those cases, it is appropriate to examine separately and in addition to Article 8 ECHR, whether domestic law provides an effective remedy as guaranteed by Article 13 ECHR.[419]

A further problem arose in *Segerstedt-Wilberg and others v. Sweden*. The ECtHR had to examine whether the existence of a specific Swedish data inspection board and a so-called record board, a body particularly empowered to monitor on a daily basis the security police's entry and storage of information and to assess compliance with the Swedish Police Data Act, fulfilled the criteria of an effective remedy in cases where individuals seek the erasure or rectification of their police entries.[420] The applicants mainly based their argumentation on the fact that neither the record board nor the data inspection board had the competence to order destruction, rectification or erasure of information kept in the secret police files. The Court accepted the reasoning of the applicant and found in *Germany* addition to the violation of Article 8 ECHR that the Swedish law did not assure direct access to any legal remedy as regards the erasure of the information in question and consequently it did not meet the requirements of an effective remedy guaranteed by Article 13 ECHR.[421] The deficits could have been outweighed by any other possibility to seek compensation, but the Swedish data protection system did not provide for it. In consequence, by invoking Article 13 ECHR, the ECtHR underlines the importance of effective erasure and notification rights which should not only exist on paper, but have to be efficiently enforced in practice. It does not prescribe the details of an effective remedy system, though it stipulates that the absence of the latter violates Article 13 ECHR.

In addition to the requirement of provisions assuring rectification and erasure rights, the right to notification and appeal is often examined within the framework of Article 8 ECHR. Both rights can also be a part of the right to effective

[416] *Klass v. Germany*, Application no. 5029/71, judgment of 6 September 1978, para 63. Ovey and White (2006), p. 460.

[417] See for instance the *Weber and Saravia v. Germany* admissibility decision dealing with the same subject matter as *Klass v. Germany*: *Weber and Saravia v. Germany*, Application no. 54934/00, admissibility decision of 29 June 2006, para 156.

[418] *Peck v. the United Kingdom*, Application no. 44647/98, judgment of 28 January 2003, paras 91–114; *Kirov v. Bulgaria*, Application no. 5182/02, judgment of 22 May 2008, paras 48–58.

[419] Where the essence of the principal complaint is the absence of an appropriate remedy required by another provision of the ECHR, it is unnecessary to consider Article 13 ECHR, see Ovey and White (2006), p. 460.

[420] *Segerstedt-Wiberg and others v. Sweden*, Application no. 62332/00, judgment of 6 June 2006, paras 108–122.

[421] Ibid, para 121.

remedy.[422] Even in secret surveillance cases, a limited remedy system has to assure the rights of the persons monitored. Examples can be found in *Klass v. Germany* where individuals believing themselves to be under surveillance could bring an action to the commission overseeing the system of surveillance (or to the German Federal Constitutional Court).[423] The lack of notification of individuals after the termination of surveillance measures additionally violates Article 13 ECHR, as those concerned are unable to seek redress in respect of the use of the secret surveillance measures against them.[424]

e) Conclusion: Procedural Rights Slightly Underpinning the Protection of Article 8 ECHR

All things considered, in addition to the guarantees of Article 8 ECHR, there are several procedural rights including data protection elements contained in Articles 5, 6, 10 and 13 ECHR. In some cases, they complete the protection stemming from Article 8 ECHR, in others they are closely interlinked with the scope of the Article on which they are based.[425] An example of the latter is the access right to court files which refers to the fair trial concept of Article 6 ECHR and can, as a matter of course, only be invoked within the scope of Article 6 ECHR. Insofar as regards the last category, it is difficult to draw generalising data protection principles out of the analysis of other provisions apart from Article 8 ECHR. In this case, the procedural data protection guarantees rather represent additional protection in particular situations than pure data protection rights. They often arise from a further development of another right of the Convention and are "annexed" to it.

The rights enshrined in Article 13, such as the rights to notification, appeal, erasure or rectification represent important guarantees completing the protection of Article 8 ECHR. It remains to be seen whether the development towards the recognition of a right of access to information within the framework of Article 10 ECHR will continue.

Both categories, however, represent vital data protection elements which are essential to develop further the protection under Article 8 ECHR.

---

[422] *Association for European Integration and Human Rights and Ekimdzhiev v. Bulgaria*, Application no. 62540/00, judgment of 28 June 2007, paras 96–103; *Kirov v. Bulgaria*, Application no. 5182/02, judgment of 22 May 2008, paras 48–58; *Klass v. Germany*, Application no. 5029/71, judgment of 6 September 1978, paras 69–70; *Weber and Saravia v. Germany*, Application no. 54934/00, admissibility decision of 29 June 2006, para 157; *Rotaru v. Romania*, Application no. 28341/954, judgment of 4 May 2000, para 57.

[423] *Klass v. Germany*, Application no. 5029/71, judgment of 6 September 1978, para 70.

[424] *Association for European Integration and Human Rights and Ekimdzhiev v. Bulgaria*, Application no. 62540/00, judgment of 28 June 2007, para 101.

[425] See Siemen (2006), p. 210.

3. *Convention No. 108 for the Protection of Individuals with Regard to Automatic Processing of Personal Data*

In contrast to the economically oriented OECD Guidelines mentioned in the introduction,[426] the Council of Europe Convention No. 108 for the Protection of Individuals with regard to Automatic Processing of Personal Data is oriented on a fundamental rights perspective.[427] From the point of view of the Council of Europe, Convention No. 108 is a consistent further development of Article 8 ECHR.[428] After ratification by France, Norway, Sweden, Spain and Germany, the instrument entered into force in 1985. During the first years, it was legally binding only for these five Member States, whereas in the meanwhile, Convention No. 108 has been ratified by 41 States of the Council of Europe.[429] The European Communities acceded Convention No. 108 in June 1999.[430] It is referred to in various EU instruments dealing with the exchange of data on the EU level.[431] While Convention No. 108 is regarded as a "non-self-executing" act by the vast majority of scholars, signifying that no individual rights can be directly deduced from it,[432] it nevertheless represents the first legally binding European instrument in the data protection field and is promoted by some authors and governments to provide a possible basis for an international data protection convention seeing that Convention No. 108 is open to accession to States which are not members of the Council of Europe since July 2008.[433]

---

[426] OECD Recommendation concerning Guidelines governing the protection of privacy and transborder flows of personal data of 23 September 1980.

[427] Convention for the Protection of Individuals with regard to Automatic Processing of Personal Data, 28 January 1981, CETS No. 108. In the following: Convention No. 108; to the history and the details, see Henke (1985–1986).

[428] Simitis (2006), p. 130, para 184.

[429] Albania, Andorra, Austria, Belgium, Bosnia, Bulgaria, Croatia, Cyprus, Czech Republic, Denmark, Germany, Estonia, Finland, France, Georgia, Greece, Hungary Iceland, Ireland, Italy, Latvia, Liechtenstein, Lithuania, Luxemburg, the former Yugoslav Republic of Macedonia, Malta, Moldova, Montenegro, Netherlands, Norway, Poland, Portugal, Romania, Sweden, Switzerland, Serbia, Slovakia, Slovenia, Spain and the United Kingdom (February 2011).

[430] Amendments to Convention No. 108 allowing the accession of the European Communities, 15th June 1999.

[431] Recital (11) of Directive 95/46/EC of the European Parliament and the Council of 24 October 1995 on the protection of the individuals with regard to the processing of personal data and on the free movement of such data, OJ 1995, L-281/31; Article 14 of Council Decision 2009/426/JHA of 16 December 2008 on the strengthening of Eurojust and amending Decision 2002/187/JHA setting up Eurojust with a view to reinforcing the fight against serious crime, OJ 2009, L-138/4; Article 27 Council Decision of 6 April 2009 establishing the European Police Office, OJ 2009, L-121/37 etc.

[432] Petri (2001), p. 141; Henke (1985–1986), p. 60 et seq. with further references.

[433] See the goals of the French government in: Besson (2008); critical: Kuner (2009), pp. 307–317, p. 313; For the decision to open accession to non-member states, see Council of Europe, Committee of Ministers, 1031st meeting of 2 July 2008, Decision, Item 10.2, (CM/Del/Dec (2008)1031 4 July 2008).

a) The Principles of Convention No. 108

In order to ensure minimum coherence between the Members of Convention No. 108, domestic legislation has to be adapted to general data protection principles which it stipulates. Following the example of the OECD Guidelines, it applies to data processing in the public as well as the private sector and is limited to automatic data processing. Convention No. 108 entails broad common principles including five "basic" data protection standards which represent common core values in European data protection law. For the first time in European history, Convention No. 108 specifies from a fundamental rights point of view, principles referring to the quality of data and to data processing. Data must be:

1. Obtained and processed fairly and lawfully,
2. Stored for specific and legitimate purposes and not used in a way incompatible with those purposes,
3. Adequate, relevant and not excessive in relation to the purposes for which they are stored,
4. Accurate and, where necessary, kept up to date and finally,
5. Preserved in a form which permits identification of the data subjects for no longer than is required for the purpose for which those data are stored.[434]

In addition to these five principles, Members of Convention No. 108 are required to establish provisions regarding "special categories" of data and a sanction and remedy system for persons concerned.[435] The notion of "special categories" has an anti-discriminatory function and therefore refers to data revealing racial origin, political opinions, religious or other beliefs, as well as personal data concerning health or sexual life or criminal convictions. According to the Explanatory Report No. 48 of Convention No. 108, further data categories can be added to this list. Nowadays, these data categories are often summarised by using the term "sensitive data". For the processing of these data, member states have to establish "appropriate" security measures. That means that the domestic law of the Member States of Convention No. 108 ultimately determines the level of protection of "sensitive data".

Derogation from the five basic principles is only allowed in accordance with Article 9 Convention No. 108 and must be provided for by national law. It must also constitute a "necessary measure in a democratic society in the interest of: protection state security, public safety, the monetary interest of the state or the suppression of criminal offences" or the protection of the data subjects' rights and freedoms of others.

Transparency is required by Article 8 of Convention No. 108 which sets out the rights of the individuals, consisting of information, rectification and erasure rights. Persons concerned shall be enabled to establish the existence of an automated personal data file, its main purposes, as well as the identity the habitual residence or principal place of business of the controller of the file and have a remedy if a

[434] Article 5 lit a-e Convention No. 108.

[435] Articles 6, 8 and 10 Convention No. 108.

request for confirmation or, as the case may be, communication, rectification or erasure is not complied with.[436]

In addition to these provisions, Convention 108 deals with transborder flows of personal data. While the scope of these provisions is restricted in regards to transfer across national borders of the Convention's Member States, these provisions do not regulate data transfer to third states. According to Article 12 Convention No. 108, it is prohibited to restrict data transfer for the sole purpose of the protection of privacy. Member States should not impose higher data protection standards to the recipient state than provided for in Convention No. 108.[437] However, Convention No. 108 does not replace domestic law – its purpose is restricted to offer "helpful guidance" in case of the implementation of domestic data protection acts. Therefore it is in the competence of the member states to concretise the Convention's provisions through implementation of national law.

b) The Additional Protocol Amending Convention No. 108 Regarding Supervisory Authorities and Transborder Data Flows

Since Convention No. 108 does not regulate the transfer of data to third states, the Council of Europe enacted in November 2001 an additional protocol amending Convention No. 108 regarding supervisory authorities and transborder data flows.[438] According to this protocol, the transfer to third actors is generally permitted under the condition that the third party ensures an adequate level of protection for the intended transfer.[439] Similar to Directive 95/46, the adequacy mechanism provides certain criteria which have to be taken into account when assessing the

---

[436] See Article 8 lit a and lit d Convention No. 108.

[437] In two cases the convention permits the suspension of the transfer to another member state. Article 12 para 3 lit a and b Convention No. 108 provides: Firstly, in case if the state's legislation includes specific regulations for certain categories of personal data or of automated personal data files, because of the nature of those data or those files, except where the regulations of the other Party provide an equivalent protection. Secondly, when the transfer is made from the state's territory to the territory of a non Contracting State through the intermediary of the territory of another Party, in order to avoid such transfers resulting in circumvention of the legislation of the Party referred to at the beginning of this paragraph. In the first case, as there is no common definition of sensitive data for contracting states, member states are in charge of specification of the criteria of sensitive data on their own. In the second case, transfer to another member states remains legitimate as long as the data processing takes place in the recipient member state. There are no regulations for data once received from a contracting party after the processing in the recipient state took place (i.e. transfer of the received data to third states).

[438] Additional Protocol of the Convention for the Protection of Individuals with regard to Automatic Processing of Personal Data regarding supervisory authorities and transborder data flows, 8 November 2001.

[439] Article 2 Additional Protocol of the Convention for the Protection of Individuals with regard to Automatic Processing of Personal Data regarding supervisory authorities and transborder data flows, 8 November 2001.

level of protection for each transfer. In addition to an examination of the circumstances of the transfer, in particular the type of data, the following must be taken into account: the purposes and duration of processing for which the data are transferred, the country of origin and the country of final destination, the general and sectoral rules of law applicable in the state or organisation in question and the professional and security rules which are in force there.[440] The adequacy of the data protection rules can be assessed for a whole state or organisation. Despite of the similarity to the adequacy mechanism of Directive 95/46,[441] the Explanatory Report of the Additional Protocol to Convention No. 108 from 2001 makes no explicit reference to it, but in practice the adequacy decisions of the EU Commission might serve as a helpful indication.

Member States, however, can derogate from this provision under the following circumstances: if domestic law provides for it, because of specific interest of the data subject or legitimate prevailing interest (especially important public interest) or if adequate safeguards (i.e. contractual clauses) are provided by the controller responsible for the transfer. In any case, they must respect "the principle inherent in European law that clauses making exceptions are interpreted restrictively, so that the exception does not become the rule".[442]

While the additional protocol to Convention No. 108 entered into force in 2004, no more than 25 Member States of the Convention No. 108 ratified the instrument so far, amongst them only 19 of the 27 EU Member States.[443] This limited participation highlights another weak point of Convention No. 108 when it comes to the possibility of broad interpretation of the general principles, in particular with regard to the implementation in domestic law. As a consequence thereof, the "categorical statement" for limitations on data processing is diminished in its value.[444]

Finally, another problem arises regarding the possibility to challenge a decision violating one of the rights listed in the Convention. Neither Convention No. 108, nor its additional protocol provide for such a possibility. Individuals shall have a right to be heard, but have no substantial right to lodge a complaint. Rather, personal data are protected in an "indirect way", i.e. states are obliged to comply with the provisions, but there is no individual right to file a complaint against misuse of data which could assure more effective protection on a European level.

---

[440] Explanatory Report of the Additional Protocol to Convention No. 108, point 27.

[441] Compare Sect. III 2 e bb.

[442] Article 2 para 2 lit a and b Additional Protocol to Convention No. 108; Explanatory Report of the Additional Protocol to Convention No. 108, point 31; WP 114 of Article 29 Working Party of 25th November 2005.

[443] Ratification in February 2011: Albania, Andorra, Austria, Bosnia and Herzegovina, Bulgaria, Croatia, Cyprus, Czech Republic, Estonia, France, Germany, Hungary, Ireland, Latvia, Liechtenstein, Lithuania, Luxembourg, Monaco, Montenegro, Netherlands, Poland, Portugal, Romania, Serbia, Slovakia, Spain, Sweden, Switzerland, Ukraine and the former Yugoslav Republic of Macedonia; EU Member States such as Belgium, Denmark, United Kingdom or Slovenia have not yet ratified the Protocol.

[444] Simitis (2006), p. 121, para 162.

4. *Recommendation No. R (87) 15 Regulating the Use of Personal Data in the Police Sector*

In addition to Convention No. 108, Recommendation R (87) 15 deals with the use of personal data in the police sector.[445] Whereas the binding force of this recommendation might be controversial,[446] it nevertheless specifies certain basic data protection principles in a law enforcement context and, even though it was adopted in 1987, it is still referred to by various EU instruments dealing with the use of personal data in a police context. Examples are the Europol Council Decision, the Schengen instruments and the Prüm Convention.[447]

Recommendation R (87) 15 constitutes one of the most consulted instruments of the Council of Europe elaborating the data protection implications of Article 8 ECHR[448] and the guarantees of Convention No. 108 in this special field of police data exchange by amongst others concretising the derogations made in Article 9 Convention No. 108.[449]

Every 4 years from 1994 to 2002, Recommendation R (87) 15 was reviewed by the Project Group on Data Protection of the Council of Europe's Committee of

---

[445] Recommendation R (87) 15 of the committee of ministers to member states regulating the use of personal data in the police sector, adopted on 17 September 1987.

[446] To the different wording of the binding force of Recommendation R (87) 15 in the context of Europol, see Petri (2001).

[447] Article 27 and recital 14 Council Decision of 6 April 2009 establishing the European Police Office and replacing the Europol Convention OJ 2009, L-121/37; Articles 115 and 117 Schengen Convention; Council Decision 2007/533/JHA of 12 June 2007 on the establishment, operation and use of second generation Schengen Information System, OJ 2007, L-205/63, recital 20; Article 34 Prüm Convention.

[448] Besides Recommendation R (87) 15, there are amongst others: Recommendation No. R (86) on the protection of personal data used for social security purposes of 23 January 1986; Recommendation No. R (89) 2 on the protection of personal data used for employment purposes of 18 January 1989; Recommendation No. R (90) 19 on the protection of personal data used for payment and other related operations of 13 September 1990; Recommendation No. R (95) 4 on the protection of personal data in the area of telecommunication services of 7 February 1995; Recommendation No. R (97) 5 on the protection of medical data of 13 February 1997 etc.

[449] Article 9 of Convention No. 108 – Exceptions and restrictions (1) No exception to the provisions of Articles 5, 6 and 8 of this convention shall be allowed except within the limits defined in this article; (2) Derogation from the provisions of Articles 5, 6 and 8 of this convention shall be allowed when such derogation is provided for by the law of the Party and constitutes a necessary measure in a democratic society in the interests of: (a) protecting State security, public safety, the monetary interests of the State or the suppression of criminal offences; (6) protecting the data subject or the rights and freedoms of others; (3) Restrictions on the exercise of the rights specified in Article 8, paragraphs b, c and d, may be provided by law with respect to automated personal data files used for statistics or for scientific research purposes when there is obviously no risk of an infringement of the privacy of the data subjects.

Ministers.[450] Afterwards, review was abandoned as the Project Group agreed that the Recommendation's principles are still relevant and therefore considered that it was not necessary to revise them at present.[451] New developments could be addressed by a teleological interpretation of the existing recommendation. The three reports published until 2002 mainly entail proposals for national legislators how to interpret Recommendation R (87) 15 and how to improve existing data protection rules with regard to current sociological and technological developments.

a) The Principles of Recommendation R (87) 15

The first principle of Recommendation R (87) 15 refers to independent control and supervision which should be established outside the police sector.[452] When introducing new technical means for data processing, two requirements have to be fulfilled: the responsible national supervisory body should be consulted before the introduction, and all reasonable measures have to be taken to ensure that their use complies with the "spirit" of existing data protection legislation.[453] Even though the role of the supervisory body is limited to an advisory one, the prior consultation of this body assures a certain influence on the legislative process as well as the possibility of a public debate before introducing new technologies.[454] Furthermore, notification about permanent automated files to the supervisory body should include the nature of each file declared, the body responsible for its processing, its purposes, the type of data contained in the file and the persons to whom the data are communicated.[455]

The second principle deals with a relatively strict limitation on the use of the data: "the collection of personal data for police purposes should be limited to such as is necessary for the prevention of a real danger or the suppression of a specific criminal offence".[456] The rather severe wording of this principle is restricted however in the following sentence whereupon any exception to this provision is the subject of specific national legislation. Point 43 of the explanatory memorandum to Recommendation R (87) 15 clarifies that this rule expresses a qualitative and quantitative approach by prohibiting open-ended and indiscriminate collection

[450] First evaluation of the relevance of Recommendation R (87) 15 of 1994; Second evaluation of the relevance of Recommendation R (87) 15 of 1998; Third evaluation of Recommendation R (87) 15 of 2002.

[451] Report on the third evaluation of Recommendation R (87) 15 of 2002, Appendix VI, point 4.

[452] Principle 1.1. of Recommendation R (87) 15; With regard to the principles of Recommendation R (87) 15, compare Mayer (2001), pp. 49 and 50.

[453] Principles 1.2. and 1.3. of Recommendation R (87) 15.

[454] See Points 31–35 of the explanatory memorandum of Recommendation R (87) 15.

[455] Principle 1.4. of Recommendation R (87) 15.

[456] Principle 2.1. of Recommendation R (87) 15.

of data by the police. It elucidates the wording of Article 5 (c) of Convention No. 108 which stipulates that personal data must be adequate, relevant and not excessive in relation to the purpose for which they are stored.[457] The explanatory memorandum further specifies that the second principle of Recommendation R (87) 15 attempts to fix the boundaries to the exception provided for in Article 9 (2) lit. a of Convention No. 108 which allows a derogation from the principle that personal data must be adequate, relevant and not excessive in relation to the purpose for which they are stored in respect of the "suppression of criminal offences". The instrument insists that this exception must be limited to the collection of data being necessary for the prevention of a real danger or the suppression of a specific criminal offence, unless the law clearly authorises wider police powers to gather information.[458] Real danger is described as "not being restricted to a specific offence or offender but includes any circumstances where there is reasonable suspicion that serious criminal offences have been or might be committed to the exclusion of unsupported speculative possibilities."[459] By taking into account the *Leander* judgment of the ECtHR, principle two additionally requires the *notification* of the person concerned when data about him have been collected and stored without his knowledge, as soon as the object of the police activities would no longer be jeopardised.[460]

Principle three entails an important provision. In addition to the limitation that stored data have to be accurate and necessary to perform police tasks within the framework of national and international law, principle 3.3. distinguishes between data collected for administrative purposes and data collected for police objectives. It stipulates that both categories should be held in separate files and administrative data should not be subject to rules applicable to police data.[461] Data based on fact and data based on personal opinions and assessments should be clearly distinguished.[462] In the event of unavoidable mixing, point 53 of the explanatory

[457] Point 43 of the explanatory memorandum of Recommendation R (87) 15.

[458] Ibid.

[459] Point 43 of the explanatory memorandum of Recommendation R (87) 15 additionally gives an example to clarify the notion of real danger, real danger means "reasonable suspicion that unspecified drugs were being illegally brought into a country through a port by unidentified private yachts would justify the collection of data on all such yachts using that port, but not all yachts, their owners and passengers using every port in that country".

[460] Principle 2.2. of Recommendation R (87) 15 and Point 45 of the explanatory memorandum of Recommendation R (87) 15.

[461] Point 53 of the explanatory memorandum of Recommendation R (87) 15 clarifies that it would be wrong in principle to allow the special regime for police data, with its particular approach to data protection in the police sector, to extend to data collected for an administrative purpose.

[462] Point 52 of the explanatory memorandum of Recommendation R (87) 15: "Principle 3.2 encourages the implementation of a system of data classification. It is thought that it should be possible to distinguish between corroborated data and uncorroborated data, including assessments of human behaviour, between facts and opinions, between reliable information (and the various

memorandum of Recommendation R (87) 15 insists on the full application of general data protection rules provided for administrative storage.

Principle three therefore recognises the important distinction between data collected by the police and data collected for other purposes, such as administrative requirements. In light of existing attempts and developments in connection with the increasing data exchange between private actors, administrative authorities and police agencies, this principle should be borne in mind. Currently, data protection rules, which were once applicable to data collected in an administrative or economic context (such as PNR, telecommunications or immigration data), change at the very moment where the data are transferred to police authorities. In most cases, the individual will not be informed about the transfer or the associated change in the applicable rules.

The strict approach of provision three is further developed in the *fourth principle* which codifies a severe purpose limitation principle. Data collected and stored by the police should be used exclusively for police purposes, i.e. prevention and suppression of criminal offences or the maintenance of public order.[463] However, the absolute nature of this principle can be modified partly by principle five which deals with the communication of data.[464]

According to *principle five*, transfer of data to public parties depends on a legitimate interest, respectively on the above mentioned police purposes. It is permissible when the communication is undoubtedly in the interest of the data subject, the data subject has given its consent or where there is a clear presumption of such consent as well as to prevent a serious and imminent danger.[465] As principle five attempts to regulate the different forms of transfer while at the same time providing for general principles applicable to all data transfers, only slightly stricter derogations apply to the transfer to private parties.[466] Communication of data to foreign authorities should be restricted to police bodies and should only be allowed if there is a clear legal provision under national or international law.[467] In the absence of such a provision, the communication is must be necessary for the prevention of a serious and imminent danger or essential for the suppression of

shades thereof) and conjecture, between reasonable cause to believe that information is accurate and a groundless belief in its accuracy".

[463] Principle 4. of Recommendation R (87) 15 and Point 55 of the explanatory memorandum of Recommendation R (87) 15.

[464] Point 55 of the explanatory memorandum of Recommendation R (87) 15.

[465] Principles 5.2.i.–5.3.ii. of Recommendation R (87) 15.

[466] Point 56 of the explanatory memorandum of Recommendation R (87) 15; the communication to private parties should only be permissible, if, in a particular case, there exists a clear legal obligation or authorisation, or with the authorisation of the supervisory authority; furthermore communication is exceptionally permissible if, it is undoubtedly in the interest of the data subject, the data subject has given its consent or it exists a clear presumption of such consent as well as to prevent a serious and imminent danger (principles 5.3.i. and 5.3.ii.).

[467] Principle 5.4. of Recommendation R (87) 15.

a serious criminal offence under ordinary law.[468] When communicating the data to foreign police authorities, the data should not be used for purposes other than those specified in the request for communication. [469] The use for other purposes is subject to the prior conclusion of an agreement with the other party.[470] It is worth noting that the transfer of data to third states is not bound to a very strict purpose limitation principle which would have required to link the use of the data to the purpose for which they had been originally collected.

As a result of the Schengen Agreement, the Council of Europe completed principle five by enacting Recommendation 1181 on police co-operation and protection of personal data in the police sector in 1992.[471] Recommendation 1181 proposes the drafting of a Convention enshrining the principles of Recommendation R (87) 15 and applying these principles in the context of data exchange in the police sector between member states and between member states and third countries.[472] The standards of Recommendation 1181 mainly deal with the rights of the individuals and the respect of accuracy of data and the purpose limitation principle.[473] An independent authority outside the police sector equipped with full access to all relevant files should assure compliance with the principles set out in the proposed Convention. Although data exchange between member states and between member states and third countries increased enormously since 1992 and consequently the need for regulation in this field is even greater than in the 1990s, the project of a Convention dealing with principles for police data exchange in this context was never realised.

Principle five additionally regulates the conditions for communication providing for quality control of the data prior to the transfer. Data should be verified at the time of their communication at the latest. Inaccurate or outdated data should not be

---

[468] Ibid.

[469] Principle 5.5.iii. of Recommendation R (87) 15; Furthermore should the interconnection of files with files held for different purposes be subject to the grant of an authorisation by the supervisory body or should be in compliance with a clear legal provision, Principle 5.6. of Recommendation R (87) 15.

[470] Principle 5.5.iii. of Recommendation R (87) 15.

[471] Recommendation 1181 (1992) 1 on police co-operation and protection of personal data in the police sector of 11 March 1992.

[472] Recommendation 1181, point 7.

[473] Point 7. ii. of Recommendation 1181: a. data should be accurate, relevant, not exceed the purpose for which they are stored and, where necessary, kept up to date; b. they should be screened before they are stored; c. an individual should have the right to know whether personal data concerning him are kept; d. he should have an appropriate right of access to such data; e. he should have the right to challenge such data and, if necessary, have them rectified or erased; f. individuals who are denied access to files relating to them should have a right to appeal to an independent authority which has full access to all relevant files and which can and should weigh the conflicting interests involved; g. there should be an independent authority outside the police sector responsible for ensuring respect of the principles laid down in such a convention; iii. appeal to member states to ensure that data in the police sector may only be exchanged with other member states and with Interpol on the lines provided for in the proposed draft convention.

transferred. If data have been transmitted in spite of this, the communicating body must immediately inform the recipients of the incorrectness of the transferred data.

The *sixth principle* gives individuals a right of access, rectification and erasure. However, it entails certain restrictions such as the performance of the legal task of the police, the protection of the data subject and the rights and freedoms of others.[474] Where access is refused, the individual should have the possibility to appeal to an independent body.

Time limits for the storage and deletion of the data if they are no longer necessary for the purposes for which they were stored are provided for in *principle seven*. Several criteria should be taken into account when fixing the time limit: the need to retain data in light of the conclusion of an inquiry into a particular case, a final judicial decision, in particular an acquittal, rehabilitation, spent convictions, amnesties, the age of the data subject and particular categories of data.[475] In addition to regular checks on the quality of the data, *principle eight* provides for the general establishment of "necessary measures to ensure the appropriate physical and logical security of the data and prevent unauthorised access, communication or alteration".[476]

Especially the age criterion in principle seven could play a central role in future discussions about time limits of vast databases. Bearing in mind the decision *S. and Marper v. the United Kingdom* in which the ECtHR underlined the importance of a time limit to the storage in particular for data of younger persons, this criterion seems to become increasingly important.[477] Stigmatisation effects which can be the consequence of an entry in a police database might have a strong influence on the future life of young people. The United Kingdom violated Article 8 ECHR as it neither provided a time limit for the storage, nor for provisions making a distinction between the nature or gravity of the offence and the age of the suspected person.[478] With the increasing amount of various databases at national as well as at EU level, the time limit of entries and the age criterion provided for in Recommendation R (87) 15 and derived from the ECtHR case law, are important corrective factors to be considered in future projects of large databases.

b) Conclusion: Recommendation R (87) 15 – Essential Data Protection Principles for Police Cooperation at European Level

All in all, Recommendation R (87) 15 entails important and basic data protection principles for the police sector. Far too often those principles are restricted in the

---

474 Principle 6.4. of Recommendation R (87) 15.

475 Principle 7.1. of Recommendation R (87) 15.

476 Principles 7.2. and 8. of Recommendation R (87) 15.

477 *S. and Marper v. the United Kingdom*, Application nos. 30562/04 and 30566/04, judgment of 4 December 2008.

478 Ibid, para 119.

case that a specific national or international law provides for a derogation.[479] However, three aspects deserve special attention:

Stipulated in principle one, comprehensive independent control and supervision established outside the police sector seems to be the most important tool to guarantee compliance with the principles. This principle regulates in detail the tasks necessary to fulfil effective oversight. In accordance with its wording, it refers only to supervisory authorities of the Member States, but bearing in mind the various references of EU instruments to Recommendation R (87) 15 and in light of present day conditions, the same principles should apply to supervisory authorities at the EU level.

Secondly, the strict limitation of the collection of data to police purposes for reasons such as the prevention of a real danger or the suppression of specific criminal offences is certainly more restrictive than the open scopes of today's data exchange mechanisms. Several examples are, amongst others, the Data Retention Directive, the Europol-US agreement on data and related information exchange, as well as the PNR agreement between the EU and the US.[480] More examples are given in Chap. C. A severe application of this principle excludes vague formulations and paraphrases of the purpose which can be found in more and more instruments dealing with the collection of (police) data. The explanatory memorandum expressly clarifies that this provision should prohibit the open-ended and indiscriminate collection of data by the police.[481]

A third important aspect concerns restrictions to the transfer of personal data. The data transferred to other public bodies, private parties and foreign authorities should not be used for purposes other than those specified in the request for communication.[482] This provision applies to all of the EU's police data exchange systems referring to Recommendation R (87) 15. Problems in this context may arise in two situations: Firstly, in particular third states do not always agree to a limited

[479] See e.g. principles 2.1.; 3.1.; 5.4. or 5.6.

[480] Directive 2006/24/EC of the European Parliament and of the Council of 15 March 2006 on the retention of data generated or processed in connection with the provision of publicly available electronic communications services or of public communications networks and amending Directive 2002/58/EC, OJ 2006, L-105/54; Agreement between the European Union and the United States of America on the processing and transfer of Passenger Name Record (PNR) data by air carriers to the Unites States Department of Homeland Security (DHS), OJ 2007, L-204/18, in the following: EU-US PNR-Agreement of August 2007, OJ 2007, L-204/18; Europol-US Agreement on the exchange of personal data and related information of 2002.

[481] Point 43 of of the explanatory memorandum of Recommendation R (87) 15.

[482] Principle 5.5.iii. of Recommendation R (87) 15; Furthermore should the interconnection of files with files held for different purposes be subject to the grant of an authorisation by the supervisory body or should be in compliance with a clear legal provision, Principle 5.6. of Recommendation R (87) 15.

use of data once received.[483] Secondly, the purpose is described in a very broad manner not specifying the exact use.[484]

5. *Conclusion: Towards Basic ECHR Principles for Security-Related Data Processing*

The analysis of the Council of Europe's instruments, particularly the ECtHR's case law, shows that the protection of personal data is of fundamental importance to an individual's enjoyment of his or her right to respect for private and family life.[485] The protection of personal data within the framework of the Council of Europe has become commonly accepted and much more explicit in recent years. Above all, the case law of the ECtHR assures relatively comprehensive protection which is conducive to extracting principles of general application. When examining the justification of interferences with this right, the discretion conferred to the Member States has become narrower over the years and rights of individuals increasingly predominate over the interests of the State. Instruments such as the Convention No. 108 and Recommendation R (87) 15 complement the protection granted by Article 8 ECHR, even though they are limited in scope and not ratified by all EU Member States. In particular the principles of Recommendation R (87) 15 are of fundamental importance in respect to the references to this instrument made by almost all EU instruments dealing with the exchange of personal data in the police sector.[486]

The exemplary function of the ECtHR's case law is all the more important at the EU level, particularly in view of the previously limited competences of the European Courts in the former third pillar.[487] Seeing that the scope of the ECHR covered

---

483 See for instance EU-US PNR-Agreement of August 2007, OJ 2007, L-204/18.

484 Examples: EU-US PNR-Agreement of August 2007, OJ 2007, L-204/18; Europol-US Agreement on the exchange of personal data and related information of 2002, in particular Article 5 accessible at http://www.europol.europa.eu/index.asp?page=agreements (accessed February 2011) and Eurojust-US Agreement of November 2006, in particular Article 2, accessible at http://www.eurojust.europa.eu/official_documents/eju_agreements.htm (accessed February 2011).

485 *Z. v Finland*, Application no. 22009/93, judgment of 25 February 1997, para 95; *Peck v. United Kingdom*, Application no. 44647/98, judgment of 28 January 2003, para 78; *L.L. v France* Application no. 7508/02, judgment of 10 October 2006, para 43; *Biriuk v Lithuania*, Application no. 23373/03, judgment of 25 November 2008, para 39; *I v Finland* Application no. 20511/03, judgment of 17 July 2008, para 38; *S. and Marper v the United Kingdom*, Application nos. 30562/04 and 30566/04, judgment of 4 December 2008, para 103; *C.C. v. Spain*, Application no. 1425/06, judgment of 6 October 2009, para 31; see also: Breitenmoser (1986), p. 245; Kugelmann (2003), p. 16 et seq.; Meyer-Ladewig (2006), Article 8, para 11; Moreham (2008), pp. 44–79.

486 Exemplarily: Article 27 Council Decision of 6 April 2009 establishing the European Police Office, OJ 2009, L-121/37 etc.

487 Compare Lenaerts (2010), in particular pp. 261–264.

the respect of fundamental rights in the law enforcement sector since its beginnings, the jurisdiction of the ECtHR could develop important principles over the last years while not being inhibited by the legal structure of the EU.

Whereas the analysis of the case law has shown that in general the ECtHR admits a wide margin of discretion to the Member States when national security is at stake, the interests of the parties however have to be reasonably balanced. Moreover, to be in accordance with the law, the measure in question must be "foreseeable", which means formulated with sufficient precision to enable an individual to regulate his conduct.[488] In the judgments related to governmental data collection and the implementation of surveillance measures in the framework of Article 8 ECHR, certain criteria stand out and must be fulfilled in order to guarantee proportionality and thus strive for a balance between the interests at stake. These criteria include the limitation on the categories of individuals against whom surveillance measures may be taken as well as the clear definition of the circumstances and limits of the storing and the use of the information before processing.[489] Time limits for storing are essential and the age of the person concerned must be taken into account to avoid indiscriminate storing of personal data in governmental databases.[490] Prior to surveillance measures and the collection of data in security-related data processing, it is crucial to determine which kind of data are to be stored and for which purposes the data should be used afterwards (purpose limitation principle).[491] Independent review and adequate and effective safeguards against abuse, including effective remedies, must exist to assure compliance with the rule of law.[492] Detailed provisions concerning the persons authorised to consult the files, the nature of the files, the procedure to be followed

---

[488] *Sunday Times v. the United Kingdom*, Application no. 6538/74, judgment of 26 April 1979, para 49; *Liberty and others v. the United Kingdom*, Application no. 58234/00, judgment of 1 July 2008, para 68; *Silver v. the United Kingdom*, Application no. 5947/72 and others, judgment of 25 March 1983, paras 85–88.

[489] *Segerstedt-Wiberg and others v. Sweden*, Application no. 62332/00, judgment of 6 June 2006, paras 88–92; *Liberty and others v. the United Kingdom*, Application no. 58234/00, judgment of 1 July 2008, para 68; *Rotaru v. Romania*, Application no. 28341/954, judgment of 4 May 2000, para 57; *Weber and Saravia v. Germany*, Application no. 54934/00, admissibility decision of 29 June 2006, paras 116 and 127.

[490] *S. and Marper v. the United Kingdom*, Application nos. 30562/04 and 30566/04, judgment of 4 December 2008, para 119; *Segerstedt-Wiberg and others v. Sweden*, Application no. 62332/00, judgment of 6 June 2006, paras 89–92.

[491] *Weber and Saravia v. Germany*, Application no. 54934/00, admissibility decision of 29 June 2006, para 116, *Rotaru v. Romania*, Application no. 28341/954, judgment of 4 May 2000, para 57; see also *Association for European Integration and Human Rights and Ekimdzhiev v. Bulgaria*, Application no. 62540/00, judgment of 28 June 2007.

[492] *Rotaru against Romania*, Application no. 28341/95, judgment of 4 May 2000, paras 55–63; *Segerstedt-Wiberg and others v. Sweden*, Application no. 62332/00, judgment of 6 June 2006, para 121.

or the use that might be made of the information thus obtained are essential requirements which have to be fulfilled before ordering surveillance.[493]

In *Weber and Saravia v. Germany*, the ECtHR clarified amongst other, that the Bundesverfassungsgericht (German Federal Constitutional Court) only adequately counterbalanced an interference, provoked by the collection and transmission of security-related personal data to another authority, by strictly limiting the types of offences on behalf of which data transmission was permitted.[494] The restriction referred to the order of the Bundesverfassungsgericht that the law in question could only be applied and data could only be transmitted, if specific facts – as opposed to mere factual indications – aroused the suspicion that someone had committed one of the limited offences listed in a special article of challenged act.[495] In order to transmit data to other authorities, there is a requirement that the data be marked and remain connected to the purposes which had justified their collection[496] and that the transmission be recorded in minutes.[497] Explicit and detailed provisions relating to the hand out procedure, including a list of the authorities to which information may be communicated as well as the circumstances in which such communication may take place and the procedure to be followed were already important criteria applied in transfer cases, since the *Leander v. Sweden* case.[498]

With regard to the subsequent notification of individuals subject to surveillance measures, the ECtHR emphasises that this question is closely linked to the effectiveness of remedies before the courts and therefore to the existence of effective safeguards against the abuse of monitoring powers.[499] Again, in the case *Weber and Saravia v. Germany*, the ECtHR adds: "As soon as notification can be carried out without jeopardising the purpose of the restriction after the termination of the surveillance measure, [. . .], information should be provided to the persons concerned".[500]

What often appears to be lost in the discussion about a common legislative data protection standard at the EU level is the absolutely central role played by ECtHR in Europe. The activity of the ECtHR in the context of national security and the prevention of disorder or crime the latter circumstances is of fundamental importance and plays a elementary role also in view of the instruments which have to be

[493] *Rotaru v. Romania*, Application no. 28341/954, judgment of 4 May 2000, para 57.

[494] *Weber and Saravia v. Germany*, Application no. 54934/00, admissibility decision of 29 June 2006, para 129.

[495] Ibid, para 127.

[496] Ibid, para 121.

[497] Ibid, para 127.

[498] *Leander v. Sweden*, Application no. 9248/81, judgment of 26 March 1987, para 55.

[499] *Weber and Saravia v. Germany*, Application no. 54934/00, admissibility decision of 29 June 2006, para 125: "since there is in principle little scope for recourse to the courts by the individual concerned unless the latter is advised of the measures taken without his or her knowledge and thus able to challenge their legality retrospectively".

[500] *Weber and Saravia v. Germany*, Application no. 54934/00, admissibility decision of 29 June 2006, para 135.

implemented at the EU level in former third pillar matters as demanded by Article 16 (2) TEU.[501] The Court creates an overarching standard and often has a role model character for both EU courts.[502] Due to the increasingly intense connection between EU law and the ECHR mentioned in the introduction (para I), the rules laid down by the ECtHR can be seen as a minimum data protection standard within the EU. Consequently, the European legislator can not step back and lag behind the criteria previously developed by the ECtHR.

Within the limits of the EU's competences, this responsibility applies as well in positive obligation cases as regards access, rectification and erasure rights. The case law regarding positive obligations visibly demonstrates that the ECtHR undoubtedly proceeds on the assumption that there are positive obligations to secure respect for private life by means of a system of data protection rules and safeguards.[503] Additionally, it has become less reluctant concerning the individual's right for a better understanding of the decisions which are taken to his or her detriment.

Finally, the combination of the different instruments of the Council of Europe – predominantly the case law of the ECtHR – assures the most comprehensive data protection approach in security-related data processing in Europe. The ECtHR specifies fundamental data protection principles when processing, storing and using personal information, thereby it increasingly abandons its case-by-case approach by stipulating more general principles which could be afterwards applied in similar cases and which serve as guiding principles for the EU and the Member States when enacting or reviewing their data protection legislation. This basic standard will be later used to assess the existing as well as the proposed instruments and measures of the actors in the AFSJ of the EU.

III European Union Standards

After having illustrated the ECHR data protection standards in security related data processing, the EU principles merit further attention. It is worth noting in advance that the EU data protection rules are to a great extent diversified and that the AFSJ

[501] Article 16 (2) TEU: "The European Parliament and the Council, acting in accordance with the ordinary legislative procedure, shall lay down the rules relating to the protection of individuals with regard to the processing of personal data by Union institutions, bodies, offices and agencies, and by the Member States when carrying out activities which fall within the scope of Union law, and the rules relating to the free movement of such data. Compliance with these rules shall be subject to the control of independent authorities. The rules adopted on the basis of this Article shall be without prejudice to the specific rules laid down in Article 39 of the Treaty on European Union".

[502] Compare with regard to the model character of the ECtHR case-law for Europol: Esser (2008); Case C-465/00, *Rechnungshof v. Österreichischer Rundfunk and Others*, judgment of 20 May 2003, para 10 and 19.

[503] *I. v. Finland*, Application no. 20511/03, judgment of 17 July 2008, para 37; *Segerstedt-Wiberg and others v. Sweden,* Application no. 62332/00, judgment of 6 June 2006 etc.

consists of a patchwork of different applicable rules making it difficult to illustrate the data protection instruments and principles in this area. However, it is worth noting that the EU's development of fundamental rights protection arose out of a case concerning the protection of private life interests.[504] The former pillar structure considerably influenced the scopes of the existing data protection instruments[505] as well as it limited the competence of the European Courts. As the power of the EU Courts in former Titles V and VI (common foreign security policy and police and judicial cooperation in criminal matters) of the EU Treaty was curtailed[506], far less case law with reference to security related data processing exists when comparing it to the ECHR. The few existing decisions are further elaborated in the following.

Another heritage of the former pillar structures relates to the fact that the main piece of legislation in EU data protection law, Directive 95/46, is not applicable to security related data processing. However, its principles represent fundamental data protection values and are often used as the framework of reference when adopting new data protection legislation in the EU. Thus, the following section focuses in a first section on the scopes of the instruments in force and analyses in a second section the principles applying to the whole or only to a part of the AFSJ. Differences between the scope and the guarantees of the diverse sources are duly considered. Included in the first section is the discussion of the important changes in relation to data protection brought by the entry into force of the Lisbon Treaty.

1. Main Data Protection Instruments in the AFSJ and Their Scope

a) Former First Pillar Protection

The Council of Europe developments in private life concerns and data protection rights influenced the efforts taken at EU level to adopt harmonised data protection standards. Even though, in contrast to the fundamental rights basis of the ECHR, the economic aspect of introducing unified standards to establish an internal market played an important role when adopting the key instrument of legislation regarding

---

[504] The *Stauder v. City of Ulm* case concerned a community scheme for the distribution of butter at reduced prices on the disclosure of the name of the recipient. *Stauder* complaint against the disclosure of his name and the Court of Justice interpreted that the community's scheme was not requiring such disclosure. The respect of Stauder's fundamental right to privacy constituted a general principle of community law and set forth to itself to annul an EC rules which went contrary to such principle, see Case 29–69, *Erich Stauder v. City of Ulm*, judgement of 12 November 1969.

[505] The scopes of the instruments are limited to specific contexts and different data protection principles apply in different situations; compare also Van den Wyngaert (2004), in particular p. 295; for a general overview of the AFSJ structure refer to Borchardt (2010), pp. 570–596.

[506] Compare Lenaerts (2010) in particular pp. 261–264.

data protection in Community law, the Data Protection Directive 95/46 in October 1995. The legal basis of Article 95 EC Treaty[507] (Article 114 TFEU) assured the participation of the European Parliament trough the co-decision procedure. Although having its roots in the harmonisation of the internal market, Directive 95/46 has a strong fundamental rights approach and was supposed to give "substance to and amplify" the principles contained in the Council of Europe Convention No. 108.[508]

Directive 95/46 covers data processing by automatic and non automatic means[509] by the Member States in (former) first pillar policies (for instance the VIS) and created the Article 29 Data Protection Working Party which examines questions relating to the interpretation of Directive 95/46 with the aim of contributing to a uniform application of the Directive.[510] Due to its pioneer character, the definitions and principles of Directive 95/46 are often a reference instrument for data protection provisions in other EU instruments. Later, the protection of personal data within the first pillar of the EU was reinforced by the adoption of the Directive on the protection of privacy in the telecommunications sector.[511] In 1997, the Amsterdam Treaty added Article 286 EC Treaty (Article 16 TFEU) which extended the application of the data protection principles contained in Directive 95/46 to personal data processed by European Community institutions and bodies. Based on this Article, Regulation 45/2001 was adopted which guarantees data protection in an EU-internal former first pillar context and established the European Data Protection Supervisor (EDPS)[512] as the authority responsible for overseeing data processing of the institutions an bodies at

[507] With regard to Article 95 EC Treaty, compare Bieber et al. (2006), pp. 264–268.

[508] Recital (11) of Directive 95/46/EC of the European Parliament and the Council of 24 October 1995 on the protection of the individuals with regard to the processing of personal data and on the free movement of such data, OJ 1995, L-281/31, in the following: Directive 95/46, OJ 1995, L-281/31; the two approaches (fundamental rights and internal market) are reflected in the title of the Directive referring to the free flow of data as well as to the protection of individuals.

[509] Article 3 (1) Directive 95/46 covers not only data processing by automatic and non automatic means of personal data which form part of a filing system or are intended to form part of a filing system, it includes also data processing otherwise than by automatic means.

[510] Article 29 and 30 of Directive 95/46. OJ 1995, L-281/31.

[511] Directive 97/66/EC of the European Parliament and of the Council of 15 December 1997 concerning the processing of personal data and the protection of privacy in the telecommunications sector OJ 1998 L-24/1; replaced by Directive 2002/58/EC of the European Parliament and of the Council of 12 July 2002 concerning the processing of personal data and the protection of privacy in the electronic communications sector (Directive on privacy and electronic communications) OJ 2002, L-201/37 and amended by Directive 2006/24/EC of the European Parliament and of the Council of 15 March 2006 on the retention of data generated or processed in connection with the provision of publicly available electronic communications services or of public communications networks and amending Directive 2002/58/EC, OJ 2006, L-105/54.

[512] Hereafter referred to as EDPS.

Community level.[513] As a result of their first pillar status, AFSJ databases such as the VIS, Eurodac and partially the SIS (II) are monitored by the EDPS. Such as Directive 95/46, Regulation 45/2001 does not apply to legal persons.[514]

b) Scope of Directive 95/46 and Regulation 45/2001

Directive 95/46 as well as Regulation 45/2001 are pure (former) first pillar instruments. Regulation 45/2001 therefore exclusively relates to "the processing of personal data by all Community institutions and bodies insofar as such processing is carried out in the exercise of activities all or part of which fall within the scope of Community law".[515] Directive 95/45 equally excludes Titles V and VI former TEU (common foreign and security policy and police and judicial cooperation) from the scope of Directive 95/46.[516]

Over the course of time, the scope of Directive 95/46 was further clarified by the case law of the Court of Justice. Initially ruling that the rights of Directive 95/46 go further than the mere exercise of economic activities (*Österreichischer Rundfunk/ Lindqvist*[517]), the Court of Justice later restricted the Directive's scope to pure first pillar subjects by confirming the inapplicability of Directive 95/46 in cases of processing data for law enforcement purposes (*PNR case*).[518] The cases determining the scope of Directive 95/46 are briefly discussed in the following in chronological order.

In *Österreichischer Rundfunk,*[519] the Court of Justice not only underlined that the provisions of Directive 95/46 were to be interpreted in the light of Article

[513] European Parliament and Council Regulation (EC) 45/2001 of 18 December 2000 on the protection of individuals with regard to the processing of personal data by the Community institutions and bodies and on the free movement of such data, OJ 2001, L-8/1 (referred to as Regulation 45/2001, OJ 2001, L-8/1 in the following).

[514] See case T-189/03, *Bank Austria Creditanstalt AG v. Commission*, judgment of 30 May 2006, para 95.

[515] Article 3 (1) Regulation 45/2001, OJ 2001, L-8/1, Article 3 (2) of Regulation 45/2001 adds that the "Regulation shall apply to the processing of personal data wholly or partly by automatic means, and to the processing otherwise than by automatic means of personal data which form part of a filing system or are intended to form part of a filing system".

[516] Article 3 (2) Directive 95/46. OJ 1995, L-281/31.

[517] Case C-465/00, *Rechnungshof v. Österreichischer Rundfunk and Others*, judgment of 20 May 2003; Case C-101/01, *Lindqvist* of 6 November 2003.

[518] Joined cases C-317/04 and C-318/04, *Parliament v. Council*, judgment of 30 May 2006.

[519] In *Rechnungshof v. Österreichischer Rundfunk and Others* the Austrian Constitutional and Supreme Court requested a preliminary ruling on the questions: first, whether Directive 95/46 precludes national legislation requiring a public body (the ORF, a broadcasting organisation governed by public law) to collect and communicate data on income for the purpose of publishing the names and incomes of state employees and second, whether the provisions precluding national the legislation are directly applicable, in the sense that the persons obliged to disclose may rely on them to prevent the application of national provisions. The answer to the first question was that

8 ECHR[520] and that the Article 8 ECHR guarantees form part of the general principles of Community law,[521] the Court additionally emphasised that the Directive applies to a wide range of data processing cases without the need to prove in each specific case the connection to the internal market.[522]

The *Lindqvist* case[523] highlighted the wide scope of data protection in the (former) first pillar matters by restricting the scope of the exceptions provided for by Article 3 (2) of Directive 95/46. The exceptions apply to "the processing of personal data outside the scope of Community law, such as Titles V and VI of the Treaty on European Union[524] and in any case to processing operations concerning public security, defence, State security (including the economic well-being of the State when the processing operation relates to State security matters) and the activities of the State in areas of criminal law" as well as to processing "by a natural person in the course of a purely personal or household activity".[525] The Court of Justice underlined that, according to the first indent of Article 3 (2) Directive 95/46, the processing of data ouside of the scope of Community law only applies to those activities by the state mentioned by way of example in Article 3 (2) Directive 95/46 unrelated to the fields of an activity of individuals[526]: the "exception applies only to the activities which are expressly listed there or which can be classified in the same category (*ejusdem generis*)".[527] The Court of Justice

---

"Articles 6(1)(c) and 7(c) and (e) of Directive 95/46 do not preclude national legislation such as that at issue in the main proceedings, provided that it is shown that the wide disclosure not merely of the amounts of the annual income above a certain threshold of persons employed by the bodies subject to control by the Rechnungshof but also of the names of the recipients of that income is necessary for and appropriate to the objective of proper management of public funds pursued by the legislature, that being for the national courts to ascertain" and to the second question: "Article 6 (1)(c) and 7(c) and (e) of Directive 95/46 are directly applicable, in that they may be relied on by an individual before the national courts to oust the application of rules of national law which are contrary to those provisions", case C-465/00, *Rechnungshof v. Österreichischer Rundfunk and Others*, judgment of 20 May 2003, paras 94 and 101.

[520] Case C-465/00, *Rechnungshof v. Österreichischer Rundfunk and Others*, judgment of 20 May 2003, paras 10, 71 et seq.

[521] To the concepts of general principles, refer to Herdegen (2010), pp. 166–170.

[522] Case C-465/00, *Rechnungshof v. Österreichischer Rundfunk and Others*, judgment of 20 May 2003, para 42.

[523] In *Lindqvist*, Mrs. Lindqvist was charged with criminal violations of Swedish data protection law because she had published, on grounds of charitable and religious reasons, on the internet names, jobs, telephone numbers, medical problems etc. of her colleagues although she removed data in case somebody objected, case C-101/01, *Lindqvist*, judgment of 6 November 2003.

[524] Title V (Common Foreign and Security Policy) and Title VI (Police and Judicial Cooperation) former TEU.

[525] Article 3 (2) Directive 95/46.

[526] Case C-101/01, *Lindqvist*, judgment of 6 November 2003, paras 42–43.

[527] Ibid, para 43.

further held that the scope of Directive 95/46 includes the loading of personal data on a website as it constitutes processing by automatic means.[528]

In light of this relatively wide interpretation of the scope of Directive 95/46, the *PNR judgement* in 2006 was unexpected by many scholars.[529] The case dealt with a request for annulment by the European Parliament of a Council as well as a Commission Decision allowing for the transfer of flight passenger data (passenger name record (PNR)) from airlines to US American security authorities. The two decisions taken together approved the conclusion of an agreement with the USA in this regard (EU-US PNR agreement) and based on the first pillar legal basis of Article 95 EC Treaty (Article 114 TFEU) implying the application of Directive 95/46.

In contrast to the foregoing case-law, the Court of Justice came to a restrictive interpretation of the scope of Directive 95/46 and ruled that, although the data are collected and transferred by an economic operator (the airlines), the use and the purpose of processing of the data, and not the purpose initially justifying their collection, should decide about the legal basis allowing for conclusion of the EU-US PNR Agreement. It stipulated: "the transfer of PNR data [...] constitutes processing operations concerning public security and the activities of the State in areas of criminal law".[530] Therefore, the PNR data transfers were regarded as security-related third pillar data processing, excluding three important things: the participation of the European Parliament in the legislative process, the possibility to challenge fundamental rights violations before the Court of Justice and finally, the application of the data protection guarantees of Directive 95/46 to the PNR transfers.

By extending the exemption entailed in Article 3 (2) Directive 95/46 to the transfer of data of economic actors when they fall under a framework established by public security authorities,[531] the *PNR judgement* of the Court raises important questions regarding the protection of data collected by economic actors and later used for law enforcement purposes. The Court however decided not to address these questions.[532]

[528] Ibid, para 19.

[529] Hijmanns and Scirocco (2009), in particular p. 1503.

[530] Joined cases C-317/04 and C-318/04, *Parliament v. Council*, judgment of 30 May 2006, para 56; the Court added: "While the view may rightly be taken that PNR data are initially collected by airlines in the course of an activity which falls within the scope of Community law, namely sale of an aeroplane ticket which provides entitlement to a supply of services, the data processing which is taken into account [...] is, however, quite different in nature", as a result, the PNR transfers did not concern "data processing necessary for a supply of services, but data processing regarded as necessary for safeguarding public security and for law-enforcement purposes", see Joined cases C-317/04 and C-318/04, *Parliament v. Council*, judgment of 30 May 2006, para 57.

[531] Joined cases C-317/04 and C-318/04, *Parliament v. Council*, judgment of 30 May 2006, para 58.

[532] Compare Chap. D III 2 a.

The distinction between law enforcement data and data serving other purposes was confirmed in *Heinz Huber v. Germany* delivered by the Court of Justice in December 2008.[533] The Court clarified that data collected for a register serving public security, defence and fight against crime purposes do not profit from the protection of Directive 95/46.[534] Processing of personal data for the purposes of the application of legislation relating to the right of residence and for statistical purposes however falls within the scope of application of Directive 95/46.[535]

The understanding of the scope of Directive 95/46 in law enforcement related activities was again subject in the data retention case, *Ireland v. Parliament and Council* in 2009, where the choice of the legal basis of the Data Retention Directive 2006/24 was at stake.[536] Comparable to the *PNR case*, the Data Retention Directive, which harmonises the obligations of electronic providers to store and hold available traffic data for the (possible) later use for crime prevention purposes, was adopted on the basis of Article 95 EC Treaty (Article 114 TFEU).

Taking into account the EU-US PNR Agreement case, Ireland, supported by Slovakia, challenged the first pillar legal basis and asked the central question whether Directive 2006/24 should not have been based on a third pillar legal basis, because it regulates the data retention for law enforcement purposes, or whether the Parliament and the Council chose Article 95 EC Treaty as the correct legal basis. Article 95 EC Treaty can be generally invoked "when disparities exist between national rules which are such as to obstruct the fundamental freedoms or to create distortions of competition and thus have a direct effect on the functioning of the internal market".[537]

The Court rejected Ireland's argument and ruled that Directive 2006/24 regulates operations which "are independent of the implementation of any police and judicial cooperation in criminal matters"[538] and exclusively relate to the harmonization of the activities of service providers in the relevant sector of the internal market.[539] Despite of Article 1 of Directive 2006/24 which expressly states that it harmonises the Member States' provisions concerning the obligation of electronic communication service providers to store the "traffic and location data on both legal entities and natural persons" and "the related data necessary to

---

[533] Case C-524/06, *Heinz Huber v. Germany*, judgment of 16 December 2008, discussed in Sect. III 2 a aa.

[534] Case C-524/06, *Heinz Huber v. Germany*, judgment of 16 December 2008, para 45.

[535] Ibid.

[536] Case C-301/06, *Ireland v. Parliament and Council*, judgment of 10 February 2009; Directive 2006/24/EC of the European Parliament and of the Council of 15 March 2006 on the retention of data generated or processed in connection with the provision of publicly available electronic communications services or of public communications networks and amending Directive 2002/58/EC, OJ 2006, L-105/54.

[537] Case C-301/06, *Ireland v. Parliament and Council*, judgment of 10 February 2009, para 63.

[538] Ibid, para 83.

[539] Ibid, para 84.

identify the subscriber or registered userclient data" processed by them, "in order to ensure that the data are available for the purpose of the investigation, detection and prosecution of serious crime",[540] the Court decided against Ireland. It distinguished between the retention and the storing of the data and its subsequent use and the access to them.[541] Only the retention and the storing determined the legal basis. Consequently, the Court of Justice approved the first pillar choice of Article 95 EC Treaty as the correct legal basis for the directive.

The two judgments taken together do not necessarily result in a consistent legal approach to law enforcement access to data collected for economic purposes[542] and have aroused substantiated criticism.[543] However, the case-law is kept legally simple and might bring more clarity on the dividing line between (former) first pillar data processing protected by Directive 95/46 and (former) third pillar data processing excluded from the Directive's scope.[544] The result is that on the one hand, instruments directly obliging private actors to transfer their data to law enforcement authorities are excluded from the scope of Directive 95/46 and on the other hand, instruments not directly regulating the access from law enforcement authorities, but the retention of economic data (even if they are intended to be subsequently used for other than economic purposes) can be included in the Directive's scope.

Finally, in *Tietosuojavaltuutettu v. Satakunnan Markkinapörssi Oy and Satamedia Oy* the Court of Justice clarified once more that data serving an economic purpose fall under the protection of Directive 95/46. It stipulates: "The scope of application of Directive 95/46 on the protection of individuals with regard to the processing of personal data and on the free movement of such data extends to the processing of personal data which consists in transferring onward on CD-ROM, in order for them to be used for commercial purposes, data on the earned and unearned income and the assets of natural persons which has been collected from documents in the public domain held by the tax authorities and processed for publication and which has already been published in the media. The scope of application of the directive also extends to the processing of such data for the purposes of a text-messaging service whereas mobile telephone users can, by sending a text message containing details of an individual's name and municipality of residence to a given number, receive those data."[545]

---

[540] Article 1 (1) and (2) Directive 2006/24/EC of the European Parliament and of the Council of 15 March 2006 on the retention of data generated or processed in connection with the provision of publicly available electronic communications services or of public communications networks and amending Directive 2002/58/EC, OJ 2006, L-105/54.

[541] Case C-301/06 *Ireland v. Parliament and Council*, judgment of 10 February 2009, para 84.

[542] Discussed in the Chap. D III 2.

[543] Simitis (2009); Hijmanns and Scirocco (2009).

[544] Hijmanns and Scirocco (2009), in particular p. 1506.

[545] Case C-73/07, *Tietosuojavaltuutettu v. Satakunnan Markkinapörssi Oy and Satamedia Oy*, judgment of 16 December 2008, summary of the judgment, para 3.

Summarising, the scope of Directive 95/46 is relatively comprehensibly defined in Article 3 of Directive 95/46. One issue requiring special attention so far relates to the interpretation of the exemptions with regard to the retention of data later used for law enforcement purposes. As long as the instrument only requires the retention of the data, without regulating the access to them, Directive 95/46 remains applicable. If an instrument directly obliges private actors to transfer their data to law enforcement authorities, the exemption of Article 3 (2) Directive 95/46 is applicable.

c) Framework Decision Governing Data Processing in Police and Cooperation

Data processing in former third pillar matters was for a long time exclusively governed by the aforementioned public international law instruments of the Council of Europe (Convention No. 108, Recommendation R (87) 15 and the ECHR standard).[546] After years of discussions and debates, the Data Protection Framework Decision 2008/977/JHA on personal data processed in the framework of police and judicial cooperation in criminal matters (FDPJ) was finally adopted in November 2008 with the intention to cover data processing in (former) third pillar matters.[547] Its provisions had to be transposed into national law by November 2010. The FDPJ is based on Article 30 (1) (b) EU Treaty (replaced by Articles 87 and 88 TFEU) requiring that collection and transfers of law enforcement information shall be subject to appropriate data protection measures.

The opportunity to create a legal data protection framework in the (former) third pillar was however missed.[548] This is mainly due to the restricted scope of the instrument which is neither applicable to the data processing of most of the AFSJ law enforcement agencies, such as Europol and Eurojust,[549] nor to other AFSJ

[546] With regard to the beginnings of the cooperation in criminal law, see Cullen and Jund (2002), pp. 23–34; with regard to the necessity to strengthen the judiciary in the EU, compare Braum (2009a).

[547] Council Framework Decision 2008/977/JHA of 27 November 2008 on the protection of personal data processed in the framework of police and judicial cooperation in criminal matters, OJ 2008, L-350/60 (in the following referred to as FDPJ, OJ 2008, L-350/60), equivalent to Directive 95/46, the processing refers to automatic and non-automatic processing of personal data, Article 2 (a) FDPJ.

[548] Hijmanns and Scirocco (2009), in particular pp. 1493–1496.

[549] Europol considers in recital (12) of Council Decision of 6 April 2009 establishing the European Police Office, OJ 2009, L-121/37: "A Council Framework Decision on the protection of personal data processed in the framework of police and judicial cooperation in criminal matters will be applicable to the transfer of personal data by Member States to Europol. The relevant set of data-protection provisions in this Decision will not be affected by that Framework Decision and this Decision should contain specific provisions on the protection of personal data regulating these matters in greater detail because of the particular nature, functions and competences of Europol"; the equivalent at Eurojust is recital (13) Council Decision 2009/426/JHA of 16 December 2008 on

exchange systems, i.e. the SIS or the CIS.[550] The reason for this inapplicability is explained in Recital 39 FDPJ and relates to the fact that the aforementioned data exchange systems were adopted under Title VI of the TEU and "constitute a complete and coherent set of rules covering all relevant aspects of data protection".[551] Additionally excluded from the scope is the internal processing of the Member States in police and criminal matters. The FDPJ exclusively applies in a cross-border context, although for instance not in case of the Treaty of Prüm[552] establishing cross-border DNA information exchange between Member States.

Hijmans and *Scirocco* rightly raise the question how these limitations work in practice.[553] At the time of collection of the data by the Member State, the subsequent possible cross-border transfer of such data will often not be foreseeable. The standards of the FDPJ therefore do not have general application. In addition to the scope, there are several other shortcomings, discussed below, and principally involving the level of protection (e.g. specific conditions enacted prior to the FDPJ take precedence over the provisions of the FDPJ[554]) and the lack of specific rules in police and criminal cooperation.[555]

d) The Impact of the Lisbon Treaty on the AFSJ

The entry into force of the Lisbon Treaty influenced the aforementioned EU data protection framework in several ways. One of the major changes relates to the abolition of the pillar structure putting an end to the structural separation between

---

the strengthening of Eurojust and amending Decision 2002/187/JHA setting up Eurojust with a view to reinforcing the fight against serious crime, OJ 2009, L-138/4, stating that: "Council Framework Decision 2008/977/JHA of 27 November 2008 on the protection of personal data processed in the framework of police and judicial cooperation in criminal matters is applicable to the processing by the Member States of the personal data transferred between the Member States and Eurojust. The relevant set of data protection provisions of Decision 2002/187/JHA will not be affected by Framework Decision 2008/977/JHA and contains specific provisions on the protection of personal data regulating these matters in more detail because of the particular nature, functions and competences of Eurojust".

550 FDPJ, OJ 2008, L-350/60, recital 39.

551 FDPJ, OJ 2008, L-350/60, recital 39.

552 The Treaty of Prüm was signed in May 2005 by seven Member States (Belgium, Germany, Spain, France, Luxembourg, the Netherlands and Austria), outside of the framework of the EU-Treaty and contains provisions about enhanced cross-border cooperation, particularly in combating terrorism and cross-border crime; in the meanwhile the provisions of the treaty have been transposed in EU law by Council Decision 2008/615/JHA of 23 June 2008 on the stepping up of cross-border cooperation, particularly in combating terrorism and cross-border crime, OJ 2008, L-210/1.

553 Hijmanns and Scirocco (2009), in particular p. 1494.

554 Article 28 FDPJ, OJ 2008, L-350/60.

555 See Sect. III 2.

"European Community" actions and "European Union" activities, a development which will largely influence data protection policy in the AFSJ.[556]

aa) Article 16 TFEU and Its Delayed Effects on the AFSJ

One important change for data protection law in the EU relates to the introduction of Article 16 TFEU stipulating a special legal basis which provides a subjective right to data protection being also applicable in the AFSJ.[557] Prominently placed in Title II on "provisions of general application", Article 16 provides in its paragraphs one and two that "everyone has the right to the protection of personal data concerning them" and that "compliance with these rules shall be subject to the control of independent authorities".[558] The European Parliament and the Council will "lay down the rules relating to the protection of individuals with regard to the processing of personal data by Union institutions, bodies, offices and agencies, and by the Member States when carrying out activities which fall within the scope of Union law, and the rules relating to the free movement of such data".[559]

Although the wording of Article 16 TFEU might be of very general nature, it expressly recognises for the first time in European history at primary law level the need for rules on data protection, not only as it regards data processing within the European Institutions (former Article 286 EC Treaty), but also as regards processing by Member States. Requiring independent supervision and prescribing the ordinary legislative procedure, where Parliament and Council act as co-legislators, democratic principles are respected to a greater extent than before.[560] Article 16 TFEU applies to all data processing in public and private matters, including the AFSJ.

---

[556] For the general changes in the AFSJ, compare the excellent overview by Müller-Graff (2009); for an overview of the historical development of the AFSJ, see Streinz (2005), pp. 377–383; Schaper (2009), pp. 27–66.

[557] Scirocco (2008); a brief comment on Article 16 TFEU can be found in Lenz and Borchardt (2010), Commentary with regard to Article 16 TFEU, pp. 363–377; Geiger et al. (2010), pp. 211 and 212; Fischer (2010), pp. 221 and 222.

[558] Article 16 (1) and (2) TFEU.

[559] Full text of Article 16 TFEU: (1) Everyone has the right to the protection of personal data concerning them; (2) The European Parliament and the Council, acting in accordance with the ordinary legislative procedure, shall lay down the rules relating to the protection of individuals with regard to the processing of personal data by Union institutions, bodies, offices and agencies, and by the Member States when carrying out activities which fall within the scope of Union law, and the rules relating to the free movement of such data. Compliance with these rules shall be subject to the control of independent authorities. The rules adopted on the basis of this Article shall be without prejudice to the specific rules laid down in Article 39 of the Treaty on European Union.

[560] Replacing Article 251 EC, which lays down the current co-decision procedure, the *ordinary legislative procedure* in Article 294 TFEU assures compulsory participation of the European Parliament, as well as of the Council acting by a qualified majority in the legislative process.

Its paragraph (2) however refers to Article 39 TEU.[561] This reference could nonetheless darken the expectations of the European Parliament and data protection authorities as regards a harmonised data protection approach to all former pillars, as it provides that in the common foreign and security policy (former second pillar), solely the Council will "adopt a decision laying down the rules relating to the protection of individuals with regard to the processing of personal data by the Member States when carrying out activities".[562] Consequently, the decision making procedure in this area will not include the European Parliament where data processing by Member States is concerned. According to the provision's wording, Article 16 TFEU seems however to remain fully applicable as regards data processing by European Institutions in the common foreign and security policy.[563]

Although, when turning to the effects of Article 16 TFEU on the AFSJ, despite of the clear advantage of having only one reference data protection standard disregarding the former (first or third) pillar specifics at first glance, there are regrettably several restrictions applying to the coherent application of Article 16 TFEU in the AFSJ. The obligation of Article 16 TFEU on the European Parliament and the Council to lay down the rules relating to data protection includes the AFSJ. However, various transitional provisions delay the effects of the full enforcement of Article 16 TFEU in this area. They are illustrated in the following.

Declaration 20 annexed to the Lisbon Treaty shows a certain hesitation as regards the application of Article 16 TFEU when it touches upon national security. The Declaration restrains Article 16 TFEU insofar as where rules on protection of personal data are be adopted on the basis of Article 16 which "could have direct implications for national security", due account needs "to be taken of the specific characteristics of the matter".[564] Declaration 21 goes even further and states that "the Conference acknowledges that specific rules on the protection of personal data and the free movement of such data in the fields of judicial cooperation in criminal matters and police cooperation based on Article 16 of the TFEU Union may prove necessary because of the specific nature of these fields".[565] It becomes clear from reading these Declarations that the Member States reserved a "back door" in national security matters as well as in police and judicial cooperation to enact other data protection rules in the AFSJ than those being possibly applicable to former first pillar matters.

Moreover, certain Member States exclude in a complicated way the application of Article 16 TFEU in specific cases. Protocol No. 21 annexed to the Lisbon Treaty

---

[561] Article 16 (2) TFEU stipulates that "the rules adopted on the basis of this Article shall be without prejudice to the specific rules laid down in Article 39 of the Treaty on European Union".

[562] Article 39 TEU.

[563] Hijmanns and Scirocco (2009) in particular p. 1515 and Scirocco (2008).

[564] Declaration 20 of the Declarations annexed to the Final Act of the Intergovernmental Conference which adopted the Treaty of Lisbon, OJ 2010, C-83/335.

[565] Compare Declaration 21 of the Declarations annexed to the Final Act of the Intergovernmental Conference which adopted the Treaty of Lisbon, OJ 2010, C-83/335 (emphasis added).

provides for derogations for the United Kingdom and Ireland. Article 6 (a) of Protocol No. 21 states that both countries shall not be bound by the rules adopted on the basis of Article 16 TFEU "which relate to the processing of personal data by the Member States when carrying out activities which fall within the scope of Chapter 4 or Chapter 5 of Title V of Part Three of that Treaty[566] where the United Kingdom and Ireland are not bound by the rules governing the forms of judicial cooperation in criminal matters or police cooperation which require compliance with the provisions laid down on the basis of Article 16".[567] This means if the United Kingdom or Ireland do not participate in specific aspects of police and judicial cooperation, they do not have to protect data in these areas either.[568]

A very complicated exception procedure applies additionally to Denmark. Article 2 (a) of Protocol No. 22 on the position of Denmark[569] refers to Article 2 of Protocol No. 22 and excludes that none of the provisions of Title V of Part Three of the TFEU[570] ("[...] no measure adopted pursuant to that Title, no provision of any international agreement concluded by the Union pursuant to that Title, and no decision of the Court of Justice of the European Union interpreting any such provision or measure or any measure amended or amendable pursuant to that Title [...]") shall be binding upon or applicable in Denmark.[571] This Article shall also apply in respect of the rules laid down on the basis of Article 16 TFEU which relate to the processing of personal data by the Member States.[572] As the United Kingdom and Ireland, Article 7 of the annex to Protocol No. 22 clarifies that Denmark is not bound by the rules of Article 16 when they relate to Chapter 4 or Chapter 5 of Title V of Part Three of the TFEU.[573]

Another important obstacle leading to a delay in the full application of the guarantees set out by Article 16 TFEU is stipulated in Protocol No. 36 on transitional provisions.[574] Its Title VII relates to transitional provisions concerning acts

---

566 Chapter IV and V of Title V of Part III of the TFEU relate to judicial cooperation in criminal matters and police cooperation.

567 Article 6 (a) Protocol No. 21 annexed to the Lisbon Treaty on the position of the United Kingdom and Ireland in respect of the Area of Freedom, Security and Justice, OJ 2010, C-83/201.

568 With regard to the opt-outs compare Monar (2009), in particular pp. 773–776.

569 Protocol No. 22 annexed to the Lisbon Treaty on the position of Denmark, OJ 2010, C-83/201.

570 Title V of Part III of the TFEU includes the AFSJ.

571 Article 2 Protocol No. 22 annexed to the Lisbon Treaty on the position of Denmark, OJ 2010, C-83/201.

572 Ibid.

573 Article 7 of the annex of Protocol No. 22 annexed to the Lisbon Treaty on the position of Denmark, OJ 2010, C-83/201 stipulates that: "Denmark shall not be bound by the rules laid down on the basis of Article 16 of the Treaty on the Functioning of the European Union which relate to the processing of personal data by the Member States when carrying out activities which fall within the scope of Chapter 4 or Chapter 5 of Title V of Part Three of that Treaty where Denmark is not bound by the rules governing the forms of judicial cooperation in criminal matters or police cooperation which require compliance with the provisions laid down on the basis of Article 16".

574 Protocol No. 36 annexed to the Lisbon Treaty on transitional provisions, OJ 2010, C-83/201.

adopted on the basis of Titles V and VI of the former TEU (common foreign and security policy and police and judicial cooperation in criminal matters) prior to the entry into force of the Lisbon Treaty. Article 9 of the Protocol No. 36 provides that the legal effects of the acts adopted before the entry into force of the Lisbon Treaty shall be preserved until those acts are repealed, annulled or amended.[575] A deadline to adapt the old instruments to the new Treaty provisions, for instance in case they do not comply with Article 16 TFEU, is not given.[576]

With respect to acts in the field of police cooperation and judicial cooperation in criminal matters adopted before the entry into force of the Treaty of Lisbon, the powers of the Commission under Article 258 TFEU (the Commission's right to enact infringement proceedings) as well as the limited powers of the Court of Justice under Title VI of the former TEU shall remain the same.[577] In this case, the transitional measure shall cease to have effect 5 years after the date of entry into force of the Treaty of Lisbon.[578]

The result of these transitional provisions is that the rules and instruments adopted prior to the Lisbon Treaty (as long as they are not modified) as well as the former situation as regards the curtailed power of judicial control in the former third pillar matters (for a maximum period of 5 years) remain untouched.[579] Having this in mind, from the perspective of the Member States, one understands the enormous legislative activity having taken place shortly prior to the entry into force of the Lisbon Treaty which led to the adoption of partially questionable decisions in terms of data protection in former third pillar matters.[580] Many instruments in the AFSJ (Europol and Eurojust Decisions, including their implementing measures, Decision allowing for law enforcement access to the VIS etc.[581]) were quickly adopted before the new provisions stipulated in the

---

[575] Article 9 Protocol No. 36 annexed to the Lisbon Treaty on transitional provisions, OJ 2010, C-83/201 states that: "The legal effects of the acts of the institutions, bodies, offices and agencies of the Union adopted on the basis of the Treaty on European Union prior to the entry into force of the Treaty of Lisbon shall be preserved until those acts are repealed, annulled or amended in implementation of the Treaties. The same shall apply to agreements concluded between Member States on the basis of the Treaty on European Union".

[576] A five years deadline is only mentioned in Article 10 (3) Protocol No. 36 referring exclusively to the powers of the Commission and the European Court of Justice.

[577] Article 10 (1) Protocol No. 36 annexed to the Lisbon Treaty on transitional provisions, OJ 2010, C-83/201.

[578] Ibid.

[579] Only Member States that made a declaration according to Article 35 (2) former TEU accepting the jurisdiction of the European Court of Justice, can continue to request a preliminary ruling relating to the validity or interpretation of an instrument enacted in this area before the entry into force of the Lisbon Treaty.

[580] This point is further discussed in the analysis of the legal basis of the AFSJ actors, in particular in Chap. B II 1 and B II 2.

[581] This is further discussed in the analysis of the legal basis of the AFSJ actors in Chaps. B II 1, B II 2 and C II 2.

Lisbon Treaty, providing for more democratic control as well as for improved legislative procedures, entered into force. In consequence, even instruments not complying with the data protection guarantees of Article 16 TFEU in the AFSJ, will remain applicable until they are modified, repealed or annulled. This affects for instance instruments such as the FDPJ which is inapplicable to domestic data processing in police and judicial matters.

Taking the above-mentioned into account, the (legal) dimension of Article 16 TFEU in terms of its exemplary effect should nevertheless not be underestimated. Its position in the principles of general application underlines the respect of data protection principles in future legislation, including proposals in the AFSJ. *Hijmans* and *Scirocco* highlight the possible direct effect Article 16 (1) TFEU could have[582] and conclude this will limit the margin of appreciation of the legislature and would lead to the possibility to invoke this right before a court. The mandate of the Parliament (and the Council) to enact data protection rules in the AFSJ will hopefully accelerate the development towards effective and harmonised data protection rules in the AFSJ.

Finally, even though Article 16 TFEU constitutes an enormous step towards the recognition of essential data protection principles in the AFSJ, its guarantees have to be specified to help enforcing the rights of the individuals in the AFSJ. The interpretation of such broad principles, as carried out by the ECtHR in recent years with regard to data protection, could support this process in a valuable way.

bb) Important Changes in Respect of the Entire AFSJ

Keeping the mentioned restrictions in mind, with respect to the entire AFSJ, regulated in Title V, Articles 67–89 TFEU, the Lisbon Treaty brings a number of important developments briefly summarised in the following[583]:

- The introduction of the ordinary legislative procedure in the entire AFSJ reinforces the long demanded democratic control by strengthening the role of the European Parliament. In contrast to the former third pillar, Council and Parliament act as co-legislators in the AFSJ. Article 87 (2) (a) expressly states that the European Parliament and the Council shall act together in accordance with the ordinary legislative procedure to establish measures concerning "the collection, storage, processing, analysis and exchange of relevant information" in police cooperation.

[582] The authors compare the direct wording of Article 16 (1) TFEU with the direct wording in Article 18 (1) EC Treaty (the right of the EU citizen to move and reside freely within the territory of the Member States, now Article 21 TFEU) to which the Court acknowledged a direct effect and conclude that Article 16 (1) is formulated in the same precise manner allowing also to concede a direct effect to it, see Hijmanns and Scirocco (2009), in particular pp. 1517–1518; with regard to the direct effect of EU primary law, compare Herdegen (2010), pp. 164–166.

[583] A good overwiev on the changes in the AFSJ is made by: Niemeier (2010); Müller-Graff (2009); Callies (2010), pp. 431–452.

- The expansion of the decisions taken by qualified majority in the Council and the reinforcement of the right of initiative of the Commission raise hopes that decisions less frequently base on the lowest common denominator in data protection matters. However, Article 76 TFEU (general provisions in the AFSJ) maintains the right of initiative of the Member States with regard to acts ensuring administrative cooperation in the AFSJ, although a threshold of one quarter of the Member States applies.
- Article 82 (3) and 83 (3) TFEU concerning judicial cooperation however introduce a so-called emergency brake[584]: Where a member of the Council considers that a draft directive would affect fundamental aspects of its criminal justice system, it may request that the draft directive be referred to the European Council. In that case, the ordinary legislative procedure shall be suspended. After discussion, and in case of a consensus, the European Council shall, within 4 months of this suspension, refer the draft back to the Council, which shall terminate the suspension of the ordinary legislative procedure.[585]
- Articles 86 (1), 87 (3) and 89 (1) TFEU additionally provide for unanimity decisions of the Council when it comes to the adoption of a European Public Prosecutor's Office, when measures concerning the operational cooperation between police authorities should be established and when the conditions and limitations regarding the extent to which national enforcement agencies can operate on the territory of another Member State are laid down.
- The reinforcement of the role of national Parliaments stipulated in Articles 12 TEU and 69 TFEU in the AFSJ leads to additional democratic accountability. Article 12 (c) TEU explicitly mentions the role of the national Parliaments in the framework of the AFSJ by taking part in "the evaluation mechanism for the implementation of the Union policies in that area" and "through being involved in the political monitoring of Europol and the evaluation of Eurojust's activities".[586] Articles 85 (1) and 88 (2) TFEU specify these tasks by referring to the involvement of the national Parliaments in the legislative process determining Eurojust's and Europol's structure, operation, field of action and tasks. The control of Eurojust's and Europol's activities by the EP and the national Parliaments will therefore increase and shall be established in the future in form of Regulations amending the current Council Decisions.
- The removal of the restrictions relating to the judicial control by the Court of Justice[587] and the possibility to enact infringement proceedings[588] in the area of

[584] Hijmanns and Scirocco (2009), in particular p. 1522.

[585] Articles 82 (3) and 83 (3) TFEU.

[586] Article 12 (c) TEU.

[587] Compare case C-160/03, *Spain v. Eurojust*, judgment of 15 March 2005, in which the Court confirmed that the acts of (former) third pillar bodies (in this case, Eurojust) did not fall within its competence.

[588] Articles 258 and 259 TFEU.

police and judicial cooperation, considerably increase procedural legitimacy and will certainly support the enforcement of decisions taken in the AFSJ.[589]

- After the transition period has expired, judicial control of the AFSJ's actors, in particular the control of the AFSJ agencies will be considerably improved by the Lisbon Treaty. The former restricted area of actions (infringement proceedings, action for annulment, complains for failure to act) which may be brought before the European Union Courts will be extended to the AFSJ.[590]
- It is also worth pointing out that the competences of the European Ombudsman which include the investigation of maladministration of the activities of EU institutions, bodies and agencies[591] will refer to bodies such as Europol and Eurojust. Every citizen of the EU or any natural or legal person residing (or having its registered office) in a Member State can address its complaint to this body.
- A further and very important improvement concerns the adoption of international Agreements in the AFSJ. They will be subject to a reinforced democratic control. According to Article 218 (6) (a) (v) TFEU the European Parliament has to give its consent to international agreements in all fields where the ordinary legislative procedure applies. Consequently, the European Parliament will have the possibility to examine in the area of police and judicial cooperation, if a third state (or organisation) agreement complies with satisfying data protection standards as well as to block such agreements in case they fail to ensure a sufficient level of protection. Such agreements will additionally fall within the competence of the Courts of the EU, establishing the opportunity to obtain an opinion of the Court on the compatibility of envisaged provisions of the agreement with the Treaties.[592]
- The establishment of the permanent standing committee, COSI (Comité de sécurité intérieur) in Article 71 TFEU coordinating the internal security policy

[589] The protocol (No 36) on transitional provisions delays can delay the entry into force of some of the provisions mentioned above, especially Article 9 and 10.

[590] Article 263 (1) TFEU provides for the possibility of legal review of the acts of EU bodies, offices and agencies "intended to produce legal effects vis-à-vis third parties" (action for annulment) and Article 265 (1) TFEU regulates the action for a failure to act for the mentioned actors. Article 267 (1) (b) TFEU which permits preliminary rulings on the validity and interpretation of acts of the institutions, bodies, offices and agencies, paves the way for a reinforced external control in the future. And, although Article 263 (5) TFEU restricts the review of the legality of the legal acts by stipulating that "acts setting up bodies, offices and agencies of the Union may lay down specific conditions and arrangements concerning actions brought by natural or legal persons against acts of these bodies, offices or agencies intended to produce legal effects in relation to them", the general situations of individuals concerned has been significantly ameliorated, not least because Article 16 TFEU is now applicable to the entire data processing of the AFSJ.

[591] Article 228 (1) TFEU.

[592] Hijmanns and Scirocco (2009), in particular p. 1522.

could contribute to a more harmonised approach to decisions taken in the AFSJ, including harmonised proposals on data protection in this area.[593]

Especially with regard to the former third pillar area, decision making under the Lisbon Treaty will in future pave the way for the adoption of a hopefully satisfying general fundamental rights framework in the AFSJ.[594] Prior to the adoption of the Treaty, the Council's unanimity power with bare consultation rights of the European Parliament in this area, often resulted in compromises on the "lowest common denominator" hindering the implementation of clear and effective data protection provisions.[595] The transitional provisions applying in the AFSJ however represent the concerns of the Member States regarding the transfer of powers to the EU in this special area and will delay the positive effects of Article 16 TFEU for some time.

Therefore, regardless of the adoption of the Lisbon Treaty, the current legal framework of data protection provisions in the EU is (still) characterised by the former pillar structure. It will take some time to overcome the traditional separation between the protection of personal data in former Community matters and police and judicial cooperation matters. However, the chances to improve the current framework are better than ever before.

All things considered, despite these shortcomings, the adoption of the Lisbon Treaty was an important step forward towards the respect of data protection rights in the AFSJ. The mandate of the Parliament and the Council to adopt data protection rules will require a thorough analysis of the existing data protection framework in the AFSJ and may lead in future to a general framework for data protection in this area. The elements laid down in Article 16 clearly need specification. The analysis of the data protection systems in the current AFSJ carried out in Chap. B may provide some assistance in this respect.

e) Charter of Fundamental Rights and Guarantees of the ECHR

In addition to Article 16 TFEU, the new statuses of the European Charter of Fundamental Rights[596] (Charter) and the ECHR enforce the role of data protection as a fundamental right. Additionally, the new Article 6 (1) TEU clearly concedes binding value to the Charter by stating that the Charter "shall have the same legal value as the Treaties".[597] The same article read together with Protocol No. 8 annexed to the Lisbon Treaty additionally lays down the Union's obligation to

---

[593] The first meeting of COSI took place in March 2010, further meetings are planned.

[594] Scirocco (2008).

[595] Scirocco (2008); the analysis of instruments prior to the adoption of the Lisbon Treaty is carried out in Sect. III.

[596] A general overview of the Charter gives Craig and De Burca (2008), pp. 412–417.

[597] For details and the historical background, compare Wentrup Große (2003), pp. 31–47; Gebauer (2007); Pache (2009); Heusel (2002); Kokott and Sobotta (2010).

accede to the ECHR.[598] Both instruments refer to the necessity of protection of personal data, whereas the Charter specifies in a slightly more detailed manner than Article 8 ECHR, the core values of the European data protection consensus.

As mentioned in the introduction, Article 8 (1) of the Charter ascertains that "everyone has the right to the protection of personal data concerning him or her". Its paragraph (2) specifies that "data must be processed fairly for specified purposes and on the basis of the consent of the person concerned or some other legitimate basis laid down by law". Everyone must have the right of access and the right of rectification.[599] Compliance with these rules shall be subject to control by an independent authority.[600]

The Charter is applicable to the institutions, bodies, offices and agencies of the EU and the Member States when they are implementing EU law.[601] Data protection is therefore recognised as a fundamental right in the entire European Union, regardeless of the former pillar strucutures.[602] Thus the Charter and the guarantees of its Article 8 are the first provision extending the respect of data protection rights also to former second and third pillar matters. Fomer third pillar agencies such as Europol and Eurojust are therefore subject to the provisions of the Charter.[603]

Comparable to the restrictions applying to Article 16 TFEU, certain Member States exclude the application of the Charter to them. Protocol No. 30 limits the extension of the rights of the Charter in Poland and in the United Kingdom.[604] As with regard to Article 16 TFEU, both countries may retrieve their submission under the Charter's regime, although Poland – in contrast to the United Kingdom – has not excluded the application of the data protection provisions of Article 16 TFEU in the AFSJ. Consequently, there is some contradiction in Poland's approach as regards data protection guarantees. From the remaining applicability of Article 16 TFEU follows however that Poland will necessarily accept the instruments enacted based on Article 16 TFEU.

It is worth noting that data protection is stipulated as a right in itself and is not annexed to the right to private life which is additionally mentioned in Article 7 of the Charter. Data protection is to be understood as an element of the right to private

[598] Article 6 (2) TEU and Protocol No. 8 annexed to the Lisbon Treaty relating to Article 6 (2) of the Treaty on European Union on the accession of the Union to the European Convention on the Protection of Human Rights and Fundamental Freedoms, OJ 2010, C-83/201.

[599] Article 8 (2) Charter of Fundamental Rights, OJ 2010, C-83/02.

[600] Article 8 (3) Charter of Fundamental Rights, OJ2010, C-83/02; for a general overview of the guarantees of Article 8 of the Charter, see Rengeling and Szczekalla (2004), § 16, pp. 453–496; Callies and Ruffert (2007), pp. 2563–2568.

[601] Article 51 (1) 52 of the Charter of Fundamental Rights, OJ 2010, C-83/02; Jarass (2010), Article 8, para 3; for details compare Wentrup Große (2003), pp. 44 and 49.

[602] Meyer (2011), Article 8, para 1.

[603] The relevance of the Chater for the activities of Europol and OLAF is emphasised by Paeffgen (2006), in particular p. 78.

[604] Protocol No. 30 annexed to the Lisbon Treaty on the application of the Charter of Fundamental Rights of the European Union to Poland and to the United Kingdom, OJ 2010, C-83/201.

life which is however particulary important and it therefore needs to be mentioned in a proper article.[605] Article 8 of the Charter is consequently described as the *lex specialis* of Article 7 of the Charter.[606]

The guarantees inherent to Article 8 of the Charter are based on Article 286 EC Treaty, Directive 95/46, Article 8 ECHR and Convention No. 108.[607] The explanation of the Praesidium specifies that the right to the protection of personal data is to be exercised under the conditions of Directive 95/46 and may be limited under the general conditions set out by Article 52 of the Charter. The article lays down that the limitations on the rights and freedoms of the Charter "must be provided for by law and respect the essence of those rights and freedoms".[608] "Subject to the principle of proportionality, limitations may be made only if they are necessary and genuinely meet objectives of general interests recognised by the Union or the need to protect the rights and freedoms of others".[609]

Article 52 of the Charter additionally underlines the close connection of the rights stipulated in the Charter and the rights of the ECHR. In so far as the Charter contains rights which correspond to the rights of the ECHR, "the meaning and the scope of those rights shall be the same as those laid down by the Convention [ECHR]".[610] With regard to the data protection guarantees in EU law, the recent judgment of the European Court of Justice in the case *Schecke v. Land Hessen*[611] confirmed the close relationship between Article 8 ECHR and Article 8 of the Charter. The case concerned the legality of several regulations in the area of the common agricultural policy[612] which obliged national authorities to publish a set of personal data belonging to beneficiaries of EU agricultural subsidies in order to improve the transparency of the Union's financial support system. In Germany, the

605 Meyer (2011), Article 8, para 6.

606 Meyer (2011), Article 8, para 13; Jarass (2010), Article 8, para 4.

607 Note from the Praesidium of the Convention, Explanation on the Charter of Fundamental Rights of the European Union, Draft Charter of Fundamental Rights, CHARTE 4473/00 CONVENT 49 of 11 October 2000; Jarass (2010), Article 8, para 1.

608 For a deepened understanding of Article 52 (3) of the Charter and of the influence of the ECHR on the Charter of Fundamental Rights, Ziegenhorn (2009); Schneiders (2010).

609 Article 52 (1) of the Charter of Fundamental Rights, OJ 2010, C-83/02; with regard to Europol and its possibility to justify interferences with regard to Article 8 of the Charter, compare Kistner-Bahr (2010), pp. 227–232.

610 Article 52 (3) of the Charter of Fundamental Rights, OJ 2010, C-83/02.

611 Joined cases C-92/09 and C-93/09, *Volker and Markus Schecke GbR and Hartmut Eifert v. Land Hessen*, judgement of 9 November 2010.

612 Council Regulation (EC) No 1290/2005 of 21 June 2005 on the financing of the common agricultural policy, OJ 2005, L-209/1, as amended by Council Regulation (EC) No 1437/2007 of 26 November 2007, OJ 2007, L-322/1 and Commission Regulation (EC) No 259/2008 of 18 March 2008 laying down detailed rules for the application of Regulation No 1290/2005 as regards the publication of information on the beneficiaries of funds deriving from the European Agricultural Guarantee Fund (EAGF) and the European Agricultural Fund for Rural Development (EAFRD), OJ 2008, L-76/28.

Federal Office for Agriculture and Food therefore made names, postcodes and amounts received public on a (searchable) website. The farmers and agricultural firms concerned claimed that the publication requirement violated their rights to private life of Article 7 of the Charter and to the protection of personal data of Article 8 of the Charter.

The Court states that: "Finally, according to Article 52 (3) of the Charter, in so far as it contains rights which correspond to rights guaranteed by the Convention, the meaning and scope of those rights are to be the same as those laid down by the Convention. Article 53 of the Charter further states that nothing in the Charter is to be interpreted as restricting or adversely affecting the rights recognised inter alia by the Convention".[613] More specifically, in the context of the legal standards following from the new Articles 7 and 8 of the Charter, the Court stipulates that: "[. . .] it must be considered that the right to respect for private life with regard to the processing of personal data, recognised by Articles 7 and 8 of the Charter, concerns any information relating to an identified or identifiable individual [. . .] and the limitations which may lawfully be imposed on the right to the protection of personal data correspond to those tolerated in relation to Article 8 of the Convention".[614]

Without going into the details of the *Schecke* case, it is worth noting the Court applies the ECtHR method and examines first, the existence and second, the justification of an interference with the rights to private life and data protection stipulated in the Charter. In essence, the Court observes that the publication of the data of the beneficiaries of EU subsidies "with no distinction being drawn according to the duration, frequency or nature and amount of the aid received" did not succeed in striking the right balance between the interests involved.[615] Institutions are obliged to balance, before disclosing information relating to individuals, "the European Union's interests in guaranteeing transparency of its actions and the infringements of the rights recognised by Articles 7 and 8 of the Charter".[616] The respective provisions of the regulations were for that reason declared void.

As follows from the foregoing, the data protection principles and guarantees of Article 8 ECHR and Directive 95/46, which are specified in the case law of the EU Courts and the ECtHR, are therefore of utmost importance when the principles mentioned in Articles 7 and 8 of the Charter should be further clarified by the EU Courts in future. For that reason, the case law of the ECtHR was illustrated in detail above.

This statement and the intended accession to the ECHR will therefore change the acceptance of the right to data protection in future European Union fields of action.[617] European Union Institutions will be directly bound by the provisions of the ECHR and their acts will be subject to critical scrutiny of the ECtHR. Besides,

---

[613] Joined cases C-92/09 and C-93/09, *Volker and Markus Schecke GbR and Hartmut Eifert* v. *Land Hessen*, judgement of 9 November 2010, para 51.

[614] Ibid, para 52.

[615] Ibid, paras 79–89.

[616] Ibid, para 85.

[617] With regard to the general changes, compare Lock (2010), pp. 777–798.

Article 6 (3) states that fundamental rights, "as guaranteed by the ECHR" and "as they result from the constitutional traditions common to the Member States, shall constitute general principles of the Union's law".[618]

Even though in *Rechnungshof v. Österreichischer Rundfunk and Others*, the European Court of Justice already recognised that the provisions of Directive 95/46 were to be interpreted in the light of Article 8 ECHR and that the guarantees of Article 8 ECHR form part of the general principles of Community law, European Union Courts will have to respect the principles laid down in the ECHR more than ever before. Thus far the ECtHR could only assess EU law indirectly by ruling on the implementation of EU law in a Member State. When the EU accedes to the ECHR, individual challenges of the acts of EU institutions and even of judicial decision of the European Union Courts before the ECtHR become possible. Although the accession is important, it will not lead to a substantial change of the case law of the EU Courts in data protection matters.[619] As stipulated above, the ECHR and the guarantees of the ECHR and the case law of the ECtHR are already incorporated into EU law (*Rechnungshof v. Österreichischer Rundfunk and Others*).

2. *EU Data Protection Principles in the AFSJ*

The following section focuses on the brief analysis of the existing data protection principles in the EU which are relevant in the AFSJ context.[620] There is no conclusive or definite set of EU data protection principles.[621] Therefore the following section orientates on the main piece of legislation in the EU, Directive 95/46. As demonstrated above, it has to be recalled that the scope of Directive 95/46 is however limited and does not refer to security-related data processing in the AFSJ. Its principles, which are a further development of the principles of Convention No. 108, are nevertheless worth mentioning, taking into consideration that they lay down the foundations of EU data protection rules and that they are applicable to instruments such as the VIS or Eurodac. The other instruments including data protection provisions relevant in the AFSJ are Regulation 45/2001 and the FDPJ. Regulation 45/2001, covering data processing at the Community institutions and bodies, mirrors most of the principles of Directive 95/46. The FDPJ equally bases on the Directive's principles, although it refers to them in a very mitigated way as the following analysis will demonstrate.

---

[618] For a detailed analysis of the meaning of the term "general principles" of EU law, refer to Schneiders (2010), pp. 44–95.

[619] Hijmanns and Scirocco (2009), in particular p. 1523.

[620] It will not consider all the details of the history of EU data protection law. This would go beyond the interest of this research. For an excellent overview of the origins of Directive 95/46, see Dammann and Simitis (1997); for a general overview of EU data protection law, refer to Siemen (2006).

[621] Brouwer (2008a), p. 204.

a) Quality Standards

Quality standards of European data protection rules are central to the processing of personal data. They are enumerated in Article 6 of Directive 95/46 and mainly contain the principles of Article 5 Convention No. 108. Personal data must be "processed fairly and lawfully, collected for specified, explicit and legitimate purposes and not further processed in a way incompatible with those purposes; adequate, relevant and not excessive in relation to the purposes for which they are collected and/or further processed; accurate and, where necessary, kept up to date". Further, "every reasonable step must be taken to ensure that data which are inaccurate or incomplete, having regard to the purposes for which they were collected or for which they are further processed, are erased or rectified; kept in a form which permits identification of data subjects for no longer than is necessary for the purposes for which the data were collected or for which they are further processed".

These criteria are specified in the aforementioned case law of the Court of Justice, which takes into account particularly the principle of proportionality[622] and the respect of fundamental rights as stipulated in Article 6 EU Treaty, especially Article 8 ECHR.[623]

aa) Lawfulness and Fairness

The requirement to process personal data lawfully is not only mentioned in Directive 95/46,[624] but also in Regulation 45/2001 and the FDPJ.[625] It signifies that data processing is based on the condition of lawfulness and requires from the Member States the enforcement of existing data protection rules as well as the enactment of new rules, if necessary.[626] Some criteria for making data processing legitimate are

[622] For details, see Koch (2003); Von Arnauld (2008) and Case C-275/06, *Productores de Música de España Promusicae vs. Telefónica de España*, judgment of 29 January 2008, paras 68–70. In *Promusicae vs. Telefónica de España* the Court of Justice stipulated that when transposing intellectual property directives, Member States must interpret them in a form "which allows a fair balance to be struck between the various fundamental rights protected by the Community legal order. Further, when implementing the measures transposing those directives, the authorities and courts of the Member States must not only interpret their national law in a manner consistent with those directives but also make sure that they do not rely on an interpretation of them which would be in conflict with those fundamental rights or with the other general principles of Community law, such as the principle of proportionality" (para 70).

[623] Case C-465/00, *Rechnungshof v Österreichischer Rundfunk and Others*, judgment of 20 May 2003, paras 66, 70, 71, 93 and 99. The Directive refers to the European Convention on Human Rights to "give substance to and amplify" the principles contained in the Council of Europe Convention of 28 January 1981 for the Protection of Individuals with regard to Automatic processing of Personal Data (recitals 10 and 11 of Directive 95/46, OJ 1995, L-281/31).

[624] Article 6 (1) (a) Directive 95/46, OJ 1995, L-281/31.

[625] Article 3 (1) FDPJ, OJ 2008, L-350/60 and Article 4 (1) (a) Regulation 45/2001, OJ 2001, L-8/1.

[626] Dammann and Simitis (1997), Article 6, para 2.

further detailed in Article 7 of Directive 95/46 and Article 5 of Regulation 45/2001.[627] Data processing is for instance legitimate, if the data subject has unambiguously given his consent, the processing is necessary in order to protect the vital interests of the data subject or the processing is necessary for the performance of a task carried out in the public interest or in the exercise of official authority vested in the controller or in a third party to whom the data are disclosed.[628] There is no requirement that the data processing must in any case have a legal basis, but it must always be in accordance with the applicable law. It is worth reminding that the ECtHR's case law, however, provides for stricter criteria with regard to the legal basis of data processing to ensure foreseeability.[629]

Nonetheless, the Court of Justice also stipulated certain criteria relating to the lawfulness of data processing. In *Huber v. Germany*, the Court of Justice makes clear that the concept of necessity in Article 7 of Directive 95/46 cannot have a meaning which varies between the Member States.[630] It has its own independent meaning in Community law and "must be interpreted in a manner which fully reflects the objective of that directive".[631]

---

[627] "Member States shall provide that personal data may be processed only if: (a) the data subject has unambiguously given his consent; or (b) processing is necessary for the performance of a contract to which the data subject is party or in order to take steps at the request of the data subject prior to entering into a contract; or (c) processing is necessary for compliance with a legal obligation to which the controller is subject; or (d) processing is necessary in order to protect the vital interests of the data subject; or (e) processing is necessary for the performance of a task carried out in the public interest or in the exercise of official authority vested in the controller or in a third party to whom the data are disclosed; or (f) processing is necessary for the purposes of the legitimate interests pursued by the controller or by the third party or parties to whom the data are disclosed, except where such interests are overridden by the interests for fundamental rights and freedoms of the data subject which require protection under Article 1 (1)", (compare Article 7 Directive 95/46, OJ 1995, L-281/31) and Article 5 Regulation 45/2001, OJ 2001, L-8/1: "Personal data may be processed only if: (a) processing is necessary for the performance of a task carried out in the public interest on the basis of the Treaties establishing the European Communities or other legal instruments adopted on the basis thereof or in the legitimate exercise of official authority vested in the Community institution or body or in a third party to whom the data are disclosed, or (b) processing is necessary for compliance with a legal obligation to which the controller is subject, or (c) processing is necessary for the performance of a contract to which the data subject is party or in order to take steps at the request of the data subject prior to entering into a contract, or (d) the data subject has unambiguously given his or her consent, or (e) processing is necessary in order to protect the vital interests of the data subject".

[628] Article 7 (a) (d) and (e) Directive 95/46, OJ 1995, L-281/31.

[629] Compare Sect. II 1 d aa (3) and *Valenzuela Contreras v. Spain*, Application no. 27671/95 judgment of 30 July 1998, para 57; *Weber and Saravia v. Germany*, Application no. 54934/00, admissibility decision of 29 June 2006, para 95; *Huvig v. France*, Application no. 11105/84, judgment of 24 April 1990, para 34, and *Kruslin v. France*, Application no. 11801/85, judgment of 24 April 1990, para 35.

[630] Case C-524/06, *Heinz Huber v. Germany*, judgment of 16 December 2008, para 52.

[631] Case C-524/06, *Heinz Huber v. Germany*, judgment of 16 December 2008, para 52.

Mr. Huber, an Austrian national who resided in Germany, requested the deletion of personal data stored in the German Central Register of Foreign Nationals (Ausländerzentralregister, AZR). The AZR is a centralised register used for statistical purposes which contains personal data, similar to the VIS,[632] relating to foreign nationals who are resident in Germany on a basis which is not purely temporary.[633] Besides the statistical purposes, these data may additionally be used for security, police and judicial purposes.[634] Germany claimed therefore to use *Mr. Huber's* data "for the performance of a task carried out in the public interest or in the exercise of official authority vested in the controller or in a third party to whom the data are disclosed" in accordance with Article 7 (e) of Directive 95/46.

Due to the restricted scope of Directive 95/46 mentioned above,[635] only data relating to the right of residence and to statistical purposes were subject to the Court of Justice proceedings.[636] The Court of Justice examined different questions relating to the existence and the use of the content of this database.[637] While the case additionally had a strong emphasis on the discriminatory function of the database,[638] with regard to the questions whether such treatment was compatible with the requirement of necessity under Article 7(e) of Directive 95/46, the Court of Justice concluded that:

> A system for processing personal data relating to Union citizens who are not nationals of the Member State concerned, [...] having as its object the provision of support to the

---

[632] Data stored in the AZR are: the name of the authority which provided the data, the reference number allocated by the Bundesamt; the grounds of registration; surname, surname at birth, given names, date and place of birth, sex and nationality; previous and other patronymics, marital status, particulars of identity documents, the last place of residence in the country of origin, and information supplied on a voluntary basis as to religion and the nationality of the spouse or partner; particulars of entries into and exits from the territory, residence status, decisions of the Federal Employment Agency relating to a work permit, refugee status granted by another state, date of death; decisions relating, inter alia, to any application for asylum, any previous application for a residence permit, and particulars of, inter alia, any expulsion proceedings, arrest warrants, suspected contraventions of the laws on drugs or immigration, and suspected participation in terrorist activities, or convictions in respect of such activities; and search warrants (Case C-524/06, *Heinz Huber v. Germany*, judgment of 16 December 2008, para 20).

[633] Case C-524/06, *Heinz Huber v. Germany*, judgment of 16 December 2008, para 19.

[634] Case C-524/06, *Heinz Huber v. Germany*, judgment of 16 December 2008, paras 19–29.

[635] Compare Sect. III 1 b.

[636] Case C-524/06, *Heinz Huber v. Germany*, judgment of 16 December 2008, para 45.

[637] The questions referred to whether: (1) the general processing of personal data of foreign citizens of the Union in a central register of foreign nationals is compatible with the prohibition of discrimination on grounds of nationality against citizens of the Union who exercise their right to move and reside freely within the territory of the Member States (Article 12(1) EC Treaty, in conjunction with Articles 17 EC and 18(1) EC Treaty)? (2) such processing is compatible with the prohibition of restrictions on the freedom of establishment of nationals of a Member State in the territory of another Member State (first paragraph of Article 43 EC Treaty)? (3) such treatment is compatible with the requirement of necessity under Article 7(e) of Directive 95/46?

[638] Gonzalez Fuster et al. (2010).

> national authorities responsible for the application of the law relating to the right of residence does not satisfy the requirement of necessity laid down by Article 7(e) of Directive 95/46 [. . .], interpreted in the light of the prohibition on any discrimination on grounds of nationality, unless:
> – it contains only the data which are necessary for the application by those authorities of that legislation, and
> – its centralised nature enables the legislation relating to the right of residence to be more effectively applied as regards Union citizens who are not nationals of that Member State.
>
> It is for the national court to ascertain whether those conditions are satisfied in the main proceedings. The storage and processing of personal data containing individualised personal information in a register such as the Central Register of Foreign Nationals for statistical purposes cannot, on any basis, be considered to be necessary within the meaning of Article 7(e) of Directive 95/46.[639]

It is Interesting to note, with regard to the processing of personal data for crime fighting purposes, that the Court of Justice emphasised the discriminatory effect of a database containing only data of non-German EU citizens whereas a similar register on German citizen was not in place. The Court of Justice followed the opinion of Advocate General *Poiares Maduro* who pointed out that "the existence of two separate data processing systems casts an unpleasant shadow over Union citizens, whom the German Government monitors much more strictly and systematically than German citizens".[640] The Court concluded that the fight against crime necessarily involves the prosecution of crimes and offences committed, irrespective of the nationality of their perpetrators, but, "it follows that as regards a Member State, the situation of its nationals cannot, as regards the objective of fighting crime, be different from that of Union citizens who are not nationals of that Member State and who are resident in its territory".[641] Therefore the difference in treatment between non-German EU citizens and German citizens which arises in consequence of systematic processing of personal data relating only to Union citizens, who are not nationals of the Member State concerned for the purposes of fighting crime, constituted a discrimination which is prohibited by Article 12 (1) EC Treaty (now Article 18 TFEU).[642]

Summarising, besides the pure data protection issue of Article 7 (e) Directive 95/46, the Court of Justice put emphasis on the important question of the discriminatory effect on a specific group of persons whose data are stored in a database used for crime fighting purposes.[643] The judgement additionally takes into account that the purpose of processing of the data is changing (data are originally collected for

---

[639] Case C-524/06, *Heinz Huber v. Germany*, judgment of 16 December 2008, para 82.

[640] Opinion of Advocate General Poiares Maduro, delivered on 3 April 2008 in case C-524/06, *Heinz Huber v. Germany*, judgment of 16 December 2008, para 15.

[641] Case C-524/06, *Heinz Huber v. Germany*, judgment of 16 December 2008, paras 78 and 79.

[642] Case C-524/06, *Heinz Huber v. Germany*, judgment of 16 December 2008, para 80.

[643] Compare also: Martin (2009), pp. 95–108.

statistical purposes and later used for other purposes) and warns against the suspicion which may arise out of the inclusion in this specific database.[644]

Against this background, it is worth noting that the FDPJ does not provide any specifications with regard to the lawfulness of the processing. This might be partly due to the fact that one of the most important requirements of lawfulness relates to the consent of the individual for the processing.[645] This criterion can reasonably only be used restrictively in a law enforcement context. Nonetheless, even in context of the FDPJ, lawfulness requires the respect of both, of basic principles such as the rule of law as well as of fundamental data protection principles subsequently specified in the FDPJ.

The criterion of a fair processing is only stipulated in Directive 94/45 and Regulation 45/2001.[646] It underlines the importance of the lawfulness of the processing. Even in absence of clear rules on data processing, the possibility to qualify data processing as illegal should not be excluded because of the applicability of unclear rules on the lawfulness.[647] Regrettably, this criterion is not mentioned in the FDPJ.

bb) Purpose Limitation

As already illustrated in the framework of the Council of Europe's instruments, purpose limitation is central to data protection law. It guarantees transparency and is therefore an important aim of Directive 95/46.[648] Data must be "collected for specified, explicit and legitimate purposes and not further processed in a way incompatible with those purposes".[649] Regulation 45/2001 and the FDPJ include similar provisions.[650] The purpose must be clearly defined before the processing which should exclude, on the one hand, processing for unspecified and unknown purposes and, on the other hand, the possibility to subsequently change the original purpose.[651] This is, at the first glance, a quite restrictive provision which

[644] Compare Gonzalez Fuster et al. (2010).

[645] Article 7 (a) Directive 95/46, OJ 1995, L-281/31 and Article 5 (d) Regulation 45/2001, OJ 2001, L-8/1.

[646] Mentioned in Article 6 (1) (a) Directive 95/46, OJ 1995, L-281/31 and Article 4 (1) (a) Regulation 45/2001, OJ 2001, L-8/1.

[647] The reason for this criterion is that the use of secret devices, for instance telephone tapping, should be excluded, compare Dammann and Simitis (1997), Article 6, para 3.

[648] According to Article 6 (1) (b), data must be "collected for specified, explicit and legitimate purposes and not further processed in a way incompatible with those purposes. Further processing of data for historical, statistical or scientific purposes shall not be considered as incompatible provided that Member States provide appropriate safeguards".

[649] Article 6 (1) (b) Directive 95/46, OJ 1995, L-281/31.

[650] Article 3 (1) FDPJ, OJ 2008, L-350/60 and Article 4 (1) (b) Regulation 45/2001, OJ 2001, L-8/1.

[651] Compare Ehmann and Helfrich (1999), Article 6, paras 6–15.

nevertheless allows for some derogation. Directive 95/46 for instance does not specify which purposes are incompatible with the original purpose and Regulation 45/2001 and the FDPJ allow for broad exceptions. Regulation 45/2001 allows changing the original purpose if "the change of purpose is expressly permitted by the internal rules of the Community institution or body".[652]

The most far reaching derogation from this principle is however contained in the FDPJ. Further processing for another purpose is permitted in so far as:

(a) It is not incompatible with the purposes for which the data were collected;
(b) The competent authorities are authorised to process such data for such other purpose in accordance with the applicable legal provisions; and
(c) Processing is necessary and proportionate to that other purpose.[653]

According to Article 11 FDPJ, when complying with the aforementioned principles, processing of data received or made available by another Member State may be additionally further processed for the following purposes:

(a) The prevention, investigation, detection or prosecution of criminal offences or the execution of criminal penalties other than those for which they were transmitted or made available;
(b) Other judicial and administrative proceedings directly related to the prevention, investigation, detection or prosecution of criminal offences or the execution of criminal penalties;
(c) The prevention of an immediate and serious threat to public security; or
(d) Any other purpose only with the prior consent of the transmitting Member State or with the consent of the data subject, given in accordance with national law.[654]

As follows from the reading of these exceptions, FDPJ allows for broad derogations from the purpose limitation principle. Solely the consent of the transmitting authority of the Member States is sufficient to fundamentally change the initial purpose of processing. The individual whose data are processed is completely left out of this decision. This shift towards the exclusive decision right of the authority processing the data with regard to the whereabouts and the subsequent use of the data clearly reverses the aim of the purpose limitation principle, which is also the protection of the individual against data processing for unspecified and unknown purposes.[655] To what extent this far reaching

---

[652] Article 6 (1) Regulation 45/2001, OJ 2001, L-8/1.

[653] Article 3 (2) FDPJ, OJ 2008, L-350/60; additionally, just as in Directive 95/46, data processing for historical, statistical or scientific purposes is allowed if the Member States provide for appropriate safeguards, such as making the data anonymous.

[654] Article 11 FDPJ, OJ 2008, L-350/60.

[655] For critical remarks on this provision, compare De Busser (2009), pp. 103–105, and third opinion of the EDPS on the proposal for a Council Framework Decision on the protection of personal data processed in the framework of police and judicial co-operation in criminal matters, OJ 2007, C-139/1 (in the following: EDPS opinion on the FDPJ, OJ 2007, C-139/1), paras 20–25.

exemption is still in compliance with the foreseeability criterion developed by the ECtHR and its case law regarding the collection of data in security-related data processing[656] is very questionable.

cc) Adequate and Not Excessive in Relation to the Purposes for Which the Data Are Collected and/or Further Processed

Data processing for adequate and not excessive purposes in relation to the original purpose of collection is provided for in Article 6 (1) (c) Directive 95/46, in Article 4 (1) (c) Regulation 45/2001 and in Article 3 (1) FDPJ.[657] The provisions restrict the amount of processed data and subject the way of their processing to the purpose for which the data were collected.[658] As we have seen before, the requirement of purpose limitation is however largely derogated from in the FDPJ. Article 11 of the FDPJ, mentioned above, therefore contradicts the limitation of the purpose provided for in Article 3 (1) FDPJ when it allows for processing for "any other purpose". Although Article 3 (1) FDPJ represents a prerequisite for the application of Article 11 FDPJ,[659] the contradiction between these Articles is obvious.

dd) Data Must Be Accurate and Where Necessary, Kept up to Date

The accuracy of the data relates to the requirement that the data must represent correct and truthful facts.[660] Related to the accuracy are the completeness and the up to date nature of a set of data. Article 6 (1) (d) Directive 95/46 and Article 4 (1) (d) Regulation 45/2001 thus add that "every reasonable step must be taken to ensure that data which are inaccurate or incomplete, having regard to the purposes for which they were collected or for which they are further processed, are erased or

---

[656] Compare *Weber and Saravia v. Germany*, Application no. 54934/00, admissibility decision of 29 June 2006, para 116; *Rotaru v. Romania*, Application no. 28341/954, judgment of 4 May 2000, para 57; see also: *Association for European Integration and Human Rights and Ekimdzhiev v. Bulgaria*, Application no. 62540/00, judgment of 28 June 2007.

[657] Article 6 (1) (c) Directive 95/46, OJ 1995, L-281/31; Article 4 (1) (c) Regulation 45/2001, OJ 2001, L-8/1 and Article 3 (1) FDPJ, OJ 2008, L-350/60.

[658] Dammann and Simitis (1997), Article 6, para 11.

[659] Article 11 provides that: "Personal data received from or made available by the competent authority of another Member State may, *in accordance with the requirements of Article 3(2)*, be further processed only for the following purposes other than those for which they were transmitted or made available [. . .]"(emphasis added).

[660] Dammann and Simitis (1997), Article 6, para 13.

rectified".[661] This second requirement symbolises both, first, incomplete data can lead to an inaccurate set of data and, second, when assessing the accuracy of processing, the purpose for which the data were collected must be taken into account.[662] While Directive 95/46 and Regulation 45/2001 explicitly refer to the accuracy and the up to date nature of data, the FDPJ only indirectly mentions these two obligations.

Article 4 (1) FDPJ provides that police and judicial "data shall be rectified if inaccurate and, where this is possible and necessary, completed or updated". As the wording of Article 4 (1) FDPJ already suggests, the enforcement of accuracy and completeness appears to be less restrictive than the formulations used in Directive 95/46 and Regulation 45/2001. The personal data shall not only be completed and updated when this is necessary, it must also be possible. The decision when it appears to be possible is left to the authority processing the data and therefore risks to be applied in a rather subjective way.

The provisions relating to the transmission to other Member States in the FDPJ are however slightly more restrictive. They do not include a subjective criterion and provide that "the competent authorities shall take all reasonable steps to provide that personal data which are inaccurate, incomplete or no longer up to date are not transmitted or made available".[663] Although important in police work, the FDPJ unfortunately does not entail a provisions – similar to principle 3 Recommendation R (87) 15 – which refers to the accuracy of the data and distinguishes, on the one hand, between data collected for administrative purposes and data collected for police objectives and, on the other hand, between data based on facts and data based on opinions or personal assessments.[664] The EDPS in its opinion on the FDPJ rightly points to the risk that the difference between evidences, facts and opinions or assessments (soft intelligence) disappears when transferring such data to another authority.[665]

No distinction is further made between the different categories of data subjects such as criminals, suspects, victims or witnesses. When recalling the ECtHR's case law in *S. and Marper v. the United Kingdom* where the ECtHR clearly insists on a different treatment of data of convicted and not convicted persons,[666] the introduction of a provision taking such separation into consideration would have been advantageous in order to harmonise essential data protection rules in EU and ECHR law.

---

[661] Article 6 (1) (d) Directive 95/46, OJ 1995, L-281/31; Article 4 (1) (d) Regulation 45/2001, OJ 2001, L-8/1.

[662] Dammann and Simitis (1997), Article 6, para 15.

[663] Article 8 (1) FDPJ, OJ 2008, L-350/60.

[664] Compare above, Sect. II 4 a.

[665] EDPS opinion on the FDPJ, OJ 2007, C-139/1, para 32.

[666] *S.* and *Marper v. the United Kingdom*, Application nos. 30562/04 and 30566/04, judgment of 4 December 2008, para 122, to the stigmatisation of innocent individuals, see Gonzalez Fuster et al. (2010).

ee) Time Limit

According to Directive 95/46 and Regulation 45/2001, data "must be kept in a form which permits identification of data subjects for no longer than is necessary for the purposes for which the data were collected or for which they are further processed".[667] The FDPJ provides that "personal data shall be erased or made anonymous when they are no longer required for the purposes for which they were lawfully collected or are lawfully further processed".[668] If at the time of expiry of the time limit the data are needed for "a current investigation, prosecution of criminal offences or the enforcement of criminal penalties", this obligation shall not apply.[669]

In both cases, the time limit is intrinsically linked to the purpose of collection or processing and therefore assures some degree of foreseeability for persons concerned, at least, as long as the purpose of processing remains unchanged. The main difference between both formulations however is the use of *shall* in the FDPJ instead of *must* in Directive 95/46 and Regulation 45/2001. The use of *shall* indicates a slightly mitigated obligation to erase data or to make them anonymous. Combined with the exhaustive possibilities to derogate from the purpose limitation principle, the time limit in the FDPJ still raises some questions. In case the purpose is changing during the processing, the time limit can easily be adapted to the new purpose. Theoretically, the time limit can be indefinitely extended. This possibility highlights the close relationship between the purpose and the duration of the storage and shows the practical effects which a derogation from the purpose limitation principle may have.

b) Special Categories of Data

The provisions prohibiting the processing of "sensitive or special categories of data" have the same anti-discriminatory function as the provision on sensitive data in Convention No. 108 and refer for that reason to almost the same categories.[670] Directive 95/46 and Regulation 45/2001 explicitly prohibit to process data revealing racial or ethnic origin, political opinions, religious or philosophical

---

[667] Article 6 (1) (e) Directive 95/46, OJ 1995, L-281/31; Article 4 (1) (e) Regulation 45/2001, OJ 2001, L-8/1.

[668] Article 4 (2) FDPJ, OJ 2008, L-350/60.

[669] Article 9 (1) FDPJ, OJ 2008, L-350/60.

[670] Directive 95/46 and Regulation 45/2001 additionally mention data on ethnic origin and trade union membership.

beliefs, trade-union membership or personal data concerning health or sex life.[671] Data processing relating to criminal offences, convictions or security measures "shall be carried out only under the control of official authority, or if suitable safeguards are provided under national law [...]"[672] or, in case of processing by the EU, "only if authorised by the Treaties establishing the European Communities or other legal instruments adopted on the basis thereof or, if necessary, by the European Data Protection Supervisor, subject to appropriate specific safeguards".[673] Although data themselves (as such) can not be sensitive, contextual criteria, which may make personal data sensitive data according to the context in which they are processed, such as economic, social or psychological circumstances of processing, are not included.[674]

Several exceptions nonetheless apply to this general prohibition. For instance, when the data subject has given its consent or the processing is necessary for a medical diagnosis, necessary for the purposes of complying with the specific rights and obligations of the controller in the field of employment law or the processing relates to data which are manifestly made public by the data subject or is necessary for the establishment, exercise or defence of legal claims.[675]

The latter exception was recently evaluated in a case before the General Court. In *Esch-Leonhardt and Others v. ECB*,[676] the General Court dismissed an application for annulment of a decision to include in the applicants' personnel files a letter concerning their use of the internal electronic mail system for transmitting union information. The background of the case is briefly summarised: the director of the human resources at the ECB prohibited the applicants, who were members of trade unions, to distribute trade union information to their colleagues by using the internal ECB e-mail system. The respective e-mail was thereupon added to the personal files of the applicants. Against this decision, the applicants enacted legal

[671] Article 8 (1) Directive 95/46, OJ 1995, L-281/31; Article 10 (1) Regulation 45/2001, OJ 2001, L-8/1.

[672] Article 8 (5) Directive 95/46, OJ 1995, L-281/31, data relating to administrative sanctions or judgments in civil cases *may be* also processed under the control of an official authority.

[673] Article 10 (5) Regulation 45/2001, OJ 2001, L-8/1.

[674] Compare for criticism on this provision, Dammann and Simitis (1997), Article 8, para 3 and for general criticism on the term "sensitive data", compare Simitis (1999).

[675] Further exceptions refer amongst others to the processing of data in the framework of organisations such as trade unions or non-profit-seeking organisations, or the processing is necessary to protect the vital interests of the data subject or of another person where the data subject is physically or legally incapable of giving his or her consent, or the processing relates to data which are manifestly made public by the data subject or is necessary for the establishment, exercise or defence of legal claims, compare Article 8 (2) and (3) Directive 95/46, OJ 1995, L-281/31; Article 10 (2) and (3) Regulation 45/2001, OJ 2001, L-8/1.

[676] T-320/02, *Esch-Leonhardt and Others v. ECB*, judgment of 18 February 2004.

proceedings by basing themselves on Articles 2 (a), (b) and (c)[677] and Article 10 (1) of Regulation 45/2001.[678]

Due to the facts that, in both cases the applicants themselves declared in the respective e-mail to be members of the trade-union and that a shortened version, blacking out the trade union membership, of the respective e-mail would not have been sufficient to a proper management of the personal files, the General Court dismissed the application for annulment and concluded that the exception provided for in Article 10 (2) (b) Regulation 45/2001[679] is applicable.

In contrast to the detailed provisions of Directive 95/46 and Regulation 45/2001, the FDPJ does not stipulate a similar list including the exceptions. It simply reverses the general prohibition of the processing of sensitive data into the opposite. Article 6 FDPJ permits the processing of data revealing racial or ethnic origin, political opinions, religious or philosophical beliefs, trade-union membership and personal data concerning health or sex life when the processing is "strictly necessary and when the national law provides adequate safeguards". Although the FDPJ is an instrument in police and judicial cooperation, it does not refer to data relating to criminal offences, convictions or security measures. Questions arising out of the fast changing technology in the framework of the processing of biometric data including DNA – subject of the ECtHR case *S. and Marper v. the United Kingdom*, discussed above – are not even mentioned.

c) Rights of the Individual

aa) Information, Notification and Transparency

One of the elements of a fair processing of data is the information provided to the data subject. Knowing that one's personal data are processed guarantees transparency

---

[677] Article 2 (a), (b), (c) of Regulation 45/2001 entails the definitions of the instrument (Article 2 (a) '*personal data*' shall mean any information relating to an identified or identifiable natural person hereinafter referred to as 'data subject'; an identifiable person is one who can be identified, directly or indirectly, in particular by reference to an identification number or to one or more factors specific to his or her physical, physiological, mental, economic, cultural or social identity; (b) '*processing of personal data*' hereinafter referred to as 'processing' shall mean any operation or set of operations which is performed upon personal data, whether or not by automatic means, such as collection, recording, organisation, storage, adaptation or alteration, retrieval, consultation, use, disclosure by transmission, dissemination or otherwise making available, alignment or combination, blocking, erasure or destruction; (c) '*personal data filing system*' hereinafter referred to as 'filing system' shall mean any structured set of personal data which are accessible according to specific criteria, whether centralised, decentralised or dispersed on a functional or geographical basis (emphasis added)).

[678] Article 10 (1) Regulation 45/2001explicitly prohibits to process data revealing racial or ethnic origin, political opinions, religious or philosophical beliefs, trade-union membership or personal data concerning health or sex life.

[679] The processing relates to data which are manifestly made public by the data subject.

and enables the person concerned to assess its own position and to adapt its behaviour to a given situation.[680] Foreseeability and the control of the use of personal information play an essential role in data protection law. Moreover, as the ECtHR in *Weber and Saravia v. Germany* emphasised, the question of information of the individual concerned is directly linked to the effectiveness of remedies before the courts and for that reason to the existence of effective safeguards against the abuse of governmental monitoring powers.[681]

Directive 95/46 and Regulation 45/2001 distinguish two situations with regard to information rights: first, data which have been obtained from the data subject and second, data which have been obtained by other means.[682] In both cases, information has to be provided irrespective of whether the individual applies for access to the data.[683] The information includes (a) the identity of the controller and of his representative, (b) the purposes of the processing for which the data are intended and (c) any further information[684] in so far as such further information is necessary having regard to the specific circumstances in which the data are collected and to guarantee fair processing in respect of the data subject.[685] Information on the categories of data must be additionally provided in the case that the information is not obtained from the data subject.[686]

Regulation 45/2001 adds information on the legal basis of the processing operation for which the data are intended, the time-limits for storing the data and the right to have recourse at any time to the EDPS and the origin of the data, except where the controller cannot disclose this information for reasons of professional secrecy[687] in so far as such further information is necessary, having regard to the

680 Dammann and Simitis (1997), Article 10, para 1; Ehmann and Helfrich (1999), Article 10, paras 25–28.

681 *Weber and Saravia v. Germany*, Application no. 54934/00, admissibility decision of 29 June 2006, para 135: "since there is in principle little scope for recourse to the courts by the individual concerned unless the latter is advised of the measures taken without his or her knowledge and thus able to challenge their legality retrospectively".

682 Articles 10 and 11 Directive 95/46, OJ 1995, L-281/31; Articles 11 and 12 Regulation 45/2001, OJ 2001, L-8/1.

683 Articles 10 and 11 Directive 95/46, OJ 1995, L-281/31; Articles 11 and 12 Regulation 45/2001, OJ 2001, L-8/1.

684 Such as the recipients or categories of recipients of the data, the existence of the right of access to and the right to rectify the data concerning the individual concerned.

685 Articles 10 (1) and 11 (1) Directive 95/46, OJ 1995, L-281/31; Articles 11 (1) and 12 (1) Regulation 45/2001, OJ 2001, L-8/1; in the event that the information is obtained from the data subject, additional information on the fact whether replies to the questions are obligatory or voluntary, as well as the possible consequences of failure to reply must be given.

686 Article 11 (1) Directive 95/46, OJ 1995, L-281/31; Articles 12 (1) Regulation 45/2001, OJ 2001, L-8/1.

687 Information on the origin of the data is only provided if the information is not obtained from the data subject.

specific circumstances in which the data are collected and to guarantee fair processing in respect of the data subject.[688]

Derogations exist in the event of processing for statistical purposes, historical or scientific research.[689] When the information is not obtained from the data subject, the information does not to be given, if the "provision of such information proves impossible or would involve a disproportionate effort or if recording or disclosure is expressly laid down by law".[690] Although the provision on the disproportionate effort allows for a certain discretion,[691] Member States must nonetheless provide appropriate safeguards in these cases.

In contrast to Directive 95/46 and Regulation 45/2001, a clear obligation to provide the data subject with information on the processing does regrettably not exist in the FDPJ. The wording of the provision on the information of the data subject appears to be more a possibility rather than an obligation.[692] Recital (26) FDPJ mentions that "[...] it may be necessary to inform data subjects regarding the processing of their data [...]". Article 16 further details that "Member States shall ensure that the data subject is informed regarding the collection or processing of personal data by their competent authorities, in accordance with national law".[693] Member States may additionally ask another Member State not to inform the data subject about data transferred from this first Member State to the other.[694]

None of the FDPJ provisions stipulates a clear obligation to inform the person concerned about the processing.

bb) Access

The right to obtain access to personal data serves similar purposes as the right to be informed about the data processing. Control about the whereabouts of personal data plays a crucial role. Similar to the access right in Convention No. 108, Directive 95/46 and Regulation 45/2001 include different aspects of the access right. Individuals have the right to obtain information from the controller relating to the confirmation as to whether or not data related to him or her are being processed; information at least as to the *purposes* of the processing operation, the categories

---

[688] Article 12 (1) (f) Regulation 45/2001, OJ 2001, L-8/1.

[689] Articles 10 (2) and 11 (2) Directive 95/46, OJ 1995, L-281/31; Articles 11 (2) and 12 (2) Regulation 45/2001, OJ 2001, L-8/1.

[690] Article 11 (2) Directive 95/46, OJ 1995, L-281/31; Articles 12 (2) Regulation 45/2001, OJ 2001, L-8/1.

[691] Compare also Chap. B II 1 d cc.

[692] EDPS opinion on the FDPJ, OJ 2007, C-139/1, para 37.

[693] Article 16 (1) FDPJ, OJ 2008, L-350/60.

[694] Article 16 (2) FDPJ, OJ 2008, L-350/60.

of data concerned, the recipients[695] or categories of recipients to whom the data are disclosed, communication in an intelligible form of the data undergoing processing and of any available information as to the source of data and knowledge of the logic involved in any automated decision process concerning him or her.[696] Regulation 45/2001 additionally provides that the controller of the data has to provide the requested information within a 3 month period.[697] The detailed wording of the aforementioned provisions should assure that the Member States, when transposing the Directive into national law, respect the different aspects of the access right and do not chose a very broad access provision susceptible to different interpretations.[698]

Recent case-law on the right of access in the framework of Directive 95/46, such as *College van burgemeester en wethouders van Rotterdam v. M.E.E. Rijkeboer,*[699] confirms that Member States indeed enjoy a certain margin of discretion in implementing the access right of Directive 95/46, which is, however, limited by proportionality elements. In *College van burgemeester en wethouders van Rotterdam v. M.E.E. Rijkeboer* the Court made clear that the access rights of Directive 95/46 not only relates to the present but also to the past. In this case, *Mr. Rijkeboer* requested in 2005 the College to notify him of all instances in which data relating to him from the local authority personal records had, in the 2 years preceding the request, been disclosed to third parties.[700] The College complied with the request only partially by notifying *Mr. Rijkeboer* that only the data relating to a period of 1 year preceding his request could be released.[701] Data dating from more than 1 year prior to his request had been, according to Dutch law, erased automatically.[702]

The question referred to the Court was whether pursuant to the access right of Directive 95/46, an individual's right of access to information on the recipients or the content of the data communicated may be limited to a period of 1 year preceding his request for access.[703] The Court concluded that, "it is for Member States to fix a time-limit for storage of information and to provide for access to information

695 It should be noted that the term "recipients" in the framework of Directive 95/46 and Regulation 45/2001 does not include "authorities which may receive data in the framework of a particular inquiry shall not be regarded as recipients" (Article 2 (g) of Directive 95/46, OJ 1995, L-281/31 and Regulation 45/2001, OJ 2001, L-8/1).

696 Article 12 (a) Directive 95/46, OJ 1995, L-281/31; Article 13 (a) to (d) Regulation 45/2001, OJ 2001, L-8/1.

697 Article 13 Regulation 45/2001, OJ 2001, L-8/1.

698 Dammann and Simitis (1997), Article 12, para 3.

699 Case C-553/07, *College van burgemeester en wethouders van Rotterdam v. M.E.E. Rijkeboer*, judgment of 7 May 2009.

700 Ibid, para 23.

701 Ibid, para 24.

702 Ibid, para 25.

703 Ibid, para 31.

which constitutes a fair balance between, on the one hand, the interest of the data subject in protecting his privacy, in particular by way of his rights to object and to bring legal proceedings and, on the other, the burden which the obligation to store that information represents for the controller".[704] Nonetheless, in the present case, the rules limiting the storage of information on the recipients and the content of the data related to a period of 1 year and correspondingly limited access to that information. Basic data however were stored for a much longer period, which did not constitute a fair balance, "unless it can be shown that longer storage of that information would constitute an excessive burden on the controller".[705]

Compared to the detailed provisions of Directive 95/46 and Regulation 45/2001, the right of access in the FDPJ is limited to information on the confirmation from the controller or from the national supervisory authority as to whether or not data relating to him have been transmitted or made available, information on the recipients or categories of recipients to whom the data have been disclosed and communication of the data undergoing processing or at least confirmation from the national supervisory authority that all necessary verifications have taken place.[706] Information relating to the purpose of processing, the source or the communication in an intelligible form are not provided.[707] In addition to the already limited information, various exceptions apply. Member States may restrict the access right (a) to avoid obstructing official or legal inquiries, investigations or procedures, (b) to avoid prejudicing the prevention, detection, investigation and prosecution of criminal offences or for the execution of criminal penalties, (c) to protect public security, (d) to protect national security, (e) to protect the data subject or the rights and freedoms of others.[708] When restricting the access, the measure must be necessary and proportional and Member States must take the legitimate interests of the person concerned into account.[709] In all of these cases the person concerned "shall be advised that he may appeal to the competent national supervisory authority, a judicial authority or to a court".[710]

cc) Erasure, Blocking, Deletion and Notification to Third Parties

In addition to the right of access, Directive 95/46, Regulation 45/2001 and FDPJ contain the right to erasure, blocking and deletion of data whose processing do not comply with the provisions of the relevant instrument, in particular because of the

[704] Ibid, para 70.
[705] Idem.
[706] Article 17 (1) FDPJ, OJ 2008, L-350/60.
[707] For criticism, compare EDPS opinion on the FDPJ, OJ 2007, C-139/1, para 37.
[708] Article 17 (2) FDPJ, OJ 2008, L-350/60.
[709] Ibid.
[710] Ibid.

incomplete or inaccurate nature of the data.[711] Where Directive 95/46 gives Member States a wide discretion relating to the implementation of these rights and remains rather vague as regards the concrete content of such provisions, Regulation 45/2001 offers more detailed rules. The right to obtain the blocking of data should for instance apply where (a) their accuracy is contested by the data subject, for a period enabling the controller to verify the accuracy, including the completeness, of the data, (b) the controller no longer needs them for the accomplishment of its tasks but they have to be maintained for purposes of proof, or (c) the processing is unlawful and the data subject opposes their erasure and demands their blocking instead.[712] Nonetheless, also in the framework of Directive 95/46, certain criteria apply. The rectification is closely related to the accuracy of the data (Article 6 (1) (d) Directive 95/46) and refers to the truthfulness of the data, which, in turn, depends on the context in which the data are stored.[713]

The FDPJ includes similar provisions and specifies that Member States shall lay down whether the person concerned may request its rights directly at the controller or through the intermediary of the national DPA.[714] Unlike the foregoing rather limited provisions with regard to the protection of the individual, the FDPJ stipulates further guarantees in case the controller refuses rectification, erasure or blocking. Each "refusal must be communicated in writing to the data subject who must be informed of the possibilities provided for in national law for lodging a complaint or seeking judicial remedy".[715]

To complete the protection of the individual, Directive 95/46 and Regulation 45/2001 provide for a sort of "aftercare". The person concerned has the right to obtain from the controller the notification to third parties to whom the data have been disclosed of any rectification, erasure or blocking carried out in line with the relevant instruments, unless this proves impossible or involves a disproportionate effort.[716] The FDPJ does not provide for an individual right of the person concerned to ask for the notification to third parties, but in case that incorrect data have been transmitted or data have been unlawfully transmitted, the recipient of the data "must be notified without delay".[717] The individual is however not notified.

---

[711] Article 12 (b) Directive 95/46, OJ 1995, L-281/31; Articles 14, 15 and 16 Regulation 45/2001, OJ 2001, L-8/1 and Articles 4 and 18 FDPJ, OJ 2008, L-350/60.

[712] Compare Article 15 (1) (a) to (c) Regulation 45/2001, OJ 2001, L-8/1.

[713] Dammann and Simitis (1997), Article 12, para 15.

[714] Articles 4 and 18 FDPJ, OJ 2008, L-350/60.

[715] Article 18 (1) FDPJ, OJ 2008, L-350/60, in addition "Upon examination of the complaint or judicial remedy, the data subject shall be informed whether the controller acted properly or not. Member States may also provide that the data subject shall be informed by the competent national supervisory authority that a review has taken place. If the accuracy of an item of personal data is contested by the data subject and its accuracy or inaccuracy cannot be ascertained, referencing of that item of data may take place", Article 18 (1) and (2) FDPJ, OJ 2008, L-350/60.

[716] Article 12 (c) Directive 95/46, OJ 1995, L-281/31; Article 17 Regulation 45/2001, OJ 2001, L-8/1; to criticism related to the term "disproportionate effort", compare Chap. B II 1 d cc.

[717] Article 8 (2) FDPJ, OJ 2008, L-350/60.

dd) The Right to Object

The right to object to the processing of personal data in Directive 95/46 and in Regulation 45/2001 is divided into two cases.

The first case concerns the possibility to object with regard to data processing on compelling grounds relating to the particular situation of the data subject "at least" in cases as described in Article 7 (e) and (f) of Directive 95/46. These provisions refer to data processing necessary for the performance of a task carried out in the public interest or in the exercise of official authority vested in the controller or in a third party to whom the data are disclosed or to the processing necessary for the purposes of the legitimate interests pursued by the controller or by the third party or parties to whom the data are disclosed.[718] In relation to Regulation 45/2001 the right to object is formulated in a broader way involving in general the objection to data processing on compelling grounds relating to the particular situation of the data subject.[719] Excepted cases are situations in which the processing is necessary for compliance with a legal obligation to which the controller is subject, or necessary for the performance of a contract to which the data subject is party or in order to take steps at the request of the data subject prior to entering into a contract or the data subject has unambiguously given his or her consent.[720] The second case in which objection is possible concerns the right to oppose data processing for the purposes of direct marketing.[721] Directive 95/46 and Regulation 45/2001 include similar provisions.

Taking the relatively secret nature of police and judicial data processing into account, it is not particular astonishing that the FDPJ does not involve a right to object. However, in this context, it is important to highlight that security related data processing does not only involve data on criminals. Data of possible suspects, victims and witnesses are equally processed. With regard to the protection of this particular sensitive group of persons, the complete exclusion of the right to object the data processing in certain situation for data processed in the framework of police and judicial data processing seems less obvious.[722] It is likely that there are situations where a victim or witness might oppose (on compelling grounds relating to his particular situation the processing) of his personal data, for instance rape victims. Situations in which a victim or witness may have legitimate grounds to object should therefore also be considered in a police and judicial context.

---

718 Article 7 (e) and (f) Directive 95/46, OJ 1995, L-281/31.

719 Article 18 (a) Regulation 45/2001, OJ 2001, L-8/1.

720 Ibid.

721 Article 14 (b) Directive 95/46, OJ 1995, L-281/31; Article 18 (b) Regulation 45/2001, OJ 2001, L-8/1.

722 Against the right to object in security related data processing, see Alonso Blas (2010), Issue 11, No. 2, pp. 233–250.

ee) Legal Prohibition on Automated Decision Making

The danger of a misuse of automatic means when making a decision, including the assessment of the personality of a person, should be encountered by a more or less strict ban on automated individual decisions. The risk of automatic decisions relates to the fact that their result might seem objective at the first glance (because no subjective impressions are considered) and therefore decision makers may tend to trust the alleged objective result more than another result which might base on subjective criteria. Therefore, Directive 95/46, Regulation 45/2001 and FDPJ protect individuals against decisions which base solely on automatic processing of data.[723] Individuals equipped with personal responsibility and not computers should be accountable for the (possibly detrimental) decision on other persons.[724]

Considerable exceptions however exist. Directive 95/46 and Regulation 45/2001 prohibit automated decision making. An exception applies if the decision is authorised by law.[725] FDPJ generally permits automated decisions if they are authorised by law.[726] In all cases the law must lay down "measures to safeguard the legitimate interests of the data subject",[727] but further guarantees in order to ensure the quality of the protective measures are not necessary. Compared to the provisions in Directive 95/46 and Regulation 45/2001, the wording of Article 7 FDPJ, which regulates automated decision making, raises concern. Instead of the general approach chosen by Directive 95/46 and Regulation 45/2001 to prohibit automated decisions, the FDPJ generally permits them.[728] This wording does not put real obstacles for Member States to enact legislation permitting automated decision making.

[723] Article 15 Directive 95/46, OJ 1995, L-281/31; Article 19 Regulation 45/2001, OJ 2001, L-8/1 and Article 7 FDPJ, OJ 2008, L-350/60.

[724] Dammann and Simitis (1997), Article 15, para 2.

[725] Article 15 (2) (b) Directive 95/46, OJ 1995, L-281/31; Article 19 Regulation 45/2001, OJ 2001, L-8/1; Directive 95/46 additionally allows for automatic decision making when entering into or fulfilling a contract, compare Article 15 (2) (a) Directive 95/46; in case of Regulation 45/2001 automatic decisions are permitted if authorised by national or Community legislation.

[726] Article 7 FDPJ, OJ 2008, L-350/60.

[727] Article 15 (2) (b) Directive 95/46, OJ 1995, L-281/31; Article 19 Regulation 45/2001, OJ 2001, L-8/1 and Article 7 FDPJ, OJ 2008, L-350/60.

[728] Article 7 FDPJ, OJ 2008, L-350/60 stipulates: "A decision which produces an adverse legal effect for the data subject or significantly affects him and which is based solely on automated processing of data intended to evaluate certain personal aspects relating to the data subject shall be permitted only if authorised by a law which also lays down measures to safeguard the data subject's legitimate interests".

ff) Independent Supervision and Article 29 Data Protection Working Party

Supervision is an essential requirement to guarantee the effective enforcement of data protection requirements.[729] Independence of this supervision is therefore acore element contributing to this aim. Directive 95/46 and the FDPJ include further specifications with regard to the powers with which the supervisory authorities should be equipped. In addition to consultation duties[730] foreseen in Directive 95/46, investigative powers,[731] effective powers of intervention[732] and powers to engage in legal proceedings or to bring infringements to the attention of the judicial authorities where the national provisions adopted pursuant to the Directive 95/46 or the FDPJ have been violated are included in both instruments (Directive 95/46 and FDPJ). The supervisory bodies shall hear claims lodged by persons and shall inform the person concerned about the outcome of the claim.[733] Decisions taken by the supervisory authorities may be appealed against through the courts.[734] Directive 95/46 additionally provides for the drawing up and the publishing of an activity report.[735]

Regulation 45/2001 establishes the EDPS as the independent supervisory authority responsible for monitoring the data processing carried out by the Community institutions and bodies. Detailed provisions lay down the legal framework of the EDPS. Its appointment, its powers and duties, conditions for the performance of its duties, staff and financial resources and guarantees relating to its independence are subject to Articles 41–48 of Regulation 45/2001. According to Article 46 of Regulation 45/2001 the duties of the EDPS involve, amongst others, the investigation of complaints, the conduction of inquiries, the prior checking of processing notified to the EDPS, the monitoring of the application of the provisions of Regulation 45/2001 and of relevant developments and the cooperation with national DPAs.[736]

In addition, the EDPS disposes of important powers stipulated in Article 47 of Regulation 45/2001. It may, inter alia, order the rectification, blocking, erasure or

---

[729] Article 28 Directive 95/46, OJ 1995, L-281/31; Articles 41–48 Regulation 45/2001, OJ 2001, L-8/1 and Article 25 FDPJ, OJ 2008, L-350/60.

[730] Article 28 (2) Directive 95/46, OJ 1995, L-281/31.

[731] Investigative powers are powers such as powers of access to data forming the subject-matter of processing operations and powers to collect all the information necessary for the performance of its supervisory duties (Article 28 (3) Directive 95/46 and Article 25 (2) (a) FDPJ).

[732] Intervention powers are powers such as, for example, that of delivering opinions before processing operations are carried out, and ensuring appropriate publication of such opinions, of ordering the blocking, erasure or destruction of data, of imposing a temporary or definitive ban on processing, of warning or admonishing the controller, or that of referring the matter to national parliaments or other political institutions (Article 28 (3) Directive 95/46 and Article 25 (2) (b) FDPJ).

[733] Article 28 (4) Directive 95/46, OJ 1995, L-281/31 and Article 25 (3) FDPJ, OJ 2008, L-350/60.

[734] Article 28 (3) Directive 95/46, OJ 1995, L-281/31 and Article 25 (2) (c) FDPJ, OJ 2008, L-350/60.

[735] Article 28 (4) Directive 95/46, OJ 1995, L-281/31.

[736] Compare Article 46 Regulation 45/2001, OJ 2001, L-8/1 and Hijmans (2006).

destruction of the data processed in breach with Regulation 45/2001, impose a ban on the processing, intervene in actions before the Court of Justice or refer the matter to the institution or body concerned, and if necessary to the Parliament, the Council and the Commission.[737] The EDPS additionally advises on policy affecting data protection matters and cooperates with national DPAs to guarantee consistent protection of personal data interests. Over the years, the EDPS has become an important actor in the field of European data protection law.[738] In the AFSJ, former first pillar databases, such as Eurodac and the VIS are monitored by the authority. Supervision of the SIS II is intended in future.[739]

The criterion of independence was recently subject to an infringement action against Germany which transposed Article 28 (1) of Directive 95/46 (which stipulates that the national DPAs shall act with complete independence in exercising their functions) by subjecting the national DPAs at federal level, responsible for supervising the processing of data outside the public sector, to state scrutiny.[740] Supported by the EDPS, the Commission considered this supervisory model as an infringement of the independence requirement of Directive 95/46 and decided to bring the action before the Court of Justice. Germany argued that the DPAs are not exposed to external influences, but rather to an "administration's internal monitoring mechanism, implemented by the authorities attached to the same administrative machinery".[741]

Against these relatively vague arguments, the Court came to a clear statement and interpreted the terms "with complete independence" in a broad way. It pointed out that "the mere risk that the scrutinising authorities could exercise a political influence over the decisions of the supervisory authorities is enough to hinder the latter authorities' independent performance of their tasks. First, as was stated by the Commission, there could be 'prior compliance' on the part of those authorities in the light of the scrutinising authority's decision-making practice. Secondly, for the purposes of the role adopted by those authorities as guardians of the right to private life, it is necessary that their decisions, and therefore the authorities themselves, remain above any suspicion of partiality".[742]

Due to this interpretation, the Court of Justice held that the German legal framework to regulate data processing oversight outside the public sector was not consistent with the independence requirement of Article 28 (1) of Directive 94/46. The unambiguous statement in favour of an undoubtful interpretation of the term "complete independence" requires the Member States to establish a legal

[737] Compare the powers listed in Article 47 Regulation 45/2001, OJ 2001, L-8/1.

[738] An excellent overview of the functions of the EDPS gives Hijmans (2006).

[739] Compare Chap. B III 1 e bb.

[740] Case C-518/07, *Commission v. Germany*, judgment of 9 March 2010, para 10; annotations with regard to this case are made by Schild (2010); Bull (2010); Roßnagel, (2010); Petri and Tinnefeld (2010).

[741] Case C-518/07, *Commission v. Germany*, judgment of 9 March 2010, para 16.

[742] Case C-518/07, *Commission v. Germany*, judgment of 9 March 2010, para 36.

framework for national DPAs which remains entirely free from any external influence, including indirect influence. Any other interpretation would have left room for discretion of the Member States and would have permitted other Member States to equally subject their DPAs to whatsoever form of supervision.

In addition to independent supervision, Directive 95/46 established the Article 29 Data Protection Working Party which coordinates the cooperation of the national DPAs at EU level.[743] The Working Party is composed of a representative of the national DPA and of a representative of the authority or authorities established for the Community institutions and bodies, and of a representative of the Commission.[744] The group acts independently and has advisory status. Over the years, it offered valuable support in interpreting the application of Directive 95/46.[745] The tasks of the Article 29 Data Protection Working Party are stipulated in Article 30 Directive 95/46. They relate to the promotion of a uniform application of the general principles of Directive 95/46 through the cooperation between national DPAs. In addition, the group advises the Commission on questions of data protection and on the level of protection in the EU and in third states, makes recommendations to the EU institutions and the public on data protection matters and gives opinions on codes of conducts drawn up at Community level.[746]

gg) Security

Security requirements should protect the personal data against destruction, loss, alteration or unauthorised access or disclosure. Article 17 Directive 95/46 requires to establish "appropriate technical measures" to protect personal data against all unlawful forms of processing.[747] The level of security must be appropriate to the risks represented by the processing and the nature of the data to be protected.[748] Further details of the kind of measures which should be taken are stipulated in Regulation 45/2001 and FDPJ. Article 22 Regulation 45/2001 and Article 22 FDPJ stipulate 11 measures which shall be implemented to protect personal data in automated data processing systems: Equipment access control[749] and control of

[743] Article 29 Directive 95/46, OJ 1995, L-281/31.

[744] Article 29 (2) Directive 95/46, OJ 1995, L-281/31.

[745] The opinions and document of the Article 29 Data Protection Working Party can be found on the webpage: http://ec.europa.eu/justice/policies/privacy/workinggroup/index_en.htm (accessed February 2011).

[746] Compare Article 30 (1) (a)–(d) of Directive 95/46, OJ 1995, L-281/31 and http://ec.europa.eu/justice/policies/privacy/workinggroup/index_en.htm (accessed February 2011).

[747] Article 17 (1) Directive 95/46, OJ 1995, L-281/31.

[748] Article 17 (2) Directive 95/46, OJ 1995, L-281/31.

[749] Which means to deny unauthorised persons access to data-processing equipment used for processing personal data.

data media,[750] storage,[751] users,[752] data access,[753] communication,[754] input,[755] and transport[756] should improve security. Recovery,[757] reliability[758] and integrity[759] of the data processing add additional protection.[760]

hh) Accountability

Remedies, liability and sanctions play an important role for the effective enforcement of data protection rights. In case that a person has suffered damage as a result of an unlawful processing operation or of any act incompatible with the instruments in force, he must be entitled to receive compensation from the controller or another authority.[761] The person concerned must dispose of a right to a judicial remedy for the breach of the right guaranteed to him.[762] Directive 95/46, Regulation 45/2001 and FDPJ indiscriminately grant these rights to "any person", irrespectively of the categories of persons concerned.[763] Any natural person or individual consequently may invoke these rights in front of national or European Courts. At European level, at least in the framework of Regulation 45/2001, an individual may lodge a

---

[750] Includes the prevention of unauthorised reading, copying, modification or removal of data media.

[751] Member States should prevent the unauthorised input of data and the unauthorised inspection, modification or deletion of stored personal data.

[752] Which means to prevent the use of automated data-processing systems by unauthorised persons using data communication equipment.

[753] Member States must ensure that persons authorised to use an automated data-processing system only have access to the data covered by their access authorisation.

[754] Member States must guarantee that it is possible to verify and establish to which bodies personal data have been or may be transmitted or made available using data communication equipment.

[755] Control of the input means to ensure that it is subsequently possible to verify and establish which personal data have been input into automated data-processing systems and when and by whom the data were input.

[756] Transport control means to prevent the unauthorised reading, copying, modification or deletion of personal data during transfers of personal data or during transportation of data media.

[757] Recovery should ensure that installed systems may, in case of interruption, be restored.

[758] Reliability ensures that the functions of the system perform, that the appearance of faults in the functions is reported.

[759] Integrity means that stored data cannot be corrupted by means of a malfunctioning of the system.

[760] Compare Articles 22 (2) (a)–(j) of Regulation 45/2001, OJ 2001, L-8/1 and FDPJ, OJ 2008, L-350/60.

[761] Article 23 (1) Directive 95/46, OJ 1995, L-281/31, Article 32 (4) Regulation 45/2001, OJ 2001, L-8/1 and Article 19 (1) FDPJ, OJ 2008, L-350/60.

[762] Article 22 Directive 95/46, OJ 1995, L-281/31, Articles 22 (1) and (2) Regulation 45/2001, OJ 2001, L-8/1 and Article 20 FDPJ, OJ 2008, L-350/60.

[763] Dammann and Simitis (1997), Article 22, para 2; Brouwer (2008), p. 221.

complaint with the EDPS.[764] Actions against decisions of the EDPS may be brought before the Court of Justice.[765] Sanctions to be imposed in case of infringement of the data protection provisions of Directive 95/46, Regulation 45/2001 and FDPJ should additionally ensure the full and effective implementation of these instruments.[766]

d) Exceptions

Despite the relatively comprehensive protection described above, Directive 95/45 and Regulation 45/2001 include various restrictions to the rights included in both instruments[767]: (a) the prevention, investigation, detection and prosecution of criminal offences, (b) an important economic or financial interest of a Member State or of the European Communities, including monetary, budgetary and taxation matters, (c) the protection of the data subject or of the rights and freedoms of others, (d) the national security, public security or defence of the Member States and (e) the monitoring, inspection or regulatory task connected, even occasionally, with the exercise of official authority in the cases referred to in (a) and (b).[768] Article 13 (2) Directive 95/46 further restricts the right to access, rectification, erasure and blocking "where there is clearly no risk of breaching the privacy of the data subject" when data are processed solely for purposes of scientific research or are kept in personal form for a period which does not exceed the period necessary for the sole purpose of creating statistics.[769] Regulation 45/2001 however insist on the requirement of informing the data subject of the principal reason on which the application of the restriction is based and of his right to have recourse to the EDPS.[770]

When invoking such restrictions, Member States, Community institutions and bodies must however establish that the measures are necessary.[771] A general

---

[764] Article 32 (2) Regulation 45/2001, OJ 2001, L-8/1.

[765] Ibid.

[766] Article 24 Directive 95/46, OJ 1995, L-281/31, Article 49 Regulation 45/2001, OJ 2001, L-8/1 and Article 24 FDPJ, OJ 2008, L-350/60.

[767] Concerned are the rights relating to the quality of the data, the information rights, access, rectification, erasure and blocking as well as the publicizing of processing operations and the erasure of traffic and billing data (Articles 6 (1), 10, 11 (1), 12 and 21 of Directive 95/46, OJ 1995, L-281/31 and Articles 4 (1), 11, 12 (1), 13 to 17 and 37 (1) of Regulation 45/2001, OJ 2001, L-8/1).

[768] Article 13 (1) Directive 95/46, OJ 1995, L-281/31 and Article 20 (1) Regulation 45/2001, OJ 2001, L-8/1; Article 13 (1) Directive 95/46 adds the monitoring, inspection or regulatory function connected, even occasionally, with the exercise of official authority in case of public security.

[769] Article 13 (2) Directive 95/46, OJ 1995, L-281/31.

[770] Article 20 (4) Regulation 45/2001, OJ 2001, L-8/1.

[771] Article 13 (1) Directive 95/46, OJ 1995, L-281/31 and Article 20 (1) Regulation 45/2001, OJ 2001, L-8/1.

exemption for specific authorities or bodies would therefore neither be in accordance with Directive 95/46,[772] nor with Regulation 45/2001.

Exceptions for the processing of personal data solely for journalistic purposes or the purpose of artistic or literary expression "if they are necessary to reconcile the right to privacy with the rules governing freedom of expression" may additionally be provided.[773] Activities may be classified as "journalistic" if their sole objective is the disclosure to the public domain of information, opinions or ideas, irrespective of the medium used to distribute them.[774]

Exceptions in the framework of the FDPJ are not specified in one general provision as in Directive 95/46 or Regulation 45/2001. They are regulated in the relevant Articles which grant rights to individuals and which were already discussed above.

e) Transfer of Personal Data

Provisions on the transfer of personal data can be found in all three instruments. Depending on the scope of the instruments,[775] different rules on the transfer of personal data apply. Directive 95/46 exclusively refers to the protection of data in the framework of the transfer from Member States to third parties in an economic context, Regulation 45/2001 involves the transmission between Community institutions, bodies and/or other recipients outside the Community order and FDPJ includes rules on the transfer of data to authorities of third states, international

---

[772] Dammann and Simitis (1997), Article 13, para 4.

[773] Article 9 Directive 95/46, OJ 1995, L-281/31.

[774] For the exception as regards the processing for journalistic purposes, compare case C-73/07, *Tietosuojavaltuutettu v. Satakunnan Markkinapörssi Oy and Satamedia Oy*, judgment of 16 December 2008, in which the Court of Justice interpreted the exception as regards the processing for journalistic purposes according to Article 9 of Directive 95/46, which governs the relationship between the protection of such data and freedom of expression, as follows: Article 9 Directive 95/46 is to be interpreted "as meaning that an activity in which data on the earned and unearned income and the assets of natural persons are: (1) collected from documents in the public domain held by the tax authorities and processed for publication, (2) published alphabetically in printed form by income bracket and municipality in the form of comprehensive lists, (3) transferred onward on CD-ROM to be used for commercial purposes, and, (4) processed for the purposes of a text-messaging service whereby mobile telephone users can, by sending a text message containing details of an individual's name and municipality of residence to a given number, receive in reply information concerning the earned and unearned income and assets of that person, must be considered as activities involving the processing of personal data carried out 'solely for journalistic purposes', within the meaning of that provision, if the sole object of those activities is the disclosure to the public, irrespective of the medium which is used to transmit them, of information, opinions or ideas. Whether that is the case is a matter for the national court to determine. In any event, those activities are not limited to media undertakings and may be undertaken for profit-making purposes" (para 65 of the judgment).

[775] Compare above Sect. III 1.

bodies or the transfer to private parties in Member States.[776] The following analysis will show that while the transfer of personal data in the context of Directive 95/46 and Regulation 45/2001 is regulated in an exhaustive manner, the rules of the FDPJ fall considerably behind as regards the protection of individual rights in the context of third state data transfer. Having in mind that in the AFSJ as well as in the former first pillar increasingly more data are transferred to third states, the provisions regulating third state data transfer are demonstrated slightly more detailed than the aforementioned rules.

aa) Transfer to Recipients Governed by Directive 95/46 and Regulation 45/2001

Until the entry into force of the Amsterdam Treaty in 1997, which added Article 286 EC Treaty (Article 16 TFEU) to the Community order, the data processing of the institutions and bodies of the Community was not subject to official regulation. First Regulation 45/2001 stipulated rules on the data processing of the Community institutions and bodies. As already seen above, its rules mirror the rules of Directive 95/46 and are equally limited to former first pillar institutions and bodies. It is worth remembering, that, even after the adoption of the Lisbon Treaty, the rules of Regulation 45/2001 are not applicable to the data processing of former third pillar actors or databases, such as Europol, Eurojust or the CIS.[777]

Regulation 45/2001 distinguishes between transmission of data by the Community institutions or bodies and other recipients.

In the first case, personal data processing of the recipient is entirely covered by the rules of Regulation 45/2001 (for instance data processing at OLAF) and data shall only be transferred "if the data are necessary for the legitimate performance of tasks covered by the competence of the recipient".[778] Consequently, the sending party must ensure (1) that the recipient has the appropriate competence and (2) that the transfer is necessary. This assessment should be made on a case-by-case basis.[779] The recipient is bound by the purpose of the transfer when processing the data.[780] When data are transferred following a request from the recipient, both, the recipient and the controller are responsible for the legitimacy of the transfer.[781] Additional safeguards relating to the lawfulness of the transfer include the requirement that the controller should verify the competence of the recipient and make

[776] Articles 25 and 26 Directive 95/46, OJ 1995, L-281/31, Articles 7–9 Regulation 45/2001, OJ 2001, L-8/1 and Articles 13 and 14 FDPJ, OJ 2008, L-350/60.

[777] Compare above Chap. B III 1.

[778] Article 7 (1) Regulation 45/2001, OJ 2001, L-8/1.

[779] EDPS, opinion on a notification for prior checking received from the data protection officer at the European Anti-Fraud Office on Criminal assistance cases, Brussels, 12 October 2007 (Case 2007–203), p. 8.

[780] Article 7 (3) Regulation 45/2001, OJ 2001, L-8/1.

[781] Ibid.

a provisional evaluation of the necessity of the transfer of the data.[782] The recipient must ensure that the necessity of the transfer of the data can be subsequently verified.[783]

In the second case (other recipients), data are either transferred to other recipients subject to Directive 95/46 or to other recipients not subject to Directive 95/46. If Directive 95/46 is applicable to the data processing of the recipient, the latter must establish that the data are necessary for the performance of a task carried out in the public interest or subject to the exercise of public authority, or the recipient establishes the necessity of the transfer and there is no reason to assume that the data subject's legitimate interests might be prejudiced.[784]

Transfer of personal data to recipients who are not governed by the regime of Directive 95/46 necessarily requires more protection. It is analysed in the next section.

bb) Third State Transfer in the Framework of Directive 95/45 and Regulation 45/2001

In contrast to the transfer to recipients governed by Directive 95/46 and Regulation 45/2001, transfer to third states is however regulated in much more detail. Chapter IV of Directive 95/46 and Article 9 of Regulation 45/2001 govern the conditions of the transmission of data to a third state in an economic context.[785] Third state data transfer occupies an increasingly important place in EU data sharing. To avoid that the protection guaranteed in the EU is not considerably weekend when transferring the data to third states and to avoid the by-passing of EU data protection rules by establishing data processing servers in countries applying a low level of data protection, both instruments provide for the so called "adequacy mechanism".

(1) Adequate Level of Protection

In general, according to Articles 25 (1) and (2) of Directive 95/46 and Article 9 of Regulation 45/2001, the transfers to a third state of personal data may take place only if the third state in question ensures an adequate level of protection. To assess the adequacy, the following procedure takes place:

First, the national DPA of the country which intends to transfer the data considers if the third country ensures – or does not ensure – an adequate level of

[782] Article 7 (2) Regulation 45/2001, OJ 2001, L-8/1, if doubts arise as to this necessity, the controller shall seek further information from the recipient.

[783] Article 7 (2) Regulation 45/2001, OJ 2001, L-8/1.

[784] Ibid.

[785] Third States are states that are neither Member States of the EU nor members of the European Economic Area (EEA); besides of the Member States of the EU, Iceland, Liechtenstein and Norway are members of the EEA.

protection.[786] If the national DPA considers that the third country does not ensure an adequate level of protection, according to Article 25 (3) Directive 95/46 the Member State is obliged to inform the European Commission or the EDPS (the latter only in case of Regulation 45/2001).[787] Second, when the Commission agrees that the third country does not ensure an adequate level of protection, Member States shall take the measures necessary to prevent any transfer of data of the same type to the third country in question.[788]

In general, Article 25 (2) of Directive 95/46 and Article 9 (2) of Regulation 45/2001 establish the criteria to be applied when evaluating the level of protection provided by a third state. The adequacy of the level shall be assessed in the light of *all* the circumstances surrounding a data transfer operation. Particular consideration shall be given to the nature of the data,[789] the purpose and duration of the proposed processing operation,[790] the country of origin and country of final destination,[791] the rules of law, both general and sectoral, in force in the third country in question and the rules and security measures which are complied with in that country.[792] The indication of "the rules and security measures which are complied with in that country" refers to economic self-regulation measures outside of the legal order that nevertheless have a binding force for the members of the organisation concerned.[793] Therefore, legal commentators postulate that Directive 95/46 follows a practice-oriented and functional approach.[794]

---

[786] The control could also be ensured by the processor itself (e.g. in Germany, § 4 b II, V BDSG).

[787] Article 9 (3) of Regulation 45/2001, OJ 2001, L-8/1.

[788] Article 25 (4) of Directive 95/46, OJ 1995, L-281/31.

[789] Especially the content of the data [e.g. sensitive data, and the possibility of the identification of the person concerned; compare Dammann and Simitis (1997), Article 25, para 10, and Engel (2003), accessible at Dissertationen of the Freie Universität Berlin online: http://www.diss.fu-berlin.de/diss/receive/FUDISS_thesis_000000001587 (accessed February 2011), pp. 110–111 (referred to as Engel (2003)].

[790] The long duration of the data demands a more intensive protection of data subjects as a short processing time, compare Engel (2003) p. 112.

[791] The indication of the country of origin is very important in the context of the import of data from a non-European country into the EU. The indication shall prevent that the data protection authorities do not make high demands to the level of protection in case of the re-import of the data into the third country. The indication of the country of final destination shall ensure that data protection authorities do not makehigh demands to the level of protection to a transit country, compare Engel (2003), pp. 112–113; *Dammann/Simitis* assume that transit countries, as well as the country of final destination, which could be different from the direct receiving country should be also considered, compare Dammann and Simitis (1997), Article 25, para 10.

[792] Article 25 (2) of Directive 95/46, OJ 1995, L-281/31; Article 9 (2) of Regulation 45/2001, OJ 2001, L-8/1.

[793] Document adopted by the Article 29 Working Party, WP 12 of 24 July 1998 on the transfers of personal data to third countries: applying Articles 25 and 26 of the EU data protection directive, pp. 11 et seq.

[794] Siemen (2006), p. 299; Brühann (2007), Article 25, para 15; Engel (2003), pp. 115 et seq.

The wording "in the light of all the circumstances surrounding a data transfer operation" suggests that the third country is not obliged to guarantee an adequate level of protection in general, but adequate guarantees must be given in the specific case of the transfer.[795] Nevertheless the Commission can adopt a decision whereupon the entire country guarantees an adequate protection of personal data.[796] Moreover, it shall be given "particular" consideration to certain circumstances, i.e. that other criteria apart from the mentioned ones could also influence the adequacy decision. Further criteria to assess the level of adequacy are not contained in Directive 95/46 or Regulation 45/2001. Such criteria are however of utmost importance considering the far reaching consequence of an adequacy decision of the Commission. A country providing an adequate level of protection profits from economic and convenient advantages when it comes to data transfer. Personal data of EU citizens may then be easily transmitted to the respective country. With regard to these advantages and the implications on the rights of individuals, it seems to be crucial to interpret in detail the meaning of the notion "adequate". When taking into account that, pursuant to its recital 11, Directive 95/46 shall give substance to and amplify the provisions contained in the Convention No. 108, it seems to be reasonable to draw a comparison between the wording used in Convention No. 108 and the wording of Directive 95/46.[797]

(2) Recourse to Convention No. 108

Pursuant to Article 12 (3) (a) of Convention No. 108, referring to the transfer of data across the borders of the member states of the Convention, the transfer of data across national borders is permitted if the receiving party provides an equivalent protection. The abovementioned additional protocol of May 2001[798] governs the transfer of data to third states. Its Article 2 (1) stipulates: "Each Party shall provide for the transfer of personal data to a recipient that is subject to the jurisdiction of a State or organisation that is not Party to the Convention only if that State or organisation ensures an adequate level of protection for the intended data

---

[795] Dammann and Simitis (1997), Article 25, para 9; Engel (2003), p. 89–90.

[796] View Commission decision with regard to: Switzerland, Hungary, Canada, Argentina, Guernsey and the Isle of Man, http://ec.europa.eu/justice/policies/privacy/thridcountries/index_en.htm (accessed February 2011).

[797] Recital 11 of the Directive 95/46: "Whereas the principles of the protection of the rights and freedoms of individuals, notably the right to privacy, which are contained in this Directive, give substance to and amplify those contained in the Council of Europe Convention of 28 January 1981 for the Protection of Individuals with regard to Automatic Processing of Personal Data".

[798] Additional Protocol to the Convention for the Protection of Individuals with regard to Automatic Processing of Personal Data, regarding supervisory authorities and Transborder Data Flows, 8 November 2001, entered into force the 1st of July 2004.

transfer".[799] When comparing the two formulations, the different wording is remarkable. The clear distinction between the words adequate and equivalent indicates that there must be a different standard regarding on the one hand the transfer of data to member states of the Convention No. 108 and on the other hand as regards the transfer to third states. It follows that a full equivalence of the level of protection between the EU and third states is not required to transfer data to another country. Instead, a lower level of protection – compared to the level of protection of the member states of the Convention – could be sufficient to guarantee an adequate level of protection in terms of the Convention No. 108 and its additional protocol.[800] Due to the close relationship between Directive 95/46 and Convention No. 108 mentioned above,[801] both adequacy criteria could be interpreted congruently. Consequently, according to this comparison, adequate does mean that the level of protection must be necessarily equivalent.

Siemen explains this conclusion also by the fact that the Explanatory Report of the Additional Protocol of 23 May 2003 interprets the adequacy of the level of protection in "the light of all the circumstances surrounding a data transfer".[802] The same wording is used in Article 25 (2) of Directive 95/46. Therefore the identical wording of the Directive 95/46 and the Explanatory Report of the Additional Protocol additionally indicates an identical understanding of both instruments.[803] *Dammann/Simitis* assume that the wording "adequate" has been chosen for flexibility reasons. With regard to potential negotiations with a third country about the guaranteed level of protection, the wording leaves a wide margin.[804] *Engels* argues in the same way and pleads for an interpretation of the wording adequacy in the sense of "functionally adequate".[805] She proposes that the protection of the personal right of the person concerned should correspond to the circumstances of the transfer.

In conclusion, it can be assumed that the wording adequate level of protection shall be interpreted in the light of the surroundings of the transfer, i.e., that in

---

[799] Article 2 (1) of the additional Protocol to the Convention for the Protection of Individuals with regard to Automatic Processing of Personal Data, regarding supervisory authorities and Transborder Data Flows, 8 November 2001, entered into force the 1st of July 2004 (emphasis added).

[800] Dammann and Simitis (1997), Article 25, para 8; Siemen (2006), p. 299.

[801] See Sect. III 1 a.

[802] Explanatory report to the additional Protocol to the Convention for the Protection of Individuals with regard to Automatic Processing of Personal Data, regarding supervisory authorities and Transborder Data Flows, 8 November 2001, entered into force the 1st of July 2004, ETS No. 181, para 26.

[803] Dammann and Simitis (1997), Article 25, para 8; Siemen (2006), pp. 300–301.

[804] Dammann and Simitis (1997), Article 25, para 8.

[805] Engel (2003), p. 91.

general Directive 95/46 accepts a lower level of protection in the third country compared to the level in the EU.[806] However, when balancing the different interests at stake the "core principles" of Directive 95/46 and Regulation 45/2001 relating to the quality standards and the individual rights must be preserved.[807]

(3) Basic Principles of the Article 29 Data Protection Working Party Regarding the Data Transfer to Third States

Due to its advisory function towards the European Commission, the Article 29 Data Protection Working Party developed guidelines to improve the coherent application of the provisions regulating the transfer of data to third states.[808] In the meantime, various documents of the Article 29 Data Protection Working Party regarding the transfer of data to third states exist.[809] These principles are briefly analysed in following.

The working papers of the Article 29 Data Protection Working Party may not be formally binding, but they are important with regard to the practical application of Directive 95/46. The Commission often refers to the arguments of the Article 29 Data Protection Working Party when substantiating its own decisions.[810] To ensure an adequate protection, the Article 29 Data Protection Working Party establishes six core data protection content principles followed by procedural requirements. Compliance with these principles "could be seen as a minimum requirement for protection to be considered adequate".[811]

[806] Dammann and Simitis (1997), Article 25, para 8; Siemen (2006), p. 299; Engel (2003), p. 93. Tinnefeld et al. (1995), pp. 110 and 122.

[807] Dammann and Simitis (1997), Article 25, para 8.

[808] Document adopted by the Article 29 Working Party, WP 4 of 26 June 1997, first orientations on the transfer of personal data to third countries – possible ways forward in assessing adequacy.

[809] Document adopted by the Article 29 Working Party, WP 12 of 24 July 1998 on the transfers of personal data to third countries: applying Articles 25 and 26 of the EU data protection directive, combined the working papers WP 4 of 26 June 1997, first orientations on the transfer of personal data to third countries – possible ways forward in assessing adequacy, WP 7 of 14 January 1998 on the judging of industry self regulation: when does it make a meaningful contribution to the level of data protection in a third country?, WP 9 of 22 April 1998 on preliminary views on the use of contractual provisions in the context of transfers of personal data to third countries and WP 114 of 25 November 2005 on a common interpretation of Article 26 (1) of Directive 95/96.

[810] Compare Commission Decision of 26 July 2000 pursuant to Directive 95/46/EC of the European Parliament and of the Council on the adequate protection of personal data provided in Switzerland, OJ L-215/1, 25 August 2000; Commission Decision of 30 June 2003 pursuant to Directive 95/46/EC of the European Parliament and of the Council on the adequate protection of personal data in Argentina, OJ L- 168/19, 5 July 2003 and Commission Decision of 21 November 2003 on the adequate protection of personal data in Guernsey, OJ L-308/27, 25 November 2003.

[811] Document adopted by the Article 29 Working Party, WP 12 of 24 July 1998 on the transfers of personal data to third countries: applying Articles 25 and 26 of the EU data protection directive, p. 5.

The content principles are summarised in six essential points:

(1) The purpose limitation principle[812]
(2) The data quality and proportionality principle[813]
(3) The transparency principle[814]
(4) The security principle[815]

---

[812] The only exemptions to the purpose limitation principle should be the grounds listed in Article 13 of the Directive 95/46: a restriction to the purpose principle is permitted if "such a restriction constitutes (a) a necessary measure to safeguard national security, (b) defence, (c) public security, (d) the prevention, investigation, detection and prosecution of criminal offences or of breaches of ethics for regulates professions, (e) an important economic or financial interest of a Member State or of the EU, (f) a monitoring, inspection or regulatory function connected with the exercise of official authority in cases referred to in (c), (d) and (e) or (g) the protection of the data subject or the rights and freedoms of others, compare Document adopted by the Article 29 Working Party, WP 12 of 24 July 1998 on the transfers of personal data to third countries: applying Articles 25 and 26 of the EU data protection directive, p. 6.

[813] The principle of *data quality* (2) should ensure that data ought to be accurate and, where necessary, kept up to date. The *proportionality principle* (2) guarantees that the data are "adequate, relevant and not excessive in relation to the purposes for which they are transferred or further processed"; these two principles should guarantee the regularly verification of the stored data, i.e., that the protection of the person concerned extends beyond the first control of; since, according to Article 2 (b) of Directive 95/46, the storage of data is also a form of data processing, *Engel* assumes that these two principles in conjunction with the purpose limitation entail the obligation to delete the data when the original purpose of the processing changes afterwards, compare (2003), pp. 97–98.

[814] The *transparency principle* (3) contains that individuals should be provided with information as to the purpose of the processing and the identity of the data controller in the third country, and other information insofar as this is necessary to ensure fairness; the only exemptions permitted should be in line with Articles 11 (2) (exceptions for statistical purposes or for the purposes of historical or scientific research) and 13 of Directive 95/46 (includes exceptions for national security, (b) defence, (c) public security, (d) the prevention, investigation, detection and prosecution of criminal offences or of breaches of ethics for regulates professions, (e) an important economic or financial interest of a Member State or of the EU, (f) a monitoring, inspection or regulatory function connected with the exercise of official authority in cases referred to in (c), (d) and (e) or (g) the protection of the data subject or the rights and freedoms of others.), compare Document adopted by the Article 29 Working Party, WP 12 of 24 July 1998 on the transfers of personal data to third countries: applying Articles 25 and 26 of the EU data protection directive, p. 6; the transparency principle should permit the person concerned to assess the risk of data processing in the third country, compare Simitis(2000), in particular pp. 472 and 477.

[815] The *security principle* (4) required that "technical and organisational security measures should be taken by the data controller that are appropriate to the risks presented by the processing". Any person operating under the authority of the data controller, including a processor, must not process data except on instructions from the controller. This principle is to counteract the fast technical development by developing normative limits to retain control about automated data processing. The need for technical security measures increases with regard to the rapid development in the information and communication technology. As compliance with this principle depends indeed on the development of automated data security systems, it is difficult to asses the level of protection regarding this criteria, compare Document adopted by the Article 29 Working Party, WP 12 of 24 July 1998 on the transfers of personal data to third countries: applying Articles 25 and 26 of the EU data protection directive, p. 6 and Simitis (2000), in particular p. 478.

(5) The rights of access, rectification and opposition[816] and
(6) Restrictions on onward transfers.[817]

The principles are strongly influenced by the provisions of Directive 95/46, but the Article 29 Data Protection Working Party stresses that the list "should not be set in stone".[818] In some cases "there will be a need to add to the list, while for others it may even be possible to reduce the list of requirements".[819] To specific types of processing, additional principles have to be applied.

In case of the processing of sensitive data, for instance, for those categories listed in Article 8 of Directive 95/46, "additional safeguards should be in place, such as a requirement that the data subject gives his/her explicit consent for the processing".[820] Also in case of the transfer of data for the purpose of direct marketing, "the data subject should be able to 'opt-out' from having its data used for such purposes at any stage".[821] Lastly, "where the purpose of the transfer is the taking of an automated decision in the sense of Article 15 of Directive 95/46, the individual should have the right to know the logic involved in this decision, and other measures should be taken to safeguard the individual's legitimate interest".[822]

---

[816] The *rights of access, rectification and opposition* (5) should ensure "the right to obtain a copy of all data relating to the data subject that are processed, and a right to rectification of those data where they are shown to be inaccurate". In certain situations the data subject should also be able to object to the processing of the data relating to him/her. The only exceptions to these rights should be in accordance with Article 13 of the Directive 95/46. This principle is closely related to the transparency principle and requires a reliable, regularly and comprehensible information accessible to the data subject, compare Document adopted by the Article 29 Working Party, WP 12 of 24 July 1998 on the transfers of personal data to third countries: applying Articles 25 and 26 of the EU data protection directive, p. 6; Dammann and Simitis (1997), introduction, p. 80 and Simitis (1997), in particular 281.

[817] The *transfer of personal data to other third states* (6) means that transfer to states different from the first recipient country should be only permitted if the other third state (the recipient of the onward transfer) ensures an adequate level of protection. The only exceptions permitted should be in line with Article 26 (1) of the Directive 95/46, compare Document adopted by the Article 29 Working Party, WP 12 of 24 July 1998 on the transfers of personal data to third countries: applying Articles 25 and 26 of the EU data protection directive, p. 6.

[818] Document adopted by the Article 29 Working Party, WP 12 of 24 July 1998 on the transfers of personal data to third countries: applying Articles 25 and 26 of the EU data protection directive, p. 5.

[819] Ibid.

[820] Document adopted by the Article 29 Working Party, WP 12 of 24 July 1998 on the transfers of personal data to third countries: applying Articles 25 and 26 of the EU data protection directive, p. 7. Article 8 of Directive 95/46 concerns for example data revealing racial or ethic origin, political opinions, religious or philosophical beliefs, trade-union membership, and the processing of data concerning health or sex life, or data relating to offences, criminal convictions or security measures.

[821] Document adopted by the Article 29 Working Party, WP 12 of 24 July 1998 on the transfers of personal data to third countries: applying Articles 25 and 26 of the EU data protection directive, p. 7.

[822] Ibid.

In general, the principles of the Article 29 Data Protection Working Party are not as detailed as the provisions of the Directive 95/46 itself, so that a flexible application of the criteria becomes possible.

Procedural mechanisms such as sanctions for data processors in case of non-compliance with data protection rules, a right to redress for individuals or the establishment of supervisory authorities with monitoring and complaint investigation functions are further guarantees necessary to ensure an adequate protection.[823] Usually the procedural instruments assure the compliance with the aforementioned content principles. Outside the EU structures, such procedural instruments are not always part of the legal order. Therefore, a comparison between the European and the third country data protection standards may be difficult. In consequence, to provide a basis for the assessment of the adequacy of the protection in the third country, it is crucial to identify the essential objectives of a data protection procedural system and on this basis "to judge the variety of different judicial and non-judicial procedural mechanisms used in third countries".[824]

The Article 29 Data Protection Working Party proposes three objectives:

Firstly, a good level of compliance with the data protection rules should be ensured. This criterion is generally characterised "by a high degree of awareness among data controllers of their obligations, and among data subjects of their rights and the means of exercising them".[825] The existence of effective and dissuasive sanctions can also play an important role in ensuring compliance with the procedural rules supported by an effective supervisory system.[826] In this context, instead of considering only the legal and organisational instruments, the crucial point is the effective implementation of the rights and freedoms of the individual in practice.[827]

Secondly, support and help to individual data subjects in the exercise of their rights also plays an important role. Data subjects must be able to enforce their rights rapidly and effectively, and without excessive cost.[828] Furthermore there must be "some sort of institutional mechanism allowing independent investigation of complaints".[829] This independent control authority must be able to investigate and to guarantee redress where necessary.[830]

[823] Ibid.

[824] Ibid.

[825] Ibid.

[826] Ibid.

[827] Dammann and Simitis (1997), Article 25, para 28.

[828] Document adopted by the Article 29 Working Party, WP 12 of 24 July 1998 on the transfers of personal data to third countries: applying Articles 25 and 26 of the EU data protection directive, p. 7.

[829] Ibid.

[830] Brühann (1998).

Thirdly, appropriate redress to the injured party where rules are not complied with must be guaranteed. A "system of independent adjudication or arbitration which allows compensation to be paid and sanctions imposed where appropriate" should exist.[831]

(4) Brief Summary

The working papers of the Article 29 Data Protection Working Party regarding the transfer of data to third states create an adequacy profile whose content principles orientate on the provisions of Directive 95/46, although the main focus constitutes the effective enforcement of the rights in practice. This practical approach guarantees a decision closely related to the individual case, without sticking to predetermined criteria ("to be set in stone"). This means that, as long as the underlying objectives – which might be achieved trough mutual concessions – will be respected, the procedural mechanisms in third states may be different from the European ones.

In addition, the content principles set limits to the procedural objectives and prevent their ambiguous interpretation. This rather practical and less theoretical approach allows to react flexibly to changing data protection conditions of third countries. Finally the approach of the Article 29 Data Protection Working Party affirms the result discussed in the framework of the comparison with the European Council Convention No. 108 mentioned above.[832]

Summarising, the wording "adequacy" has to be interpreted in the sense of "functionally adequate", which means that the fundamental rights protection of the person concerned should be assessed in accordance with the concrete situation in the respective third country. Thereby, the purpose limitation principle is the most important, but at the same time the most problematic element. It is susceptible to abuse and should therefore be handled with care.[833] Respecting the purpose limitation principle assures a legitimate processing and therefore plays an important role in assessing whether the protection is adequate.

The content principles and the procedural mechanisms developed by the Article 29 Data Protection Working Party assure effective data protection regarding the transfer of data to third states. However, these principles and mechanisms only refer to Article 25 Directive 95/46. Exemptions to the principles are stipulated in Article 26 of the Directive 95/46. They will be illustrated in following.

---

[831] Document adopted by the Article 29 Working Party, WP 12 of 24 July 1998 on the transfers of personal data to third countries: applying Articles 25 and 26 of the EU data protection directive, p. 7.

[832] See Sect. III 2 e bb (2).

[833] To the possibilities of abuse, see Simitis (2000), in particular p. 476; Weichert (2006) and Dix and Gardain (2006), in particular 346.

cc) Derogations According to Article 26 Directive 95/46 and Article 9 (6) Regulation 45/2001

The derogations from the adequacy requirement listed in Article 26 Directive 95/46 and Article 9 (6) Regulation 45/2001 mainly refer to situations arising in the context of private data transfer and international economic transactions. Analysing this topic in details would go far beyond the objectives of this research. For that reason, the derogations are only briefly mentioned in the following.

In terms of Article 26 Directive 95/46 and Article 9 (6) Regulation 45/2001, the transfer to third countries not providing an adequate level of protection should be allowed under the condition that:

(a) The data subject has given his consent unambiguously to the proposed transfer; or
(b) The transfer is necessary for the performance of a contract between the data subject and the controller or the implementation of precontractual measures taken in response to the data subject's request; or
(c) The transfer is necessary for the conclusion or performance of a contract concluded in the interest of the data subject between the controller and a third party; or
(d) The transfer is necessary or legally required on important public interest grounds, or for the establishment, exercise or defence of legal claims; or
(e) The transfer is necessary in order to protect the vital interests of the data subject; or
(f) The transfer is made from a register which according to laws or regulations is intended to provide information to the public and which is open to consultation either by the public in general or by any person who can demonstrate legitimate interest, to the extent that the conditions laid down in law for consultation are fulfilled in the particular case.

The derogations usually concern cases where legally protected interests of third parties play a role or where there is a small risk to interfere with the right to privacy. Nevertheless, the derogations have to be interpreted restrictively and in view of the fundamental rights considering Article 1 (1) of Directive 95/46.[834]

Article 26 (2) Directive 95/46 and Article 9 (7) Regulation 45/2001 authorise Member States or the EDPS to transfer personal data (or a set of personal data) to a third country which does not ensure an adequate level of protection, where the controller adduces adequate safeguards with respect to the protection of the privacy and fundamental rights and freedoms of individuals and as regards the exercise of the corresponding rights. Such safeguards may in particular result from appropriate contractual clauses.[835]

---

[834] Wuermeling (2000), p. 142.

[835] Article 26 (3) of Directive 95/46 provides a reporting requirement for the Member States about the authorisations they grant pursuant to paragraph 2. If a Member State or the Commission objects

dd) Data Transfer in the Framework Decision Governing Data Processing in Police and Judicial Cooperation

Quite contrary to the rather detailed provisions and the additional documents regulating and specifying personal data transfer in the framework of Directive 95/46 and Regulation 45/2001, the FDPJ includes far less guidelines. Its provisions refer to the data transfer to third states and to private parties.[836] While the former first pillar Regulation 45/2001 ensures the application of the data protection principles of Directive 95/46 in former first pillar EU institutions and bodies, the FDPJ does not regulate EU-internal personal data transfer in the framework of police and judicial cooperation.

Recital (23) of the FDPJ stipulates that where personal data are transferred from a Member State to third states or international bodies, these data should, *in principle*, benefit from an adequate level of protection.[837] Article 13 (1) FDPJ specifies that personal data may be transferred only, if (a) it is necessary for the prevention, investigation, detection or prosecution of criminal offences or the execution of criminal penalties (b) the receiving authority in the third tate or receiving international body is responsible for the prevention, investigation, detection or prosecution of criminal offences or the execution of criminal penalties (c) the Member State from which the data were obtained has given its consent to the transfer in compliance with its national law[838] and (d) the third state or international body concerned ensures an adequate level of protection for the intended data processing.

on justified grounds involving the protection of the privacy and fundamental rights and freedoms of individuals, the Commission shall take appropriate measures in accordance with the procedure laid down in Article 31 (2) Directive 95/46. Member States shall take the necessary measures to comply with the Commission's decision.

Pursuant to the last paragraph the Commission can decide that certain standard contractual clauses offer sufficient safeguards as required by Article 26 (2) Directive 95/46. So far there a three Commission decisions according to standard contractual clauses, compare 2001/497/EC: Commission Decision of 15 June 2001 on standard contractual clauses for the transfer of personal data to third countries, under Directive 95/46/EC, OJ 2001, L-181/19; 2002/16/EC: Commission Decision of 27 December 2001 on standard contractual clauses for the transfer of personal data to processors established in third countries, under Directive 95/46/EC, OJ L-6/52 and 2004/915/EC: Commission Decision of 27 December 2004 amending Decision 2001/497/EC as regards the introduction of an alternative set of standard contractual clauses for the transfer of personal data to third countries, OJ 2004, L-385/74.

[836] Articles 13 and 14 FDPJ, OJ 2008, L-350/60.

[837] Recital (26) FDPJ, OJ 2008, L-350/60.

[838] Transfer without prior consent in accordance with paragraph 1(c) shall be permitted only if transfer of the data is essential for the prevention of an immediate and serious threat to public security of a Member State or a third state or to essential interests of a Member State and the prior consent cannot be obtained in good time; the authority responsible for giving consent shall be informed without delay, compare Article 13 (2) FDPJ, OJ 2008, L-350/60.

Article 13 (4) FDPJ uses the same formulation as Directive 95/46 when is comes to the specification of the adequacy of the level of protection.[839] However, whether or not the term *adequate* refers to the same strict criteria stipulated in the framework of Directive 95/46 is not further specified. Moreover, broad exceptions to these conditions apply. Personal data may be transferred if (a) the national law of the Member State transferring the data so provides because of: (i) legitimate specific interests of the data subject or (ii) legitimate prevailing interests, especially important public interests or (b) the third state or receiving international body provides safeguards which are deemed adequate by the Member State concerned according to its national law.[840] Consequently, personal data relating to police and judicial purposes can be transferred to third states or international organisations for various reasons. Member States may assess the level of adequacy on their own. Very vague and far reaching derogations to the criteria stipulated in Article 13 (1) FDPJ, such as public interests, apply. Additionally, Article 26 FDPJ permits further derogations in case that Member States or the EU have already concluded (at the time of the adoption of the FDPJ) bilateral or multilateral agreements with third states which provide for other rules.[841]

Another provision which aroused criticism[842] is Article 14 FDPJ referring to the transmission of personal data to private parties. Personal data collected for police and judicial purposes can be transferred to private parties if (a) the competent authority of the Member State from which the data were obtained has consented to transmission in compliance with its national law, (b) no legitimate specific interests of the data subject prevent transmission, and (c) in particular cases transfer is essential for the competent authority transmitting the data to a private party for: (i) the performance of a task lawfully assigned to it, (ii) the prevention, investigation, detection or prosecution of criminal offences or the execution of criminal penalties, (iii) the prevention of an immediate and serious threat to public security or (iv) the prevention of serious harm to the rights of individuals.[843] The party transmitting the data shall inform the private party of the purposes for which the data may exclusively be used.[844]

---

[839] The level of protection shall be assessed in the light of all the circumstances surrounding a data transfer operation or a set of data transfer operations. Particular consideration shall be given to the nature of the data, the purpose and duration of the proposed processing operation or operations, the state of origin and the state or international body of final destination of the data, the rules of law, both general and sectoral, in force in the third state or international body in question and the professional rules and security measures which apply (compare Article 13 (4) FDPJ, OJ 2008, L-350/60).

[840] Article 13 (4) FDPJ, OJ 2008, L-350/60.

[841] Ibid.

[842] Compare EDPS opinion on the FDPJ, OJ 2007, C-139/1, paras 34–36.

[843] Article 14 (1) FDPJ, OJ 2008, L-350/60.

[844] Ibid.

When reading these provisions, it becomes clear that personal data can be transferred to private parties for various reasons. It is not required that the purpose of collection is maintained. In fact, the transmitting party may establish a new purpose for which the data may then be processed by the private party. Additional supervision in this sensitive area is not provided for in this context. Although the FDPJ regulates the transfer of law enforcement data to private parties, it regrettably remains silent on the topic of rules regulating the access of law enforcement bodies to data stored in private databases. Recent developments such as the Data Retention Directive or the PNR agreements with the USA[845] clearly show the need for regulation in this currently unregulated field.

f) Transparency and Data Protection

The balance between transparency and the right of individuals for the protection of their personal data is not only important in the ECHR context,[846] it was also recently subject to the famous EU case *Bavarian Lager Co. Ltd v. Commission.*[847] In a nutshell, *Bavarian Lager*, a German trade association for beer, requested the annulment of a Commission decision rejecting its request for full access to the minutes of a meeting organised by the Commission. Based on Article 4 (1) (b) Regulation 1049/200 on access to documents,[848] the Commission had refused access to the names of 5 members of trade associations attending the meeting on grounds of the protection of their personal data following from the application of Regulation 45/2001.[849] While the Court of First Instance (now General Court) in

[845] For an overview of the transfer of data to the United States, compare, Bellanova and De Hert (2009).

[846] The case *Társaság a Szabadságjogokért v. Hungary*, Application no. 37374/05, judgment of 14 April 2009 of the ECtHR is worth remembering here, compare above Sect. II 2 c.

[847] Cases: T-194/04, *Bavarian Lager Co. Ltd v. Commission*, judgment of 8 November 2007, reversed in appeal in case C-28/08, *Bavarian Lager Co. Ltd v. Commission*, judgment of 29 June 2010; compare Sanner (2010); Wägenbaur (2001).

[848] Regulation No. 1049/2001 of the European Parliament and of the Council of 30 May 2001 regarding public access to European Parliament, Council and Commission documents, OJ 2001, L-145/43, Article 4 (1) (b) stipulates that: "the institutions shall refuse access to a document where disclosure would undermine the protection of privacy and the integrity of the individual, in particular in accordance with Community legislation regarding the protection of personal data."

[849] The fundamental difference between the right of access to documents and the right of individuals for the protection of their personal data is excellently summarised by the Court of First Instance (General Court) in para 98 of the judgment *Bavarian Lager Co. Ltd v. Commission*: Regulation 1049/2001 is "designed to ensure the greatest possible transparency of the decision-making process of the public authorities and the information on which they base their decisions. It is thus designed to facilitate as far as possible the exercise of the right of access to documents, and to promote good administrative practices". Regulation 45/2001 "is designed to ensure the protection of the freedoms and fundamental rights of individuals, particularly their private life, in the handling of personal data", T-194/04, *Bavarian Lager Co. Ltd v. Commission*, judgment of 8 November 2007, para 98.

2007 obliged the Commission to disclose the names of the attendants arguing that the disclosure would not undermine the privacy of the relevant persons (mainly because they attended the meeting in their role as an official representative of a collective body and not as a private person),[850] the Court of Justice in 2010 repealed this decision.

It ruled that the General Court correctly held that surnames and forenames may be regarded as personal data and that the communication of personal data in response to a request for access of documents falls within the definition of processing for the purpose of Regulation 45/2001.[851] However, it held that the General Court disregards the wording of the exception provided for in Article 4 (1) (b) of Regulation 1049/2001,[852] which requires that any undermining of privacy and the integrity of an individual must be examined and assessed in conformity with the legislation of the EU, in particular with Regulation 45/2001.[853] The General Court mainly focused on Article 8 and the case law of the ECtHR to assess the conformity. The Court of Justice made clear that the reference to Article 8 ECHR and the case-law of the ECtHR indeed applies to processing carried out by Community institutions and bodies falling outside the scope of Regulation 45/2001 (activities relating to police and judicial cooperation and common foreign and security policy),[854] but not to the activities covered by Regulation 45/2001.[855]

It follows that "where a request based on Regulation No. 1049/2001 seeks to obtain access to documents including personal data, the provisions of Regulation No 45/2001 become applicable in their entirety, including Articles 8 and 18 thereof".[856] Consequently, the Commission was right to verify whether the attendants had given their consent to disclosure of personal data concerning them. The Commission correctly based its reasoning on Article 4 (1) (b) of Regulation 1049/2001 and Regulation 45/2001 and succeeded in establishing an equilibrium

---

[850] T-194/04, *Bavarian Lager Co. Ltd v. Commission*, judgment of 8 November 2007, paras 145–158.

[851] Ibid.

[852] "The institutions shall refuse access to a document where disclosure would undermine the protection of privacy and the integrity of the individual, in particular in accordance with Community legislation regarding the protection of personal data" (Regulation No. 1049/2001 of the European Parliament and of the Council of 30 May 2001 regarding public access to European Parliament, Council and Commission documents, OJ 2001, L-145/43, Article 4 (1) (b)).

[853] C-28/08, *Bavarian Lager Co. Ltd v. Commission*, judgment of 29 June 2010, para 59.

[854] Compare recital (15) of Regulation No. 1049/2001 of the European Parliament and of the Council of 30 May 2001 regarding public access to European Parliament, Council and Commission documents, OJ 2001, L-145/43.

[855] C-28/08, *Bavarian Lager Co. Ltd v. Commission*, judgment of 29 June 2010, para 62.

[856] Ibid, para 63. Article 8 (b) of Regulation 45/2001 refers to the transfer of personal data to recipients, other than Community institutions and bodies, subject to Directive 95/46 "if the recipient establishes the necessity of having the data transferred and if there is no reason to assume that the data subject's legitimate interests might be prejudiced". Article 18 of Regulation 45/2001 refers to the data subject's right to object.

between the two regulations in question.[857] As provided for in Article 8 (b) of Regulation 45/2001,[858] it rightly required that *Bavarian Lager* must establish the necessity for transfer of the relevant personal data. As the necessity was not convincingly demonstrated, the Commission was right to reject the application for access to the full minutes.[859]

The importance of the case lies in the balance between the issues of transparency/ access to documents and the protection of personal data. Critical voices feared that data protection arguments risks to be invoked in order to minimise transparency of the institutions.[860] The EDPS, supporting the applicant, argues that the reasoning of the Commission that information can only be disclosed after the attendants have given their consent or if *Bavarian Lager* proves the necessity of having the data transferred (Article 8 (b) Regulation 45/2001) risks to become counterproductive to data protection objectives.[861] An interpretation of the Article 8 (b) of Regulation 45/2001[862] which would deprive the access Regulation 1049/2001 of its main content should be avoided.[863] Article 6 of Regulation 1049/2001 underlines that the applicant for access to a document is not obliged to state reasons for the application.[864]

The interpretation of Article 8 (b) of Regulation 45/2001 according to which the applicant must justify its request would therefore be contrary to the objective of Regulation 1049/2001.[865] The EDPS refers to the *Borax v. Commission* case in which the Court of First Instance (General Court) confirmed that names can be disclosed to the applicant without the consent of the person concerned if the privacy

---

[857] C-28/08, *Bavarian Lager Co. Ltd v. Commission*, judgment of 29 June 2010, paras 65 and 67.

[858] Article 8 (b) of Regulation 45/2001 refers to the transfer of personal data to recipients, other than Community institutions and bodies, subject to Directive 95/46 "if the recipient establishes the necessity of having the data transferred and if there is no reason to assume that the data subject's legitimate interests might be prejudiced".

[859] C-28/08, *Bavarian Lager Co. Ltd v. Commission*, judgment of 29 June 2010, para 79.

[860] Compare the Pleadings of the EDPS of 16 June 2009 at the hearing of the Court in case C-28/08, *Bavarian Lager Co. Ltd v. Commission*, accessible at: http://www.edps.europa.eu/EDPSWEB/edps/lang/en/Consultation/Court (accessed February 2011).

[861] Ibid.

[862] Article 8 (b) of Regulation 45/2001 refers to the transfer of personal data to recipients, other than Community institutions and bodies, subject to Directive 95/46 "if the recipient establishes the necessity of having the data transferred and if there is no reason to assume that the data subject's legitimate interests might be prejudiced".

[863] Pleadings of the EDPS of 16 June 2009 at the hearing of the Court in case C-28/08, *Bavarian Lager Co. Ltd v. Commission*, p. 2, accessible at: http://www.edps.europa.eu/EDPSWEB/edps/lang/en/Consultation/Court (accessed February 2011).

[864] Article 6 (1) Regulation No. 1049/2001 of the European Parliament and of the Council of 30 May 2001 regarding public access to European Parliament, Council and Commission documents, OJ 2001, L-145/43.

[865] Pleadings of the EDPS of 16 June 2009 at the hearing of the Court in case C-28/08, *Bavarian Lager Co. Ltd v. Commission*, p. 4, accessible at: http://www.edps.europa.eu/EDPSWEB/edps/lang/en/Consultation/Court (accessed February 2011).

is not effectively undermined by such disclosure.[866] The EDPS refers to the risk of censoring the public debate if persons acting in public decision-making could themselves decide in the name of their personality rights whether or not to publish information. It refers to the ECtHR case *Társaság a Szabadságjogokért v. Hungary*, briefly discussed above,[867] in which the ECtHR insisted that "it would be fatal for the freedom of expression if public figures could censor the press and public debate in the name of their personality rights".[868] A similar reasoning could be applied in the *Bavarian Lager* case.

The dispute in this case clearly demonstrates that the balance between transparency and data protection is not always easy to find. The dangers of a possible misuse of data protection arguments to restrict public access to documents are real and require a sophisticated solution. Taking this risk into account, the solution can not be the supremacy of data protection provisions in any potential case, as postulated by the Court of Justice in the *Bavarian Lager* case. As we have seen above, according to the Court's reasoning, whenever personal data is involved, the rules on data protection apply, even to the detriment of transparency.[869] This, however, does not constitute a real balance. One of the solutions therefore could be the strict application of proportionality requirements following from Article 5 (4) TEU.[870] In case that two rights conflict, the usual balance relates to the application of the principle of proportionality.[871] For that reason, data protection concerns could not generally override the interest in public access to documents. On the contrary the interest of the individual in keeping its data secret and the interest of the applicant of public access must be critically weighted. Excluding this assessment from the outset, by arguing that if based on Regulation No. 1049/2001 an applicant seeks access to documents containing personal data, the provisions of Regulation 45/2001

[866] Compare case T-121/05, *Borax Europe Ltd. v. Commission*, judgment of 11 March 2009, paras 40–42, and Pleadings of the EDPS of 16 June 2009 at the hearing of the Court in case C-28/08, *Bavarian Lager Co. Ltd v. Commission*, p. 5, http://www.edps.europa.eu/EDPSWEB/edps/lang/en/Consultation/Court (accessed February 2011).

[867] Compare above Sect. II 2 c.

[868] *Társaság a Szabadságjogokért v. Hungary*, Application no. 37374/05, judgment of 14 April 2009, para 37.

[869] Compare the reasoning in para 63 of the *Bavarian Lager* judgment in which the Court of Justice stipulated: "It follows that where a request based on Regulation No. 1049/2001 seeks to obtain access to documents including personal data, the provisions of Regulation No 45/2001 become applicable in their entirety, including Articles 8 and 18 thereof", C-28/08, *Bavarian Lager Co. Ltd v. Commission*, judgment of 29 June 2010, para 63.

[870] Compare for an excellent analysis: EDPS background paper series, July 2005, n°1, "public access to documents and data protection", in particular pp. 32–40, accessible at: http://www.edps.europa.eu/EDPSWEB/edps/site/mySite/Papers (accessed February 2011).

[871] *Koch* (2003), pp. 158–172, and EDPS background paper series, July 2005, n°1, "public access to documents and data protection", in particular pp. 32–40, accessible at: http://www.edps.europa.eu/EDPSWEB/edps/site/mySite/Papers (accessed February 2011).

become applicable in their entirety,[872] the full respect of the proportionality principle is denied. The aforementioned *Schecke* case[873] in which the Court obliged the EU legislator to balance the different interests involved (namely transparency and the infringements of the rights to data protection and private life) by carrying out a detailed proportionality test can serve as an example for the method to be applied in similar cases.

g) Common Foreign and Security Policy

With regard to the common foreign and security policy, there is no harmonised standard or general framework governing data processing in this area.[874] However, it should be briefly mentioned that the European Union Courts established case law on the legitimacy of some activities of the common foreign and security policy regarding the management of so called terrorists' blacklists.

In the cases *Sison v. Council, Organisation des Modjahedines de people d'Iran (OMPI) v. Council* and *PKK and KNK v. Council,*[875] the Tribunal of First Instance annulled two Council Decisions implementing Article 2 (3) of Regulation No. 2580/2001 on specific restrictive measures directed against certain persons and entities with a view to combating terrorism and repealed the Council Decision placing the applicants on the list of terrorist organisations. Some of the applicants achieved their erasure from the blacklist and, consequently, the Council agreed in April 2007 to a new policy regarding the way in which individuals and groups are added to the list, taking into consideration the *Modjahedines* judgement.[876] This policy includes "that the parties concerned will be informed that the Council intends to maintain them on the list and will be informed via a "statement of reasons" of the specific information that forms the basis for the Council's decision".[877] "The persons, groups and entities concerned will also be informed about the opportunity to make their views known and present observations".[878] The Council will also "consider any reaction by the parties concerned before taking

---

[872] C-28/08, *Bavarian Lager Co. Ltd v. Commission*, judgment of 29 June 2010, para 63.

[873] Compare Sect. III 1 e.

[874] Hijmanns and Scirocco (2009), in particular p. 1447.

[875] Cases T-228/02, *Organisation des Modjahedines de people d'Iran v. Council*, judgment of 12 December 2006; T-284/08, *Organisation des Modjahedines de people d'Iran v. Council*, judgment of 4 December 2008; Case T-47/03, *Sison v. Council*, judgment of 11 July 2007; C-266/05 P, *Sison v. Council*, judgment of 1 February 2007 and C-229/05 P, *PKK and KNK v. Council*, judgment of 18 January 2007.

[876] See Council press release 8425/07 (Presse 80), p. 34, 35; for further information see Guild (2008), in particular p. 189; with regard to the protection against the placing on the lists, see Feinäugle (2010), pp. 188–190; Gless and Schaffner (2009).

[877] Council press release 8425/07 (Presse 80), p. 35.

[878] Ibid.

a final decision".[879] Member States are therefore required to provide information concerning the reasons of the placement of certain persons on the list.

In the aforementioned cases,[880] the Court of Justice used elements of data protection to guarantee the protection of other fundamental rights, such as the right to defence and judicial protection.[881] Although the Court of Justice in *Sison v. Council* made clear that Regulation 1049/2001[882] does not include a right to access personal data, the Court however refers to the possibility that the applicant may have a right to be informed about the nature and cause of the accusations against him and that this right may involve the access to documents held by the Council.[883] In *Organisation des Modjahedines de people d'Iran v. Council,*[884] the rights of defense were violated because the Council did not comply with the requirement to duly inform the applicants about the processing of their personal data.[885] In *PKK and KNK v. Council,*[886] the Court of Justice underlines the importance of periodical reviews of the situation which lead to the inclusion of the persons in the blacklists.[887] In other words, the principle to keep personal data accurate and up to date was duly considered.[888]

Although none of the aforementioned cases directly mention data protection guarantees, the case-law shows that even in common foreign and security policy[889] certain minimum legal requirements, which include data protection elements, apply in the context of personal data processing in this area. With the entry into force of the Lisbon Treaty, the situation for individuals in the area of common foreign and security policy has additionally improved. Although, in general, the Court of Justice shall not have jurisdiction with respect to the provisions relating to the common foreign and security policy or with respect to acts adopted on the basis of those

---

[879] Ibid.

[880] Cases C-266/05 P, *Sison v. Council*, judgment of 1 February 2007, T-284/08, *Organisation des Modjahedines de people d'Iran v. Council*, judgment of 4 December 2008 and C-229/05 P, *PKK and KNK v. Council*, judgment of 18 January 2007.

[881] For an excellent analysis of this case law and its data protection elements, see Hijmanns and Scirocco (2009), in particular p. 1509.

[882] Regulation 1049/2001 (of the European Parliament and of the Council of 30 May 2001 regarding public access to European Parliament, Council and Commission documents, OJ 2001, L-145/43) gives the general public a right of access to documents of the institutions and should not be confused with the right to access to personal data subject to Regulation 45/2001.

[883] Case C-266/05 P, *Sison v. Council*, judgment of 1 February 2007, para 48, and Hijmanns and Scirocco (2009), in particular p. 1510.

[884] Case T-284/08, *Organisation des Modjahedines de people d'Iran v. Council*, judgment of 4 December 2008.

[885] Ibid.

[886] Case C-229/05 P, *PKK and KNK v. Council*, judgment of 18 January 2007.

[887] Ibid.

[888] Hijmanns and Scirocco (2009), in particular p. 1511.

[889] A good overview of the recent developments in the Common Foreign and Security Policy is made by Oppermann et al. (2009), pp. 684–701.

provisions, Article 275 TFEU stipulates that the Court of Justice has jurisdiction in proceedings "reviewing the legality of decisions providing for restrictive measures against natural or legal persons adopted by the Council on the basis of Chapter 2 of Title V [specific provisions on the common foreign and security policy] of the Treaty on European Union".[890]

3. *Conclusion: Data Protection Rules in the AFSJ are Still a Patchwork*

The patchwork of data protection rules in the AFSJ leads to a complex situation in EU data protection law in which the former pillar structures still have a great impact on the current post-Lisbon area.[891] Nonetheless, the impact of the Lisbon Treaty is important and can lead to the adoption of a comprehensive data protection framework for future data processing in this area. The *status quo* however is not yet sufficient in terms of data protection rules. The restricted scopes of the main instruments in force (Directive 95/46, Regulation 45/2001 and FDPJ) and the lack of principles for security related data processing developed through EU case-law constitute a major problem. The FDPJ with its vague provisions and broad exceptions can unfortunately not fill this gap.

The case law in the framework of the former first pillar, in particular in the case *Huber v. Germany*, nonetheless shows the willingness of the EU Courts to establish a data protection regime which goes beyond the former third pillar structure. By recognizing the discriminatory effect of a database used for crime fighting purposes which contained only the data of a particular group of persons, the Court of Justice raised hopes for the indiscriminate application of data protection principles also in the former third pillar. This tendency needs to be confirmed in future judgments in this area.

The described patchwork situation is additionally reflected in rather weak data protection quality standards and individual rights guarantees included in the FDPJ. The purpose limitation principle is extended to a point where the authorities processing the data can decide about the change of the purpose. The initial aim of the purpose limitation principle, which is the protection of individual rights against the indiscriminate use of personal data, is therefore reversed. In addition to the purpose limitation principle, important guarantees, such as the accuracy and adequacy of data, the respect of time limits, the protection of sensitive data and the up to date nature of data are included in all three instruments. But again, the guarantees in the FDPJ are formulated in a mitigated way.

---

[890] Compare Article 275 TFEU.

[891] For a brief and general overview of the data protection provisions in Europe, refer to Holznagel and Werthmann (2010), pp. 2001–2019.

The rights of the individuals, including notification, access, erasure, blocking, deletion, objection and independent supervision, are additionally granted in the analysed instruments. The obligation to notify the individuals about the data processing in the framework of the FDPJ is however not compulsory and is left to the discretion of the Member States. Additionally, the right to get access to personal data is regulated more exhaustively in Directive 95/45 and Regulation 45/2001 when comparing it to the access right in the FDPJ. In the framework of Directive 95/46 it even includes in certain cases that states must be able to inform the applicant not only about data processing currently taking place, but also about the extent to which personal data have been disclosed to third parties in the past.[892]

The right to object to the processing of personal data is only stipulated in Directive 95/46 and Regulation 45/2001. The FDPJ does not include a similar provision, although, as previously mentioned, there may be situations in which persons concerned by data processing in a police and judicial context (e.g. victims or witnesses) have legitimate grounds to object. These situations should therefore also be considered in a police and judicial context. The requirement of independent supervision applies to all of the analysed instruments. In this context, the term "supervision" is interpreted in a broad way which includes that the mere risk that authorities may be subject to political influence violates the independence requirement of Directive 95/45.[893]

Provisions restricting the transfer of personal data to third parties are regulated in detail in Directive 95/46 and Regulation 45/2001. In particular the adequacy requirement of Directive 95/46, including its interpretations by the Article 29 Data Protection Working Party, establish a quite comprehensive data protection regime with regard to the transfer of personal data to third states. The opposite however is true in respect of the FDPJ which includes far reaching derogations for Member States when it comes to data transfer to third states. Crucial subjects such as the access by law enforcement authorities to data stored in private databases are not regulated in the FDPJ.

There is no data protection framework governing the common foreign and security policy. According to Article 39 TEU, the Council shall however adopt in future a decision laying down data protection rules in this area.[894] So far, the Court of Justice in its case law on the so called terrorist blacklists[895] however used

[892] Case C-553/07, *College van burgemeester en wethouders van Rotterdam v. M.E.E. Rijkeboer*, judgment of 7 May 2009.

[893] Case C-518/07, *Commission v. Germany*, judgment of 9 March 2010, para 36.

[894] Article 39 TEU.

[895] For instance Cases C-266/05 P, *Sison v. Council*, judgment of 1 February 2007, T-284/08 *Organisation des Modjahedines de people d'Iran v. Council*, judgment of 4 December 2008 and C-229/05 P, *PKK and KNK v. Council*, judgment of 18 January 2007.

elements of data protection to guarantee the protection of other fundamental rights, such as the right to defence and judicial protection.[896]

To sum up, the formulations used and the guarantees stipulated in the FDPJ are to a great extent less strict in terms of data protection rights than the rules contained in Directive 95/46 and Regulation 45/2001. In addition, the restricted scope of the FDPJ considerably limits its application the AFSJ. Due to these shortcomings, the legal instruments establishing the AFSJ actors play an important role in the analysis of the data protection guarantees applicable in the AFSJ. Their data processing framework is analysed in the next section.

[896] For an excellent analysis of this case law and its data protection elements, see Hijmanns and Scirocco (2009), in particular p. 1509.

Chapter B
AFSJ Actors in the Light of the European Data Protection Standard

Chapter B seeks to present the data processing and data protection framework of the different European actors in the AFSJ in order to assess their compliance with the data protection guarantees developed in Chap. A. As demonstrated in Chap. A, the general data protection rules in the AFSJ are diversified and reflect the former pillar structure. Therefore, specific data protection rules are additionally entailed in the legal bases of the AFSJ actors itself. To analyse to which extent personal data are protected at the AFSJ actors, a first subdivision studies the legal framework of the agencies Europol, Eurojust Frontex as well as the Commission's anti fraud unit OLAF. A second section involves the analysis of the data processing activities of the information systems SIS, CIS, VIS and Eurodac in the AFSJ. The data protection standards of the Council of Europe, specified in Convention No. 108, Recommendation R (87) 15 and particularly within the ECtHR's interpretation of Article 8 ECHR as well as the EU principles demonstrated above are duly considered in this analysis. The following Chapter therefore critically reviews the data processing activities as well as the data protection mechanisms of the main AFSJ actors.

Chapter B presents essential background information necessary to the understanding of the extent as to which the AFSJ actors collect and exchange personal data. Without knowing the field of activity, the data processing framework, the supervisory structure and the exact amount of personal data which are processed at the relevant actors, the dimension of the interlinks between them are difficult to grasp. Therefore, Chap. B critically examines the data processing activities of the AFSJ actors.

F. Boehm, *Information Sharing and Data Protection in the Area of Freedom, Security and Justice*, DOI 10.1007/978-3-642-22392-1_3,

I Brief Background Information

The Hague Programme, an achievement plan for the AFSJ from December 2004 stipulates that:

> The European Council is convinced that strengthening freedom, security and justice requires an innovative approach to the cross-border exchange of law-enforcement information. The mere fact that information crosses borders should no longer be relevant.[1]

As mentioned in the introduction, law enforcement related data exchange in the AFSJ was from then on governed by the so called "availability principle" which inevitably led to reinforced cooperation and increased data sharing of the existing actors in this field. However, the Hague programme also called for the respect of data protection standards which should have been "*strictly observed*".[2] It provided for the implementation of measures protecting individuals from abuse of data as well as the development of "common standards for access to the data" and "supervision of respect for data protection".[3] Additionally individuals should have the right to seek correction of incorrect data and "appropriate control prior to and after the exchange".[4]

However the question of what has become of the promised coherent and protective data protection framework since 2005, which should have accompanied the process of reinforced cooperation in the AFSJ, is still not answered. Whether the aforementioned goals and the promised coherent data protection standard have been achieved is to be analysed in the following.

To facilitate the assessment of the actors operating in the field of security-related data processing and data exchange in the AFSJ, connections between them will be made visible when dividing them into the main groups of actors exchanging personal data in the AFSJ: European agencies, OLAF and the European Information Systems.

The first group consists of the European agencies and OLAF increasingly exchanging data for law enforcement purposes. Europol, Eurojust, Frontex and OLAF are thereby the most active ones in this field. Their main tasks and their data processing framework is therefore briefly analysed hereinafter in Sect. II.

The second group is represented by the European Information Exchange Systems, whose function and data processing and protection structures are equally studied in Sect. III.

[1] The Hague Programme, Council doc. 16054/04 of 13 December 2004, point 2.1, p. 18.

[2] Ibid, point 2.1, pp. 18–19 (emphasis added).

[3] Ibid, point 2.1., pp. 18 and 19.

[4] Ibid, point 2.1, p. 19.

II European Agencies and OLAF

1. Europol

Being the actor with the largest amount of connections to other agencies, to OLAF and to the other European data exchange systems as well as to third states, this section firstly focuses on the general data protection framework at Europol, including a brief analysis of the relevant provision in the new Europol Decision which entered into force in January 2010.[5] While Europol is the biggest of the AFSJ agencies, its legal framework will serve as an example for the data protection standard of European agencies as well as background information for the subsequent scrutiny of the data protection standard of the cooperation between the different AFSJ actors. Europol's legal basis is therefore illustrated slightly more detailed than those of the other AFSJ actors.

a) Competences and Tasks

Europol is a European law enforcement organisation which aims at improving the cooperation of the competent authorities in the Member States by collecting, storing, analysing and exchanging information.[6] Europol prepares threat assessments, strategic analyses and general reports based on information provided by the Member States[7] while also offering expertise and technical support for investigations and operations carried out within the EU which take place under the supervision of the Member States.[8] One of the goals of Europol's work is the harmonisation of investigative techniques in the Member States. Cooperation with the Member States principally occurs through the establishment of Europol national

[5] Council Decision of 6 April 2009 establishing the European Police Office, OJ 2009, L-121/37.

[6] Article 88 TFEU and Article 5 (1) lit. a of the Council Decision of 6 April 2009 establishing the European Police Office, OJ 2009, L-121/37; for a deepend understanding of Europol and ist tasks, compare also Kistner-Bahr (2010), pp. 29–34; background information on Europol can be found in Engel (2006); Milke (2003); Gleß et al. (2001); for a brief overview refer to Borchardt (2010), pp. 593 and 596.

[7] Article 5 (1) lit. f Council Decision of 6 April 2009 establishing the European Police Office, OJ 2009, L-121/37; see for instance the threat assessment relating to organised crime: "OCTA 2009, EU organised crime threat assessment", http://www.europol.europa.eu/publications/European_Organised_Crime_Threat_Assessment_(OCTA)/OCTA2009.pdf (accessed February 2011).

[8] Article 5 of the Council Decision of 6 April 2009 establishing the European Police Office, OJ 2009, L-121/37.

units in each Member State while each one seconds a liaison officer to Europol.[9] Additionally Member States may also allow direct contacts between competent national authorities.[10]

Europol's legal framework was profoundly changed in January 2010. The Europol Convention (1999–2010), which was accompanied by an assortment of legal provisions progressively extending Europol's competences,[11] was replaced by a Council Decision intended to be more "flexible" by reducing the duration of the ratification process for potential changes to it in comparison to the process provided for in the former Europol Convention and also by transforming Europol into an agency.[12]

However, in addition to the procedural change, the Council Decision also contains substantive changes regarding the extension of Europol's mandate[13] as well as provisions regarding the exchange of data with third parties, illustrated

---

[9] Article 8 and 9 Council Decision of 6 April 2009 establishing the European Police Office, OJ 2009, L-121/37, note that currently 121 liaison officers work at Europol, compare Europol Review, annual general report on Europol activities 2009, p. 6.

[10] Article 8 (2) Council Decision of 6 April 2009 establishing the European Police Office, OJ 2009, L-121/37.

[11] The amendments include protocols, Council Decisions and acts implementing the Europol Convention, see examples: Protocol drawn up on the basis of Article K.3 of the Treaty on European Union, on the interpretation, by way of preliminary rulings, by the Court of Justice of the European Communities of the Convention on the establishment of a European Police Office, OJ 1996, C-299/2; Protocol drawn up, on the basis of Article K.3 of the Treaty on European Union and Article 41 (3) of the Europol Convention, on the privileges and immunities of Europol, the members of its organs, the deputy directors and employees of Europol, OJ 1997, C-221/2; Council Act of 30 November 2000 drawing up on the basis of Article 43(1) of the Convention on the establishment of a European Police Office (Europol Convention) of a Protocol amending Article 2 and the Annex to that Convention, OJ 2000, C358/1; Council Decision of 3 December 1998 supplementing the definition of the form of crime 'traffic in human beings' in the Annex to the Europol Convention, OJ 1999, C-26/21; Council Decision of 3 December 1998 instructing Europol to deal with crimes committed or likely to be committed in the course of terrorist activities against life, limb, personal freedom or property, OJ 1999, C-26/22; Council Decision of 29 April 1999 extending Europol's mandate to deal with forgery of money and means of payment, OJ 1999, C-149/16; Council Decision of 6 December 2001 extending Europol's mandate to deal with the serious forms of international crime listed in the Annex to the Europol Convention, OJ 2001, C-362/1; Council Decision 2005/511/JHA of 12 July 2005 on protecting the euro against counterfeiting, by designating Europol as the Central Office for combating euro counterfeiting, OJ 2005, L-185/35; Protocol – amending the Convention on the establishment of a European Police Office (Europol Convention) and the Protocol on the privileges and immunities of Europol, the members of its organs, the deputy directors and the employees of Europol, OJ 2002, C-312/2; Protocol – Drawn up on the basis of Article 43(1) of the Convention on the Establishment of a European Police Office (Europol Convention), amending that Convention, OJ 2004, C-2/3.

[12] Opinion of the EDPS on the proposal for a Council Decision establishing the European Police Office (Europol) – COM(2006) 817 final, OJ 2007, C-255/13, point I.(2); Den Boer et al. (2008), p. 111; for an overview of the new regulatory framework of Europol: De Moor and Vermeulen (2010).

[13] To the continually extended competences of Europol see Den Boer et al. (2008).

further below.[14] Europol also became more "communautarised" and thus more independent from the contributions of Member States as, in contrast to the Europol Convention, the funding of Europol is now financed by the Community budget and Europol's staff is subject to EU staff regulations.

According to the new Council Decision, Europol has the following principal tasks[15]:

1. To collect, store, process, analyse and exchange information and intelligence;
2. To notify the competent authorities of the Member States without delay via the national unit referred to in Article 8 Europol Decision of information concerning them and of any connections identified between criminal offences;
3. To aid investigations in the Member States, in particular by forwarding all relevant information to the national units;
4. To ask the competent authorities of the Member States concerned to initiate, conduct or coordinate investigations and to suggest the setting up of joint investigation teams in specific cases;
5. To provide intelligence and analytical support to Member States in connection with major international events and
6. To prepare threat assessments, strategic analyses and general situation reports relating to its objective, including organised crime threat assessments.

According to Article 5 (3) of the Europol Decision, Europol has additional tasks including developing specialised knowledge of the investigative procedures of the national authorities and providing advice on investigations and strategic intelligence. Further, it shall assist the Member States by providing support, advice and research in the training of members of national authorities, organising and equipping those authorities as well as promoting crime prevention methods and technical and forensic methods and analyses.

The Europol Decision was hastily adopted before the entry into force of the Lisbon Treaty in order to avoid inter alia the mandatory participation of the European Parliament in the adoption process required by the Treaty's new provisions.[16] The consequence of this rushed timing is that the legal effects of the TEU and the TFEU on Europol have been delayed for a 5 year period regarding the jurisdiction of the Court of Justice[17] (no infringement procedures and references

[14] See Sect. II 1 g.

[15] Article 5 (1) Council Decision of 6 April 2009 establishing the European Police Office, OJ 2009, L-121/37.

[16] See House of Lords Europol report, European Union Committee, 29th report of session 2007–2008, "Europol: coordinating the fight against serious and organised crime", published 12 November 2008, p. 15, paragraph 23 and Article 88 TFEU.

[17] As Europol's judicial control was one of the most discussed issues since its establishment, a protocol on the interpretation, by way of preliminary rulings, by the Court of Justice of the EC of the Convention on the establishment of a European Police Office was introduced in 1996 (Council Act of 23 July 1996 drawing up, on the basis of Article K.3 of the Treaty on European Union, the Protocol on the interpretation, by way of preliminary rulings, by the Court of Justice of the

only from 17 national Courts) and the powers of the Commission to bring a matter before the Court of Justice.[18]

However, regarding future amendments of the Europol Decision under the new Lisbon Treaty, it has to be taken into account that upcoming measures in the field of police and judicial cooperation in criminal matters will now be subject to the usual effects of EU law (direct effect and supremacy) and legislative acts will have the form of Directives and Regulations adopted by using the so called "ordinary legislative procedure" which combines the decisions of the Council and the European Parliament and forms the basis of the jurisdiction of the Court of Justice.[19] So far, parliamentary scrutiny is restricted to two areas: general informational duties in the form of a general report forwarded to the European Parliament after endorsement of the Council, and consultation requirements concerning the adoption of implementing rules dealing with details of Europol's data processing systems in cooperation with third states.[20]

Article 88 TFEU regulates Europol's future mission and tasks including Europol's competence to coordinate, organise and implement "investigative and operational action carried out jointly with the Member States' competent authorities or in context of joint investigations teams, where appropriate in liaison with Eurojust".[21] These tasks relate to "serious crime affecting two or more Member States" as well as "forms of crime which affect a common interest covered by a Union policy".[22] The focus therefore remains on supportive tasks. Whereas the aforementioned wording might allow a future concession of operational powers[23] to Europol, Article 88 (3) TFEU stipulates that the application of coercive measures remains the exclusive responsibility of the competent national authorities.[24] As the meaning of the term is not further detailed, *Ladenburger* argues that it would not exclude the granting of the power to Europol to instruct national authorities to apply

European Communities of the Convention on the establishment of a European Police Office, OJ 1996, C-299/1), but its acceptance by the Member States depended on an additional declaration accepting the Court's jurisdiction in case of preliminary rulings on the interpretation of Europol Convention which made at least a partial judicial control of Europol subject to the political choice of the Member States, see Mitsilegas (2009), p. 177.

[18] Articles 9 and 10 of the protocol no. 36 on transitional provisions, annexed to the Lisbon Treaty, OJ 2010, C-83/201, to the details see Chap. A III 1 d.

[19] Peers (2009).

[20] Articles 37 (10) (c), 14 (1), 26 (1) or 28 (1) Council Decision of 6 April 2009 establishing the European Police Office, OJ 2009, L-121/37.

[21] Article 88 (2) (b) TFEU.

[22] Article 88 (1) TFEU.

[23] The term "operational power" is not further defined but might best be described as "capable of being involved in operations" as well as carrying out investigative and field work activities, including coordinative tasks in terms of law enforcement, criminal prosecution and preventive police work, compare also: Gärditz (2008), in particular pp. 213–214.

[24] Article 88 (3) TFEU.

coercive measures.[25] In any case, the wording of Article 88 TEU suggests that supporting and operational tasks will become increasingly indistinguishable.

In order to expand Europol's current tasks (analysed hereinafter) to the extent permitted by the Lisbon Treaty, the European Parliament and the Council have to determine Europol's future structure, operation, field of action and tasks by means of regulations adopted in accordance with the ordinary legislative procedure.[26] Therefore, Article 88 TFEU has improved democratic control over Europol which is exercised on one hand by the European Parliament, and on the other by the national parliaments which "contribute actively" to the AFSJ by being "involved in the political monitoring of Europol".[27]

However, to come back to the current legal framework, the scope of the Europol Decision does not yet cover crime affecting a common interest covered by a Union policy, but organised crime, terrorism and "other forms of serious crime" affecting two or more Member States.[28] An annex to the Europol Decision lays down 24 wide

---

[25] To the details of coercive measures see Amelung (2008); Ladenburger (2008), p. 39; see also Mitsilegas (2009), p. 229.

[26] Article 88 TFEU: "1. Europol's mission shall be to support and strengthen action by the Member States' police authorities and other law enforcement services and their mutual cooperation in preventing and combating serious crime affecting two or more Member States, terrorism and forms of crime which affect a common interest covered by a Union policy. 2. The European Parliament and the Council, by means of regulations adopted in accordance with the ordinary legislative procedure, shall determine Europol's structure, operation, field of action and tasks. These tasks may include: (a) the collection, storage, processing, analysis and exchange of information, in particular that forwarded by the authorities of the Member States or third countries or bodies; (b) the coordination, organisation and implementation of investigative and operational action carried out jointly with the Member States' competent authorities or in the context of joint investigative teams, where appropriate in liaison with Eurojust. These regulations shall also lay down the procedures for scrutiny of Europol's activities by the European Parliament, together with national Parliaments. 3. Any operational action by Europol must be carried out in liaison and in agreement with the authorities of the Member State or States whose territory is concerned. The application of coercive measures shall be the exclusive responsibility of the competent national authorities".

[27] Article 12 (c) TEU: "National Parliaments contribute actively to the good functioning of the Union: by taking part, within the framework of the area of freedom, security and justice, in the evaluation mechanisms for the implementation of the Union policies in that area, in accordance with Article 70 of the Treaty on the Functioning of the European Union, and through being involved in the political monitoring of Europol and the evaluation of Eurojust's activities in accordance with Articles 88 and 85 of that Treaty" and 70 TFEU: "Without prejudice to Articles 258, 259 and 260, the Council may, on a proposal from the Commission, adopt measures laying down the arrangements whereby Member States, in collaboration with the Commission, conduct objective and impartial evaluation of the implementation of the Union policies referred to in this Title by Member States' authorities, in particular in order to facilitate full application of the principle of mutual recognition. The European Parliament and national Parliaments shall be informed of the content and results of the evaluation", see also Article 88 (2) lit. b TFEU.

[28] Article 3 Council Decision of 6 April 2009 establishing the European Police Office, OJ 2009, L-121/37.

ranging forms of crime which Europol is competent to deal with.[29] Six legal definitions of specific crimes, such as "illegal immigrant smuggling" and "motor vehicle crime" are provided to substantiate the content of some of the listed crimes.[30] The existence of an organised criminal structure, as was the requirement for Europol's actions in the Europol Convention, is no longer a limiting element.[31]

b) Databases

Europol processes personal data in three ways: in the Europol Information System (EIS), the analysis work files and the index system.[32] In addition, a secure information exchange tool, SIENA (Secure Information Exchange Network), connects the Member States via the Europol national units and the Europol liaison bureaus[33] but does not routinely involve Europol.[34] SIENA has been in use since 2009, replacing the information exchange application (Info-Ex) that had been in use since 1996. It is currently used to share sensitive data between the Member States (303,613 operational messages in 2009), but in later stages the functionalities of SIENA should be expanded and its availability extended to competent authorities and cooperation partners such as Eurojust, Norway, Switzerland, Australia, Canada, USA and Interpol.[35] Currently, third parties have indirect access to SIENA via Europol's operation centre.

The following section focuses on Europol's three information systems.

---

[29] Namely: unlawful drug trafficking, illegal money-laundering activities, crime connected with nuclear and radioactive substances, illegal immigrant smuggling, trafficking in human beings, motor vehicle crime, murder, grievous bodily injury, illicit trade in human organs and tissue, kidnapping, illegal restraint and hostage taking, racism and xenophobia, organised robbery, illicit trafficking in cultural goods, including antiquities and works of art, swindling and fraud, racketeering and extortion, counterfeiting and product piracy, forgery of administrative documents and trafficking therein, forgery of money and means of payment, computer crime, corruption, illicit trafficking in arms, ammunition and explosives, illicit trafficking in endangered animal species, illicit trafficking in endangered plant species and varieties, environmental crime; illicit trafficking in hormonal substances and other growth promoters.

[30] Annex to the Council Decision of 6 April 2009 establishing the European Police Office, OJ 2009, L-121/37; for an overview of the databases, refer to Engel (2006), pp. 46–54.

[31] De Moor and Vermeulen (2010), in particular p. 1097.

[32] A brief overwiev and description of Europols' information systems could be found at: Weßlau (2008).

[33] Offices established in the 27 European capitals to link Europol's headquarter in The Hague with the Member States, compare Europol Review, annual general report on Europol activities 2009, p. 6.

[34] House of Lords, submission by Europol, Select Committee on European Union, Call for Evidence, File no. 3100–174, 28 April 2008, section 1.3., p. 9; to the subject of data processing at Europol, see also: Cali (Spring 2000).

[35] Europol Review, annual general report on Europol activities 2009, pp. 8 and 51.

aa) EIS

The EIS interconnects the computer networks of the national authorities of the Member States with Europol and allows introducing and retrieving data from it. It became fully operable in 2005, but was not used by all of the Member States before 2008.[36] As a result, the number of objects stored in the EIS in December 2009 increased by 57% compared to December 2008.[37] In December 2009 it included 29,964 "person objects", 135,154 relationships and 135,489 objects.[38]

According to Article 12 (1) of the Europol Decision, the data introduced in the EIS must be necessary for the performance of Europol's tasks and relate to persons who are suspected of having committed, having taken part in or have been convicted of criminal offences pursuant to the national law of the Member State which provided the information concerned and in respect of which Europol is competent.[39] Additionally, even in case of "factual indications or reasonable grounds" under a Member State's law "to believe that a person will commit criminal offences", entry in the EIS is possible.[40]

The wording of Article 12 (1) lit. b of the Europol Decision constitutes a remarkable broadening of the requirements to be fulfilled in order to enter personal data into the EIS, compared to the more restrictive formulation of Europol Convention Article 8 (2) which required "serious grounds" for entering personal information in the EIS.[41]

To the extent the wording in subparagraph 1 of Article 12 of the Europol Decision has been widened, the maximum quantity of particulars of persons whose data may be entered into the EIS has also been considerably extended. Added to the list of basic personal information (name, place of birth, nationality and sex), allowed under the Europol Convention are particulars concerning social security data (social security number, driving licence, identification documents, passport data), the whereabouts, profession and "where necessary", biometric information such as fingerprints and DNA profiles.[42] When exactly it seems to be necessary to input biometric data is not clarified more precisely. There are

---

[36] Mitsilegas (2009), p. 173; House of Lords, submission by Europol, Select Committee on European Union, Call for Evidence, File no. 3100–174, 28 April 2008, section 5.1.3., p. 18; the first users have been France, Germany, Portugal, Sweden, United Kingdom, the last once Romania and Bulgaria.

[37] Europol Review, annual general report on Europol activities 2009, p. 7.

[38] Ibid.

[39] Article 12 Council Decision of 6 April 2009 establishing the European Police Office, OJ 2009, L-121/37.

[40] Ibid, Article 12 (1) lit. b.

[41] Article 8 (2) of the Europol Convention reads as follows: "persons who there are serious grounds under national law for believing will commit criminal offences for which Europol is competent under Article 2".

[42] Article 12 (2) lit. a-g Council Decision of 6 April 2009 establishing the European Police Office, OJ 2009, L-121/37.

additional possibilities to include particulars relating to specifics of criminal offences, the means used to commit such offences, the suspected membership of a criminal organisation or convictions of the past.[43]

When comparing the quite detailed information of the Europol Decision to the more restricted possibilities of the Europol Convention and the low threshold to pass when entering data in the EIS, one understands why the participation of the European Parliament was avoided by all means during the legislative process. It is more than likely that such wide-ranging extensions of Europol's competences and data processing possibilities would not have passed the European Parliament without fundamental amendments.

According to the current Europol Decision, it is possible to store data for a 3 year period regarding individuals who potentially will commit a crime in the future, based on factual indications.[44]

Considering that data stored in the EIS could be investigated, accessed by all 27 Member States and liaison officers from third states,[45] as well as transmitted to third parties (analysed in Sects. II 1 c aa and II 1 g), the entry of data from individuals based on factual indications that this person might one day commit a crime, seems to be extremely far reaching. As a consequence of the entry, investigations against the persons might be instituted. This situation fundamentally challenges ECtHR's foreseeability criterion and the its jurisdiction in *Weber and Saravia v. Germany* and *Association for European Integration and Human Rights and Ekimdzhiev v. Bulgaria* in which the ECtHR tolerated data transfer to other law enforcement authorities only under the condition that specific facts – as opposed to mere factual indications – aroused the suspicion that someone had committed one of the offences.[46]

According to the formulations, everyone in principle seems to be suspicious. The categories of people liable to have their data entered in Europols' databases are therefore far from being clear. It seems impossible to predict whether an individual has his data entered or not. With regard to foreseeability, the question arises how an individual should regulate his behavior and foresee the consequences which a given action may entail. While the German solution in *Weber and Saravia v. Germany* (requiring specific facts – as opposed to mere factual indications) might constitute

[43] Ibid, Article 12 (3).

[44] Ibid, Article 20 (1).

[45] From the US (from the FBI, the US secret service, the drug enforcement administration and the US postal inspection), Australia, Canada, Colombia, Croatia, Iceland, Norway Switzerland, and Interpol working at Europol in Den Hague, see Article 9 Council Decision of 6 April 2009 establishing the European Police Office, OJ 2009, L-121/37; Europol annual report 2008, p. 45; House of Lords, European Union Committee, 29th report of session 2007–2008, "Europol: coordinating the fight against serious and organised crime", published 12 November 2008, p. 51, paragraph 193; Den Boer et al. (2008), p. 110.

[46] *Weber and Saravia v. Germany*, Application no. 54934/00, admissibility decision of 29 June 2006, para 127, and *Association for European Integration and Human Rights and Ekimdzhiev v. Bulgaria*, Application no. 62540/00, judgment of 28 June 2007, para 89.

only one possibility to limit the circle of persons concerned by surveillance measures and governmental data mining, the ECtHR leaves no doubt that the collection of personal data in absence of any suspicion would certainly contradict the guarantees of Article 8 ECHR.[47] Having this judgment in mind, it remains to be seen whether additional safeguards restricting the use of these data as well as the possible accessing actors (analysed in Sect. II 1 g) are entailed in the Europol Decision.

Besides challenging ECtHR case law, the far reaching entry possibilities also contradict to principle 2 of Recommendation R (87) 15 which limits data collection for police purposes to the extent necessary for the prevention of a real danger or the suppression of a specific criminal offence.[48] Point 43 of the explanatory memorandum of Recommendation R (87) 15 indisputably clarifies that this rule attempts to prohibit an open-ended and indiscriminate collection of data by the police. In this context, Recommendation R (87) 15 refers to the wording of Article 5 (c) of Convention No. 108 and Article 9 (2) lit. a of Convention No. 108 which allow for a derogation from the principle that personal data must be adequate, relevant and not excessive in relation to the purpose for which they are stored in regard to the "suppression of criminal offences". Recommendation R (87) 15 insists that this exception must be limited to the collection of data being necessary for the prevention of a real danger or the suppression of a specific criminal offence, unless the law clearly authorises wider police powers to gather information.[49] Real danger is thereby explained as "not being restricted to a specific offence or offender but includes any circumstances where there is reasonable suspicion that serious criminal offences have been or might be committed to the exclusion of unsupported speculative possibilities."[50] The latter sentence obviously excludes data collection due to mere "factual indications" that an individual might become a criminal in the future.

Further the storage of data of criminals and possible criminals in the same database also opposes to principle 3.2 of Recommendation R (87) 15 specifying that data based on facts should be distinguished from data based on opinions or personal assessments. When analysing whether or not an individual represents a possible criminal, an assessment based on evaluations of several facts has to be

---

[47] ECtHR, *Weber and Saravia*, Application no. 54934/00, admissibility decision of 29 June 2006, paras 125–129; for an excellent overview of Europol's possibility to pre-emptively process personal data and the violation of the German "Recht auf informationelle Selbstbestimmung", see Schubert (2008).

[48] Principle 2.1. of Recommendation R (87) 15.

[49] Point 43 of the explanatory memorandum of Recommendation R (87) 15.

[50] Point 43 of the explanatory memorandum of Recommendation R (87) 15, compare also the example given in point 43 of the explanatory memorandum: "real danger" means "reasonable suspicion that unspecified drugs were being illegally brought into a country through a port by unidentified private yachts would justify the collection of data on all such yachts using that port, but not all yachts, their owners and passengers using every port in that country".

made. By its very nature the results of this assessment are the outcome of an opinion made by analysts, but these data are not stored in a separate database.

Consequently, it is highly questionable whether Article 12 (1) lit. b Europol Decision complies with its own reference instrument, Recommendation R (87) 15. The rules allowing for derogation from principle 2 of Recommendation (87) 15 were adopted lacking democratic control of the European Parliament and the risks of prejudgment and stigmatisation stemming from a Europol record are not necessarily outweighed by the possibility of probably finding a criminal under various possible suspects. Moreover, it is extremely doubtful whether the pre-emptive entry of possible criminals due to factual indications correctly balances fundamental rights, above all the presumption of innocence against the interest of the Member States to detect criminals.[51]

Article 12 (5) of the Europol Decision at least stipulates that in case Europol entered the information itself and gives filing reference, Europol has to specify the source of the information[52] and that the entries have to be deleted, if proceedings against the person concerned are "definitively dropped or if that person is definitively acquitted"[53]; however, most importantly, Europol Decision Article 12 does not include a provision protecting the data related to possible criminals who have never committed a crime and may never be subject to investigations or court proceedings. Once more, it is extremely questionable whether the processing of the data, including biometric information, on a 3 years basis[54] complies with the presumption of innocence and the guarantees of Article 8 ECHR which provides for a difference of treatment of the data of criminals and that of possible suspects (compare *S. and Marper v. the United Kingdom*).[55]

bb) Analysis Work Files

The second possibility for Europol to store and process information is regulated in a far reaching manner in Article 14 of the Europol Decision. In addition to information about persons referred to in Europol Decision Article 12 (1) (criminals and possible criminals) which may be "stored, modified and used" in the analysis work files, data about witnesses, victims, contacts, associates as well as data about persons who can provide information on the criminal offences under consideration

---

[51] To the missing separation between preventive and repressive police work at Europol, compare Kistner-Bahr (2010), pp. 110–115.

[52] Article 12 (4) Council Decision of 6 April 2009 establishing the European Police Office, OJ 2009, L-121/37.

[53] Ibid, Article 12 (5).

[54] Ibid, Article 20 (1).

[55] *Marper v. the United Kingdom*, Application nos. 30562/04 and 30566/04, judgment of 4 December 2008, para 122, compare Chap. A II 1 d cc (1).

can be included in the analysis work files. What exactly has to be understood by "storing, modifying and using" is not further elucidated.

By contrast, the meaning of processing is elaborated in the Council Decision 2009/936 of adopting the implementing rules for Europol analysis work files which was also adopted on 30 November 2009, 1 day before the entry into force of the Lisbon Treaty, which would have demanded a mandatory participation of the European Parliament that previously rejected the draft implementing decision on 24 November 2009 (640 votes against, 12 in favour, 10 abstentions).[56] The Council Implementing Decision 2009/936 covers almost all possible forms of processing, namely: "any operation or set of operations which is performed upon personal data, whether or not by automatic means, such as collection, recording, organisation, storage, adaptation or alteration, retrieval, consultation, use, disclosure by transmission, dissemination or otherwise making available, alignment or combination, blocking, erasure or destruction".[57]

When processing the data in the aforementioned ways, it is also permissible to deal with data revealing racial or ethnic origin, political opinions, religious or philosophical beliefs or trade union membership or data concerning health or sex life. They could be processed under the requirement that they are "strictly necessary for the purposes of the file concerned and supplement other personal data already input in that file".[58] As a minimum constraint it is not allowed to select a particular group of persons solely on the basis of the mentioned criteria.[59]

Thus, analysis work files may contain information about criminals but also about innocent persons such as victims, witnesses or possible criminals. When looking at the mixture of these two types of data, it is very doubtful that these provisions comply with the requirements stipulated by the ECtHR in *S. and Marper v. the United Kingdom*, where the ECtHR clearly insisted on a different treatment of data of persons who have been convicted of an offence and those who have never been.[60] This provision obviously contradicts the message relating to the EIS contained in Article 12 (5) Europol Decision according to which the collected data have to be deleted in case of dropping of the proceedings or an acquittal. Two Articles before Article 14 Europol Decision, the legislator obviously took into consideration that the person concerned has to be treated in a different way. One could argue that analysis work files are different from the EIS, in particular with regard to the

[56] http://www.europarl.europa.eu/oeil/FindByProcnum.do?lang=en&procnum=CNS/2009/0810 (accessed February 2011); Council Decision 2009/936/JHA of 30 November 2009 adopting the implementing rules for Europol analysis work files, OJ 2009, L-325/14.

[57] Article 1 (e) Council Decision 2009/936/JHA of 30 November 2009 adopting the implementing rules for Europol analysis work files, OJ 2009, L-325/14.

[58] Article 14 (1) after lit. e Council Decision of 6 April 2009 establishing the European Police Office, OJ 2009, L-121/37.

[59] Ibid.

[60] See Chap. A II 1 d cc (1); *S. and Marper v. the United Kingdom*, Application nos. 30562/04 and 30566/04, judgment of 4 December 2008, para 122.

category of persons having access to the analysis work files,[61] however, this does not change the fact that data about totally innocent persons who have never been suspected of having committed a crime are "stored, modified and used" in the same analysis work file system as data about persons in terms of Article 12 (1) Europol Decision, mostly being suspects or offenders.

In contrast to the EIS, it is not further specified directly in the Europol Decision which kind of data can be entered in the analysis work files. Article 16 Europol Decision simply provides for an "order opening" containing some essential information about the content of the file which the director has to implement before setting up an analysis work file.[62] Details, particularly regarding the categories of data referred to in Article 14 Europol Decision, are laid down in the aforementioned hurriedly adopted Council Implementing Decision 2009/936.[63]

When looking at the enormous amount of categories possible to input in the analysis work file (69 different categories containing subcategories) according to Article 6 (2) Council Implementing Decision 2009/936, it becomes clear why all these categories are not listed directly in the Europol Decision.[64]

---

[61] See Sect. II c aa.

[62] According to Article 16 Europol Decision the order opening must contain: the file name, the purpose of the file, the groups of persons concerning whom data are stored the nature of the data to be stored and personal data revealing racial or ethnic origin, political opinions, religious or philosophical beliefs or trade-union membership and data concerning health or sex life which are strictly necessary; the general context leading to the decision to open the file; the participants in the analysis group at the time of opening the file; the conditions under which the personal data stored in the file may be communicated, to which recipients and under what procedure; the time limits for examination of the data and the duration of storage; the method of establishment of the audit log.

[63] Council Decision 2009/936/JHA of 30 November 2009 adopting the implementing rules for Europol analysis work files, OJ 2009, L-325/14.

[64] See full list of Article 6 (2) Council Decision 2009/936/JHA of 30 November 2009 adopting the implementing rules for Europol analysis work files, OJ 2009, L-325/14: "The following categories of personal data, including associated administrative data, may be processed on the categories of persons referred to in Article 14(1) (a) of the Europol Decision: (a) Personal details: 1. Present and former surnames, 2. Present and former forenames, 3. Maiden name, 4. Father's name (where necessary for the purpose of identification), 5. Mother's name (where necessary for the purpose of identification), 6. Sex, 7. Date of birth, 8. Place of birth, 9. Nationality, 10. Marital status, 11. Alias, 12. Nickname, 13. Assumed or false name, 14. Present and former residence and/or domicile, (b) Physical description: 1. Physical description, 2. Distinguishing features (marks/scars/tattoos etc.), (c) Identification means: 1. Identity documents/driving licence, 2. National identity card/passport numbers, 3. National identification number/social security number, if applicable, 4. Visual images and other information on appearance, 5. Forensic identification information such as fingerprints, DNA profile, (established from the non-coding part of DNA), voice profile, blood group, dental information, (d) Occupation and skills: 1. Present employment and occupation, 2. Former employment and occupation, 3. Education (school/university/professional), 4. Qualifications, 5. Skills and other fields of knowledge (language/other), (e) Economic and financial information: 1. Financial data (bank accounts and codes, credit cards etc.), 2. Cash assets, 3. Share holdings/other assets, 4. Property data, 5. Links with companies, 6. Bank and credit contacts, 7. Tax position, 8. Other information revealing a person's management of their financial

At first glance, the data to be introduced in an analysis work file seem to distinguish between information which can be collected about persons according to Article 12 (1) Europol Decision (criminals, suspects or possible suspects) and data which can be stored relating to other groups (witnesses, victims, contacts, associates as well as data about persons who can provide information on the criminal offences) pursuant to Article 14 (1) Europol Decision. In respect of the first group, criminals, suspects and persons regarding whom "factual indications or reasonable grounds" suggest that they will commit criminal offences, in addition to typical personal details, data regarding the DNA profile, voice profile, dental information, occupation and skills, the economic and financial situation (all financial data, links with companies, tax position etc), behavioural data, contacts and associates, means of communication and transport used, information related to criminal activities for which Europol is competent, references to other databases in which information on the person is stored including private entities and information on legal persons associated with the economic and financial situation as well as with criminal activities for which Europol has competence, can be input in the analysis work file.[65]

In connection with contacts and associates, the 69 categories of data listed in paragraph 2 of Article 6 Council Implementing Decision 2009/936 relating to criminals, suspects and potential/alleged suspects may also be stored "as necessary, provided there is reason to assume that such data are required for the analysis of the role of such person as contacts or associates".[66]

---

affairs, (f) Behavioural data: 1. Lifestyle (such as living above means) and routine, 2. Movements, 3. Places frequented, 4. Weapons and other dangerous instruments, 5. Danger rating, 6. Specific risks such as escape probability, use of double agents, connections with law enforcement personnel, 7. Criminal-related traits and profiles, 8. Drug abuse, (g) Contacts and associates, including type and nature of the contact or association, (h) Means of communication used, such as telephone (static/mobile), fax, pager, electronic mail, postal addresses, Internet connection(s), (i) Means of transport used, such as vehicles, boats, aircraft, including information identifying these means of transport (registration numbers), (j) Information relating to criminal activities for which Europol has competence under Article 4 of the Europol Decision: 1. Previous convictions, 2. Suspected involvement in criminal activities, 3. Modi operandi, 4. Means which were or may be used to prepare and/or commit crimes, 5. Membership of criminal groups/organisations and position in the group/organisation, 6. Role in the criminal organisation, 7. Geographical range of criminal activities, 8. Material gathered in the course of an investigation, such as video and photographic images, (k) References to other databases in which information on the person is stored: 1. Europol, 2. Police/customs agencies, 3. Other enforcement agencies, 4. International organisations, 5. Public entities, 6. Private entities, (l) Information on legal persons associated with the data referred to in points (e) and (j), 1. Designation of the legal person, 2. Location, 3. Date and place of establishment, 4. Administrative registration number, 5. Legal form, 6. Capital, 7. Area of activity, 8. National and international subsidiaries, 9. Directors, 10. Links with banks".

[65] See full list of Article 6 (2) Council Decision 2009/936/JHA of 30 November 2009 adopting the implementing rules for Europol analysis work files, OJ 2009, L-325/14; compare footnote before.

[66] Article 6 (3) Council Decision 2009/936/JHA of 30 November 2009 adopting the implementing rules for Europol analysis work files, OJ 2009, L-325/14.

Contacts and associates are persons for whom "there is sufficient reason to believe that information which relates to the persons under paragraph 2 [criminals, suspects and possible suspects] and which is relevant for the analysis can be gained through them".[67] Further, "associates" are persons who have regular contact with the (alleged) suspects while "contacts" are persons who have irregular contact with (alleged) suspects.[68] Therefore, even persons with remote links to a person covered by Article 12 (1) Europol Decision may find themselves in a situation where their own data are entered into an analysis work file.

As a minimum protective requirement, Article 6 (3) lit. a Council Implementing Decision 2009/936, imposes that the relationship of contacts and associates shall be clarified as soon as possible and in case that a clarification is not possible, this shall be considered when deciding on the need and the extent of storage for further analysis.[69] If it turns out that the persons concerned can not be regarded as contacts or associates, the data about them shall be deleted immediately.[70]

With regard to victims or to persons "who certain facts give reason to believe could be victims", in addition to typical personal data,[71] other data relating to crime related information (including information on their relationship with other persons) or the reasons for victimisation or the damage may be stored as well. Data about witnesses may also include information on their relationship with other persons included in the analysis work file. The most astonishing provision in context with victim or witness data however is the wording of Article 6 paragraph 4 and 5 making it possible to process all categories of data listed in paragraph 2 of Article 6 Council Implementing Decision 2009/936. This paragraph refers to the list of 69 different data categories "provided there is reason to assume that such data are required for the analysis of a person's role as victim [witnesses] or potential victim".[72]

The same applies to persons who can provide information on the criminal offences under consideration.[73] It is only restricted by the euphemistic obligation

---

[67] Ibid.

[68] Ibid.

[69] Article 6 (3) lit. a and e Council Decision 2009/936/JHA of 30 November 2009 adopting the implementing rules for Europol analysis work files, OJ 2009, L-325/14; With regard to the former Council Act of 3 November 1998 adopting rules applicable to Europol analysis files, OJ 1999 C-26/01, *Thomas Bernhard Petri* assumes that this provision provides no effective protection at all for contacts and associates ("faktisch schutzlos"), Petri (2001).

[70] Article 6 (3) lit. b Council Decision 2009/936/JHA of 30 November 2009 adopting the implementing rules for Europol analysis work files, OJ 2009, L-325/14.

[71] Data in terms of Article 6 paragraph 2 lit. a (1) to 2 lit c (3); compare footnote 64 of this chapter.

[72] Article 6 (4) and (5) Council Decision 2009/936/JHA of 30 November 2009 adopting the implementing rules for Europol analysis work files, OJ 2009, L-325/14; for the full list of possible data to be stored about victims and potential victims, compare footnote 64 of this chapter.

[73] Article 6 (5) and (6) Council Decision 2009/936/JHA of 30 November 2009 adopting the implementing rules for Europol analysis work files, OJ 2009, L-325/14; for the full list of possible data to be stored about victims and potential victims, compare footnote 64 of this chapter.

to delete the stored data if they are not required for further analysis.[74] Persons providing information can be identified as a confidential police informant when reading together Article 6 paragraph 6 lit. b-h Council Implementing Decision 2009/936 which stipulates inter alia that, information about the type of information supplied, a new identity or financial rewards can be additionally stored about a person providing information.

In order to place a person in a different category, "serious and corroborating indications" must exist.[75] Data processing in this case is thus restricted to the data processing which is permitted according to the new category. In respect of the aforementioned exception of the existence of a "reason to assume that such data are required for the analysis of a person's role" as a victim, witness or confidential informant, this requirement has been emptied of its meaning and does not provide protection. The second sentence of Article 6 (7) Council Implementing Decision 2009/936 affirms this observation by clarifying that if, on the basis of the mentioned indications, it turns out that "a person could be included in two or more different categories [...], all data allowed under such categories may be processed by Europol".[76]

Summarising, legal concerns arise in context of the low threshold to surmount when including new persons into the analysis work files as well as the amount of data elements stored, in particular regarding to persons whose data are introduced due to their victim or witness status. Through the adoption of the Council Implementing Decision 2009/936, which specifies the rules on analysis work files, without the participation of the European Parliament, restrictions on the processing as well as the amount of data are regrettably not foreseen. The combination of different types of data in only one file raises further concerns.

cc) Index Function

The index system gives the Director of Europol, the Deputy Directors, "duly empowered" Europol staff, liaison officers[77] and "duly empowered" members of

[74] Article 6 (4), (5) and (6) Council Decision 2009/936/JHA of 30 November 2009 adopting the implementing rules for Europol analysis work files, OJ 2009, L-325/14.

[75] Ibid, Article 6 (7).

[76] Ibid.

[77] As of December 2009, liaison officers from each of the Member States, the US (from the FBI, the US secret service, the drug enforcement administration and the US postal inspection), Australia, Iceland and Norway work at Europol in The Hague, see Article 9 Council Decision of 6 April 2009 establishing the European Police Office, OJ 2009, L-121/37; House of Lords, European Union Committee, 29th report of session 2007–2008, "Europol: coordinating the fight against serious and organised crime", published 12 November 2008, p. 51, paragraph 193; Den Boer et al. (2008), p. 110.

national units the possibility to find out whether or not the data stored in an analysis work file are of interest for them.[78] It is not further specified what exactly is to be understood by the condition "duly empowered" or which data are exactly contained in the index system. Article 15 (3) Europol Decision simply states that it shall be possible to determine "whether or not an item of information is stored in an analysis work file, but not to establish connections or further conclusions regarding the content of the file".[79] The Management Board which consists of one representative of each Member State plus one envoy of the Commission shall define the access conditions and the design of the index system.[80]

dd) Additional Data Exchange

Additionally to the existing requirement to transmit the aforementioned categories of data to Europol, in the post 9/11 efforts the Council enacted a specific obligation to target potential terrorists. The Council Decision 2005/671/JHA on the exchange of information and cooperation concerning terrorist offences, obliges Member States to designate a specialised service within its police services which collects relevant information related to these offences for transferring them to Europol (and Eurojust).[81] When looking at the transmitted information, which does not go beyond the already established data categories in the Europol Decision, it seems that the Council Decision rather aims at emphasising policy priorities in this field than enlarging the amount of data elements stored at Europol.[82]

ee) New Data Processing Systems

A further interesting provision in the new Europol Decision is Article 10 allowing for the establishment of other data processing systems in near future, under the condition that the new data processing system complies with the data protection

[78] Article 15 (2) Council Decision of 6 April 2009 establishing the European Police Office, OJ 2009, L-121/37.

[79] Ibid, Article 15 (3).

[80] Ibid, Article 37; to the structure of Europol compare Seong (2005), pp. 115–124.

[81] Council Decision 2005/671/JHA of 20 September 2005 on the exchange of information and cooperation concerning terrorist offences, OJ 2005, L 253/22.

[82] Article 2 (4) Council Decision 2005/671/JHA of 20 September 2005 on the exchange of information and cooperation concerning terrorist offences, OJ 2005, L 253/22; the data relate to data identifying the persons, the acts under investigation, the offences concerned as well as the link with other cases, the use of communication technologies and the threat posed by the possession of weapons of mass destruction.

provisions contained in the Europol Decision. The final decision about this possible system is subjected to the approval of the Council. Parliamentary consultation or similar control is not provided for. However, as mentioned above, this will change with regard to the Lisbon Treaty.[83] Another important modification in contrast to the Europol Convention involves Europol's new capacity to include information and intelligence transmitted by private parties in the mentioned databases, analysed in more detail in Sect. II 1 f.

In addition to a possible new data processing system, Europol may also process data outside the three existing systems for the purpose of figuring out whether the processed data are relevant to its data processing systems and whether they can be included in them.[84]

Rules regarding the conditions of this processing are laid down by the Council in an once more rashly adopted Council Decision from 30 November 2009, 1 day before the European Parliament would have had the right to participate in the decision process according to the Lisbon Treaty.[85]

The Decision is intended to concretise access, use, the rules on data protection and the time limit of storage, but it remains vague, mainly repeating the provisions of the Europol Decision and is therefore susceptible to broad interpretation. Persons who are allowed to access these data are for instance described as "duly authorised Europol staff" which is defined as "Europol staff designated by the Director to process personal data in accordance with this decision" which does not necessarily specify whether these persons have to be qualified or otherwise experienced in handling such data. Additional data protection guarantees for this special data category exceeding those of the Europol Decision are not offered.

The time limit for data during the pre-processing process should not exceed 6 months. Whether it is proportional to process data for a timespan of 6 months, which might later not be included in one of Europol's databases since they do not correspond to the tasks of Europol, seems to be doubtful. The risk of using the data for the simple reason that they are available, before sending them back to the party which inputted the information can not be denied. These data should be included in a separate database which is subject to control of a competent and independent authority. Further, before the establishment of such a database, the European Parliament should be involved in the decision process.

---

[83] See Chap. A III 1 d.

[84] Article 10 (4) Council Decision of 6 April 2009 establishing the European Police Office, OJ 2009, L-121/37.

[85] Decision of the Europol Management Board on the conditions related to the processing of data on the basis of Article 10 (4) of the Europol Decision, 15942/09, adopted the 30 November 2009, OJ 2009, L-348/1.

c) Use of Europol's Databases

aa) Accessing Actors

National Europol units, liaison officers, the Director, Deputy Directors and "duly empowered Europol staff" shall have direct access to the information stored in the EIS.[86] 121 Liaison officers are seconded from each of the Member States, from the US (the FBI, the US Secret Service, the Drug Enforcement Administration and the US Postal Inspection), Australia, Canada, Colombia, Croatia, Iceland, Norway, Switzerland, and Interpol. All of them are currently working at Europol.[87] Moreover, Canada and Russia seconded temporary local staff to Europol.[88]

On 1 April 2008, 1,479 persons using the EIS were known to Europol, whereby the largest amount of users came from Germany (502) compared to Belgium which is the second largest user (150) or France (62).[89]

Access to analysis work files is however more limited and only granted to the participants of the relevant analysis group which may consist of the Europol staff participating in this analysis work file, liaison officers and invited "experts" from the Member States, whereby, in any case, information resulting of the analysis shall be given to all Member States when it is of general nature and of a strategic type.[90] "Experts" from OLAF can also be associated to a work file when the latter concerns fraud.[91] Eurojust's participation in the establishment of analysis work files was increasingly facilitated by the adoption of a new Europol-Eurojust cooperation agreement from January 2010.[92] Finally, experts from third parties may be involved in the activities of an analysis work file.[93] Working arrangements which

[86] Article 13 (1) Council Decision of 6 April 2009 establishing the European Police Office, OJ 2009, L-121/37.

[87] As of December 2009, liaison officers from each of the Member States, the US (from the FBI, the US secret service, the drug enforcement administration and the US postal inspection), Australia, Canada, Colombia, Croatia, Iceland, Norway Switzerland, and Interpol work at Europol in The Hague, see Article 9 Council Decision of 6 April 2009 establishing the European Police Office, OJ 2009, L-121/37; Europol Review, annual general report on Europol activities 2009, p. 6; Den Boer et al. (2008), p. 110.

[88] Europol annual report 2008, p. 45.

[89] Submission by Europol, House of Lords, Select Committee on European Union, Call for Evidence, File no. 3100–174, 28 April 2008, section 5.1.1., pp. 16–17.

[90] Article 14 (2) and (4) Council Decision of 6 April 2009 establishing the European Police Office, OJ 2009, L-121/37.

[91] Ibid, Article 14 (8).

[92] Agreement between Europol and Eurojust which entered into force the 1 January 2010, the agreement is discussed in detail in Chap. C I 1 b.

[93] Article 14 (8) Council Decision of 6 April 2009 establishing the European Police Office, OJ 2009, L-121/37.

regulate the details have to be concluded with the third party, whereas Europol's supervisory body has to be consulted as regards the details of those agreements. However, the final decision lies with the Management Board, after approval of the Council.[94]

It is worth mentioning that the clause contained in the Europol Convention limiting access of national units to personal data relating to possible criminals in the EIS[95] to certain details relating to the identity, has been deleted in the Europol Decision.[96] Now, access to all data elements of persons who have not (yet) committed a crime is granted to the national units, the liaison officers, the Director, Deputy Directors, other Europol staff and "experts" without being restricted by the former restriction. In the light of this extension, compliance with the ECtHR case law, especially with the findings in *S. and Marper v. the United Kingdom* where the Strasbourg Court refers to the presumption of innocence and clearly demands a different treatment of personal data of persons convicted of criminal offences and those who are suspected, but were never convicted, is very doubtful.[97]

Additionally, full access to data of innocent persons also contradicts the aforementioned ECtHR approach of the cases *Weber and Saravia v. Germany* and *Association for European Integration and Human Rights and Ekimdzhiev v. Bulgaria*, in which the ECtHR only tolerated data transfer to other law enforcement authorities under the condition that specific facts – as opposed to mere factual indications – aroused the suspicion that someone had committed one of the offences.[98] Remembering the wording of Article 12 (1) lit. b Europol Decision which permits storing of data of persons "regarding whom there are factual indications" to "believe that they will commit a crime" and the aforementioned deletion of the former access restriction for personal data of those persons combined with the access to the data in question by 27 European law enforcement authorities plus the liaison officers from third states and international organisations, the conditions of the Europol Decision under which data of innocent individuals are stored do not correspond to the requirements stipulated in the ECtHR jurisprudence.

---

[94] Ibid, Article 23 (2).

[95] Persons referred to in Article 12 (1) lit. b Council Decision of 6 April 2009 establishing the European Police Office, OJ 2009, L-121/37.

[96] Article 7 (1) Europol Convention.

[97] *S. and Marper v. the United Kingdom*, Application nos. 30562/04 and 30566/04, judgment of 4 December 2008, para 122.

[98] *Weber and Saravia v. Germany*, Application no. 54934/00, admissibility decision of 29 June 2006, para 127, and *Association for European Integration and Human Rights and Ekimdzhiev v. Bulgaria*, Application no. 62540/00, judgment of 28 June 2007, para 89.

bb) Time Limits for Storing

In general, Europol stores data for as long "as it is necessary for the performance of its tasks".[99] Whereas the need for continued storage was reviewed on a yearly basis and had to be documented according to the Europol Convention, the decision about the continuing storage in the Europol Decision should be taken for the first time after 3 years.[100] A review on a yearly basis is not carried out. Bearing in mind that even data of innocent people are entered into Europol's databases, the extension to a 3 years review interval and the abolishment of the duty to document the need for continued storage certainly does not constitute an improvement for persons concerned compared to the former Europol Convention.

After the first 3 years, in the case that storing is still necessary from the point of view of the Member States or Europol, the inputting party (which decides on data entered in the EIS), or Europol (deciding on all other files) determines a prolongation of 3 years. If no decision is taken, the data will be deleted automatically. In case a Member State deletes data once transferred to Europol from its national database, Europol shall be informed, although it can nonetheless decide to continue the storage when it "has further interest" in them based on intelligence information going beyond the Member State's knowledge.[101] In particular this last sentence illustrates Europol's possibility to store data for an indefinite period of time, independently from the Member State's national investigations. In this case, it becomes extremely difficult for persons concerned to trace back in which of the existing databases his data were actually introduced and to which authority he might request access.

d) Individual Rights

According to Article 27 of the Europol Decision, Europol "shall take account" of the principles of Convention No. 108 and of Recommendation R (87) 15, in particular when processing and storing personal data.[102]

---

[99] Article 20 (1) Council Decision of 6 April 2009 establishing the European Police Office, OJ 2009, L-121/37.

[100] Compare Article 21 (3) Europol Convention with Article 20 (1) Council Decision of 6 April 2009 establishing the European Police Office, OJ 2009, L-121/37.

[101] Ibid, Article 20 (3).

[102] Ibid, Article 27 and recitals (11) and (14); with regard to a first analysis of the data protection standard of Europol compare Mayer (2001).

aa) Right of Access

Any person interested in knowing whether Europol processes his or her data may make a request to that effect to the authority appointed for that purpose in the relevant Member State.[103] The Member State's authority then has to send the request to Europol which must reply within a 3 month limit.

Under the former Europol Convention, one main problem arising in this context was related to Europol's hesitation to inform people whether their data had been processed at Europol.[104] Even in cases where data were not contained in one of Europol's information systems, applicants were kept in suspense by referring to the possible negative effects to the prevention and detection of crime.[105] As a result, the Europol annual report 2009 refers to over 300 responses to data subjects requests for access in 2009[106] without however specifying whether the requested information was given or not. This policy is partly understandable when taking into account that criminals could otherwise easily figure out whether their data are stored at Europol and in this way whether there are ongoing investigation on them, on the other hand, in case of requests from people not suspected of a crime or victims, a possibility to inform those groups would certainly enhance transparency at Europol in this regard.

Whether the restricted information policy vanishes within the new regulatory framework seems to be doubtful when looking at the vague formulation of the derogations under the Europol Decision. Access to information processed by Europol is only granted under several conditions: unless revealing this information does not contradict the fulfillment of the tasks of Europol, the protection of security and public order in the Member States, the prevention of crime, the protection of the rights and freedoms of third parties and the guarantee that any national investigation will not be jeopardised.[107] Therefore it is to be expected that even under the Europol Decision, Europol will find good reasons to reject a citizen's request.

Contradictory to principle 2.2. Recommendation R (87) 15 and the ECtHR case *Weber and Saravia v. Germany*, notification of the individuals whose data are stored at Europol as soon as police activities are no longer likely to be prejudiced is not foreseen.[108]

---

[103] Article 30 (1) and (2) Council Decision of 6 April 2009 establishing the European Police Office, OJ 2009, L-121/37.

[104] House of Lords, European Union Committee, 29th report of session 2007–2008, "Europol: coordinating the fight against serious and organised crime", published 12 November 2008, questions to the head of the JSB, p. 176, Q426.

[105] Ibid.

[106] Europol Review, annual general report on Europol activities 2009, p. 16.

[107] Article 30 (5) lit. a-d Council Decision of 6 April 2009 establishing the European Police Office, OJ 2009, L-121/37.

[108] *Weber and Saravia v. Germany*, Application no. 54934/00, admissibility decision of 29 June 2006, para 135.

bb) Supervision and Appeal

If Europol denies access or there has been no response to the request, judicial review is possible by appealing to the Joint Supervisory Body (JSB).[109] The members of the JSB are delegated from the data protection authorities from the Member States and meet four or five times a year.[110] A maximum of two members or representatives of each national supervisory body is appointed for 5 years by each Member State.

In cases relating to the requested access to data input by Europol in the EIS or data stored in the analysis work files (or in another system which can be established by Europol according to Article 10 Europol Decision), the JSB has the power to overrule a Europol decision by a majority of two-thirds of its members.[111] Regrettably, this possibility does not exist in appeal decisions related to the deletion or correction of data.[112]

In this context, it has to be taken into consideration that the main task of the JBS does not refer to the assurance of the access right of individuals. The JSB issues opinions and is responsible for various other tasks: additionally to the review of compliance with individual data protection rights at Europol, the JSB should monitor the permissibility of the transmission of data to third bodies as well as reviewing the activities of Europol in its exercise of its right to access and search data in databases such as the SIS II or the VIS.[113] The JSB must also produce a report after having carried out an annual inspection at Europol.[114] While, the JSB describes inspection as a key part of its work, it also functions as the aforementioned appeal committee. In this role, the JSB functions as a "quasi-judicial body", in particular regarding the fact that the rulings of the JSB's appeal committee are

---

[109] Article 32 (1) Council Decision of 6 April 2009 establishing the European Police Office, OJ 2009, L-121/37, overview of the possibilities to obtain judicial review against the acts of Europol, compare Kistner-Bahr (2010), pp. 139–188.

[110] House of Lords, European Union Committee, 29th report of session 2007–2008, "Europol: coordinating the fight against serious and organised crime", published 12 November 2008, questions to the head of the JSB, p. 171, Q411.

[111] Article 32 (4) Council Decision of 6 April 2009 establishing the European Police Office, OJ 2009, L-121/37.

[112] See House of Lords, European Union Committee, 29th report of session 2007–2008, "Europol: coordinating the fight against serious and organised crime", published 12 November 2008, questions to the head of the JSB, p. 174, Q417; the question referred to the Europol Convention, but Article 19 (7) Europol Convention regulating the right to overrule Europol decisions has not profoundly changed in the Europol Decision (Articles 31 and 32 (4) thereof).

[113] See Article 41 (5) (e) Council Decision 2007/533/JHA of 12 June 2007 on the establishment, operation and use of the second generation Schengen Information System (SIS II), OJ 2007, L-205/63.

[114] Article 34 (1) Council Decision of 6 April 2009 establishing the European Police Office, OJ 2009, L-121/37 and House of Lords, European Union Committee, 29th report of session 2007–2008, "Europol: coordinating the fight against serious and organised crime", published 12 November 2008, questions to the head of the JSB, p. 171, Q411.

final. However, an appeal against this decision should be possible if the conditions of Article 263 TFEU are fulfilled.[115] Additionally, the JSB also interprets and examines the implementation of the Europol Decision.[116]

The amount of tasks shows that only a minor part of the JSB's tasks is the examination of appeal decisions.[117] *Bernhard Petri* therefore doubts the impartiality of the JBS which is simultaneously involved in the establishment process of a file at Europol whereby it has an access right to documents, paper and data files, as well as being competent to examine questions concerning implementation and interpretation as regards Europol's data use and processing.[118] This might explain the low number of appeal decisions, amounting to not more than six, made from 2002 to 2008.[119] *Petri* assumes that, even if not directly mentioned in the Europol Convention (Article 27, now Article 36 Europol Decision), that the JSB acts like one of the organs of Europol and is integrated into the administration of Europol. One argument supporting this opinion might be that the JSB is financed by the budget of Europol.[120] He concludes that the JSB's "double function" as an integrated administrative organ as well as a supervisory body, influences the quality of the judicial review carried out by the JSB as the JSB may take part in the initial decision (the establishment of the file) leading to the interference.[121]

The JSB's involvement in the establishment process as well as in appeal decisions might also be seen as the exercise of double control at various levels which would not be exercised when limiting the JSB's responsibility to that of a mere appeal body. Data protection authorities often exercise multi leveled control:

---

[115] Article 34 (8) Council Decision of 6 April 2009 establishing the European Police Office, OJ 2009, L-121/37 and House of Lords, European Union Committee, 29th report of session 2007–2008, "Europol: coordinating the fight against serious and organised crime", published 12 November 2008, questions to the head of the JSB, p. 172, Q411; With regard to legal review after the Lisbon Treaty and the inclusion of Agencies within the scope of Article 263 TFEU, see Everling (2009), in particular pp. 77–78; Thiele (2010); Sauer (2010).

[116] Article 34 (3) Council Decision of 6 April 2009 establishing the European Police Office, OJ 2009, L-121/37; See also The fourth activity report of the Joint Supervisory Body of Europol, November 2006 – November 2008 and House of Lords, European Union Committee, 29th report of session 2007–2008, "Europol: coordinating the fight against serious and organised crime", published 12 November 2008, questions to the head of the JSB, p. 171, Q411.

[117] See Sect. II 1 d bb.

[118] Thomas Bernhard Petri refers to former Article 24 (2) and (3) Europol Convention which today is the amended Article 34 (2) and (3) Council Decision of 6 April 2009 establishing the European Police Office, OJ 2009, L-121/37; see Petri (2001), p. 147; see also Article 1 of the rules of procedure of JSB: http://www.eurojust.europa.eu/jsb-legalframework.htm#jsb-rules (accessed February 2011).

[119] http://europoljsb.consilium.europa.eu/ (accessed February 2011).

[120] Article 34 (10) Council Decision of 6 April 2009 establishing the European Police Office, OJ 2009, L-121/37 and The fourth activity report of the Joint Supervisory Body of Europol, November 2006–November 2008, point II.2.3, p. 31.

[121] Petri (2001), p. 147.

they participate in particular in notification procedures, in the legislative process as well as in appeal decisions.[122]

However, the JSB is composed of (only) two members of the national DPAs which have to exercise their functions at a national as well as a European level and shall nonetheless "not receive instructions from any other body".[123] This seems to be difficult especially in cases where the power of national DPAs and that of the JSB conflict. In general the JSB is only responsible for data held and used by Europol. When Member States use data on Europol's premises for bilateral exchanges, the JSB is not competent as the data are not subject to Europol's data protection rules.[124] Regarding the input and the retrieval of data in Europol's databases or from Europol's databases as well as the monitoring of Europol's national units and of the liaison officers, the national DPAs are competent to monitor compliance with the national data protection rules.[125] Moreover, there are significant differences regarding the monitoring powers of DPAs at the national level.[126] Some DPAs, for instance, do not have the power to audit the bodies they are monitoring, only when carrying out their responsibilities as a member of the JSB.[127]

The House of Lords report on Europol from November 2008 rightly points to the tension arising due to the separation of the relevant tasks of the Member States authorities and those of Europol.[128] The report shows that there were cases in which

[122] Articles 10 (2) and (4), 14 (1) and (8), 15 (4), 16 (2) and (3), 18, 22 (2) etc. Council Decision of 6 April 2009 establishing the European Police Office, OJ 2009, L-121/37.

[123] Article 34 (1) Council Decision of 6 April 2009 establishing the European Police Office, OJ 2009, L-121/37.

[124] House of Lords, European Union Committee, 29th report of session 2007–2008, "Europol: coordinating the fight against serious and organised crime", published 12 November 2008, p. 57, paragraph 225.

[125] Article 33 (1) Council Decision of 6 April 2009 establishing the European Police Office, OJ 2009, L-121/37.

[126] Answer given by the British Information Commissioner when he was asked whether a simplification of the supervision of the third pillar protection arrangements appears to be necessary, in: House of Lords report: 5th report of session 2004–05, "After Madrid: the EU's response to terrorism", published 8 March 2005, p. 22, para 45.

[127] Ibid.

[128] House of Lords, European Union Committee, 29th report of session 2007–2008, "Europol: coordinating the fight against serious and organised crime", published 12 November 2008, pp. 57 and 58, paras 225 and 226; the report gives the following example: "The Deputy Information Commissioner explained that information on a group of 33 young women was in the Europol information system. They were a ring of prostitutes and the information indicated that they were suspects of criminal activity. When we traced it back to the Member State, it appeared that actually they were probably victims of people trafficking, though it was possible that amongst the 33 one or two were part of the criminal ring behind the people trafficking. There was not sufficient evidence to hold them in the Europol system as suspects. Our report asked for those data to be deleted. When we came to do the inspection this year, those data were still in the system. We wrote to the data protection authority for the Member State, because the inputting of data is a matter for the Member State rather than Europol, and we also wrote to the Director reminding him that Europol have some responsibility as well. We set a time limit and those data were then quickly removed from the system".

the JSB asked to delete information entered by a Member State as it came to the conclusion that there were not sufficient facts to store this specific information in the EIS, but the relevant information stayed for over 1 year in the EIS due to the fact that neither Europol nor the relevant Member State felt responsible in this case.[129] This also means that Europol can dissociate itself from data protection liability when Europol is "only" providing the technology on which the data are transmitted from one Member State to another, as in this case, the legal responsibility stays with the Member States.[130] The example illustrates that supervision through the JSB does not extend to all of the data input in Europol's data systems. The twofold supervisory system is therefore inconsistent and does not guarantee the full respect of the data protection rights for all the data stored at Europol.

This situation, which stands exemplary for the cooperation in AFSJ information exchange, reflects the problems occurring in multi-level cooperation systems[131] in which fragmented responsibilities with an unclear distribution of powers can easily lead to the violation of individual rights. An intensified cooperation between the national DPAs and Europol's JSB is necessary to improve the current situation.

Further problems arise as regards the internal communication between Europol and the JSB concerning the information about the work in so called "target groups" which are specific groups within analysis work files in which a smaller number of Member States cooperate looking at particular characteristics of criminal activity.[132]

Finally, supervision of Europol is further carried out by an internal Data Protection Officer (DPO) whose mandate was elevated to a statutory basis by the Europol Decision.[133] Article 28 Europol Decision introduced this post, which already existed under the Europol Convention although it was not a requirement. The DPO, as an employee of Europol, is appointed by Europol's Management Board on the proposal of Europol's Director and consequently does not exercise external control.

Although his work may play an important part in the daily work of Europol, particularly in situations where quick decisions on data security are necessary, it is debatable whether an internal DPO acts totally independently from the orders of those who appointed him and provide his remuneration. Therefore and because of

---

[129] See example in footnote before.

[130] House of Lords, European Union Committee, 29th report of session 2007–2008, "Europol: coordinating the fight against serious and organised crime", published 12 November 2008, questions to the head of the JSB, p. 175, Q425.

[131] To the problems arising out of data protection issues in relation to cooperation between Europol and Member States, compare Gusy (2008), in particular p. 272.

[132] Article 34 (3) Council Decision of 6 April 2009 establishing the European Police Office, OJ 2009, L-121/37 and House of Lords, European Union Committee, 29th report of session 2007–2008, "Europol: coordinating the fight against serious and organised crime", published 12 November 2008, questions to the head of the JSB, p. 175, Q423.

[133] Articles 28 and 34 Council Decision of 6 April 2009 establishing the European Police Office, OJ 2009, L-121/37; he is supported by 8 staff members.

the fact that his annual appraisal will be done by the Director, the head of the JSB considers the DPO as a "quasi-independent" body, which excludes total independence from orders of the Director.[134]

Regrettably, guarantees regarding his independence, such as safeguards for appointment and dismissal are not included in the Europol Decision.[135] According to Article 28 (5) of the Europol Decision, the Management Board is urged to adopt implementing rules concerning these questions.[136] However, the fact that, the body towards the DPO shall gain independence, adopts those rules contradicts by its very nature the independency requirement demanded by Article 8 Charter of Fundamental Rights, principle 1.1. Recommendation R (87) 15 as well as by the EU Commission[137] and stipulated in the ECtHR's and the EU's case law[138] which calls for an independent supervisory body established outside the police sector.

When considering the phrasing of these implementing rules, independency is granted within the limits of the performance of his duties which includes that he "may not receive any instructions that would interfere" with his functions.[139] In this context, it must taken into account that "according to the organisational interest of Europol, the Data Protection Officer may also assume other functions/duties within Europol, providing arrangements for the conduct of these separate issues are made so as to avoid any conflict of interest".[140] Even if these "arrangements" should uphold the principle of independence,[141] a closer examination having regard to all of the Articles of the implementing rules, does not allow to qualify the internal DPO as independent.

Principally, the so called "escalation procedure", the procedure to be followed in case the DPO detects that a data protection provision of the Europol Decision has not been complied with, reveals the DPO's dependence on Europol's director as well as the Management Board.[142] For instance, in case of a discovery of nonconformity with the Europol Decision, before getting in contact with the JSB, the

---

[134] House of Lords, European Union Committee, 29th report of session 2007–2008, "Europol: coordinating the fight against serious and organised crime", published 12 November 2008, questions to the head of the JSB, p. 178, Q437.

[135] See to this point: opinion of the European Data Protection Supervisor on the proposal for a Council Decision establishing the European Police Office (Europol) – COM(2006) 817 final, OJ 2007, C-255/13, para 60.

[136] Implementing rules concerning the Data Protection Officer, Europol Management Board, The Hague 23 September 2009.

[137] See case C-518/07, *Commission v. Germany*, judgment of 9 March 2010.

[138] See for instance ECtHR case *Segerstedt-Wilberg and others v. Sweden*, Application no. 62332/00, judgment of 6 June 2006, paras 62–68 and 103, and C-518/07, *Commission v. Germany*, judgment of 9 March 2010.

[139] Article 4 Implementing rules concerning the Data Protection Officer, Europol Management Board, The Hague 23 September 2009.

[140] Ibid, Article 2 (3).

[141] Ibid, Article 2 (3).

[142] Ibid, Article 11.

DPO must first inform the Director, requiring him to resolve the non-compliance within a specific time. Providing that this attempt fails, he should secondly inform the Management Board and agree on a specified time for response. In the end, only under the condition that the Management Board does not resolve the non-compliance, the DPO is allowed to refer the matter to Europol's JSB.[143]

Another astonishing provision is entailed in Article 10 of the implementing rules: in case of "obvious misuse of the right to request an inquiry, in particular in cases of repeated requests of the same data subject with similar content", the DPO is not obliged to report back to an individual making a request to perform an inquiry in a specific case.[144] Regrettably, it is not further elucidated what else, apart from repeated requests, an obvious misuse could be, but the simple reading of this provision seems to indicate a certain risk of arbitrariness.

Finally, guarantees referring to his dismissal exist to the extent that he may be only dismissed by Europol's Management Board if he no longer fulfils the conditions required for the performance of his duties.[145] Regrettably, the JSB has no right to object the possible dismissal decision of the Management Board; its Members are only notified in advance about it.

cc) Data Security

Article 35 Europol Decision stipulates specific rules relating to data security involving the "necessary technical and organisational measures to ensure the implementation of this Decision".[146] Like the wording of this first paragraph of Article 35 of the Europol Decision suggests, the implementation of data security measures depends on the necessity of these measures. The latter are considered as "necessary where the effort they involve is proportionate to the objective they are designed to achieve in terms of protection".[147] Thus, data security rules are subjected to a necessity criterion whose content leaves open certain questions. Which body within Europol decides about the effort to be made and about the proportionality of this effort? Europol's JSB is not mentioned in this context, but Article 10 (3) Europol Decision refers to the Management Board which shall ensure that the measures and principles referred to in Article 35 Europol Decision are properly implemented. Consequently, the Management Board decides about the implementation of data security rules and in this way about the question to what extent the effort appears to be proportionate and as a result about the effort to be

[143] Ibid, Article 11.

[144] Ibid, Article 10 (1).

[145] Ibid, Article 2 (1).

[146] Article 35 (1) Council Decision of 6 April 2009 establishing the European Police Office, OJ 2009, L-121/37.

[147] Ibid, Article 35 (1).

made to adopt a specific security measure. The internal DPO or the JSB are not involved.

Under the condition of having met this unconvincing necessity criterion, Article 35 (2) details important measures Europol has to implement. Among others, it has to deny unauthorised persons access to data processing equipment, prevent all forms of unauthorised use, modification, transfer or inspection of stored data and control the users and the access to the data.[148] Additionally, Europol has to ensure communication control by making it possible to verify and establish to which bodies personal data might be or have been transmitted, to control the input and to ensure recovery of the data in the event of interruption of one of the data processing systems.[149] Reliability and integrity of the system must additionally be guaranteed.[150] A provision according to which it is possible to verify what data has been retrieved from the databases, when, by whom and for what purpose (control of data recording) is unfortunately missing in the list of data security rules.

e) Access of Europol to European, National and International Databases

Article 21 Europol Decision regulating the access to data from other information systems has been newly introduced through the Europol Decision.[151] It supports the interlinks between the European, national and international databases and involves possible computerised access to databases such as the other European information systems (VIS, CIS, SIS etc.) and the national databases of the Member States.[152] As a general rule, Europol is allowed to retrieve data directly from these systems "by such means if that is necessary for the performance of its tasks".[153] It is worth mentioning that additional specifications regarding the conditions of access to and use of data from other information systems are not entailed in the Europol Decision.

Although Article 21 Europol Decision is embedded in Chapter III of the Europol Decision relating to "common provisions on information sharing", the largest part of the provisions entailed in this chapter refers to the relation between Member States and Europol, not including Europol's access to other European, national or international information systems. In consequence, according to the logic of the Europol Decision, all questions related to the inclusion of data from other information systems in Europol's databases have to be stipulated in the relevant instruments regulating the exchange of the information concerned. To what extent these

[148] Ibid, Article 35 (2) (a)-(e) and (h).

[149] Ibid, Article 35 (2) (f), (g) and (i).

[150] Ibid, Article 35 (2) (j).

[151] Ibid, Article 21.

[152] See further below in Chap. C II.

[153] Article 21 Council Decision of 6 April 2009 establishing the European Police Office, OJ 2009, L-121/37.

instruments (principally exchange agreements or Council Decisions allowing for exchange) effectively entail such provisions is examined in Chap. C.

As regards Europol's access to international or other national databases, this provision mainly seems to be directed to the access to Interpol's database. Direct access to a third state's police or judicial database seems to be rather questionable. Existing international agreements are restricted to mutual data exchange while excluding direct computerised access to a third party's database.[154]

All in all, Article 21 Europol Decision is a very wide and general formulated provision permitting systematic and broad access to other law enforcement related information systems. The potential factual and legal problems arising out of the fact that the concrete access to, the use of the mentioned systems and the respective data protection provisions shall be governed by the applicable rules of the relevant exchange instruments, are analysed in more detail in Chap. C in context of the data exchange partners of Europol.[155] In the same context, the details of Europol's agreements enabling access to other databases are additionally considered.

f) Processing of Information Originating from Private Parties and Private Persons

The use of information originating from private parties or natural persons is a further innovation of the Europol Decision and follows the general tendency in police cooperation to use data collected by private actors for law enforcement purposes which causes fundamental data protection problems regarding the purpose limitation principle, discussed in Chap. D III 2.[156]

According to Article 25 Europol Decision, the purpose for which Europol may process data coming from private parties is formulated in the same broad terms as the access to other databases, namely: Europol may process the relevant data "in so far as it is necessary for the legitimate performance of its tasks". Private parties are described as bodies governed by private law, in particular companies, firms, business associations or non-profit organisations which might be credit card companies or similar actors in possession of possible valuable data. The Europol Decision mainly distinguishes three categories of private parties from which Europol may receive information: private parties established under the law of a Member State, private parties governed by the law of a third state with which

[154] See further below Chap. C II 1–4.

[155] See Chap. C II 1–4.

[156] Chapter D III 2 and Opinion of the European Data Protection Supervisor on the proposal for a Council Decision establishing the European Police Office (Europol) – COM(2006) 817 final, OJ 2007, C-255/13, para 17.

Europol has concluded a cooperation agreement and private parties established under the law of a third state with which Europol has no cooperation agreement.[157]

Personal data originating from the first and the second category of private parties may only be processed when they were transmitted from the Member States national unit or the third state's contact point and are in accordance with the national law of the Member State or with the third state's cooperation agreement.[158] A similar provision exists for information originating from individuals meaning private persons.[159] Whereas Europol is not allowed to contact private parties of the Member Sates directly to retrieve information, there is no such provision regarding private parties of third states.[160] However, a teleological interpretation must come to the conclusion that if it is forbidden to contact private parties of the Member Sates, it must all the more be forbidden to make contact with private parties in third countries.

To obtain data from private parties of a third state with which Europol has no cooperation agreement, Europol must either conclude so called memoranda of understanding confirming the legality of the collection and transmission or the private party must be on a list drawn up by the Europol Management Board (after having obtained the opinion of the JSB).[161]

Despite the low data protection level of countries which are for that reason not qualified to conclude a data exchange agreement with Europol, special independent internal control through the Data Protection Officer or the JSB is not provided for by the Europol Decision. Certainly, one of the JSB's tasks relate to the general monitoring of the permissibility of the data originating from Europol, but there are no additional tasks concerning this particularly sensitive area. However, it is not possible to gather completely new information via this dubious method, given that use of these data is restricted to information which relates to other data already available in Europol's processing systems or to a query made by a national unit within one of the systems.[162]

---

[157] Article 25 (3) Council Decision of 6 April 2009 establishing the European Police Office, OJ 2009, L-121/37; additionally, Article 25 (4) Europol Decision allows to store and process data from publicly available sources, such as media, public data or commercial intelligence providers.

[158] Article 25 (3) lit. a and b Council Decision of 6 April 2009 establishing the European Police Office, OJ 2009, L-121/37.

[159] Ibid, Article 25 (5).

[160] Compare Article 25 (3) lit. a with lit. b Council Decision of 6 April 2009 establishing the European Police Office, OJ 2009, L-121/37.

[161] Article 25 (3) lit. c Council Decision of 6 April 2009 establishing the European Police Office, OJ 2009, L-121/37; the Management Board is composed of one representative of each Member State and one of the Commission, compare Article 37 Council Decision of 6 April 2009 establishing the European Police Office, OJ 2009, L-121/37.

[162] Article 25 (6) Council Decision of 6 April 2009 establishing the European Police Office, OJ 2009, L-121/37.

Nonetheless, it seems to be hard to imagine that received information which might be significant but is not yet included in Europol's databases will be sent back to the private party in the third state which provided the information, pretending that Europol never took notice of possibly interesting information. Supplementary supervision of these activities would therefore be useful to control this sensitive activity open to abuse.

At least, the data protection responsibility, meaning the legality of the collection, of the transmission and of the input, the accuracy, the up-to-date nature as well as the verification of storage time-limits, related to data originating from third states (second and third category), lies with Europol.[163] For data originating from private parties or persons in Member States, the responsibility lies with the Member States.[164]

Besides the mentioned concerns as regards the purpose limitation principle in this context, the data protection provisions of the use of data originating from private parties seem to be inadequate. The question of how the Member States could guarantee and control conformity with data protection provisions as regards data coming from private parties or persons entered in Europol's information systems is worth mentioning.

Further problems arise concerning the data protection provisions which shall be applicable in this context: the rules governing the private sector of the relevant Member State (because the data were taken from a private actor) or the data protection rules regulating law enforcement measures in the Member States? The influence of national data protection authorities designated to monitor data transfer in this context is very limited which may lead to serious data protection gaps regarding this special category of affected data.

Finally *de Moor* and *Vermeulen* add for consideration that the Europol Decision in itself does not constitute a sufficient legal basis for private parties to transmit information to Europol.[165]

g) Transmission of Data to Third Bodies

In 2007, Europol exchanged 21,028 messages with third parties.[166] Generally, Europol can transfer the data stored in its information systems to third parties

[163] Article 25 (6) referring to Article 29 (1) b Council Decision of 6 April 2009 establishing the European Police Office, OJ 2009, L-121/37.

[164] Article 29 (1) b regulating the responsibility in data protection matters only refers to data originating from private parties, not private persons, but in very general terms, Europol should be responsible for data communicated to it "by third parties" which may include data coming from private persons.

[165] De Moor and Vermeulen (2010), in particular p. 1108.

[166] Submission by Europol, House of Lords, Select Committee on European Union, Call for Evidence, File no. 3100–174, 28 April 2008, section 6.1., pp. 20–21; an overview about the cooperation with third states provide Gless and Zerbes (2008).

with which it has concluded an exchange agreement.[167] Expressly mentioned in Articles 22 and 23 of the Europol Decision are European Union institutions, bodies or agencies, such as Eurojust, OLAF, Frontex, CEPOL, the European Central Bank and the EMCDDA[168] as well as third states[169] and international organisations such as Interpol. Prior to the transfer, Member States have to give their consent concerning data entered by them. This consent may be given in general terms or can be subject to specific conditions. Regrettably, these consent arrangements are not published or otherwise available. When transferring the data, Europol shall be responsible for the legality of the transmission, assuring that the use of the transferred data is restricted to the purpose of transmission, not however to the purpose for which they were collected, i.e when applying a strict purpose principle, violations of this principle cannot be excluded.[170]

Hitherto, Europol distinguished two classes of agreements with third parties, so called strategic and operational agreements.

The first category includes agreements concerning the exchange of strategic and technical data not allowing for personal data exchange.[171] Operational agreements additionally provide for personal data exchange.[172]

So far, strategic agreements are concluded with EU bodies such as the European Central Bank, the Commission, EMCDDA, OLAF and Frontex[173] and with third states and international organisations such as Albania, Bosnia and Herzegovina, Colombia, Former Yugoslav Republic of Macedonia (FYROM), Moldova, Russia, Turkey, the World Customs Organisation as well as the United Nations Office on Drugs and Crime.[174] Operational agreements exist with Australia, Canada, Colombia, Croatia, Iceland, Norway, Switzerland, the United States of America as well as with Eurojust and Interpol.[175] Operational Agreements with Israel, Russia and Monaco are projected.[176]

[167] Derogations are provided for in Articles 22 (3), 23 (3), (4) and (8) Council Decision of 6 April 2009 establishing the European Police Office, OJ 2009, L-121/37.

[168] European Monitoring Centre for Drugs and Drug Addiction (EMCDDA).

[169] Currently, Europol has concluded 14 agreements with third states: Australia, Canada, Croatia, Iceland, Norway, Switzerland, United States of America, Albania, Bosnia and Herzegovina, Colombia, Former Yugoslav Republic of Macedonia, Moldova, Russia and Turkey.

[170] Article 24 (2) Council Decision of 6 April 2009 establishing the European Police Office, OJ 2009, L-121/37.

[171] Article 1 (g) Council Decision 2009/934/JHA of 30 November 2009 adopting the implementing rules governing Europol's relations with partners, including the exchange of personal and classified information, OJ 2009, L-325/6.

[172] Ibid, Article 1 (h).

[173] See Chap. C I 3.

[174] http://www.europol.europa.eu/index.asp?page=agreements (accessed February 2011).

[175] http://www.europol.europa.eu/index.asp?page=agreements (accessed February 2011).

[176] See report 51st meeting of the JSB of Europol, Brussels 12 October 2009, points 6 and 12.

The Europol Decision, in so far as it regards third states or international organisations, obliges the Council to determine a list of states and organisations with which Europol should conclude agreements which may include the exchange of personal data.[177] Additionally, the Council has adopted implementing rules governing Europol's relation with partners.[178] Prior to the conclusion of the agreement and after having consulted the Management Board as well as having obtained the opinion of the JSB (as far as the agreement concerns personal data exchange), the Council must give its approval.[179]

Like the Council Implementing Decision 2009/936 on analysis work files, the Council's list of states and organisations with which Europol shall conclude agreements as well as the implementing rules governing Europol's relation with partners[180] were also adopted 1 day before the entry into force of the Lisbon Treaty which would have demanded a mandatory participation of the European Parliament in the legislative process.[181] The European Parliament previously rejected the draft list of states and organisations with 633 votes against, 17 in favour and 7 abstentions, but, ultimately subjected to the rules of the EU Treaty, it could not avoid the adoption of the list.[182] This list expressly refers to the aforementioned states and organisations with which Europol has already concluded an operational agreement, although it additionally mentions countries not necessarily having the same data protection standard as the European Union, such as: Bolivia, Bosnia and Herzegovina, China, Colombia, India, Israel, Liechtenstein, Moldova, Monaco, Montenegro, Morocco, Peru, Russia, Serbia, Turkey, Ukraine, ICPO-Interpol, United Nations Office on Drugs and Crime (UNODC) and the World Customs Organisation.[183]

Before Europol is allowed to transfer personal data to third states or international organisations, it must be satisfied that an "adequate level of data protection" is

[177] Article 23 (2) Council Decision of 6 April 2009 establishing the European Police Office, OJ 2009, L-121/37 and Council Decision 2009/935/JHA of 30 November 2009 determining the list of third states and organisations with which Europol shall conclude agreements, OJ 2009, L-325/12.

[178] Council Decision 2009/934/JHA of 30 November 2009 adopting the implementing rules governing Europol's relations with partners, including the exchange of personal and classified information, OJ 2009, L-325/6.

[179] Article 23 (2) Council Decision of 6 April 2009 establishing the European Police Office, OJ 2009, L-121/37.

[180] Council Decision 2009/934/JHA of 30 November 2009 adopting the implementing rules governing Europol's relations with partners, including the exchange of personal and classified information, OJ 2009, L-325/6.

[181] Council Decision 2009/935/JHA of 30 November 2009 determining the list of third states and organisations with which Europol shall conclude agreements, OJ 2009, L-325/12.

[182] http://www.europarl.europa.eu/oeil/FindByProcnum.do?lang=en&procnum=CNS/2009/0809 (accessed February 2011).

[183] See Council Decision 2009/935/JHA of 30 November 2009 determining the list of third states and organisations with which Europol shall conclude agreements, OJ 2009, L-325/12.

ensured by this entity.[184] At first glance, the adequacy assessment seems to be very similar to its parallel provision of Directive 95/46[185] which takes into account the circumstances of the transfer, the nature of the data as well as the purpose and the duration of the intended processing; however, the data protection standards in reality are lower than the first reading might indicate which is due to the fact that the adequacy assessment refers to the guarantees given by the third body and varies thus from one agreement to another. Additionally, Europol has to consider the data protection provisions of the entity concerned as well as whether or not the entity has agreed to "specific conditions required by Europol concerning the data".[186]

The Europol Decision does not clearly specify which body (Management Board, Council or Commission) is responsible to asses the level of data protection, though, in any case, the JSB's role is limited to an advisory one.[187] However, unfettered transfer is not permitted: Article 9 (4) (a) of the implementing rules governing Europol's relations with partners requires that the transmission to third parties shall only be permissible, where it is "necessary in *individual cases* for the purpose of preventing or combating criminal offences".[188] Transmission of information to third parties which are not included in the Council list might nevertheless take place, in so far as "it is absolutely necessary in individual cases for the purpose of preventing or combating criminal offences in respect of which Europol is competent".[189]

The provisions regarding data exchange agreements, or so called "working arrangements", concluded with EU bodies according to Article 22 Europol Decision, are even less strict. They can be concluded after approval of the Management Board which, in case the agreement concerns personal data exchange, has to consult the JSB.[190] Europol can generously derogate from this rule "in so far as that is necessary for the performance of its tasks" which opens a back door for data exchange without having concluded agreements regulating data protection issues in this context.[191]

---

[184] Article 23 (6) lit. b Council Decision of 6 April 2009 establishing the European Police Office, OJ 2009, L-121/37.

[185] Article 25 (2) of Directive 95/46.

[186] This wording does not necessarily refer to data protection guarantees. Europol can also derogate from the former provision and transmit data or classified information in cases where the director considers the transmission to be absolutely necessary to safeguard the essential interest of a Member State or to prevent an "imminent danger associated with crime or terrorist offences"; in this case, the Director assesses the adequacy of the level of data protection.

[187] See Articles 23 (2) and (9) Council Decision of 6 April 2009 establishing the European Police Office, OJ 2009, L-121/37.

[188] Article 9 (4) (a) Council Decision 2009/934/JHA of 30 November 2009 adopting the implementing rules governing Europol's relations with partners, including the exchange of personal and classified information, OJ 2009, L-325/6; emphasis added.

[189] Article 13 Council Decision 2009/934/JHA of 30 November 2009 adopting the implementing rules governing Europol's relations with partners, including the exchange of personal and classified information, OJ 2009, L-325/6.

[190] Article 22 (2) Council Decision of 6 April 2009 establishing the European Police Office, OJ 2009, L-121/37.

[191] Ibid, Article 22 (3).

Finally, an agreement on confidentiality is required for the transmission of classified information to EU bodies or to third states or organisations.[192]

Some basic specifications of Europol's transfer provisions in terms of data protection arrangements applicable to third party agreements are nonetheless contained in the implementing rules governing Europol's relations with partners. These rules are in some cases astonishingly detailed although formulated with a certain hesitation as regards the enforcement of the self-imposed standards. A good example is the careful wording used in Article 17 (2) of the implementing rules: "In negotiating agreements, Europol *shall make* every *effort* to ensure that, *where possible*, a third State designates one competent authority to act as the national contact point [. . .]" to carry out mutual data exchange.[193] The implementing rules are planned to apply to future data exchange with possible partners and were therefore not yet considered in the current agreements analysed in Chap. C I. However, its provisions are the first rules intended to regulate inner AFSJ data exchange and are for that reason are worth mentioning.

Referring to Europol's responsibility for the transmission, the implementing rules lay down for instance that in both cases (transmission to EU bodies or other third parties), Europol should insist that the recipients of the data give a commitment obliging them to use the transferred data only for the purposes for which they were transmitted as well as that further transmission of the data remains limited to the authorities mentioned in the agreement and takes place only under the same conditions as applicable in the agreement.[194] Personal data requested without any indication as to the purpose of, and reason for the requests, shall not be transmitted.[195] Further the undertaking shall oblige the third party to correct or delete inaccurate, incorrect or outdated data or data which should not have been transmitted by Europol.[196] The undertaking shall further provide that onward transmission of the received data shall only take place with the consent of Europol and only in exceptional cases, after the authorisation of the Director, if he considers transfer as absolutely necessary to guarantee the essential interests of the Member States concerned or the interests of preventing imminent danger associated with crime or terrorist offences.[197]

As follows from the foregoing, Europol has various possibilities to transfer data to third states and bodies. The list of states with which Europol should conclude agreements was adopted against the votes of the European Parliament, but will nevertheless build the framework for future cooperation in this area. The

---

[192] Ibid, Article 23 (7).

[193] Article 17 (2) Council Decision 2009/934/JHA of 30 November 2009 adopting the implementing rules governing Europol's relations with partners, including the exchange of personal and classified information, OJ 2009, L-325/6; emphasis added.

[194] Ibid, Articles 10 and 17 (3).

[195] Ibid, Article 15 (1).

[196] Ibid, Article 16 (1).

[197] Ibid, Article 18 (2).

implementing rules governing Europol's relations with partners are going in the right direction, although its provisions are sometimes formulated with a certain hesitation in terms of creating binding rules and do still need to undergo a "reality check".

h) Conclusion: Data Protection at Europol – Still Some Efforts to Make

The assessment of the regulatory framework of the most important actor in the AFSJ has shown that the data protection standard and the supervision as regards data processing in the AFSJ sometimes significantly lags behind the criteria stipulated in the Charter of Fundamental Rights, the ECtHR's and the EU's case law, the Council of Europe Convention No. 108 and Recommendation R (87) 15.

The extension of Europol's powers regarding the collection as well as the processing and transmission of data in the new Europol Decision of 2010 did not keep pace with important improvements in its data protection framework. The rapid adoption of the new Europol Decision, including several implementing decisions, before the entry into force of the Lisbon Treaty, was clearly used to avoid the participation of the European Parliament in the legislative process. Although having been adopted in this rather undemocratic way, this instrument governs Europol's current legislative framework. Future amendments to it will nonetheless be subject to the ordinary legislative procedure in which the Parliament has to give its consent to possible modifications. However, the non participation of the European Parliament is reflected in the relatively weak data protection rules stipulated in the Europol Decision.

Particular concerns are raised by the far reaching entry conditions in the databases of Europol. The fact that the inclusion in the EIS is already possible in case of factual indications or reasonable grounds to believe that a person will commit criminal offences,[198] challenges the ECtHR's foreseeability criterion and its jurisdiction in *Weber and Saravia v. Germany* and *Association for European Integration and Human Rights and Ekimdzhiev v. Bulgaria* in which the Strasbourg Court tolerated data transfer to other law enforcement authorities only under the condition that specific facts – as opposed to mere factual indications – aroused the suspicion that someone had committed one of the offences.[199]

In view of the far reaching access possibilities and the various actors using the EIS (national units, over 120 liaison officers, the Director, Deputy Directors, other Europol staff and "experts"), the inclusion of possible criminals in the EIS contradicts the ECtHR jurisprudence in *S. and Marper v. the United Kingdom* in

---

[198] Article 12 (1) lit. b Council Decision of 6 April 2009 establishing the European Police Office, OJ 2009, L-121/37.

[199] *Weber and Saravia v. Germany*, Application no. 54934/00, admissibility decision of 29 June 2006, para 127, and *Association for European Integration and Human Rights and Ekimdzhiev v. Bulgaria*, Application no. 62540/00, judgment of 28 June 2007, para 89.

which the Strasbourg Court emphasised a different treatment of data of persons who have been convicted of an offence and those who have never been.[200]

Against this background, the non separation of data of victims and witnesses from data of criminals in Europol's analysis work files raises further concern. Europol stores up to 69 different data categories about different persons in the same analysis work file. The new Europol Decision permits the establishment of new data processing systems which will hopefully include greater specifications with regard to the different categories of persons stored in their files.

Europol's hesitation to inform people whether their data had been processed at Europol is another shortcoming with regard to the enforcement of individual rights. As additionally no notification of the person concerned is foreseen that personal data are included in Europol's databases, the enforcement of data protection rights remains fictional.

Supervisory problems occur due to the outdated organisation of supervision. The JSB should fulfil various tasks at the same time (appeal body, supervise the data exchange, deal with access requests, review Europol's databases etc.). In addition, tension between their work at national as well as at EU level may arise. A new supervisory structure is therefore urgently needed.

The access of Europol to other databases was newly regulated in a far reaching manner in the new Europol Decision. Europol is allowed to retrieve data directly from these systems "by such means if that is necessary for the performance of its tasks".[201] Further restrictions are not applicable. Europol's possibilities to transfer data to third states and bodies are equally extensive. The list of states with which Europol should conclude agreements was even adopted against the votes of the European Parliament, but will nevertheless build the framework for future cooperation in this area.

Summarising, as Europol's databases play a central role in exchanging and distributing information, in particular as it is the actor having the most connections to the other AFSJ agencies and to the European information systems, the examples given by the illustration of Europol's legal framework shall serve as background information when looking at the other agencies and bodies as well as at the connections between the AFSJ agencies, and in this context, at the data protection standard in the agreements concluded between different AFSJ agencies (Chap. C I) as well as between the AFSJ agencies and the European information systems (Chap. C II).

---

[200] *S. and Marper v. the United Kingdom*, Application nos. 30562/04 and 30566/04, judgment of 4 December 2008, para 122.

[201] Article 21 Council Decision of 6 April 2009 establishing the European Police Office, OJ 2009, L-121/37.

2. *Eurojust*

Eurojust was established in 2002 by a Council Decision (Eurojust Decision 2002) as a judicial coordination unit and now functions as an agency.[202] Its mandate and especially its data processing provisions and control mechanisms were changed in 2009 and are briefly illustrated below.

a) Tasks and Mandate

Pursuant to Article 3 Council Decision 2009/426 (the Eurojust Decision), Eurojust's main objectives are:

- To stimulate and improve the coordination between the competent authorities of the Member States during investigations and prosecutions in those States, taking into account any request emanating from a competent authority of a Member State and any information provided by any body competent by virtue of provisions adopted within the framework of the Treaties;
- To improve cooperation between the competent authorities of the Member States, in particular by facilitating the execution of requests for, and decisions on, judicial cooperation, including decisions regarding instruments giving effect to the principle of mutual recognition;
- To otherwise support the competent authorities of the Member States in order to render their investigations and prosecutions more effective.[203]

According to the amended Eurojust Decision, Eurojust's mandate refers to "the types of crime and the offences in respect of which Europol is at all times competent to act".[204] Thus the far-reaching list of crimes for which Europol is responsible and which is laid down in Article 3 of the Europol Decision as well as in its annex expressly applies additionally to Eurojust.[205]

Provisions about the specific crimes expressly mentioned in the 2002 Eurojust Decision were deleted according to the 2009 Eurojust Decision, most probably not least of all to calm the simmering conflict between two agencies, OLAF and

[202] Council Decision 2002/187/JHA of 28 February 2002 setting up Eurojust with a view to reinforcing the fight against serious crime, OJ 2002, L-63/1, in the following: Eurojust Decision 2002; the first steps to establish Eurojust were already taken in 1999 at the Tampere summit, but Eurojust's final legal framework was not adopted before 2002; to the development and the tasks of Eurojust, see Fawzy (2005); Mitsilegas (2009), pp. 187–192; Haratsch et al. (2010), pp. 507 and 508; Borchardt (2010), pp. 589–590. Seong (2005), pp. 66–80.

[203] Article 3 Council Decision 2009/426/JHA of 16 December 2008 on the strengthening of Eurojust and amending Decision 2002/187/JHA setting up Eurojust with a view to reinforcing the fight against serious crime, OJ 2009, L-138/4, in the following: Eurojust Decision.

[204] Article 4 (1) Eurojust Decision.

[205] Compare above Sect. II 1 a.

Eurojust, relating to the competence to examine fraud affecting the Community's financial interests.[206] Even though this offence is not particularly mentioned any longer, the prosecution of fraud still constitutes an important element of Eurojust's work.[207]

The members of Eurojust are prosecutors, judges or police officers seconded by each Member State principally supporting the coordination and cooperation of investigations and prosecutions of crime which affect two or more Member States.[208] Its members, who operate in the form of a College (consisting of national members[209]) or in their role as a national member, can not oblige Member States to undertake investigations. However Member States have to justify their decision when refusing to comply with a request of Eurojust.[210] The division of responsibilities between Eurojust as a College and Eurojust's national members is clarified in Articles 5, 6 and 7 of the Eurojust Decision: Eurojust acts as a College when it is requested by the Member States, when the case involves investigations or prosecution affecting the Union level or when a general question relating to the achievement of its objectives is involved, as well as when it is specially provided for in the Eurojust Decision. National members are primarily involved in bilateral cases.[211]

In this context, it is noteworthy that since the entry into force of the Lisbon Treaty, Article 85 (1) TFEU has significantly reinforced the role of Eurojust by enlarging its future functions from merely those of a coordinative mission to the initiation of criminal investigations and dispute settlement as regards conflicts of jurisdiction.[212]

---

[206] Article 4 (1) (b) Eurojust Decision 2002 referred to computer crimes, fraud and corruption and any criminal offences affecting the European's financial interests, laundering of the proceeds of crime, environmental crime and participation in a criminal organisation.

[207] Compare Eurojust's annual report 2008, in particular pp. 16–17, http://www.eurojust.europa.eu/press_releases/annual_reports/2008/Annual_Report_2008_EN.pdf (accessed February 2011).

[208] Article 2 Eurojust Decision; according to the aforementioned Council Decision on the exchange of information and cooperation concerning terrorist offences which leads to the entering to information related to terroristic offences into the databases of Europol, national correspondent for terrorism matters are additionally seconded to Eurojust, Article 2 (2) of Council Decision 2005/671/JHA of 20 September 2005 on the exchange of information and cooperation concerning terrorist offences, OJ 2005, L 253/22, compare Sect. II 1 b dd.

[209] Article 10 (1) Eurojust Decision.

[210] Article 8 Eurojust Decision and Article 5 (1) (a) and (b) Eurojust Decision (not amended). The College is composed of 27 national member of Eurojust (one from each Member State).

[211] According to Articles 6 (1) (a) and 7 (1) (a) Eurojust Decision national members, as well as Eurojust as a College may ask the competent authorities of the Member States concerned, giving its reasons, to: (i) undertake an investigation or prosecution of specific acts; (ii) accept that one of them may be in a better position to undertake an investigation or to prosecute specific acts; (iii) coordinate between the competent authorities of the Member States concerned; (iv) set up a joint investigation team in keeping with the relevant cooperation instruments; (v) provide it with any information that is necessary for it to carry out its tasks; Eurojust's national members my additionally asks Member States to give its reasons to take special investigative measures as well as to take any other measure justified for the investigation or prosecution.

[212] Article 85 (1) (a) TFEU.

However, before Eurojust's tasks are extended, a further important provision of Article 85 TFEU relates to the legislative procedure establishing Eurojust's legislative framework and restricts over-ambitious changes in Eurojust's competences: whereas according to the EU Treaty the Council alone could decide on modifications of Eurojust's tasks and structure, Article 85 TFEU now provides for mandatory participation of the European Parliament by using the ordinary legislative procedure (comparable to the provisions concerning future modifications in Europol's legislative framework) when adopting future changes in the legislative framework concerning Eurojust.

An additional significant change arises through the integration of the former third pillar in the TFEU. Eurojust became a body of the European Union to which the provisions of general application of the TFEU, in particular Article 16 TFEU, fully apply.

Additionally, the possibility to transform Eurojust into a European Public Prosecutor's Office, an intensely disputed topic during the last years, is now provided for in Article 86 TFEU.[213] Its establishment would further clarify Eurojust's relation to OLAF which partially has an overlapping mandate.[214]

However, before the European Parliament could exercise its control functions over the former third pillar body, similar to Europol, Eurojust's legal basis was hastily adopted in the end of 2008 and entered into force in June 2009 shortly before the Lisbon Treaty took effect, a fact which delays the full application of important changes such as the judicial control by the European Court of Justice[215] or parliamentary scrutiny.

b) Data Processing and Time Limit for Storing

Eurojust manages the so called Case Management System (CMS) which involves Eurojust's temporary work files and an index system, both containing personal data.[216] The CMS is intended to support and coordinate investigations and prosecutions including Eurojust's participation, "in particular by cross-referencing

[213] To the development of the European Public Prosecutor's Office and its overlaps with OLAF's functions, see Staicu et al. (2008), pp. 177–192; Callies (2010), pp. 451 and 452; Mitsilegas (2009), pp. 229–232; White (2010), in particular 92–94; Nilsson (2000); Fawzy (2005), pp. 113–119; Seong (2005), pp. 80–95.

[214] To this problem, see Chap. C I 4.

[215] To the question of limited judicial control of the European Court of Justice, see case C-160/03 *Spain v. Eurojust*, judgment of 15 March 2005, were the Court dismissed the action as inadmissible as it did not find itself competent to judge over a call for applications issued by Eurojust and concluded that this call could not be the subject of an action for annulment under Article 230 EC (whereby the Court did not follow the alternative opinion of AG *Poiares Maduro*).

[216] Article 16 Eurojust Decision.

of information".[217] Additionally, it shall facilitate the Member States' access to information on ongoing investigations and prosecutions.

The data elements contained in the CMS were subject to significant changes in the Eurojust Decision amended in 2009.[218] A good example is the modification of Article 15 (1) of the Eurojust Decision: in contrast to the former Eurojust Decision of 2002 according to which only data of persons who were already subject of criminal investigations or prosecution could be processed, it is now allowed to process personal data in Eurojust's CMS from individuals *suspected* of having committed or having taken part in a criminal offence.[219]

Further, in addition to the already quite elaborate list of data elements[220] which could be processed by Eurojust, new types of information, such as DNA profiles, fingerprints or data related to internet connections, have been added in Article 15 of the Eurojust Decision embracing now up to 30 data elements.[221] Noticeably, after criticism from the EDPS, the proposition to introduce an open list not even specifying the data elements to be stored, provided for in the draft Eurojust Decision, was abandoned.

The processing of personal data of witnesses and victims, however, is restricted to a smaller number of components. Only in exceptional cases may Eurojust also process more than the 11 listed data elements.[222] Such a decision shall be taken jointly by at least two national members, and the data protection officer has to be informed.[223] To introduce witness or victim data in the CMS, the College must decide about the inclusion.[224]

---

[217] Ibid, Article 16 (2).

[218] See EDPS opinion on the Council Decision concerning the strengthening of Eurojust and amending Decision 2002/187/JHA of 5 December 2008, OJ 2008, C-310/1, p. 3, para 13, which makes references to Articles 9 (4), 9a, 12 (15), 13a, 15, 26 (1) (a) and 27a Eurojust Decision.

[219] Compare amendment of Article 15 (1) Eurojust Decision.

[220] Article 15 Eurojust Decision lists: name(s), date and place of birth, nationality, sex, place of residence, profession and whereabouts of the person concerned, social security number, driving licences, information concerning legal persons if it includes information relating to the individual who is subject of the investigation or prosecution, bank accounts and other accounts and the description, the nature and the date of the offences involving them as well as the facts pointing to an international extension of the case and details relating to alleged membership of a criminal organisation.

[221] Compare Article 15 of the Eurojust Decision 2002 with Article 15 of the Eurojust Decision of 2009.

[222] Article 15 (2) Eurojust Decision lists: (a) surname, maiden name, given names and any alias or assumed names; (b) date and place of birth; (c) nationality; (d) sex; (e) place of residence, profession and whereabouts of the person concerned; (f) the description and nature of the offences involving them, the date on which they were committed, the criminal category of the offences and the progress of the investigations.

[223] Article 15 (3) Eurojust Decision.

[224] Article 17 (2) rules of procedure on the processing and the protection of personal data at Eurojust, OJ 2005, C-68/1.

Similar to Europol, data at Eurojust shall generally be stored for only "as long as it is necessary for the achievement of its objectives".[225] Data may not be stored beyond the date on which the persons was acquitted and the decision became final, 3 years after the date on which the judicial decision of the last Member State concerned by the investigation or prosecution became final or the date on which Eurojust and the Member States concerned agreed or established that it was no longer necessary for Eurojust to coordinate investigations and prosecutions (unless there is an obligation to provide Eurojust with this information)[226] and finally 3 years after the transmission from the Member States.[227] However, when the mentioned deadlines expire, Eurojust has to carry out a review examining whether the storage period should be extended in order to enable it "to achieve its objectives".[228] Such reviews shall be carried out on a 3-year basis.[229] Regrettably, as a maximum time limit for storage is not given, persons concerned are not able to foresee the maximum length of the storage period.

c) Individual Rights (Access, Correction and Information)

While gradually more data elements are entered and processed in Eurojust's database according to the new Eurojust Decision from 2009, the right of access to data stored therein as well as the correction and deletion rights have not been changed.[230] This is more than astonishing as this would have been a possibility to harmonise Eurojust's different data protection provisions which are currently applicable and additionally laid down in the rules of procedure regarding the processing and protection of personal data from 2005 as well as in the additional rules defining some specific aspects of the application of the latter rules from 2006.[231]

As a result of the various applicable rules, individuals depend on not always enforceable provisions stipulated in multiple sources. In relation to Europol, particularly Eurojust's rules of procedure on the processing of personal data include a relatively extensive, but complicated data protection framework.[232] Besides

[225] Article 21 (1) Eurojust Decision (not amended).

[226] Compare Article 21 (2) Eurojust Decision.

[227] Ibid, Article 21 (2) (d).

[228] Ibid, Article 21 (3) (b).

[229] Ibid, Article 21 (3).

[230] Compare Articles 19 and 20 Eurojust Decision 2002 with the Eurojust Decision of 2009.

[231] Rules of procedure on the processing and the protection of personal data at Eurojust, OJ 2005, C-68/1 and additional rules defining some specific aspects of the application of the rules on the processing and protection of personal data at Eurojust to non-case related operation, http://www.eurojust.europa.eu/official_documents/eju_dp_rules.htm (accessed February 2011).

[232] Rules of procedure on the processing and the protection of personal data at Eurojust, OJ 2005, C-68/1.

provisions on the purpose limitation of the processed data, the lawfulness and fairness of the processing and the data quality, the rules of procedure regulate individual access and correction rights.[233]

When considering that the legal value of these rules can not be compared to the status of the Eurojust Decision, the non inclusion of the data protection rights of the rules of procedure in the amended Eurojust Decision is regrettable and may hinder in certain cases the effective enforcement of individual data protection rights. The legal value of these rules of procedure should be taken into consideration when looking at the provisions entailed therein in the following. Firstly, however, the rights entailed in the Eurojust Decision will be briefly illustrated.

The access procedure, provided for in Article 19 of the 2002 Eurojust Decision, was maintained in the amended Eurojust Decision. When reading this article, the process to access documents stored in Eurojust's database seems to be rather complex since Eurojust almost completely delegated the access procedure to the Member States: individuals wishing to exercise their access right have to make a request to the "authority appointed for this purpose in that Member State" (normally the national DPA) and that authority should then refer to Eurojust.[234] The applicable law in this context is the law of the Member State in which the individual has made its request or in the case that Eurojust can determine which authority in a state originally transmitted the data, this Member State is able to require that the right of access is exercised in compliance with law of the relevant Member State.[235] The national member seconded from the Member State concerned by the request shall then deal with the request and "reach a decision on Eurojust's behalf" and shall inform the data protection officer.[236] Only if this assessment fails can the matter be referred to Eurojust's College which needs a two-third majority to make a decision on the request.[237] The data protection officer shall carry out additional checks and inform the national member of its findings. Finally, the data protection officer communicates the final decision taken by the national member to the applicant who may, when he is not satisfied with the given answer, appeal before Eurojust's supervisory body (JSB).[238]

In addition to the already fairly complicated access procedure, there are three very general reasons to deny access to the data: access can be denied when such

[233] Articles 5–9, rules of procedure on the processing and the protection of personal data at Eurojust, OJ 2005, C-68/1.

[234] Article 19 (2) Eurojust Decision; Article 21 (1) of the rules of procedure on the processing and the protection of personal data at Eurojust, OJ 2005, C-68/1 however states that individuals "wishing to exercise their rights as a data subject" may also address their request directly to Eurojust which then transmits the request to the national member.

[235] Article 19 (3) Eurojust Decision.

[236] Article 19 (6) Eurojust Decision and Article 21 (3) rules of procedure on the processing and the protection of personal data at Eurojust, OJ 2005, C-68/1.

[237] Article 19 (6) Eurojust Decision.

[238] See next Sect. II 2 d.

access may jeopardise one of Eurojust's activities, any national investigation or the rights and freedoms of third parties.[239]

It has to be added that the rules of procedure on data processing from 2005 also allow individual requests to be addressed directly to Eurojust, but this improvement was for some inexplicable reason not integrated in the Eurojust Decision from 2009, creating doubts on the binding force as well as the application of this provision.[240]

In the case that an individual succeeds in obtaining the information that Eurojust is in possession of his data, he can ask Eurojust to correct, block or delete the relevant data under the condition that they are incorrect or incomplete or their input or storage contravenes the Eurojust Decision.[241] If Eurojust corrects, blocks or deletes the data of an applicant, it must notify the requesting person.[242] When the requesting person is not satisfied with Eurojust's reply, he may also appeal to Eurojust's JSB.

A Member State's competent authority or a national member may also request to correct, block or delete data processed at Eurojust when the data were transmitted or entered by the relevant Member State.[243] In the case that Eurojust notices that data being processed at Eurojust are incorrect or incomplete or that their input or storage is in breach of the Eurojust Decision, it must also block, delete or correct the data. In the last two cases, Eurojust has the obligation to notify the suppliers and addressees instantaneously.[244]

A welcomed provision which has regrettably not found its way into the amended Eurojust Decision is entailed in Article 8 of the rules of procedure on data processing at Eurojust. It refers to a right of information of the data subject including information on the purpose of processing, the identity of the data controller, the recipients, the right of access and rectification and even further information under the following circumstances[245]: information must generally be provided at the moment of collection of the data from the data subject, when receiving data from a third party, when recording the personal data or if general disclosure or disclosure to a third party are envisaged and as soon as the "purpose of the processing, national investigations and prosecutions and the rights and freedoms of third parties are not likely to be jeopardised".[246] Additional restrictions

[239] Article 19 (4) Eurojust Decision.

[240] Article 21 rules of procedure on the processing and the protection of personal data at Eurojust, OJ 2005, C-68/1.

[241] Article 20 (1) Eurojust Decision.

[242] Ibid, Article 20 (2).

[243] Ibid, Article 20 (4).

[244] Ibid, Article 20 (5).

[245] Article 8 rules of procedure on the processing and the protection of personal data at Eurojust, OJ 2005, C-68/1.

[246] Article 8 rules of procedure on the processing and the protection of personal data at Eurojust, OJ 2005, C-68/1.

nevertheless apply to this right when dealing with case-related data processing.[247] Pursuant to Article 19 (1) rules of procedure on data processing at Eurojust, information can only be provided as soon as it is apparent that its disclosure does not undermine the fulfilment of Eurojust's tasks, prosecutions in which Eurojust assists, a monitoring inspection or regularly tasks connected with the exercise of an official prosecuting or judicial authority. All in all, although this right is restricted, its mere existence constitutes an improvement when comparing it to Europol's data protection structure. It nevertheless would have been desirable if this provision had been introduced in the 2009 amended Eurojust Decision to clarify its importance and to meet ECtHR requirements stipulated *Weber and Saravia v. Germany*[248] or in Principle 2.2. of Recommendation R (87) 15 which relate to a right to be informed when police activities are no longer to be prejudiced.

d) Supervision

Monitoring at Eurojust is organised in a twofold way: external supervision is carried out by Eurojust's JSB and internal supervision by the data protection officer.

The external supervisory body of Eurojust, the JSB, is composed of three permanent members appointed by an assembly of judges. Each judge in the assembly is nominated by a Member State.[249] When the JSB first started to operate, there was criticism that JSB members must be members of the judiciary and might not necessarily have enough data protection expertise to fulfil their tasks.[250] However in the meantime, when looking at the various tasks of the JSB of Eurojust which are similar to those of Europol's, the main problem of the body seems to be the fate of being understaffed.[251] It seems to be very questionable how three judges who meet approximately four times a year could be able to monitor the following responsibilities provided for in the Eurojust Decision: supervise Eurojust's activities, ensure proper data processing, hear appeals, inspect Eurojust, assess the adequate data

---

[247] Case related means when the data are linked to the operational tasks of Eurojust (Articles 5, 6 and 7 Eurojust Decision); the definition can be found in the rules of procedure on the processing and the protection of personal data at Eurojust, OJ 2005, C-68/1, Article 3 (2).

[248] *Weber and Saravia v. Germany*, Application no. 54934/00, admissibility decision of 29 June 2006, para 135.

[249] Article 23 Eurojust Decision and Act of the Joint Supervisory Body of Eurojust of 23 June 2009 laying down its rules of procedure, Article 3, http://www.eurojust.europa.eu/official_documents/eju_jsb_act.htm (accessed February 2011).

[250] House of Lords Eurojust report, European Union Committee, 23rd report of session 2003–04, "Judicial cooperation in the EU: the role of Eurojust", published 21 July 2004, p. 24.

[251] See annual report 2008 of Eurojust's JSB, pp. 5–12, and House of Lords Eurojust report, European Union Committee, 23th report of session 2003–04, "Judicial cooperation in the EU: the role of Eurojust", published 21 July 2004, p. 24; for the JSB report, see http://www.eurojust.europa.eu/press_releases/annual_reports/JSB/JSB_ActivityReport2008.pdf (accessed February 2011).

protection standard with regard to third parties, issue opinions on cooperation agreements and supervise compliance with the data protection provisions of the agreements as well as monitor the liaison officers posted to third states.[252]

The restricted personal resources might be the explanation for its rather slim annual report of 2008 embracing only 12 pages whereby only one very short section vaguely criticises "difficulties in complying with some rules in the CMS [Case Management System], some instances of non-compliance with Eurojust's security rules and non-compliance in the processing of manual files".[253] Serious problems may be hidden behind such a phrase, but details of the mentioned difficulties are not further specified in the annual report. Although the JSB generally recommends an increased awareness of the right of the data subjects to access their data,[254] it does not publish its inspection report which is the source of these observations and whose publication might help to contribute to a better respect of individual rights at Eurojust by urging the agency to explain its criticised access policy.

The awareness of individuals regarding the tasks of Eurojust's JSB also seems to be very low, especially when considering that the body received no appeals in 2008 and only one in 2007, but registered 1,193 cases in 2008.[255] The fact that Eurojust's JSB neither has a webpage, nor publishes its opinions or appeal decisions does not raise hopes for a future awareness increase in awareness.

However, the mandate of the three permanent members of the JSB was extended in the new Eurojust Decision from 18 months to 3 years assuring at least more personal stability.[256]

Since the establishment of Eurojust in 2002, the body is additionally supervised by an internal Data Protection Officer whose tasks are regulated in Article 17 of Eurojust Decision 2009 (Article 17 of Eurojust Decision 2002). As the latter provision served as an example for the statutory introduction of a Data Protection Officer at Europol in 2010, most of the aforementioned criticism applies as well to this function.[257] Identical to Eurojust's JSB, the Data Protection Officer neither has a webpage nor publishes information on the internet about data protection rights at

[252] The Act of the Joint Supervisory Body of Eurojust of 23 June 2009 laying down its rules of procedure, Article 7, http://www.eurojust.europa.eu/official_documents/eju_jsb_act.htm (accessed February 2011) stipulates that for carrying out checks on Eurojust locations, Eurojust's JSB may be assisted by experts, however it is not specified to what extent such cooperation has already taken place or how many external experts may be designated.

[253] Annual report 2008 of Eurojust's JSB, pp. 6–7, http://www.eurojust.europa.eu/press_releases/annual_reports/JSB/JSB_ActivityReport2008.pdf (accessed February 2011).

[254] Annual report 2008 of Eurojust's JSB, pp. 6–7, http://www.eurojust.europa.eu/press_releases/annual_reports/JSB/JSB_ActivityReport2008.pdf (accessed February 2011).

[255] Annual report 2008 of Eurojust's JSB, p. 12 and annual report of Eurojust 2008, p. 13, http://www.eurojust.europa.eu/press_annual.htm (accessed February 2011).

[256] Article 23 (1) Eurojust Decision.

[257] With regard to Europol, see above Sect. II 1 d bb.

Eurojust. Cooperation between Eurojust's JSB and the data protection officer is foreseen "where appropriate".[258]

All in all, there are quite a few possibilities to reinforce supervision at Eurojust. The introduction of an internal Data Protection Officer can be seen as a step in the right direction, but has to be accompanied by guarantees relating to her independency. Personnel resources at Eurojust's JSB should be increased in order to effectively monitor the amount of tasks with which it is entrusted. The publication of its inspection report would contribute to an increased transparency as it regards the respect of data protection rights at Eurojust. Considering the increased amount of data processed at Eurojust as well as the 1,372 cases dealt with in 2009 at Eurojust,[259] the current supervisory situation does not offer an effective protection against the abuse of personal data.

e) Relation to Third Parties

The capacity of Eurojust to establish relations with other EU bodies was also revised and is now regulated in Articles 26 to 27a of the Eurojust Decision. These provisions are very similar to the provisions in the Europol Decision regulating third party relations, with one exception: the Eurojust Decision from 2009 does not include provisions regulating the computerised access to data from other information systems.[260]

According to Article 26 (2) of the Eurojust Decision, Eurojust shall conclude agreements or working arrangements with Europol, OLAF, Frontex as well as the Council's Joint Situation Centre[261] regulating the exchange of information, including personal data. A new Article 26 (a) Eurojust Decision has been introduced referring to the conclusion of data exchange agreements with third states and international organisations, in particular Interpol. These agreements mainly deal with information exchange and the secondment of liaison officers from third states to Eurojust and vice versa.[262] In the case that cooperation agreements deal with personal data exchange, they may only be concluded when the body concerned is subject to Convention No. 108 of the Council of Europe or when "an adequate level of protection" is ensured by the third party. Further requirements are the prior consultation with the JSB of Eurojust concerning the data protection provisions and the approval by the Council acting by qualified majority.[263] An important

258 Article 6 (6) Act of the Joint Supervisory Body of Eurojust of 23 June 2009 laying down its rules of procedure, http://www.eurojust.europa.eu/official_documents/eju_jsb_act.htm (accessed February 2011).

259 Eurojust annual report 2009, p. 50.

260 The analysis of Europol's relation to third parties can be found in Sect. II 1 e–g.

261 The Council's Joint Situation Centre is briefly analysed in Sect. II 5.

262 Article 26a (2) and 27a Eurojust Decision, see also: Coninsx and da Mota (2009).

263 Article 26a (2) Eurojust Decision.

improvement compared to previously concluded agreements is the introduction of provisions on the monitoring of the implementation, "including implementation of the rules on data protection", of the concluded agreements within the text of the agreements.[264]

Whereas the mentioned provisions on data exchange in the context of previously concluded agreements entail the obligation to respect basic data protection principles, there is a great uncertainty in the context of data exchange taking place in the absence of a formerly concluded agreement.

Article 26a (5) to (9) together with Article 27 (1) of the Eurojust Decision regulate cases relating to the receipt of information from third parties in so far "as this is necessary for the legitimate performance" of Eurojust's tasks. The transmission of personal data in this case is indeed generally prohibited, however two exemptions to this general rule are made: first, Eurojust may transmit personal data to third states after having concluded an agreement and transfer "is necessary in individual cases for the purposes of preventing or combating criminal offences for which Eurojust is competent"[265] and the Member State which originally provided the information has given its consent to the transfer[266] and secondly, if the aforementioned conditions are not fulfilled, "a national member may, acting in his capacity as a competent national authority and in conformity with the provisions of his own national law, by way of exemption and with the sole aim of taking urgent measures to counter imminent serious danger threatening a person or public security, carry out an exchange of information involving personal data".[267] In the latter case, the national member shall be responsible for the legality of authorising the transmission and in both cases the recipient should give an undertaking obliging him to use the data only for the purpose for which they were communicated.[268]

As follows from the foregoing, the responsibility of personal data transmission without the prior conclusion of an agreement is completely shifted to the national member of Eurojust, which usually excludes the supervision of such sensitive transfers by the JSB. As, in addition, no notification of the national DPA is provided in this case, it remains questionable how this kind of data transfer is actually supervised. Whereas in the case of failure or likelihood of failure to comply with the minimum data protection requirement in an existing agreement Eurojust's JSB has to be immediately informed and the JSB may then prevent further data exchange,[269] in case of exceptional data exchange this information requirement is missing. A simple provision providing for a notification of the JSB in case of an

[264] Ibid, Article 26a (4).

[265] Ibid, Article 26a (7) (a).

[266] Ibid, Article 27 (1).

[267] Ibid, Article 26a (9).

[268] Ibid, Articles 26a (9) and 27 (2).

[269] Ibid, Article 26a (8).

exceptional data exchange (which then could contact the national DPA) would assure effective control of the data transfer even in such an extraordinary situation.

All in all, as regards the relation to third states, in comparison with the 2002 Eurojust Decision, the Eurojust Decision of 2009 considerably extended the possibilities to exchange personal data with third states.[270] Unfortunately, the competences of Eurojust's JSB as well as the data protection officer in this context were not modified to the same extent. Both actors do not dispose of "real" rights in terms of the right to oppose Eurojust's decisions or to make final decisions about issues concerning data protection. Mere consultation constraints instead of co-decision duties characterise their influence.

f) Conclusion: Eurojust's Complicated Data Protection Framework – No Tool to Channel Increasing Operational Powers

The ongoing extension of Eurojust's tasks and responsibilities, which lead to the implication of Eurojust in investigations as well as to increasing data processing and data exchange with third bodies, follows Europol's expansion trend and reveals an alarming development which is not accompanied by corresponding progresses regarding the data protection rights of the individuals concerned.

As in the case of Europol, Eurojust's legal framework was recently changed in 2009. The adoption of the Lisbon Treaty, in particular its Article 85 (1) TFEU, has additionally reinforced the role of Eurojust by extending its future functions from merely those of a coordinative mission to the initiation of criminal investigations and dispute settlement as regards conflicts of jurisdiction.[271]

The changes in 2009 related amongst others to the enlargement of Eurojust's data processing possibilities. The agency is now allowed to process personal data in its CMS from individuals suspected of having committed or having taken part in a criminal offence.[272]

As the expansion trend with regard to Europol has shown, gradually more data elements are entered and processed in Eurojust's database according to the new Eurojust Decision. In contrast, data protection rights, such as the right of access to data stored in the CMS or the correction and deletion rights have not been changed.[273] Important data protection rights are still stipulated in the rules of procedure regarding the processing and protection of personal data of Eurojust and in the additional rules defining some specific aspects of the application of the latter rules from 2006. These rules have not found their way into the new Eurojust

---

[270] See EDPS opinion on the Council Decision concerning the strengthening of Eurojust and amending Decision 2002/187/JHA of 5 December 2008, OJ 2008, C-310/1, p. 3, para 13, which makes references to Articles 9 (4), 9a, 12 (15), 13a, 15, 26 (1) (a) and 27a Eurojust Decision.

[271] Article 85 (1) (a) TFEU.

[272] Compare amendment of Article 15 (1) Eurojust Decision.

[273] Compare Articles 19 and 20 Eurojust Decision 2002 with the Eurojust Decision of 2009.

decision of 2009. This is regrettable as this would have been a possibility to harmonise Eurojust's different data protection rules which are currently applicable.

In relation to the supervisory structure, similar problems as with regard to Europol arise. The same outdated JSB approach applies also in context with Eurojust. Three judges who meet approximately four times a year should monitor Eurojust. Its tasks relate to the supervision of Eurojust's activities (ensure proper data processing, hear appeals, inspect Eurojust) and the assessment of the adequate data protection standard with regard to third parties. In addition, the JSB is supposed to issue opinions on cooperation agreements and supervise compliance with the data protection provisions of the agreements as well as monitor the liaison officers posted to third states.[274] As the relation to third states and the possibility to exchange data with third bodies was considerably extended by the Eurojust Decision of 2009, this particular task will increase in future. In view of this amount of tasks, a revision of the supervisory structure is urgently required. The personal as well as procedural underpinning of the current JSB should be reconsidered.

In summary, the enthusiasm of the Council in combination with the Commission to adopt the mentioned wide ranging modifications before the entry into force of the Lisbon Treaty clearly demonstrates the political will to expand Eurojust without being "disturbed" by civil rights admonishers. The inclusion of broader data protection rights, still stipulated in the rules of procedure on data processing within the next Eurojust Decision plus a personal as well as procedural reinforcement of Eurojust's JSB would be desirable steps towards a more efficient and enforceable data protection framework for Eurojust.

3. *OLAF*

OLAF, the European Anti-Fraud Office, was established in 1999 by a Commission Decision in response to the failure of the Santer Commission due to the internal mismanagement of Community funds in the same year.[275] As mentioned in the introduction, it is affiliated to the Commission and consequently not constituted as an agency such as Europol or Eurojust analysed above, although it fulfils investigative tasks and exchanges data with the mentioned agencies and is therefore analysed hereinafter.

---

[274] The Act of the Joint Supervisory Body of Eurojust of 23 June 2009 laying down its rules of procedure, Article 7, http://www.eurojust.europa.eu/official_documents/eju_jsb_act.htm (accessed February 2011) stipulates that for carrying out checks on Eurojust locations, Eurojust's JSB may be assisted by experts, however it is not specified to what extent such cooperation has already taken place or how many external experts may be designated.

[275] Commission Decision 1999/352/EC of 28 April 1999 establishing the European Anti-Fraud Office (OLAF), OJ 1999 L-136/20; for details on OLAF's history and current framework, see Murawska (2008); Cullen (2004); Hecker (2010), pp. 129; Seong (2005), pp. 56–65.

a) Tasks

A range of legal bases including regulations, decisions, and sectoral legal bases regulate OLAF's tasks.[276] Over the years, the list of regulations and decisions allowing external and internal investigations as well as data transfer was progressively extended and eventually became hardly comprehensible.[277]

The "basic" instruments however are Commission Decision 1999/352/EC establishing OLAF as well as Regulation 1073/1999 dealing with investigations conducted by OLAF.[278] Pursuant to the latter, OLAF shall investigate internal and external fraud and any other illegal activity affecting the financial interest of the European Community. For carrying out external "administrative investigations"[279] OLAF thereby exercises the Commission's power in this field.[280] Whereas OLAF

---

[276] Some examples are: Commission Decision 1999/352/EC of 28 April 1999 establishing the European Anti-Fraud Office (OLAF), OJ 1999, L-136/20; Regulation (Euratom) No. 1074/99 of the European Parliament and of the Council of 25 May 1999 concerning investigations by the European Anti-Fraud Office (OLAF), OJ 1999 L-136/8; Council Regulation (Euratom, EC) No 2185/96 of 11 November 1996 concerning on-the-spot checks and inspections carried out by the Commission in order to protect the European Communities' financial interests against fraud and other irregularities, OJ 1996, L-292/2; Regulation (EC) No. 1073/1999 of the European Parliament and of the Council of 25 May 1999 concerning investigations conducted by the European Anti-Fraud Office (OLAF), OJ 1999, L-136/31; Council Regulation (EC, Euratom) No 2988/95 of 18 December 1995 on the protection of the European Communities financial interests, OJ 1995, L-312/1; Regulation (EC) No. 766/2008 of the European Parliament and of the Council of 9 July 2008 amending Council Regulation (EC) No 515/97 on mutual assistance between the administrative authorities of the Member States and cooperation between the latter and the Commission to ensure the correct application of the law on customs and agricultural matters, OJ 2008, L-218/48; Article 37 of Council Regulation (EC) No. 1290/2005 of 21 June 2005 on the financing of the common agricultural policy, OJ 2005, L-209/1; Article 72 of Council Regulation (EC) No. 1083/2006 of 11 July 2006 laying down general provisions for the European Regional Development Fund, the European Social Fund and the Cohesion Fund, repealing Regulation (EC) No 1260/1999, OJ 2006, L-210/25; Article 87 of the financial regulation on contractual provisions, OJ 2002, L-248/1; Regulation (Euratom) No. 1074/99 of the European Parliament and of the Council of 25 May 1999 concerning investigations by the European Anti-Fraud Office (OLAF), OJ 1999, L-136/1.

[277] Van den Wyngaert (2004), in particular p. 295.

[278] Commission Decision 1999/352/EC of 28 April 1999 establishing the European Anti-Fraud Office (OLAF), OJ 1999 L-136/20 and Regulation (EC) No. 1073/1999 of the European Parliament and the Council of 25 May 1999 concerning investigation conducted by the European Anti-Fraud Office (OLAF), OJ 1999, L-136/31.

[279] Which means "all inspections, checks and other measures undertaken by employees of the Office in performance of their duties [. . .]" of OLAF, Article 2 Regulation (EC) No. 1073/1999 of the European Parliament and the Council of 25 May 1999 concerning investigation conducted by the European Anti-Fraud Office (OLAF), OJ 1999, L-136/31.

[280] Article 2 (1) of Commission Decision 1999/352/EC of 28 April 1999 establishing the European Anti-Fraud Office (OLAF), OJ 1999, L-136/20 and Council Regulation (Euratom, EC) No. 2185/96 of 11 November 1996 concerning on-the-spot checks and inspections carried out by the Commission in order to protect the European Communities' financial interests against fraud and other irregularities, OJ 1996, L-292/2.

forms a special unit within the Commission, its legal basis provides for complete independence when exercising its investigative powers.[281] The term "external investigations" refers to "on-the-spot" inspections and checks carried out in the Member States as well as in third countries, whereby the latter depend on a cooperation agreement in force.[282]

Internal investigations are carried out within all the European institutions, bodies, offices and agencies, including the EU's Central Bank as well as the European Investment Bank.[283] A further important task of OLAF relates to the forwarding of information obtained in the course of external or internal investigations to the competent (administrative and judicial) authorities of the Member States[284] as well as the operation of the so called Customs Information System (CIS) to detect administrative offences in former first pillar legislation (customs and agriculture).[285]

b) Judicial Review and Individual Rights

In respect of the analysis regarding OLAF's data processing in the following, a particular problem at OLAF concerning its judicial accountability will be briefly discussed in order to identify the framework in which OLAF processes personal data.

Due to OLAF's attachment to the Commission and its simultaneous mission to conduct internal investigations, its legislative framework and "hybrid status of

[281] Article 3 of Commission Decision 1999/352/EC of 28 April 1999 establishing the European Anti-Fraud Office (OLAF), OJ 1999, L-136/20.

[282] Article 3 Regulation (EC) No. 1073/1999 of the European Parliament and the Council of 25 May 1999 concerning investigation conducted by the European Anti-Fraud Office (OLAF), OJ 1999, L-136/31; for details on external investigations, see Murawska (2008), pp. 103–110.

[283] Article 4 Regulation (EC) No 1073/1999 of the European Parliament and the Council of 25 May 1999 concerning investigation conducted by the European Anti-Fraud Office (OLAF), OJ 1999, L-136/31; For the power to conduct investigations at the EU's Central as well as at the European Investment Bank, see cases C-13/00, *Commission v. European Investment Bank*, judgment of 10 July 2003 and C-11/00, *Commission v. European Central Bank*, judgment of 10 July 2003. For details on internal investigations, see Murawska (2008), pp. 111–113.

[284] Gonzalez-Herrero Gonzalez (2009).

[285] Article 10 Regulation (EC) No. 1073/1999 of the European Parliament and of the Council of 25 May 1999 concerning investigations conducted by the European Anti-Fraud Office (OLAF), OJ 1999, L-136/31 and Regulation (EC) No. 766/2008 of the European Parliament and of the Council of 9 July 2008 amending Council Regulation (EC) No 515/97 on mutual assistance between the administrative authorities of the Member States and cooperation between the latter and the Commission to ensure the correct application of the law on customs and agricultural matters, OJ 2008, L-218/48.

investigative autonomy"[286] has raised criticism since OLAF's beginnings.[287] Additionally its investigative powers together with its alleged "untouchable" judicial status, which was affirmed in several cases, particularly in the *Tillack v. Commission* case,[288] cast further doubts on OLAF's compliance with the rule of law.[289] The question whether OLAF's investigations form part of an administrative or rather of a criminal procedure is part of an ongoing legal dispute.[290] Additionally, the lack of access to OLAF's files at any stage during the investigation procedure has raised several problems during the last years.[291]

OLAF's ambiguous judicial responsibility regarding its accountability in investigative acts was moderately reversed in the last years in cases such as *Nikolaou v. Commission*, *Yves Franchet and Daniel Byk v. Commmision*[292] as well as *Violetti and others v. Commission*.[293] The central problem arising in those cases always involves the question whether OLAF's decision to forward possible incriminating information to national judicial authorities constitutes a challengeable act or a mere preparatory act which does not lead to a distinct change in the legal position of the applicant and consequently does not produce adverse effects.

In *Violetti and others v. Commission* the Civil Service Tribunal took an interesting approach by making a distinction between EU officials and other applicants, such as *Tillack*:

> However, those decisions were given in relation to a person who did not have the status of Community official, in cases brought on the basis of Article 230 EC [*Tillack*] and not under Article 236 EC [*Violetti*]. Both the Court of Justice and the Court of First Instance, which

[286] House of Lords, European Union Committee, "Financial Management and Fraud in the European Union: Perceptions, Facts and Proposals", 50th report of session 2005–2006, published 13 November 2006, p. 142, para 140 and House of Lords, European Union Committee, "Strengthening OLAF, the European Anti-Fraud Office", 24th report with evidence of session 2003–2004, published 21 July 2004, p. 16, para 29.

[287] House of Lords, European Union Committee, "Strengthening OLAF, the European Anti-Fraud Office", 24th report with evidence of session 2003–2004, published 21 July 2004, pp. 16–18, para 29–36; Quirke (2009, 2010); White (2009, 2010); an excellent overview of the recent developments offers: Groussot and Popov (2010).

[288] T-193/04, *Tillack v. Commission*, judgment of 4 October 2006 and C-521/04 P (R) *Tillack v. Commission*, judgment of 19 April 2005 and compare with ECtHR judgment *Tillack v. Belgium*, Application no. 20477/05, judgment of 27 November 2007, which is discussed in the Chap. A II 2 c; see also T-215/02, *Gomez-Reino v. Commission*, order of 18 December 2003 and T-29/03, *Comunidad Autonoma de Andalucia v. Commission*, order of 13 July 2004.

[289] Hetzer (2006); Balogava (2008), p. 143, Wakefield (2008); see also Jansen and Lanbroek (2007), pp. 21–38 (study ordered by OLAF).

[290] Murawska (2008), p. 119; Gleß and Zeitler (2001).

[291] White (2009); White (2010), in particular pp. 87–89.

[292] T-48/05, *Yves Franchet and Daniel Byk v. Commission*, judgment of 8 July 2008; see White (2008), and Niestedt and Boekmann (2009).

[293] T-259/03, *Nikolaou v. Commission*, judgment of 12 September 2007; see also T-309/03, *Camos Grau v. Commission*, judgment of 6 April 2006; F-23/05, *Giraudy v. Commission*, judgment of 2 May 2007 and F-5/05 and 7/05, *Violetti and others v. Commission*, judgment of 28 April 2009.

> did not have before them the question of the scope of Article 90a of the Staff Regulations, pointed out that the applicant had sufficient procedural safeguards before the national court and that the act of forwarding, by OLAF, of information concerning him was merely a preparatory act. However, that situation is unrelated to the situation in this case. Since it concerned a third party in relation to the Communities, whose career and material circumstances do not depend directly on measures adopted by the Community authorities, the Community judicature does not have a particular authority enabling it to guarantee, on behalf of the national court, the observance of fundamental rights and of the requirements of a fair trial.[294]

The Civil Service Tribunal further stipulates that, in order to be effective, the judicial review of an act such as the decision to forward the information:

> [. . .] would contribute to full observance by OLAF of the legality of investigations and of the fundamental rights of persons to whom they relate, in accordance with the legislature's intention.[295]

It has to be taken into consideration that the mentioned decisions were given in the context of individuals working for the EU institutions or EU agencies and do not affect individuals not having the status of Community officials. In that regard, the Civil Service Tribunal interpreted the scope of Article 90a Staff Regulations differently from the scope of Article 230 EC and declared the claim admissible. In the following, it came to the conclusion to annul OLAF's decision to forward the information to the national judicial authorities due to the non-respect of the applicant's defence rights seeing that he was not heard before the transmission of the possible incriminating documents.[296]

Although this jurisdiction clearly points to a much-anticipated and more effective judicial control of OLAF's transmission activities, it was annulled in the appeal decision by the Court of First Instance (General Court) due to the same arguments as in the Tillack case. According to the General Court, OLAF's decision to forward the information to national law enforcement authorities forms part of an administrative and not a criminal procedure constituting a preparatory act which does not have adverse effects providing grounds of complaint in terms of Article 90 Staff Regulations.[297] Only the decision of the national authorities to open criminal

[294] F-5/05 and 7/05, *Violetti and others v. Commission*, judgment of 28 April 2009, para 94.

[295] F-5/05 and 7/05, *Violetti and others v. Commission*, judgment of 28 April 2009, para 82.

[296] F-5/05 and 7/05, *Violetti and others v. Commission*, judgment of 28 April 2009, paras 104–115; the Civil Service Tribunal further observes that "in this case, OLAF did not reply to the complaints which the applicants in Case F-5/05 had submitted to it under Article 90a of the Staff Regulations until 21 February 2005, that is, after the action had been brought, and that only the Commission, which was not the author of the act in question, explicitly replied to the complaints which had been submitted to it. Such a situation, in which the author of a contested decision does not comment on the criticisms made against that decision, is hardly compatible with the principle of sound administration and reveals the problems to which an absence of clearly affirmed and effective judicial supervision is liable to give rise. The analysis of the action as to its merits is not such, in the present case, as to invalidate that finding", para 82.

[297] T-261/09 P, *Commission v. Violetti and others*, judgment of 20 May 2010, paras 62–65.

investigations at the national level is able to change the legal position of the person concerned.[298]

While the first *Violetti* judgment of the Civil Service Tribunal could have been an impulse to extend this jurisdiction to applicants subjected to external investigations, which would have been a desired move towards OLAF's judicial responsibility also in the context of individuals outside the EU structures, acknowledging that potential damages on an individual's reputation through the forwarding of incriminating information to national authorities are able to justify a complaint, the General Court went back to the point of departure.

A judgment to the detriment of OLAF would have eventually forced OLAF to take appropriate measures to ensure that information about alleged suspicions is not disclosed to the public, a fact increasingly raising concerns.[299] Once it has reached the public sphere, such information could have serious consequences for the status of a person concerned as well as for its economic and legal situation. The insistence of the General Court on mere preparatory acts as regards OLAF's activities regrettably does not provide helpful guidance in solving this problem. The question of judicial review during OLAF's investigations therefore remains unsolved.

Apart from information which reaches the public sphere, OLAF information policy regarding the individual's right of access was quite often subject to cases handled by the European Ombudsman.[300] From the 35 cases dealt with from 2001 to 2009, the most prominent case however dealt with a leak of confidential information in connection with the *Tillack* affair, mentioned above, in which OLAF "made incorrect and misleading statements in its submissions to the Ombudsman" as it tried to justify the reasons for its activities.[301]

Finally, in *Nikolaou v. Commission*, the General Court made an essential statement, which is of utmost importance in the AFSJ data exchange: the court stipulates that the rule of law requires that a person concerned shall be informed as soon as possible of the existence of an investigation, as long as the information does not prejudice the ongoing investigation.[302]

---

[298] Ibid, paras 65 and 73.

[299] T-193/04, *Tillack v. Commission*, judgment of 4 October 2006 and C-521/04 P (R) *Tillack v. Commission*, judgment of 19 April 2005; T-48/05, *Yves Franchet and Daniel Byk v. Commission*, judgment of 8 July 2008; T-259/03, *Nikolaou v. Commission*, judgment of 12 September 2007; T-309/03, *Camos Grau v. Commission*, judgment of 6 April 2006; F-23/05, *Giraudy v. Commission*, judgment of 2 May 2007.

[300] Examples are: 18/12/2009, Decision of the European Ombudsman closing his inquiry into joined complaints 723/2005/OV and 790/2005/OV against the European Anti-Fraud Office or 15/10/2009, Decision of the European Ombudsman concerning complaint 2930/2008/JMA against the European Anti-Fraud Office, compare http://www.ombudsman.europa.eu/cases/home.faces (accessed February 2011).

[301] Special Report from the European Ombudsman to the European Parliament following the draft recommendation to the European Anti-Fraud Office in complaint 2485/2004/GG.

[302] T-259/03, *Nikolaou v. Commission*, judgment of 12 September 2007, paras 263–264.

c) Data Processing and Time Limits for Storing

Another critical issue concerns OLAF's data processing embracing particularly sensitive information which can be stored for 20 years, including data concerning suspected offences, offences or criminal convictions.[303]

OLAF principally has three main data processing systems: the Mail Registration System (MRS), the Case Management System (CMS) and the Anti Fraud Information System (AFIS). Whereby the first handles incoming, internal and outgoing correspondence, the second and the third (CMS and AFIS) contain rather sensitive information. The CMS is an electronic case management database, including a complete electronic version of each OLAF case file and the AFIS provides the infrastructure to communicate with national authorities and third states after the conclusion of cooperation agreements.[304] The CMS was initially created as a register of OLAF cases, but today functions as a database entailing different modules which serve diverse purposes.[305] Amongst others, it entails an "intelligence request module" managing the requests to intelligence units or a "legal and judicial advice module" recording and managing requests for legal advice, but also a "data protection module" to manage notifications to data subjects.[306]

The AFIS is a secure communication and e-mailing system used as a platform for the exchange of information between the Member States and between the latter and the OLAF. It consists of several functions (databases, communication modules, coordination, intelligence tools) and is used by different user groups[307] utilising electronic forms (modules) to enter information in the different databases of the AFIS concerning specific potential fraud activities and irregularities.[308]

AFIS, for instance, includes the Customs File Identification Database (FIDE)[309] and the CIS. Two databases which were newly regulated in Regulation 766/2008

[303] Opinion of the European Data Protection Supervisor on the proposal for a regulation of the European Parliament and of the Council amending Regulation (EC) No 1073/1999 of the European Parliament and the Council of 25 May 1999 concerning investigation conducted by the European Anti-Fraud Office (OLAF), OJ 2007, C-91/1, para 4.

[304] See OLAF manual on operational procedures of 1 December 2009, p. 9, to be found at: http://ec.europa.eu/dgs/olaf/legal/index_en.html (accessed February 2011).

[305] See Case Management Systems – Principles, accessible at: http://ec.europa.eu/dgs/olaf/legal/index_en.html (accessed February 2011).

[306] See Case Management Systems – Principles, accessible at: http://ec.europa.eu/dgs/olaf/legal/index_en.html (accessed February 2011).

[307] OLAF annual report 2009, ninth activity report for the period 1 January 2008 to 31 December 2008, section 4.2.1, p. 55.

[308] OLAF manual of 25 February 2005, p. 133, para 4.3; the term is not explained in the new manual on operational procedures of 1 December 2009, although used on p. 81.

[309] Article 41a-d Regulation (EC) No. 766/2008 of the European Parliament and of the Council of 9 July 2008 amending Council Regulation (EC) No 515/97 on mutual assistance between the administrative authorities of the Member States and cooperation between the latter and the Commission to ensure the correct application of the law on customs and agricultural matters, OJ 2008, L-218/48; FIDE stands for the French acronym "Fichier d'identification des dossiers d'enquêtes douanières".

which also established a new "European Data Directory" database having the purpose "to detect movements of goods that are the object of operations in potential breach of customs and agriculture legislation by means of transport including containers, used for that purpose".[310]

The CIS operated by OLAF is part of the customs cooperation in the EU and therefore closely connected to an almost identical information exchange system also entitled CIS established by a Convention to detect criminal offences in customs cooperation in former third pillar matters, analysed in Sect. III 3.[311] However, although sharing the name, both CIS databases are separate databases managed by different actors and based on different legal instruments.[312] In order to ensure their use for different purposes, they are made available to different bodies.[313] Regrettably, due to the fact that the Council repealed the CIS Convention on 30 November 2009 and replaced it by Council Decision 2009/971 on the use of information technology for customs purposes, the impact of the Lisbon Treaty on the twofold CIS structure (which is based on former first as well former third pillar legislation) could not be further clarified.[314] The entry into force of the Lisbon Treaty definitely would have significantly affected the legal framework as well as the supervision composition governing the third pillar CIS, but as a result of the Council's hurry in adopting the new decision, the previous twofold arrangement with all its legal difficulties was maintained. Criticism of the EDPS was constantly ignored.[315] Council Decision 2009/971 is analysed in more detail in Sect. III 3.

When returning to the first pillar CIS operated by OLAF, the Commission (OLAF) and the Member States have access to the (first pillar) databases CIS and

---

[310] Article 18a (1) Regulation (EC) No. 766/2008 of the European Parliament and of the Council of 9 July 2008 amending Council Regulation (EC) No 515/97 on mutual assistance between the administrative authorities of the Member States and cooperation between the latter and the Commission to ensure the correct application of the law on customs and agricultural matters, OJ 2008, L-218/48.

[311] The CIS with regard to criminal offences is analysed in Sect. III 3.

[312] Compare Regulation (EC) No. 766/2008 of the European Parliament and of the Council of 9 July 2008 amending Council Regulation (EC) No 515/97 on mutual assistance between the administrative authorities of the Member States and cooperation between the latter and the Commission to ensure the correct application of the law on customs and agricultural matters, OJ 2008, L-218/48 (former first pillar instrument) and Convention drawn up on the basis of Article K.3 of the Treaty on European Union, on the use of information technology for customs purposes, OJ 1995, C-316/34 (former third pillar instrument).

[313] Opinion of the EDPS on the proposal for a regulation of the European Parliament and of the Council of 9 July 2008 amending Council Regulation (EC) No 515/97 on mutual assistance between the administrative authorities of the Member States and cooperation between the latter and the Commission to ensure the correct application of the law on customs and agricultural matters (COM(2006) 866 final), OJ 2007, C-94/3.

[314] Council Decision 2009/971 on the use of information technology for customs purposes is further analysed in Sect. III 3.

[315] Opinion of the EDPS on the initiative of the French Republic for a Council Decision on the use of information technology for customs purposes (5903/2/09 REV 2), OJ 2009, C-229/12, para 27.

FIDE established by Regulation 515/97, recently amended by Regulation 766/2008.[316] The Information delivered is entered via the "AFIS Terminal" which is a system installed on a computer in the Member States as well as in the relevant third states.[317] Different modules, for instance modules for the exchange of operational intelligence or for the monitoring of movements of sensitive goods as well as for the reporting of irregularities in Community funds shall facilitate the exchange of information regarding a specific topic. The CIS, for instance, contains details of potential contraventions of Community law (former first pillar) in the area of customs or agriculture.[318]

The AFIS system is additionally used as a platform to exchange information during so called "joint surveillance operations" which are operations of different Member States related to surveillance of maritime, container or road traffic and allows the participating countries to collect and exchange information on subjects under their control in one record virtually stored and accessible by the participating countries.[319]

However, when trying to find out which specific data elements are actually stored in OLAF's databases, in particular in the CMS, individuals concerned will neither find answers in the Commission Decision 1999/352/EC nor in Regulation 1073/1999 although these instruments build OLAF's legal basis.

A puzzling assortment of diverse Commission Decisions, Council Regulations, the OLAF manual as well as non binding "privacy statements" issued by OLAF itself, were intended to shed more light on this issue, however a closer look on them challenges the readers perceptive ability to understand interlinked references (which additionally do not necessarily point to the "correct" regulation[320]) and complicated legal structures.[321] Even after having read and identified the various

[316] Regulation (EC) No. 766/2008 of the European Parliament and of the Council of 9 July 2008 amending Council Regulation (EC) No 515/97 on mutual assistance between the administrative authorities of the Member States and cooperation between the latter and the Commission to ensure the correct application of the law on customs and agricultural matters, OJ 2008, L-218/48.

[317] OLAF annual report 2009, ninth activity report for the period 1 January 2008 to 31 December 2008, section 4.2.1, p. 55.

[318] According to OLAF annual report 2009, the use of the CIS does not match the expectations (800 cases stored in 2008); the cases are accessible to over 1600 users; OLAF annual report 2009, ninth activity report for the period 1 January 2008 to 31 December 2008, section 4.2.2, p. 56.

[319] OLAF manual of 25 February 2005, pp. 133–135, para 4.3.; not mentioned in the new manual on operational procedures of 1 December 2009.

[320] For instance privacy statement for internal investigations (OLAF DPO-7), section 1 which refers to Article 4 of Regulation 1073/2001, which deals with tenders for the export of oats; see Commission Regulation (EC) No 1073/2001 of 31 May 2001 concerning tenders notified in response to the invitation to tender for the export of oats issued in Regulation (EC) No 2097/2000, OJ 2001, L-148/06; presumably meant was Regulation (EC) No. 1073/1999 of the European Parliament and of the Council of 25 May 1999 concerning investigations conducted by the European Anti-Fraud Office (OLAF), OJ 1999, L-136/31.

[321] Compare the various instruments entailing data processing rules, such as Regulation (EC) No. 766/2008 of the European Parliament and of the Council of 9 July 2008 amending Council

instruments relating to data processing at OLAF, the concrete amount of data elements which finally can be stored by OLAF nevertheless remains untold. OLAF's so called "privacy statements" refer to wide-ranging terms such as identification data, professional data and case involvement data which could embrace a great number of data elements.[322] While embracing more than 130 pages, OLAF's manual dated 1 December 2009 unfortunately does not refer to the data components stored at OLAF.[323]

The only regulation specifying to a certain extent the data categories entered in OLAF's databases is the abovementioned Regulation 766/2008 on mutual assistance between the Member States and the Commission in the framework of CIS cooperation referring in its Article 25 to passport data, such as names, place of birth, nationality and address, but also to categories relating to permanent physical characteristics or the registration number of the means of transport.[324] Data revealing racial or ethnic origin, political opinions, religious or philosophical beliefs, trade union membership as well as health data or sex life related data are not allowed to be included.[325]

It is worth pointing out that compared to the former Regulation 515/97 not only the list of data elements in Article 25 Regulation 766/2008 was enlarged, but also

Regulation (EC) No 515/97 on mutual assistance between the administrative authorities of the Member States and cooperation between the latter and the Commission to ensure the correct application of the law on customs and agricultural matters, OJ 2008, L-218/48; Council Regulation (Euratom, EC) No 2185/96 of 11 November 1996 concerning on-the-spot checks and inspections carried out by the Commission in order to protect the European Communities' financial interests against fraud and other irregularities, OJ 1996, L-292/2; Council Regulation (EC, Euratom) No 2988/95 of 18 December 1995 on the protection of the European Communities financial interests, OJ 1995, L-312/1; privacy statement for internal investigations (OLAF DPO-7); privacy statement for external investigations (OLAF DPO-6, 8, 9, 10, 11 and 13); privacy statement for coordination cases (OLAF DPO-143); privacy statement for criminal assistant cases (OLAF DPO-15); privacy statement for monitoring cases (OLAF DPO-16); privacy statement for non-cases and prima facie non-cases (OLAF DPO-129); privacy statement for follow-up (OLAF DPO-1, 2, 3, 4 and 5); privacy statement for fraud notification system (OLAF DPO-133); privacy statement for investigations by the OLAF DPO (OLAF DPO-111) etc., accessible at: http://ec.europa.eu/dgs/olaf/data/index_en.html (accessed February 2011) as well as OLAF's manual of 25 February 2005, in which it is regrettably not specified which data elements are processed by OLAF.

[322] Privacy statement for internal investigations (OLAF DPO-7), section 2, and privacy statement for external investigations (OLAF DPO-6, 8, 9, 10, 11 and 13), section 2; accessible at: http://ec.europa.eu/dgs/olaf/data/index_en.html (accessed February 2011).

[323] OLAF manual on operational procedures of 1 December 2009.

[324] Regulation (EC) No. 766/2008 of the European Parliament and of the Council of 9 July 2008 amending Council Regulation (EC) No 515/97 on mutual assistance between the administrative authorities of the Member States and cooperation between the latter and the Commission to ensure the correct application of the law on customs and agricultural matters, OJ 2008, L-218/48.

[325] Ibid, Article 25.

the possible use of these data has become a broader one, including operational analysis[326] and discreet surveillance.[327] Regulation 766/2008 additionally derogates from the "prior authorisation" principle set out in Regulation 515/97 according to which personal data entered by a Member State could be copied from CIS into other data-processing systems only with the prior authorisation of the CIS partner which entered them.[328] Article 35 Regulation 766/2008 now allows for copying in "systems of risk management used to direct national customs controls or in an operational analysis system used to coordinate actions at Community level".[329]

The above mentioned European Data Directory,[330] also regulated in Regulation 766/2008, embraces data related to the name, maiden name, forenames, former surnames, aliases, date and place of birth, nationality, sex and address.[331] Personal data elements contained in the FIDE are separately regulated through Regulation 766/2008. The purpose of the FIDE is to prevent operations in breach of customs and agriculture legislation "applicable to goods entering or leaving the customs territory of the Community and to facilitate and accelerate their detection and prosecution".[332] Similar to the CIS, the FIDE can also be used in the framework of police cooperation while the Commission's role is to assure the technical management of the database.[333] Consequently, FIDE entails first pillar and third

[326] According to Article 1 (1) Regulation 766/2008 operational analysis means "analysis of operations which constitute, or appear to constitute, breaches of customs or agricultural legislation, involving the following stages in turn: (a) the collection of information, including personal data, (b) evaluation of the reliability of the information source and the information itself, (c) research, methodical presentation n and interpretation of links between these items of information or between them and other significant data, (d) the formulation of observations, hypotheses or recommendations directly usable as risk information by the competent authorities and by the Commission to prevent and detect other operations in breach of customs or agricultural legislation and/or to identify with precision the person or business implicated in such operation".

[327] Opinion of the EDPS on the proposal for a Regulation of the European Parliament and of the Council amending Council Regulation (EC) No 515/97 on mutual assistance between the administrative authorities of the Member States and cooperation between the latter and the Commission to ensure the correct application of the law on customs and agricultural matters (COM(2006) 866 final), OJ 2007, C-94/3, para 26.

[328] Recital 7 Regulation 766/2008.

[329] Ibid, Article 35.

[330] Compare Sect. II 3 c (at the beginning).

[331] Article 18a (3) (c) Regulation (EC) No. 766/2008 of the European Parliament and of the Council of 9 July 2008 amending Council Regulation (EC) No 515/97 on mutual assistance between the administrative authorities of the Member States and cooperation between the latter and the Commission to ensure the correct application of the law on customs and agricultural matters, OJ 2008, L-218/48.

[332] Ibid, Article 41a (2).

[333] Ibid, Article 41a (5).

pillar data which are indeed treated as separated data, however the database is operated by users as if it were a single database.[334]

The personal data entered by the Member States according to the first pillar Regulation (EC) No. 766/2008 in the FIDE relating to persons "which are or have been subject of administrative enquiries or criminal investigations" are "suspected of committing or of having committed a breach of customs or agriculture legislation or of participating in or of having participated in an operation in breach of such legislation" as well as to persons which have been "the subject of a finding relating to such operation" or "have been subject of an administrative penalty or judicial penalty for such operations".[335] The data elements are restricted to name, maiden name, forenamed, former surnames, aliases, date and place of birth, nationality and sex.[336]

However, the AFIS entails more personal data than those mentioned in Regulation 766/2008. "OLAF's register of processing operations of personal data", containing the notifications of controllers to OLAF's data protection officer on their processing, gives some indication of the terms aforementioned in the privacy statements (identification data, professional data and case involvement data).[337]

Nevertheless the 76 notification reports thus far, each including up to 30 pages, are definitively not the easiest accessible source for persons seeking information about the data elements processed at OLAF. Further information about the data elements stored by OLAF are also given by the EDPS in its opinions on the notifications for prior checking on OLAF's data processing (pursuant to Article 27 Regulation 45/2001). The EDPS clarifies that OLAF processes data about the persons subject to investigations, informants, witnesses, EU staff Members or whistleblowers including data such as name, address as well as profession, but also evidence mentioning the person and comments regarding the relation of the

[334] Annual report of OLAF 2009 for the period 1 January 2008 to 31 December 2008, p. 38, para 4.2.2.

[335] Article 41b (1) (a-c) Regulation (EC) No. 766/2008 of the European Parliament and of the Council of 9 July 2008 amending Council Regulation (EC) No 515/97 on mutual assistance between the administrative authorities of the Member States and cooperation between the latter and the Commission to ensure the correct application of the law on customs and agricultural matters, OJ 2008, L-218/48.

[336] Ibid, Article 41b (2) (a).

[337] Accessible at: http://ec.europa.eu/anti_fraud/dataprotectionofficer//register/index.cfm?TargetURL=D_REGISTER (accessed February 2011); See for instance: external investigations and operations master, notification to the data protection officer from OLAF's former director Franz Hermann Brüner, version 2, DPO 6 of 10 December 08, which explains that identification data, professional data and case involvement data in principle consists of name, address, telephone number, e-mail address, date of birth, nationality, employer, marital status, children, professional position, statements made regarding events under investigation by the person or about the person, evidence mentioning the person and notes regarding the relation of the person to the events under investigation.

person to the events under investigation (e.g. possibility of a conflict of interest).[338] The EDPS document moreover describes that according to an internal document issued by OLAF,[339] the body in principle does not process data revealing racial or ethnic origin, political opinions, religious or philosophical beliefs, trade-union membership or data concerning health or sex life, unless "they are directly relevant to the matter under investigation".[340]

Finally, it is surprising that, compared to the former third pillar organisations Eurojust and Europol which regulate in detail the data categories that are stored in their data processing systems, at OLAF a list specifying the data stored in its databases does not exist. Clear rules identifying which data elements are exactly stored, in particular in the AFIS and the CMS, are essential, not at least because of the fact that the deficiency leads to exceptionally non-transparent databases containing a vague content and eventually opening various possibilities of misuse for erroneous entries.

d) Data Protection and Supervision

Although OLAF is part of the Commission and hence the provisions of Article 16 TFEU and Regulation 45/2001 apply to data processing at OLAF, the transfer of information between OLAF and the national judicial authorities has raised several questions in particular concerning the use of this information in national proceedings, the judicial control of this transfer as well as the fundamental rights of the individuals concerned since its establishment.[341] The OLAF manual refers to allegedly non binding "data protection guidelines for OLAF staff" which are

[338] For example: Opinion of the EDPS on five notifications for prior checking received from the data protection officer of the European Anti-Fraud Office (OLAF) on external investigations of 4 October 2007 (cases 2007–47, 2007–48, 2007–50, 2007–72), pp. 5–6, paras 2.2.4. and 2.2.5.

[339] Compare Opinion of the EDPS on five notifications for prior checking received from the data protection officer of the European Anti-Fraud Office (OLAF) on external investigations of 4 October 2007 (cases 2007–47, 2007–48, 2007–50, 2007–72), p. 2, para 2.1. together with p. 6, para 2.2.5, which refers to the internal document issued by the Director General of OLAF and addressed to OLAF staff "Instructions to staff conducting investigations following from opinion of European Data Protection Supervisor (EDPS) on prior checking on internal investigations".

[340] Opinion of the EDPS on five notifications for prior checking received from the data protection officer of the European Anti-Fraud Office (OLAF) on external investigations of 4 October 2007 (cases 2007–47, 2007–48, 2007–50, 2007–72), p. 6, para 2.2.5.

[341] To the latter, see Court of First Instance judgment T-193/04, *Tillack v. Commission*, judgment of 4 October 2006 and European Court of Justice confirmation C-521/04 P (R), *Tillack v. Commission*, judgment of 19 April 2005 and compare to ECtHR judgment *Tillack v. Belgium*, Application no. 20477/05, judgment of 27 November 2007 as well as Court of First Instance, T-48/05, *Yves Franchet and Daniel Byk v. Commission*, judgment of 8 July 2008; see also pending case: Civil Service Tribunal, F-118/07, *Strack v. Commission*, action brought on 22 October 2007 regarding amongst others the communication of personal data of an whistle blower to the public.

contained in annex 5 of the manual specifying the applicable data protection rules, but these guidelines mainly repeat the provisions of Regulation 45/2001 and explain to OLAF staff, amongst other, that "data protection is a fundamental right".[342] While, of course, more detailed examples are given in the following, which explain the concrete application of the principles of the regulation in the daily work at OLAF, the guidelines are nevertheless not necessarily binding.[343]

As regards supervision, it is noteworthy that the office is monitored at the EU level by the EDPS but also by a special supervisory committee regularly examining OLAF's investigations and consisting of five independent experts broadly monitoring compliance with fundamental rights and issuing (non binding) recommendations.[344] Its last activity report in 2009 reveals serious problems, particularly related to five rather alarming key issues:

- In addition to inexplicable delays in investigations procedures, "serious quality problems" in the so called 9-month reports, which are the reports setting out the reasons for non completion of investigations and the expected time for closing a case, have arisen (9 months were exceeded in 78% of cases in a period from January 2007–December 2008).[345]
- The supervisory committee further notes "an inadequate level of supervision and control of the day to day management of investigations" lacking investigation plans, timeframes as well as systems of assessing the results.[346]
- Further criticism refers to the unresolved issue of the division of tasks between OLAF and the Commission's Investigation and Disciplinary Office which forms part of the Directorate General for personnel and administration and is also entrusted with the conduct of internal administrative inquiries.[347]
- Two additional points of disapproval concern the lacking transparency and the obviously intentional omitted notification of the supervisory committee in two important situations: firstly, circumstances requiring the transmission of a case to national judicial authorities and secondly, situations in which OLAF received

[342] Guidelines for OLAF staff regarding practical implementation of data protection requirements of December 2008, p. 5, point 1.2, http://ec.europa.eu/dgs/olaf/legal/manual-annexes.html (accessed February 2011).

[343] Compare Guidelines for OLAF staff regarding practical implementation of data protection requirements of December 2008, http://ec.europa.eu/dgs/olaf/legal/index_en.html (accessed February 2011).

[344] Article 4 of Commission Decision 1999/352/EC of 28 April 1999 establishing the European Anti-Fraud Office (OLAF), OJ 1999, L-136/20; Mitsilegas (2009), p. 224.

[345] Activity Report of OLAF Supervisory Committee, June 2008 – May 2009, September 2009, p. 20, paras II and III, accessible at: http://ec.europa.eu/anti_fraud/reports/sup-com_en.html (accessed February 2011).

[346] Ibid, p. 20, para IV.

[347] Activity Report of OLAF Supervisory Committee, June 2008 – May 2009, September 2009, p. 20, para VII; to this problem, see also White (2010), in particular p. 89.

complaints of alleged abuse of fundamental rights and procedural guarantees.[348] In both cases the surveillance committee should have been informed according to the ruling of the Court of First Instance/General Court in *Yves Franchet and Daniel Byk v. Commission.*[349]

- Finally the supervisory committee criticised that as far as personal data protection is concerned, an agreement on equal access to OLAF's CMS for the supervisory committee is still outstanding.[350]

The results of this report are worrisome and seem to confirm the concerns of scholars and institutions constantly criticising OLAF's lack of accountability as well as its legislative framework and demanding a strengthening of the rights of individuals in investigations along with a reinforcement of OLAF's supervisory committee.[351]

The aforementioned problems may partly result from the fact that data protection provisions at OLAF are neither regulated in the Commission Decision, nor in the aforementioned regulation as OLAF forms part of the Commission and therefore underlies the general data protection rules of Regulation 45/2001 (including the rights to rectification, access, notification etc.[352]) and the access rules of Regulation 1049/2001.[353] Beside these rules however, OLAF insists that "throughout OLAF's operation activities the person concerned (or its legal counsel) has no specific right of direct access to the OLAF investigation file".[354]

Moreover, the compliance with the Regulation 45/2001 in OLAF's rather specific judicial context dealing with very sensitive crime related information[355] seems not always to be guaranteed.[356] The positive consequence of Regulation 45/2001

---

[348] Activity Report of OLAF Supervisory Committee, June 2008 – May 2009, September 2009, p. 21, paras IX and X.

[349] T-48/05, *Yves Franchet and Daniel Byk v. Commission*, judgment of 8 July 2008.

[350] Activity Report of OLAF Supervisory Committee, June 2008 – May 2009, September 2009, p. 17, para III (1).

[351] Compare House of Lords, European Union Committee, "Strengthening OLAF, the European Anti-Fraud Office", 24th report with evidence of session 2003–2004, published 21 July 2004, in particular pp. 25–27, paras 60–70; Gleß and Zeitler (2001); Hetzer (2006).

[352] Articles 13–19 Regulation 45/2001.

[353] See Article 8 of Regulation (EC) No 1073/1999 of the European Parliament and the Council of 25 May 1999 concerning investigation conducted by the European Anti-Fraud Office (OLAF), OJ 1999, L-136/31.

[354] OLAF manual on operational procedures of 1 December 2009, p. 123, para 5.1.3.2.

[355] In contrast to Directive 95/46 which excludes data processing in police and judicial cooperation matters from its scope, Regulation 45/2001 is applicable to the processing of personal data by all Community institutions and bodies, including OLAF, but was originally not designed to handle the particularly sensitive area of personal data exchange embracing criminal related information.

[356] Opinion of the European Data Protection Supervisor on the proposal for a regulation of the European Parliament and of the Council amending Regulation (EC) No 1073/1999 of the European Parliament and the Council of 25 May 1999 concerning investigation conducted by the European Anti-Fraud Office (OLAF), OJ 2007, C-91/1, para 46.

however is, that it assures the important participation of the EDPS and of a data protection officer[357] at the surveillance of OLAF activities under a broader Union umbrella. Data processing likely to present specific risks to data protection rights is thus subject to prior checking by the EDPS according to Article 27 of Regulation 45/2001. So far the EDPS issued 23 opinions in this context illustrating in more detail data protection issues relating to specific activities of OLAF, such as external or internal investigations.[358]

However, despite the cooperation with the EDPS and after years of discussions and several attempts to amend OLAF's framework,[359] it is all the more astonishing that the Commission's proposal to amend Regulation 1073/1999 in 2006[360] does not meet the minimum data protection standard contained in Regulation 45/2001.[361] According to the EDPS opinion dealing with the proposal to amend Regulation 1073/1999,[362] in case the proposal takes precedent over the application of Regulation No. 45/2001, this situation would constitute "an unacceptable watering down of the data protection standards in the context of OLAF's investigations".[363] Although the Commission's proposal,[364] contradictory to Regulation 1073/1999, entails at least some provisions on data protection and on the rights of data subjects, the EDPS particularly criticised shortcomings regarding the right of information, the right of access and the right of rectification in the context of OLAF's investigations.[365] Even OLAF's former director addressed criticism

[357] Article 24 (1) of Regulation 45/2001 provides that "each Community institution and Community body shall appoint at least one person as data protection officer".

[358] EDPS opinions on OLAF's activities' can be found at: http://ec.europa.eu/dgs/olaf/data/index_en.html (accessed February 2011).

[359] Annual report of OLAF 2009 for the period 1 January 2008 to 31 December 2008, p. 14, para 1.3. and Staicu (2008).

[360] Proposal for a Regulation of the European Parliament and the Council amending Regulation (EC) No 1073/1999 concerning investigation conducted by the European Anti-Fraud Office, COM (2006) 244 final of 24 May 2006, see also critical remarks from OLAF's former director in: Brüner and Spitzer (2008).

[361] Opinion of the European Data Protection Supervisor on the proposal for a regulation of the European Parliament and of the Council amending Regulation (EC) No 1073/1999 of the European Parliament and the Council of 25 May 1999 concerning investigation conducted by the European Anti-Fraud Office (OLAF), OJ 2007, C-91/1, para 46.

[362] Opinion of the European Data Protection Supervisor on the proposal for a regulation of the European Parliament and of the Council amending Regulation (EC) No 1073/1999 of the European Parliament and the Council of 25 May 1999 concerning investigation conducted by the European Anti-Fraud Office (OLAF), OJ 2007, C-91/1.

[363] Ibid, para 46.

[364] Proposal for a regulation of the European Parliament and of the Council amending Regulation (EC) No 1073/1999 of the European Parliament and the Council of 25 May 1999 concerning investigation conducted by the European Anti-Fraud Office (OLAF), COM(2006) 244.

[365] Opinion of the European Data Protection Supervisor on the proposal for a regulation of the European Parliament and of the Council amending Regulation (EC) No 1073/1999 of the European Parliament and the Council of 25 May 1999 concerning investigation conducted by the European Anti-Fraud Office (OLAF), OJ 2007, C-91/1, paras 11–35.

regarding the weak judicial review provisions in context of OLAF's investigations which are provided for in the Commission's proposal.[366] Taking into consideration the different opinions and improvement suggestions from the actors involved, so far, the final adoption of the Commission's proposal to amend Regulation 1073/1999 is not yet in sight.

Finally, one exception to the rather worrisome data protection and supervision situation at OLAF seems to be the supervision carried out by the EDPS in context with the CIS. Regulation 766/2008 undoubtedly refers to the EDPS being the responsible authority to assure compliance of the CIS with Regulation 45/2001.[367] After criticism by the EDPS,[368] Article 37 (4) Regulation 766/2008 now even refers to the coordination of supervision between the relevant national DPAs and the EDPS by including a paragraph urging the EDPS to convene a meeting at least once a year with the national DPAs competent for CIS-related supervisory issues. The individual access right and its limits are expressly regulated in Articles 36 and 37 Regulation 766/2008 and can be exercised by complaining to the supervisory authority, the EDPS or the national DPAs depending on whether the data concerned have been entered in the CIS by a Member States or by the Commission.

e) Transmission of Data to Third Bodies

Since Regulation 45/2001 applies to OLAF's data processing, the general transfer provisions of Article 7 and 8 Regulation 45/2001, analysed in Chap. A III 2 e, regulate the transfer between Community institutions and OLAF as well as between OLAF and recipients in Member States which are subject to the data protection rules of Directive 95/46.[369] At European Union level, agreements with actors such as Europol and Eurojust have been concluded to manage the data exchange in this area. Their functioning is analysed in Chap. C I 2 and C I 4.

Article 9 Regulation 45/2001 deals with addressees outside the scope of Directive 95/46, for instance police authorities of the Member States or third states which have to comply with the adequacy requirement prior to the transfer and which have succeeded in receiving a positive adequacy decision by the Commission allowing for data exchange as well as for the conclusion of a data exchange agreement.[370]

---

[366] Brüner and Spitzer (2008).

[367] Article 37 (3) (a) Regulation 766/2008.

[368] Opinion of the EDPS on the proposal for a Regulation of the European Parliament and of the Council amending Council Regulation (EC) No 515/97 on mutual assistance between the administrative authorities of the Member States and cooperation between the latter and the Commission to ensure the correct application of the law on customs and agricultural matters (COM(2006) 866 final), OJ 2007, C-94/3, para 35.

[369] Article 7–8 Regulation 45/2001.

[370] See Articles 7–9 Regulation 45/2001 and Chap. A III 2 e.

Data exchange with countries or organisations which have not received an adequacy decision of the Commission must assure in the form of contractual arrangements (which have to be approved by the EDPS) that an adequate level of data protection is ensured for the transfer.[371]

OLAF however seems to apply its own adequacy criterion by concluding in its "data protection guidelines for OLAF staff" that all countries having ratified Convention No. 108 provide an adequate level of protection.[372] Regrettably, OLAF does not consider that the adequacy requirement of Regulation 45/2001 does not automatically correspond to that of Convention No. 108. Disregarding this important difference, the guidelines list, amongst others, the following countries as adequate recipients of personal data: Albania, Andorra, Bosnia and Herzegovina, Croatia, Georgia, Moldova, Montenegro, Serbia as well as Macedonia.[373]

In addition to these already legally doubtful data transfers, "occasional transfers" are also possible.[374] OLAF staff is advised in such cases to "rely on the derogation in Article 9 (6) (d) of the Regulation [45/2001] that the transfer is necessary or legally required on important public interest grounds, or for the establishment, exercise or defence of legal claims."[375] A sheet about the data protection standards should be annexed to the standard letter to refer to the EU data protection standard.[376] With regard to OLAF's daily work, which does not seem not require an extremely quick decision to prevent an immediate threat, it is barely understandable why it should not be possible to agree on data protection requirements prior to such transfers involving personal data.

More detailed rules on OLAF's data transfer to third actors are difficult to find. Article 10 Regulation 1073/1999 generally allows for forwarding of information obtained in the course of external or internal investigations "at any time" to the competent authorities of the Member States as well as the forwarding of information obtained through internal investigations to the institutions, bodies, offices or

---

[371] The following third country authorities have already signed such arrangements: Inspecteur général des finances du Sénégal, National Procecution Authority of South Africa (Scorpions), Inspecteur général d'Etat de Djibouti, La Commission nationale de lutte contre la corruption du Congo Brazzaville, forum des inspections générales d'état d'Afrique (FIGE), L'administration des douanes et impots indirectes (ADII) du royaume du Maroc, L'inspection générale des finance du Maroc, Guidelines for OLAF staff regarding practical implementation of data protection requirements of December 2008, annex 5, http://ec.europa.eu/dgs/olaf/legal/manual-annexes.html (accessed February 2011).

[372] Guidelines for OLAF staff regarding practical implementation of data protection requirements of December 2008, p. 15, point 1.7.3. and annex 5, http://ec.europa.eu/dgs/olaf/legal/manual-annexes.html (accessed February 2011).

[373] Ibid, compare list in annex 5.

[374] Ibid, p. 15, point 1.7.3.

[375] Ibid, p. 16, point 1.7.3.

[376] Ibid, p. 16, point 1.7.3.

agencies concerned, although it does not take third states into consideration. Regulation 766/2008 on mutual assistance in customs and agricultural matters further includes data exchange provisions regarding the administrative authorities of the Member States and the Commission, particularly in the framework of the CIS.[377] The agreements with Europol and Eurojust are based on the regulations concerning OLAF's investigations, the Convention on Mutual Assistance in Criminal Matters and on the Council Framework Decision on joint investigation teams.[378] Whether their provisions comply with Regulation 45/2001 is examined in Chap. C I 2 and C I 4.

In addition to the cooperation with the Member States, OLAF concluded a range of agreements on mutual administrative assistance in customs matters based on Article 300 and 310 EC Treaty (Articles 217 and 218 TFEU) with third states partially providing for the exchange of personal data.[379]

---

[377] Regulation (EC) No. 766/2008 of the European Parliament and of the Council of 9 July 2008 amending Council Regulation (EC) No 515/97 on mutual assistance between the administrative authorities of the Member States and cooperation between the latter and the Commission to ensure the correct application of the law on customs and agricultural matters, OJ 2008, L-218/48; Regulation 766/2008 amended the former Council Regulation (EC) No 515/97 on mutual assistance and cooperation between the Member States and the Commission in 2008 to derogate amongst other from the "prior authorisation" principle set out in Regulation 515/97 according to which personal data entered by a Member State could be copied from CIS into other data-processing systems only with the prior authorisation of the CIS partner which entered them (compare recital 7 Regulation 766/2008); Article 35 Regulation 766/2008 now allows for copying in "systems of risk management used to direct national customs controls or in an operational analysis system used to coordinate actions at Community level", but regrettably, Regulation 766/2008 does not exactly indicate whether the "operational analysis system" at Community level remains restricted to OLAF or may also include other systems such as, for instance, Europol (Article 2 (1) Regulation 766/2008 indeed defines the term "operational analysis", however, the term used in context with the Community level is not clarified).

[378] Convention on Mutual Assistance in Criminal Matters between the Member States of the European Union, OJ 2000, C-197/3; Council Framework Decision of 13 June 2002 on joint investigation teams, OJ 2002, L-162/1; Regulation (Euratom) n° 1074/99 of the European Parliament and of the Council of 25 May 1999 concerning investigations by the European Anti-Fraud Office (OLAF), OJ 1999, L-136/8, and Regulation (EC) No. 1073/1999 of the European Parliament and of the Council of 25 May 1999 concerning investigations conducted by the European Anti-Fraud Office (OLAF), OJ 1999, L-136/31.

[379] Albania, Algeria, Andorra, Antigua and Barbuda, Armenia, Azerbaijan, Bahamas, Barbados, Belize, Bosnia and Herzegovina, Canada, Chile, China, Croatia, Dominica, Dominican Republic, Egypt, Faroe Islands, Georgia, Grenada, Guyana, Hong Kong, Iceland, India, Israel, Jamaica, Japan, Jordan, Kazakhstan, Kyrgyzstan, Lebanon, Liechtenstein, Macedonia, Mexico, Moldova, Montenegro, Morocco, Norway, Palestinian Authority, Republic of Korea, Russian federation, Saint Christopher and Nevis, Saint Lucia, Saint Vincent ant the Grenadines, San Marino, Serbia, South Africa, Suriname, Switzerland, Tajikistan, Trinidad and Tobago, Tunisia, Turkey, Ukraine, USA and Uzbekistan; available at: http://ec.europa.eu/dgs/olaf/assist_3rd/index_en.html (accessed February 2011).

f) Conclusion: OLAF – Multiple Data Protection Sources Versus Effective Enforcement of Individual Rights

Since OLAF's beginnings, its attachment to the Commission and its simultaneous mission to conduct internal investigations were described as a "hybrid status of investigative autonomy"[380] and have raised criticism.

In addition, its judicial responsibility was often subject to Court rulings. Cases such as *Nikolaou v. Commission, Yves Franchet and Daniel Byk v. Commmision*[381] as well as *Violetti and others v. Commission*[382] illustrate the legal problems arising in context with OLAF. The core problem arising in those cases always involves the question whether OLAF's decision to forward possibly incriminating information to national judicial authorities constitutes a challengeable act or a mere preparatory act. The Civil Service Tribunal's jurisprudence in this regard constituted a first step towards the recognition of OLAF's legal accountability, but it was regrettably not followed up by the General Court. Therefore, OLAF's accountability as well as its judicial responsibility for its activities needs to be strengthened.

Further criticism relates to the amount of legal sources applicable to OLAF which considerably hinders the understanding as well as the enforcement of data protection rights at OLAF. It is not clear how many and which data elements are exactly included in OLAF's different databases. As mentioned above, a puzzling assortment of diverse Commission Decisions, Council Regulations, the OLAF manual as well as non binding "privacy statements" issued by OLAF itself, challenge the understanding of applicable data protection rules. The so called "privacy statements" refer to wide-ranging terms such as identification data, professional data and case involvement data which could embrace a great number of data elements.[383] The concrete amount of data elements which can be stored by OLAF remains untold. To assure compliance with Article 12 (c) Regulation 45/2001 individuals concerned essentially need to know which data elements are to be stored at OLAF. Transparent and, above all binding, rules on the CMS would solve this problem.

With regard to these shortcomings, it is not surprising that the last activity report of OLAF's special supervisory committee in 2009 revealed serious problems,

---

[380] House of Lords, European Union Committee, "Financial Management and Fraud in the European Union: Perceptions, Facts and Proposals", 50th report of session 2005–2006, published 13 November 2006, p. 142, para 140 and House of Lords, European Union Committee, "Strengthening OLAF, the European Anti-Fraud Office", 24th report with evidence of session 2003–2004, published 21 July 2004, p. 16, para 29.

[381] T-48/05, *Yves Franchet and Daniel Byk v. Commission*, judgment of 8 July 2008; see White (2008) and Niestedt and Boekmann (2009).

[382] T-259/03, *Nikolaou v. Commission*, judgment of 12 September 2007; see also T-309/03, *Camos Grau v. Commission*, judgment of 6 April 2006; F-23/05, *Giraudy v. Commission*, judgment of 2 May 2007 and F-5/05 and 7/05, *Violetti and others v. Commission*, judgment of 28 April 2009.

[383] Privacy statement for internal investigations (OLAF DPO-7), section 2 and privacy statement for external investigations (OLAF DPO-6, 8, 9, 10, 11 and 13), section 2; accessible at: http://ec.europa.eu/dgs/olaf/data/pst_en.html (accessed February 2011).

particularly relating to the inadequate level of supervision and control of the day to day management of investigations, missing transparency and inexplicable delays in investigations procedures.

The relation to third states raises particular concern as OLAF presumes that all countries having ratified Convention No. 108 provide an adequate level of protection.[384] This understanding of the adequacy criterion does not correspond to legal reality considering that the adequacy requirement of Regulation 45/2001 does not automatically correspond to that of Convention No. 108.

In conclusion, OLAF's legal framework needs to be profoundly reconsidered. Clear data protection rules, transparency and accountability need to be strengthened.

4. *Frontex*

Frontex was established by Regulation 2007/2004 in 2004 to be the EU's external border agency.[385]

a) Tasks

Frontex focuses on the coordination of operational cooperation between the Member States in the field of external border management[386] by performing the following main tasks[387]:

- Assisting Member States in training of national border guards, including the establishment of common training standards Eurojust's
- Carrying out risk analyses
- Following up on the development of research relevant for the control and surveillance of external borders
- Assisting Member States in circumstances requiring increased technical and operational assistance at external borders
- Providing Member States with the necessary support in organising joint return operations, e.g. an alien's deportation to its home country.

---

[384] Guidelines for OLAF staff regarding practical implementation of data protection requirements of December 2008, p. 15, point 1.7.3. and annex 5, http://ec.europa.eu/dgs/olaf/legal/manual-annexes.html (accessed February 2011).

[385] Council Regulation (EC) No. 2007/2004 of 26 October 2004 establishing a European Agency for the Management of Operational Cooperation at the External Borders of the Member States of the European Union, OJ 2004, L-349/1, in the following: Regulation 2007/2004.

[386] Article 1 (2) Regulation 2007/2004.

[387] Compare Article 2 (1) (a)-(f) Regulation 2007/2004; further information in: Tohidipur and Fischer-Lescano (2008–2009); Möllers (2009).

b) Data Processing

Theoretically, Frontex's current legal framework excludes personal data processing. However, in the course of the adoption of Regulation (EC) No. 863/2007 in 2007 Frontex obtained executive competences permitting the creation of so called "Rapid Border Interventions Teams" (RABITs) which could now be established by Frontex recruiting staff from the Member States to exercise border checks and surveillance tasks for a limited period of time.[388] The introduction of the RABITs has raised criticism,[389] principally concerning their comprehensive responsibilities, but also as it regards their possibilities to use national as well as European databases. During their operations, members of the RABITs, which are seconded from the Member States, can be authorised by the host Member State to consult national as well as European databases for border checks and surveillance. When doing so they shall consult those data "which are required for performing their tasks and exercising their powers".[390] Frontex shall be *informed* about the consultation. This nonetheless leads to a schizophrenic situation: on the one hand, Frontex itself, unlike Europol and Eurojust, has a "limited mandate", which does not allow gathering or analysis of personal data from people that have been arrested. On the other hand, members of Frontex's RABITs consult databases and use the relevant data for the performance of their tasks based on the national law of the host Member State.

All in all, apart from the RABIT's activities, Frontex's current legal framework does not allow for gathering or processing of personal data by the agency. Nonetheless, a House of Lords report adds that Europol has worked "informally" with Frontex since 2006.[391] An external report evaluating Frontex's work and published on Frontex's webpage sheds light on this issue and reveals further problems. According to the report, Frontex collects data in the framework of joint operations

---

[388] Regulation (EC) No. 863/2007 of the European Parliament and of the Council of 11 July 2007 establishing a mechanism for the creation of Rapid Border Intervention Teams and amending Council Regulation (EC) No. 2007/2004 as regards that mechanism and regulating the tasks and powers of guest officers, OJ 2007, L-199/30.

[389] Marischka (2009); Löhr (2008); Tohidipur and Fischer-Lescano (2008–2009), in particular pp. 510–511; on the accountability of Frontex see Pollak and Slominski (2009); Neal (2009); Weinzierl (2008–2009).

[390] Regulation (EC) No. 863/2007 of the European Parliament and of the Council of 11 July 2007 establishing a mechanism for the creation of Rapid Border Intervention Teams and amending Council Regulation (EC) No. 2007/2004 as regards that mechanism and regulating the tasks and powers of guest officers, OJ 2007, L-199/30, Article 6 (8); see also Regulation (EC) No 562/2006 the European Parliament and of the Council of 15 March 2006 establishing a Community Code on the rules governing the movement of persons across borders (Schengen Borders Code), OJ 2006, L-105/1, Article 7 (2).

[391] House of Lords Europol report, European Union Committee, 29th report of session 2007–2008, "Europol: coordinating the fight against serious and organised crime", published 12 November 2008, p. 80.

in order to send them to other agencies, such as Europol for threat analysis.[392] Joint operations are described as a "good example of integrated analyses by Europol and Frontex" and are regarded as a working practice in which intelligence and operations are brought together as closely as possible".[393] Pursuant to the report, 10% percent of the detained persons during a joint operation are interviewed by Frontex staff,[394] which means in the end that in addition to the RABITs, Frontex itself also collects personal data notwithstanding its restrictive legal framework at present. Consequently, Frontex acts in absence of a legal basis allowing for the collection and processing as well as the transfer of personal data.

c) Judicial Review

Judicial review against such measures seems to be very difficult to obtain. Certainly, a request to verify a decision taken by Frontex to deny access to documents pursuant to Regulation 1049/2001 could be brought before the Ombudsman or could be challenged by lodging an action for annulment to the European Court of Justice,[395] but at least the first option is restricted to individuals with EU citizenship or having their place of residence within the EU.[396] Judicial review by the Ombudsman is therefore excluded for third state nationals who are for the most part affected by Frontex measures.[397]

An applicant invoking the second possibility will meet the same problems as emerged in the *Tillack* case[398]: a complaint according to Article 263 TFEU[399] requires an act addressed to the individual or an act "which is of direct and individual concern" to him and produces legal effects "affecting the interests of the applicant by bringing about a distinct change in his legal position".[400] However, the possibility of Frontex processing data, including its data collection, its related operational activities and the data transfer between the agency and Europol, does

---

[392] Final report of COWI (European consulting group) of January 2009 preparing an external evaluation of Frontex provided for in Article 33 of the Council Regulation (EC) No 2007/2004 of 26 October 2004 establishing Frontex, p. 48, available at: http://www.frontex.europa.eu/specific_documents/other/(accessed February 2011); to the cooperation between Europol and Frontex, see Holzenberger (2006).

[393] Final report of COWI (European consulting group) of January 2009 preparing an external evaluation of Frontex provided for in Article 33 of the Council Regulation (EC) No 2007/2004 of 26 October 2004 establishing Frontex, p. 48, available at: http://www.frontex.europa.eu/specific_documents/other/ (accessed February 2011).

[394] Ibid.

[395] Article 28 (5) Regulation 2007/2004.

[396] Article 228 (1) TFEU.

[397] See Tohidipur and Fischer-Lescano (2008–2009), in particular pp. 513–514.

[398] See Chap. A II 2 c and Sect. II 3 b.

[399] To the possibility of judicial review against Agencies in the Lisbon Treaty, see Everling (2009).

[400] T-193/04, *Tillack v. Commission*, judgment of 4 October 2006, para 67.

not directly change the position of an individual and could therefore be seen as preparatory acts not fulfilling the requirement of an action for annulment in terms of Article 263 TFEU, even if they may have serious consequences for individuals, for example regarding their future chances to ask for asylum.

A complaint to the EDPS would theoretically be possible according to Article 32 (2) Regulation 45/2001 although there is no reference in the Frontex instruments to the regulation due to the fact that the agency does not officially process data.

Judicial review before national courts might be possible when national members of Frontex act on the basis of national law, but it can neither be invoked in case of data processing at Frontex, nor in situations which concern data transfer to Europol.

d) Amending the Frontex Regulation

The mentioned inconsistencies might be the reason for Commission proposal to amend the Frontex regulation providing for a broad extension of the mission of Frontex including the collection, storage, processing and transfer of personal data in context of the detection of criminal networks organising illegal immigration.[401] Since the question of whether the final regulation shall include the transfer of data to third countries it is not yet decided,[402] the proposal additionally aims at enabling Frontex to analyse operational risks and requirements in the Member States, to coordinate joint return operations, to allow the agency to finance and implement technical assistance projects in third countries and to second liaison officers in third countries as well as to award Frontex a "co-leading role for the implementation of joint operations".[403] Compulsory contributions of equipment as well as of human resources, such as border guards on detachment from the Member States, shall further strengthen Frontex's mandate.[404]

An intended information system would enable exchanges of information concerning "emerging risks at the external borders including the Information and

[401] Proposal for a Regulation of the European Parliament and the Council amending Council Regulation (EC) No. 2007/2004 of 26 October 2004 establishing a European Agency for the Management of Operational Cooperation at the External Borders of the Member States of the European Union (FRONTEX) of 24 February 2010, COM(2010) 61 final, Article 2.

[402] Impact assessment accompanying the proposal for a Regulation of the European Parliament and the Council amending Council Regulation (EC) No. 2007/2004 of 26 October 2004 establishing a European Agency for the Management of Operational Cooperation at the External Borders of the Member States of the European Union (FRONTEX) of 24 February 2010, COM (2010) 61 final, pp. 34–36.

[403] Explanatory memorandum of the Proposal for a Regulation of the European Parliament and the Council amending Council Regulation (EC) No. 2007/2004 of 26 October 2004 establishing a European Agency for the Management of Operational Cooperation at the External Borders of the Member States of the European Union (FRONTEX) of 24 February 2010, COM(2010) 61 final, p. 4.

[404] Ibid.

Coordination Network".[405] The system would establish a secure web-based information and coordination line for the exchange of information on irregular migration, illegal entry and immigration and the return of illegal residents. Frontex shall provide assistance to the development and operation of a European border surveillance system as well as to the establishment of a common information sharing environment.[406] Within the framework of joint operations, Frontex shall gather and use personal data for the purpose of carrying out risk analyses.[407]

The risk analysis procedure at Frontex would entail the "process of information, collection and consolidation" as well as the analysis of information and the conclusion on the results which it shall send to the Council and the Commission.[408] Specific factors, such as the "multi angle (legal, operational, political perspective) analysis of intelligence information" and the efficient gathering of "reliable surveillance information and intelligence" shall thereby support Frontex's work to achieve a "tailored and detailed risk analysis".[409]

So far, the lack of Frontex's mandate to collect personal data has hampered the inclusion of Frontex data in such analyses, but the Commission's impact assessment on the Frontex proposal notes that "the risk analysis carried out by the agency could be substantially enriched if it could collect and process certain types of personal data".[410] Consequently, if the proposal enters into force, future risk

[405] Proposal for a Regulation of the European Parliament and the Council amending Council Regulation (EC) No. 2007/2004 of 26 October 2004 establishing a European Agency for the Management of Operational Cooperation at the External Borders of the Member States of the European Union (FRONTEX) of 24 February 2010, COM(2010) 61 final, Article 2 (3) (iii) (h); the Information and Coordination Network bases on Council Decision of 16 March 2005 establishing a secure webbased Information and Coordination Network for Member States' Migration Management Services, OJ 2005, L-83/48.

[406] Proposal for a Regulation of the European Parliament and the Council amending Council Regulation (EC) No. 2007/2004 of 26 October 2004 establishing a European Agency for the Management of Operational Cooperation at the External Borders of the Member States of the European Union (FRONTEX) of 24 February 2010, COM(2010) 61 final, Article 2 (3) (iii) (i).

[407] Impact assessment accompanying the proposal for a Regulation of the European Parliament and the Council amending Council Regulation (EC) No. 2007/2004 of 26 October 2004 establishing a European Agency for the Management of Operational Cooperation at the External Borders of the Member States of the European Union (FRONTEX), COM(2010) 61 final, of 24 February 2010, p. 34.

[408] Description of the risk analysis process at Frontex in: Deloitte, study on the feasibility of establishing specialised branches of Frontex, final report, 11 December 2009, p. 18, para 4.1.1., http://www.frontex.europa.eu/specific_documents/other/ (accessed February 2011), see also House of Lords, European Union Committee, 9th report of session 2007–2008, "Frontex: the EU external borders agency", published 5 March 2008, pp. 25–27, paras 66–70, and Pollak and Slominski (2009) pp. 911–912.

[409] Description of the risk analysis process at Frontex in: Deloitte, study on the feasibility of establishing specialised branches of Frontex, final report, 11 December 2009, p. 18, para 4.1.1., http://www.frontex.europa.eu/specific_documents/other/ (accessed February 2011).

[410] Executive summary of the impact assessment accompanying the proposal for a Regulation of the European Parliament and the Council amending Council Regulation (EC) No. 2007/2004 of 26

analyses carried out by Frontex will also include the analysis of personal data. In this case, the Commission recognises that only a stringent data protection regime could balance the impact this measure would have on the rights of individuals concerned.[411] Unfortunately, the Commission's qualms expressed in the impact assessment are not further reflected in its own proposal, according to which the European Parliament would not be involved in the risk analysis assessment and only one short reference to the generally applicable data protection rules of Regulation 45/2001 and the appointment of a data protection officer is made in Article 11a of the proposal.[412]

Further data processing provisions are not entailed in the proposal. It is not specified whether and under which circumstances, conditions, limitations and safeguards data processing at Frontex shall take place.[413] The proposal neither contains a specific legal basis allowing Frontex to process personal data, nor provisions guaranteeing individual rights, such as provisions referring to access to, correction or deletion of personal data. This serious omission must be corrected in the following adoption process of the proposal.

Finally, all things considered, the adoption of the proposal including the reference to Regulation 45/2001 would – besides the extended competences of Frontex and its inherent possibilities to use and process personal data – also lead to a slightly improved legal certainty. When taking into account the current ambiguous situation with regard to data processing at Frontex, the application of Regulation 45/2001 would underline Frontex's legal responsibilities in this regard. The entire data processing would fall under an established data protection framework due to Frontex's status as a Community agency. Supervision would be carried out by the EDPS and restrictions would apply to the transfer of personal data to third parties as well as to recipients which are not subject to Directive 95/46 such as Europol or Eurojust. A formal complaint to the EDPS in case of misuse of data would be possible.

October 2004 establishing a European Agency for the Management of Operational Cooperation at the External Borders of the Member States of the European Union (FRONTEX) of 24 February 2010, p. 2, para 1.

[411] Impact assessment accompanying the proposal for a Regulation of the European Parliament and the Council amending Council Regulation (EC) No. 2007/2004 of 26 October 2004 establishing a European Agency for the Management of Operational Cooperation at the External Borders of the Member States of the European Union (FRONTEX) of 24 February 2010, p. 36, para 5.5.4.

[412] Proposal for a Regulation of the European Parliament and the Council amending Council Regulation (EC) No. 2007/2004 of 26 October 2004 establishing a European Agency for the Management of Operational Cooperation at the External Borders of the Member States of the European Union (FRONTEX) of 24 February 2010, COM(2010) 61 final, Article 11a.

[413] Compare also: Opinion of the European Data Protection Supervisor on the proposal for a Regulation of the European Parliament and the Council amending Council Regulation (EC) No. 2007/2004 establishing a European Agency for the Management of Operational Cooperation at the External Borders of the Member States of the European Union (FRONTEX) of 17 May 2010.

However, in any case, it is necessary that the data processing framework be included in the Commission's proposal to specify the extent and the limits of Frontex's currently unregulated data processing.

The details of the provided data exchange with EU bodies and third states in the new Frontex regulation are discussed in Chap. C I 3 and C I 5.

e) Conclusion: Frontex's Legal Framework Versus Reality

The results of the analysis of the legal framework and the data processing activities of Frontex are worrisome. Although the current legal framework of Frontex does not allow for personal data processing, Frontex takes part in joint operations in which it collects personal data and sends them to Europol for threat analyses.[414] These joint operations are regarded as a "working practice in which intelligence and operations are brought together as closely as possible".[415] Ten percent of the detained persons during a joint operation are interviewed by Frontex staff.[416]

In addition to the data collection during joint operations, Frontex has established so called RABITs which have full access to national as well as European databases. Although their members are seconded from the Member States and underlie national law, Frontex is nonetheless informed about the outcomes of possible searches, which means that Frontex partly circumvents its legal basis which does not permits personal data processing. This situation can be best described as schizophrenic: on the one hand, Frontex itself (in contrast to Europol and Eurojust) has a "limited mandate", which does not allow gathering or analysis of personal data from people that have been detained. On the other hand, members of Frontex's RABITs consult and use databases, simply based on the national law of the host Member State.

As follows from the foregoing, Frontex's legal basis does not cover its actual tasks. This situation has further consequences, which lead inter alia to difficulties as regards the judicial review for the persons concerned which are principally third state nationals. The same difficulties as emerged in the OLAF cases are likely to arise. As Frontex limits its activities to the forwarding of data to Europol, it is questionable whether this forwarding is a mere preparatory act or whether it produces adverse legal effects affecting the position of the individual. Only in the last case, a complaint according to Article 263 TFEU would be available.

---

[414] Final report of COWI (European consulting group) of January 2009 preparing an external evaluation of Frontex provided for in Article 33 of the Council Regulation (EC) No 2007/2004 of 26 October 2004 establishing Frontex, p. 48, available at: http://www.frontex.europa.eu/specific_documents/other/ (accessed February 2011); for the cooperation between Europol and Frontex, see Holzenberger (2006).

[415] Final report of COWI (European consulting group) of January 2009 preparing an external evaluation of Frontex provided for in Article 33 of the Council Regulation (EC) No 2007/2004 of 26 October 2004 establishing Frontex, p. 48, available at: http://www.frontex.europa.eu/specific_documents/other/ (accessed February 2011).

[416] Ibid.

Finally, the planned amendment of the Frontex regulation includes further inconsistencies. While on the one hand, data processing should now be included in Frontex's tasks, specific data protection rules are not provided in the proposal. Nonetheless, in case the proposal enters into force, the general rules of Regulation 45/2001 would be applicable to data processing carried out by Frontex. This would certainly improve the rather unregulated data processing which is currently taking place.

In summary, Frontex's legal framework, in particular its legal basis with regard to its data processing activities, needs to be reconsidered. Currently, Frontex is violating its own legal framework by collecting and transferring personal data to other agencies such as Europol.

5. *Joint Situation Centre of the Council*

The Joint Situation Centre (SitCen) is a body resembling an EU "intelligence agency" composed of seconded national intelligence experts based in Brussels making counter-terrorism assessments and subsequently briefing the Council and other policy makers about terrorist trends and risks.[417] Its establishment can be traced back to 1999 when the Office of the EU High Representative was created.[418] The SitCen as a distinct entity was created through an administrative decision by the Secretary General/High Representative in 2000 and formed part of the General Secretariat of the Council.[419]

After the entry into force of the Lisbon Treaty the SitCen has been integrated into the European External Action Service (EEAS)[420] provided for in Article 27 (3) TEU which assists the High Representative for Foreign Affairs and Security Policy, Catherine Ashton.[421] It has no particular legal basis although it has a staff of around 110 people.[422]

Due to its rather secret status and its establishment largely unnoticed by the public, it is not entirely clear whether SitCen processes personal data. The unit admittedly works together with Europol and even concluded an agreement with the agency in 2005 (which is not published and can not be found on Europol's webpage

---

[417] House of Lords, European Union Committee, report "Civil Protection and Crisis Management in the European Union", seventh report of session 2008–2009, examination of witnesses, 21 January 2009, questions 92–99 to Johnny Engel-Hansen, Head of Operations Unit at SitCen, General Secretariat of the Council of the EU.

[418] Ibid.

[419] Ibid.

[420] Outcome of proceedings of CATS on 11 February 2010, Council doc. 6557/10, CATS 18/ COMIX 138 p. 4, II Items, para 4.

[421] Council Decision of 20 July 2010 establishing the organisation and functioning of the European External Action Service, Council Doc. 11665/1/10, REV 1/POLGEN 104/INST 243, see annex, Policy Units.

[422] Compare article in the EU observer, "EU diplomats to benefit from new intelligence hub", 22 February 2010, http://euobserver.com/?aid=29519 (accessed February 2011).

where all agreements are usually published),[423] but its work is exercised in a clandestine way.

SitCen undertakes situation monitoring (24 h a day, 7 days a week), situation assessment and provides facilities and organisational infrastructure for the crisis task forces and Brussels-based support and assistance to the EU field activities, including those of the Secretary General/High Representative, EU Special Representatives etc.[424] Seconded national experts in analytical functions work together with Council officials.[425] Information is thereby exchanged with the Member States' diplomatic services, intelligence as well as security services.[426]

While the role of the SitCen in personal data processing and exchange is far from clear, its influence on the access of intelligence services and law enforcement actors to European databases should not be underestimated. Some authors assume that the body's reports and recommendations in the context of the movement of suspected terrorists "have been a driving force" behind the legislative measures allowing for such access.[427]

When looking at the tasks of SitCen and the Europol-SitCen Agreement, the SitCen seems to fuse (former) third and second pillar information exchange. It is worth noting here, that the SitCen describes itself as a cross-pillar body and pays attention to the fact that is it not only seen as a second pillar actor.[428] There is, however, no information about its data processing activities.

6. *European Judicial Network*

The European Judicial Network (EJN) was established by the Joint Action 98/428 in 1998 to better coordinate judicial cooperation in criminal matters.[429] The EJN is

---

[423] Compare Europol's publications: Anniversary publication: 10 years of Europol 1999-2009 referring to the agreement of 26 October 2005 concluded with the SitCen, p. 56 and EU Terrorism Situation and Trend Report TE-SAT 2010, pp. 5 and 8, to be found on Europol's webpage: http://www.europol.europa.eu/index.asp?page=publications&language= (accessed February 2011).

[424] House of Lords, European Union Committee, report "Civil Protection and Crisis Management in the European Union", seventh report of session 2008–2009, examination of witnesses, 21 January 2009, questions 92–99 to Johnny Engel-Hansen, Head of Operations Unit at SitCen, General Secretariat of the Council of the EU.

[425] Ibid.

[426] Ibid; see also EU Terrorism Situation and Trend Report TE-SAT 2010, p. 8, footnote 3, the report can be consulted on Europol's webpage: http://www.europol.europa.eu/index.asp?page=publications&language= (accessed February 2011).

[427] Van Buuren (2009); the access and the interactions between the actors discussed in Chap. B are further analysed in Chap. C.

[428] Van Buuren (2009); House of Lords report: 5th report of session 2004–2005, "After Madrid: the EU's response to terrorism", published 8 March 2005, p. 61.

[429] Joint Action of 29 June 1998 adopted by the Council on the basis of Article K.3 of the Treaty on European Union, on the creation of a European Judicial Network (98/428/JHA), OJ 1998, L-191/4 (in the following: European Judicial Network Decision 2008).

a network of over 300 national contact points[430] supplying the judicial authorities of the Member States with information on judicial cooperation requests and assists in bilateral cases requiring cooperation of the national judicial authorities, predominantly in actions to combat forms of serious crime.[431] While the link to Eurojust's remit is evident, both actors maintain "privileged relations"[432] and collaborate closely whereby a clear distinction between their areas of responsibility seems not to be possible in each and every case.[433] The EJN secretariat forms part of Eurojust's staff yet functions as a separate unit within Eurojust.[434] The EJN supports mutual legal assistance in criminal matters in the course of the establishment of direct contacts between the national judicial authorities.[435] In contrast to Eurojust, which was designed to deal with multilateral cases, the EJN should be primarily involved in bilateral cases; however this distinction does not correspond with the reality of the case work of Eurojust.[436] Both the new EJN Decision from 2008 as well as Eurojust Annual Report 2008 propose a clarification of the relationships between the two bodies.[437]

As so far the EJN does not process personal data, it is not further analysed. However it is worth mentioning that it makes available to Eurojust its information tool and a secure telecommunication connection which initially served as a communication tool for the operational work of the EJN's national contact points but may also be used for operational work by Eurojust's national correspondents, Eurojust's national correspondents for terrorist matters as well as the national members of Eurojust and liaison magistrates appointed by Eurojust.[438] The secure telecommunication connection may also be linked to Eurojust's CMS (Case Management System).[439]

As the mandates of the Eurojust and the EJN partly overlap, the EJN Secretariat was integrated in the structure of the Eurojust Secretariat leading to a "certain

---

[430] http://www.ejn-crimjust.europa.eu/about-ejn.aspx (accessed February 2011).

[431] Article 4 European Judicial Network Decision 2008.

[432] Recital (5) and Article 10 European Judicial Network Decision 2008.

[433] Compare the references made in the Eurojust Decision vis-à-vis the Council Decision 2008/976/JHA of 16 December 2008 on the European Judicial Network, OJ 2008, L-348/130 and vice versa, examples are Articles 12 (5) (b), 16 (3) and in particular 25 (a) of the Eurojust Decision and Articles of the European Judicial Network Decision 2008, see also Fawzy (2005), pp. 95–102.

[434] Article 25a (b) Eurojust Decision.

[435] See Recital (2) European Judicial Network Decision 2008 making reference to the Convention on Mutual Assistance in Criminal Matters between the Member States of the European Union, OJ 2000, C-197/3.

[436] Mitsilegas (2009), p. 191, and annual report of Eurojust 2008, pp. 13 and 52, according to which Eurojust dealt with 956 bilateral cases and only 237 multi-lateral cases in 2008, http://www.eurojust.europa.eu/press_annual.htm (accessed Februar 2011).

[437] Recital (6) European Judicial Network Decision 2008 and annual report of Eurojust 2008, p. 41 http://www.eurojust.europa.eu/press_annual.htm (accessed Februar 2011).

[438] Articles 7, 9 and 10 (a) European Judicial Network Decision 2008.

[439] Article 9 (3) European Judicial Network Decision 2008 and Article 16 (3) Eurojust Decision.

degree of oversight by the President of Eurojust" whereby the legal basis for this supervision is not clearly defined.[440]

7. *Conclusion: Fragmented Data Protection Framework Versus Increasing Powers of the AFSJ Agencies and OLAF*

Detecting the data protection shortcomings of the AFSJ agencies as well as OLAF is fundamental to understanding their framework before analysing their cooperation with the European information exchange systems and amongst each other.

The results are rather worrisome from a data protection point of view. The foregoing analysis has revealed several tendencies, briefly illustrated hereinafter.

The threshold to enter data about a person in the databases of Europol or Eurojust was considerably lowered in recent years.[441] Pre-emptive entries, such as the entry of personal data based on mere factual indications[442] that a person might become a criminal in the future, clearly contradict ECtHR case law and the principles of Recommendation (87) 15.[443] This infringement is regrettably not outweighed by other provisions providing for the protection of individuals concerned by such entries.

While on the one hand, gradually more actors profit from the use of the databases of Europol or Eurojust, on the other hand, the amount of data elements stored, including information on victims or witnesses, increases noticeably. New types of information, such as DNA profiles, fingerprints or data related to internet connections, have been added in the recent Eurojust Decision.[444]

At the same time, the review period as well as the access to information at Europol was extended when comparing it to the previous regulation (Europol Convention)[445] and comprises now even the information regarding persons whose data were entered as a result of factual indications that they might become criminal one day.

---

[440] Mitsilegas (2009), p. 201; see also Article 26 (2) (b) Eurojust Decision.

[441] Compare Article 15 (1) Eurojust Decision and Article 12 (1) lit. b Council Decision of 6 April 2009 establishing the European Police Office, OJ 2009, L-121/37.

[442] Article 12 (1) lit. b Council Decision of 6 April 2009 establishing the European Police Office, OJ 2009, L-121/37.

[443] *Weber and Saravia v. Germany*, Application no. 54934/00, admissibility decision of 29 June 2006, para 127; *Association for European Integration and Human Rights and Ekimdzhiev v. Bulgaria*, Application no. 62540/00, judgment of 28 June 2007, para 89; Principle 2.1. of Recommendation R (87) 15; Point 43 of the explanatory memorandum of Recommendation R (87) 15.

[444] Compare Article 15 of the Eurojust Decision 2002 with Article 15 of the Eurojust Decision of 2009.

[445] Article 7 (1) Europol Convention.

This development can be partly traced back to the undemocratic way in which important choices specifying the Europol Decision were made. Against the votes of the European Parliament and only 1 day before the Lisbon Treaty came into force, four Council Implementing Decisions regulating the details of the analysis work files, the possibility of Europol to process data prior to the actual data processing for 6 month, the rules governing the relation to partners as well as a list of third states with which Europol shall conclude agreements, were approved by the Council.[446]

Taking into account the foregoing observations, the rather weak position of the JSB in both cases as well as the maintenance of the same data processing supervisory structure, even after the above mentioned enlargements of data processing possibilities, does not necessarily contribute to an effective control. Both JSBs have to fulfil a huge amount of tasks while their few members have a "double function" at national as well as at the European level. In some cases, their supervisory function does not relate to all data processed at the databases[447] and in case of Eurojust, only three judges should monitor the whole personal data processing at the agency.

The introduction of an internal DPO at both agencies constitutes an important improvement guaranteeing an additional control, but he/she is, from a data protection point of view, not totally independent from the agency he/she should supervise.[448]

A further point illustrating the weakness of the JSB relates to Europol's implementation of data security measures which depend on the "necessity" of such measures. Without involving the JSB or the internal DPO in the final decision about the necessity, the Management Board alone decides about their establishment.[449]

Reinforcing the supervisory structure of both supervisory bodies in terms of human as well as financial resources accompanied by the "upgrading" of their functions would lead to an effective monitoring as demanded by the ECtHR.[450] Either their influence could be improved by replacing the current consulting requirements through more effective approval provisions, or a replacement of the

---

[446] Council Decision 2009/936 of 30 November 2009 adopting the implementing rules for Europol analysis work files, OJ 2009, L-325/14; Council Decision 2009/935/JHA of 30 November 2009 determining the list of third states and organisations with which Europol shall conclude agreements, OJ 2009, L-325/12; Council Decision 2009/934/JHA of 30 November 2009 adopting the implementing rules governing Europol's relations with partners, including the exchange of personal and classified information, OJ 2009, L-325/6; Decision of the Europol Management Board on the conditions related to the processing of data on the basis of Article 10 (4) of the Europol Decision, 15942/09, adopted the 30 November 2009, OJ 2009, L-348/1; With regard to the continually extending powers of the EU agencies in general, compare Griller and Orator (February 2010).

[447] See for instance the example of Europol, above in Sect. II 1 d bb.

[448] Compare Sect. II 1 d bb.

[449] Article 10 (3) and 35 (1) Council Decision of 6 April 2009 establishing the European Police Office, OJ 2009, L-121/37.

[450] *Rotaru v. Romania*, Application no. 28341/95, judgment of 4 May 2000, para 59.

current JSB structure by another, more effective, monitoring system should also be considered.[451]

A notification of individuals concerned in case police activities are no longer to be prejudiced would contribute to an improved monitoring as well as to an enhanced awareness of Europol's and Eurojust's data processing activities. This notification should include a reference to the JSB/the monitoring body which would have two positive effects: individuals concerned could better enforce their rights and the JSB/the monitoring body could focus their activities on specific cases.

While in sum, the data protection rules of Eurojust are more comprehensive than those of Europol, the most common criticism relates to the structuring of the data protection rules at Eurojust which are not only regulated in the Eurojust Decision, but also in two additional instruments not automatically having the same binding force as the Eurojust Decision.[452] These rules, which are often more advantageous for people concerned, were not introduced in the newly regulated Eurojust framework in 2009; a fact which is creating doubts on the applicability as well as on the enforceability of such provisions.

Concerning OLAF's data processing, information is difficult to obtain. OLAF's doubtful accountability and legal responsibility for personal information disclosed to the public raises concerns. Far too many different sources consisting of instruments with doubtful legal value (manual, privacy statements etc.) hinder the understanding of the data processing structures and do not include further information about, for instance, the data elements stored therein. In contrast to Europol or Eurojust, a detailed list of the data kept at OLAF does not exist. Regrettably, the proposal to amend OLAF Regulation 1073/1999 does not raise hopes for amelioration in this regard.[453]

In addition to the aforementioned serious problems, OLAF's transfer of data to third countries is also legally doubtful. Transfer is already assessed as adequate if third countries have ratified Convention No. 108.[454] Even transfers without any data protection guarantees are possible.[455]

The situation at Frontex is however different from that of the aforementioned actors, in regard to that its legal framework does not (yet) allow for personal data

---

[451] Discussed in Chap. D IV.

[452] Eurojust Decision; Rules of procedure on the processing and the protection of personal data at Eurojust, OJ 2005, C-68/1 and additional rules defining some specific aspects of the application of the rules on the processing and protection of personal data at Eurojust to non-case related operation, http://www.eurojust.europa.eu/official_documents/eju_dp_rules.htm (accessed February 2011).

[453] Proposal for a regulation of the European Parliament and of the Council amending Regulation (EC) No 1073/1999 of the European Parliament and the Council of 25 May 1999 concerning investigation conducted by the European Anti-Fraud Office (OLAF), COM(2006) 244.

[454] Guidelines for OLAF staff regarding practical implementation of data protection requirements of December 2008, p. 15, point 1.7.3. and annex 5, http://ec.europa.eu/dgs/olaf/assist_3rd/index_en.html (accessed Ferbruary 2011).

[455] Ibid, p. 16, point 1.7.3.

processing. In reality, reports reveal that the agency indeed deals with personal data.[456] The current ambiguous situation of Frontex in this regard is reflected in the Commission's proposal for an amendment of the Frontex regulation,[457] which would, if adopted, considerably enlarge the tasks of Frontex, but entails, in its current version, no data protection guarantees applying to the specific situation in which Frontex is working.

Although both actors, OLAF and Frontex, are former first pillar actors, large efforts need to be made to significantly improve transparency as well as data protection rights.

In the light of the foregoing considerations, it appears that the analysis of the data processing framework of the AFSJ agencies and OLAF has revealed serious data protection shortcomings. Whether these shortcomings also exist in the framework of the AFSJ information exchange systems remains to be seen and is analysed in the next section.

III Data Processing in European Information Exchange Systems

In addition to the information gathering by the AFSJ agencies and OLAF, further information systems in the framework of policing, custom- and border control as well as immigration control have been established in recent years and will be gradually linked to the databases of the AFSJ agencies. The following section illustrates the data protection framework and the use of the Schengen Information System (SIS), the Visa Information System (VIS), the Customs Information System (CIS) and Eurodac, by reference to six key factors relating to the use of the respective system, the data stored therein, the accessing agencies, the individual rights framework, the supervision structure and the time limits for the storage of the data.

---

456 Final report of COWI (European consulting group) of January 2009 preparing an external evaluation of Frontex provided for in Article 33 of the Council Regulation (EC) No 2007/2004 of 26 October 2004 establishing Frontex, p. 48, available at: http://www.frontex.europa.eu/specific_-documents/other/ (accessed February 2011) and House of Lords Europol report, European Union Committee, 29th report of session 2007-2008, "Europol: coordinating the fight against serious and organised crime", published 12 November 2008, p. 80.

457 Proposal for a Regulation of the European Parliament and the Council amending Council Regulation (EC) No. 2007/2004 of 26 October 2004 establishing a European Agency for the Management of Operational Cooperation at the External Borders of the Member States of the European Union (FRONTEX) of 24 February 2010, COM(2010) 61 final.

1. *The Schengen Information System*

The SIS, the first Europe-wide database in the framework of immigration, policing and criminal law for the purpose of law enforcement and immigration control,[458] became operable in 1995 with the entry into force of the Schengen Convention[459] and applies to Member States which fully participate in the Schengen *Acquis*.[460] While Iceland, Norway and Switzerland are associated to the SIS, the UK, Liechtenstein and Ireland do not fully participate in it. More specifically, the UK

---

[458] House of Lords, European Union Committee, 9th report of session 2006–2007, "Schengen Information System II (SIS II)", published 2 March 2007, foreword; for a detailed overview of the SIS and the SIS II, see Brouwer (2008a) and Kabera Karanja (2008); De Hert and Vandamme (September 2004).

[459] Convention implementing the Schengen Agreement of 14 June 1985 between the Governments of the States of the Benelux Economic Union, the Federal Republic of Germany and the French Republic on the gradual abolition of checks at their common borders, OJ 2000, L-239/19, articles 38 (2), 94 (3), 115 (1), 117 (1), especially title VI, article 126 (1); to the background of the Schengen integration, see Monar (2009), in particular pp. 778; Bracke (2002); Oppermann et al. (2009), pp. 657–661; Hailbronner and Weil (1999); Breitenmoser et al. (2009). The Schengen Convention has been transferred to EU law trough the Treaty of Amsterdam, see Council Decision of 20 May 1999 concerning the definition of the Schengen acquis for the purpose of determining, in conformity with the relevant provisions of the Treaty establishing the European Community and the Treaty on European Union, the legal basis for each of the provisions or decisions which constitute the acquis OJ 1999, L-176/1. The Convention implementing the Schengen Agreement was amended by Council Regulation (EC) No. 871/2004 of 29 April 2004 concerning the introduction of some new functions for the Schengen Information System, including in the fight against terrorism, OJ 2004, L-162/29 and Council Decision 2005/211/JHA of 24 February 2005 concerning the introduction of some new functions for the Schengen Information System, including in the fight against terrorism, OJ 2005, L-68/44. See also Council Decision 2006/228/JHA of 9 March 2006 fixing the date of application of certain provisions of Decision 2005/211/JHA concerning the introduction of some new functions for the Schengen Information System, including the fight against terrorism, OJ 2006, L-81/45 and Council Decision 2006/229/JHA of 9 March 2006 fixing the date of application of certain provisions of Decision 2005/211/JHA concerning the introduction of some new functions for the Schengen Information System, including in the fight against terrorism, OJ 2006, L-81/46.

[460] The Schengen acquis – Convention implementing the Schengen Agreement of 14 June 1985 between the Governments of the States of the Benelux Economic Union, the Federal Republic of Germany and the French Republic on the gradual abolition of checks at their common borders, OJ 2000, L-239/19, Article 92-119 (in the following: Schengen Convention, OJ 2000, L-239/19); to the participation of UK, Ireland, Iceland, Norway, Switzerland and Liechtenstein, see Council Regulation amending Decision 2008/839/JHA on migration from the Schengen Information System (SIS 1+) to the second generation Schengen Information System (SIS II), OJ 2008, L-299/1, recitals 21-27, and exemptions in: Commission Proposal for a Council Regulation on migration from the Schengen Information System (SIS 1) to the second generation Schengen Information System (SIS II) COM/2008/0197 final of 16 April 2008, recitals 22-29; for details see House of Lords, European Union Committee, 9th report of session 2006–2007, "Schengen Information System II (SIS II)", published 2 March 2007; an analysis of the background of the Schengen *Aquis* can be found in Fungueirino-Lorenzo (2002); Hailbronner (1996).

and Ireland do not have access to immigration data, but to those data related to police and criminal cooperation.[461] Liechtenstein was due to implement the SIS in 2010. Currently, the SIS is fully applicable in 22 Member States, not including Bulgaria and Romania which are expected to implement the SIS in 2011. Cyprus has signed the Schengen Convention, but has not yet implemented it.

A second generation of the SIS, the SIS II, should have become operational in 2007,[462] but its implementation was considerably delayed in the last years as a result of technical problems.[463]

a) Purpose and Use: From SIS to SIS II

Originally, the SIS was a hit/no hit system allowing for a simple technical request whether data related to certain persons or objects are included in the database or not.[464] It contains a national section (N-SIS) which is connected to a central EU system (C-SIS).[465] Since its implementation in 1995, more than 31.6 million records have been created and the amount of registered data is increasing quickly.[466] However, already in the beginnings of the SIS, the information entered in the SIS was supposed to serve two rather wide ranging purposes related to "public policy and public security".[467] On the one hand the SIS shall be used for border checks as well as for "other police and customs checks" and on the other, for the purpose of issuing visas, residence permits and the administration of legislation

[461] Council Decision of 29 May 2000 concerning the request of the United Kingdom of Great Britain and Northern Ireland to take part in some of the provisions of the Schengen acquis, OJ 2000, L-131/43 and Council Decision of 28 February 2002 concerning Ireland's request to take part in some of the provisions of the Schengen acquis, OJ 2002, L-64/20; basically the UK and Ireland do not enter data related to third country nationals who should be denied entry to any of the Schengen State according to Article 96 of the Schengen Convention, OJ 2000, L-239/19.

[462] The Hague Programme, Council doc. 16054/04 of 13 December 2004, point 1.7.1., p. 15.

[463] To the reasons for the delay, see House of Lords, European Union Committee, 9th report of session 2006–2007, "Schengen Information System II (SIS II)", published 2 March 2007, paras 22–27, pp. 12–14; to the SIS II in general see Christou (2008).

[464] Busch (2006), p. 30.

[465] Article 92 (2) Schengen Convention, OJ 2000, L-239/19.

[466] Council document 6162/10 of 5 February 2010, note to the SIS-TECH Working Party/Mixed Committee (EU-Iceland/Norway/Switzerland/Liechtenstein); compare for the increasing amount of data Council SIS Database Statistics of 1 January 2008, 5441/08, 30 January 2008 and Council Doc. 5171/09 of 19 February 2009 on the staff shortage and workload SIS II, SIRIS 7, COMIX 22, Annex 3, spreadsheet p. 11; Hayes (2005).

[467] Article 93 Schengen Convention, OJ 2000 L-239/19.

relating to third-country nationals.[468] A list of the competent authorities having access to the SIS is entailed in a Council document.[469]

The legal basis of the SIS is shared between the former first and the former third pillar as a result of the exhaustive scope of the SIS, embracing subjects of both former pillars.[470] The legal basis for visa and immigration policy within the Schengen framework can be found in Community Law,[471] whereas the police and judicial cooperation is based on the rules of the former third pillar. For the same reason, the Council adopted not one, but three instruments to amend the SIS in preparation of the SIS II: Council Decision 2007/533 on the establishment, operation and use of the SIS II covering issues of the former third pillar, Regulation 1987/2006 of the European Parliament and the Council on the establishment, operation and use of the SIS II and Regulation 1986/2006 of the European Parliament and the Council regarding access to the SIS II by the services in the Member States responsible for issuing vehicle registration certificates.[472] Although the SIS II constitutes one single information system that should operate as such, a triple legal basis is intended to regulate it (the Council Decision and two Regulations).

Originally, the main purpose of the SIS II was twofold: the functioning of the system should have gone hand in hand with the enlargement of the Schengen area in 2007 by having prepared the participation of the new Member States within the SIS, additionally it should have paved the way for the inclusion of new categories of data, particularly biometric data.[473] As the SIS II had not entered into force in 2007, Portugal put forward a proposal called "SIS one4all" enabling the Member States which joined the Schengen area in 2007 to participate in the original SIS.[474] At the

---

[468] Articles 92 (1) and 101 (1) and (2) Schengen Convention, OJ 2000 L-239/19. A list of the authorities having access to the SIS is entailed in Council doc. 6073/3/07, REV 3 of 23 July 2007, List of competent authorities which are authorised to search directly the data contained in the Schengen Information System pursuant to Article 101(4) of the Schengen Convention.

[469] Council doc. 6073/3/07, REV 3 of 23 July 2007, List of competent authorities which are authorised to search directly the data contained in the Schengen Information System pursuant to Article 101(4) of the Schengen Convention.

[470] Braum (2008). With regard to the fundamental rights implications of this shared legal basis, compare also Geyer (2008).

[471] EC Treaty (Treaty of Rome, as amended) Title IV.

[472] SIS II Council Decision 2007/533 of 12 June 2007 on the establishment, operation and use of the second generation Schengen Information System (SIS II), OJ 2007, L-205/63; Regulation (EC) No 1986/2006 of the European Parliament and of the Council of 20 December 2006 regarding access to the Second Generation Schengen Information System (SIS II) by the services in the Member States responsible for issuing vehicle registration certificates, OJ 2006, L-381/1; Regulation (EC) No 1987/2006 of the European Parliament and of the Council of 20 December 2006 on the establishment, operation and use of the second generation Schengen Information System (SIS II), OJ 2006, L-381/4.

[473] House of Lords, European Union Committee, 9th report of session 2006–2007, "Schengen Information System II (SIS II)", published 2 March 2007, para 20, p. 12.

[474] See Council Conclusions on the SIS II, the SIS 1+ and the enlargement of the Schengen area, doc. 16324/06 of 5 December 2006 referring to the "feasibility study - SIS one 4all-Schengen Information System", doc. 13540/06 of 12 October 2006.

end of 2009, however, the Council emphasised that the SIS II should become operational soon, although tests to run the SIS II have failed.[475] In the meanwhile, the adoption of an enormous amount of intermediary instruments intended to regulate the migration from the SIS to the SIS II has lead to an immense confusion regarding the currently applicable rights.[476] Due to this legal mix, only the main instruments of the SIS and the SIS II are analysed in turn.

The general scope of the SIS II is stipulated in an even broader manner than the SIS.[477] Regulation 1987/2006 as well as Council Decision 2007/533 refer to the purpose of ensuring “a high level of security” within the AFSJ including the “maintenance of public security and public policy and the safeguarding of security in the territories of the Member States”.[478] Specifications of the scope depend on the legal bases of the instruments. Formulations such as “for the purpose of police and judicial cooperation” in case of Council Decision 2007/533 and “for the purpose of refusing entry into or a stay in, a Member State” in case of Regulation 1987/2006 should specify the field of application.[479] However, the wide ranging description of the purpose has already raised criticism, particularly when

[475] Press release, 2979th Council meeting, Justice and Home Affairs, Brussels, 30 November and 1 December 2009, 16883/1/09 REV 1 (Presse 35 5), p. 10 and outcome of proceedings of CATS on 12 and 13 April 2010, Council Doc. 9371/10 of 4 May 2010, p. 8.

[476] Council Decision 2008/839/JHA of 24 October 2008 on migration from the Schengen Information System (SIS 1+) to the second generation Schengen Information System (SIS II), OJ 2008, L-299/43; Council Regulation (EC) No 1104/2008of 24 October 2008 on migration from the Schengen Information System (SIS 1+) to the second generation Schengen Information System (SIS II), OJ 2008, L-299/1; Commission Decision 2009/720/EC of 17 September 2009 laying down the date for the completion of migration from the Schengen Information System (SIS 1+) to the second generation Schengen Information System (SIS II) (1st pillar); OJ 2009, L-257/26; Commission Decision 2009/724/JHA of 17 September 2009 laying down the date for the completion of migration from the Schengen Information System (SIS 1+) to the second generation Schengen Information System (SIS II) (3rd pillar), OJ 2009, L-257/41; Proposal for a Council Regulation amending Regulation (EC) No 1104/2008on migration from the Schengen Information System (SIS 1+) to the second generation Schengen Information System (SIS II) (1st pillar) [COM (2009) 508 final – not published in the Official Journal]; Proposal for a Council Regulation amending Decision 2008/839/JHA on migration from the Schengen Information System (SIS 1+) to the second generation Schengen Information System (SIS II) [COM(2010) 15 final – not published in the Official Journal].

[477] Compare also: opinion of the European Data Protection Supervisor on the Proposal for a Council Decision on the establishment, operation and use of the Second Generation Schengen Information System (SIS II) (COM(2005)230 final); the Proposal for a Regulation of the European Parliament and of the Council on the establishment, operation and use of the Second Generation Schengen Information System (SIS II) (COM(2005)236 final), and the Proposal for a Regulation of the European Parliament and of the Council regarding access to the Second Generation Schengen Information System (SIS II) by the services in the Member States responsible for issuing vehicle registration certificates (COM(2005)237 final) OJ 2006, C-91/38, point 3; hereinafter referred to as: Opinion of the EDPS on the SIS II proposals OJ 2006, C-91/38.

[478] Regulation (EC) No 1987/2006, Article 1 and SIS II Council Decision 2007/533, OJ 2007, L-205/63, Article 1.

[479] Ibid, Article 2.

considering that neither an explanatory memorandum nor an impact assessment study, which might have given further indications identifying the purpose, has been published.[480]

Due to the delay in the implementation of the SIS II and in order to show the differences between the SIS and the SIS II, the provisions relevant for the rights of individuals in a data protection context are briefly illustrated for both systems in the following sections.

b) Gathered Data

aa) SIS

The SIS lists five categories of personal data regulated in Articles 95–99 of the Schengen Convention, the so called alerts, defined as a set of data "allowing the competent authorities to identify a person with a view to taking specific action".[481] They relate to:

- Data about persons wanted for arrest or extradition (Article 95),
- Third country nationals to be refused entry into the Schengen territory (Article 96),
- Missing persons including minors or persons temporarily to be placed under police protection for their protection or in order to prevent threats (Article 97),
- Data on witnesses and persons convened to appear before judicial authorities in connection with criminal proceedings (Article 98) and
- Data on persons under discreet surveillance or specific checks (Article 99).

Relatively limited data elements, such as the names and aliases, specific objective physical characteristics, date and place of birth, sex, nationality, whether the persons concerned are armed or violent, the reason for the entry and the action to be taken, are mentioned in the Schengen Convention.[482] Following a hit in the SIS,[483] the participating states therefore exchange supplementary information, such as photographs and fingerprint information,[484] by using the SIRENE (Supplementary Information Request at the National Entry) system which is not expressly

[480] Opinion of the EDPS on the SIS II proposals OJ 2006, C-91/38, points 1.2. and 3.

[481] Regulation (EC) No 1986/2006 of the European Parliament and of the Council of 20 December 2006 regarding access to the Second Generation Schengen Information System (SIS II) by the services in the Member States responsible for issuing vehicle registration certificates, OJ 2006, L-381/1, Article 3 (a).

[482] Article 94 (2) Schengen Convention, OJ 2000, L-239/19.

[483] Kabera Karanja (2008), p. 206.

[484] SIRENE manual, doc. 12802/02 of 7 March 2008, compare pp. 18, 20 and 30 and Kabera Karanja (2008), p. 207.

mentioned in the Schengen Convention and whose exact content is not made public.[485] Originally it had no legal base,[486] Article 108 Schengen Convention only provides for the establishment of an authority responsible for the national section of the SIS in each SIS Member State. Via these contact points, the so called SIRENE bureaus, extensive and not standardised additional information is exchanged without restriction[487] and may include also information about "future crimes" or threats to public policy and security.[488] Although the SIRENE system had been in operation long before, it was first officially introduced in the Schengen Convention in February 2005.[489]

Data about objects in the SIS relate to vehicles, boats, aircrafts and containers for the purpose of discrete surveillance or specific checks as well as to objects sought for the purpose of seizure or use as evidence in criminal proceedings.[490] Examples are stolen vehicles, firearms, official documents or passports, identity cards or driving licences.[491]

bb) SIS II

The SIS II instruments refer to the similar categories of alerts, but they introduce new functions.[492] The data categories processed relate now to alerts on:

- Third-Country nationals for the purpose of refusing entry and stay (Article 20 Regulation 1987/2006)
- Persons wanted for arrest or surrender purposes (Article 26 Council Decision 2007/533)
- Missing persons (Article 32 Council Decision 2007/533)
- Person sought to assist with a judicial procedure (Article 34 Council Decision 2007/533)

---

485 Compare the "not declassified" annexes in the SIRENE manual, doc. 12802/02 of 7 March 2008; Articles 39-46 Schengen Convention refer to a reinforced police cooperation, but do not mentioned directly the SIRENE cooperation; details to SIRENE can be found in: Kabera Karanja (2008) pp. 202–208.

486 House of Lords, European Union Committee, 9th report of session 2006-2007, "Schengen Information System II (SIS II)", published 2 March 2007, paras 54 and 55, p. 19.

487 Kabera Karanja (2008), p. 207.

488 Article 46 Schengen Convention, OJ 2000, L-239/19.

489 Council Decision 2005/211/JHA of 24 February 2005 concerning the introduction of some new functions for the Schengen Information System, including in the fight against terrorism, OJ 2005, L-68/44 introduced a new Article 92 to integrate the SIRENE system in the Schengen Convention.

490 Articles 45 (2), 99 and 100 Schengen Convention, OJ 2000, L-239/19.

491 Ibid, Article 100 (3).

492 Chapter IV Regulation 1987/2006 and Chapters V, VI, VII, VIII SIS II Council Decision 2007/533, OJ 2007, L-205/63.

- Persons and objects for discreet checks or specific checks (Article 36 Council Decision 2007/533) and
- Objects sought for the purpose of seizure or use as evidence in criminal proceedings (Article 38 Council Decision 2007/533).

The SIS II now explicitly mentions the exchange of supplementary information via the SIRENE bureaus in its Articles 7 and 8 of Council Decision 2007/533, although the provisions are vague and refer to a SIRENE manual which is not entirely published.[493] At least, since the SIRENE bureaus are now mentioned in the SIS II instruments, the data protection rules of the SIS II apply to data exchanges in the framework of SIRENE exchanges.

An interesting amendment of the SIS clearly shows that the SIS II is developing more and more towards becoming a police investigative tool: Member States may now make use of the possibility to interlink alerts creating a relationship between two or more alerts.[494] A Council document gives 45 examples of the possible combination of the entries, such as: Articles 95–99 Schengen Convention: husband wanted terrorist + wife suspected accomplice, Articles 96–98 Schengen Convention: persons to be refused entry + witness in an illegal immigration case, Articles 95–96 Schengen Convention, EU national offender + convicted companion to be refused entry etc.[495]

Connecting two alerts can have a major impact on the rights and the status of the persons concerned.[496] The status of an individual in the SIS II no longer depends solely on his or her personal actions, but, when connected to the actions of other people, the person concerned might be treated with more suspicion than before.[497] This can easily lead to a situation in which a previously innocent individual is linked to an alert of a criminal, having as a consequence that the status of the relevant person will be negatively influenced. Moreover, the possibility to make associations between different alerts is not easy to bring in line with Article 46 (1) Council Decision 2007/533 whereupon the processing of the data provided for in Articles 20, 26, 32, 34 and 38 is restricted to the purpose laid down for each type of alerts referred to in those Articles.[498] When linking two alerts, the purpose of processing may become a new one, differing from the initial purpose of the alert.

---

[493] The SIRENE manual for the SIS II was subject to a not published opinion of the JSA, see Schengen Joint Supervisory Authority, activity report – December 2005-December 2008 (in the following: JSA report 2005–2008), pp. 28–30.

[494] Article 37 Regulation 1987/2006 and Article 52 SIS II Council Decision 2007/533, OJ 2007, L-205/63.

[495] Council document no. 12537/3/04 on the SIS II functions of 30 November 2004, p. 3.

[496] Opinion of the EDPS on the SIS II proposals, OJ 2006, C-91/38, point 4.3.

[497] Ibid.

[498] Article 46 (1) SIS II Council Decision 2007/533, OJ 2007, L-205/63.

The decision to link the alerts is based on national law of the Member States and should however only be used "when there is a clear operational need",[499] but only a strict application and supervision of this new function can avoid negative consequences for individuals concerned. Finally, due to previous criticism regarding the adoption of the SIS II instruments,[500] the authorities with no right of access to certain categories of alerts shall not be able to see the link to an alert to which they do not have access.[501]

While it has already been possible to use the SIRENE bureaus, the SIS II now introduces the possibility to process biometric data such as fingerprints and photographs directly in the SIS II.[502] Because of the very specific and permanent nature of biometric data, they shall only be used after a hit in the SIS II system and only be entered following a special quality check, but exceptions for certain data categories, for instance for witnesses or minors, do not exist.[503] Statistics show that intense use is made of this new function.[504] In February 2009 the entries of pictures and fingerprints increased to 256, 260.[505]

In this context, it is worth considering that the introduction of biometric data was heavily disputed. Hence, it is all the more astonishing that the SIS II proposals are not accompanied by an impact assessment or an explanatory memorandum. The dangers arising out of the use of biometric data were subject to several studies[506] and criticism referred to the storage of data having a "quasi-absolute distinctiveness" and permanent nature.[507] Additionally, when taking the *S. and Marper v. the United Kingdom* judgment of the ECtHR into account in which the Strasbourg Court demands a different treatment of data, in particular biometric data, of persons

[499] Article 37 (4) Regulation 1987/2006 and Article 52 (4) and (5) SIS II Council Decision 2007/533, OJ 2007, L-205/63.

[500] Opinion of the EDPS on the SIS II proposals, OJ 2006, C-91/38, point 4.3.

[501] Article 37 (3) Regulation 1987/2006 and Article 52 (3) SIS II Council Decision 2007/533, OJ 2007, L-205/63.

[502] Article 20 (2) (e) and (f) Regulation 1987/2006 and SIS II Council Decision 2007/533, OJ 2007, L-205/63.

[503] Article 22 (a) and (b) Regulation 1987/2006 and SIS II Council Decision 2007/533, OJ 2007, L-205/63.

[504] Council Doc. 5171/09 of 19 February 2009 on the staff shortage and workload SIS II, SIRIS 7, COMIX 22, Annex 3, spreadsheet p. 12.

[505] Ibid.

[506] De Hert (2005); Article 29 Working Party: Working documents on biometrics, WP 80 of 1 August 2003 and Opinion No. 7/2004 of the Article 29 Data Protection Working Party on the inclusion of biometric elements in residence permits and visas taking into account of the establishment of the European information system on visas (VIS) of 11 August 2004; EDPS Opinion on the proposal for a Regulation of the European Parliament and the Council concerning the Visa Information System (VIS) and the exchange of data between Member States on short stay-visas (COM(2004)835 final), OJ 2005, C-181/13, para 3.4.

[507] EDPS Opinion on the proposal for a Regulation of the European Parliament and the Council concerning the Visa Information System (VIS) and the exchange of data between Member States on short stay-visas (COM(2004)835 final); OJ 2005, C-181/13, para 3.4.2.

who have been convicted of an offence and those who have never been as well as the respect of the age of the person whose data are entered in the database,[508] further safeguards relating to the protection of witness data as well as to data of minors should have been included in the SIS II instruments. The preparation of an impact assessment or of an explanatory memorandum would have forced the participating actors (Council, Commission European Parliament) to face these problems. A comprehensive discussion surrounding the inclusion of biometric data in the SIS II would have definitely hindered the indiscriminate collection of biometric data and would have led to the introduction of additional safeguards of certain groups of persons. The SIS II instruments in their current indistinctive version regarding the treatment of data of witnesses and minors are therefore not obviously compliance with ECtHR case law.

A further enlargement of the SIS II, compared to the SIS, involves the storage of additional data on alerts concerning persons wanted for arrest and surrender or extradition.[509] Data referred to in Article 8 (1) of Framework Decision 2002/584 on the European Arrest Warrant as well as a copy of the original of the European Arrest Warrant now form part of the supplementary information to be entered into the SIS II.[510]

A welcomed change however concerns the provisions which protect the data of victims of stolen identity. Additional data for the purpose of differentiating between victims whose identity has been misused by persons intended as the subject of an alert shall – under the condition of the person's explicit consent – be introduced by the Member State in order to avoid the consequences of misidentification.[511]

---

[508] Compare Chap. A II 1 d cc (1) and *S. and Marper v. the United Kingdom*, Application nos. 30562/04 and 30566/04, judgment of 4 December 2008, paras 66–125.

[509] Articles 27 and 28 SIS II Council Decision 2007/533, OJ 2007, L-205/63.

[510] Council Framework Decision 2002/584/JHA of 13 June 2002 on the European arrest warrant and the surrender procedures between Member States – Statements made by certain Member States on the adoption of the Framework Decision, OJ 2002, L-190/1; its Article 8 (1) contains the following data: (a) the identity and nationality of the requested person; (b) the name, address, telephone and fax numbers and e-mail address of the issuing judicial authority; (c) evidence of an enforceable judgment, an arrest warrant or any other enforceable judicial decision having the same effect, coming within the scope of Articles 1 and 2; (d) the nature and legal classification of the offence, particularly in respect of Article 2; (e) a description of the circumstances in which the offence was committed, including the time, place and degree of participation in the offence by the requested person; (f) the penalty imposed, if there is a final judgment, or the prescribed scale of penalties for the offence under the law of the issuing Member State; (g) if possible, other consequences of the offence.

[511] Articles 36 Regulation 1987/2006 and Article 51 SIS II Council Decision 2007/533, OJ 2007, L-205/63. This provision has been introduced in reaction to a JSA opinion (Opinion 98/2 of 3 February 1998 on entering an alert in the SIS on individuals whose identity has been usurped) recommending the change.

c) Accessing Actors

As a general rule access depended (and still depends) on the different category of alerts.

aa) SIS

Back in 1995, the Schengen Convention restricted access to border authorities, the national police and custom authorities as well as to authorities responsible for issuing or examining visas and residence permits of the Member States.[512]

Over the years, the restricted access was extended. For example, in 2004, Regulation 871/2004 granted broader access to authorities responsible for issuing or examining visas and residence permits.[513] The same regulation also extended access to the judicial authorities of the Member States. A Council Decision issued 1 year later[514] additionally permitted the EU actors Europol and Eurojust to directly search and access certain SIS data. From then on, Europol could access data of persons wanted for extradition, persons or vehicles placed under surveillance or subjected to specific checks as well as data related to objects sought for the purpose of seizure or use in criminal proceedings.[515] The access granted to Eurojust covered data of persons wanted for extradition, persons wanted as witnesses, or for the

---

[512] Article 101 Schengen Convention OJ 2000, L-239/19.

[513] Council Regulation (EC) No 871/2004 of 29 April 2004 concerning the introduction of some new functions for the Schengen Information System, including in the fight against terrorism, OJ 2004, L-162/29, Article 1, and Council Decision 2005/451/JHA of 13 June 2005 fixing the date of application of certain provisions of Regulation (EC) No 871/2004concerning the introduction of some new functions for the Schengen Information System, including in the fight against terrorism, OJ 2005, L-158/26.

[514] Council Decision 2005/211/JHA of 24 February 2005 concerning the introduction of some new functions for the Schengen Information System, including in the fight against terrorism, OJ 2005, L-68/44, Article 1.

[515] Council Decision 2005/211/JHA of 24 February 2005 concerning the introduction of some new functions for the Schengen Information System, including in the fight against terrorism, OJ 2005, L-68/44, Article 1, referring to Articles 95, 99 and 100 Schengen Convention, OJ 2000, L-239/19; see also Council Decision 2005/719/JHA of 12 October 2005 fixing the date of application of certain provisions of Decision 2005/211/JHA concerning the introduction of some new functions for the Schengen Information System, including in the fight against terrorism, OJ 2005, L-271/54; Council Decision 2005/727/JHA of 12 October 2005 fixing the date of application of certain provisions of Decision 2005/211/JHA concerning the introduction of some new functions for the Schengen Information System, including the fight against terrorism, OJ 2005, L-273/25; Council Decision 2006/228/JHA of 9 March 2006 fixing the date of application of certain provisions of Decision 2005/211/JHA concerning the introduction of some new functions for the Schengen Information System, including the fight against terrorism, OJ 2006, L-81/45; Council Decision 2006/229/JHA of 9 March 2006 fixing the date of application of certain provisions of Decision 2005/211/JHA concerning the introduction of some new functions for the Schengen Information System, including in the fight against terrorism, OJ 2006, L-81/46.

purposes of prosecution or the enforcement of sentences.[516] Moreover, Regulation 1160/2005 permitted access to authorities issuing registration certificates for vehicles.[517] Finally, national security services are also allowed to access the SIS.[518]

bb) SIS II

While access of the already accessing authorities remains unchanged,[519] the SIS II instruments further enlarge the access to authorities "responsible for the identification of third-country nationals" (asylum authorities).[520] In 2009, over a half million access terminals already existed in the Schengen area.[521] Third parties such as third states or international organisations shall not be able to have access to the SIS II database.[522] One explicit exception should apply to the exchange of data on passports with Interpol.[523] An agreement between the EU and Interpol shall be concluded in the future regulating the mutual exchange of data including the passport number, country of issuance and the document type of stolen, misappropriate, lost or invalidated passports by establishing a connection between SIS II and the Interpol database.[524] This agreement shall entail provisions regulating that the transmission of data entered by a Member State is subject to the consent of the Member State and that the data communicated "shall only be accessible to members of Interpol from countries that ensure an adequate level of protection of personal

---

[516] Council Decision 2005/211/JHA of 24 February 2005 concerning the introduction of some new functions for the Schengen Information System, including in the fight against terrorism, OJ 2005 L-68/44, Article 1 referring to Articles 95 and 96 Schengen Convention, OJ 2000, L-239/19.

[517] Regulation (EC) No 1160/2005 of the European Parliament and of the Council of 6 July 2005 amending the Convention implementing the Schengen Agreement of 14 June 1985 on the gradual abolition of checks at common borders, as regards access to the Schengen Information System by the services in the Member States responsible for issuing registration certificates for vehicles, OJ 2005, L-191/18, Article 1.

[518] This follows from a report of the Schengen Joint Supervisory Authority, activity report – December 2005–December 2008, p. 13, hereinafter referred to as: JSA report 2005–2008; compare also Peers (2006), p. 549 and Brouwer (2008a), pp. 78 and 100; a list of the accessing authorities can be found in: Council doc. 6073/3/07, REV 3 of 23 July 2007, List of competent authorities which are authorised to search directly the data contained in the Schengen Information System pursuant to Article 101(4) of the Schengen Convention.

[519] Regulation No. 1987/2006, Article 27 (1) and (2) and SIS II Council Decision 2007/533, OJ 2007, L-205/63, Article 40 (2).

[520] Regulation No. 1987/2006, Article 27 (3).

[521] Interinstitutional file 2009/0089 (COD), no. 13350/09, note from the French delegation on the legislative package establishing an agency for the operational management of large-scale IT systems in the area of freedom, security and justice of 15 September 2009, p. 3.

[522] Regulation No. 1987/2006, Article 39 and SIS II Council Decision 2007/533, OJ 2007, L-205/63, Article 54.

[523] Article 55 (2) SIS II Council Decision 2007/533, OJ 2007, L-205/63.

[524] Ibid, Article 55.

data".[525] Before concluding such an agreement, the Commission must assess Interpol's level of protection as well as the level of protection of countries having delegated members at Interpol.

The indirect way for third states to gain access to data stored in the SIS II, is discussed in Chap. C II 1 and C II 5.

A worrisome change concerns Eurojust's extended access conditions. The general access restriction relating to specific categories of data is indeed maintained, but Eurojust can access new categories of data, now additionally including the access to alerts on missing persons (Article 32 Council Decision 2007/533) and on objects for seizure or use as evidence in criminal proceedings (Article 38 Council Decision 2007/533).

In the cases of both Eurojust and Europol, access to the SIS II is exercised within their "mandate" which was considerably enlarged for both of them in the recent past.[526] Compared to the former regulation, the absence of any specification of their access purpose leads to a devaluation of the relatively strict purpose limitation principle of the Schengen Convention. Whereas in general the authorities having access to the SIS II data are bound to the specific purpose of each alert when using the SIS II data,[527] Europol's and Eurojust's access seems not to be governed by the same restriction. Linking the purpose of access to their mandate, which could be changed whenever it seems appropriate, contradicts the protection the purpose limitation principle intends to offer. To consider the effects of this problem in more detail, the particulars of the access of Europol and Eurojust to the SIS II are analysed in Chap. C II.

d) Individual Rights

aa) SIS

The data protection framework of the SIS is governed by a special set of provisions mainly oriented on the rules of Convention No. 108 and Recommendation (87) 15 of the Council of Europe. Member States have to adopt national law in order to achieve a level of protection at least equal to these to instruments.[528]

Specific rules governing the processing of personal data and the rights of individuals whose data are processed in the SIS are regulated in Articles 102–118 Schengen Convention. The relation between national law and the Convention's rules is defined in Article 140 (2) Schengen Convention: "In so far as this

---

[525] Ibid, Article 55 (2).

[526] Ibid, Articles 41 and 42; for details see Sects. II 1 a and II 2 a.

[527] This follows from the definition of "alert" in Article 3 (a) SIS II Council Decision 2007/533, OJ 2007, L-205/63 and Regulation 1987/2006 according to which an alert is a set of data "allowing the competent authorities to identify a person with a view to taking specific action".

[528] Article 117 (1) Schengen Convention, OJ 2000, L-239/19.

Convention does not lay down specific provisions, the law of each Contracting Party shall apply to data entered in its national section of the Schengen Information System".

The data processing principles in the SIS relate at first to the purpose limitation principle, more precisely to the interdiction against using the data in Articles 95–100 for other purposes than the purpose laid down in each category of alert.[529] An exemption in case of an "imminent serious threat to public policy and public security, on serious grounds of national security or for the purpose of preventing a serious criminal offence" could be made, whereby prior authorisation from the party issuing the alert must be obtained.[530] Any use of the data which does not comply with the mentioned rules "shall be considered a misuse under the national law of each contracting party".[531]

A great number of provisions refer to the responsibility of the Member States providing for instance for a record of approximately every tenth transmission of personal data in the N-SIS for the purpose of checking whether the search is admissible or not. Similarly, there is a provision for the responsibility of the contracting states to guarantee that the data entered in the SIS are accurate, up to date and lawful.[532] Article 106 (1) establishes the "owner principle",[533] signifying that only the state originally entering the data has permission later to change, modify or delete them.[534]

The liability for an injury caused to a person through the use of a national file, rules regarding access to the data and how to correct or delete inaccurate or unlawfully stored data are additionally provided for in Articles 109–111 and Article 116 of the Schengen Convention. The exercise of these rights is governed by national law, whereby the right of access is restricted by Article 109 (2) Schengen Convention. Access could be refused if necessary "for the performance of a lawful task in connection with the alert or for the protection of the rights and freedoms of third parties".[535] In any case, it shall be refused concerning alerts for the purpose of discreet surveillance.[536] A data subject has the possibility to refer to the national

---

529 Ibid, Article 102 (1).

530 Ibid, Article 102 (3); Article 102 (4) Schengen Convention further provides that "data may not be used for administrative purposes", by way of derogation, data entered under Article 96 [third country nationals to be refused entry into the Schengen territory] may be used in accordance with the national law of each Contracting Party for the purposes of Article 101(2) only [Article 101 (2) regulates the access from immigration authorities to the SIS].

531 Article 102 (5) Schengen Convention, OJ 2000, L-239/19.

532 Ibid, Articles 103 and 105.

533 JSA report 2005–2008, p. 15.

534 If a party has evidence that the data of another party are incorrect, it "shall advise" the party originally entering the data, Article 106 (2) Schengen Convention, OJ 2000, L-239/19.

535 Article 109 (2) Schengen Convention, OJ 2000, L-239/19.

536 Ibid, Article 109 (2); to the details of the access rights, see Kabera Karanja (2008), pp. 224–229.

DPA according to Article 114 (2) of the Schengen Convention to have his data checked. Thereupon, the national DPA has to coordinate this check, if necessary together with DPAs of other Member States, in case that the data were entered by another Member State.

Article 111 Schengen Convention gives an individual the right to bring an action to correct, delete or obtain information or compensation related to its data in the SIS before the courts or a competent authority under national law. According to Article 111 (2) final decisions must be mutually enforced in the Schengen states. Since this right is of fundamental nature, it seems that the enforcement of such decision meets serious practical problems.[537] A report of the joint supervisory authority Schengen (JSA) published in 2008 reveals that "there is sufficient doubt whether Article 111 (2) functions in practice".[538]

bb) SIS II

As a general rule, the individual rights standard acknowledged in the SIS is in principle maintained in the SIS II.[539]

The rights of data subjects are mainly in Articles 56–59 Council Decision 2007/533 and Articles 40–43 Regulation 1987/2006. The SIS II instruments refer to Directive 95/46, Convention No. 108 and Regulation 45/2001. According to the EDPS, this system is based on the combined application of *lex generalis* and *lex specialis*.[540] It is determined partly in the SIS II instruments themselves, as a *lex specialis* and complimented by a different legislation of reference (*lex generalis*) for each sector. In fact, different rules are applicable depending on the bodies which are responsible.[541] Data Protection Directive 95/46 represents the *lex generalis* for

---

[537] See next Sect. III 1 e and JSA report 2005–2008, pp. 14 and 15; see also Case C-503, *Commission v. Spain*, judgment of 31 January 2006 and Brouwer (2008b).

[538] JSA report 2005–2008, p. 16, for a comprehensive analysis of the SIS; for an excellent overview, see Brouwer (2008a).

[539] Opinion of the European Data Protection Supervisor on the Proposal for a Council Decision on the establishment, operation and use of the Second Generation Schengen Information System (SIS II) (COM(2005)230 final); the Proposal for a Regulation of the European Parliament and of the Council on the establishment, operation and use of the Second Generation Schengen Information System (SIS II) (COM(2005)236 final), and the Proposal for a Regulation of the European Parliament and of the Council regarding access to the Second Generation Schengen Information System (SIS II) by the services in the Member States responsible for issuing vehicle registration certificates (COM(2005)237 final), OJ 2006, C-91/38, in the following refered to as: Opinion of the EDPS on the SIS II proposals, OJ 2006, C-91/38; see also 2010 Schengen Catalogue, recommendations and best practices, data protection, Council doc. 9768/10 of 10 May 2010, pp. 10–12.

[540] Opinion of the EDPS on the SIS II proposals OJ 2006, C-91/38, point 1.2.3.

[541] The Article 29 Data Protection Working Party warns against this structure which would lead to a watering down of the level of data protection, compare opinion 6/2005 of the Article 29 Data Protection Working Party on the Proposals for a Regulation of the European Parliament and of the

data processing by Member States in case of Regulations 1987/2006 and 1986/2006, Convention No. 108 of the Council of Europe is the *lex generalis* for data processing in the framework of the Council Decision 2007/533 and data processing through the Commission (be it in the Regulation or in the Decision) is covered by Regulation 45/2001.[542]

Taking into account this rather complicated structure, the EDPS rightly points to the risk of leading to a watering down of the level of data protection or to unjustified discrepancies between the data protection of the individuals concerned, according to the type of data processed about them due to the application of different levels of protection depending on the relevant legislation of reference and the interaction of *lex generalis* and *lex specialis*.

Beside the criticism, there is also an important improvement relating to the right of information of third country nationals who are subject to an alert in accordance with Articles 10 and 11 of Directive 95/46 explicitly foreseen in Article 42 Regulation 1987/2006. Third country nationals subject to an alert are to be informed about, amongst others, the identity of the controller, the recipients of data, the existence of the right of access and rectification as well as about the purpose of processing.[543] Regrettably, a number of exceptions apply to this right,[544] such as the exclusion of information when the provision of the information "proves impossible or would involve a disproportionate effort".[545] It would have been favorable to include provisions acting as rules regulating on which initiative (controller or data subject) this right should be exercised as well as rules providing for a time limit to make the information available or additionally information explaining the duration of the retention period, the existence of the right to request a review or appeal of the decision to issue an alert or the possibility to obtain assistance from the DPA.[546] Finally, it remains to be seen how the right is to be enforced in practice, but the general introduction of a right of information might be the beginning of a development towards an improved protection of third-states nationals in the SIS II.[547]

Regrettably, a similar provision concerning EU-nationals subject to an alert entered according to Council Decision 2007/533 does not exist. They have to exercise their right of access provided for in Article 58 Council Decision 2007/

Council (COM(2005) 236 final) and a Council Decision (COM(2005) 230 final) on the establishment, operation and use of the second generation Schengen information system (SIS II) and a Proposal for a Regulation of the European Parliament and of the Council regarding access to the second generation Schengen Information System (SIS II) by the services in the Member States responsible for issuing vehicle registration certificates (COM(2005) 237 final), Working Paper 116, p. 22.

[542] Opinion of the EDPS on the SIS II proposals, OJ 2006, C-91/38, points 2.2.1–2.2.3.

[543] Articles 10 and 11 Directive 95/46.

[544] Article 42 Regulation 1987/2006.

[545] Ibid, Article 42 (2) (a) (ii).

[546] Opinion of the EDPS on the SIS II proposals, OJ 2006, C-91/38, point 6.1.

[547] For more details and criticism, see Brouwer (2008b).

533 to be informed about their inclusion in the SIS II. Article 19 of Council Decision 2007/533 merely provides for an information campaign notifying the public about the rights of persons, but does not establish a general right to be informed. A solution according to which an automatic notification is given to the persons concerned, above all to persons whose data are stored owing to their witness function, would be preferable and at the same time in compliance with Article 16 of the FDPJ.[548]

The provisions allowing as well as restricting the access to the data kept in the SIS II are largely oriented on the rights of the Schengen Convention. A 60 day time limit is newly introduced to reply to a demand for access and the individual shall be informed in no more than 3 months about the follow-up given to the exercise of his rights.[549] Similar to Article 111 of the Schengen Convention, actions to access, correct, delete data or obtain compensation could be brought before the courts or the competent authorities by any person under the law of the Member State.[550] Presumably due to the problems related to the enforcement of these rights in practice, the SIS II instruments stipulate that the Commission shall evaluate the rules on remedies.[551]

e) Supervision

aa) SIS

Supervision of the individual rights guaranteed in the SIS is divided between the Member States being responsible for the supervision of the N-SIS and, similar to Europol, a special supervisory authority, the JSA, which supervises compliance with the data protection rules relating to the C-SIS.[552] Consisting of two representatives of each Member State's national supervisory authority, the JSA fulfils tasks similar to the supervisory bodies of Europol and Eurojust.[553] The main responsibilities of the JSA include inspecting the C-SIS, examining difficulties of

---

[548] Council Framework Decision 2008/977/JHA on the protection of personal data in the framework of police and judicial cooperation, OJ 2008, L-350/60.

[549] Article 58 SIS II Council Decision 2007/533, OJ 2007, L-205/63 and Article 41 Regulation 1987/2006.

[550] Ibid, Articles 59 and 43.

[551] Article 59 (3) SIS II Council Decision 2007/533, OJ 2007, L-205/63 and Article 43 (3) Regulation 1987/2006; the evaluation should have been taken place in 2009, but due to the delays in connection with the SIS II implementation, it has not yet taken place.

[552] Articles 114 and 115 Schengen Convention, OJ 2000, L-239/19.

[553] Ibid, Article 115; the similarity between the tasks of the joint supervisory authorities of the SIS, Europol and Eurojust is not entirely coincidental as the JSA was the first supervisory authority coordinating supervision as regards a large-scale EU database in the law enforcement sector and therefore served as an example for the establishment of the supervisory authorities at Europol and partially at Eurojust.

application or interpretation of the SIS and ensuring compliance with the provisions on data protection.[554] As a result of these tasks, the JSA is regularly issuing reports and opinions.[555] Regrettably, not all of them are published and the JSA does not have the power to intervene in conflicts between States concerning questions of data entered in the SIS. The role of the JSA is rather limited to an advisory one, restricted to delivering non-binding opinions.[556]

Compliance with some of the mentioned individual rights has already been subject to control by the JSA. So far, the JSA has inspected the use of Article 96 (alerts on third country nationals) as well as the use of Article 99 (alerts on persons or vehicles for the purpose of discreet surveillance) of the Schengen Convention. Moreover a survey relating to the use of Article 111 Schengen Convention (action to correct, delete or obtain information or compensation) was also carried out.[557] The worrying results were published in 2008 (regarding Articles 99 and 111), respectively in 2005 (regarding Article 96). The most important findings can be summarised as follows[558]:

- The reasons for issuing an Article 96 as well as an Article 99 alert were not harmonised throughout the Schengen area, having as a consequence that in some Member States alerts on nationals from other EU Member States were entered under Article 96 Schengen Convention.
- A definition of the types of crimes that could lead to an Article 99 alert does not exist.
- A discrepancy in retention periods for Article 96 of the Schengen Convention emerged between the Member States which sometimes led to an incorrect retention period or to an automatical renewal of the provided 3 year period without having examined whether the prolongation was justified.
- There were no formal written procedures developed by the national DPAs ensuring that Article 96 and Article 99 data were accurate, up to date and lawful.
- Control and inspections in the context of Article 99 alerts should take place every 6 months through the national DPAs.
- In countries where different DPAs were responsible for the quality and integrity of the data, they were not sufficiently interlinked to carry out an effective control.
- Some Member States entered contact persons in the SIS by using the Article 99 alert which is contradictory to the wording of Article 99 (2) Schengen Convention.

[554] Article 115 Schengen Convention, OJ 2000, L-239/19.

[555] Reports and opinions can be found at: http://www.schengen-jsa.dataprotection.org/ (accessed February 2011).

[556] Compare Article 115 Schengen Convention, OJ 2000, L-239/19.

[557] JSA report 2005–2008 and Report of the Schengen Joint Supervisory Authority, activity report – January 2004-December 2005 (in the following: JSA report 2004–2005).

[558] Compare JSA report 2004–2005, pp. 8–10 and JSA report 2005–2008, pp. 11–17.

- Article 111 final decisions are not equally enforced by the Schengen Member States and they were often not communicated to the national DPAs.
- There is no follow-up procedure of the execution of a final decision taken under Article 111 of the Schengen Convention.
- The control of the execution of final decisions in another Member State is left to the individual.
- A variety of authorities is responsible to deal with Article 111 decisions, but only in one country (Austria) is the national DPA competent to give a final decision.
- Not in all Schengen States national DPAs are informed of an Article 111 complaint.
- Not all Schengen States provide a formal procedure to consult the other state (or involve them) in cases of Article 111 proceedings.
- Only 17 cases in which Article 111 Schengen Convention was applicable were reported in a period covering December 2005 to December 2008.
- In all cases, the cooperation between the national DPAs was not sufficiently developed.

A follow-up by the JSA in 2008 of the Article 96 inspection showed certain improvements concerning the Article 96 alert on EU-nationals as well as the establishment of internal guidelines regarding case handling and control procedures for the processing of cases.[559] Further information relating to possible improvements in connection with the mentioned data retention period problems or the lacking national DPAs procedure ensuring that Article 96 data were accurate, up to date and lawful, are not given.

The JSA report in 2008 revealed further problems related to the non respect of the recording duty of Article 103 of the Schengen Convention. Usually, according to this article, every tenth transmission of personal data shall be recorded in the N-SIS by the data file managing authority for the purpose of checking the admissibility of the searches.[560] Apparently, there was a lack of control of the access of vehicle certification services[561] which led to the violation of Article 103 of the Schengen Convention.[562] Some Member States even performed checks on vehicle registration certificates and entered the data into the SIS before the entry into force of the Council Decision allowing for access of vehicle certification services.[563]

[559] JSA report 2005–2008, p. 18.

[560] Article 103 Schengen Convention, OJ 2000, L-239/19.

[561] Council Decision 2006/228/JHA of 9 March 2006 fixing the date of application of certain provisions of Decision 2005/211/JHA concerning the introduction of some new functions for the Schengen Information System, including the fight against terrorism, OJ 2006, L-81/45.

[562] JSA report 2005–2008, p. 25.

[563] Ibid, p. 26.

bb) SIS II

Supervision of the SIS II is structured differently from the rules of the Schengen Convention. Article 62 of Council Decision 2007/533 establishes a layered supervision based on cooperation between the EDPS and the national DPAs whereby the latter remain responsible for the N-SIS. Regulation 1987/2006 concedes broader powers than Article 114 of the Schengen Convention to the national DPAs by referring to Article 28 Directive 95/46.[564] Council Decision 2007/533 does not entail a similar provision, which is attributable to its scope restricted to police and judicial cooperation typically excluding the application of Directive 95/46, whereas this does not mean that national DPAs are limited in the exercise of these powers at a national level when the national law provides for it. The EDPS on the other hand checks the personal data processing activity of the Management Authority which is responsible for the operational management of the C-SIS II.[565] The duties and relatively wide ranging powers referred to in Article 46 and 47 of Regulation 45/2001 apply to the EDPS in this context.[566] A welcomed provision is Article 47 of Regulation 1987/2006 as well as Article 15 (7) of Council Decision 2007/533 regulating the supervision of the EDPS in the case of delegation of the powers of the Commission. The latter sometimes delegates its tasks to another organisation or entity (such as a private company) in the management and development of a new system and its communication structures. The mentioned articles assure that during the delegation phase the EDPS has "the right and is able to fully exercise his tasks, including carrying out on-the-spot checks, and to exercise any other powers conferred on him by Article 47 of Regulation 45/2001".[567]

The national DPAs and the EDPS meet at least twice a year to improve their cooperation, more specifically to study common problems, draw up harmonised proposals for joint solutions and assist each other in carrying out audits and inspections. A joint report of activities is to be sent to the European Parliament, the Council, the Commission and the Management Authority every 2 years.[568] So far, EDPS reports examining the SIS II are not yet published. The general responsibility of the EDPS for CIS-SIS II data processing operations as well as the cooperation approach with the national DPAs however could considerably contribute to a more effective supervision of the SIS II. In particular the application of Article 46 and 47 of Regulation 45/2001 to the tasks of the EDPS represents a welcome improvement compared to the former SIS structure.

---

[564] The powers for example entail investigative powers, intervention as well as checking the lawfulness and engaging in legal proceedings, compare Chap. A III 2 c ff.

[565] Article 15 SIS II Council Decision 2007/533, OJ 2007, L-205/63.

[566] Compare Chap. A III 2 c ff.

[567] Article 63 SIS II Council Decision 2007/533, OJ 2007, L-205/63.

[568] Articles 46 (3) Regulation 1987/2006 and 62 (3) SIS II Council Decision 2007/533, OJ 2007, L-205/63; data processing during the transitional period is regulated in Articles 47 Regulation 1987/2006 and 63 SIS II Council Decision 2007/533, OJ 2007, L-205/63.

f) Time Limits for Storing

The Schengen Convention and the SIS II instruments are based on the central retention principle that an alert on persons shall be kept only for the time required to achieve the purpose for which it was entered.[569] Both the Schengen Convention and the SIS II instruments provide for a review of the need to continue storage not later than 3 years after the date of introduction into the SIS.[570] Alerts on persons must be automatically erased after the review period expires except in cases where a Member State has decided to keep the alert longer.[571] According to the SIS II instruments, this decision shall be based on a "comprehensive individual assessment".[572]

Alerts on objects for discreet checks or specific checks (Article 36 Council Decision 2007/533) should be kept for a maximum of 5 years and data objects sought for the purpose of seizure or use as evidence in criminal proceedings (Article 38 Council Decision 2007/533) for a maximum period of 10 years, unless an extension proves necessary for the purpose for which the alert was issued.[573]

SIRENE data shall be kept for such time as may be required to achieve the purposes for which they were supplied and in any event be deleted at the latest 1 year after the related alert has been deleted from the SIS II.[574]

g) Conclusion: Extended Functionalities of the SIS Versus Minor Improvements in Its Data Protection Framework

The foregoing analysis of the SIS and the SIS II reveals an important tendency: whereas over the years essential changes have taken place relating to the extension of the functions of the SIS, to the enlargement of the accessing actors and the access conditions as well as to the increasing amount of data stored in the database, the data protection framework mainly remained the same in comparison to the beginnings of the SIS. Only minor improvements have taken place. In view of the enormous amount of data – more than 31.6 million records have been created so far[575] – the importance of data protection rights in the SIS is equally increasing.

---

[569] Article 112 (1) Schengen Convention; Article 44 (1) SIS II Council Decision 2007/533, OJ 2007, L-205/63 and Article 29 (1) Regulation 1987/2006.

[570] Article 112 (1) Schengen Convention, OJ 2000, L-239/19.

[571] Article 44 (4) and (5) SIS II Council Decision 2007/533, OJ 2007, L-205/63 and Article 29 (4) and (5) Regulation 1987/2006.

[572] Article 44 (4) SIS II Council Decision 2007/533, OJ 2007, L-205/63 and Article 29 (4) Regulation 1987/2006.

[573] Article 45 SIS II Council Decision 2007/533, OJ 2007, L-205/63.

[574] Article 53 (2) SIS II Council Decision 2007/533, OJ 2007, L-205/63 and Article 38 (2) Regulation 1987/2006.

[575] Council document 6162/10 of 5 February 2010, note to the SIS-TECH Working Party/Mixed Committee (EU-Iceland/Norway/Switzerland/Liechtenstein); compare for the increasing amount

New functions, such as the interlinking of alerts, influence the legal position of the individual. Its status no longer depends solely on his or her personal actions, but, when connected to the actions of other people, this individual might be treated with more suspicion than before.[576] This might lead to a situation in which an alert of a previously innocent individual is linked to an alert of a criminal, having as a consequence that the status of the relevant person will be negatively influenced.

In addition to the new functions, the analysis revealed that the access to the SIS II is enlarged when comparing it to the access to the SIS. The amount of over a half million access terminals in the Schengen area will therefore soon increase. This development raises concern, in particular with regard to the data protection shortcomings which were detected by the JSA with regard to the SIS so far.[577]

The SIS II provides an enhanced supervisory structure compared to the Schengen Convention. However, the unchanged layered structure of applicable data protection rights neglects the developments in former third pillar matters which have taken place in recent years such as the adoption of the Framework Decision on the protection of personal data processed in the framework of police and judicial cooperation in criminal matters.

A further irritating outcome involves the observation that whereas in its beginnings the SIS was restricted to a hit/no hit database, it is continually developing towards a general intelligence database used as a police investigative tool by more than 30 actors in the near future for different purposes.[578]

2. *The Visa Information System*

The decision to establish a Visa Information System (VIS) is based on Council conclusions after the 9/11 attacks.[579] Following several Council meetings between 2001 and 2004, the Council Decision 2004/512 in June 2004 represents the first step in order to create a legal framework to create the VIS as a system for the exchange of visa data between the Member States.[580] It mandates the Commission to organise

---

of data Council SIS Database Statistics of 1 January 2008, 5441/08, 30 January 2008 and Council Doc. 5171/09 of 19 February 2009 on the staff shortage and workload SIS II, SIRIS 7, COMIX 22, Annex 3, spreadsheet p. 11; Hayes (2005).

[576] Opinion of the EDPS on the SIS II proposals, OJ 2006, C-91/38, point 4.3.

[577] Compare JSA report 2004–2005, pp. 8–10 and JSA report 2005–2008, pp. 11–17.

[578] Compare Council Doc. 5171/09 of 19 February 2009 on the staff shortage and workload SIS II, SIRIS 7, COMIX 22, Annex 3, spreadsheets p. 10 and p. 11.

[579] Compare recital 1, Regulation No. 767/2008 of the European Parliament and of the Council of 9 July 2008 concerning the Visa Information System (VIS) and the exchange of data between Member States on short-stay visas (VIS Regulation), OJ 2008, L-218/60, in the following: VIS Regulation 767/2008, OJ 2008, L-218/60; see also Herberlein (2009), p. 168.

[580] Council Decision of 8 June 2004 establishing the Visa Information System (VIS), OJ 2004, L-213/5; with regard to the history and the origins of visa and asylum policy in the EU, compare Fungueirino-Lorenzo (2002); Schmidt (2001).

the technical development of the VIS. Following two and a half years of negotiations between the European Parliament and the Council, in September 2008 VIS Regulation 767/2008 entered into force regulating the conditions and data exchange procedure between the Member States.[581] A dual legal basis ensures compliance with the EC Treaty.[582] As the VIS entails provisions of the former first pillar, it had to be adopted by using the co-decision procedure (now ordinary legislative procedure) where Parliament and Council decide together. Like the SIS, the VIS builds up on the Schengen *Acquis*[583] having as a consequence that the states participating in the Schengen cooperation also contribute to the VIS.[584]

a) Purpose, Use and Technical Aspects

Whereas the SIS II processes data from EU and third state nationals, the VIS is principally restricted to third state individuals underlying a visa requirement to enter the EU.[585] It contains information relating to every visa application made in the EU, irrespective whether the visa was issued, revoked, annulled, extended or refused.[586] The visa statistics in the EU/Schengen countries for 2008 refer to 12 million visas issued and over 10 million further visas applied for.[587] Besides, the VIS also entails data of EU citizens provided they act as a person issuing an invitation for a third country national or in case they pay the visa applicant's subsistence costs during his stay.[588]

The purpose of the VIS was initially restricted to coordinate and control immigration, but Article 2 of the new VIS Regulation 767/2008 embraces a more comprehensive approach by describing seven purposes of the VIS and linking the

581 VIS Regulation 767/2008, OJ 2008, L-218/60.

582 Article 66 and Article 62 (2) (b) (ii) EC Treaty, now Articles 74 and 77 TFEU.

583 The Schengen acquis – Schengen Convention, OJ 2000, L-239/19, Article 92-119; to the participation of UK, Ireland, Iceland, Norway, Switzerland and Liechtenstein, see Council Regulation amending Decision 2008/839/JHA on migration from the Schengen Information System (SIS 1+) to the second generation Schengen Information System (SIS II), OJ 2008, L-299/1, recitals 21-27; for details see House of Lords, European Union Committee, 9th report of session 2006–2007, "Schengen Information System II (SIS II)", published 2 March 2007.

584 See Sect. III 1.

585 Council Regulation No. 539/2009 of 15 March 2001 listing the third countries whose nationals must be in possession of visas when crossing the external borders and those whose nationals are exempt from that requirement, OJ 2001, L-81/1, amended by Council Regulation No. 1932/2006 of 21 December 2006 amending Regulation (EC) No 539/2001 listing the third countries whose nationals must be in possession of visas when crossing the external borders and those whose nationals are exempt from that requirement, OJ 2006, L-405/23.

586 Articles 10-14 VIS Regulation 767/2008, OJ 2008, L-218/60.

587 Council doc. 12493/09 of 31 July 2009 on the exchange of statistical information on uniform visas issued by Member States' diplomatic missions and consular posts, p. 95.

588 Article 9 (4) VIS Regulation 767/2008, OJ 2008, L-218/60.

improvement of the common visa policy with security interests of the Member States and of the EU. In order to facilitate the data exchange between the Member States and to improve the implementation of the common visa policy, consular cooperation and consultation between central visa authorities, the VIS shall[589]:

- Facilitate the visa application procedure;
- Prevent the bypassing of the criteria for the determination of the Member State responsible for examining the application (so called visa shopping);
- Facilitate the fight against fraud;
- Facilitate checks at external border crossing points and within the territory of the Member States;
- Assist in the identification of any person who may not, or may no longer, fulfil the conditions for entry to, stay or residence on the territory of the Member States;
- Facilitate the application of Regulation (EC) No 343/2003 (which determines the Member State responsible for examining an asylum application lodged in one of the Member States by a third-country national); and
- Contribute to the prevention of threats to the internal security of any of the Member States.

It is worth taking into consideration that the express inclusion of the last purpose, the prevention of threats to the internal security, considerably broadens the original purpose of the VIS consisting of the improvement of the common visa policy. The explicit reference to this particular purpose paves the way for the use of the VIS data beyond the framework of visa policy which is also reflected in the range of accessing actors, later discussed.

Moreover, synergies as well as interconnections between the VIS and the SIS were envisaged from its beginning.[590] Both systems are based on a centralised architecture consisting of a central information system (C-VIS), a central European database and an interface in each Member State building the national part (N-VIS) of the VIS and connecting the national authorities with the C-VIS.[591] As the central database of both systems is located in Strasbourg, the Commission suggested to use a common technical platform which can be additionally extended to Eurodac, although access to data should nevertheless remain separated.[592]

---

[589] Ibid, Article 2.

[590] Communication from the Commission to the Council and the European Parliament – Development of the Schengen Information System II and possible synergies with a future Visa Information System (VIS), COM(2003) 771 final.

[591] Article 1 Council Decision of 8 June 2004 establishing the Visa Information System (VIS), OJ 2004, L-213/5.

[592] Communication from the Commission to the Council and the European Parliament – Development of the Schengen Information System II and possible synergies with a future Visa Information System (VIS), COM(2003) 771 final and Interinstitutional file 2009/0089 (COD), no. 13350/09, note from the French delegation on the legislative package establishing an agency for the operational management of large-scale IT systems in the area of freedom, security and justice of

b) Gathered Data

Data collected for VIS purposes are gathered for five categories of visas: short-stay visas, transit visas, airport transit visas, visas with limited territorial validity and long stay visas.[593] Member States are responsible for long stay visas and data gathered in this context are therefore stored at the national level, except for national long stay visas valid concurrently as a short stay visa.[594] After having received a visa application, every visa authority creates an application file including a particular set of data referred to in Articles 8 and 9 of VIS Regulation 767/2008 and checks whether the applicant has previously been registered elsewhere.[595] At an initial stage, the visa authority introduces information relating to the application number, the authority with which the application has been lodged and to the status of the visa application in a common application form.[596]

The first record is linked with a possible previous application file and with application files of persons travelling together (group, spouse, children).[597] The data in the application form include: names, sex, date, place and country of birth, current nationality and nationality at birth, type and number of the travel document, the authority which issued it and the date of issue and of expiry, place and date of the application, type of visa requested, details of the person issuing an invitation and/or liable to pay the applicant's subsistence costs during the stay,[598] main destination and duration of the intended stay, purpose of travel, intended date of arrival and departure, intended border of first entry or transit route, residence, current occupation and employer; for students: name of school, in the case of minors, surname and first name(s) of the applicant's father and mother.[599] A photograph and fingerprints are additionally added.[600]

---

15 September 2009, p. 4; to this development compare Proposal for a Regulation (EU) No . . ./. . . of the European Parliament and of the Council on establishing an agency for the operational management of large-scale IT systems in the area of freedom, security and justice, COM(2010) 93 final of 19 March 2010 discussed in Sect. III 5.

[593] Articles 11 (1) (a), 11 (1) (b), 11 (2), 14 and 16 Schengen Convention and Article 4 (1) (a)–(e) VIS Regulation 767/2008, OJ 2008, L-218/60.

[594] Article 18 Schengen Convention and Article 4 (1) (e) VIS Regulation 767/2008, OJ 2008, L-218/60.

[595] Article 8 (2) VIS Regulation 767/2008, OJ 2008, L-218/60.

[596] Article 9 (1)-(3) VIS Regulation 767/2008, OJ 2008, L-218/60; more details on the procedures and conditions for issuing visas can be found in Regulation (EC) No. 810/2009 of the European Parliament and of the Council of 13 July 2009 establishing a Community Code on Visas (Visa Code), OJ 2009, L-243/1.

[597] Article 8 VIS Regulation 767/2008, OJ 2008, L-218/60.

[598] In the case of a natural person, the surname and first name and address of the person, in the case of a company or other organisation, the name and address of the company/other organisation, surname and first name of the contact person in that company/organisation, Article 9 (4) VIS Regulation 767/2008, OJ 2008, L-218/60.

[599] Article 9 (4) VIS Regulation 767/2008, OJ 2008, L-218/60.

[600] Ibid, Article 9 (5) and (6).

While the integration of the photo in the application file has already been subject to Regulation 1683/95,[601] the inclusion of fingerprints is rather a new element of the EU's visa policy.[602] The processing of biometric data should enable the Member States to clearly verify and identify the visa applicants, particularly to prevent illegal immigration. Fingerprints mainly serve two purposes: first, in case of a subsequent control of the applicant, the comparison of fingerprints with the relevant fingerprints in the visa application form should facilitate the finding whether the person showing the visa corresponds to the person who has originally obtained the visa; second, the comparison of fingerprints with all of the VIS data serves the purpose to identify a person not being in possession of identification papers or trying to use false identification data.[603] Member States are allowed to copy fingerprints from an application file already registered in the VIS into a new application file within the first 5 years of storage of the fingerprint.[604]

Once the decision about the visa is taken, additional data depending on the result of this decision are added to the VIS record relating to the status of the visa, the issuing authority and the type of the visa.[605]

c) Entering and Accessing Actors

In the first place, visa authorities of the Member States enter the relevant information in the VIS. Article 4 (3) Regulation 767/2008 defines the visa authorities as authorities responsible for "examining and for taking decisions on visa applications or for decision whether to annul, revoke or extend visas, including the central visa authorities and the authorities responsible for issuing visas at the borders".[606] Access to the VIS for entering, amending or deleting the data shall be reserved exclusively to the "duly authorised" staff of the visa authorities designated by the Member States.[607]

Access for consulting the VIS data is however open to a broader circle of authorities, competent for the purposes laid down in Articles 15 to 22 of Regulation

[601] Council Regulation (EC) No 1683/95 of 29 May 1995 laying down a uniform format for visas, OJ 1995, L-164/1.

[602] Herberlein (2009), p. 169.

[603] Ibid, pp. 169–170.

[604] Commission Decision of 30 November 2009 adopting technical implementing measures for entering the data and linking applications, for accessing the data, for amending, deleting and advance deleting of data and for keeping and accessing the records of data processing operations in the Visa Information System, OJ 2009, L-315/30, annex, paras 2.1. and 2.3.1.

[605] Articles 10-14 VIS Regulation 767/2008, OJ 2008, L-218/60.

[606] Article 4 (3) VIS Regulation 767/2008, OJ 2008, L-218/60, this article refers to Council Regulation No. 415/2003 of 27 February 2003 on the issue of visas at the border, including the issue of such visas to seamen in transit, OJ 2003, L-64/1.

[607] Article 6 (1) and (3) VIS Regulation 767/2008, OJ 2008, L-218/60.

767/2008, although restricted to the "extent that the data are required for the performance of their tasks in accordance with those purposes, and proportionate to the objectives pursued".[608] Once a year, a list of these authorities specifying the purpose for which the respective authority may process the data is to be communicated to the Commission.[609] Pursuant to Regulation 767/2008, the authorities consulting the VIS include:

- The competent visa authority for the purposes of examination of applications, the decisions relating to those applications and the reporting and statistics including the decision whether to annul, revoke, extend or shorten the validity of the visa in accordance with the relevant provisions shall be given access to parts of the application file and for the first two purposes to the whole application file if the applicant is recorded in the VIS (Articles 15 and 17 Regulation 767/2008);
- The competent authorities for carrying out checks at external border crossing points for the purpose of verifying the identity of a person, the visa holder and the authenticity of the visa and whether the conditions for entry to or stay on or residence in the territory of the Member States are fulfilled or are no longer fulfilled, shall have access to the VIS to search by using the number of the visa sticker in combination with verification of fingerprints of the visa holder (Articles 18 and 20 Regulation 767/2008). Broader access to data can be given if the search indicates that data on the applicant are recorded in the VIS (Articles 18 (4) and 20 (2) Regulation 767/2008 allow among others for the use of photographs);
- The authorities competent for carrying out checks within the territory of the Member States as to whether the conditions for entry to, stay or residence on the territory of the Member States are fulfilled for the purpose of verifying the identity of the visa holder or the authenticity of the visa or whether the conditions for entry to, stay or residence in the territory of the Member States are fulfilled, shall have access to search with the number of the visa sticker in combination with verification of fingerprints of the visa holder, or the number of the visa sticker (Article 19 Regulation 767/2008). Broader access to data can be given if the search indicates that data on the applicant are recorded in the VIS (Article 19 (2) Regulation 767/2008);
- The competent asylum authorities for the purpose of examining an asylum application or of determining the Member State responsible for an asylum application shall have access to search with the fingerprints of the asylum seeker (Articles 21 and 22 Regulation 767/2008). Broader access to data can be given under the circumstances listed in Articles 21 (2) and 22 (2) of Regulation 767/2008.

---

[608] Ibid, Article 6 (2).

[609] Ibid, Article 6 (3).

When reading the aforementioned articles, the definition of authorities having access seems not always precise. The authorities competent for carrying out checks within the territory of the Member States may refer to immigration authorities, but can also include other authorities not further specified. Clarifications in this regard would have been desirable, although they seem to have been intentionally not included as already in 2005 the EDPS pointed to the unclear wording of such formulations.[610] All in all, Regulation 767/2008 nevertheless distinguishes between the different authorities and admits access to different data for different purposes which generally represents a welcomed approach complying with the purpose limitation principle. The list communicated to the Commission including the relevant authorities may give more detailed indications about the exact description of the accessing authorities.[611]

Nonetheless, in addition to the authorities listed in Regulation 767/2008, the amount of authorities having access to the VIS was increasingly extended in 2008 by Council Decision concerning the access for consultation of the VIS by "designated authorities of Member States and by Europol for the purposes of the prevention, detection and investigation of terrorist offences and of other serious criminal offences".[612]

Designated authorities in this context refer to "authorities responsible for the prevention, detection or investigation of terrorist offences or of other serious criminal offences",[613] usually including law enforcement authorities and intelligence services.[614] The access of the latter becomes particularly evident in view of the formulations of the initial proposal referring to "authorities of the Member States responsible for internal security".[615] Article 3 (1) of Regulation 767/2008 specifies the access conditions of the national authorities in this regard that access

[610] EDPS opinion on the proposal for a regulation of the European Parliament and of the Council concerning the Visa Information System (VIS) and the exchange of data between Member States on short stay visas (COM(2004)835 final), OJ 2005, C-181/13, para 3.7.2.

[611] The list is not yet published.

[612] Council Decision 2008/633/JHA of 23 June 2008 concerning access for consultation of the Visa Information System (VIS) by designated authorities of Member States and by Europol for the purposes of the prevention, detection and investigation of terrorist offences and of other serious criminal offences, OJ 2008, L-218/129.

[613] Article 2 (1) (e) Council Decision 2008/633/JHA of 23 June 2008 concerning access for consultation of the Visa Information System (VIS) by designated authorities of Member States and by Europol for the purposes of the prevention, detection and investigation of terrorist offences and of other serious criminal offences, OJ 2008, L-218/129.

[614] Brouwer (2008a), p. 132; EDPS Opinion on the proposal for a Council Decision concerning access for consultation of the Visa Information System (VIS) by the authorities of Member States responsible for internal security and by Europol for the purposes of prevention, detection and investigation of terrorist offences and of other serious criminal offences (COM(2005) 600 final), OJ 2006, C-97/6, para 2.5. (b).

[615] Compare Opinion of the EDPS on the proposal for a Council Decision concerning access for consultation of the Visa Information System (VIS) by the authorities of the Member States responsible for internal security and by Europol for the purposes of the prevention, detection

should be restricted to "reasonable grounds to consider that consultation of VIS data will substantially contribute to the prevention, detection or investigation of terrorist offences and of other serious criminal offences".[616] Member States must create one or more central access points to organise the VIS consultation. Following a reasoned written or electronic request the access shall be granted. In urgent exceptional cases, an oral request, whose compliance with the access conditions can be verified *ex-post*, is sufficient.[617] Comparable to the SIS provisions, Europol's access to the VIS is not further detailed in Regulation 767/2008 and depends again on its mandate restricted to "the performance of its tasks".[618] The exact features and the extent of Europol's access will be amplified in Chap. C II 2.

In order to prove the identity of a third country national, including return to his home state, communication of the VIS data to third states or international organisations (UN organisations, International Organisation for Migration, Red Cross) is possible.[619] Besides the consent of the Member State entering the data, transfer to third states is based on the adequacy decision requirement of Article 25 (6) Directive 95/46, the conditions of Article 26 of Directive 25/46 or the requirement of a readmission agreement in force.[620] Further, the data transferred must be in compliance with the relevant EU data protection provisions and the third country or international organisation has to agree to use the data only for the purpose for which they were provided.[621]

The data obtained by the designated agencies and by Europol according to Article 3 of Regulation 767/2008 shall not be transferred or otherwise made available to third countries or international organisations. One exception applies in case of urgency. The data could then be transferred for the purpose of the prevention and detection of terrorist offences and of other serious offences under the conditions of Council Decision 2008/633 whose provisions are analysed in Chap. C II 2.

d) Data Protection Framework and Individual Access, Correction and Deletion Rights

Due to the former first pillar status of the VIS Regulation 767/2008, references are made to the Charter of Fundamental Rights of the European Union and to secondary

---

and investigation of terrorist offences and of other serious criminal offences (COM(2005) 600 final), OJ 2006, C-97/6.

[616] Article 3 (1) VIS Regulation 767/2008, OJ 2008, L-218/60.

[617] Ibid, Article 3 (2).

[618] Ibid, Article 3 (1).

[619] Ibid, Article 31.

[620] Ibid, Article 31 (2) (a) and (d).

[621] Ibid, Article 31 (2) (b) and (c).

law such as Directive 95/46 and Regulation 45/2001 which establish the general data protection framework of the VIS.[622]

The data protection structure covering the law enforcement access of Europol and the "designated authorities" mentioned in Article 3 of Regulation 767/2008 is unfortunately not further elucidated in Regulation 767/2008. Only Council Decision 2008/633 concerning the access for consultation of the Visa Information System (VIS) by designated authorities of Member States and by Europol includes rules regulating this subject. According to the latter, Member States must ensure that their data protection level corresponds to Convention No. 108[623] and the "corresponding case law pursuant to Article 8" ECHR.[624] Additionally they have to take Recommendation R (87) 15 into account and the FDPJ.[625] Compliance with these rules is considered in more detail in Chap. C II 2.

Regarding the data processing apart from law enforcement access within the VIS, specific data protection and data security rules are provided for in Chapter VI of Regulation 767/2008.[626] Particularly mentioned are the rights of information, access, correction and deletion.[627]

Article 37 of Regulation 767/2008 includes the right of information which goes even beyond the requirements of Article 10 of Directive 95/46 (information which has to be given to the data subject). Visa applicants and persons issuing an invitation or liable to pay the applicant's subsistence cost during the stay are informed of the identity of the controller, the purpose of the data processing in the VIS, the categories of recipients of the data, including Europol and the "designated authorities" of the Member States, the data retention period, the existence of their right to access and the right to request rectification or deletion of their data, as well as of the right to receive information on the procedures for exercising those rights and even of the contact details of the national DPA responsible for hearing their claims.[628]

Although this provision constitutes an essential right for the visa applicants and the other persons concerned, the information duty remains restricted to data

---

[622] Recitals (17)-(19) and Articles 31 (2) (a), 37 (3), 38 (1), 39, 41, 42 and 44 VIS Regulation 767/2008, OJ 2008, L-218/60.

[623] For those Member States which have ratified it, the Additional Protocol of 8 November 2001 to Convention No. 108 should also be taken into account.

[624] Recital (9) Council Decision 2008/633/JHA of 23 June 2008 concerning access for consultation of the Visa Information System (VIS) by designated authorities of Member States and by Europol for the purposes of the prevention, detection and investigation of terrorist offences and of other serious criminal offences, OJ 2008, L-218/129.

[625] Recital (9) Council Decision 2008/633/JHA of 23 June 2008 concerning access for consultation of the Visa Information System (VIS) by designated authorities of Member States and by Europol for the purposes of the prevention, detection and investigation of terrorist offences and of other serious criminal offences, OJ 2008, L-218/129.

[626] Article 32 and 37-44 VIS Regulation 767/2008, OJ 2008, L-218/60.

[627] Ibid, Articles 37 and 38.

[628] Ibid, Article 37.

processing in the VIS and does not include information about the purpose of the processing of the accessing law enforcement authorities (Europol and the national "designated authorities"). This aspect is governed by national law. Applicants are only informed about the fact that Europol or a national law enforcement authority or intelligence service may receive the data. A more detailed information duty including the exact purpose of processing and use of the accessed data by Europol and the other national actors would enable the individual to identify the possible consequences of his application. It is worth pointing out in this context that the visa applicants are usually not suspected of any crime justifying their inclusion in law enforcement databases and therefore this aspect should be taken into account when informing the applicants about the details of their data processing.

The rules for individuals to obtain access to the data stored in the VIS and to have them corrected and deleted are subjected to national law, though the formulation of the respective Article seems to be rather complicated: according to Article 38 (1) of Regulation 767/2008 "the access to data may be granted only by a Member State".[629]

It can be assumed that this means that the law of the respective Member State is applicable and that access can only be requested in one of the Member States and not directly at the central VIS database. However, the formulation relating to the rights to request correction or deletion of the data seems to clarify the situation. Article 38 (2) and (3) of Regulation 767/2008 allow that these rights can be invoked in any Member State which subsequently has to contact the responsible Member State originally entering the data in the VIS.[630] In case the Member State corrects or deletes the data, it has to notify the person concerned that is has taken the relevant action.[631]

Cooperation between the Member States to ensure the enforcement of the mentioned rights is provided for in Article 39 of Regulation 767/2008. National DPAs shall assist and advise the persons concerned in exercising their rights, and shall remain available throughout possible proceedings against the Member State refusing the right of access, correction or deletion.[632]

Finally, the liability for damages as a result of unlawful data processing is also governed by national law.[633]

---

[629] Compare EDPS opinion on the proposal for a regulation of the European Parliament and of the Council concerning the Visa Information System (VIS) and the exchange of data between Member States on short stay visas (COM(2004) 835 final), OJ 2005, C-181/13.

[630] Article 38 (3) VIS Regulation 767/2008, OJ 2008, L-218/60.

[631] Ibid, Article 38 (4).

[632] Ibid, Article 39 (2) and 40.

[633] Ibid, Article 33.

e) Supervision

Monitoring of the VIS is shared between the national DPAs and the EDPS. The national part of the VIS, including the monitoring of the transmission of data to and from the VIS is carried out by the national DPAs.[634] Member States should designate one authority considered to be the controller pursuant to Article 2 (d) of Directive 95/46 which has the central responsibility for the data processing in the relevant Member State. National DPAs enjoy the rights stipulated in Directive 95/46 and Member States must further ensure that the national DPAs are equipped with the necessary resources to fulfil their tasks, the latter including an audit of the data processing operations of the national VIS at least every 4 years.[635]

In order to monitor the lawfulness of the processing of personal data by the Management Authority responsible for the management of the central VIS and the national interfaces,[636] the rights and duties of Articles 46 and 47 of Regulation 45/2001[637] apply to the EDPS.[638] At least every 4 years, like the national DPAs, the EDPS shall carry out an audit of the data processing activities of the Management Authority of the VIS and send the respective report to the European Parliament, the Council, the Commission and the national DPAs.[639] The Management Authority shall provide the EDPS with requested information, give him access to all documents and to its records and allow him access to all its premises.[640]

Meetings at least twice a year to coordinate mutual assistance and to examine difficulties of interpretation of the Regulation between the national DPAs and the EDPS should support comprehensive supervision.[641] A joint report of activities shall be sent to the European Parliament, the Commission and the Management Authority every 2 years.[642]

f) Time Limits for Storing

The general retention period for data kept in the VIS amounts to a maximum of 5 years and includes all data entered by the visa authorities of the Member States including data relating to applications which have been withdrawn, closed or

---

[634] Ibid, Article 41.

[635] Ibid, Article 41 (2) and (3).

[636] Ibid, Article 42 (1).

[637] Compare Chap. A III 2 c ff.

[638] Article 26 (1) VIS Regulation 767/2008, OJ 2008, L-218/60.

[639] Ibid, Article 42 (2).

[640] Ibid, Article 42 (3).

[641] Ibid, Article 43 (1).

[642] Ibid, Article 43 (3).

discontinued.[643] A record of each VIS entry shall be kept at the Member State and at the Management Authority of the VIS for 1 year after the deletion of the data in the VIS.[644] While it is stipulated that the records may only be used to monitor data protection, data processing and date security, the retention period can nevertheless be extended in case the data are required for "monitoring procedures which have already begun".[645] Once an applicant acquired the nationality of a Member State or the Member State entering the data decides to delete the data, the data and the links shall be removed without delay.[646]

Beyond that, there is no time limit for data retrieved from the VIS and then kept in national files. This possibility exists in individual cases for "no longer than necessary in that individual case" and should correspond to the purpose of the VIS.[647] A welcomed stipulation in this context relates to the provision according to which any use of the data not corresponding to purpose of the VIS shall be considered as misuse under the national law of the Member State.[648]

g) Conclusion: Changing Purpose – from Visa Applicants to Potential Criminals

Whereas on one hand the original purpose of the VIS has been enlarged to crime detecting purposes by Regulation 767/2008, the provisions relating to the relatively precise access rules restricted to a specific set of data combined with a definite purpose of the processing on the other hand, contribute to a certain restriction of the access to the VIS by the listed authorities. Unfortunately, this approach does not affect the provisions involving the access for consultation of the VIS by national law enforcement and security authorities of Member States and Europol.

The details of this access have been left to the regulations of Council Decision 2008/633,[649] which – in contrast to the VIS Regulation 767/2008 – did not require the participation of the European Parliament in the legislative adoption process. While the particulars of this decision are analysed in Chap. C II 2, the participation

[643] Ibid, Article 23 (1).

[644] Article 34 VIS Regulation 767/2008, OJ 2008, L-218/60; the record entails the purpose of access referred to in Article 6(1) and in Articles 15 to 22, the date and time, the type of data transmitted as referred to in Articles 9–14, the type of data used for interrogation as referred to in Articles 15(2), 17, 18(1) to (3), 19(1), 20(1), 21(1) and 22(1) and the name of the authority entering or retrieving the data.

[645] Article 34 (2) VIS Regulation 767/2008, OJ 2008, L-218/60.

[646] Ibid, Articles 23 (1), 24 and 25.

[647] Ibid, Article 30.

[648] Ibid, Article 30 (3).

[649] Council Decision 2008/633/JHA of 23 June 2008 concerning access for consultation of the Visa Information System (VIS) by designated authorities of Member States and by Europol for the purposes of the prevention, detection and investigation of terrorist offences and of other serious criminal offences, OJ 2008, L-218/129.

of the European Parliament in the law-making procedure of Regulation 767/2008 could be seen as a missed opportunity to regulate the law enforcement access in a more constrained way. Instead of using the standard access formulations, such as "access shall be granted for the performance of Europol's tasks", concrete conditions such as the requirement that the access must *substantially* contribute to law enforcement purposes or that access could only be granted in very exceptional cases, should have been introduced. Regrettably, the European Parliament failed to work towards such conditions during the negotiations.

More precise formulations specifying the conditions and the exact purpose of law enforcement access in Regulation 767/2008 would have also contributed to a better comprehension of these provisions by the individuals concerned. In its current state of play, Regulation 767/2008 does not necessarily enable an applicant to regulate his behavior and to foresee the consequences which his application may entail, in particular regarding the possible use of the data through law enforcement agencies.

Conversely to the aforementioned criticism, the introduction of a relatively comprehensive right of information is very likely owed to the involvement of the European Parliament in the VIS negotiations and represents a considerable improvement when comparing it to the rather limited guarantees of the SIS II and the databases of the law enforcement agencies such as Europol, Eurojust and OLAF.

3. *The Customs Information System*

The CIS is based on a third pillar Convention on the use of information technology custom purposes from 1995 entering into force only in 2005 after the ratification of all of the participating Member States.[650] Prior to 2005, the Convention applied in those Member States which ratified the Agreement on provisional application of the CIS Convention.[651] A protocol on the jurisdiction on preliminary rulings by the Court of Justice assured the Court's competence to interpret the Convention on reference from the national courts.[652]

[650] Convention drawn up on the basis of Article K.3 of the Treaty on European Union, on the use of information technology for customs purposes, OJ 1995, C-316/34.

[651] Agreement on provisional application between certain Member States of the European Union of Convention drawn up on the basis of Article K.3 of the Treaty on European Union, on the use of information technology for customs purposes, OJ 1995, C-316/58.

[652] Council Act of 29 November 1995 drawing up, on the basis of Article K.3 of the Treaty on European Union, the Protocol on the interpretation, by way of preliminary rulings, by the Court of Justice of the European Communities of the Convention on the use of information technology for customs purposes, OJ 1997, C-151/15; further protocols are: Council Act of 12 March 1999 drawing up, on the basis of Article K.3 of the Treaty on European Union, the Protocol on the scope of the laundering of proceeds in the Convention on the use of information technology for

As we have already seen above in context of Europol, 1 day before the entry into force of the Lisbon Treaty, the Convention was replaced by the third pillar CIS Decision 2009/917 basing on Articles 30 (1) (a) and 34 (2) (c) EU Treaty which was intended to bring in line the third pillar instrument with the first pillar one, previously discussed.[653]

However, the adoption prior to the Lisbon Treaty legally maintained the twofold CIS structure differentiating between the "first pillar" and the "third pillar CIS" mentioned above.[654] An adoption after the Lisbon Treaty would have logically better contributed to the Council's "alignment aim" and would have significantly affected the legal framework as well as the supervision governing the CIS, but then the European Parliament would have also been involved in the legislative process and this would have possibly hindered the achievement of the second important objective of the Convention's replacement: the granting of Europol and Eurojust access to the CIS.[655]

Nonetheless, both CIS systems are nearly identical[656] and operate by using the same search engine whereas the data involved remain separated between information entered based on the first pillar Regulation 766/2008, discussed in Sect. II 3 c, and data entered based on the third pillar CIS Decision 2009/917 which is subject to closer analysis in the following.

a) Purpose and Use

The aim of the CIS is to offer assistance "in preventing, investigating and prosecuting serious contraventions of national law by making information available more rapidly, thereby increasing the effectiveness of the cooperation and control procedures" of the customs authorities of the Member States.[657] More precisely, the CIS shall reinforce "cooperation between customs administrations, by laying down procedures under which customs administrations may act jointly and exchange personal and other data concerned with illicit trafficking activities, using new technology for the management and transmission of such information".[658] To achieve this objective, new functions such as the possibility to conduct strategic

customs purposes, OJ 1999, C-91/1 and Council Act of 8 May 2003 drawing up a Protocol amending, as regards the creation of a customs files identification database, the Convention on the use of information technology for customs purposes, OJ 2003, C-139/1.

[653] Council Decision 2009/917/JHA of 30 November 2009 on the use of information technology for customs purposes, OJ 2009, L-323/20, in the following: CIS Council Decision 2009/917, OJ 2009, L-323/20.

[654] See Sect. II 3.

[655] CIS Council Decision 2009/917, OJ 2009, L-323/20.

[656] Peers (2006), p. 550.

[657] Article 1 (2) CIS Council Decision 2009/917, OJ 2009, L-323/20.

[658] Ibid, Recital (3).

and operational analysis were added.[659] The system is technically managed by the Commission supported by a special CIS Committee consisting of representatives from the national customs authorities which is responsible for the implementation and application of CIS Decision 2009/917 and the functioning of the CIS.[660]

b) Gathered Data and Purpose of Processing

The CIS consists of a central database accessible via terminals in each Member State, the CIS, and a newly created Customs Files Identification Database (FIDE) mirroring the construction of the FIDE in the first pillar Regulation 766/2008.

aa) CIS

According to the CIS Convention, the CIS comprises data necessary to achieve the CIS's aim previously mentioned, such as commodities, means of transport, businesses, persons, fraud trends, availability of expertise. The new CIS Decision 2009/917 added two new categories: items detained, seized or confiscated and cash detained, seized or confiscated.[661] The Member States determine the items to be included relating to the each of the mentioned categories whereby the data elements which can be entered relate to a closed list of personal data and are divided into two groups depending on the aforementioned categories.

With regard to the four first categories (commodities, means of transport, businesses and persons), eleven data elements can be stored including: names, date and place of birth, nationality, sex, number and place and data of issue of the identity papers, address, any particular objective and permanent physical characteristics, reasons for entering the data, suggested action, a warning code indicating any history of being armed, violent or of escaping, registration number of the means of transport.[662]

Data elements relating to the newly introduced last two categories (items detained, seized or confiscated and cash detained, seized or confiscated) refer to names, date and place of birth, nationality, sex and address.[663] Personal data revealing racial or ethnic origin, political opinions, religious or philosophical beliefs or trade-union membership or data concerning health or sex life are excluded in any case from processing.[664]

---

[659] Ibid, Recitals (10) and (11).

[660] Ibid, Articles 3 (2) and 27.

[661] Ibid, Article 3 (1).

[662] Ibid, Article 4 (2).

[663] Ibid, Article 4 (4).

[664] Ibid, Article 4 (5).

The threshold to enter the data for the relevant purposes into the CIS seems not to be a very high one: according to Article 5 (2) CIS Decision 2009/917, the CIS is rather based on suspicions than on convictions[665] by stipulating that the data may be entered in the CIS if there are "real indications", in particular (but not exclusively) on the basis of prior illegal activities, "to suggest that the person concerned has committed, is in the act of committing or will commit serious contraventions of national law".[666] Consequently, similar to the databases of Europol and Eurojust it is possible to introduce data in the CIS based on indications suggesting that an individual will commit "serious contraventions of national law".[667] The term serious contraventions is defined in context with the FIDE database and refers to contraventions that are punishable in national law "by deprivation of liberty or a detention order for a maximum period of not less than 12 months or by a fine of at least EUR 15 000".[668]

According to Articles 5 and 8 (2) of Council Decision 2009/91, the purpose of processing of the stated data categories by the national authorities designed by each Member State[669] shall serve the aim of the CIS Decision and involves "sighting and reporting, discreet surveillance, specific checks and strategic or operational analysis".[670] Only the use of the data referring to the last category (cash detained, seized or confiscated) is restricted to the purpose of strategic or operational analysis.[671]

The term strategic analysis is defined in Article 2 (5) Council Decision 2009/91 and refers to "research and presentation of general trends in breaches of national law through an evaluation of the threat, scale and impact of certain types of operation in breach of national law, with a view to setting priorities, gaining a better picture of the phenomenon or threat, reorienting action to prevent and detect fraud and reviewing departmental organisation".[672] Operational analysis is described as "analysis of operations which constitute, or appear to constitute, breaches of national law" involving amongst others the collection of personal data, research, presentation and interpretation of links between the items of information as well as the formulation of observations, hypotheses or recommendations directly usable as risk information.[673] When taking the definitions and the criteria to

[665] Compare Opinion of European Data Protection Supervisor on the Initiative of the French Republic for a Council Decision on the use of information technology for customs purposes (5903/2/09 REV 2), OJ 2009, C-229/12, para 33.

[666] Article 5 (2) CIS Council Decision 2009/917, OJ 2009, L-323/20.

[667] Ibid, Article 5 (2).

[668] Article 15 (3) CIS Council Decision 2009/917, OJ 2009, L-323/20.

[669] Each Member State shall send the other Member States and the CIS Committee a list of the competent authorities it has designated, Article 8 (3) CIS Council Decision 2009/917, OJ 2009, L-323/20.

[670] Article 5 (1) CIS Council Decision 2009/917, OJ 2009, L-323/20.

[671] Ibid, Article 5 (1).

[672] Ibid, Article 2 (5).

[673] Ibid, Article 2 (4).

enter the data in the CIS into account, the term operational analysis embraces a range of police work activities, including the interlinking of data of people which are only suspected of planning a crime. Whether this far reaching possibility to process and to make available data of innocent people is accompanied by a supervision scheme as well as strong safeguards in term of data protection rights, remains to be seen in the following.

Besides the purpose named in Article 5 CIS Decision 2009/917, Article 8 (1) of CIS Decision 2009/917 includes a very astonishing provision which additionally expands the subsequent use of the data, creating strong doubts on its compliance with the purpose limitation principle: Member States including Europol and Eurojust may use the CIS data in order to achieve the aim of the CIS and for "administrative purposes or other purposes" subject to the conditions and the prior consent of the Member State entering the data.[674] Such other use shall be in compliance with Article 3 (2) of the FDPJ as well as with Principle 5.2.i of Recommendation R (87) which "should be taken into account".[675]

Article 3 (2) of the FDPJ refers to rather general principles of lawfulness, proportionality and purpose and allows processing for another purpose in so far as (a) it is not incompatible with the purposes for which the data were collected, (b) the competent authorities are authorised to process such data for such other purpose in accordance with the applicable legal provisions and (c) processing is necessary and proportionate to that other purpose.[676]

Principle 5.2.i. of Recommendation R (87), to which CIS Decision 2009/917 makes reference in slightly mitigated terms by using the formulation "taking into account" instead of "being in accordance with", involves to some extent stricter rules on the use for other purposes:

> Communication of data to other public bodies should only be permissible if, in a particular case: (a) there exists a clear legal obligation or authorisation, or with the authorisation of the supervisory authority, or if (b) these data are indispensable to the recipient to enable him to fulfil his own lawful task and provided that the aim of the collection or processing to be carried out by the recipient is not incompatible with the original processing, and the legal obligations of the communicating body are not contrary to this.[677]

Despite these relatively broad restrictions, it can not be ignored that Article 8 (1) of CIS Decision 2009/917 allows for the use of the CIS data for *any possible use*, not further specified in the instrument as long it is somehow compatible with the provisions of two other not especially detailed provisions which are far from regulating the use of the CIS data. More specific rules on the subsequent use of the latter as well as a clear and limited purpose within CIS Decision 2009/917

---

674 Ibid, Article 8 (1).

675 Ibid, Article 8 (1).

676 Article 3 (2) Council Framework Decision 2008/977/JHA of 27 November 2008 on the protection of personal data processed in the framework of police and judicial cooperation in criminal matters, OJ 2008, L-350/60; compare above Chap. A II 1 c.

677 Principle 5.2.i of Recommendation R (87).

would prevent using the data for purposes not further identified or even to be determined in future. Additionally, compared to the first pillar CIS not allowing for data processing for undefined "other purposes", the aim to harmonise both instruments seems to be missed.

bb) FIDE

Article 15 of CIS Decision 2009/917 creates a special database within the CIS, the Customs File Identification Database (FIDE) which mirrors the creation of the FIDE in the first pillar CIS previously addressed[678] and which is generally based on the same provisions applicable to the CIS.[679] Special rules, for instance in relation to the retention period and the interdiction of the copying of the FIDE data to national files, are provided for in Articles 15 and 19 of CIS Decision 2009/917.

The FIDE serves the purpose of enabling the national customs authorities, Europol and Eurojust, when investigating or opening a file on a person or business, "to identify competent authorities of other Member States which are investigating or have investigated" cases involving such persons or businesses and which therefore are in possession of relevant investigation files.[680] The information of investigations and files includes only serious infringements which are punishable either by a deprivation of liberty or a detention order for a maximum period of not less than 12 month or by a fine of at least 15,000 Euro.[681]

Consequently the (third pillar) FIDE entails information on a person or a business which is or has been subject of a national investigation file and fulfills one of the three following conditions[682]:

- Is, according to the national law of the Member State, suspected of committing or having committed or participating or having participated in the commission of a serious infringement of national law;
- Has been the subject of a report establishing that such infringement has taken place, or;
- Has been the subject of an administrative or judicial sanction for such infringement.

When comparing the (third pillar) FIDE data entering conditions to those of the CIS, the FIDE data are to a great extent more restrictive. This fact is also reflected in the data categories referring to the mentioned information which additionally

---

678 Compare Sect. II 3 c.

679 Article 15 (1) CIS Council Decision 2009/917, OJ 2009, L-323/20.

680 FIDE stands for Fichier d'Identification des Dossiers d'Enquête Douanière.

681 Article 15 (3) (a) and (b) CIS Council Decision 2009/917, OJ 2009, L-323/20.

682 Ibid, Article 16 (a) (i)–(iii).

include the field covered by the investigation file and the name, nationality and contact information of the national authority handling the case.

Personal data to be stored about the persons or the business concerned consist of persons of names, former names and aliases, place of birth, nationality and sex. Data on a business include business name, name under which trade is conducted, address, VAT identifier and excise duties identification number.

c) Entering and Accessing Actors Including Transfer

Whereas Article 18 (1) CIS Decision 2009/917 entails a decision stipulating the entering authorities in the FIDE database, an equivalent provision with regard to the CIS is missing. According to this article, the authorities referred to in Article 15 (2) of CIS Decision 2009/917 may enter and consult the FIDE database. Expressly mentioned therein are national authorities responsible for carrying out customs investigations pursuant to Article 7 (which includes "other authorities competent to act"), Europol and Eurojust.[683]

In absence of a provision clearly stipulating CIS entering authorities – CIS Decision 2009/917 only mentions the "supplying Member State" – the wording of Article 7 (1) together with Article 3 (1) of CIS Decision 2009/917 suggests that the data are entered by the Member States via the terminals of the national authorities, including customs administration but also other national authorities competent to act under the law of the Member States.[684] A list, which each Member State has to send to the other Member States and to the CIS Committee containing the competent authorities which have been designated to have direct access to the CIS, is regrettably not published.[685]

The entry of the data into the CIS is governed by the respective national law of the supplying Member State.[686] Only the latter has the right to amend, supplement, rectify and erase the data which it has entered into the CIS.[687] In case a Member State remarks that the entered data are factually inaccurate or stored contrary to the CIS Decision, it shall amend, supplement, rectify or erase the data.[688] The same

683 Article 15 (2) CIS Council Decision 2009/917, OJ 2009, L-323/20.

684 Article 7 (1) CIS Council Decision 2009/917, OJ 2009, L-323/20, reads as follows: "Direct access to data entered into the Customs Information System shall be reserved to the national authorities designated by each Member State. Those national authorities shall be customs administrations, but may also include other authorities competent, according to the laws, regulations and procedures of the Member State in question, to act in order to achieve the aim stated in Article 1(2)". Article 3 (1) CIS Council Decision 2009/917, OJ 2009, L-323/20 refers to the terminals in each Member State.

685 Article 7 (2) CIS Council Decision 2009/917, OJ 2009, L-323/20.

686 Ibid, Articles 7 (1) and 9 (1).

687 Ibid, Article 13 (1).

688 Ibid, Article 13 (2).

applies if another Member State, Europol or Eurojust notice inaccuracies and inform the Member State concerned thereof.[689]

Access to the CIS is granted to the authorities referred to, plus Europol and Eurojust.[690] Articles 11 and 12 CIS of Decision 2009/917 refer to the usual wording when it comes to granting access to both actors: access to the CIS will be permitted within the respective mandate and for the fulfilment of Europol's or Eurojust's tasks.[691] Europol or Eurojust's national members, their deputies, assistants and specialised authorised staff are allowed to search the CIS and the FIDE whereby any use of the information depends on the consent of the Member State which made the entry.[692] Once this consent is given, the rules of Europol or Eurojust apply.[693] The conditions and the problems arising in context with this particular from of access are discussed in Chap. C II 3 and C II 6.

Moreover, the transfer provisions in CIS Decision 2009/917 are far from being restrictive: dependent on the prior authorisation of, and the conditions imposed by the Member State which entered the information, CIS data may be transferred to national authorities other than the mentioned ones, to third countries and to international and regional organisations "wishing to make use of them".[694] Pursuant to Article 8 (4) of CIS Decision 2009/917, each Member State is responsible for taking measures to ensure the security of the transferred data and must communicate the details of such measures to the Joint Supervisory Authority (JSA) monitoring compliance with the CIS Decision.[695] The Council may even, by a unanimous decision, allow access to the CIS by international and regional organisations.[696] Thereby it shall "take into account", but is not obliged to follow, reciprocal agreements and the opinion on the adequacy of data protection measures by the JSA.[697] References to a possible opinion of the European Parliament or the EDPS are not made and the JSA's participation remains limited to an advisory one.

Considering that no further safeguards are provided in CIS Decision 2009/917, Article 8 (4) offers an insufficient level of data protection as it regards the onward transfer of and the access by international and regional organisations to CIS data. Although Articles 11 and 13 of the FDPJ are applicable in this context, they do not replace specific provisions regulating the conditions under which CIS data may be transferred to third parties and which protection measures apply in such circumstances to the respective data.

---

[689] Ibid, Article 13 (3).

[690] Ibid, Articles 11 and 12.

[691] Ibid, Articles 11 (1) and 12 (1).

[692] Ibid, Articles 11 (3) and 12 (2).

[693] Ibid, Articles 11 (3) and 12 (2).

[694] Ibid, Article 8 (4).

[695] Ibid, Article 8 (4).

[696] Ibid, Articlc 7 (3).

[697] Ibid, Article 7 (3).

At this point, it is worth remembering that CIS Decision 2009/917 was adopted at the Council meeting 1 day before the adoption of the Lisbon Treaty and, when considering the wording of Article 8 (4) CIS Decision 2009/917, the swift adoption seems to be explicable from the Council's point of view. Compliance with the first pillar CIS, where Regulation 45/2001 is applicable to third state data transfer, was in any event not the reason for the rapid adoption.

d) Individual Data Protection and Access Rights

The general standard for data processing at the CIS includes Convention No. 108, Recommendation R (87) and the FDPJ.[698]

Special provisions are entailed in Article 21 CIS Decision 2009/917 and involve for instance that CIS data may not be copied in into a national data file.

However, broad exceptions apply to the CIS, although not to the FIDE data [699]: copies stored in risk management systems, used to direct customs controls, or held in an operational analysis system used to coordinate actions, may be copied "to the extent necessary for specific cases or investigations".[700]

Thus, CIS data may be copied in national files for various purposes of police work. The term risk management system is not further explained and no indication is given about the systems involved,[701] but Member States have nonetheless the obligation to send a list of the risk management departments whose analysts are authorised to copy and process CIS data for the other Member States and the CIS Committee.[702] This obligation neither implies the publication of the list, nor does it apply to the operational analysis departments. The data copied from the CIS shall only be kept for the time necessary to achieve the purpose for which they were copied and their need shall be annually reviewed whereby the storage period shall not surpass 10 years. Personal data not necessary any longer for operational analysis shall be deleted immediately or have any identifying factors removed.[703] The conditions however under which circumstances data are permitted to be copied to national files are not further detailed.

The right of access, rectification and erasure or blocking of personal data as well as liability is governed by the national law of the Member States which should have ideally implemented the rules of the FDPJ. Requests invoking one of the mentioned

---

[698] Ibid, Recital (3).

[699] Article 15 (1) CIS Council Decision 2009/917, OJ 2009, L-323/20 excludes the applicability of Article 21 (2) CIS Council Decision 2009/917, OJ 2009, L-323/20 to the FIDE.

[700] Article 21 (2) CIS Council Decision 2009/917, OJ 2009, L-323/20.

[701] Compare Opinion of the Customs Joint Supervisory Authority with respect to the draft Council Decision on the use of information technology for customs purposes (Opinion 09/03) of 24 March 2009, p. 6.

[702] Articles 27 and 21 (4) CIS Council Decision 2009/917, OJ 2009, L-323/20.

[703] Ibid, Article 21 (5).

rights have to be directed to the national DPA whereas, similar to the SIS II rules, the Member States shall mutually enforce the final decisions taken by a court or other competent authority relating to the rectification or erasure of factually inaccurate data or to the access to personal data.[704] Whether the rights might be invoked in every Member State, is not further explained. Although the EDPS in its opinion on the CIS Decision presumes that the procedure of the CIS Convention for data subjects is maintained which would enable the persons concerned to choose the Member States in which they want to complain.[705] Other claims, such as a compensation claim must be invoked in the State entering the data.[706]

The common arguments for denying access, such as the reason for refusing access when the refusal seems to be necessary and proportionate in order not to jeopardise ongoing investigations or surveillance, can be invoked by the Member States.[707] Although it is worth mentioning that the general refusal to deny access "in any event during the period of discreet surveillance or sighting and reporting" entailed in the CIS Convention[708] was slightly mitigated in favour of a more access friendly provision taking into better account the interest of the persons concerned.[709] The future will show whether the improved access provision in reality leads to the granting of broader access to CIS data.

e) Supervision

In contrast to the SIS II and VIS where the supervision is shared between the EDPS and the national DPAs, the CIS follows the rather outdated approach of the original SIS and is monitored by a Joint Supervisory Authority (JSA) consisting of two representatives from each Member State's respective national DPA.[710] The supervisory functions of the EDPS are restricted to the activities of the Commission regarding the CIS, a fact which would have been the case anyhow when taking the provisions of Regulation 45/2001 into account.[711] Consequently the powers referred to in Articles 46 and 47 Regulation 45/2001 apply to the EDPS in this context.[712]

---

[704] Ibid, Articles 13 (5) and 23 (2).

[705] Opinion of European Data Protection Supervisor on the Initiative of the French Republic for a Council Decision on the use of information technology for customs purposes (5903/2/09 REV 2), OJ 2009, C-229/12, para 44.

[706] Article 30 CIS Council Decision 2009/917, OJ 2009, L-323/20.

[707] Ibid, Article 22.

[708] Article 15 (2) Convention drawn up on the basis of Article K.3 of the Treaty on European Union, on the use of information technology for customs purposes, OJ 1995, C-316/34.

[709] Article 22 CIS Council Decision 2009/917, OJ 2009, L-323/20.

[710] Ibid, Article 25 (1).

[711] Ibid, Article 26 (1).

[712] See above Chap. A III 2 c ff.

Proposals from the EDPS, according to which the amendment of the CIS Convention should have been used as an opportunity to align the supervisory structure of the CIS with that of the other large scale systems such as the SIS II, VIS and Eurodac and in particular with that of the first pillar CIS and FIDE, were regrettably ignored.[713] The uniform and coordinated supervisory model of the other systems based on the three-layered structure: DPAs at national level, EDPS at central level and coordination between both, would have certainly better contributed to more coherency and less legal uncertainty in particular with regard to the Lisbon Treaty and the abolition of the third pillar. As the EDPS is already entrusted with the monitoring of the other information systems as well as with the first pillar CIS and first pillar FIDE, synergies and experience as well as the personal resources of the EDPS could have used to coordinate effective supervision. Moreover considering that the first pillar and the third pillar parts of the FIDE and the CIS are operated by users as if they were a single database,[714] the divided supervision seems to be rather artificial. While now being limited to the monitoring of the Commission, the EDPS shall harmonise its restricted monitoring activities with that of the JSA by issuing common recommendations.[715]

The JSA, however, is responsible for the examination of "difficulties of application and interpretation" during the operation of the CIS. Problems relating to the exercise of access rights as well as the exercise of independent supervision by the national DPAs form also part of its spectrum of tasks. The JSA is also involved in the operation of the system as it shall draw up proposals "for the purpose of finding joint solutions to problems".[716] Contrary to the EDPS, in order to fulfill these tasks, a right to access to the CIS is therefore granted to the JSA. The reports of the latter shall be transferred to the authorities to which the national DPAs submit their report, to the Council and to the European Parliament.

f) Time Limits for Storing

Apart from the provisions relating to the rectification and erasure of data in case of inaccurate or wrongly entered data,[717] retention in the CIS is not limited. Data can be kept for the "time necessary to achieve the purposes for which they were entered"[718] An annual review by the supplying Member State is carried out to

[713] Opinion of European Data Protection Supervisor on the Initiative of the French Republic for a Council Decision on the use of information technology for customs purposes (5903/2/09 REV 2), OJ 2009, C-229/12, paras 56–63.

[714] Annual report of OLAF 2009 for the period 1 January 2008–31 December 2008, p. 38, para 4.2.2, see above, Sect. II 3 c.

[715] Article 26 (2) CIS Council Decision 2009/917, OJ 2009, L-323/20.

[716] Ibid, Article 25 (3).

[717] Ibid, Article 13 (3).

[718] Ibid, Article 14 (1).

examine the need for continued retention.[719] During the review period, the Member State can decide to keep the data until the next review if the retention is necessary for the purpose for which the data were entered.[720] In case that no decision regarding the continued storage is taken, the data are automatically transferred to a special section of the CIS where they are retained for another year and which is only accessible by a representative of the CIS Committee or the supervisory authorities for the purpose of checking their accuracy and lawfulness.[721]

It is worth pointing out that, although the entering conditions as well as the data elements contained in the FIDE are less infringing than the corresponding CIS provisions, the retention period and the erasure obligation for FIDE data are more restrictive. The time limits are governed by the national law of the Member States, even though pursuant to Article 19 (1) (a)-(c) they are not allowed to exceed:

- A period of 3 years when data relate to current investigations are stored and no infringement has taken place in the provided period, before the expiry of 3 years the data shall be erased if 12 month have passed since the last investigative act;
- A period of 6 years when the data refer to investigation files which have established that an infringement has taken place but which has not led to a conviction or to a imposition of a fine;
- A period of 10 years if the data relate to investigation files which have led to a conviction or fine.

All data relating to a person or a business have to be erased from the FIDE in two situations: first, as soon as a person or a business is removed from an investigation referred to in points one and three, and second, the data shall be automatically removed from the FIDE when the aforementioned retention period expires.[722]

g) Conclusion: Underregulated and Uncontrolled? Serious Data Protection Gaps in the CIS

To conclude, some problems with regard to data protection rights are worth mentioning.

Particularly striking is the fact that the data in the CIS may be entered based on suspicions rather than convictions while at the same time the purpose of processing is a rather wide one and not clearly described. Similar to the databases of Europol and Eurojust it is possible to introduce data in the CIS based on indications suggesting that an individual will commit "serious contraventions of national law".[723]

---

[719] Ibid, Article 14 (1) CIS Council Decision 2009/917, OJ 2009, L-323/20.

[720] Ibid, Article 14 (2).

[721] Ibid, Article 14 (2) and (4).

[722] Ibid, Article 19 (2) and (3).

[723] Ibid, Article 5 (2).

In addition, various purposes of processing are possible when interpreting the different terms describing the purpose. In addition to sighting and reporting, discreet surveillance, specific checks and strategic or operational analyses are described as the aims of the CIS.[724] Member States, as well as Europol and Eurojust may even use the CIS data for "other purposes".[725] Ultimately, the CIS data are available for almost any possible use.

Further shortcomings relate to the missing provisions clearly stipulating the authorities allowed to enter data in the CIS. National authorities responsible for carrying out customs investigations, Europol and Eurojust but also "other authorities competent to act"[726] may include data and make use of the CIS.

Moreover, further concern arises regarding the transmission of CIS data to third countries as well as to regional or international organisations which might even include access to all of the CIS data. There is almost no restriction as regards the use of data by other actors. CIS data may be transferred to national authorities, to third countries and to international and regional organisations "*wishing to make use of them*".[727]

A last regrettable point concerns the supervisory structure which unfortunately neither reaches the aim of a coordinated approach between the first and the third pillar CIS, nor brings in line the CIS supervision mechanism with those of the other large scale systems such as SIS II, VIS and Eurodac. As in the case of Europol and Eurojust, the CIS is still supervised by the rather outdated JSA approach which was criticised above. With regard to the unlimited storage period of the CIS data, a more effective and coherent monitoring approach would be desirable.

In summary, the CIS is the database with the most data protection shortcomings analysed in this research. In addition, although the CIS has the most far reaching entry possibilities and allows for the use of the data for various purposes, the supervisory structure is outdated and far from being effective. A considerable rework of its legal framework is therefore necessary to bring it in line with the data protection requirements illustrated in Chap. A.

4. *Eurodac*

Eurodac Regulation 2725/2000 was adopted in 2000 and has been in operation since January 2003.[728] It was enacted to implement the Dublin II

---

[724] Ibid, Article 5 (1).

[725] Compare Sect. III 3 c.

[726] Article 15 (2) CIS Council Decision 2009/917, OJ 2009, L-323/20.

[727] Ibid, Article 8 (4).

[728] Council Regulation (EC) No 2725/2000of 11 December 2000 concerning the establishment of 'Eurodac' for the comparison of fingerprints for the effective application of the Dublin Convention, OJ 2000, L-316/1, in the following: Eurodac Regulation, OJ 2000, L-316/1; the Eurodac

Regulation,[729] which aims at determining the Member State[730] responsible for examining an asylum application in the EU and in this way hindering asylum seekers from making multiple asylum applications in different Member States. In addition to taking the fingerprints of asylum seekers for the purpose of comparison with the fingerprint data previously (and subsequently) transmitted to the Eurodac database, the Eurodac Regulation additionally obliges the Member States to take the fingerprints of illegal border crossers for checking them against those subsequently taken from asylum seekers.[731] Besides, fingerprints of "persons found illegally present" in a Member State might also be checked against the entries in the Eurodac database.[732]

Currently, the Eurodac legal framework is undergoing a comprehensive revision. In 2009 and 2010 the Commission adopted two proposals intended to amend Eurodac's current framework. The first proposal refers to a Regulation aiming at the amendment of the Eurodac Regulation (Eurodac proposal)[733] and the second proposal relates to a Council Decision enabling national law enforcement authorities and Europol access to the Eurodac data which is later discussed in Chap. C II 4.[734]

a) Purpose and Use

The purpose of Eurodac is "to assist in determining which Member State is to be responsible pursuant to the Dublin Convention for examining an application for

Regulation is implemented by Council Regulation (EC) No 407/2002 of 28 February 2002 laying down certain rules to implement Regulation (EC) No 2725/2000 highlighting concerning the establishment of 'Eurodac' for the comparison of fingerprints for the effective application of the Dublin Convention, OJ 2002, L-62/1; compare also Rogowicz (2010).

729 Council Regulation (EC) No 343/2003of 18 February 2003 establishing the criteria and mechanisms for determining the Member State responsible for examining an asylum application lodged in one of the Member States by a third-country national, OJ 2003, L-50/1 and Commission Regulation (EC) No 1560/2003of 2 September 2003 laying down detailed rules for the application of Council Regulation (EC) No 343/2003 establishing the criteria and mechanisms for determining the Member State responsible for examining an asylum application lodged in one of the Member States by a third-country national, OJ 2003, L-222/3.

730 In the context of Eurodac, Member State means any state participating in Eurodac.

731 Chapters II–III Eurodac Regulation, OJ 2000, L-316/1.

732 Chapter IV Eurodac Regulation, OJ 2000, L-316/1.

733 Amended proposal for a Regulation of the European Parliament and of the Council concerning the establishment of 'Eurodac' for the comparison of fingerprints for the effective application of Regulation (EC) No [.../...] establishing the criteria and mechanisms for determining the Member State responsible for examining an application for international protection lodged in one of the Member States by a third-country national or a stateless person (recast version), COM(2010) 555 of 11 October 2010, in the following: Eurodac Proposal, COM(2010) 555 of 11 October 2010.

734 Proposal for a Council Decision on requesting comparisons with Eurodac data by Member States' law enforcement authorities and Europol for law enforcement purposes, COM(2009) 344.

asylum lodged in a Member State, and otherwise to facilitate the application of the Dublin Convention".[735] Therefore, fingerprint data of asylum applicants are compared with the fingerprint data transmitted by other participating Member States previously or subsequently stored in the Eurodac database, the so called central database.[736] This process enables the authorities to check whether an asylum seeker has already lodged an application in another Member State. According to Article 25 of the Eurodac Regulation, Member States shall ensure that the use of data recorded in the central database contrary to the mentioned purpose is subject to appropriate penalties.

A specific purpose relates to the data of irregular border crossers which shall be recorded for the sole purpose of comparison with data on applicants for asylum transmitted subsequently to the central database. Comparison with any data previously recorded in the central database is not permitted nor with data from illegal border crossers subsequently transmitted.[737]

Data of illegal residents are checked against the central database, but not recorded at Eurodac and underlie otherwise the same restrictions as the data of irregular border crosser.[738]

While the purpose of the current Eurodac Regulation is limited to data processing for purposes relating to an asylum procedure, the Eurodac proposal enabling national law enforcement authorities and Europol access to the Eurodac data provides for a noticeable extension of the use of Eurodac data.[739] Access would thereby be granted to national law enforcement authorities and Europol, later discussed in Chap. C II 4.

b) Gathered Data

The central database contains fingerprint information of asylum seekers as well as of immigrants who are arrested for crossing the EU's borders illegally and are at least 14 years of age.[740] In addition to these two groups of individuals, Eurodac also allows for the comparison of fingerprint data of persons found illegally present in a participating Member State with fingerprint data of asylum applicants already stored at Eurodac.[741]

Information on asylum seekers and irregular border crossers includes all of the ten fingerprints as well as data on the Member State of origin, place and date of

---

[735] Article 1 (1) Eurodac Regulation, OJ 2000, L-316/1.

[736] Ibid, Article 4 (3).

[737] Ibid, Article 9 (1).

[738] Ibid, Article 11 (3).

[739] Proposal for a Council Decision on requesting comparisons with Eurodac data by Member States' law enforcement authorities and Europol for law enforcement purposes, COM(2009) 344.

[740] Chapters II–III Eurodac Regulation, OJ 2000, L-316/1.

[741] Ibid, Chapter IV.

application for asylum/apprehension, sex, reference number used by the Member State of origin and the date on which the fingerprints were taken as well as the date on which the data were transferred to the so called Central Unit (responsible for the management of the central database), details in respect of the recipient(s) of the data transmitted and the date(s) of transmission(s).[742] As mentioned, the system does not allow the storing of data of illegal residents.[743]

In case of a hit in the Eurodac system, an additional data exchange is likely to take place via a system called DubliNet allowing for the exchange of data such as name, data of birth, nationality, photos as well as of particulars of family members and addresses.[744]

In 2008 the Central Unit received 357.421 sets of fingerprints from asylum seekers, 61.945 sets from illegal border crossers and 75.919 sets from illegal residents.[745] The total content of the Eurodac Central Unit's database in 2008 amounted to 1.323.363 fingerprint sets.[746]

Such as it is the case in the SIS II and the VIS, the Eurodac proposal[747] intends to replace the Central Unit and introduce a Management Authority for the operational management of Eurodac.[748] The latter shall be responsible for the three mentioned systems, in particular as it regards the supervision, security and coordination of relations between the Member States and the provider.[749]

c) Entering and Accessing Actors and Transfer of Data

Participating states include the 27 EU Member States plus Iceland,[750] Norway and Switzerland[751] as well as Liechtenstein in the near future.[752] The fingerprints are

[742] Ibid, Article 5 and 8.

[743] Ibid, Article 11 (5) (a).

[744] Eurodac Supervision Coordination Group, Second Inspection Report, Brussels 24 June 2009, p. 5.

[745] Report from the Commission to the European Parliament and the Council, annual report to the Council and the European Parliament on the activities of the Eurodac Central Unit in 2008, COM (2009) 494 final of 25 September 2009, pp. 5–6, para 3.1.

[746] Ibid, p. 10, Table 1.

[747] Rogowicz (2010), in particular pp. 564.

[748] Article 4 Eurodac Proposal, COM(2010) 555 of 11 October 2010.

[749] Ibid, Article 4 (2) and (7).

[750] Agreement between the European Community and the Republic of Iceland and the Kingdom of Norway concerning the criteria and mechanisms for establishing the State responsible for examining a request for asylum lodged in a Member State or in Iceland or Norway – Declarations, OJ 2001, L-93/40.

[751] Agreement between the European Community and the Swiss Confederation concerning the criteria and mechanisms for establishing the State responsible for examining a request for asylum lodged in a Member State or in Switzerland – Final Act – Declarations, OJ 2008, L-53/5.

[752] Proposal for Council Decision on the conclusion of a Protocol between the European Community, the Swiss Confederation and the Principality of Liechtenstein on the accession of the Principality of Liechtenstein to the Agreement between the European Community and the Swiss

entered by the asylum authorities of the Member States and sent to the central database based within the EU Commission and responsible for operating a computerised database equipped with an automated fingerprint identification system (AFIS) which compares the data to already stored fingerprint data transmitted by other Member States.[753]

In theory, only national authorities dealing with asylum should have access to the database, although in 2007 the EDPS and the national DPAs in their first coordinated inspection report on Eurodac noted that in some Member States Eurodac was entirely operated by national police services being characteristically not involved in asylum procedures.[754] Occasionally, even tax authorities had access to Eurodac's database.[755] Whether this particular situation has changed in the meanwhile is regrettably not further mentioned in the more recent second coordinated inspection report from 2009 subsequently discussed.[756]

In any case, with regard to the planned proposal enabling national law enforcement authorities and Europol to access the VIS data, the group of assessing actors will be soon considerably expanded by, when entering into force, allowing all authorities designated by the Member States as well as Europol's specialised unit, to have access to the Eurodac data.[757]

Unless specifically authorised in a Community agreement, transfer of the data to third States by Central Unit is prohibited.[758]

d) Individual Rights

While the rules of Directive 95/46 are applicable as a *lex generalis* to the data processing at the central database, at first glance, special rules entailed in Article 15–18 of the Eurodac Regulation seem to establish a relatively compact protection system.

Member States may for instance not conduct searches in or receive data transferred by another Member State apart from the data resulting from the

---

Confederation concerning the criteria and mechanisms for establishing the State responsible for examining a request for asylum lodged in a Member State or in Switzerland, COM(2006) 754 final, conclusion pending.

753 Articles 3 and 4 (3) Eurodac Regulation, OJ 2000, L-316/1.

754 Eurodac Supervision Coordination Group, report of the first coordinated inspection, Brussels, 17 July 2007, pp. 12–13.

755 Ibid.

756 Compare Sect. III 4 d and Eurodac Supervision Coordination Group, Second Inspection Report, Brussels 24 June 2009.

757 Proposal for a Council Decision on requesting comparisons with Eurodac data by Member States' law enforcement authorities and Europol for law enforcement purposes, COM(2009) 344, the proposal is discussed in Chap. C II 4.

758 Article 15 (5) Eurodac Regulation, OJ 2000, L-316/1.

comparison.[759] Only the Member State or the Central Unit on request of the Member State entering the data has the right to amend or erase them.[760] Mutual information duties apply in case the Central Unit or the Member State suggest that data recorded in the central database are inaccurate or entered contrary to the Eurodac Regulation.

If a Member State does not agree that the data stored in the central database are factually incorrect or unlawfully recorded, it must explain to the person concerned "without excessive delay" the reasons for its decision including information explaining the steps to be taken if the person concerned does not accept the explanation given (how to bring a complaint before court, financial or other assistance provided etc.).[761] The national DPA shall assist in this process and cooperate when necessary with DPAs of other Member States.[762]

The Central Unit is obliged to keep records of all data processing operations within the Central Unit showing the purpose of access, the data, the time, the data transmitted, the data used for interrogation and the name of the unit entering or retrieving the data as well as the persons responsible. Such records may only be used for monitoring purposes.[763]

In addition to the rights of access, correction and/or deletion in accordance with Directive 95/46, the rights of the persons concerned include a relatively broad information right in Article 18 of the Eurodac Regulation, including the right to be informed about the identity of the controller,[764] the purpose for processing, the recipients of the data, the existence of the right of access and rectification of data and the obligation to have fingerprints taken.[765]

The information is generally to be provided when the fingerprints are taken.[766] An exception however applies to illegal residents: whereby in general such information is to be provided when the data of the illegal residents are transmitted to the Central Unit, in case the provision of such information proves impossible or involves a "disproportionate effort", the obligation can be dropped.[767]

Liability is governed by national law. The Member State responsible shall be liable for damages as a result of unlawful processing or any other act incompatible with the provisions of the Eurodac Regulation, even if the damage occurred at the

---

[759] Ibid, Article 15 (3).

[760] Ibid, Article 15 (1).

[761] Ibid, Article 18 (6).

[762] Ibid, Article 18 (9) and (10).

[763] Ibid, Article 16.

[764] The Eurodac Proposal slightly improves the information right by providing for a right to receive information on the procedures for exercising the rights of access, correction and deletion including the contact details of the controller and the respective national DPA, see Article 24 (1) (e) Eurodac Proposal, COM(2010) 555 of 11 October 2010.

[765] Article 18 (1) (a)-(c) Eurodac Regulation, OJ 2000, L-316/1.

[766] Ibid, Article 18 (1).

[767] Ibid, Article 18 (1).

central database, "unless and insofar as the Commission failed to take reasonable steps to prevent the damage from occurring".[768]

While at first glance the protective provisions seem to be rather far reaching, some practical enforcement problems are worth mentioning.

A specific problem concerns the data protection guarantees of the aforementioned DubliNet system which allows for additional data exchange: the mentioned rights refer to the central database and do not automatically include the DubliNet system. Indeed, rules on DubliNet exist in Regulation 1560/2003[769] but they are limited to the technical details of the establishment of DubliNet and do not refer to data protection questions such as the exact purpose of processing, access rights, security, storing or deletion.[770] The need for data protection rules dealing with the details of the data processed via the DubliNet is evident and all the more astonishing is that this topic is not included in the Commission's proposal for an amendment of the Eurodac Regulation.[771]

In addition to the shortcomings concerning the DubliNet system, a Commission report on the evaluation of the Dublin system in 2007 observes that the enforcement of the individual rights contained in the Eurodac Regulation sometimes lags behind the rather strict criteria stipulated in the instrument.[772] The problems mainly occur in the context of the negligence of the deletion requirements due to the Member States' hesitation to inform each other of the status of the asylum seeker as well as in context of an unclear specification of the national authorities having access to the Eurodac data hindering the monitoring of the Commission and the EDPS.[773]

More detailed criticism is raised however in the latest common inspection report of the EDPS together with the national DPAs. It was issued in June 2009 and principally dealt with two issues: the enforcement of the rights of information of asylum seekers, in particular their right of access to data stored at Eurodac and the methods for assessing the age of young asylum seekers in view of their registration in the system.[774]

---

[768] Ibid, Article 17 (2).

[769] Commission Regulation (EC) No 1560/2003of 2 September 2003 laying down detailed rules for the application of Council Regulation (EC) No 343/2003 establishing the criteria and mechanisms for determining the Member State responsible for examining an asylum application lodged in one of the Member States by a third-country national, OJ 2003, L-222/3.

[770] Compare Article 18-21 of Regulation 1560/2003, OJ 2003, L-222/3.

[771] Eurodac Proposal, COM(2010) 555 of 11 October 2010.

[772] Report from the Commission to the European Parliament and the Council on the evaluation on the Dublin system, COM(2007) 299 final of 6 June 2007.

[773] Ibid, pp. 9–10.

[774] Eurodac Supervision Coordination Group, Second Inspection Report, Brussels 24 June 2009, p. 6; apart from data protection issues briefly considered hereinafter, ethical and reliability problems also occur in connection with the methods for determining the age of asylum seekers especially in context of the harmonisation of systems assessing the age; for more details, see pp. 15–23.

With regard to data protection related subject matters, the results of the inspection are worrying and show that the above mentioned individual rights contained in the Eurodac regulation are not necessarily enforced in practice. The outcome can be summarised as follows: the information of asylum seekers about their rights and the use of their data seems to be deficient, specifically as it regards information concerning the consequences of being fingerprinted as well as the right to access to and rectification of their data.[775]

The information provided by the report regarding the treatment among the Member States of asylum seekers and illegal immigrants differed widely. In general, illegal immigrants received far less information than asylum seekers if they received any at all.[776]

In some countries, the information about the rights of the asylum applicant is only given orally and no effort is made to verify whether the applicant has understood the significance of the provided information.[777] Only one third of the examined countries (which were all 27 Member States plus Iceland, Norway and Switzerland) clearly indicated that asylum authorities make sure that the applicant understands the given information.[778] At least, among all studied countries, only one does not provide a copy of the information to the person concerned.[779]

More astonishing however is that only 27% of the inspected countries qualify the information on data protection (access, rectification and erasure rights, the consequences of having its fingerprints taken and the possibility of data transfer to other countries) as a specific aspect of the application procedure.[780] In most countries, the information on data protection issues is included in the whole asylum procedure and given together with a huge amount of other information involving the risk of being not understood.[781] A significant number of countries does not provide any information at all relating to the consequences of being fingerprinted as well as the exchange of the data with other countries, and only a minority considered the information provided as being fully in accordance with the Eurodac Regulation.[782] The worst cases however concern those countries which limit their information to an oral procedure and in which it was therefore *per se* nearly impossible to assess the information provided.[783] But even in countries giving written information, the majority of the DPAs emphasises that the information is

---

[775] Compare Eurodac Supervision Coordination Group, Second Inspection Report, Brussels 24 June 2009, pp. 14–15.

[776] Ibid, pp. 14–15.

[777] Ibid, p. 11.

[778] Ibid, p. 11.

[779] Ibid, p. 11.

[780] Ibid, p. 12.

[781] Ibid, p. 12.

[782] Ibid, p. 12.

[783] Ibid, pp. 12–13.

"insufficient", "incomplete", "too general", "not fully appropriate" or "not clear enough".[784]

The common inspection report issues several important recommendations, naturally including the postulation for an improvement of the quality of information on data protection to meet the requirements stipulated in Article 18 Eurodac Regulation (the right to be informed about the identity of the controller). Regrettably, neither the EDPS nor the national DPAs dispose of powerful and effective tools to enforce their proposals in the examined countries.

At this point, the ECtHR ruling in *Segerstedt-Wiberg and others v. Sweden* is worth remembering, in particular as regards the importance of effective data protection rights which should not only exist on paper, but have to be efficiently enforced in practice.[785] Finally, with regard to the fact that the majority of examined countries has not yet received any requests for access to data,[786] the low level of information actually provided to the persons concerned seems to be an explanation for this.

A slight improvement, yet only on paper, is nevertheless included in the Eurodac proposal. The information on individual rights and data protection issues shall now be given in writing and only "where appropriate" orally as well as in a language the person concerned understands or may reasonably be presumed to understand.[787]

e) Supervision

Supervision over the data processing of the Central Unit is carried out by the EDPS.[788] The national DPAs are responsible for monitoring the collection and transmission of the fingerprint information to the Central Unit at national level.[789] Coordination between the EDPS and the national DPAs is ensured by the Eurodac Supervision Coordination Group, composed of representatives from the EDPS and the national DPAs meeting two or three times a year and issuing inspections and activity reports.[790] The proposal amending the Eurodac Regulation puts this cooperation on a legal basis and brings it in line with the layered supervision structure of

[784] Ibid, p. 13.

[785] Compare Chap. A II 2 d and *Segerstedt-Wiberg and others v. Sweden*, Application no. 62332/00, judgment of 6 June 2006, para 121.

[786] Eurodac Supervision Coordination Group, Second Inspection Report, Brussels 24 June 2009, p. 13.

[787] Article 24 (1) Eurodac Proposal, COM(2010) 555 of 11 October 2010.

[788] The EDPS replaced a provisional Joint Supervisory Body in 2004 according to Article 20 (11) Eurodac Regulation, OJ 2000, L-316/1.

[789] Articles 13 and 19 Eurodac Regulation, OJ 2000, L-316/1.

[790] Compare Coordinated Supervision of Eurodac, Activity Report 2008–2009 of March 2010.

the other databases such as the VIS and the SIS II previously discussed.[791] The proposal also explicitly refers to the EDPS and the application of Articles 46 and 47 of Regulation 45/2001 in this context while it is worth noting that a reference to the supervision activities of the EDPS in case that the Commission delegates its powers to another entity – which is for instance included in the SIS II instruments[792] – is lacking.

f) Time Limits for Storing

The maximum time limit for data storage is 10 years for asylum seekers.[793] The data have to be erased as soon as the applicant has acquired citizenship of a Member State and they must be blocked as soon as the applicant is recognised and admitted as refugee.[794] The storage period for illegal border crossers generally is 2 years.[795] In case the person acquires citizenship, obtains a residence permit or leaves the EU territory, the data shall be erased.[796]

It is worth pointing out that the proposal amending the Eurodac Regulation entails an astonishing provision which limits the storage of data of illegal border crossers to 1 year, contradicting therefore the tendency observed in relation to the storage period in other European databases constantly extending their time limits for storage.

The fingerprints of illegal residents in a Member State are not allowed to be stored in the central database.[797]

g) Conclusion: Legal Guarantees of Eurodac Challenged in Practice

The shortcomings as regards the practical enforcement of the data protection rights guaranteed on paper mainly concern the Eurodac database. As the provisions of Directive 95/46 are applicable as *lex generalis* to the data processing at Eurodac, the legal data protection framework appears to be better adapted to the data processing actually taking place than the legal framework of the other analysed databases SIS, CIS and VIS. The legal provisions including access, correction and

---

791 Article 27 Eurodac Proposal, COM(2010) 555 of 11 October 2010; for the VIS and the SIS II, see Sects. III 1 e and III 2 e.

792 Compare Sect. III 1 a bb.

793 Article 6 Eurodac Regulation, OJ 2000, L-316/1.

794 Articles 7 and 12 Eurodac Regulation, OJ 2000, L-316/1 (Article 10 Eurodac Proposal, COM (2010) 555 of 11 October 2010.

795 Article 10 (1) Eurodac Regulation, OJ 2000, L-316/1.

796 Ibid, Article 10 (1).

797 Ibid, Article 11 (3).

deletion rights as well as the requirements of the information of the persons concerned are satisfactory at least in the context of pure Eurodac data processing.

However, the data protection guarantees of the DubliNet system which allows for additional data exchange are not yet sufficiently developed. The Regulation establishing the DubliNet includes technical details of the organisation of DubliNet, but regrettably does not refer to data protection guarantees. The need for data protection rules in this context is evident.

As mentioned above, the enforcement of data protection rights in practice constitutes the essential shortcoming of Eurodac. The inspection report of the Eurodac supervisory group revealed that the information of asylum seekers about their rights and the use of their data is deficient, in particular as regards information concerning the consequences of being fingerprinted as well as the right to access to and rectification of their data.[798] The procedure to inform the asylum applicants about their rights varies from country to country. Sometimes, this important information was only given orally with a large amount of other information. Improvements with regard to the practical enforcement of data protection rights in this regard are therefore necessary.

The problems arising out of the access of law enforcement authorities and Europol to Eurodac, as provided for in the proposal for a Council Decision in 2009,[799] are discussed from a data protection point of view in Chap. C II 4.

5. *Proposal for an Agency Managing Large IT Systems (SIS II, VIS and Eurodac) from a Data Protection Point of View*

In June 2009 the Commission adopted a proposal for a Regulation of the European Parliament and the Council establishing an agency for the operational management of large-scale IT systems in the AFSJ which was in the meanwhile replaced by an amended proposal in March 2010 (proposal for an agency managing large-scale IT systems).[800] The provided regulatory agency shall be responsible for the long-term operational management of the SIS II, the VIS and Eurodac including potential other large-scale IT systems in the framework of the AFSJ (Title V TFEU) and will

[798] Compare Eurodac Supervision Coordination Group, Second Inspection Report, Brussels 24 June 2009, pp. 14–15.

[799] Proposal for a Council Decision on requesting comparisons with Eurodac data by Member States' law enforcement authorities and Europol for law enforcement purposes, COM(2009) 344.

[800] Proposal for a regulation of the European Parliament and the Council establishing an agency for the operational management of large-scale IT systems in the area of freedom, security and justice COM(2009) 293 of 24 June 2009, in the meanwhile replaced by the amended Proposal for a Regulation (EU) No . . ./. . . of the European Parliament and of the Council on establishing an agency for the operational management of large-scale IT systems in the area of freedom, security and justice, COM(2010) 93 final of 19 March 2010; in the following: proposal for an agency managing large-scale IT systems COM(2010) 93 final of 19 March 2010.

have legal personality.[801] The aim of the proposal is to achieve synergies by creating one entity to benefit "from economics of scale, creating critical mass and ensuring the highest possible utilisation rate of capital and human resources".[802]

The agency shall perform the tasks of the Management Authority by which all of the existing instruments are or shall be administered and which is responsible for the operational management of the system.[803] The monitoring of the developments in research relevant for the operational management of the SIS II, VIS and Eurodac and other large-scale IT systems in the AFSJ as well as implementing pilot schemes for the development or operation of large-scale IT systems in this area are additional tasks of the new agency.[804] Its administrative and management structure is provided to be composed of a Management Board, consisting of one representative of each Member State and two representatives of the Commission, an Executive Director and Advisory Groups.[805] While being technical responsible, the specific rules involving the purpose of processing, access rights, security measures and further data protection requirements applicable to each of the systems shall not be affected.[806] The data processing of the agency itself would base on Regulation 45/2001 and therefore the EDPS.[807] An internal DPO is intended to additionally supervise the agency.[808]

The influence of Europol and Eurojust is intended to be assured by involving them in the agency's work at several stages. Europol shall for instance be granted observer status at the meetings of the Management Board in the framework of questions relating to the SIS II and the VIS.[809] Eurojust may profit from the same status but only in relation to the SIS II.[810] Both actors may also appoint a representative in the SIS II advisory group while Europol is additionally allowed to appoint

[801] Explanatory memorandum of the proposal for an agency managing large-scale IT systems COM(2010) 93 final of 19 March 2010, p. 2.

[802] Recital (5) proposal for an agency managing large-scale IT systems COM(2010) 93 final of 19 March 2010; compare also Articles 2-4 proposal for an agency managing large-scale IT systems COM(2010) 93 final of 19 March 2010.

[803] Article 15 SIS II Council Decision 2007/533, OJ 2007, L-205/63; Article 42 (1) VIS Regulation 767/2008, OJ 2008, L-218/60 and Article 4 Eurodac Proposal, COM(2010) 555 of 11 October 2010.

[804] Articles 5 and 6 proposal for an agency managing large-scale IT systems COM(2010) 93 final of 19 March 2010.

[805] Ibid, Articles 8 and 10.

[806] Ibid, Recital (10).

[807] Ibid Article 25.

[808] Ibid, Article 9 (1) (0).

[809] Ibid, Article 12 (4).

[810] Ibid, Article 12 (4).

one in the VIS advisory group.[811] If the previously mentioned proposal on law enforcement access to Eurodac[812] enters into force, the power of Europol will probably also relate to the same functions with regard to Eurodac.[813] The Commission originally considered letting Frontex manage the three systems or alternatively letting Europol manage the SIS II whereas the Commission should be responsible for the VIS and Eurodac,[814] although after criticism from the EDPS and a comparative analysis of the various options, these two possibilities are no longer going to be pursued.

General concerns relate to the interoperability of the different IT systems and the possible creation of a "big brother agency" which risks to lead to a so called function creep, referring to the way in which information that has been collected for one limited purpose, is gradually allowed to be used for other purposes which might not approved of.[815] The concerns of the EDPS in this context refer to the idea that the new agency might be able to create and combine on its own motion the already existing and new large-scale IT systems to an extent which is unforeseen at the moment.[816] He therefore calls for a limitation of the scope of the agency clearly defined in its legal basis.[817] The current proposal from March 2010 however refers to rather wide ranging tasks including the operational management of the three mentioned systems and the development and management of other large-scale IT systems in application of Title V TFEU (AFSJ).[818] However, according to Article 6 (1) proposal for an agency managing large-scale IT systems interoperability is not provided for. The initiative for the development of new databases in the AFSJ lies with the Commission and the new agency is not allowed to act on its own proposal, a specific and precise request of the Commission for the development of a new system is required before developing new databases.[819]

Two main concerns in this context nevertheless arise relating to the absence of a definition of the large-scale IT system in the proposal and to the wider scope,

---

811 Ibid Article 16.

812 See Chap. C II 2.

813 Opinion of the EDPS of 7 December 2009 on the proposal for a Regulation establishing an agency for the operational management of large-scale IT systems in the area of freedom, security and justice, and on the proposal for a Council Decision conferring upon the agency tasks regarding the operational management of SIS II and VIS in application of Title VI of the EU Treaty, OJ 2010, C-70/13, para 7, Fn. 10 (in the following: EDPS opinion on the agency managing large-scale IT systems, OJ 2010, C-70/13).

814 Impact assessment of the proposal for an agency managing large-scale IT systems COM(2010) 93 final of 19 March 2010, pp. 7–8.

815 EDPS opinion on the agency managing large-scale IT systems, OJ 2010, C-70/13, para 24; compare definition of function creep in, Oxford Business English Dictionary, Oxford University Press, November 2005.

816 EDPS opinion on the agency managing large-scale IT systems, OJ 2010, C-70/13, para 26.

817 Ibid.

818 Article 1 proposal for an agency managing large-scale IT systems COM(2010) 93 final of 19 March 2010.

819 Ibid, Article 6 (1).

referring to Title V TFEU which embraces different policies such as rules on border checks, asylum and immigration as well as judicial cooperation in civil and criminal matters and police cooperation.

So far, the notion of large-scale IT systems is neither defined in the proposal (not even in the amended one from March 2010), nor in any of the other instruments referring to databases in the AFSJ, although the scope of the proposal clearly relates to this term. When applying a broader interpretation, various databases might soon be managed by the provided agency. The EDPS thus doubts whether only centralised databases such as the VIS, SIS II and Eurodac, might be included in the scope of additionally decentralised data exchange systems, for instance the Prüm system or the ECRIS (European Criminal Records Information System).[820] A report dealing with the different European databases carried out by the European Biometrics Forum on behalf of the Commission's Joint Research Centre agreed with regard to big biometric databases that "large scale not only applies to the potential size of the database or, more specifically, to the number of people whose biometric details are enrolled in the system, but equally to the number of searches that are carried out".[821] Pursuant to this definition, almost all European databases would fall under this definition and a limitation to centralised databases seems not to be evident.

Regarding the wide ranging scope of the agency, which could hypothetically include the management of all databases in the AFSJ, the risks of errors and abuse should be taken into account when considering that gradually more large-scale IT systems are handled by only one operational manager. At the same time, focused knowledge and sufficient personal resources might be an advantage in the daily work with the systems including the monitoring of only one operator instead of three different databases. In any case, the risk that one day the different systems are interconnected since they are using the same infrastructure and it would be technically feasible to do so, should be considered.

To sum up, the proposal for an agency managing large-scale IT systems does not provide so far for interoperability of the systems. Each system should keep its different rules regarding the purpose of processing, access rights, security measures and the data protection requirements applicable to each of the systems. The planned agency therefore does not directly affect the legal framework previously criticised. However, if the Commission once decides to ask the agency to develop an interoperability scheme, data protection and purpose limitation considerations would be two of the crucial points of discussion arising during in the legislative process, now, after the adoption of the Lisbon Treaty, luckily involving the European Parliament.

---

[820] EDPS opinion on the agency managing large-scale IT systems, OJ 2010, C-70/13, para 32.

[821] Report "Security & Privacy in Large Scale, Biometric Systems", based on an experts meeting held in Brussels on 25 September 2006, produced by the European Biometrics Forum, author: *Max Snijder*, commissioned by the EC – Commission's Joint Research Centre (JRC)/Institute for Prospective Technological Studies (IPTS), p. 9.

6. *Conclusion: Stagnating Data Protection Framework in Contrast to Increasing Functionalities of the EU Information Systems*

Several tendencies observed in Sect. II with regard to the agencies and OLAF can be confirmed also in context of the information exchange systems in the AFSJ. The scope of the analysed databases was significantly enlarged in all cases. Increasingly more data elements are allowed to be stored, including biometric data, and gradually more actors have access to databases originally established for a limited and specific purpose. Information systems, such as the SIS (II) continually develop towards a general intelligence database operated as a police investigative tool. New functions such as the linking of alerts in the SIS II could have negative consequences on the status of the person concerned.[822] Databases initially established in the framework of immigration control (VIS) are used for complete different purposes such as "the prevention of threats to internal security".[823]

Whereas over the years these important changes have taken place, the data protection framework mainly remained the same in comparison to the beginnings of the databases.

A further outcome of the foregoing analysis relates to the observation that the access of Europol and Eurojust to the above mentioned databases is often based on less restrictive provisions compared to the access conditions of Member States' law enforcement or security authorities and is regulated in a far reaching manner, regrettably not describing the access conditions in detail. In light of this shortcoming, some improvements are suggested relating to more restrictive formulations to regulate the law enforcement access.[824] In light of this significant tendency, the next section will go into the details of this access.

Regarding the entry conditions of personal data into the databases, the CIS regulation deserves particular attention: whereas entry in the databases is based on specific conditions in case of the SIS II, the VIS and Eurodac, the threshold to enter the data into the CIS is a regrettable reminder of the low entry requirements applying to the databases of Europol or Eurojust. Entry simply bases on the suspicion that an individual might one day commit serious contraventions of national law.[825] In case of the CIS, not only are the entry conditions broadly regulated, but the conditions applying to the use of the data by Europol and Eurojust are not even specified.[826] The same applies in the framework of third party transfer.[827]

---

[822] Compare Sect. III 1 b bb.

[823] Article 2 VIS Regulation 767/2008, OJ 2008, L-218/60.

[824] Compare Sect. III 2 c and Chap. D VI 4 and 5.

[825] Article 5 (2) CIS Council Decision 2009/917, OJ 2009, L-323/20.

[826] See Sect. III 3 c.

[827] See Sect. III 3 c.

In the light of these unsatisfactory conditions, the CIS supervisory structure is unfortunately not adapted to the developments which have taken place with regard to the other analysed databases. The shared monitoring between the EDPS and the national DPAs in case of the SIS, VIS and Eurodac assures an improvement when compared to the rather redundant CIS approach consisting of a joint supervisory body outside the EU structures.

Section III has established that the data processing and protection framework of the examined databases can be essentially improved when considering the increased access possibilities as well as the enlargement of the scopes of the databases. So far, the growing opportunities to process and analyse personal data are not sufficiently reflected in growing powers of their supervisory bodies. Old monitoring structures such as the JSA at the CIS should be replaced by the shared supervisory structure of the other databases. When now analysing the cooperation of the AFSJ agencies, OLAF and the information systems in the next chapter, the data processing framework illustrated in Chap. C should be kept in mind.

Chapter C
Cooperation and Data Exchange of the AFSJ Actors and Their Compliance with the European Data Protection Standard

As has already been established in the present contribution, the data protection frameworks of the AFSJ actors show several shortcomings and inconsistencies. Having this in mind, it is now worth pointing out that the data processing by these actors is not limited to the actors themselves; most of them are additionally interlinked with each other. Consequently, it is interesting to evaluate how and if at all, personal data are protected when it comes to the cooperation and the exchange of personal data amongst the different AFSJ actors.

This chapter will demonstrate the difficulty of controlling personal data once it has been entered into one of the systems and then interlinked and transferred to other AFSJ authorities or even to third states. In doing so, this chapter will take into account that the agencies Europol, Eurojust and Frontex as well as the Commission's anti-fraud unit OLAF do not only cooperate amongst themselves, some of them additionally have access to the European information systems (SIS, CIS, VIS or Eurodac), which are not necessarily connected to the field of activity of the accessing actors. The powers of Europol and Eurojust in this regard are particularly wide-ranging and deserve special attention.

By analysing both the agreements concluded for this purpose and the European legal instruments, principally Council decisions which were implemented in the last few years or were to be implemented in the near future in order to establish a basis for data exchange among AFSJ actors, the complexity of the cooperation structures will be made visible. While illustrating the interlinks between the parties involved, the general data protection framework of the AFSJ actors illustrated in Chap. B should be kept in mind.

For a detailed analysis of the data protection problems arising in this context, this chapter is divided into the illustration of the cooperation between the AFSJ agencies and OLAF on the one hand and the access of AFSJ agencies to the European information systems SIS, CIS, VIS and Eurodac on the other hand.

F. Boehm, *Information Sharing and Data Protection in the Area of Freedom, Security and Justice*, DOI 10.1007/978-3-642-22392-1_4,

I Inter-Agency Data Exchange and OLAF

1. Europol-Eurojust

Primary (Article 85 (1) TFEU) as well as secondary law (Article 26 of the Eurojust Decision) provide for a close cooperation between Europol and Eurojust. Both agencies exchange data based on agreements and are working together in so called Joint Investigation Teams (JITs), discussed in the first subdivision (a).[1] Eurojust is also associated with some of Europol's analysis work files, whereas a connection with all of Europol's work files is likely in the future.[2] Hence, a secure channel for information exchange was introduced in 2008.[3] A new cooperation agreement which entered into force in January 2010 replaced the former agreement concluded in 2004 and regulates in particular the exchange of information and the participation of Eurojust in Europol's analysis work files. It is examined in a second subdivision.

a) Joint Investigation Teams

According to Article 88 (2) (b) TFEU, the role of Europol includes the "coordination, organisation and implementation of investigative and operational action carried out jointly with the Member States' competent authorities or in context of Joint Investigation Teams, where appropriate in liaison with Eurojust". The European Parliament and the Council are empowered to adopt rules regulating this matter.

Until the entry into force of the Lisbon Treaty, the role of Europol and Eurojust in JITs was restricted to a supporting and coordinating function rather than to a party initiating investigations as Article 88 (2) (b) TFEU stipulates. Therefore, so far the main responsibilities of Europol and Eurojust related to JITs were rather of an organising and supportive nature,[4] acting on the basis of the Council Decisions which established them, reviewed above.[5]

---

[1] For the JITs see Joint Investigation Teams Manual of 23 September 2009 prepared by Europol and Eurojust, Council doc. 13598/09; Rijken (2006); Gualtiere (2007); for Europol's and Eurojust's participation, see de Buck (2007); Helmberg (2007).

[2] See annual report of Eurojust 2008, p. 41, http://www.eurojust.europa.eu/press_annual.htm (accessed February 2011); in 2008, Eurojust was involved in 12 of Europol's analysis work files.

[3] See annual report of Eurojust 2008, p. 41, http://www.eurojust.europa.eu/press_annual.htm (accessed February 2011); in 2008, Eurojust received 140 messages from Europol via this channel.

[4] Compare recital 9 and Articles 5 (1) (d), 5 (5), 6, 8 (7) c and 54 Council Decision of 6 April 2009 establishing the European Police Office, OJ 2009, L-121/37 as well as Articles 6 (b) (iv), 9 (f), 12 (2) (d), 13 (2) (5) and 25 (a) (2) Eurojust Decision.

[5] Article 6 Europol Decision and Article 7 (4) Eurojust Decision.

The role of Europol and Eurojust in JITs is described in a Joint Investigation Teams Manual from 23 September 2009 (The JIT manual). According to this manual, only the national members of Eurojust acting on the basis of their national law can be members of the JIT; officials from Europol and Eurojust[6] may participate but are not allowed to be a member of the JIT.[7] Article 6 of the Europol Decision and the JIT manual restrict their function to the involvement in the operation of the JIT, and exclude participation in any coercive measures.[8] These general rules may however be subject to further specific arrangements in form of particular agreements between the participating Member States and the bodies concerned, annexed to the initial agreement setting up the JIT, which may confer more rights on Europol or Eurojust.[9]

Considering the formulations in the JIT manual, in practice it seems to be hard to distinguish between the "participation in the operation of the JIT" on the one hand and the exclusion of coercive measures on the other, in particular when taking Article 6 (2) of the Europol Decision into account, which stipulates that Europol staff should "assist in *all* activities and exchange information with all the members" of the JIT.[10]

While the concept of JITs was introduced in 2000 by the Convention on Mutual Assistance in Criminal Matters and later reaffirmed by a Framework Decision on JITs,[11] the role of Europol and Eurojust in JITs has continually evolved over the last years. The Framework Decision on JITs specifies that two or more Member States can set up a JIT for a specific purpose and a limited period of time to carry out investigations while Eurojust and Europol may participate in the JITs.[12] For this purpose, participating Member States conclude mutual agreements and organise information events and publish manuals on the concept of JITs. In their aforementioned joint JIT manual from 2009, both agencies encourage Member States to set

[6] Lopes da Mota (2009).

[7] Joint Investigation Teams Manual of 23 September 2009, Council Doc. 13598/09, p. 10 and Eurojust Decision, Article 9 (f).

[8] Joint Investigation Teams Manual of 23 September 2009, Council Doc. 13598/09, p. 10; see also Article 6 (1) Council Decision of 6 April 2009 establishing the European Police Office, OJ 2009, L-121/37.

[9] Joint Investigation Teams Manual of 23 September 2009, Council Doc. 13598/09, pp. 26 and 27 suggesting a model agreement for the participation of Europol, Eurojust or OLAF.

[10] Article 6 (1) Council Decision of 6 April 2009 establishing the European Police Office, OJ 2009, L-121/37 (emphasis added); with regard to this problem, see de Buck (2007), pp. 260–261.

[11] Council Act of 29 May 2000 establishing in accordance with Article 34 of the Treaty on European Union the Convention on Mutual Assistance in Criminal Matters between the Member States of the European Union, OJ 2000, C-197/1, Article 13; to the initiation of the JIT project, see Horvatis and de Buck (2007), and Rijken and Vermeulen (2006).

[12] Article 1 and recital (9) of Council Framework Decision of 13 June 2002 on joint investigation teams, OJ 2002, L-162/1 and Article 13 Council Act of 29 May 2000 establishing in accordance with Article 34 Treaty on European Union the Convention on Mutual Assistance in Criminal Matters between the Member States of the European Union, OJ 2000, C 197/1.

up JITs to better coordinate cases involving several Member States.[13] A JIT consist of law enforcement officers, prosecutors, judges or other law enforcement related personnel and is established in the Member State in which investigations are supposed to be principally carried out.[14] Other European Union bodies, particularly the Commission (OLAF) as well as law enforcement bodies from third states such as the FBI may additionally be involved, however just as Europol and Eurojust, they may participate in the operation of a JIT, but they cannot lead or be a member of it.[15] They are associated via an agreement between the agency/administration of a Member State as a party to the agreement and the relevant European Union or third state body.[16]

Rules on information exchange in the JITs follow a *local* solution and are generally attached to the national law. They are vaguely mentioned in Article 6 (4) and (5) of the Europol Decision and Article 13 (9) and (10) of the Convention on Mutual Assistance in Criminal Matters as well as Article 1 (9) and (10) of the Framework Decision on JITs (which literally repeats the aforementioned Articles of the Convention) and stipulate that information could be shared *within the limits of the national law* of the national members seconded to the JIT.

Usually, the use of this information is restricted to the purpose for which the JIT has been set up and subject to the prior consent of the Member State where the information became available.[17] Information can further be used for preventing an immediate and serious threat to public security, for initiating criminal investigations or for other purposes to the extent that this is agreed between the Member States setting up the team.[18] Further details regarding the exchange of information and data protection issues are entailed in the specific arrangements of the agreements setting up the JIT,[19] but the specifics of these arrangements are not published and depend on the agreed compromise between the Member State and the relevant European actor in a particular case. Rules of general application regulating this nevertheless rather informal data exchange would definitely lead to more legal certainty as well as to a transparent way to deal with data protection rights in this

---

[13] Joint Investigation Teams Manual of 23 September 2009, Council Doc. 13598/09.

[14] Explanatory report on the Convention on Mutual Assistance in Criminal Matters between the Member States of the European Union, OJ 2000, C-379/7, Article 13 and Joint Investigation Teams Manual of 23 September 2009, Council Doc. 13598/09, p. 6.

[15] Joint Investigation Teams Manual of 23 September 2009, Council Doc. 13598/09, pp. 9 and 10.

[16] A model agreement can be found in Joint Investigation Teams Manual of 23 September 2009, Council Doc. 13598/09, pp. 26–27.

[17] Article 1 (10) (b) of Council Framework Decision of 13 June 2002 on joint investigation teams, OJ 2002, L-162/1.

[18] Ibid, Article 1 (10) (a)–(d).

[19] See the example of a model agreement in Joint Investigation Teams Manual of 23 September 2009, Council Doc. 13598/09, p. 24.

context, independent of secret agreements concluded between Member States and Europol or Eurojust.[20]

However, most importantly, Europol may provide the JIT members with information stemming from the EIS or from an analysis work file whereby it has to inform the Member State which originally provided the information thereof.[21] Europol thereby grants access to both systems "by means of a Europol mobile office located where the JIT is operating".[22] JIT members are allowed to have direct access to Europol's information systems, facilitating in particular the access to information of Member States which do not participate in the JIT as well as to information of third States cooperating with Europol.[23] When a Europol staff member participating in a JIT obtains information, he can include the information in Europol's data processing systems, after having obtained the prior consent of the relevant Member State.[24]

The active participation of Europol in information exchange with the JIT nevertheless risks conflicting with the aforementioned local approach chosen in the Convention on Mutual Assistance in Criminal Matters as well as in the Framework Decision on JITs when considering that the information may only be shared within the boundaries of the national law of the national members seconded to the JIT. As a result, the assortment of different domestic rules on data exchange and data protection may conflict with each other and additionally with the Europol rules, which could finally lead to a considerable lack of legal certainty.

Whereas the Europol Decision entails rules allowing for the exchange between its data processing systems and the JITs, data exchange between Eurojust and the JITs is not regulated. Although Article 7 (a) (iv) of the Eurojust Decision refers to the participation of Eurojust in JITs and the JIT manual clearly speaks of a participation of Eurojust officials in JIT operations[25] (excluding coercive measures), information exchange or data protection rules in this regard are missing. The redraft of the Eurojust Decision in 2009 could have closed this regulatory gap, but either it was not detected or intentionally not regulated, whereby it seems to be possible that information obtained in course of JITs is entered by the national Members of Eurojust acting on the basis of national law and not by Eurojust officials in the Case Management System of Eurojust. This possibility would also lead to a non-regulated transfer of data from the Case Management System to the

[20] To this problem, see Rijken and Vermeulen (2006), pp. 110–118; Mitsilegas (2009), p. 171.

[21] Council Decision of 6 April 2009 establishing the European Police Office, OJ 2009, L-121/37, Article 6 (4).

[22] De Buck (2007), p. 263.

[23] Information from third States can be obtained by using the so called Virtual Private Network (VPN) connecting Europol's national units and offering encrypted lines with third States, see de Buck (2007), p. 263.

[24] Compare Council Decision of 6 April 2009 establishing the European Police Office, OJ 2009, L-121/37, Article 6 (4) and (5).

[25] Joint Investigation Teams Manual of 23 September 2009, Council Doc. 13598/09, p. 10.

other JIT members considering that national law does not apply in this rather European context. Additionally, in case that only the national members of Eurojust supply Case Management Information to the JIT or information stemming from Eurojust's own analysis, the question of information transfer from Eurojust's Case Management System to the JIT through a member acting on behalf of Eurojust involved in the JIT is left unanswered.[26]

Rules comparable to the Europol Decision which clarify the transfer of data between Eurojust and the JITs as well as the specifics of the information entered in the Case Management System are necessary to regulate this specific problem.

b) The Europol-Eurojust Agreement

The Europol-Eurojust Agreement[27] mainly regulates Eurojust participation in Europol's analysis work files which is a new development linking the legal framework of the two bodies, hence affecting data protection questions related to the sharing of the files with another agency. Problems regarding the accountability of processing and supervision might arise. The EDPS in its opinion to the amendment of the Eurojust Decision rightly points to the questions of "who will be the processor?" and "who will be the controller?" within this new collaboration structure.[28] Details to these questions are unfortunately not regulated in the Europol-Eurojust Agreement as it indeed provides for mutual association, but it neither clarifies questions of supervision in case of Eurojust's participation in Europol's analysis work files, nor regarding the transmission of personal data. The data protection particulars of the agreement of 2010 between Europol and Eurojust, including a comparison to the former agreement, are therefore briefly analysed hereinafter.

At first glance, the Europol-Eurojust Agreement entails considerable changes regarding the communication and the exchange of information between the two bodies. Whereas the former agreement based on information exchange upon request, the new agreement stipulates in Articles 7 and 8 that both Europol and Eurojust shall "of its own motion" *or* upon request, provide each other with analysis results including interim analysis results. When the information communicated matches the information stored in the respective processing systems, Europol or

[26] To the general data protection problems arising out of JITs, see Gusy (2008), in particular pp. 274–278.

[27] Agreement between Europol and Eurojust which entered into force the 1 January 2010, Articles 7 (2) and 8 (2), in the following: Europol-Eurojust Agreement; this Agreement replaced the Agreement between Europol and Eurojust of 9 June 2004.

[28] EDPS opinion on the Council Decision concerning the strengthening of Eurojust and amending Decision 2002/187/JHA of 5 December 2008, OJ 2008, C 310/1, p. 6, para 34.

Eurojust shall additionally provide each other with data linked to the information provided.[29]

This evidently leads to merging of the data still stored separately either in the Europol or in Eurojust databases. Article 8 (3) of the Europol-Eurojust Agreement further provides for a regular transmission of relevant data stored at Eurojust for the purpose of using them in Europol's analysis work files. The same applies to other information, in particular information on cases, provided that they fall within Europol's competence.[30] It is worth mentioning here that both actors are principally competent to deal with the same criminal offences.[31]

In addition to the exchange of information as regards the analysis work files, there is a further profound and important change as regards the possibilities of Eurojust to play a part in Europol's analysis work files.

According to Article 9 (2) of the Europol-Eurojust Agreement, Eurojust has the right to take the initiative to open an analysis work file or even to establish a target group, if Eurojust is associated with the analysis work file concerned.[32] Whereas direct access by Eurojust to Europol's analysis work files was excluded under the former cooperation agreement, Article 11 (1) of the Europol-Eurojust Agreement goes one step further: Europol shall associate experts of Eurojust to participate within the activities of Europol's analysis work files, in particular when Eurojust has initiated the opening of the respective file. Eurojust may also request to be associated with the activities of a particular analysis group.[33]

When Europol associates Eurojust to its analysis work files, according to Article 11 (3) of the Europol-Eurojust Agreement, Eurojust's experts will have the following privileges: they can attend the analysis group meetings, are informed of the development of the respective work file, receive analysis data and results, including interim results and are entitled to transfer the received data onward with the prior consent of the provider while respecting the conditions regulated in Article 14 of Europol-Eurojust Agreement. This Article indicates the general rules which have to be respected in case of data transfer. Spontaneous data transmission as well as transmission upon request must be accompanied by an indication of the purpose for which the relevant information is transferred. When restrictions apply to the use, access or deletion of the transmitted data, the transmitting party must indicate this. Transmission to third parties, apart from the member State's prior consent, is possible when allowed under the legal framework of the transmitting party (Europol or Eurojust Decision including its reference instruments) and when respecting the conditions or restrictions indicated by the transmitting party.[34] The

[29] Articles 7 (2) and 8 (2), Europol-Eurojust Agreement.

[30] Ibid, Article 8 (3).

[31] Eurojust's mandate refers to a list of crimes for which Europol is responsible and which is laid down in Article 3 Europol Decision, compare Article 4 (1) Eurojust Decision.

[32] Article 9 (2) Europol-Eurojust Agreement.

[33] Ibid, Article 11 (2).

[34] Ibid, Article 14 (6).

Eurojust Decision additionally provides, in case of third state data transfer, for the consent of the national member of the Member State which originally submitted the information.[35] Further, in case that transmitted data are deleted or corrected, the transmitting party must inform the third party thereof.[36]

c) Conclusion: Europol and Eurojust – Close Cooperation in Absence of Effective Supervision

The fact that Eurojust participates in the activities of an analysis work file and an analysis group at Europol is astonishing, in particular with regard to Article 14 (2) of the Europol Decision whereupon the access to analysis work files is strictly restricted to analysts, designated Europol staff, liaison officers or experts from the Member States. This Article moreover provides that only analysts are authorised to enter data into the file and modify such data. Taking into account that Article 13 of the Europol-Eurojust Agreement stipulates that the transmission shall be in accordance with the establishing act of the parties and additionally considering the enormous variety (information about criminals, victims, witnesses, contacts etc.) as well as amount of personal data (up to 69 data elements) which can be stored in Europol's analysis work file, each widening of the circle of persons having access to the relevant information should be accompanied with additional safeguards against abuse as well as effective tools of supervision.[37]

Remembering the conditions under which the ECtHR's in *Weber and Saravia v. Germany* accepted the transmission to other authorities (only allowed when particularly supervised and restricted to the transmission of data arousing the suspicion that specific facts, as opposed to mere factual indications, pointing to the fact that this person has committed a crime), the non-regulation of supervision as well as the transfer provisions in this context, in particular regarding data of victims or witnesses, seems to be very doubtful.[38]

Article 13 of the Europol-Eurojust Agreement provides for some "general terms and conditions" requiring that each party has to indicate the source of information as well as stipulating the obligation to record the transfer and its grounds. However, it does not refer to supervision or additional safeguards in case of data transfer to the analysis work files. It simply states that transmitted data shall be limited to the purposes for which they were communicated, which does not mean that they are

---

[35] Article 27 (1) Eurojust Decision.

[36] Article 18 (5) Europol-Eurojust Agreement.

[37] Compare Chap. B II 1 b bb.

[38] *Weber and Saravia v. Germany*, Application no. 54934/00, admissibility decision of 29 June 2006, paras 42–43 and 123–129, see Chap. A II 1 d cc (2); Article 14 (4) Europol-Eurojust Agreement however lays down that the transmission of data revealing racial origin, political opinions or religious or other beliefs, or concerning health and sexual life shall be restricted to absolutely necessary cases and that such data shall only be transmitted in addition to other data.

limited to the purpose for which they were collected. A strict interpretation of the purpose limitation principle, as it was applied by the ECtHR in *Weber and Saravia v. Germany,*[39] would here come to a violation of this principle.

Nevertheless, the Europol-Eurojust Agreement lays down access as well as correction and deletion rights.[40] Disappointingly, although the participation of Eurojust in Europol's work files was newly introduced, the data protection provisions were not adapted to the new circumstances. Rules requiring information of witnesses, victims or persons requesting access about the transfer of their data as well as rules relating to the information of Europol's or Eurojust's JSB about the transfer, are missing. Provisions regulating the competence for access request once Eurojust's data are included in Europol's analysis work files are additionally not provided for in the agreement, not to mention provisions relating to the supervision of the data generated in this way.

All in all, especially the participation Eurojust in Europol's analysis work files demands further protections for individuals, in particular regarding the rights of victims or witnesses to know whether and to whom their data are transferred. The JSB and the data protection officers of both agencies should be informed in any case in order to guarantee at least minimum supervision. In addition, when taking the enormous amount of data into account with which both agencies are dealing,[41] it is worth considering the establishment of an independent authority for the sole purpose of monitoring the data transfer between them.

The Europol-Eurojust Agreement further provides for an annual duty to report to the Council and the Commission, in particular as regards the cooperation in analysis work files.[42] With regard to the entry into force of the Lisbon Treaty and its abandoning of the pillar structure as well as its strengthening of democratic control, this obligation should be additionally extended to the European Parliament.

---

[39] *Weber and Saravia v. Germany*, Application no. 54934/00, admissibility decision of 29 June 2006, para 121.

[40] According to Article 18 (3) Europol-Eurojust Agreement, transmitted data shall be deleted when they are no longer necessary for the purpose for which they were transferred or when they are not necessary for the tasks of the receiving party or when no decision has been taken within 3 month after receipt (Article 16 (4)); a retention review must take place within the first three years of storage and when the storage exceeds three years, an annual review has to be implemented, see Article 18 (5) Europol-Eurojust Agreement.

[41] Eurojust registered 1372 new cases in 2009, compare Eurojust annual report 2009, p. 50 and Europol had 88419 objects stored in the EIS and initiated 8377 cases in 2008, compare Europol annual report 2008, pp. 33–35.

[42] Article 22 Europol-Eurojust Agreement.

2. *Europol-OLAF*

Compared to the wide-ranging cooperation between Europol and Eurojust, that of Europol and OLAF seems to be far less developed. Although both actors deal with fraud-related activities, normally calling for a clear and aligned cooperation to avoid overlapping effects, the existing cooperation provisions are based on different legal instruments making it difficult to understand the collaboration mechanism. Especially OLAF's provisions give reason for concern. While Europol's data exchange rules with third parties are stipulated in its legal basis and have been analysed in Chap. B II 1 e, OLAF's role is illustrated below.

a) Joint Investigation Teams

OLAF can be associated to JITs under the same conditions as Europol and Eurojust (illustrated in Sect. I 1 a) signifying that OLAF officials may participate, but are not allowed to have a member status or leading function in the JIT whereas the details of the cooperation may be specified in an additional agreement between the contributing Member States and OLAF.[43]

Although the participation at JIT in the case of Europol and Eurojust is stipulated in their legal bases as well as even in the TFEU (Article 88 (2) (b)), OLAF's different legal bases give no indication of its inclusion in JITs.[44] While OLAF officials proceed on the assumption that the second protocol from 1999 to the Convention on the protection of the EC's financial interests[45] – broadly dealing with the cooperation between the Member states and the Commission in fraud related matters, active and passive corruption and money laundering – taken together with the Convention on Mutual assistance in Criminal Matters enables OLAF to participate in JITs,[46] none of these instruments explicitly refers to this sensitive subject matter. On the contrary, OLAF is not even mentioned.

---

[43] Joint Investigation Teams Manual of 23 September 2009, Council Doc. 13598/09, pp. 9, 10 and 22.

[44] Compare Commission Decision 1999/352/EC of 28 April 1999 establishing the European Anti-Fraud Office (OLAF), OJ 1999, L-136/20 and Regulation (EC) No 1073/1999 of the European Parliament and the Council of 25 May 1999 concerning investigation conducted by the European Anti-Fraud Office (OLAF), OJ 1999, L-136/31; Article 2 (6) Commission Decision 199/352 broadly regulates that "the office shall be in direct contact with the police and judicial authorities" and Article 1 (2) Regulation 1073/1999 only refers to "assistance" from the Commission to the Member States in organising close cooperation between the competent authorities of the Member States.

[45] Second Protocol, drawn up on the basis of Article K.3 of the treaty on European Union, to the Convention on the protection of the European Communities' financial interests – Joint Declaration on Article 13 (2) – Commission Declaration on Article 7, OJ 1997, C-221/12.

[46] De Moor (2009), p. 97; see also: Riegel (2009).

Indeed the Convention provides for "operational assistance" including exchange of personal data in fraud-related offences between the Commission and the Member States, but it does not specify the instruments to be used in this context. With regard to the potential far reaching information exchange in the JITs framework, it is extremely worrisome that OLAF acts in absence of a clear legal basis, in absence of rules specifying which information OLAF may disclose or collect when participating in JITs. Additionally keeping in mind Europol's extensive data exchange possibilities in the JITs, particularly the inclusion of information obtained in the JIT framework in the analysis work files and vice versa, OLAF's role within the JIT structure certainly has to be clarified. In this context, special attention has to be paid to the fact that the cooperation of these two bodies is so far based on an agreement not allowing for personal data exchange (see following section). The participation of OLAF and Europol in common JITs unavoidably leads to personal data exchange and would therefore contradict OLAF's existing legal bases as well as the cooperation agreement between Europol and OLAF, discussed hereafter.

b) The Europol: OLAF Administrative Arrangement

The cooperation between Europol and OLAF is based on an administrative agreement, signed in 2004, restricted to the exchange of strategic information.[47] Plans to conclude an agreement allowing for personal data exchange have existed for a long time: in 2005, the Commission's legal service concluded that the transmission of personal data between Europol and OLAF could only take place based on an (international) agreement between Europol and the European Community (not OLAF, as it is part of the Commission).[48] Currently, negotiations discussing an administrative arrangement similar to that concluded with Eurojust which allows for personal data exchange, are taking place.[49]

However, it is worth noting that, after the entry into force of the new Europol Decision on 1 January 2010, Article 22 (3) of Europol Decision permits Europol to directly receive, use and transmit information, including personal data from OLAF, even prior to the conclusion of a formal exchange agreement "in so far as it is necessary for the legitimate performance of Europol's or OLAF's tasks". In case the

[47] Administrative Arrangement between the European Police Office (Europol) and the European Anti-Fraud Office (OLAF) of 8 April 2004, http://www.europol.europa.eu/legal/agreements/Agreements/52153.pdf (accessed February 2011).

[48] Council Document 13424/2/06, rev. 2, ENFOCUSTOM 64, Action Plan to implement the Strategy for Customs Co-operation in the Third Pillar and Council Document 11216/1/08, rev 1 EUROPOL 63 on customs cooperation at Europol, section 3.1.2.1.

[49] OLAF annual report 2009, ninth activity report for the period 1 January 2008 to 31 December 2008, section 4.6.2, p. 59.

transmitted data were originally introduced by a Member State, Europol has to ask the Member State for prior consent.[50]

Taking into account the different existing provisions, on one hand a valid agreement not allowing for personal data exchange and on the other, the rules stipulated in the Europol Decision, the legal basis for personal data exchange between OLAF and Europol is far from being clear. Theoretically, according to its legal basis, Europol could transmit and receive personal data stored in OLAF's databases, although it has to be taken into account that OLAF's provisions in this context are less revealing, apart from the fact that they must be generally in accordance with the provisions of Regulation 45/2001.[51]

Regrettably, neither Commission Decision 1999/352/EC establishing OLAF nor Regulation 1073/1999 include transfer provisions regulating personal data exchange with third states or agencies such as Europol.[52] The first pillar CIS Regulation 766/2008 refers to third State data transfer, ignoring the exchange with European agencies such as Europol.[53] Articles 18a, 29 (1), 41a and 41c of CIS Regulation 766/2008 restrict the access to data included in the CIS and the FIDE databases as well as in the European Data Directory to national authorities of the Member States and the departments designated by the Commission.[54] Rules on the transfer to agencies are nowhere to be found in OLAF's instruments.

c) Conclusion: Europol and OLAF – Information Exchange in Absence of a Clear Legal Basis for OLAF

Summarising, the legal bases regulating personal data exchange between Europol and OLAF are not sufficiently developed. Whilst the Decision establishing Europol was recently amended and now allows for personal data exchange with different actors, OLAF's legal framework lags considerably behind. Neither is OLAF's cooperation in JITs based on an appropriate legal basis, nor is the possible mutual transfer of personal data according to the Europol Decision reflected in OLAF's legal instruments.

[50] Article 24 (1) Europol Decision.

[51] Compare Chap. B II 3 c; Regulation 45/2001 is restricted in scope and refers only to personal data transfer between Community bodies which represent bodies established under the former first pillar and does not include Europol or Eurojust.

[52] Article 10 Regulation 1073/1999 refers to the forwarding obtained in course of internal investigations to the bodies, offices and agencies concerned by the investigation, however this provision does not take the data exchange in the framework of criminal or judicial cooperation into account.

[53] Article 30 (4) Regulation 766/2008.

[54] Cooperation with international or regional organisations is additionally mentioned in Article 29 (3) Regulation 766/2008.

With regard to the far reaching possibilities to exchange data during a JIT operation, OLAF's missing legal basis in this regard is particularly striking. It is however worth noting that OLAF, in contrast to Europol, has been part of the legal framework of the first pillar which would have permitted a more detailed regulation of its legal basis and its role in JITs.

OLAF's possibility to participate in JITs together with Europol raises further concern in view of the fact that the current cooperation agreement between the two bodies does not permit the exchange of personal data. How and if this legal interdiction is enforced in practice, especially during JIT operations, is questionable. In particular as Europol has extensive data exchange possibilities in the framework of JITs, analysed in Sect. I 1 a, OLAF's role urgently needs to be clarified. Otherwise, data exchange in absence of a legal basis would not be in compliance with the rule of law and the data protection requirements stipulated in Chap. A.

Moreover, the new Europol Decision permits Europol to directly receive and use information from OLAF, even in absence of an exchange agreement. This situation should be considered when OLAF's legal framework will be reconsidered in future.

The current situation, in which the provisions of the agreement between OLAF and Europol contradict OLAF's possibility to participate in JITs, however, is far from being clear. The aforementioned serious shortcomings have to be resolved before personal data between the two actors are exchanged.

3. *Europol-Frontex*

Frontex and Europol cooperate based on a "strategic agreement" concluded in 2008.[55] The agreement excludes the transmission of personal data and thus can not legalise the informal cooperation between Europol and Frontex, which almost certainly includes the transfer of personal data from Frontex to Europol. In the framework of joint operations, Frontex apparently sends data to Europol for threat analysis.[56] The proposal to amend the Frontex regulation, analysed hereinafter,

[55] Strategic co-operation agreement between the European Agency for the Management of Operational Cooperation at the External Borders of the Member States of the European Union and the European Police Office of 28 March 2008; in the following: Europol-Frontex Agreement of 28 March 2008.

[56] Compare Chap. B II 4 b and House of Lords Europol report, European Union Committee, 29th report of session 2007–2008, "Europol: coordinating the fight against serious and organised crime", published 12 November 2008, p. 80 as well as Final report of COWI (European consulting group) of January 2009 preparing an external evaluation of Frontex provided for in Article 33 of the Council Regulation (EC) No 2007/2004 of 26 October 2004 establishing Frontex, p. 48, available at: http://www.frontex.europa.eu/specific_documents/other/ (accessed February 2011).

should eventually put this exchange on a legal basis.[57] Nevertheless, even if the proposal enters into force, personal data exchange with Europol or other Union agencies or bodies would generally require the conclusion of a new cooperation agreement.[58]

a) The Europol-Frontex Agreement

The "strategic cooperation agreement" between Europol and Frontex from March 2008 is limited to the exchange of strategic and technical information[59] prohibiting the exchange of personal data, more precisely the transfer of "data related to an identified individual".[60] It mainly deals with the areas of criminality covered by the scope of this agreement (the mandate of Europol and Frontex), the exchange of expertise as well as confidentiality provisions and procedures in context with the exchange of classified information.

Astonishing, however, is the provision regulating the exchange of information. Whereas Article 1 of the agreement expressively clarifies that the agreement is not related to personal data, the wording of Article 5 reveals remarkably detailed data exchange provisions which are normally contained in agreements including personal data exchange. Examples are provisions relating to the purpose limitation principle regarding the information exchanged as well as rules on the proceeding, in case an individual makes a request to disclose information.[61] These provisions seem to make sense when personal data shall be exchanged.

---

[57] The legal basis of the proposal is Article 74 and 77 (1) (b) and (c) TFEU by using the codecision procedure.

[58] Compare Article 13 of the proposal for a Regulation of the European Parliament and the Council amending Council Regulation (EC) No. 2007/2004 of 26 October 2004 establishing a European Agency for the Management of Operational Cooperation at the External Borders of the Member States of the European Union (FRONTEX) of 24 February 2010, COM(2010) 61 final.

[59] According to Article 2 Europol-Frontex Agreement: 1. "Strategic information" includes, but is not limited to: a. enforcement actions that might be useful to suppress offences and improve the integrated border management of the Member States of the European Union; b. new methods used in committing offences, in particular, those threatening the security of external borders or facilitating illegal immigration; c. trends and developments in the methods used to commit offences; d. observations and findings resulting from the successful application of new enforcement aids and techniques; e. routes and changes in routes used by smugglers, illegal immigrants or those involved in illicit trafficking offences covered by this agreement; f. prevention strategies and methods for management to select law enforcement priorities; g. threat assessments, risk analysis and crime situation reports. 2. "Technical information" includes, but is not limited to: a. means of strengthening administrative and enforcement structures in the fields covered by this agreement; b. police working methods as well as investigative procedures and results; c. methods of training the officials concerned; d. criminal intelligence analytical methods; e. identification of law enforcement expertise.

[60] Article 1 Europol-Frontex Agreement of 28 March 2008.

[61] Article 5 para 4, 5 and 7 Europol-Frontex agreement.

Conditions on the further use and transfer of the transmitted information may also be imposed on the receiving party, just as Europol shall only supply information to Frontex "which was collected, stored and transmitted in accordance with the relevant provisions of the Europol Convention and its implementing regulations",[62] though the latter apparently deals with personal data.

Such specified provisions are exceptional and not included in similar strategic agreements Europol has concluded with other EU bodies (Central Bank, Commission, Monitoring Centre for Drugs and Drug Addiction, OLAF). A fact casting doubts on the complete exclusion of personal data from the cooperation between the two actors, in particular when taking informal cooperation of Europol and Frontex into consideration, which according to external evaluation reports[63] leads to personal data transfer from Frontex to Europol. Additionally, the agreement's exclusion of personal data exchange seems to be rather obsolete, yet disconnected to a great extent from the cooperation between Europol and Frontex in reality, also in the light of Europol's new Council decision which provides for personal data exchange even in absence of an agreement allowing for the latter (pursuant to its Article 22 (3)).

b) Frontex Proposal and Data Transfer to Europol

Above, we have seen two important facts relating to data processing by Frontex: while neither the Frontex Regulation 2007/2004 nor the Europol-Frontex agreement permit personal data processing or transfer, the reality seems to tell another story.

For this reason, clarifications in Frontex's legal framework were long overdue and have resulted in 2010 in the Frontex proposal in the Commission and the Council to amend Frontex regulation 2007/2004[64] by, amongst others, now including two important changes concerning the question of data processing at Frontex:

---

[62] Article 5 para 3 et 8 Europol-Frontex agreement.

[63] Final report of COWI (European consulting group) of January 2009 preparing an external evaluation of Frontex provided for in Article 33 of the Council Regulation (EC) No 2007/2004 of 26 October 2004 establishing Frontex, p. 48, available at: http://www.frontex.europa.eu/specific_documents/other/ (accessed February 2011) and House of Lords Europol report, European Union Committee, 29th report of session 2007–2008, "Europol: coordinating the fight against serious and organised crime", published 12 November 2008, p. 80.

[64] Proposal for a Regulation of the European Parliament and the Council amending Council Regulation (EC) No. 2007/2004 of 26 October 2004 establishing a European Agency for the Management of Operational Cooperation at the External Borders of the Member States of the European Union (FRONTEX) of 24 February 2010, COM(2010) 61 final and Council document 2010/0039 (COD), 8121/10, proposal for a regulation of the European Parliament and the Council amending Council Regulation (EC) No 2007/2004 establishing a European Agency for the Management of operational cooperation at the external borders of the Member States of the European Union (Frontex) 29 March 2010.

on the one hand, the Frontex proposal allows the collection, processing and exchange of personal data concerning the detection of criminal networks organising illegal immigration,[65] and on the other hand it supports the use and the possible recomposing of the collected data by allowing risk analysis to be carried out.[66] The latter tasks would considerably overlap with Europol's mandate. Regrettably, the proposal does not specify the details of data processing at Frontex, neither does it include individual rights.[67]

Moreover, provisions relating to the cooperation with EU agencies and bodies as well as international organisations are not very well developed within the proposal. Article 13 of the proposal refers to "working arrangements" which might be concluded with possible partners such as the explicitly named bodies Europol, the European Asylum Support Office and the Fundamental Rights Agency and which shall specify the details of this cooperation.[68] No references are made to the data categories to be exchanged, the respect of data protection rules in these situations or the conditions under which such exchange could take place, nor are there further explanations given in the Commission's impact assessment. The EDPS assumes therefore that Article 13 of the proposal does not involve the transfer of personal data.[69] This however conflicts with Article 22 (2) and (3) of the new Europol

[65] Proposal for a Regulation of the European Parliament and the Council amending Council Regulation (EC) No. 2007/2004 of 26 October 2004 establishing a European Agency for the Management of Operational Cooperation at the External Borders of the Member States of the European Union (FRONTEX) of 24 February 2010, COM(2010) 61 final, Article 2; Eurosur is the planned European Border Surveillance System; for more details, see Commission staff working paper, report on progress made in developing the European Border Surveillance System (EUROSUR) of 24 September 2009, Sec(2009), 1265 final; An analysis of the Commission communications on future development of Frontex and the creation of a European Border Surveillance System (EUROSUR), briefing paper from policy department C, citizens' rights and constitutional affairs, civil liberties, justice and home affairs, Directorate General internal policies of the Union of June 2008, PE 408.295.

[66] Impact assessment accompanying the proposal for a Regulation of the European Parliament and the Council amending Council Regulation (EC) No. 2007/2004 of 26 October 2004 establishing a European Agency for the Management of Operational Cooperation at the External Borders of the Member States of the European Union (FRONTEX) of 24 February 2010, p. 34.

[67] Compare Chap. B II 4 d and Opinion of the European Data Protection Supervisor on the proposal for a Regulation of the European Parliament and the Council amending Council Regulation (EC) No. 2007/2004 establishing a European Agency for the Management of Operational Cooperation at the External Borders of the Member States of the European Union (FRONTEX) of 17 May 2010.

[68] Proposal for a Regulation of the European Parliament and the Council amending Council Regulation (EC) No. 2007/2004 of 26 October 2004 establishing a European Agency for the Management of Operational Cooperation at the External Borders of the Member States of the European Union (FRONTEX) of 24 February 2010, COM(2010) 61 final, Article 13.

[69] Opinion of the European Data Protection Supervisor on the proposal for a Regulation of the European Parliament and the Council amending Council Regulation (EC) No. 2007/2004 establishing a European Agency for the Management of Operational Cooperation at the External Borders of the Member States of the European Union (FRONTEX) of 17 May 2010, p. 7.

Decision allowing for personal data exchange with Frontex. Article 13 of the Frontex proposal should be clarified to avoid a situation leading to personal data exchange with Frontex in absence of a legal basis.

c) Conclusion: Europol and Frontex – Cooperation Built on an Ambiguous Legal Basis

It follows from the above that the current agreement between Europol and Frontex seems not to correspond to the cooperation actually taking place between the two actors. The exchange and in particular Frontex's collection of personal data is neither covered by the Europol-Frontex agreement, nor by Frontex's current legal basis.

The amendment of the Frontex regulation will probably allow for data processing at Frontex as well as for an intensified cooperation with EU agencies/ bodies and third states,[70] but the widening of Frontex's mandate in this regard would also connect two not directly linked remits (border control and serious crime prevention) and would partly overlap with Europol's mandate.

It is important that, in contrast to Europol, the mandate of Frontex does not (and will not) cover the collection of data related to serious crime or organised immigration crime which means that the data of Europol and Frontex are definitely not collected for the same purpose. The exchange of the data could eventually lead to the connection of data of potential immigrants with data included in Europol's databases, the latter dealing for the most part with data related to persons associated to crimes. Linking these two subjects while disregarding any distinction between data of criminals and data of (possible) immigrants, contravenes the purpose limitation principle and blurs the border between criminals and immigrants.

Clear rules respecting the protection of personal data of the individuals concerned in the Frontex proposal would help to prevent the criminalisation of this specific group and should accompany the ambitions of the Council and the Commission to extend the capabilities of Frontex to exchange data.

---

[70] See also Frontex priorities in its "Programme of Work 2010", which demand an intensified cooperation between Europol and Frontex as well as between Frontex and agencies such as Community Fisheries Control Agency (CFCA), the European Maritime Safety Agency (EMSA), the European Union Satellite Centre (EUSC), and with the European Asylum Support Office that will be set up in 2010, as well as inter-institutional cooperation in particular with UNODC and OSCE, p. 116, http://www.frontex.europa.eu/gfx/frontex/files/justyna/pow2010.pdf (accessed February 2011).

4. *Eurojust-OLAF*

Since the establishment of Eurojust, the relation to OLAF was characterised by a climate of mistrust due to their overlapping mandates, specifically as both bodies are competent to cope with investigations as regards fraud affecting the Community's financial interests and additionally feel called upon to establish a European Prosecutor from their structures in the future. A House of Lords report from 2004 refers to the competition between the two bodies and the "hostile situation" with which Eurojust had to deal in the beginning of the relationship to OLAF and describes the situation in 2004 between the two bodies as "regrettable".[71] The report gives the impression that during the first years of side by side existence, the potential for cooperation relating to fraud investigations was not fully exploited, despite a Memorandum of Understanding in 2003 regulating the data exchange (excluding personal data exchange) between the two bodies.[72] Over the years, the situation seems to have improved. However, to what extent cooperation and data exchange is currently feasible, will be shown in the analysis of the new cooperation agreement concluded in 2008 replacing the restricted 2003 Memorandum of Understanding not allowing for personal data exchange.[73] Additionally the clear statement in the Lisbon Treaty that the European Public Prosecutor should be developed "from Eurojust" may have clarified an important issue of dispute.[74]

a) Joint Investigation Teams

Contradictory to the Europol-OLAF agreement, the question of joint participation in JITs is integrated in the cooperation agreement between Eurojust and OLAF. In case one party is associated to a JIT related to fraud, corruption or criminal offences affecting the EU's financial interest, it shall inform the other party about its participation and propose the Member States setting up the JIT to consider inviting the other party.[75] However, similar to the Europol-OLAF provisions in this case, details regarding the JITs cooperation, including the applicable data protection rules, are subject to the JIT agreement concluded between the participating parties.

---

[71] House of Lords Eurojust report, European Union Committee, 23th report of session 2003–04, "Judicial cooperation in the EU: the role of Eurojust", published 21 July 2004, p. 27–28; see also: Quirke (2010), in particular pp. 100–101; to the relation between Eurojust and OLAF, compare Fawzy (2005), pp. 102–113.

[72] Memorandum of Understanding between Eurojust and OLAF of 4 April 2003, http://ec.europa.eu/anti_fraud/press_room/pr/2003/memo_en.pdf (accessed February 2011).

[73] Section I 4 b.

[74] Article 86 (1) TFEU.

[75] Practical Agreement on arrangements of cooperation between Eurojust and OLAF of 24 September 2008, point 9 (1).

As seen above, in contrast to Europol, the Eurojust Decision remains silent on the subject of information exchange in the framework of JITs.[76] Whereas Europol is allowed to provide the JIT members with information from its EIS or the analysis work files and may grant access to these systems, Eurojust's role and its competences to provide JIT members with information stemming from its CMS (Case Management System) are unclear, although Eurojust's function is no longer restricted to a mere "interface" between national authorities, limited to horizontal cooperation[77] given that the Eurojust Decision visibly extended its operational tasks and Eurojust's role in JITs.[78] For instance, Eurojust's national members are allowed to participate in JITs and the Secretariat of the JIT Experts Network shall form part of the Eurojust's staff.[79] Article 16 (2) (a) of the Eurojust Decision specifies that the CMS is intended to support investigations and prosecutions by providing assistance "in particular by the cross-referencing of information" included in the CMS. *José Luis da Mota* (former president of Eurojust) clarifies that the new Eurojust Decision makes Eurojust the "focal point" as well as the "key player and centre for expertise" with regard to JITs and that "the flow of information" will allow Eurojust to receive information about the investigations carried out in the JITs and their outcomes.[80] Eurojust's purpose should not be "to accumulate information but rather to disseminate it to the practitioners".[81] Taking these arguments into consideration, the lack of regulation of the information flow within the JITs as well as from JIT members to Eurojust is more than surprising.

b) The Eurojust-OLAF Agreement

The practical agreement on arrangements of cooperation between Eurojust and OLAF from 2008 is divided into four chapters dealing with the definitions and purpose of the agreement, cooperation, data protection provisions and concluding remarks.

The agreement provides for the setting up of teams consisting of Eurojust national members as well as of OLAF officials for the purpose of exchanging case summaries (not including personal data) to reinforce common strategies on cases and coordinate activities and to indentify individual or joint activities.[82]

---

[76] See Sect. I 1 a.

[77] Vervaele (2008), p. 184.

[78] Lopes da Mota (2009), p. 88; compare also Article 13a Eurojust Decision.

[79] Articles 9f and 25a (2) Eurojust Decision.

[80] Lopes da Mota (2009).

[81] Ibid, p. 89.

[82] The exchange of case summaries should be regarded as a request to the other party to "examine the necessity for close cooperation on a specific case", but the requested party can decide not to cooperate; see Practical Agreement on arrangements of cooperation between Eurojust and OLAF of 24 September 2008, point 5.

Cooperation is also possible without exchanging case summaries beforehand, but by participating in operational and strategic meetings organised by the other organisation. Only when Eurojust and OLAF collaborate in a specific case do they exchange the necessary information spontaneously or on request, including personal data.[83] Further criteria do not have to be fulfilled. Personal data may be transmitted either to Eurojust as a College or to a national member, whereby only the latter is allowed to transfer data to OLAF.[84] Further restrictions, the conditions on the use of the data or the time of storage of the transmitted data are regrettably not given.

Onward transfer of transmitted data is generally legitimate, although provisions restricting the use or access of the transmitted information shall be communicated when transferring the information, including rules on its deletion and destruction.[85] Within the limits of its respective legal framework, the receiving party may also further process the information obtained for the purpose of detecting fraud, corruption or other criminal offences affecting the EU's financial interests. A record of the transmission and receipt of personal data communicated must be kept by each party.

Individual rights are not directly mentioned, although OLAF's data processing must usually comply with Regulation 45/2001.[86] The misleading title "rights of data subjects" of point 14 of the agreement only reveals a consultation duty for the requested party towards the other party before deciding about a request by an individual to have access to, or to demand correction, blocking or deletion of, its personal data transmitted under the agreement.[87] Apart from that provision, the agreement makes reference to the relevant data protection rights of the parties.

Further mutual information duties include the notification duty of the other party about corrections or deletions made, including the reasons therefore.[88] Additionally, regarding cases in which one of the parties assumes that information received is not accurate, not up to date or should not have been transmitted, the other party has to be warned.[89] A further important provision consists of the requirement to inform a third party to which transmitted data have been transferred about any

[83] Practical Agreement on arrangements of cooperation between Eurojust and OLAF of 24 September 2008, point 6.

[84] Ibid, points 6 (3) and (4).

[85] Ibid, points 11 (2) and 15 (4).

[86] Compare Chap. B II 3 c.

[87] Practical Agreement on arrangements of cooperation between Eurojust and OLAF of 24 September 2008, point 14.

[88] Ibid, points 15 (1).

[89] Ibid, points 15 (3).

deletions or corrections made concerning this data. In addition, the time limits of the storage are based on the respective rules of the parties.

c) Conclusion: Eurojust and OLAF – Intensive Cooperation Lacking Transparency

Whereas the Eurojust-OLAF agreement allows for extensive data exchange, less attention seems to have paid to provisions guaranteeing individual rights of the persons concerned in the transfer between Eurojust and OLAF. The mere reference to the applicable rules of the parties does not automatically assure compliance with them. Considering that the motivation to exchange personal data represents one of the main reason for the amendment of the 2003 cooperation agreement, taking additional safeguards into account the specific risks of data transfer would have illustrated the "good will" of the parties to acknowledge the importance of data protection rights in this context.

The indication of an authority exercising independent supervision of the agreement would have for instance emphasised the submission under a data protection regime while at the same time accepting its significance. Although theoretically the EDPS and possibly Eurojust's JSB are responsible for this task, it would not do any harm to the parties to mention them in the agreement.

A particular problem in this context relates to the fact that the responsibility for personal data transfer from Eurojust to OLAF lies only with the national member and not with Eurojust, having as a consequence that supervision is becoming increasingly difficult and can not usually be exercised by Eurojust's JSB. When additionally recalling the serious data protection problems mentioned in the 2009 report of OLAF's supervisory committee,[90] as well as the limited supervision of OLAF's CMS,[91] efficient and independent supervision of the data transfer between OLAF and Eurojust seems to be absolutely necessary.

A further important point concerns the possibility of transferring the received information to third parties. It is worth mentioning in this context that Eurojust's local approach[92] as it regards the possibility to get access to data stored in its database strongly conflicts with its transfer options. Taking into account that the applicable law in case of exercising the access right at Eurojust is the law of the Member State in which the applicant has made its request, supplementary safeguards in case of onward transmissions of data received from OLAF should be established.

---

[90] Compare Chap. B II 3 d.

[91] Compare Chap. B II 3 c and d.

[92] See Chap. B II 2 c.

When considering the different time limit of storage (20 years at OLAF and as long as it is necessary at Eurojust), further restrictions and conditions on the use of OLAF's data in Eurojust's CMS should be introduced.

Finally, as the agreement "may be amended by mutual consent of the parties at any time",[93] the provided evaluation of the cooperation agreement may be used to introduce clearer rules regarding the mentioned subjects.

5. *Eurojust-Frontex*

Cooperation between Eurojust and Frontex is neither explicitly foreseen in the Frontex proposal, nor does a formal cooperation agreement exist. Preliminary plans to cooperate in the future nevertheless can be found in the Eurojust work programme of 2010 as well as in Council documents relating to the cooperation of the JHA agencies.[94] Specifics of the cooperation are not yet further developed and, due to the rather different spectrum of tasks of Eurojust and Frontex, it may take some time to realise them. In the case that this cooperation should include the exchange of personal data, Regulation 45/2001 would apply.

6. *Conclusion: Unsatisfactory Data Protection Framework in AFSJ Inter-Agency Information-Sharing*

The foregoing analysis has established serious shortcomings regarding the data exchange between the AFSJ agencies as well as OLAF. It could be established that information exchange between the aforementioned actors takes place at different levels: data exchange in the framework of JITs refers to a particular case and specific cooperation agreements should assure the everyday data exchange.

Certain specific issues raise interesting questions in the Europol-Eurojust cooperation. The lack of rules governing the data exchange in JITs, in particular the lacking legal basis of Eurojust for the exchange of data between the agency and the JIT is surprising. Whereas the Europol Decision at least stipulates certain basic criteria, Eurojust's role in JITs remains untold. Questions referring to a data

---

[93] Practical Agreement on arrangements of cooperation between Eurojust and OLAF of 24 September 2008, point 18 (1).

[94] Eurojust work programme 2010, p. 12, para 7; Communication from the Commission to the Council and the European Parliament of 23 October 2007 on the role of Eurojust and the European Judicial Network in the fight against organised crime and terrorism in the European Union, COM (2007) 644 final, p. 9, para 2.4; Note from the General Secretariat to the Standing Committee on operational cooperation on internal security (COSI), final report on the cooperation between JHA agencies, Council doc. 8387/10 of 9 April 2010, para 1.4, p. 6.

protection framework going beyond the national law of the Member State organising the JIT arise and are so far not answered.

The agreement between Europol and Eurojust reveals further problems: minimum criteria for the transmission of data (for instance, only when the transfer is necessary in a specific case, or the data will contributes substantially to the detection of a crime) are completely missing. There is no particular supervision monitoring the data transferred or even generated in this way. Whether the transferred data remain connected to the purpose for which they were collected is left open. The opening of Europol's analysis work files to Eurojust is a further new tool leading to a merger of the data of both agencies and is also not especially supervised. Rights of individuals (above all victims and witnesses) to be informed about the transfer of their data to another agency should be introduced to assure the control of the data and the transparency vis-à-vis person concerned.

A further outcome of the analysis is that OLAF's involvement in the data exchange in the AFSJ is far from being regulated. OLAF's participation in JITs as well as its possible data exchange with Europol lacks a proper legal basis. Profound improvements establishing a framework for OLAF allowing for personal data exchange with agencies such as Europol are absolutely necessary to clarify the current ambiguous situation in which the Europol Decision provides for personal data transfer between the two actors, but OLAFs' legal bases remain silent on this question.

A similar observation concerns the legal framework of Frontex: whereby in reality data exchange is very likely to take place,[95] the current agreement between Europol and Frontex as well as Frontex's legal basis actually exclude personal data exchange. The proposed amendment of the Frontex regulation indeed entails provisions which would put this exchange on a legal basis, even though it can not retroactively legalise the data exchange already taking place.

In addition, the proposal still needs considerable rework because it neither refers to data protection provisions in this context, nor does it specify the conditions under which such personal data transfer could be carried out. It also completely disregards the fact that Europol and Frontex are not established for the same purpose and process data for different reasons. Before a possible extension of Frontex involving comprehensive data processing possibilities, the future role of Frontex should be better assessed to avoid possible overlapping effects with the tasks of Europol.

The combined participation of Eurojust and OLAF in JITs is indeed entailed in their cooperation agreement, although the question of personal data exchange in this particular framework is not answered. Moreover, the information exchange

[95] House of Lords Europol report, European Union Committee, 29th report of session 2007–2008, "Europol: coordinating the fight against serious and organised crime", published 12 November 2008, p. 80; Final report of COWI (European consulting group) of January 2009 preparing an external evaluation of Frontex provided for in Article 33 of the Council Regulation (EC) No 2007/2004 of 26 October 2004 establishing Frontex, p. 48, available at: http://www.frontex.europa.eu/specific_documents/other/ (accessed February 2011).

based on this agreement is not particularly supervised. The legal responsibility of the transfer lies with the national member of Eurojust and therefore usually excludes the involvement of the JSB. The cooperation agreement does regrettably not touch upon questions of the conditions on the use or the time of storage of the transmitted data.

II Data Exchange Between AFSJ Agencies and Europe's Information Systems: SIS, CIS, VIS and Eurodac

Personal data exchange is not only limited to AFSJ agencies, it is also taking place between European information systems and the AFSJ agencies. The information systems include the databases previously analysed in Chap. B III. The increasing data exchange between the mentioned actors considerably enlarges the authorities and bodies having access to personal data originally entered in only one of the databases. Thereby, attention should be paid to the rather limited purpose for which the databases were established (compare Chap. B III) and which is continually broadened when allowing various actors, not necessarily connected to this original purpose, to access. In the light of the foregoing considerations, it is therefore interesting to analyse the relation and the data exchange possibilities in the framework of AFSJ agencies and European information systems in order to understand the data protection impact of the access from the AFSJ agencies to the databases studied in Chap. B III.

1. Europol-SIS II Access

One important difference initially distinguishing the SIS and the Europol databases was that the SIS was restricted to an identification system, while Europol's databases rather had an investigative function. With the adoption of the SIS II instruments, this difference vanished increasingly.[96] The scopes of the SIS and the Europol databases have both been widened and as one consequence thereof, their objectives are slowly approaching each other. This is particularly reflected in formulations relating to the objective of both actors, such as "maintenance of public security" (SIS II) or the "safeguarding of security in the territories of the Member States" (SIS II) or the "support and strengthen action by the competent authorities of the Member States and their mutual cooperation in preventing and combating

[96] See above Chap. B III 1.

organised crime, terrorism and other forms of serious crime" (Europol Decision).[97] The tasks and functions of Europol however remain more comprehensive and the data processed in its databases entail much more elements than those stored in the SIS II.[98]

a) Access Provisions and Purpose of the Access

Europol gained access to information relating to important categories of data contained in the SIS already in February 2005.[99] In the meanwhile, we have seen that the tasks of Europol as well as the scope of the new SIS II evolve continually and the data entered in both databases is getting more and more extensive.

Technically, the databases of Europol and the SIS II are not linked – although the legal bases of the two actors provide for mutual data exchange, the Europol Decision does not directly mention the SIS II. Article 21 of the Europol Decision does however permit wide-ranging access to data of Union databases to the extent "that is necessary for the performance of its tasks". Article 41 of SIS II Decision 2007/533 mirrors this provision by stipulating that Europol has the right "within its mandate" to access and search data directly in the SIS II. The scope of access in SIS II Decision 2007/533 is equally described as relating to the data required for Europol to performance its tasks.[100]

Unfortunately, the Europol Decision limits further clarifications to the simple provision that the legal instruments of the relevant partner databases shall govern Europol's use of the data as well as its access conditions, "in so far as they provide for stricter rules on access and use" than those of the Europol Decision.[101] As follows from the foregoing,[102] all questions related to the inclusion of data from other information systems in Europol's databases are to be regulated in the relevant instruments of the information systems concerned; in this case they should be included in Article 41 of SIS II Decision 2007/533.

---

[97] Article 1 Regulation (EC) No 1987/2006 and SIS II Decision 2007/533; Article 3 Council Decision of 6 April 2009 establishing the European Police Office, OJ 2009, L-121/37.

[98] Compare Chap. B II 1 b.

[99] Council Decision 2005/211/JHA of 24 February 2005 concerning the introduction of some new functions for the Schengen Information System, including in the fight against terrorism, OJ 2005, L-68/44, Article 1 referring to Articles 95, 99 and 100 Schengen Convention, OJ 2000, L-239/19 (persons wanted for extradition, persons or vehicles placed under surveillance or subjected to specific checks as well as to objects sought for the purpose of seizure or use in criminal proceedings).

[100] Article 43 SIS II Decision 2007/533; the word "computerised" is missing in SIS II Decision 2007/533.

[101] Article 21 Council Decision of 6 April 2009 establishing the European Police Office, OJ 2009, L-121/37.

[102] See Chap. B II 1 e.

This Article allows Europol direct access and search in the SIS II database related to persons wanted for arrest or surrender purposes (Article 26 SIS II Decision 2007/533), persons and objects for discreet checks or specific checks (Article 36 SIS II Decision 2007/533) as well as objects for seizure or use as evidence in criminal proceedings (Article 38 SIS II Decision 2007/533). When a Europol search reveals an alert in the SIS II, it has to inform the Member State issuing the alert which then has to give its consent for the use of the information.[103] If the Member States agrees, according to Article 41 (3) of SIS II Decision 2007/533, the handling of the information is subsequently governed by the rules of the Europol Convention (today by the Europol Decision).[104] Only under the condition of prior consent by the Member State may Europol communicate such information to third states.[105]

Provisions relating to the protection of the information are stipulated in Article 41 (5) of SIS II Decision 2007/533 and concern the introduction of a recording duty of every access and search made by Europol as well as a provision prohibiting the connection, the transfer, the download and the copying of the SIS II data to another computer system "for data collection and processing operated by or at Europol".[106]

At first glance this seems to be a wide ranging restriction, prohibiting the introduction of SIS II data into one of Europol's databases; however, the wording of Article 41 (5) SIS II Decision 2007/533 only excludes the *direct* introduction of SIS II data in Europol's databases. The *indirect* way of asking the Member States after a hit in the SIS II to introduce the same information in Europol's data processing systems is not excluded but has the same effect.

This possibility is also reflected in Article 41 (4) SIS II Decision 2007/533 which provides that Europol may request further information from the Member State concerned "in accordance with the Europol Convention" (today Europol Decision). Eventually, this could mean in practice that SIS II information is entered in an indirect way by pretending that the information directly comes from the Member States while using the Member State concerned as an intermediary to enter originally SIS II information in one of Europol's database. Pursuant to Article 41 (3) SIS II Decision 2007/533, this information may also be given to third states (Member State's consent provided), circumventing the initial restriction of Article 54 SIS II Decision 2007/533 whereupon SIS II data should not made available to third countries.

Another possibility to integrate SIS II data into Europol's databases is to interpret Article 41 (3) SIS II Decision 2007/533 such that Europol is indeed urged to ask the Member State for consent to use this information, but afterwards,

[103] Article 41 (2) and (3) SIS II Decision 2007/533.

[104] Ibid, Article 41 (3).

[105] Ibid.

[106] Ibid, Article 41 (5) (b).

the rules of the Europol Decision apply which finally means that Europol could integrate the information in its data processing systems.

These two possibilities also influence the following restrictions of Article 41 (5) (c) and (d) SIS II Decision 2007/533 pursuant to which Europol must adopt security and confidentiality rules as well as limit access to data entered in the SIS II to specifically authorised staff. Even if the access is initially restricted to certain persons, which is generally a welcomed provision, in the case that the data are later introduced by a Member State in the EIS or used in an analysis work file, the initially restricted access only exists on paper.

Finally, in addition to its already exhaustive tasks,[107] Europol's JSB shall also review the activities of Europol in the exercise of its access to SIS II data.

The lack of provisions specifying the purpose of Europol's access was briefly discussed in Chap. B II 1 e and should now, in addition to other open questions, be further analysed in the following section.

b) Conclusion: Europol's Access to the SIS – Virtually Unfettered

After having analysed Article 41 SIS II Decision 2007/533 allowing Europol access to the SIS II, it seems to be astonishing that the purpose of the use of the transmitted data, which should usually be defined explicitly and restrictively when transferring personal data,[108] is not further explained. The fact that the use of the data for Europol's purposes considerably varies from a rather restricted use in the SIS II (in relation to Europol), is not even mentioned. Taking Europol's different tasks into consideration, the possible processing of SIS II data at Europol could have serious consequences on the social and legal situation of an individual.[109]

Allowing Europol access to the extent that is necessary "for the performance of its tasks" without restricting the use afterwards is much too far reaching and should be clarified by specifying the purpose of the access and linking it to the purpose of the subsequent use. This also has to be seen in the light of the continually evolving tasks of Europol. A concrete factor not susceptible to change over time should be used to define Europol's access conditions and the subsequent use of the data.

Also regrettably is the fact that no statements are made about Europol's need to access the SIS II, nor about the possibility to obtain the data by other less intrusive means.[110]

A further important question arises out of the fact that SIS II Decision 2007/533 does not clarify by whom and in which of Europol's databases the SIS II data are to be included. Are they introduced by Europol or by a Member State in the EIS, or

[107] Compare criticism, Chap. B II 1 d bb.

[108] Compare *Weber and Saravia v. Germany*, Application no. 54934/00, admissibility decision of 29 June 2006; Chap. A II 1 c bb (2) and A II 1 d cc (2).

[109] See the different tasks of Europol in Chap. B II 1 a–c.

[110] Opinion of the EDPS on the SIS II proposals, OJ 2006, C-91/38, point 4.2.3.

used in context of an analysis work file? What happens to the data after they have been included in one of Europol's databases? Are they marked and do they remain connected to the purposes which had justified their collection, as the ECtHR considered it appropriate in *Weber and Saravia v. Germany*?[111]

Moreover, when requesting further information from the Member States according to Article 41 (4) SIS II Decision 2007/533 and presumably asking a Member State to additionally introduce its SIS II data in the EIS or in an analysis work file, it is very likely that the time limit for storing originally provided for in the SIS II would start to run again, based on the rules of Europol. This would bypass any possible effects of the provisions providing for a time limit in the SIS II (3 years), in particular in cases in which the transferred data approach the SIS II time limit.

Another important issue relates to the circle of accessing actors: the SIS II prohibits access from states not participating in the Schengen Cooperation, but, as demonstrated in Chap. B II 1 b, the EIS as well as the analysis work files allow for access of a much wider range of other actors, such as liaison officers from third states or international organisations, invited "experts" from the third states or other European actors such as OLAF. In consequence, the circle of persons and authorities having access to the data is significantly enlarged when transferring (even if indirectly) the data in Europol's databases and could lead to investigations being instituted against the persons concerned.[112] The proposal of the EDPS and the JSA Schengen to limit searches to the individuals whose name are already contained in Europol's files, was regrettably not considered.[113]

Finally, although postulated by the ECtHR, a provision providing for notification of the transmission of the person concerned as soon as it can be carried out without jeopardising the purpose of the transmission is lacking.[114]

2. *Europol-VIS Access*

Based on the introducing observations in Chap. B III 2 c stating the access conditions of Europol entailed in VIS Regulation 767/2008 and the national law enforcement and security authorities, Europol's access to the VIS is – as in the case of the SIS II – very broadly restricted to its mandate and "the performance of its

[111] *Weber and Saravia v. Germany*, Application no. 54934/00, admissibility decision of 29 June 2006, para 121; compare Chap. A II 1 c bb (2) and A II 1 d cc (2).

[112] Compare *Weber and Saravia v. Germany*, Application no. 54934/00, admissibility decision of 29 June 2006, para 79.

[113] Opinion of the EDPS on the SIS II proposals OJ 2006, C-91/38, point 4.2.2.

[114] Compare *Weber and Saravia v. Germany*, Application no. 54934/00, admissibility decision of 29 June 2006, para 135; Chap. A II 1 d cc (2).

tasks".[115] Pursuant to the wording of Article 3 (1) of VIS Regulation 767/2008, the important limitation applying to the access conditions of national authorities, according to which they are restricted to "reasonable grounds" to consider that the consultation of the VIS data "substantially" contributes to the prevention, detection or investigation of terrorist offences and of other criminal offences, regrettably does not relate to the access of Europol.

In contrast to Europol's rather unregulated access to the SIS II, Europol's access to VIS, although previously analysed, is further detailed in Council Decision 2008/633 concerning access for consultation of the Visa Information System (VIS) by designated authorities of Member States and by Europol for the purposes of the prevention, detection and investigation of terrorist offences and other serious criminal offences.[116]

This instrument entered into fore on 2 September 2008 and was not, contrary to VIS Regulation 767/2008, adopted by using the co-decision procedure, but formed part of the "VIS legislative package" agreed between the European Parliament and the Council in 2007 after two and a half years of negotiations.[117] The reason therefore can be found in the legal basis of the instrument which is governed by Title VI of the EU Treaty dealing with police and judicial cooperation in criminal matters, more specifically the Decision is based on Article 30 (1) (b) and 34 (2) (c) of the EU Treaty. Thus the Council alone may decide on the adoption of the instrument.

The Member States consider the decision as a further development of the Schengen *acquis*, typically excluding the participation of the United Kingdom which, as a result, instituted proceedings against this decision.[118] The European Court of Justice however dismissed the action in October 2010.[119]

Due to the influence exerted by the European Parliament during the negotiations and compared to the SIS II instruments, Council Decision 2008/633 requires a more sophisticated, if not necessarily always sufficient, data protection framework analysed hereinafter.

---

[115] Article 3 (1) VIS Regulation 767/2008, OJ 2008, L-218/60.

[116] Council Decision 2008/633/JHA of 23 June 2008 concerning access for consultation of the Visa Information System (VIS) by designated authorities of Member States and by Europol for the purposes of the prevention, detection and investigation of terrorist offences and of other serious criminal offences, OJ 2008, L-218/129.

[117] Report from the Commission to the European Parliament and the Council on the development of the Visa Information System (VIS) in 2008, of 15 September 2009, COM(2009) 473 final, p. 4.

[118] Case C-482/08, *United Kingdom of Great Britain and Northern Ireland against the Council of the European Union*, judgment of 26 October 2010.

[119] Ibid.

a) Access Provisions and Purpose of the Access

While Article 3 (1) of VIS Regulation 767/2008 does not specify Europol's access conditions, Council Decision 2008/633 does not succeed in reaching comprehensive clarification in this regard either.

Its first article generally refers to the purpose of prevention, detection and investigation of terrorist offences and of other serious crimes. Terrorist offences means the offences under national law corresponding or being equivalent to the offences listed in Article 1 to 4 of Framework Decision 2002/475 on combating terrorism[120] and serious criminal offences, encompassing the forms of crimes corresponding or being equivalent to those referred to in Article 2 (2) Framework Decision 2002/584 on the European Arrest Warrant.[121]

These offences list a range of different crimes, not always corresponding to those of the Europol Decision. Article 7 of Council Decision 2008/633 therefore limits Europol's access to its mandate, indicating slightly better access conditions for Europol. The same article further refers to access for the purpose of the performance of Europol's tasks described in Article 3 (1) point 2 of the Europol Convention[122] as well as for analysis purposes according to Article 10 Europol Convention[123] (today Europol Decision). The reason for access to VIS data by Europol however remains vague when looking at the formulations used in the mentioned articles: Article 3 (1) point 2 of the Europol Convention (Article 5 (1) (a) Europol Decision) merely mentions that Europol has the task to "obtain, collate and analyse information and intelligence"[124] and Article 10 of the Europol Convention (Article 14 Europol Decision) stipulates the conditions for collection, processing and utilisation of personal data in analysis work files.[125]

In the context of the use of the VIS data in Europol's databases, Article 7 (1) of Council Decision 2008/633 only refers to the use in analysis work files. A difference is made between specific analyses and analysis of general nature or of a strategic type.[126] Only in the first case (specific analyses), Europol is not obliged to render the VIS data anonymous. In the two other situations (general analysis and analysis of strategic type), the VIS data must be anonymised and retained in a form excluding the identification of the data subject. Given the fact that these analyses are communicated to all Member States via the liaison officers and the experts,[127]

[120] Council Framework Decision 2002/475/JHA of 13 June 2002 on combating terrorism, OJ 2002, L-164/3.

[121] Council Framework Decision 2002/584/JHA of 13 June 2002 on the European arrest warrant and the surrender procedures between Member States, OJ 2002, L-190/1.

[122] Corresponding to Article 5 (1) (a) Europol Decision.

[123] Mainly corresponding to Article 14 Europol Decision.

[124] Today corresponding to Article 5 (1) (a) Europol Decision.

[125] Article 10 Europol Convention now corresponds to Article 14 Europol Decision.

[126] Article 7 (1) Council Decision 2008/633/JHA, OJ 2008, L-218/129.

[127] Compare Article 14 (4) Europol Decision.

this precaution seems to be absolutely necessary to limit the circle of recipients. The use of the VIS data in the EIS is not dealt with in Council Decision 2008/633, although it does not seems to be excluded.

Nevertheless, similar criticism as mentioned in the SIS II discussion applies also in the framework of the VIS. In both cases, access depends on a variable factor, namely the performance of Europol's tasks which are subjected to modifications at any time. A good example is the last amendment of the Europol Convention, the Europol Decision entering into force in January 2010, analysed above, which completely reversed Europol's legal framework and considerably enlarged its tasks.[128]

A further important, although regrettable aspect in this context, involves the non-application to Europol of important requirements applying to the access conditions of national "designated authorities".

Article 5 (1) Council Decision 2008/633 dictates three cumulative access conditions for national law enforcement and intelligence authorities: first, the access must be necessary for the purpose of prevention, detection and investigation of terrorist offences or other serious crime, second, necessary in a specific case and third, consultation must *substantially* contribute to the mentioned purposes.[129] Once the national authorities comply with these requirements, a two-step access to the VIS data is stipulated in Article 5 (2) and (3) of Council Decision 2008/633, which, at this stage of the procedure, also applies to Europol.[130] The two-step access limits the initial search in the VIS to 11 data elements,[131] including fingerprints. Only in the event of a hit are the other data from the visa application form, as well as photographs and the data entered in respect of any visa issued, annulled, revoked, refused or extended open to access.[132] Whereas the Member States have to fulfill all of the conditions of Article 5 Council Decision 2008/633, Europol's access seems to be regarded as less intrusive.

However, Member States as well as Europol have to establish a list with the operating units which are allowed to access the VIS.[133] These units play an important role in the access procedure as they must submit a reasoned written and electronic request to the central access point established in each Member State

---

[128] Compare Chap. B II 1.

[129] Article 5 (1) Council Decision 2008/633, OJ 2008, L-218/129.

[130] Ibid, Article 7 (2).

[131] Surname, surname at birth (former surname(s)); first name(s); sex; date, place and country of birth; current nationality and nationality at birth; type and number of the travel document, the authority which issued it and the date of issue and of expiry; main destination and duration of the intended stay; purpose of travel; intended date of arrival and departure; intended border of first entry or transit route; residence; fingerprints; type of visa and the number of the visa sticker; details of the person issuing an invitation and/or liable to pay the applicant's subsistence costs during the stay.

[132] Articles 5 (2) and (3) Council Decision 2008/633, OJ 2008, L-218/129.

[133] Ibid, Articles 3 (3) and 7 (3).

or Europol to coordinate VIS access.[134] The personnel of the access point shall verify whether the conditions of Article 5 Council Decision 2008/633 are fulfilled. When processing the access request, it should nevertheless be kept in mind that Europol's access conditions are far less strict than the Member State's obligations.

Europol's access is thus significantly wider than the access of national authorities and does not depend on a specific case, nor on the fact that the consultation has to substantially contribute to the purpose of the access. One could argue that Europol's access is indeed restricted to the aforementioned purposes of Articles 3 (1) point 2 and 10 Europol Convention[135] (Article 5 (1) (a) and 14 Europol Decision), but as we have seen above, these purposes are far reaching and can not be compared to the limitation imposed on the national authorities. In the light of this, it is interesting to note that both the Commission and the European Parliament stressed during the decisions' negotiations that "routine access" by Europol should be prevented.[136] Whereby the term "routine access" might be open to discussion, a provision according to which Europol must have reasonable grounds for considering that its access to the VIS data substantially contributes to the prevention, detection or investigation of a criminal offence for which Europol is competent to act, would certainly improve the definition of the boundaries of Europol's access while allowing stricter supervision.

In the current state of play, it is doubtful whether Europol's rather general access does not go beyond what is necessary to achieve the purpose of Council Decision 2008/633. The exceptional aspect of allowing a law enforcement authority access to a database dealing with individuals not suspected of any crime should be at least compensated through very rigid access conditions to avoid transforming the VIS into a general crime fighting database, disregarding the fundamental rights of individuals. The introduction of stricter access conditions would have been an important step in this direction.

---

[134] Article 4 (1) Council Decision 2008/633, OJ 2008, L-218/129; paragraph 2 of Article 4 Council Decision 2008/633 provides for an exception: "In an exceptional case of urgency, the central access point(s) may receive written, electronic or oral requests. In such cases, the central access point(s) shall process the request immediately and only verify ex-post whether all the conditions of Article 5 are fulfilled, including whether an exceptional case of urgency existed. The ex-post verification shall take place without undue delay after the processing of the request".

[135] Today corresponding to Article 5 (1) (a) Europol Decision and Article 10 Europol Convention now corresponds to Article 14 Europol Decision.

[136] Report of 21 Mai 2007 of the European Parliament on the on the proposal for a Council Decision concerning access for consultation of the Visa Information System (VIS) by the authorities of the Member States responsible for internal security and by Europol for the purposes of the prevention, detection and investigation of terrorist offences and of other serious criminal offences (COM(2005)600final – 2005/0323(CNS)), Committee on Civil Liberties, Justice and Home affairs, rapporteur: *Sarah Ludford*, pp. 7–8, para (7), and proposal for a Council Decision of 24 November 2005 concerning access for consultation of the Visa Information System (VIS) by the authorities of the Member States responsible for internal security and by Europol for the purposes of the prevention, detection and investigation of terrorist offences and of other serious criminal offences (COM(2005)600final – 2005/0323(CNS)), p. 5.

A welcomed provision however relates to the requirement to designate a specialised unit for VIS access within Europol, allowing for better supervision while concentrating the request accesses at one specific entity.[137] Such as in the SIS II, Europol's use of the data is subject to the consent of the Member States entering the data into the VIS.[138]

Another astonishing provision relates to the access possibility of the Member States effectively not participating at the VIS due to their limited participation in the Schengen cooperation. In addition to the access of Europol and the national authorities, Article 6 VIS Regulation 767/2008 also grants consultation to Member States to which the VIS Regulation 767/2008 does not apply. It is exercised via a participating Member State in the way that Member States not yet participating at the VIS shall make its visa data available to the participating Member States, on the basis of a "duly reasoned written or electronic request".[139] Apart from the identical problem arising in the SIS II discussion dealing with the enlargement of the circle of access of national authorities to data to which the relevant Member States originally had no access due to their non participation in the Schengen *Acquis*, discussed in the framework of Europol's SIS II access,[140] one could also asks the question whether it makes sense to limit the participation in VIS Regulation 767/2008 to Schengen Member States when non-participating Member States eventually could get access to the VIS data pursuant to Article 6 of VIS Regulation 767/2008. At least the access based on a reasoned request assures the limitation to specific cases different from the wide access allowed to Europol.

b) Protection of Personal Data and Supervision in Council Decision 2008/633

The general data protection framework of Council Decision 2008/633 for Member States is based on the level of protection of Convention No. 108 and its subsequent amendments,[141] the case law pursuant to Article 8 ECHR,[142] Recommendation R (87) 15 and on the FDPJ.[143] Regrettably, Council Decision 2008/633 does not further clarify its relation to the FDPJ. The EDPS assumes that the data protection

---

[137] Article 7 (3) Council Decision 2008/633, OJ 2008, L-218/129; see also: Opinion of the EDPS on the proposal for a Council Decision concerning access for consultation of the Visa Information System (VIS) by the authorities of the Member States responsible for internal security and by Europol for the purposes of the prevention, detection and investigation of terrorist offences and of other serious criminal offences (COM(2005)final), OJ 2006, C-97/6.

[138] Article 7 (4) Council Decision 2008/633, OJ 2008, L-218/129.

[139] Ibid, Article 6.

[140] Section II 1.

[141] For those Member States which have ratified it, the Additional Protocol of 8 November 2001 to Convention No. 108 should also be taken into account.

[142] Recital (9) Council Decision 2008/633/JHA, OJ 2008, L-218/129.

[143] Ibid, Article 8 (1) and recital (9).

provisions of Council Decision 2008/633 shall be seen as a *lex specialis* specifying the *lex generalis* (FDPJ).[144] Regarding this matter, there is some value in pointing out that the FDPJ partially entails stricter rules, in particular in context of onward transfer, discussed hereinafter.[145] This situation would reverse the general relation between *lex specialis* and *lex generalis* whereupon the *lex generalis* should naturally govern the *general* law matters and the *lex specialis*, due to its regulation of a specific subject matter, overrides the *lex generalis* rules.

Europol's data processing in the VIS-Europol data exchange on the other hand is briefly dealt with: it must be in compliance with the Europol Convention (today Europol Decision) and its implementing rules pursuant to Article 8 (2) of Council Decision 2008/633, analysed in Chap. B III 2 c. Supervision shall again be exercised by the presumably overcharged JSB of Europol.[146] Consequently, once the data are transferred to Europol, the general rules of the Europol Decision apply.

After having defined the general framework, Council Decision 2008/633 nevertheless entails a few significant provisions restricting the subsequent use of the data at Europol: personal data obtained from the VIS shall only be processed for the "purpose of the prevention, detection, investigation and prosecution of terrorist offences or other serious crime".[147] Article 8 (4) of Council Decision 2008/633 mirrors Article 3 of Regulation 767/2008 according to which the onward transfer of the obtained VIS data is prohibited. Only in an "exceptional case of urgency such data may be transferred or made available" to a third party for the purpose of the prevention and detection of terrorist offences and of other serious offences. Regrettably there is no definition of such an exceptional case, but there are three additional criteria to be fulfilled to transfer the VIS data to third parties: the data must be necessary in a specific case, the consultation must substantially contribute to the mentioned purposes and the Member States having entered the data into the VIS must have given its consent.[148] A provision similar to Article 13 (1) (d) of the FDPJ, according to which the level of data protection of the third party must be adequate for the intended data processing, does regrettably not exist.[149] Although, as the

---

[144] Opinion of the EDPS on the proposal for a Council Decision concerning access for consultation of the Visa Information System (VIS) by the authorities of the Member States responsible for internal security and by Europol for the purposes of the prevention, detection and investigation of terrorist offences and of other serious criminal offences (COM(2005)final), OJ 2006, C-97/6, point 2.5 (a).

[145] Compare Articles 13 Council Framework Decision 2008/977/JHA of 27 November 2008 on the protection of personal data processed in the framework of police and judicial cooperation in criminal matters, OJ 2008, L-350/60.

[146] Article 8 (2) Council Decision 2008/633/JHA, OJ 2008, L-218/129; compare Chap. B II 1 d bb.

[147] Article 8 (3) Council Decision 2008/633/JHA, OJ 2008, L-218/129.

[148] Ibid, Article 8 (4).

[149] Article 13 (1) (d) Council Framework Decision 2008/977/JHA of 27 November 2008 on the protection of personal data processed in the framework of police and judicial cooperation in criminal matters, OJ 2008, L-350/60.

FDPJ is applicable to Council Decision 2008/633, the latter rules must comply with those of the former.

Moreover, Article 8 (4) of Council Decision 2008/633/JHA addresses a provision to the Member States providing that, to be in accordance with national law, records have to be kept which are to be made available to national DPAs on request.

A similar condition regarding Europol and its JSB does not exist, Article 8 (7) of Council Decision 2008/633/JHA, however, refers to Europol's duty to allow its supervisory body to obtain the "necessary information to enable them to carry out their tasks". Finally, Article 8 (8) of Council Decision 2008/633/JHA stipulates that training about data security and data protection rules should be given to the staff of the authorities allowed to access the VIS.[150]

While the rules on third party data transfer apply to the Member States as well as Europol, the provisions on data security, liability and claims for compensation are governed by national law and are only addressed to the Member States. Europol relies on its own data security rules whose implementation, discussed in Chap. B II 1 d cc, is subjected to a very unconvincing necessity criterion.

Additionally, as mentioned at the same place, in contrast to the data security rules applicable to the Member States,[151] Europol's security rules do not require a provision providing for monitoring of the data recording.[152] For that reason, Article 16 of Council Decision 2008/633, which is also applicable to Europol, involves a welcomed and detailed recording duty applicable to the data transferred from the VIS to Europol. Pursuant to this provision, records of all data processing operations resulting from the VIS access shall be made for the purpose of checking whether the search is admissible or not, for the purpose of monitoring the lawfulness of data processing and for self-monitoring. The record to be made contains detailed information about the exact purpose of the access, the respective national file reference, the data and time of access, whether the urgency procedure of Article 4 (2) of Council Decision 2008/633 has been used, the data and the type of data used for consultation and the identifying mark of the person who ordered or who carried out the search.[153] Records containing personal data may only be used for data protection monitoring of the legality of data processing and to ensure data security.[154] The use of records containing personal data for other monitoring purposes is forbidden.[155]

As in Article 38 of VIS Regulation 767/2008, the right of access, correction and deletion depends on the law of the Member State in which an applicant invokes that right.[156]

[150] Article 8 (8) Council Decision 2008/633/JHA, OJ 2008, L-218/129.

[151] Ibid, Article 9 (2) (i).

[152] Compare Chap. B II 1 d cc.

[153] Article 16 (1) (a)-(g) Council Decision 2008/633/JHA, OJ 2008, L-218/129.

[154] Ibid, Article 16 (2).

[155] Ibid, Article 16 (3).

[156] Ibid, Article 14.

Individuals interested in knowing whether their VIS data have been transferred to Europol are merely informed in the framework of the right to information provided for in Article 37 of VIS Regulation 767/2008, evaluated in Chap. B III 2 d. When recalling the findings of the relevant section, it is striking that the notification of the applicant is broadly restricted to the fact that Europol *may* receive the data.[157] There is no information duty provided for in VIS Regulation 767/2008 in the very likely case that the data will be transferred to Europol *after* the visa applicant or the person issuing an invitation or liable to pay the applicant's subsistence cost, has been initially informed about Europol's ability to access VIS data. Consequently, information about the actual transfer of the information is not given. Nor do the provisions of the Europol Decision, referred to in Chap. B II 1 d, provide for help. Exhaustive exceptions in Article 30 (5) of the Europol Decision to deny access to Europol data and Europol's hesitation to inform applicants whether their data has been recently processed in their systems, hinder the effective enforcement of the right to access at Europol.[158] Nor is a notification duty towards individuals whose data are stored at Europol, as soon as police activities are no longer likely to be prejudiced, contained in the Europol Decision.[159]

In both cases, at Europol and the VIS, an access request can not be directly addressed to the actors actually processing the data. Requests have to be previously directed to the national DPAs which then forward them to the respective bodies at Europol or at the VIS.[160]

c) Conclusion: Europol's Access to the VIS – Violation of the Purpose Limitation Principle

Compared to Europol's more or less unfettered access to the SIS II, Council Decision 2008/633 allowing Europol to use the VIS data entails a few important data protection provisions involving in particular the recording duty which is however limited to an *a posteriori* control of the admissibility and lawfulness of the data transfer.

Criticism relates to Europol's access purpose and the access conditions to the VIS data which both remain rather vague for the most part. It is regrettable in this context that the relatively strict access conditions applying to the law enforcement authorities of the Member States do not affect Europol's access.

Moreover, the provisions allowing for third state data transfer are not in accordance with Article 13 (1) (d) of the FDPJ having important effects on the relation

[157] Compare Chap. B III 2 d.

[158] Compare Chap. B II 1 d aa.

[159] Compare Chap. B II 1 d aa.

[160] Compare Chap. B II 1 d bb.

between the *lex generalis* rules of FDPJ and the *lex specialis* provisions of Council Decision 2008/633. The latter entails less specific rules concerning third state data transfer than the *lex generalis* finally leading to a legally doubtful situation.

Inconsistencies further concern the supervision of Europol's access to VIS data. There is no coordinated approach such it is exercised by the EDPS and the national DPAs in context with the central VIS.[161] Meetings between the EDPS and Europol's JSB should regularly take place to guarantee a minimum of supervision. However, one may even go further to suggest that the EDPS which supervises the VIS should become responsible for the supervision of the data transfer from the VIS to Europol, including regular checks on the compliance with the provisions of Council Decision 2008/633 during the processing of the VIS data in Europol's databases. Above all, when considering that the VIS data contain data of innocent individuals who have at no point been suspected of a crime. When already allowing wide-ranging access conditions for Europol, the supervision of this access should at least be effective, independent and equipped with the necessary personal resources.

The last point of criticism refers to the non existence of provisions providing for a notification of visa applicants or of persons issuing an invitation or liable to pay the applicant's subsistence cost. In the first case, the visa applicant should be notified immediately about the data processing as soon as the notification does not prejudice the purpose of the transmission to comply with ECtHR requirements.[162] In the last two cases, when data of individuals only marginally implied in the visa process are transferred, such persons should categorically be notified.

3. *Europol-CIS Access*

In contrast to the VIS access, an agreement regulating the details of the access from Europol to the CIS data does not exist. Therefore, only Article 11 CIS Council Decision 2009/917, briefly discussed in Chap. B III 3 c provides for, at first glance, almost unfettered access to the data entered into the third pillar CIS as well as the FIDE.[163] Regrettably, as it will be demonstrated in the following, even when going into the details of the few access provisions of the CIS Council Decision 2009/917, restrictions relating to a limitation of the access or to the subsequent use of the data by Europol are hard to find.

---

[161] Compare Chap. B III 2 e.

[162] *Weber and Saravia v. Germany*, Application no. 54934/00, admissibility decision of 29 June 2006, para 135.

[163] Article 11 Council Decision 2009/917, OJ 2009, L-323/20.

a) Access Provisions and Purpose of the Access

The CIS Council Decision 2009/917 uses the general wording within its respective "mandate and the fulfilment of Europol's tasks",[164] when describing the limits of the right of Europol's access to the CIS.[165] Recital (5) of Council Decision 2009/917 specifies the reason for access in this way as it "should allow Europol to cross-check information obtained through other means with the information available in those databases, to identify new links that were so far not detectable and thus to produce a more comprehensive analysis".[166] Finally access should enable Europol to "uncover connections between cases of criminal investigations, so far unknown to Europol that have a dimension in and outside the European Union".[167]

Regrettably, no further specifications as regards the subsequent processing of the CIS data at Europol can be found in the CIS Council Decision 2009/917, apart from the obligation to ask the Member State originally entering the data for consent when using and transferring the data to third countries.[168] After having obtained the consent, the rules of the Europol Decision apply which, as shown above, do not regulate the use or the processing of data from the other European databases.[169]

Additionally, a very doubtful provision, previously discussed,[170] is Article 8 (1) of CIS Council Decision 2009/917 which allows Europol to use the CIS data for *any other purpose* as long as they are vaguely connected to policing purposes.

The only provision slightly referring to an access restriction relates to the usual interdiction to directly connect parts of the CIS to Europol's own data processing systems and to transfer, download or copy the CIS data to its systems, although Europol may also request further information from the Member State.[171]

The persons having access to the CIS shall be limited to "duly authorised" Europol staff and, reminiscent of the SIS II and the VIS access rules, Europol's JSB shall additionally monitor Europol's activities in this regard.

A responsibility to inform the supplying Member State in case that Europol has evidence to suggest that an item of data is factually inaccurate or was entered contrary to the CIS Council Decision 2009/917, applies to the body as well as the obligation to introduce security measures.[172] Two obligations which are also

[164] Ibid, Articles 11 (1).

[165] Ibid, Articles 11 (1).

[166] Ibid, Recital (5).

[167] Ibid, Recital (5).

[168] Ibid, Articles 11 (3) and 12 (2).

[169] Ibid, Articles 11 (3). compare above Chap. B II 1 e.

[170] See Chap. B III 3 b aa.

[171] Articles 11 (4) and (5) Council Decision 2009/917, OJ 2009, L-323/20.

[172] Ibid, Articles 13 (3) and 28.

stipulated in the provisions in the Europol Decision and are therefore nearly equivalent.[173]

All in all, the conditions dealing with Europol's access to the CIS, compared to the SIS II and the VIS, are even more far reaching. There are no provisions restricting the access, which leads to almost unrestrained access of Europol to the CIS data.

b) Conclusion: Europol's Access to the CIS – Violation of Basic Data Protection Principles

Based on the preceding observations, serious questions arise concerning the purpose as well as the necessity of Europol's extremely far reaching possibility to access the CIS data. A substantial assessment of proportionality and necessity, including the reason why Europol is granted such extensive access, would have been crucial to explain the added value of the measure as well as its impact on the protection of personal data.

The JSA's demand to introduce an obligation to evaluate Europol's access after 3 years in its opinion to the amendments of the CIS Convention was intentionally not granted.[174]

All in all, although the CIS processes various personal data elements,[175] Europol's access and its subsequent processing, including a specification of the purpose of the processing of the received data, are not regulated. Individual rights, applicable to the transferred data are limited to the standard Europol rules and not specifically tailored to the data received.

It seems that the transfer of CIS data to Europol was found not important enough to be accompanied by the necessary safeguards which are to be introduced when transferring personal data from a (customs) database to a law enforcement agency such as Europol whose tasks significantly vary from the CIS and whose actions might have a serious impact on the situation of an individual.

Taking Europol's powers combined with the various actors having access to their files into account, the non regulation of the personal data transfer between the CIS and Europol violates basic data protection standards.

[173] Articles 29 (4) and 35 Council Decision of 6 April 2009 establishing the European Police Office, OJ 2009, L-121/37.

[174] Opinion of the Customs Joint Supervisory Authority with respect to the draft Council Decision on the use of information technology for customs purposes (Opinion 09/03) of 24 March 2009, p. 6.

[175] See Chap. B III 3 b.

4. *Europol-Eurodac Access*

So far, law enforcement agencies and/or Europol did not have access to the Eurodac database. This will however change when the Eurodac proposal from 10 September 2009 enters into force. It entails provisions already briefly discussed in Chap. B III 4 which are now going to be analysed in more detail. As in the case of the VIS, the details of Europol's access are laid down in a proposal for a specific Council Decision enabling national law enforcement authorities and Europol access to the Eurodac data (proposal on law enforcement access to Eurodac).[176] The analysis of this instrument in the following orientates at the relevant data processing and protection provisions.

a) Intended Access Provisions

While the standard formulation – namely the "purpose of prevention, detection and investigation of terrorist offences and other serious criminal offences" – is used to describe the reason for access in the proposal on law enforcement access to Eurodac,[177] the access seems at first glance however be regulated in a slightly more restrictive way when comparing it to the previously analysed law enforcement access to the SIS II, the VIS and the CIS.

The Eurodac proposal provides that only in cases where the comparison with data stored in the national fingerprint databases as well as the access to the fingerprint databases of other Member Sates according to the Prüm Decision[178] return negative results, Member States and Europol may have recourse to the Eurodac database.[179] It is intended that the access is restricted to fingerprints, necessary in a specific case and is followed by a reasoned written or a reasoned logged electronic request.[180] A specific case exists "in particular when the request for comparison is connected to a specific and concrete situation or to a specific and

[176] Proposal for a Council Decision on requesting comparisons with Eurodac data by Member States' law enforcement authorities and Europol for law enforcement purposes, COM(2009) 344 final of 10 September 2009, in the following: Proposal on law enforcement access to Eurodac, COM(2009) 344 final of 10 September 2009; Rogowicz (2010), in particular pp. 564 and 565.

[177] Article 1 Proposal on law enforcement access to Eurodac, COM(2009) 344 final of 10 September 2009.

[178] Council Decision 2008/615/JHA of 23 June 2008 on the stepping up of cross-border cooperation, particularly in combating terrorism and cross-border crime, OJ 2008, L-210/1.

[179] Recital (11) proposal on law enforcement access to Eurodac, COM(2009) 344 final of 10 September 2009.

[180] Ibid, Article 6 (1).

concrete danger associated with a terrorist or other serious criminal offence, or to specific persons in respect of whom there are serious grounds for believing that the persons will commit or have committed terrorist offences or other serious criminal offences".[181] Thereby, the formulation seems not to restrict the search to data of suspects of crimes, victim and witness data might also be included.

Additionally, it is worth noting that the proposal on law enforcement access to Eurodac does not apply the same access conditions to the national law enforcement agencies and to Europol. Comparable to the situation in the VIS, only the national law enforcement authorities are subjected to the following three step conditions: comparison must be necessary for the prevention, detection or investigation of terrorist offences or other serious crime, necessary in a specific case and there are reasonable grounds to consider that consultation of data stored in the Eurodac central database will substantially contribute to the prevention, detection or investigation of any of the criminal offences in question.[182]

Europol's access conditions however are, for some inexplicable reason, much wider and are clearly reminiscent of the VIS access conditions. They simply relate to the "limits of its mandate and where necessary for the performance of its tasks".[183]

The reason for these far reaching access conditions might be found in the legal categorisation in which the proposal on law enforcement access to Eurodac was intended to be adopted before the adoption of the Lisbon Treaty. In contrast to the Eurodac proposal previously mentioned, the proposal on law enforcement access was intended to be adopted in form of a Council Decision without the involvement of the European Parliament. Luckily, with the entry into force of the Lisbon Treaty, the obligatory participation of the Parliament in the legislative process will hopefully lead to new assessment of the Europol access, at least to coherent rules providing for stricter access rules for Europol. This statement however does not generally mean that the provided law enforcement and Europol access to Eurodac is acceptable from a data protection and fundamental rights point of view. This question is discussed in the next section.[184]

---

[181] Ibid, Recital (11).

[182] Article 7 proposal on law enforcement access to Eurodac, COM(2009) 344 final of 10 September 2009; the comparison of fingerprints at the national level is carried out by a so called "verifying authority" whose tasks are further defined in Article 4 of the proposal on law enforcement access to the Eurodac; each Member State shall designate a single national body being responsible for the "prevention, detection and investigation of terrorist offences and other serious criminal offences" excluding agencies/units dealing especially with national security issues; only this authority shall be authorised to forward requests for comparison of fingerprints to the national contact point responsible for communicating with Eurodac's central database.

[183] Article 8 proposal on law enforcement access to Eurodac, COM(2009) 344 final of 10 September 2009.

[184] See Chap. D III 2.

Article 12 of proposal on law enforcement access to Eurodac interdicts the transfer of possible hits or the Eurodac data obtained in this way to third states, international organisations or private entities in or outside the EU, but allows the transfer to states applying the Dublin Convention when the conditions of Article 13 of the FDPJ are fulfilled.[185]

The protection of personal data is briefly dealt with. The broad guarantees of the FDPJ shall be applicable.[186] In addition, it is provided that the fingerprints obtained by the national law enforcement authorities or Europol must be erased in the respective files after a 1 month period if they are not required for a specific ongoing criminal investigation.[187] To verify and evaluate the intended law enforcement access, an ex-post control is additionally foreseen. For this purposes an annual report on the effectiveness of the comparison of fingerprint data with "statistics on the exact purpose of the comparison, including the type of a terrorist offence or a serious criminal offence, number of requests for comparison, the number and type of cases which have ended in successful identifications and on the need and use made of the exceptional case of urgency as well as on those cases where that urgency was not accepted by the ex post verification carried out by the verifying authority" shall be published.[188]

b) Conclusion: Europol's Envisaged Access to Eurodac – Serious Concerns Raising Fundamental Questions on the Protection of Fundamental Rights

Although the proposal on law enforcement access to Eurodac refers to searches only in specific cases, it nevertheless paves the way for routine requests of law enforcement agencies as well as Europol to a database concerning exclusively the data of innocent individuals very likely never convicted or suspected of a crime. If adopting the proposal in its current state of play, law enforcement agencies of 30 countries[189] as well as Europol would have access to the data of persons which were never involved in any criminal procedure.

Serious concerns going far beyond data protection concerns arise out of the planned measures. They are among others outlined by the Meijers Committee,[190]

---

[185] Article 12 proposal on law enforcement access to Eurodac, COM(2009) 344 final; the states which have already ratified the Dublin Convention apart from the 27 Member States are: Norway, Iceland and Switzerland (soon Liechtenstein).

[186] Article 10 (1) proposal on law enforcement access to Eurodac, COM(2009) 344 final.

[187] Ibid, Article 10 (4).

[188] Ibid, Article 17 (1).

[189] 27 Member States plus Norway, Iceland and Switzerland.

[190] Meijers Committee, standing committee of experts on international immigration, refugee and criminal law, Utrecht/The Netherlands, letter of 30 December 2009 to the European Parliament, Civil Liberties, Justice and Home Affairs Committee on the Proposal on law enforcement access to Eurodac, COM(2009) 344 final.

the EDPS[191] and the Working Party on Police and Justice[192] and can be summarised as follows: the proposals seriously challenge proportionality as well as purpose limitation, compliance with the ECtHR and the EU case law[193] is extremely doubtful, the principle of non-discrimination risks to be undermined and the right to asylum and protection against torture and inhuman treatment seems to be disregarded. While the arguments leading to such conclusions can be found in the respective reports,[194] the data protection and privacy shortcomings are briefly discussed in the following.

Before going into details, the *S. and Marper v. the United Kingdom* case of the ECtHR is worth remembering where the Strasbourg court was faced with the legitimacy of a fingerprint database of the United Kingdom containing fingerprint information of individuals, including minors, suspected, but not convicted of a crime.[195] When considering the scope of Eurodac as well as the proposal allowing access to it, the dimensions of the Eurodac database are even bigger and store significantly more data than the UK database. The ECtHR clarified that the retention of fingerprints without the consent of the individual concerned cannot be regarded as neutral or irrelevant[196] and that the storing and the treatment of fingerprint data of not convicted individuals, entitled to the presumption of innocence, must be distinguished from the storing of data of convicted criminals. In particular, when taking into consideration the risk of stigmatisation inherent to the assumption that all applicants for asylum are suspected to be possible criminals.

---

[191] Opinion of the European Data Protection Supervisor on the amended proposal for a Regulation of the European Parliament and of the Council concerning the establishment of 'Eurodac' for the comparison of fingerprints for the effective application of Regulation (EC) No (.../...) (establishing the criteria and mechanisms for determining the Member State responsible for examining an application for international protection lodged in one of the Member States by a third-country national or a stateless person), and on the proposal for a Council Decision on requesting comparisons with Eurodac data by Member States' law enforcement authorities and Europol for law enforcement purposes, OJ 2010, C-92/1; in the following: EDPS opinion on the proposal of law enforcement access to Eurodac, OJ 2010, C-92/1.

[192] The Working Party on Police and Justice (WPPJ) is a working party composed of experts from national DPAs and works together with the Article 29 Working Party; compare WPPJ, Draft Annual Report for the Year 2009, p. 4.

[193] For the discriminatory effect of a crime fighting database, compare case C-524/06, *Heinz Huber v. Germany*, judgment of 16 December 2008, discussed in Chap. B III 2 a aa.

[194] WPPJ, Draft Annual Report for the Year 2009, p. 4; EDPS opinion on the proposal of law enforcement access to Eurodac, OJ 2010, C-92/1 and Meijers Committee, standing committee of experts on international immigration, refugee and criminal law, Utrecht/The Netherlands, letter of 30 December 2009 to the European Parliament, Civil Liberties, Justice and Home Affairs Committee on the proposal on law enforcement access to Eurodac, COM(2009) 344 final.

[195] *S. and Marper v the United Kingdom*, Application nos. 30562/04 and 30566/04, judgment of 4 December 2008, compare Chap. A II 1 d cc (1).

[196] *S. and Marper v the United Kingdom*, Application nos. 30562/04 and 30566/04, judgment of 4 December 2008, para 84.

Before establishing a link between criminals and asylum seekers, the pure assumption of being a criminal is discriminatory.[197]

Considering the necessity of the proposal, in particular the proportionality of the planed measure, the aim and its purpose have to be taken into account. The latter refers to the prevention, detection and investigation of terrorist crime and other serious crime and is therefore completely different to the originally purpose for which Eurodac has been established and for which the data are entered and stored in its database. If however merging the data originally entered for an asylum applications with the subsequently use of the data for law enforcement purposes, the limitation of the originally purpose is rendered useless.

Moreover, the reasons for access and the extension of the purpose of processing are more than vague and not confirmed by statistics[198] or other weighty evidence or arguments. The absence of the possibility for law enforcement authorities and Europol to access Eurodac data is simply seen as a "shortcoming" hindering the "effectiveness, interoperability and synergies" among European databases in the AFSJ.[199] The Commission's explanatory memorandum accompanying the proposal does not go further into the details of this question, limiting its remarks to the statement that the proposal is in accordance with Article 8 Charter of Fundamental Rights as well as with theFDPJ.[200] Reasons for this assumption are not given.

In addition to the relatively vague arguments to allow law enforcement agencies and Europol access to Eurodac, existing provisions in the AFSJ already deal with fingerprint exchange between the Member States[201] and should generally be used in the first place to fulfil the subsidiary criterion of Article 8 (2) ECHR. The purpose of the proposal might be reached by using the existing tools. Whether the existing measures, such as the Prüm Decision as well as Framework Decision 2006/960,[202] are efficient and produce evidence on the functioning of fingerprint exchange is not

[197] Ibid, paras 116 and 117.

[198] Meijers Committee, standing committee of experts on international immigration, refugee and criminal law, Utrecht/The Netherlands, letter of 30 December 2009 to the European Parliament, Civil Liberties, Justice and Home Affairs Committee on the proposal on law enforcement access to Eurodac, COM(2009) 344 final.

[199] Explanatory memorandum of the proposal on law enforcement access to Eurodac, COM(2009) 344 final of 10 September 2009, p. 3.

[200] Ibid, p. 4.

[201] Council Decision 2008/616/JHA of 23 June 2008 on the implementation of Decision 2008/615/JHA on the stepping up of cross-border cooperation, particularly in combating terrorism and cross border crime, OJ 2008, L-210/12 (Prüm Decision) and Council Framework Decision 2006/960/JHA of 18 December 2006 on simplifying the exchange of information and intelligence between law enforcement authorities of the Member States of the European Union, OJ 2006, L-386/89.

[202] Council Framework Decision 2006/960/JHA of 18 December 2006 on simplifying the exchange of information and intelligence between law enforcement authorities of the Member States of the European Union, OJ 2006, L-386/89.

yet demonstrated and must be evaluated before establishing new access possibilities. When looking at the state of play with regard to the Prüm Decision, its full implementation, provided for June 2011, should be waited for prior to the creation of new far reaching access for law enforcement authorities and Europol.

Against this argument, the Commission counters that the Prüm Decision does not specifically relate to asylum seekers and that the use of Framework Decision 2006/960 would require different requests in at least 27 countries.[203] However, instead of supporting the establishment of a new access possibility in this area, the Commission's statements in this context seem rather to call the efficiency of their own instruments into question which are usually advertised as an effective tool against terrorism and crime. Without evaluating the existing system and showing the absolute need for a new one, the planned measures appear to be premature and ill-conceived.

A further problem deals with the storage period: compared to the law enforcement databases such as the SIS II and the CIS, the storage period in the Eurodac database is rather long and amounts to 10 years. When now exchanging the data with the national law enforcement agencies and Europol, the original already extensive storage period is once again extended and can amount to an almost indefinite storage period at Europol in the worst case when alleging that Europol requests data which are provided to be deleted soon and then transferred to Europol where they can be stored for several years only restricted by the criterion of ongoing investigations.[204]

A last issue concerns the accessibility and foreseeability of the intended proposal. Whether an asylum seeker arriving at the border of the EU or and illegal border crosser is aware of the fact that his fingerprints taken in one country during an asylum procedure might later be used to check them against fingerprint data of criminals stored in databases of 30 countries as well as at Europol, seems to be not very likely. There is no information right for persons concerned about the recipients and the purpose of processing when taking the fingerprints. And, even if it would be introduced, it might not be sufficient to explain to a person coming from a complete different legal order and cultural background the consequences of having his fingerprinted taken and stored in a large European database. This means that the consequences of this measure might not be very predictable. The provided procedure makes it additionally almost impossible for an asylum seeker to find out which authorities exactly in which countries have access to his fingerprint data and are possibly in the possession of them. The list of authorities having access to Eurodac, which the the Member States are required to keep[205] (without obligation to publish

[203] Explanatory memorandum of the proposal on law enforcement access to Eurodac, COM(2009) 344 final of 10 September 2009, p. 2.

[204] Article 10 (4) proposal on law enforcement access to Eurodac, COM(2009) 344 final of 10 September 2009.

[205] Compare Article 3 (2) proposal on law enforcement access to Eurodac, COM(2009) 344 final of 10 September 2009.

the list) might be one step in the right direction, but it does not limit the access to the data or the knowledge about a concrete access request as Member States may designate their authorities without further restrictions and without informing the person being fingerprinted.

5. *Eurojust-SIS II Access*

Eurojust's access to other databases is neither mentioned in the new Eurojust Decision, nor in any of its predecessors. Only Article 42 of SIS II Decision 2007/533 refers to the possibility of Eurojust's national Members, not including Eurojust staff, to access and search data in the SIS II.[206]

The absence of Eurojust's mandate is particularly striking when taking the remarks of the House of Lords, already made in 2003, into account which point to the lacking provisions allowing Eurojust's access: "The only provision that enables Eurojust access to SIS data appears to be an unpublished non-legally binding declaration annexed to the Eurojust Decision (which we have asked to see but have never received)".[207] The Eurojust Decision 2009 could have been an opportunity to define the conditions of Eurojust's access to the SIS II as well as the details regarding the use of the data. The non inclusion of this topic in the instrument leaves strong doubts on the political will to concretely identify Eurojust's mandate regarding the SIS II data and opens the way for a non regulated data use at Eurojust.

This should also seen in the light of Article 42 SIS II Decision 2007/533 which is similarly structured as the provision referring to Europol's access, although it permits Eurojust to access more SIS II data categories than Europol. Eurojust's access covers data about persons wanted for arrest or surrender purposes (Article 26 SIS II Decision 2007/533), missing persons (Article 32 SIS II Decision 2007/533), persons sought to assist with a judicial procedure (Article 34 SIS II Decision 2007/533) as well as persons and objects for discreet checks or specific checks (Article 36 SIS II Decision 2007/533).[208] Analogous to the Europol provision, the scope of access refers to Eurojust's mandate and the data necessary for the performance of its tasks.[209] Consequently, the same criticism referred to in the context of Europol's access applies to the access by Eurojust.

---

[206] Articles 42 (1) and (6) SIS II Decision 2007/533.

[207] House of Lords, Select Committee on European Union Written Evidence Sub-Committee F (Social Affairs, Education and Home Affairs), letter from the Chairman to Bob Ainsworth MP, Under-Secretary of State, Home Office, Schengen Information System: new functions, (9407/02 and 9408/02) of 9 April 2003.

[208] Article 42 SIS II Decision 2007/533.

[209] Ibid, Articles 42 (1) and 43.

As in the case of Europol, data transfer of the obtained data to third states is generally allowed whereby the decision to communicate the data is left to the Member State concerned which has to give its prior consent.[210] The recording duties, the security and confidentiality rules as well as the provisions concerning the interdiction to copy, download or transfer the data to Eurojust's database mirror the aforementioned provisions applied to Europol.[211]

One distinction to the provisions applying to Europol is that Article 42 of Decision 2007/533 does not involve any specification regarding Eurojust's use of the information obtained. Whereas in the case of Europol reference is at least made to the rules of the Europol Convention (today Europol Decision), Eurojust's use is not further specified at all. This might be partially due to the fact that only national members of Eurojust can access the SIS II database, then integrating the data in the Eurojust system, but it does not explain why a reference is entirely lacking. Although Decision 2007/533 entailed a provision referring to the use in the case of the transfer to Europol, this provision was not further specified, and as a consequence thereof, similar questions as already referred to in this context arise with regard to Eurojust.[212]

The entire or, in Europol's case, partial lack of provisions regulating the subsequent use of the SIS II data at Eurojust and Europol produces the situation that the responsibility of the use is to a great part shifted to the national level, having the effect that Member States decide about the introduction of the SIS II data into the databases of Europol or Eurojust as well as of the transfer to third states. Even though this might be the "heritage" of the former third pillar structures, provisions assuring that the decision of the Member States regarding the transfer of the data is supervised should have been included. Such provisions could for instance provide for a notification to the relevant national DPA about the access and transfer of the data by Europol or Eurojust. Otherwise, supervision at this stage seems to be difficult to exercise and raises concern. Once the consent is given, formerly SIS II data can be entered in the databases of Eurojust and Europol or transferred to third states.

A further possibility could be a duty to inform the individual concerned as soon as possible about the access of other authorities to the SIS II data or the transfer of them. This is currently left to the Member States and depends on the national data protection systems.[213]

---

[210] Ibid, Article 42 (2).

[211] Compare Article 41 (5) (a), (b) and (d) with Article 42 (4), (5) and (7) SIS II Decision 2007/533.

[212] See Sect. II 1 b.

[213] Compare Article 16 Council Framework Decision 2008/977/JHA of 27 November 2008 on the protection of personal data processed in the framework of police and judicial cooperation in criminal matters; OJ 2008, L-350/60.

6. *Eurojust-CIS Access*

Comparable to the situation regarding the SIS II, the Eurojust Decision remains silent on the topic of Eurojust's access to the CIS. Only the CIS Decision refers to this possibility, even though in rather vague terms which principally mirror the provisions allowing Europol the access to CIS data and which therefore provoke similar criticism.[214] It is worth highlighting that Article 8 (1) of the CIS Decision allowing for the use of the received data for "other purposes" also applies to Eurojust.

The only difference refers to the reason for access and relates to Eurojust's need "to obtain immediate information required for an accurate initial overview enabling to identify and overcome legal obstacles and to achieve better prosecution results" as well as "to receive information of ongoing and closed investigations in different Members States and thus to enhance the support of judicial authorities in the Member States".[215]

More details on Eurojust's access to the CIS are not codified which reveals a significant lack of legal shortcomings resulting in the complete absence of Eurojust's mandate to access the CIS data, the lack of provisions regulating both, the individual rights when the data are transferred as well as the technical details concerning the practical implementation of the access.

All things considered, the Eurojust-CIS data transfer is not specifically regulated, the deficiencies are fundamental and they clearly need to be corrected as soon as possible to be in accordance with basic legal requirements (such as a legal basis for the access) as well as with the case law of the ECtHR.[216]

7. *Conclusion: Unbalanced Interests – Law Enforcement Access and Respect of Data Protection Principles*

The analysis of the data exchange between AFSJ agencies and the information systems SIS, VIS, CIS and Eurodac, confirms the tendency that AFSJ agencies, with focus on Europol and Eurojust, increasingly access databases which were established outside of police and judicial cooperation. The structuring and organisation of such access thereby varies from database to database and is far

---

[214] Recital (6) and Articles 8 and 12 Council Decision 2009/917, OJ 2009, L-323/20, for criticism compare Sect. II 3.

[215] Recital (6) Council Decision 2009/917, OJ 2009, L-323/20.

[216] Compare cases *Weber and Saravia v. Germany*, Application no. 54934/00, admissibility decision of 29 June 2006; *Malone v. the United Kingdom*, Application no. 8691/79, judgment of 2 August 1984, para 84; *Klass v. Germany*, Application no. 5029/71, judgment of 6 September 1978; *Kennedy v. the United Kingdom*, Application no. 26839/05, judgment of 18 May 2010 and *Kvasnica v. Slovakia*, Application no. 72094/01, judgment of 9 June 2009.

from being unified. In some cases, the mandate to access is completely missing (e.g. Eurojust's access to the SIS II as well as to the CIS), in other cases, specific instruments regulate the access (e.g. Europol's access to the VIS) and yet others restrict the mandate to access to one specific article in the respective legal bases (e.g. Europol-SIS II or Europol-CIS access).

The scope of the law enforcement access always refers to the performance of the respective tasks of Europol or Eurojust (in case of the SIS II, VIS, CIS, Eurodac). While the performance of tasks is a variable factor susceptible to changes at any time (as illustrated above in Chap. B III 2 g and Sect. II 1 b), stricter access conditions are proposed referring to concrete conditions and requirements, similar to those referring to national law enforcement authorities entailed in the VIS Regulation.[217]

While in the case of the VIS, an additional instrument entails some specifications to the conditions of the use of the VIS data in Europols' databases (with regard to the use in analysis work files, the access restricted by a specialised unit, strict conditions on third party transfer of the received data, recording duty), such an instrument is completely missing with regard to the access of Europol or Eurojust to the SIS II or the CIS data. Although in case of the SIS II and the VIS at least some few access requirements apply (which are scarcely regulated in case of the SIS II in the SIS II Decision), access by Europol and Eurojust to the CIS seems to be regarded as self-evident. The problem that personal data are transferred from a customs database to a law enforcement database is not at all taken into account.

Regarding the CIS access, but also Europol's SIS II access, it is worrisome that no link is made between the purpose of the access and the later use of the data in a law enforcement database. This disconnection from the original purpose of collection seriously interferes with the purpose limitation principle.

It is also debatable that the whereabouts of the transferred data are often not clarified. Into which of Europols' databases the data are introduced and which third parties get access to the data should in any case be explained before the transfer. Different circles of accessing actors (for instance much more actors access Europols' databases in comparison to the SIS II) lead to a considerably extension of the persons possibly using the transferred data. A provision limiting the searches to persons already stored in a law enforcement database and the notification of persons concerned in the transfer, as soon as possible, should be introduced in particular regarding transferred VIS data and would clearly restrict over-excessive use.

Important questions additionally arise in context of the time limits provided for in the databases of origin which are significantly extended when introducing SIS II or VIS data into Europol's or Eurojust's databases. The instruments allowing for the access of law enforcement agencies remain silent on this issue.

---

[217] Article 3 (1) VIS Regulation 767/2008.

All these problems lead to the conclusion that particular supervision of this sensitive matter going beyond the (former) pillar structures is urgently needed. Currently, the interests of law enforcement authorities, which already act across the (former) pillar structure on the one hand and the interest of the person concerned, which are still not efficiently enforced because their supervisory model (e.g. the JSBs) still correspond to the former pillar structure on the other, seems to be out of balance. A coherent monitoring approach covering the protection of the data from their collection over their processing and their use in different databases would noticeably improve the situation. In practice, this could for instance mean that in case of the VIS, the EDPS should become responsible for the whereabouts and the use of the VIS data also at Europol. The current situation in which the (former) legal structures hinder the enforcement of data protection rights within the law enforcement authorities does not correspond any longer to the current challenges and developments outlines above.

A more substantive problem concerns the question of the extent to which law enforcement authorities should have access to databases established for a completely different purpose. This rather general question is discussed with regard to the intended access from Europol to Eurodac and should be seen in connection with other instruments such as the Data Retention Directive or the planned access by law enforcement authorities to flight passenger data (PNR) data.[218]

Finally, after having analysed the data protection shortcomings of the AFSJ actors in Chap. C, Chap. D reveals further problems in context of the cooperation and the data exchange between the examined actors. Indeed, these deficiencies partly result from their data protection framework previously addressed, but are also an outcome of the former pillar structures and the possibilities the pre-Lisbon area offered to the Council and the Commission. Now, after the adoption of the Lisbon Treaty, it will be interesting to study possible solutions by developing a coherent approach for the data exchange in the AFSJ.

[218] Directive 2006/24/EC of the European Parliament and of the Council of 15 March 2006 on the retention of data generated or processed in connection with the provision of publicly available electronic communications services or of public communications networks and amending Directive 2002/58/EC, OJ 2006, L-105/54 and proposal for a Council Framework Decision on the use of Passenger Name Record (PNR) for law enforcement purposes, COM(2007) 654 of 6 November 2007; with regard to the planned EU PNR system, compare McGinley (2010); with regard to the Data Retention Directive, compare Maras (2009).

Chapter D
Perspectives and Suggestions for Improvement

As follows from the foregoing analysis, information sharing in the AFSJ has become an essential tool in recent years to contribute to EU-internal security policy. Law enforcement cooperation between Member States, EU agencies, bodies and information systems is based to a large extent on the exchange of (personal) data and plays an increasing role in the AFSJ. The Hague as well as the Stockholm programme call for an increasing interoperability of the AFSJ databases which in some cases leads to a questionable connection of systems established for different purposes. In view of the authors of the Stockholm programme, interoperability constitutes a precondition for the efficiency of police and judicial cooperation in the AFSJ, whereby the interpretation of interoperability is explicitly limited to a *technical understanding*.[1] The legal dimension of interoperability is not touched upon. Data protection rules are currently (re)negotiated for each new instrument.[2] Moreover, the language used in the programmes tends to understate the crucial influence the increasing cooperation has on the fundamental rights of the individuals concerned. Implicitly linked to the technical collaboration is therefore the harmonisation of the individual rights standard. Otherwise, interoperability may be reached at the cost of a weak fundamental rights framework.

The foregoing analysis has shown that there are serious shortcomings as regards the compliance of the AFSJ actors with data protection and private life guarantees. These shortcomings are reflected in the few rules regulating the cooperation between the actors. A coherent approach for the cooperation between the AFSJ actors does not exist which leads to data exchange in absence of a comprehensive framework in which data protection and private life concerns often seem to be regarded as an obstacle hindering effective cooperation and are therefore not always respected. When balancing the interest in security-related data exchange against the rights of the persons concerned, security concerns often prevail. Whereas better

[1] To the beginnings of the use of the term "interoperability" in the EU and explicit disconnection of the technical aspects from the political and legal impacts, compare De Hert and Gutwirth (2006).

[2] Compare Chap. C and De Hert and Vandamme (September 2004), in particular p. 433.

F. Boehm, *Information Sharing and Data Protection in the Area of Freedom, Security and Justice*, DOI 10.1007/978-3-642-22392-1_5,

cooperation between the AFSJ actors might help to achieve their goals, their actions must nevertheless comply with fundamental rights. Therefore, this final Chapter summarises the key problems arising in the information sharing in the AFSJ (Sect. I) and discusses possible solution to reduce the existing deficits (Sect. II–VII).

I. Key Findings

Since the analysis of the AFSJ actors and their interactions brings about debatable outcomes in terms of their compliance with data protection rules, the main inconsistencies are worth recalling before suggesting possible improvements.

While both the Council of Europe instruments, including the ECtHR's interpretation of the ECHR as well as the EU instruments, in particular the Charter of Fundamental Rights[3] and the Lisbon Treaty, call for an increasing respect of data protection rights and the right to private life in security-related data processing and law enforcement data exchange, the recent as well as the proposed developments regarding the AFSJ data exchange seem to disregard these instruments into consideration.

The analysis in Chap. A II has shown that the ECtHR developed minimum standards for the security-related data processing as regards the foreseeability of such measures as well as criteria balancing the powers between the interests of individuals concerned and governmental data collection and the implementation of surveillance measures in the framework of Article 8 ECHR. Considering the important statements on the limitation on the categories of individuals against whom surveillance measures may be taken as well as on the clear definition of the circumstances and limits of the storing and the use of the information before the processing[4] and the time limits for storing, these criteria could serve as instruments limiting overambitious currents in EU internal security policy. Avoiding indiscriminate storing of personal data in governmental databases[5] along with determining which kind of data are to be stored and for which purposes the data should be used afterwards (purpose limitation principle)[6] are essential guarantees contributing to

[3] To the background of the Charter, see Heusel (2002).

[4] *Segerstedt-Wiberg and others v. Sweden,* Application no. 62332/00, judgment of 6 June 2006, paras 88–92; *Liberty and others v. the United Kingdom,* Application no. 58234/00, judgment of 1 July 2008, para 68; *Rotaru v. Romania,* Application no. 28341/954, judgment of 4 May 2000, para 57; *Weber and Saravia v. Germany,* Application no. 54934/00, admissibility decision of 29 June 2006, paras 116 and 127.

[5] *S. and Marper v. the United Kingdom,* Application nos. 30562/04 and 30566/04, judgment of 4 December 2008, para 119; *Segerstedt-Wiberg and others v. Sweden,* Application no. 62332/00, judgment of 6 June 2006, paras 89–92.

[6] *Weber and Saravia v. Germany,* Application no. 54934/00, admissibility decision of 29 June 2006, para 116; *Rotaru v. Romania,* Application no. 28341/954, judgment of 4 May 2000, para 57; see also *Association for European Integration and Human Rights and Ekimdzhiev v. Bulgaria,* Application no. 62540/00, judgment of 28 June 2007.

an improved protection of individuals in police and judicial related data processing. Detailed provisions concerning the persons authorised to consult the files, the nature of the files, the procedure to be followed or the use that might be made of the information thus obtained are additional important criteria which have to be fulfilled before ordering surveillance.[7] The required existence of independent review and adequate and effective safeguards against abuse, including effective remedies to assure compliance with the rule of law[8] are further parts of the protective framework established by the ECtHR.

Interestingly, the Strasbourg Court is faced with similar problems as the ones arising in the EU context. Because the power of processors increases with the ability to exchange data,[9] the ECtHR in the case *Weber and Saravia v. Germany* offered valuable suggestions in order to determine standards relating to the transmission of data between law enforcement authorities. By clarifying that the German Federal Constitutional Court only satisfactorily compensated an interference, provoked by the transmission of security-related personal data to another authority, by strictly restraining the types of offences concerned by transmission and by limiting the transmission to cases in which specific facts – as opposed to mere factual indications – aroused the suspicion that someone had committed one of the limited offences listed in a specific article of the challenged act,[10] the ECtHR underlines that restrictions to the transfer of personal data between law enforcement authorities are necessary. Explicit and detailed provisions relating to the hand out procedure, including a list of the authorities to which information may be communicated as well as the circumstances in which such communication may take place and the procedure to be followed were already important criteria applied in former transfer cases such as in the *Leander v. Sweden* case.[11]

Moreover, when requiring the notification of individuals concerned as soon as it can be carried out without jeopardising the purpose of the restrictive measure after its termination of the respective measure,[12] the ECtHR goes beyond the current EU standards.

The data protection rules in EU law in the AFSJ have been analysed in the third part of Chap. A III. In contrast to rather detailed principles for security related data processing in the ECHR framework, they were identified as a legal patchwork which leads to a complex situation in which the former pillar structures still influence the current post-Lisbon area. However, the impact of the Lisbon Treaty

---

[7] *Rotaru v. Romania*, Application no. 28341/954, judgment of 4 May 2000, para 57.

[8] *Rotaru against Romania*, Application no. 28341/95, judgment of 4 May 2000, paras 55–63; *Segerstedt-Wiberg and others v. Sweden*, Application no. 62332/00, judgment of 6 June 2006, para 121.

[9] De Hert and Gutwirth (2006), in particular p. 30.

[10] *Weber and Saravia*, Application no. 54934/00, admissibility decision of 29 June 2006, para 127.

[11] *Leander v. Sweden*, Application no. 9248/81, judgment of 26 March 1987, para 55.

[12] *Weber and Saravia v. Germany*, Application no. 54934/00, admissibility decision of 29 June 2006, para 125.

in the AFSJ should not be underestimated. Its rules will certainly influence data processing and data protection rules in the near future, in particular after the applicable transition periods will expire. The existing data protection guarantees in the AFSJ are however not yet sufficiently developed. The restricted scopes of the main legislative instruments in force (Directive 95/46, Regulation 45/2001 and FDPJ) and the weak data protection guarantees for security related data processing in the FDPJ do not assure comprehensive individual rights protection in this area. Quality standards and individual rights guarantees included in the FDPJ, as well as the guarantees relating to the purpose limitation principle, allow for broad exceptions. In some cases, law enforcement authorities themselves can decide about the change of the purpose of processing of the data. The initial aim of the purpose limitation principle, which is the protection of the individual against data processing for unspecified and unknown purposes, is therefore reversed in this instrument.

Essential data protection guarantees, such as the accuracy and adequacy of data, the respect of time limits, the protection of sensitive data and the up to date nature of data are stipulated in all three instruments (Directive 95/46, Regulation 45/2001 and FDPJ), whereas the guarantees in the FDPJ are in all cases formulated in a mitigated way. Equally included in the analysed instruments are the rights of the individuals, including notification, access, erasure, blocking, deletion, objection and independent supervision. The requirement to notify the individuals about the data processing in the framework of the FDPJ is however not obligatory and is left to the discretion of the Member States.

The importance of the right to get access to one's personal data was recently underlined by the Court of Justice in *College van burgemeester en wethouders van Rotterdam v. M.E.E. Rijkeboer.*[13] The Court stipulated that in the framework of Directive 95/46 the access right not only relates to the present but also to the past. When states store personal data for a certain period, they must also be able to inform the applicant not only about data processing currently taking place, but also about the extent to which personal data have been disclosed to third parties in the past.[14]

The right to object to the processing of personal data is only included in Directive 95/46 and Regulation 45/2001. Even though there may be situations in which persons concerned by data processing in a police and judicial context (e.g. victims or witnesses) may have legitimate grounds to object their data processing, this right is not included in the FDPJ.

However, independent supervision plays an important role in all of the analysed instruments. The Court of Justice recently interpreted this requirement in a broad

[13] Case C-553/07, *College van burgemeester en wethouders van Rotterdam v. M.E.E. Rijkeboer*, judgment of 7 May 2009.

[14] Ibid.

way which means that the mere risk that authorities may be subject to governmental influence violates the independency requirement of Directive 95/45.[15]

As it is the case with regard to most of the guarantees of the FDPJ, the provisions regulating the protection of personal data in the context of third party transfers are far less detailed than similar provisions in Directive 95/46 and Regulation 45/2001. Whereas in the former first pillar, the adequacy requirement of Directive 95/46, including its interpretations by the Article 29 Data Protection Working Party, establishes a quite comprehensive data protection regime with regard to the transfer of personal data to third states, far reaching derogations apply for Member States in the framework of the FDPJ. The access by law enforcement authorities to data stored in private databases is not regulated in the FDPJ.

With regard to the common foreign and security policy, the situation in terms of data protection rights is even less regulated than in former first in third pillar matters. Admittedly, the Court of Justice in its case law on the so called terrorist blacklists[16] used elements of data protection to guarantee the protection of other fundamental rights, such as the right to defence and judicial protection,[17] but there is no general data protection framework governing this area. Article 39 TEU nonetheless provides that the Council shall adopt a decision laying down data protection rules in this area.[18]

In summary, Chap. A III illustrated the EU data protection framework in the AFSJ. The results lead to the conclusion that the guarantees stipulated in the FDPJ are to a great extent less strict in terms of data protection rights than in Directive 95/46 and Regulation 45/2001. Moreover, the restricted scope of the FDPJ significantly limits its application in the AFSJ. The legal instruments establishing the AFSJ actors therefore play an important role in the analysis of the data protection guarantees applicable in this area. Although the case law in the framework of the former first pillar, in particular the case *Huber v. Germany*, recognizes the discriminatory effect of a crime fighting database which exclusively contains the data of a particular group of persons, specific case law on security related data processing is missing due to the restricted competences of the European Courts in the former third pillar.

Against this background, Chap. B analysed the data processing framework of the AFSJ actors and revealed serious shortcomings involving procedural as well as substantial deficiencies. Particulary striking in terms of the procedural non-respect of data protection and private life concerns in security-related data processing, was the undemocratic adoption of several Council Implementing Decisions dealing with important details of the data processing at Europol as well as of the Council

[15] Case C-518/07, *Commission v. Germany*, judgment of 9 March 2010, para 36.

[16] For instance Case C-266/05 P, *Sison v. Council*, judgment of 1 February 2007 and T-284/08 *Organisation des Modjahedines de people d'Iran v. Council*, judgment of 4 December 2008 and C-229/05P, *PKK and KNK v. Council*, judgment of 18 January 2007.

[17] For an excellent analysis of this case law, see Hijmanns and Scirocco (2009), in particular p. 1509.

[18] Article 39 TEU.

Decision 2009/917 replacing the CIS Convention and allowing Europol and Eurojust to access the CIS, one day before the Lisbon Treaty entered into force to avoid parliamentary participation.[19]

It is within the framework of the data protection standards developed in Chap. A that one of the main substantial problems following from the analysis in Chaps. B and C relates to the continual lowering of the thresholds to enter data in the AFSJ databases. This is, to the detriment of fundamental rights of the individuals concerned, not counterbalanced by equivalent supervisory structures. The lowering of the thresholds to enter data into the AFSJ databases goes hand in hand with the extension of the mandates of the AFSJ actors (compare Europol's scope which no longer refers exclusively to organised crime, but also other serious crime[20]). One could get the impression that targeted selection, finding its expression in the "select before you collect" approach[21] which restricts the collection of data to specific purposes and arises out of the purpose limitation principle, is reversed in situations in which information is no longer necessary for a specific purpose, but for variable uses which are still uncertain at the time of collection.

However, whereas the legal framework of AFSJ actors has undergone substantial changes in recent years leading to the processing of more and more (personal) data, the data protection framework mainly remained the same. New possibilities, such as the pre-emptive introduction of personal data in Europol's EIS based on factual indications to believe that a person will commit a criminal offence in future[22] are highly questionable in light of the ECtHR case-law, in particular with regard to the outcome of the case *S. and Marper v. the United Kingdom*[23] where the Strasbourg Court recently underlined the relevance of the rights of (un) suspected individuals in the field of security-related data storing and processing. The ECtHR found a severe violation of Article 8 ECHR in the case concerning the storage of DNA and fingerprint information of suspected, but not convicted individuals. The Strasbourg Court clearly opposed a data retention carried out

---

[19] Council Decision 2009/936 of 30 November 2009 adopting the implementing rules for Europol analysis work files, OJ 2009, L-325/14; Council Decision 2009/935/JHA of 30 November 2009 determining the list of third states and organisations with which Europol shall conclude agreements, OJ 2009, L-325/12; Decision of the Europol Management Board on the conditions related to the processing of data on the basis of Article 10 (4) of the Europol Decision, 15942/09, adopted the 30 November 2009, OJ 2009, L-348/1 and Council Decision 2009/917/JHA of 30 November 2009 on the use of information technology for customs purposes, OJ 2009, L-323/20.

[20] To Europol's development, see De Moor and Vermeulen (2010), in particular p. 1097.

[21] Hijmanns (2010), p. 222.

[22] Article 12 (1) lit. b Council Decision of 6 April 2009 establishing the European Police Office, OJ 2009, L-121/37.

[23] *S. and Marper v. the United Kingdom*, Application nos. 30562/04 and 30566/04, judgment of 4 December 2008.

"indefinitely whatever the nature or seriousness of the offence of which the person was suspected".[24]

In particular in the cases of Eurojust and OLAF, the complicated data protection framework of these actors hinders the transparent understanding of the data protection rules in force and the data processing actually taking place. While on the one hand the tasks and responsibilities of Eurojust and OLAF increase, on the other hand, the data protection framework does not represent an effective tool to limit the increasing powers. Accountability and judicial review of OLAF's activities are particularly alarming. The outcome of cases such as *Commission v. Violetti and others*[25] is to be seen as a missed opportunity to strengthen OLAF's legal accountability. Therefore the question of whether OLAF's decision to forward possibly incriminating information to national judicial authorities constitutes a challengeable act or a mere preparatory act is not yet resolved and requires further reflection.[26]

With regard to Frontex, its ambiguous role as regards personal data processing needs to be clarified. Apparently, although the current legal framework of Frontex does not allow for personal data processing, the agency collects personal data and sends them to Europol for threat analyses.[27] This situation raises concerns in terms of accountability and judicial responsibility. The planned amendment of the Frontex regulation does regrettably not solve this problem as it does not include data protection guarantees tailored to the specific situation arising at Frontex (control of third state nationals at the borders of the EU).

The study of the data processing framework of the European information exchange systems, such as the SIS, VIS, CIS and Eurodac confirms the tendencies observed with regard to the agencies and OLAF. Enlarged scopes which permit to enter an increasing quantity of data in the systems, more and more actors accessing the databases and data protection structures which remained unchanged in recent years despite the new challenges characterise the legal framework in this area.

The data protection shortcomings of the legal frameworks of the AFSJ actors accumulate when it comes to data exchange between AFSJ agencies and the European information systems SIS, VIS, CIS and Eurodac, analysed in Chap. C.

---

[24] *S. and Marper v. the United Kingdom*, Application nos. 30562/04 and 30566/04, judgment of 4 December 2008, para 119.

[25] T-261/09 P, *Commission v. Violetti and others*, judgment of 20 May 2010.

[26] Compare the cases discussed above: T-259/03, *Nikolaou v. Commission*, judgment of 12 September 2007; see also T-309/03, *Camos Grau v. Commission*, judgment of 6 April 2006; F-23/05, *Giraudy v. Commission*, judgment of 2 May 2007 and F-5/05 and 7/05, *Violetti and others v. Commission*, judgment of 28 April 2009.

[27] Final report of COWI (European consulting group) of January 2009 preparing an external evaluation of Frontex provided for in Article 33 of the Council Regulation (EC) No 2007/2004 of 26 October 2004 establishing Frontex, p. 48, available at: http://www.frontex.europa.eu/specific_documents/other/ (accessed February 2011); to the cooperation between Europol and Frontex, see Holzenberger (2006).

Inter-agency data exchange between Europol, Eurojust, OLAF and Frontex takes place at different levels (in JITs or via cooperation agreements) and often lacks essential legal requirements such as a legal basis (e.g. Eurojust's or OLAF's involvement in JITs) or specific data protection guarantees which compensate the risks caused by the transfer of data from one agency to another. The opening of Europol's analysis work files to Eurojust for instance leads to a mergence of the data so far stored separately in the databases of different agencies. As the transfer to another authority is in general not particularly supervised, such close connections between the agencies raise serious concerns in terms of the protection of individuals against the gradual enlargement of the circle of actors having access to personal data. In this context, it is worth mentioning that the individuals concerned, including victims or witnesses, are not notified about the transfer of their data.

Moreover, while, on the one hand, the scopes of activities of the AFSJ actors become wider, making it possible to preventively enter data of an extremely diverse nature, on the other hand, Europol and Eurojust increasingly access databases which were established outside of police and judicial cooperation, thus challenging the purpose limitation principle. Although the ECtHR allows derogations from this principle only in few restricted cases and only insofar as they are proportionate, indispensable and foreseeable and can outweigh the serious infringement caused,[28] the already existing and planned access to the databases rarely seems to take these restrictions into account.

In the absence of unified standards and due to the case-by-case approach, the current conditions for access to the databases vary extremely while being generally very favourable for the accessing actors. Whereas in some cases additional instruments exist regulating the law enforcement and judicial access, in others personal data exchange is carried out in absence of a legal basis (e.g. Eurojust-CIS). Questions concerning for instance the whereabouts of the transferred data, the access requirements or the time-limits as well as the conditions for third party transfer of the received data or the rights of individuals after the data are transferred are therefore often left open. This legal uncertainty is increased when considering that personal data exchange is often carried out without linking the purpose of the access to the later use of the data in a law enforcement or judicial database (e.g. Eurojust-CIS or Europol-SIS II access) or that different circles of accessing actors, depending on the respective database, considerably extend the circle of persons using the transferred data.

All in all, the problems in AFSJ cooperation result in a large part from the fact that no coherent approach to AFSJ personal data exchange exists. This outcome of the analysis raises numerous interesting questions. Discussion and attention could be focused on the following items: is the ever extending AFSJ data collection and exchange still lawful (Sect. II)? What are the limits of law enforcement access to databases of different nature and of the ever-widening and preventive data

[28] *Weber and Saravia v. Germany*, Application no. 54934/00, admissibility decision of 29 June 2006, paras 80 et seq.

processing possibilities of the AFSJ actors (Sect. III)? Which supervisory structure can improve the weak position of the individual and corresponds better to the post-Lisbon situation (Sect. IV)? Are there tools to improve the legal framework of the AFSJ actors to bring their data processing framework in line with the European data protection standard developed in Chap. A (Sect. V)? Is there a coherent approach based on common legal standards to replace today's confusing intra-AFSJ data exchange and case-by-case solutions (Sect. VI)? In which way is the Lisbon Treaty expected to help in this process (Sect. VII)?

II. Lawfulness of the Expanding AFSJ Functionalities

The first observation raising doubts about the legitimacy of the increasing data exchange possibilities in the AFSJ relates to the question of whether the growing data exchange is still foreseeable for the persons concerned. The widening scopes and the data protection shortcomings included in the legal bases of the AFSJ actors (Chap. B) combined with the continually extending data exchange possibilities, often described in unclear wording, jeopardise the individual's capacity to foresee the consequences a given action, such as the entry of its data into one of the AFSJ databases, might entail. Following a preventive entry in the CIS, personal data may be transmitted to Europol or to third states thereby gradually extending the circle of recipients. A visa applicant might be confronted with the entry of his data in a law enforcement database (because he might be a possible witness in a criminal case) having as a consequence that he might be treated with more suspicion than before and this, in turn, will most likely negatively influence his chances to receive a visa.[29]

Additionally, in most of the cases, the individual is neither notified about the entry of his data, nor about the transfer. This lack of knowledge generally excludes that the person concerned is able to realise to which extent his data are collected and used or how he is able to exercise his right to correction or deletion. These rights remains entirely fictional.[30] It is not exaggerated to say that he cannot even rely on the fact that his data are not used for a completely different purpose that he might have never considered at the time of recording. Therefore, foreseeability in such anonymous data exchange systems as established by the AFSJ actors over the last years seems not to be guaranteed.

[29] Compare the former practice of Spain to refuse entry into the States party to the Schengen Agreement as well as to issue a visa for the purpose of entry to a national of a third country, on the sole ground that he is a person for whom an alert was entered in the SIS, without examining the circumstances on a case-by-case bases and verifying whether the presence of that person constitutes a genuine, serious threat affecting one of the fundamental interests of society; case C-503/03 *Commission v. Spain*, judgment of 31 January 2006.

[30] Peers (2006), p. 555.

The flexibility and the hurry with which the interconnection of the AFSJ actors was pushed forward prior to the adoption of the Lisbon Treaty illustrates that the Council and the Member States, often supported by the Commission, strive for an almost unlimited and flexible functionality of the AFSJ databases. The close cooperation between Council, Commission and Member States not only challenges the usual balance of powers between the three actors, but additionally makes an end to this "data hoarding" unforeseeable. The rationale behind this development seems to be the belief that an increase in the number of (connected) databases increases security.[31]

Statistics of the results of the widening exchange and access possibilities at EU level however do not (yet) exist.[32] As in many cases no impact assessment was carried out by the Commission and existing instruments were not evaluated before the adoption of new measures, empirical findings about the effectiveness of the (interconnection of) databases do not exist. The question of whether the increasing access and exchange possibilities are effective should be evaluated before new initiatives such as Europol's intended Eurodac access are adopted. Otherwise, on behalf of security, the interferences with data protection rights increase and gradually push back the boundaries of what appears to be necessary to detect criminals. Whether this development is still adequate and necessary in a democratic society is open to discussion.

More generally, that pre-emptive storing and the entering of huge amounts of personal data in law enforcement databases actually contribute to an improved protection of individuals is so far only based on assumptions – concrete proofs are lacking. Again, evidence in form of statistics showing a connection between the entry of personal data (including the purpose of the entry) into law enforcement databases and the convicted (not the arrested) persons are urgently needed to justify the widening of the entry conditions. Moreover, a detailed evaluation of the increasing access opportunities, in particular in respect of Europol, should be carried out as soon as possible. Comprehensive impact assessments with the involvement of all actors concerned, including representatives of the persons concerned, should be carried out.

When assuming that only a clear definition of the purpose allows a correct assessment of the proportionality and adequacy of data processing,[33] the nebulous character of formulations used when describing the purpose of collection or the access to other databases (e.g. for the performance of tasks etc.) creates doubts

[31] Balzacq et al. (2006); De Hert and Gutwirth (2006), in particular p. 28.

[32] Statistics of Member States, for instance Germany on data gathering operations for crime prevention purposes do not show the necessity of massive data storing; compare Kant (2006) and De Hert and Gutwirth (2006).

[33] Opinion of the European Data Protection Supervisor on the Proposal for a Regulation of the European Parliament and of the Council concerning the Visa Information System (VIS) and the exchange of data between Member States on short stay-visas (COM(2004) 835 final), OJ 2005, C-181/13, p. 17.

regarding the legitimacy of processing for specified and explicit purposes demanded by the ECHR and Article 6 Directive 95/46.

Merging purposes of police, judicial, investigative, preventive and informational interests gradually blur the boundaries between those interests. Again, constantly expanding data exchange possibilities seem in some cases to ignore the purpose limitation principle. The fusion of data processing purposes gives the impression that law enforcement and judicial purposes are regarded as being significantly more important than the interests of the individuals in their personal data. Often missing is an impact assessment or an evaluation of the (planned) measures leading to the assumption that a balancing between the different interests as demanded by the ECtHR rarely takes place. In absence of a debate about the interests at stake, the importance of data protection rights risks to be undermined. The interests most likely remain imbalanced. This assumption is underpinned by the weakness of the data protection regimes of the AFSJ actors in connection with the missing transparency rules and guarantees in case of data exchange (compare analysis in Chaps. B and C).

As illustrated in the foregoing, in some cases, almost no control of onward transmission exists (e.g. CIS). Consequently, even if a person concerned might succeed in getting his data corrected by the national authorities or the central databases, the (wrong) data might stay in the third country database and may lead possibly to the arrest of the person when trying to cross the border of the respective third country.

Summarising, when looking at the imbalanced interests and the shortcomings as regards the foreseeability of data storing in the AFSJ, the requirements of the ECHR and the Charter of Fundamental Rights, stipulated in Chap. A, seem to be violated. Maximum discretion to law enforcement authorities with no indication of the limits of this discretion does not adequately counterbalance the interests at stake.

III. Limits of Preemptive Storing and Law Enforcement Access to Databases of a Non Law Enforcement Nature

The important tendencies observed in the foregoing analysis raise questions in relation to the preventive storing of personal data in law enforcement databases and about the extent to which law enforcement authorities should have access to databases established for a completely different purpose. In both cases, data of persons not yet suspected of a crime are concerned.

These fundamental questions relating to the legal barriers which EU law enforcement and judicial agencies face in accessing data of innocent individuals do not only arise in the context of AFSJ databases, but should be seen in connection with other instruments following the same tendency such as the Data Retention

Directive,[34] the EU-US Passenger Name Record Agreement (EU-US PNR Agreement),[35] the planned access by law enforcement authorities to Passenger Name Records (PNR) data at EU level[36] as well as the API directive.[37] In all cases, data originally collected for a different purpose (e.g. harmonising visa policy or economic purposes) of people not suspected of a crime are later used for law enforcement purposes. This shift in the purpose of processing has serious consequences for the rights of individuals, which implicitly leads to a change in the applicable data protection rights and their connected procedural guarantees such as access, appeal and correction rights. The EDPS and the Agency of Fundamental Rights additionally highlight the discriminatory effect on certain ethnic or religious groups that proactive investigation methods may have.[38] In particular, decisions taken about one individual which result from analysing patterns derived from other individuals raise fundamental rights problems and risk a high error rate.[39] An individual whose data have been linked to data of another, possibly suspicious person, might himself be treated with more suspicion than before.

1. *Pre-Emptive Storing in View of the Case-Law*

The development towards the storing of personal data in absence of a suspicion basied on a purely preventive rationale[40] is particularly problematic as illustrated on the one hand by the low thresholds to enter data into the databases of Europol,

[34] Directive 2006/24/EC of the European Parliament and of the Council of 15 March 2006 on the retention of data generated or processed in connection with the provision of publicly available electronic communications services or of public communications networks and amending Directive 2002/58/EC, OJ 2006, L-105/54.

[35] Agreement between the European Union and the United States of America on the processing and transfer of Passenger Name Record (PNR) data by air carriers to the Unites States Department of Homeland Security (DHS), OJ 2007, L-204/18.

[36] Proposal for a Council Framework Decision on the use of Passenger Name Record (PNR) for law enforcement purposes, COM(2007) 654 of 6 November 2007.

[37] Council Directive 2004/82/EC of 29 April 2004 on the obligation of air carriers to communicate passenger data, OJ 2004, L-261/24.

[38] EDPS, Opinion on the draft proposal for a Council Framework Decision on the use of Passenger Name records (PNR) for law enforcement purposes, OJ 2008, C-110/01, point 12 and Opinion of the European Union Agency for Fundamental Rights on the Proposal for a Council Framework Decision on the use of Passenger Name Record (PNR) data for law enforcement purposes, 28 October 2008. To the general concerns raised by data mining including further references, see De Hert and Bellanova (2008).

[39] EDPS, Opinion on the draft proposal for a Council Framework Decision on the use of Passenger Name records (PNR) for law enforcement purposes, OJ 2008, C-110/01, point 22.

[40] Gonzalez Fuster et al. (2010).

Eurojust or the CIS [41] and on the other by the almost unlimited access possibilities for Europol or Eurojust to databases originally not related to law enforcement or judicial activities. The phrasing usually used to enter the data or to get access to another database is "for the prevention, detection and investigation of crime". Data can be collected, stored and accessed because of the (purely preventive) belief that they could be useful in the future to detect a criminal of a crime yet to be committed.[42]

Regrettably, so far, neither the ECtHR, nor the European Court of Justice have been directly confronted with the question whether or to what extent such pre-emptive storing is legitimate.

Indeed, in *S. and Marper v. the United Kingdom,*[43] where two not convicted individuals asked for the removal of their data from a governmental DNA database, the Strasbourg Court theoretically had the possibility to discuss this questions,[44] but the ECtHR limited its findings to the nevertheless very important, statement that the retention of data must be proportionate in relation to the purpose of collection[45] and therefore declared the indefinite storing void. The Court missed the opportunity to make reference to Principle 2.1. of Recommendation R (87) 15 which restricts preventive storing to the presence of a real danger or to the principle of transparency set out in Article 8 of Convention No. 108 which requires to specify the categories of persons included in a file to enable an individual to foresee whether its data might be introduced.

Some authors argue that the ECtHR logic might be workable in cases in which the purpose of collection is the investigation of a crime, having for consequence that the data must be destroyed after the case was solved.[46] Although, if databases serve pre-emptive purposes[47] and are fed with data serving an entirely preventive function (such as for example Europol,[48] Eurojust and the CIS) or the access to

[41] See above Chaps. B II 1 b, B II 2 b and B III 3 b; more precisely: Article 12 (1) lit. b Council Decision of 6 April 2009 establishing the European Police Office, OJ 2009, L-121/37, Article 5 (2) CIS Council Decision 2009/917, OJ 2009, L-323/20 and Article 15 (1) Eurojust Decision.

[42] Gonzalez Fuster et al. (2010).

[43] *S. and Marper v. the United Kingdom*, Application nos. 30562/04 and 30566/04, judgment of 4 December 2008.

[44] Critical in this regard, Gonzalez Fuster et al. (2010) and *Peyrou-Pistouley* (2009), in particular p. 741 to the beginnings of preventive police work at EU level, see Bigo (1996), in particular pp. 333–336.

[45] *S. and Marper v. the United Kingdom*, Application nos. 30562/04 and 30566/04, judgment of 4 December 2008, para 107.

[46] Gonzalez Fuster et al. (2010).

[47] Ibid.

[48] To the attempt to assimilate the differences between preventive and repressive work at Europol, see Gärditz (2008), in particular pp. 212–215.

other databases is allowed for the *prevention of crime* (which is the standard formulation used to allow Europol or Eurojust access to different databases[49]), the retention for any desired time would completely correspond to the purpose of collection or the purpose of retrieval.[50] However, this argument does not exclude that the retention is judged as disproportionate when exceeding certain limits. It is worth noting that by approving the German solution in *Weber and Saravia v. Germany* to limit the transfer of personal data to cases where only a suspicion based on specific facts justifies the transfer of personal data to other authorities, the ECtHR made a clear statement in direction of a limited approach to the transfer of personal data. Its jurisdiction suggests that the transmission (and possibly even the collection) of personal data regardless of any suspicion in a wide range of cases would most likely contradict the guarantees of Article 8 ECHR.[51]

As follows from the foregoing, the key problem lies in the shaping and the interpretation of the term *prevention of crime* in the European law enforcement framework. Which limits are still proportional and should apply regarding the pre-emptive introduction in and retrieval of personal data from EU databases? This issue seems to be complex, although urgent and should not be regarded as insignificant, in particular in view of the development and the use of possible new databases as well as the continually growing access possibilities of law enforcement and judicial EU agencies to other databases containing data of persons not suspected of any crime as illustrated in Chap. C. Currently, a very wide interpretation of the term *prevention* seems to apply when considering the abovementioned low thresholds to pass when collecting, storing and accessing personal data in the AFSJ. More or less arbitrary criteria (introduction of personal data for the sake of preventing a future crime, perhaps never to be committed) gain ground and seem to slowly infiltrate the information management in the AFSJ.

a) Incentives by the German “Bundesverfassungsgericht”

While at European level the discussion about the storing of personal data for the benefit of the detection of not yet committed crimes (or crimes never to be committed) has just started, the need for stricter rules on the protection of innocent

---

[49] Compare for instance Article 1 of Council Decision 2008/633/JHA of 23 June 2008 concerning access for consultation of the Visa Information System (VIS) by designated authorities of Member States and by Europol for the purposes of the prevention, detection and investigation of terrorist offences and of other serious criminal offences, OJ 2008, L-218/129.

[50] To the terms prevention and repression of crime in European law, see Gärditz (2008).

[51] *Weber and Saravia*, Application no. 54934/00, admissibility decision of 29 June 2006, paras 125–129.

individuals in the framework of governmental data storing for crime prevention purposes has been recently underlined in several judgements of the German Constitutional Court (Bundesverfassungsgericht) ruling on the German act transposing the Data Retention Directive[52] as well as on the practice of governmental profiling.

The Bundesverfassungsgericht repeatedly points to the risks of intimidating effects which could have a negative impact on the exercise of fundamental rights and the "feeling of living in a surveillance state" arising out of the collection and storage of large amounts of data in governmental databases.[53] With regard to the retention of telecommunications data, the same court found that the storage without occasion is "capable of creating a diffuse feeling of being watched which can impair a free exercise of fundamental rights in many areas".[54] In view of the scope and the persons concerned by the retention of telephone data, the court considers data security as being of great importance and ruled that: "there is a need for legislation which provides for a particularly *high degree of security*, whose essential provisions are at all events *well defined and legally binding*".[55]

The main findings of the data retention judgment also relate to the use of the data which is only permitted if there is "the *suspicion of a criminal offence*, based on *specific facts*, that is *serious* even in an individual case" and "there is a sufficiently evidenced concrete danger to the life, limb or freedom of a person, to the security of [Germany] or to ward off a common danger".[56] Transparency requirements include additionally that the collection and use of personal data should be openly exercised.[57] Similar to the questions arising at EU level, the court's reflections refer to an information duty of the persons concerned in order to guarantee transparency and "counteract the diffuse sense of threat which may be conveyed to citizens by the storage and use of data which in itself is not perceptible".[58] Therefore, the Bundesverfassungsgericht applied a rather strict

---

[52] DeSimone (2010); Westphal (2010).

[53] Judgment on governmental profiling of the German Constitutional Court of 4 April 2006, Bundesverfassungsgericht, 1 BvR 518/02, para 117.

[54] Judgment on data retention of the German Constitutional Court of 2 March 2010, Bundesverfassungsgericht, 1 BvR 256/08, 1 BvR 263/08 and 1 BvR 586/08, para 212; English press release no 11/2010 of 2 March 2010, para 3.

[55] Ibid para 3 emphasis added.

[56] Ibid para 4 emphasis added.

[57] Ibid para 4.

[58] Ibid para 4, compare Gietl (2010); Petri (2010); Roßnagel (2010a); with regard to the newly introduced duty of the processor to inform the person concerned in cases of unintentional knowledge of personal data in the German Data Protection Act, compare Eckhardt and Schmitz (2010).

approach as regards the notification of individuals by subjecting the secret use of data in criminal cases to external judicial control:

> The data may be constitutionally used without the knowledge of the person affected only if otherwise the purpose of the investigation served by the retrieval of data would be frustrated. The legislature may in principle assume that this is the case for warding off danger and carrying out the duties of the intelligence services. In contrast, *in criminal prosecution there is also the possibility that data may be collected and used openly.* There may only be a provision for secret use of the data here if such use *is necessary and is ordered by a judge in the individual case*. Insofar as the use of the data is secret, the legislature must provide for a duty of information, at least subsequently. This must guarantee that the persons to whom a request for data retrieval directly applied are in principle informed, at least subsequently. Exceptions to this require *judicial supervision*.[59]

In light of the particularly serious interference caused by the storage of personal data of innocent individuals', the Bundesverfassungsgericht insists on a high standard of data security which was missing in the German act transposing the Data Retention Directive. As in the case of Europol, in which the establishment of security measures depends on the necessity of the measures,[60] German law left the introduction of specific security provisions to the discretion of the service providers depending on the adequacy of the measures.[61] The measures were regarded as adequate when the technological and economic efforts they involve are proportional to the importance of the protected rights.[62] These formulations were declared void for being too general, introducing undefined considerations of (economic) adequacy.[63] Unfortunately, the wording used in the German act strongly recalls the phrasing used by Europol, namely that security measures are "necessary where the effort they involve is proportionate to the objective they are designed to achieve in terms of protection".[64]

---

[59] Judgment on data retention of the German Constitutional Court of 2 March 2010, Bundesverfassungsgericht, 1 BvR 256/08, 1 BvR 263/08 and 1 BvR 586/08, paras 239 et seq.; English press release no 11/2010 of 2 March 2010, para 4; emphasis added.

[60] Article 35 (1) Council Decision of 6 April 2009 establishing the European Police Office, OJ 2009, L-121/37; emphasis added.

[61] Judgment on data retention of the German Constitutional Court of 2 March 2010, Bundesverfassungsgericht, 1 BvR 256/08, 1 BvR 263/08 and 1 BvR 586/08, para 271; emphasis added.

[62] Ibid para 271 emphasis added.

[63] Ibid para 271 emphasis added.

[64] Article 35 (1) Council Decision of 6 April 2009 establishing the European Police Office, OJ 2009, L-121/37.

b) Realisation at EU Level

Although the foregoing observations of the German Bundesverfassungsgericht do not directly refer to the European framework, they nevertheless provide helpful guidance when it comes to specifying the limits of such abstract formulations like the storing for the prevention of crime, persistently used in the legal bases of AFSJ actors. To ensure that personal data are not stored at random, but only on the basis of a sufficient initial suspicion, similar requirements such as the ones mentioned in the judgement of the German Bundesverfassungsgericht should also be considered in the European context. The court has additionally made clear that the access of law enforcement agencies to databases serving a different purpose should remain the exception to the general rule that the data remain connected to the purpose for which they were originally entered (which could be economic or policy related). In view of the foregoing, if accessing and using these data, high security and transparency standards involving a notification duty, at least subsequently, are important tools to guarantee proportionality.

While in Germany the exceptions to the general notification duty call for judicial supervision, at European level the creation of a general notification duty would be a first step to improve the rights of individuals in AFSJ databases in order to guarantee transparency in this sensitive field. In addition, independent review and adequate and effective safeguards against abuse[65] require a reinforced European supervisory structure to partially compensate the serious infringements caused. Enhanced control, independently exercised by a single common supervisory body, could equally monitor the notification of individuals concerned.[66]

In light of the rule of law, prevention of crime, even at European level, cannot mean that personal data can be collected based on simple assumptions in absence of any suspicion or verifiable standards. The clear definition of the circumstances and limits of the storing and the use of the information before the processing[67] as demanded by the ECtHR requires the framing and the definition of such key terms as prevention of crime and factual indications in the legal bases of the AFSJ actors. Concrete and unambiguous criteria based on a verifiable prognosis, open to scrutiny by an external supervisor, to underpin the estimation that somebody plans to commit a crime, should be established to concretise the currently broad terms. The starting point to legitimise data storing for preventive purposes

---

[65] *Rotaru against Romania*, Application no. 28341/95, judgment of 4 May 2000, paras 55–63; *Segerstedt-Wiberg and others v. Sweden*, Application no. 62332/00, judgment of 6 June 2006, para 121.

[66] As regards the need of such a body, refer to the following section in Sect. IV 1.

[67] *Segerstedt-Wiberg and others v. Sweden*, Application no. 62332/00, judgment of 6 June 2006, paras 88–92; *Liberty and others v. the United Kingdom*, Application no. 58234/00, judgment of 1 July 2008, para 68; *Rotaru v. Romania*, Application no. 28341/954, judgment of 4 May 2000, para 57; *Weber and Saravia v. Germany*, Application no. 54934/00, admissibility decision of 29 June 2006, paras 116 and 127.

must be the existence of a risk and a certain degree of probability that crimes could be committed.[68] Pure hypothetical reflections or mere individual assumptions lead to the result that in the end, personal data of everyone can be introduced. Criminalistic indicators implying the assessment by several actors in the field of crime prevention purposes would considerably improve the existing legal prerequisites. In this way, clear normative provisions, even in a pre-emptive context, would contribute to an improved protection of individuals in the AFSJ environment and a clear definition of the circumstances and limits of the storing and the use of the information before the processing.[69]

In absence of a formulated distinction between preventive and repressive storing in the AFSJ as well as in order to assess the necessity of pre-emptive storing, statistics showing the results of the data preventively entered, the cases actually initiated, the arrests obtained and the convictions achieved are urgently required. Data revealing the relation between hits in the AFSJ databases in comparison with persons convicted due to the hits might prove the need for (preventive) data storing.

However, when assuming that pre-emptive data storing primarily occurs in the context of suspected terrorists – remembering one of the main reasons for the profound changes in the legal bases of the AFSJ actors illustrated in Chaps. B and C – and considering in particular efforts made by Europol in this perspective,[70] recent statistics reveal interesting results: surprisingly in 2009 only 337 persons were convicted of terrorist activities in Europe, whereby of these 337, the prevailing majority of the verdicts relate to regional separatist activities in Spain (182) and France (77).[71] In light of these outcomes, the global threat of terrorism, to which the Stockholm programme frequently makes reference in order to justify the increasing interlinks of the information exchange systems,[72] appears to be rather exaggerated. Regrettably, statistics of how many personal data were preventively entered and

---

[68] With reference to Europol and its possibility to pre-emptively process personal data under violating the German "Recht auf informationelle Selbstbestimmung", see Schubert (2008), in particular pp. 147–151.

[69] *Segerstedt-Wiberg and others v. Sweden*, Application no. 62332/00, judgment of 6 June 2006, paras 88–92; *Liberty and others v. the United Kingdom*, Application no. 58234/00, judgment of 1 July 2008, para 68; *Rotaru v. Romania*, Application no. 28341/954, judgment of 4 May 2000, para 57; *Weber and Saravia v. Germany*, Application no. 54934/00, admissibility decision of 29 June 2006, paras 116 and 127.

[70] EU Terrorism Situation and Trend Report TE-SAT 2010, to be found on Europol's webpage: http://www.europol.europa.eu/index.asp?page=publications&language= (accessed February 2011).

[71] Compare statistics in EU Terrorism Situation and Trend Report TE-SAT 2010, pp. 16 and 17 to be found on Europol's webpage: http://www.europol.europa.eu/index.asp?page=publications&language= (accessed February 2011).

[72] Communication from the Commission to the European Parliament, the Council, the European Economic and Social Committee and the Committee of the Regions – Delivering and area of freedom, security and justice for European's citizens – Action Plan implementing the Stockholm Programme, COM(2010) 171 final, in particular p. 6.

how many of these data actually contributed to the aforementioned results do not exist.

In this context, a profound assessment of the efficiency of the existing databases and their results in terms of convictions and prevented crimes in relation to the data entered, should be made before allowing Europol or Eurojust to access further data (for instance to Eurodac). While all of the data storing, even the pre-emptive type, falls under the goals mentioned in Article 8 (2) ECHR (the interest of national security and the prevention of disorder and crime), this does not automatically mean that they are necessary in a democratic society and therefore justified. The measure must also be proportionate with regard to the interference. Therefore, statistics and assessments are essential to verify the necessity. So far, in most of the cases analysed above, sufficient evidence is lacking with regard to necessity and proportionality.

Insofar as the low thresholds to enter or to access data are retained, individual rights must counterbalance the infringements caused by reinforcing the data processing and protection framework within the AFSJ (see point IV).

2. *No Coherent Solution by the European Court of Justice for Law Enforcement Access*

The analysis in Chaps. B and C raises the question of the legal implications of a case where data which are regulated by a rather exhaustive data protection framework and which were collected and stored for a specific purpose (not connected to law enforcement objectives) are subsequently used for law enforcement purposes. This question was briefly discussed with regard to the intended access by Europol to Eurodac,[73] and should now be examined in light of the jurisdiction of the European Court of Justice.

On two occasions, the European Court of Justice was faced with this problem, but regrettably missed the opportunity to analyse the substance or opine on the fundamental rights implications of this question.[74] While both cases involved the choice of the legal basis (first or third pillar) for measures obliging private actors to hold their data available for law enforcement agencies, the European Court of Justice reached two different solutions.

[73] Compare Chap. C II 4.

[74] Joined cases C-317/04 and C-318/04, *Parliament v. Council*, judgment of 30 May 2006 and case C-301/06, *Ireland v. Parliament and Council*, judgment of 10 February 2009. To the similiarity of the cases, see Simitis (2009).

a) The Annulment of the Legal Basis of the First EU-US PNR Agreement

The first case concerned the aforementioned *PNR case*[75] dealing with legal basis for the first EU-US PNR Agreement of 2004.[76] After the 9/11 terrorist attacks, the US decided to monitor and analyse flight passenger data. Airlines were forced to transfer up to 69 different data elements of their passengers to American security authorities, such as the Department of Homeland Security, before they enter American territory.[77] Airlines not complying with this requirement had their landing rights withdrawn. At the time of conclusion, the EU-US PNR agreement was heavily disputed and criticized by many scholars.[78] Criticism focused in particular on the legal basis of the agreement, the lack of data protection guarantees by the US, and the large volume of transmitted data.

The PNR data transfers to the US and their processing were initially treated as economic related first pillar data processing because the PNR were originally collected by the airlines. Two decisions allowing for the conclusion of the agreement were based on Article 95 EC Treaty (today 114 TFEU). Against this first pillar choice, the European Parliament, assisted by the EDPS, intervening in support of the Parliament, initiated proceedings before the European Court of Justice.[79] One of the underlying questions, from a fundamental rights point of view, however, concerned the limits of the use of personal data originally stored for an economic purpose (electronic communication services) and later used for law enforcement purposes.[80]

Disappointingly, although being challenged by the Parliament as well as by the EDPS, the European Court of Justice limited its findings to the discussion of the applicable legal basis of the PNR processing and avoided the question of the data protection implications of the EU-US PNR Agreement on the rights of individuals. The European Court of Justice regarded the PNR data transfers as security-related third pillar data processing hindering the participation of the European Parliament

[75] Compare Chap. A III 1 b.

[76] Joined cases C-317/04 and C-318/04, *Parliament v. Council*, judgment of 30 May 2006.

[77] The information relates to a plane trip to the USA and entails amongst other: date of reservation/ issue of ticket, date(s) of intended travel, name(s), available frequent flier and benefit information (i.e. free tickets, upgrades, etc.), other names on PNR, including number of travelers on PNR, all available contact information (including originator information meaning address and telephone number at the final destination), all available payment/billing information linked to the travel transaction, travel itinerary for specific PNR, travel agency/travel agent, code share information, split/divided information, travel status of passenger (including confirmations and check-in status), ticketing information, including ticket number, one-way tickets and Automated Ticket Fare Quote, all baggage information, seat information, including seat number. See also Hasbrouck (2011).

[78] For a profound analysis with further references see Papakonstantinou and De Hert (2009); Mendez (2007).

[79] Joined cases C-317/04 and C-318/04, *Parliament v. Council*, judgment of 30 May 2006, paras 33–50.

[80] Simitis (2009), in particular p. 1783.

in the legislative process as well as the possibility to challenge fundamental rights violations before the European Court of Justice The first pillar decision of the Council leading to the conclusion of the agreement was therefore annulled.[81] From then on, the new PNR agreements were governed by public international law. As a result, some authors spoke about a "pyrrhic victory" of the European Parliament that brought the action against the first agreement in the name of fundamental rights protection before the European Court of Justice.[82]

b) The Legal Basis of Data Retention

The second case brought before the European Court of Justice involved the choice of the legal basis of the Data Retention Directive 2006/24.[83]

Ireland claimed the annulment of the Data Retention Directive 2006/24 arguing that, as the directive, pursuant to its Article 1, harmonises the Member States' provisions concerning the obligation of electronic communication service providers to store the "traffic and location data on both legal entities and natural persons" and "the related data necessary to identify the subscriber or registered userclient data" processed by them, "in order to ensure that the data are available for the purpose of the investigation, detection and prosecution of serious crime",[84] the directive should have been based on a third pillar legal basis instead of Article 95 EC Treaty (Article 114 TFEU) because it regulates the data retention for law enforcement purposes.

As mentioned in the Chap. A III 1 b, the Court rejected Ireland's arguments and decided that the Parliament and the Council chose Article 95 of the EC Treaty as the correct legal basis for data retention distinguishing between the retention and the storing of the data and its subsequent use and the access to them.[85]

---

[81] The Court added: "While the view may rightly be taken that PNR data are initially collected by airlines in the course of an activity which falls within the scope of Community law, namely sale of an aeroplane ticket which provides entitlement to a supply of services, the data processing which is taken into account [. . .] is, however, quite different in nature", as a result, the PNR transfers did not concern "data processing necessary for a supply of services, but data processing regarded as necessary for safeguarding public security and for law-enforcement purposes", see Joined cases C-317/04 and C-318/04, *Parliament v. Council*, judgment of 30 May 2006, para 57.

[82] Mendez (2007); Schaar (2007).

[83] Case C-301/06, *Ireland v. Parliament and Council*, judgment of 10 February 2009; Directive 2006/24/EC of the European Parliament and of the Council of 15 March 2006 on the retention of data generated or processed in connection with the provision of publicly available electronic communications services or of public communications networks and amending Directive 2002/58/EC, OJ 2006, L-105/54, compare Chap. A III 1 b.

[84] Article 1 (1) and (2) Directive 2006/24/EC of the European Parliament and of the Council of 15 March 2006 on the retention of data generated or processed in connection with the provision of publicly available electronic communications services or of public communications networks and amending Directive 2002/58/EC, OJ 2006, L-105/54.

[85] Case C-301/06, *Ireland v. Parliament and Council*, judgment of 10 February 2009, para 84.

Similar to the EU-PNR Agreement case, one of the core underlying questions however dealt with the fundamental breach of the purpose limitation principle caused by the use of personal data originally stored for an economic purpose (electronic communication services) and later used for law enforcement purposes.[86] Unfortunately, like in the EU-PNR Agreement case, the European Court of Justice totally ignored this problem and completely focussed on the choice of the legal basis.

Regardless of the clear wording of Article 1 of Directive 2006/24 cited above,[87] the Court ruled that Directive 2006/24 regulates operations which "are independent of the implementation of any police and judicial cooperation in criminal matters"[88] and exclusively relate to the harmonization of the activities of service providers in the relevant sector of the internal market.[89] The Court distinguished between the retention and the storing of the data and its subsequent use and the access to them.[90] Consequently, the European Court of Justice approved the first pillar choice of Article 95 EC Treaty as the correct legal basis for the directive.

c) Two Cases, Two Different Solutions

With the ruling in the data retention case, the European Court of Justice contradicts its own jurisprudence in the EU-PNR Agreement case, which evidently focused on the use and the access to these data as well as their purpose of processing as being the decisive factor in search of a legal basis.[91]

As a result of the rulings, both measures have completely different legal bases, despite the fact that both cases concern the interest of law enforcement agencies in the personal data stored by private actors.

While the reasons for the European Court of Justice's turnaround in the data retention case might be well-intended,[92] it again disregards the fundamental rights dimension. By disconnecting the storage of the data from its subsequent use and the access to these data as well as their purpose of processing, the European Court of

[86] Simitis (2009), in particular 1783; Braum (2009b).

[87] Compare Chap. B III 1 b; Article 1 (1) Directive 2006/24 stipulates that: "This Directive aims to harmonise Member States' provisions concerning the obligations of the providers of publicly available electronic communications services or of public communications networks with respect to the retention of certain data which are generated or processed by them, in order to ensure that the data are available *for the purpose of the investigation, detection and prosecution of serious crime, as defined by each Member State in its national law*", emphasis added.

[88] Case C-301/06, *Ireland v. Parliament and Council*, judgment of 10 February 2009, para 83.

[89] Ibid para 84.

[90] Ibid.

[91] Simitis (2009), in particular 1784.

[92] A third pillar basis would have for instance hindered a subsequent judicial control in front of the European Courts.

Justice creates an artificial distinction, which fundamentally challenges the purpose limitation principle. Only the connection of the purpose of processing with the reason for the storage allows the assurance that the data are not disproportionally used for other purposes.

Meanwhile, several national Courts, such as the German Bundesverfassungsgericht as well as the Romanian Constitutional Court, annulled the respective national acts implementing Directive 2006/24 on grounds of non-compliance with their constitutions, notably with the proportionality test and the presumption of innocence.[93] Although these judgments did not touch upon the question of the lawfulness of the provisions of Directive 2006/24 itself, they clearly demonstrate the fundamental rights implications inherent to them.

Applying the outcome of these European Court of Justice decisions to the situation of the increasing access of Europol and Eurojust to the European databases, it becomes evident that the European Court of Justice solutions circumvent the fundamental rights impact and do not solve the problem occurring at EU level. The artificial distinction between the storage and the retention of data in the data retention case on the one hand, and the access, use and processing on the other, cannot be upheld in respect of the law enforcement access to the databases analysed above. One outcome of both cases however is that the reflections on such fundamental problems should not remain limited to a formal discussion about the legal basis.

IV. Reforming the Supervisory Structure and Creating a General Notification Duty

One key finding of the foregoing considerations relates to the lack of a coherent approach in the supervision of AFSJ information exchange. The current monitoring is dispersed and is principally based on two models: the former first pillar instruments such as the VIS, Eurodac the CIS are supervised by the EDPS and the former third pillar instruments, such as Europol, Eurojust or the third pillar part of the CIS are monitored by the JSBs. To balance the infringements to the right to private life illustrated in Chaps. B and C arising out of the new developments initiated by the Hague programme, an effective supervisory system should be in

[93] Judgment on data retention of the German Constitutional Court of 2 March 2010, Bundesverfassungsgericht, 1 BvR 256/08, 1 BvR 263/08 and 1 BvR 586/08 and Curtea Constitutionala, 8 October 2009 number 1258, Romanian Official Monitor no. 789 of 23 November 2009. For more details, see de Vries et al. (2010; Manolea 2010).

place to comply with ECtHR requirements calling for independent review and adequate and effective safeguards against abuse.[94]

1. *The Need for a Central Supervisory Authority*

The current system of shared supervision between EDPS and the JSBs in the AFSJ reflects the pre-Lisbon situation, mixing former intergovernmental structures with traditional Community structures and consisting of separate arrangements and a separate supervisory authority for each former third pillar AFSJ body. So far, the external (legal) responsibility is fragmented and sometimes confusing for individuals concerned.

In light of the need for reinforced protection of individual rights as well as a simplification of the existing structures, the outdated JSBs should be replaced by one central responsible supervisory actor. Taking into account the nevertheless similar data processing and supervisory problems arising in respect of the AFSJ databases (Chap. B) and in particular the increasing cooperation between the AFSJ actors (analysed in Chap. C), the existing amount of different legal mechanisms and supervisory regimes appears to be confusing (former first and third pillar provisions as well as the various specific data processing instruments of the AFSJ actors), inflexible and "disproportionately consuming of the limited resources available to data protection authorities".[95]

When keeping the current fragmented monitoring approach, the dangers arising out of the fast growing data exchange in the AFSJ are most likely not effectively counterbalanced. On the one hand there are the increasingly cooperating AFSJ actors, on the other hand, the different JSBs, each entrusted with the tasks to monitor the data processing and exchange of its national authorities as well as of the specific databases of the AFSJ actors. No JSB currently has the power to monitor the entire AFSJ data processing, including the exchange. The general overview of the entire AFSJ data sharing is therefore missing. Whether such a fragmented system is still effective, is questionable. Arguments in favour of maintaining the current situation referring to the well appreciated experience in the last 10 years of common JSB inspection as well as the "understanding of the business" of the AFSJ actors,[96] do not necessarily consider the changing AFSJ

---

[94] Compare *Klass v. Germany*, Application no. 5029/71, judgment of 6 September 1978, para 50, or *Weber and Saravia v. Germany*, Application no. 54934/00, admissibility decision of 29 June 2006, para 135.

[95] Answer given by the British Information Commissioner when he was asked whether a simplification of the supervision of the third pillar protection arrangements appears to be necessary, in: House of Lords report: 5th report of session 2004–05, "After Madrid: the EU's response to terrorism", published 8 March 2005, p. 21, para 43.

[96] Alonso Blas (2010), in particular pp. 245–249, referring to the experiences made at Eurojust.

priorities. Whereas admittedly the expertise and experience developed over the last years by the JSB members certainly contributes to inspections and monitoring,[97] the general overview is missing. A common single AFSJ supervisory body could nevertheless profit from the knowledge of the current JSBs and add reinforced and more effective protection.

Moreover, considering the Lisbon Treaty, which extends fundamental rights to policy areas of the former third pillar, and the jurisdictions of the ECtHR in security-related data processing, there would be clear advantages in terms of harmonisation when entrusting AFSJ supervision to a single authority.

The shortcomings identified in Chaps. B and C additionally relate to the limited resources in comparison to the amount of tasks of the national DPAs. As shown above, the national DPAs, trapped in their double role at national level as well as the JSBs, cannot keep up with the rapid proliferation of data storing and again, the increasing data exchange in the AFSJ.

One organisation pooling its entire resources to provide an overview of the applicable rights, depending on the database in which the data are processed, seems to be a better response to the challenges illustrated in the foregoing. Although the rules of the existing AFSJ databases are different, they could nevertheless be monitored by a single supervisory body. Simplifying the current supervision arrangements does not mean to deny the need for the specific rules governing the respective data processing framework of the AFSJ databases.

One possibility would be to extend the EDPS' monitoring powers to the former third pillar systems. An overall responsibility[98] of the EDPS would focus expertise and personal resources while at the same time guaranteeing a coherent application of individual rights. One single forum covering former first as well as third pillar data protection matters would not only contribute to the monitoring of the AFSJ, but also to the assessment of upcoming initiatives.

While in 2007 the EDPS might not yet have seen an "immediate need" for a single JSB replacing the existing JSBs and supervising data protection in the field of police and justice,[99] in the meantime the situation has dramatically changed. The arguments made against a common supervisory authority in 2007 mainly referred to the legal implications this subject matter would have on the legislative process of the Framework Decision on data protection discussed at that time, fearing that such a proposal would only additionally complicate its adoption procedure. In general, the EDPS admits that one single supervisory system "might lead to an even more

[97] Alonso Blas (2010), in particular pp. 245–249.

[98] House of Lords report: 5th report of session 2004–05, "After Madrid: the EU's response to terrorism", published 8 March 2005, p. 21, para 44.

[99] EDPS, third opinion of 27 April 2007 on the proposal for a Council Framework Decision on the protection of personal data processed in the framework of police and judicial co-operation in criminal matters, OJ 2007, C-139/1, para 42.

efficient system of supervision, and further ensure consistency of the level of protection within the bodies established under the third pillar".[100]

Whereas the interest of the Member States to have their DPAs participate in the supervision and in the inspections is understandable and could be exercised in form of a close cooperation with them (for instance in form of regular meetings, common training opportunities and mutual information exchange), the need for one single European authority supervising the extremely fast growing data exchange in the AFSJ remains obvious.

2. *Upgrading the Rights of the Supervisory Body to Guarantee Effective Protection*

Going hand in hand with the establishment of a common supervisory authority is the reinforcement of the role of the common supervisory body in terms of a procedural underpinning. To effectively exercise control, this body should be equipped with a formal role in relation to the existing databases as well as to the legislative proposals forming the subject of the future development in the AFSJ.

The standard advisory role of the supervisory bodies (delivering of non-binding opinions, continual use of "shall take into account" when describing the role of supervisory authorities etc.) should be increased in value by giving the supervisory body "real" powers by granting co-decision rights. Examples of such powers could relate to a right to participate in decisions whether to grant access to a database or to extend the original storage period (e.g. whether the prolongation is justified). In addition, these rights could include the participation in the decision to dismiss the internal DPO or in decisions relating to the access right to an EU database of third states or organisations (e.g. as regards the CIS). Due to its sensitive nature, the supervisory bodies should be further involved in the assessment of the level of protection in case of third party transfer. In this way, the supervision of third party data transfers as well as the compliance with general data protection requirements would be effectively carried out.

Powerful and effective tools for the supervisory body to put pressure on the actors not complying with the standards set out in their own legal bases (e.g. Eurodac, OLAF) are essential. For instance, the general duty to publish the inspection reports would strengthen transparency and force the actor concerned to publicly justify the reason for non-compliance. In case of repeatedly negative inspection reports, disciplinary instruments such as the possibility to interrupt the collection or the access to a system when a specific problem persistently occurs (e.g. one country does not offer any information at all to asylum seekers about their

[100] EDPS, third opinion of 27 April 2007 on the proposal for a Council Framework Decision on the protection of personal data processed in the framework of police and judicial co-operation in criminal matters, OJ 2007, C-139/1, para 41.

data protection rights, although it is obliged to do so) would considerably improve compliance with the rules in question.

The common supervisory body would additionally simplify the current complicated access procedures to a great extent. One single access point at European level would noticeably improve the transparency as well as the accessibility to data stored in AFSJ databases. The fact that individuals concerned simply have to contact one specific institution and lodge one common access form at the central authority, which could then make contact with the responsible national DPA, would not only increase transparency, but also support public awareness-raising. The possibility to centrally assess (in cooperation with the respective national DPA) whether the conditions for (denying) access are actually fulfilled would be exercised by specialised personnel, focused on the EU background and its specifics. The common supervisory body should consider publishing on its website a best practice guide on how the individuals can exercise their rights. Additionally, a common supervisory authority would render unnecessary the currently sometimes omitted notification of the national DPAs in case of complaints received by individuals.[101] Complaints to the common supervisory body should be thereby open to EU as well as to third state nationals to avoid discrimination effects (in case of Frontex, the VIS or the SIS).

Creating a "protection network" consisting of close cooperation with the national DPAs, as already provided for in the VIS and the SIS II, should become the general standard in each AFSJ database. Regular meetings, assistance in carrying out audits and inspections, common reports as well as harmonised proposals for joint solutions would create a "protection network" responding to the challenges arising out of the increasing (technical) interoperability.[102] Seeing that the current responsibilities of the supervisory body do not relate to all of the data stored in the systems, a revision of the review mechanism should be considered in order to reinforce the rights of the supervisory body with regard to the data entered by the Member States. The supervisory body could play the role of a mediator intervening in conflicts between Member States concerning questions of data entered in the AFSJ databases. In case the suggested changes do not meet the approval of the Member States, regular and intensive cooperation with the national DPAs could counterbalance the restricted possibilities of the EU supervisory body with regard to data belonging to the Member States in the AFSJ databases. Additionally, to handle situations requiring quick decisions, the introduction of an internal DPO at each AFSJ actor would complement the aforementioned "protection network".

---

[101] Compare Chap. B II 3 d.

[102] To the beginnings of the use of the term interoperability in the EU, compare De Hert and Gutwirth (2006); to the term interoperability, see the comprehensive analysis of Wallwork and Baptista (2005).

3. *Towards a General Notification Duty*

The existence of an efficient supervisory system is closely connected to the effectiveness of possible remedies before courts and therefore to the notification of the use and the transfer of the data. Unless a person does not know that his/her data are processed and transferred, he/she is not able to challenge the legality of the processing or the transfer before a court or the supervisory authority retrospectively.[103] Therefore, the introduction of a general notification duty is an essential requirement and would bring the EU framework in line with Principle 2.2. of Recommendation R 87 (15) of the Council of Europe.[104] Persons such as witnesses, victims and also persons whose data were pre-emptively entered, under the condition that the notification does not prejudice ongoing investigations, should in any case be notified about their data being processed. Where the entry into a law enforcement database is simply based on factual indications or reasonable grounds to believe that a person will commit criminal offences,[105] the supervisory body should be involved in every notification process relating to the question of whether or not to notify. A general notification duty would increase transparency[106] and it would presumably lead to an increasing use of the access possibilities. The concrete provisions of a possible notification duty are illustrated in the next section.

V. Aligning the Data Processing Framework in the AFSJ: Improvement Suggestions

As mentioned in the introduction, the sheer number of existing instruments and the growing set of legislation in the AFSJ make it necessary to identify a core set of data protection principles to serve as a benchmark for the initiation and evaluation of future legislative measures in the AFSJ as well as for the upcoming amendments in the legal framework Europol and Eurojust required by the entry into force of the Lisbon Treaty.[107]

---

[103] Compare the arguments of the ECtHR with regard to surveillance measures in *Weber and Saravia v. Germany*, Application no. 54934/00, admissibility decision of 29 June 2006, para 135.

[104] Compare Chap. A II 4 a.

[105] Article 12 (1) lit. b Council Decision of 6 April 2009 establishing the European Police Office, OJ 2009, L-121/37.

[106] Increasing transparency in European data protection law was recently underlined by the Commission in its communication on "A comprehensive strategy on data protection in the European Union", COM(2010) 609 final of 4 November 2010, p. 6, para 2.1.2.

[107] Compare Communication from the Commission to the European Parliament and the Council, Overview of information management in the area of freedom, security and justice, COM(2010) 385 final, p. 24.

These principles build upon and seek to complement the general data protection principles illustrated in Chap. A, in particular the standards developed by the ECtHR. While the new standards could uphold the already existing tailor-made data protection standards of the AFSJ actors for a transitional period, some improvements in order to introduce harmonised basic standards in their legal bases resulting from the foregoing general analysis in Chap. B could already play a part in contributing to an enhanced enforcement of the rights of individuals relating to data processing in the AFSJ.

At a later stage, one single core set of basic and standard data protection principles covering all actors dealing with police and judicial data in the AFSJ (former third pillar actors, but also actors dealing with police or jusdicial data such as Frontex), could be established. It could be complemented by specific provisions for each of the different AFSJ actors, if necessary. The quick adoption of one single comprehensive data protection framework for the AFSJ in absence of tailor-made rules might however be favourable in terms of legal simplification,[108] although when taking the current rather specific data processing context of the nevertheless different AFSJ actors into account,[109] strong arguments could be made here in favor of maintaining, as a first step, the tailor-made solutions plus an additional basic standard of data protection principles. In a later step (taking into account the transitional period of 5 years included in Protocol No. 36), one single instrument could replace the current solutions whereby special rules, for instance with regard to the particular data processing systems (such as Europol's analysis work files or EIS, SIS II, Eurojust's Case Management System etc.) could be entailed in the legal basis of the respective actor.

Whereas the specific nature of data protection in the area of law enforcement[110] is to be recognised, the need for a comprehensive AFSJ legal framework arises not only out of the increasing transfer possibilities between former first pillar and third pillar instruments (Europol-VIS, proposed Eurodac access for Europol etc.), other arguments additionally support this view.

The main argument relates to the entry into force of the Lisbon Treaty and the abolishment of the third pillar specialties. The restricted approach of Directive 95/46 was owed to the old pillar structure and not to the completely different nature of police and judicial data.[111]Further, *Hijmanns* rightly argues that the implementing laws of Directive 95/46 are applicable to data processing by police and judicial

---

[108] Hijmanns (2010).

[109] For instance is the data processing in Europol's analysis work files or in the EIS different from data processing in the SIS II or at Eurojust's Case Management System; compare with regard to Eurojust Alonso Blas (2010), in particular pp. 236–245, with good arguments to keep the tailor-made approach.

[110] Opinion of the EDPS of 19 December 2005 on the Proposal for a Council Framework Decision on the protection of personal data processed in the framework of police and judicial co-operation in criminal matters (COM(2005) 475 final), OJ 2006, C-47/27 and Alonso Blas (2010).

[111] Hijmanns (2010).

authorities in practically all Member States.[112] Article 16 TFEU enlarges its protection to the former third pillar regime, irrespective of the area concerned. Even before the Lisbon Treaty came into force, the European Court of Justice extended the principle of loyal cooperation developed in the first pillar to former third pillar instruments, such as a Framework Decision in the famous *Pupino case*.[113] One could argue that basic data protection principles might have been developed in the first pillar, but, to guarantee a conform interpretation, these principles should also be respected in the third pillar. However, such arguments might seem rather obsolete in light of Article 16 TFEU subjecting data protection to the principles of general application in the entire Union.

When developing this core set of basic AFSJ data processing principles, the following suggestions could be taken into account.

1. *Procedural Requirements and Legal Basis*

First and foremost, in view of the particular amount of stored data and in order to comply with the rule of law as well as with the proportionality requirement, the collection, storing or other related activites involving personal data must always have a legal basis which should include the essential data protection and data processing rules (e.g. the Frontex legal basis and Frontex proposal). To ensure a high level of fundamental rights protection and data security, the data protection provisions should not be diversified and included in different instruments, such the rules of procedure[114] and/or additional data protection statements (OLAF). One common catalogue of well-defined legally binding data protection principles applying to all of the databases and exchange systems operated by the respective AFSJ actors[115] as well as by OLAF is essential to guarantee effective fundamental rights protection as well as transparency.

2. *Catalogue of Stored Data*

Each AFSJ database storing personal data, including the databases managed by OLAF, should have one clear and understandable list of the personal data which may be stored. While Eurojust and Europol as well as the information databases, VIS,

---

[112] Ibid.

[113] Case C-105/03, criminal proceedings against *Maria Pupino*, judgment of 16 June 2005.

[114] For instance the rules of procedure on the processing and the protection of personal data at Eurojust, OJ 2005, C-68/1.

[115] Some AFSJ actors operate different databases or exchange systems, for instance Eurodac, which allows additional data exchange via its DubliNet system; compare Chap. B III 4 b.

CIS, SIS (II) and Eurodac comply with this requirement, OLAF's data processing practice and the Frontex proposal should be immediately improved in this regard.

3. *Avoiding Unclear Terms and Harmonising Key Terms*

To improve the foreseeability of data processing, unclear terms such as "for the performance of the tasks" or "may use the data for other purposes"[116] should be replaced by a concrete description of the respective action. This means for instance, that Europol should be allowed to use or store data for so long as the data are necessary for the prevention,[117] detection or investigation of a specific offence described in its legal basis (instead of referring to the necessity for the performance of its tasks[118]) or that Europol or Eurojust can establish relations to other EU bodies only for the purpose of the prevention, detection or investigation of the offences stipulated in their legal basis.

Concrete definitions, conditions and limits for pre-emptive data storing and therefore for the term "prevention of crime", are urgently to be developed. To comply with transparency requirements, the existence of such purposes in individual cases should at any time be subject to external supervision.

Key terms used in almost every legal basis of an AFSJ actor such as "serious crime" or "risk management systems"[119]should be defined in the same harmonised way. The Europol Decision for example entails a similar, but not identical list of serious crimes when comparing it to the Council Decision empowering Europol to consult the VIS which refers to the list entailed in Decision on the European Arrest Warrant.[120] Creating a common definition of such important terms is an essential requirement ensuring improved foreseeability and legal certainty.

4. *Framing the Access Conditions*

With regard to the increasing amount of accessing actors, four conditions applying to the Member States as well as to EU actors when accessing an EU database could replace the current conditions of access to the databases of the analysed AFSJ actors taking into account the diverse data stored in large databases, such as the EIS or the analysis work files of Europol or the data in the SIS II. The consultation of the

---

[116] Article 8 (1) CIS Council Decision 2009/917, OJ 2009, L-323/20.

[117] The term should be further explained in the legal basis.

[118] Article 20 (1) Council Decision of 6 April 2009 establishing the European Police Office, OJ 2009, L-121/37.

[119] Article 21 (2) CIS Council Decision 2009/917, OJ 2009, L-323/20.

[120] Compare Chap. C II 2 a.

respective database should always have a concrete purpose and could be subject to conditions formulated similar to the following wording: Access should (a) be necessary for the purpose of the prevention, detection or investigation of terrorist offences or other serious criminal offences corresponding to the respective mandate of the assessing actor; (b) access for consultation should be necessary in a specific case, (c) there should be reasonable grounds to consider that consultation of the data will substantially contribute to the prevention, detection or investigation of any of the criminal offences in question, (d) there is a reasoned written or electronic request to the respective database justifying the reasons for access, in case that the grounds for access differ from the purpose of the collection of the requested data and, (e) any use of the data which does not comply with the mentioned rules shall be considered a misuse under the laws of the accessing actor.

To guarantee transparency in AFSJ data processing, the list of accessing actors, specifying the purpose for which the respective authorities may process the data in each of the AFSJ databases, should be communicated to the European Parliament, the Commission as well as the Council and should be regularly updated and published in the Official Journal. The current non-disclosure of such lists[121] hinders that individuals concerned are able to understand which national authority or EU actor actually processes their data. The knowledge remains in the hands of the respective actor (or of the Commission, if the list is sent to it) which leads to an unnecessary "secret-mongering", in particular when taking into account that the existence of the accessing law enforcement agencies is, in general, public knowledge. Few exceptions to the proposed publishing duty could be made, although as a minimum requirement the Member States should at least describe the field of action of the accessing agency.

In addition to the reinforcement of the rights of the individuals and the transparency effect, this list would also contribute to the framing of the definitions of the possibly accessing actors. As illustrated in the cases of the VIS, the actors allowed to access are often defined in a wide-ranging manner.[122]A public list would therefore facilitate the identification of the actors while additionally allowing for an enhanced control of those actors at national as well as at EU level.

5. *Improving the Protection of Victims, Witnesses and Persons Whose Data are Pre-Emptively Entered in Security Related Databases*

The introduction of clear and understandable rules on the protection of data of vulnerable persons such as victims and witnesses (Europol, Eurojust, SIS (II)), but

[121] All AFSJ actors keep the list of accessing actors secret, apart from the list provided for in the Eurodac Proposal (Article 21 (2) Eurodac Proposal, COM(2010) 555 of 11 October 2010).

[122] Compare Chap. B III 2 c.

also of persons whose data are entered pre-emptively based on factual indications to believe that a person will commit a criminal offence[123] would counteract indiscriminate data storing not tolerated by the ECtHR.[124] The current indistinctive storing should be replaced by an improved protection of these special categories of data

Protection of victims' or witnesses' data and data of possible criminals could be exercised at different levels:

- First, in addition to the aforementioned access conditions, as far as data of victims, witnesses and possible criminals[125] are concerned, a step-by-step approach when accessing the data could be applied. In a first step, access should be permitted to only a few restrictive data, such as names or date of birth, later, if the search with the (restricted) criteria reveals a hit, further information could be provided in a second step.
- Second, the protection of such data should also take place within the data processing systems in the way that those data are marked and remain connected to the purpose of collection[126] underlying the two-step access possibilities mentioned above, hindering sprawling access by various actors. When data of victims or witnesses are interlinked with other personal data (SIS II), particular supervision is needed which must assure that the status of the person concerned will not be negatively influenced by the linking. As far as the linking is not related to ongoing investigations, the person concerned should be notified about the changes in its status (e.g. persons to be refused entry + witness in an illegal immigration case[127]).
- Third, a general interdiction against the transfer of such data to third parties should be introduced. Only if it seems absolutely necessary to prevent an immediate danger or threat, an exception could be made and the data would be transmitted under the following condition: the data should always be marked and remain generally connected to the purpose of collection or, in a very specific case underlying the control (or in urgent cases the a posteriori control) of the supervisory body, to the purpose of transfer.
- Fourth, if data of victims, witnesses or possible criminals are planned to be processed in one of the information systems of the AFSJ actors, such as in

---

[123] Article 12 (1) lit. b Council Decision of 6 April 2009 establishing the European Police Office, OJ 2009, L-121/37.

[124] See for instance *S. and Marper v. the United Kingdom*, Application nos. 30562/04 and 30566/04, judgment of 4 December 2008, para 119 and principle 2.1. of Recommendation R (87) 15.

[125] Article 12 (1) lit. b Council Decision of 6 April 2009 establishing the European Police Office, OJ 2009, L-121/37.

[126] *Weber and Saravia v. Germany*, Application no. 54934/00, admissibility decision of 29 June 2006, para 121.

[127] Council document no. 12537/3/04 on the SIS II functions of 30 November 2004, p. 3.

the CMS of Eurojust,[128] the supervisory body should be informed in any case and must in doubtful cases approve this inclusion.

6. *Individual Rights*

The possibility of individuals requesting access to an AFSJ database to a common AFSJ supervisory body in order to verify their data should become the general rule. The need for, the added value of and the possible tasks of this supervisory body were analysed in Sect. IV.

In case the data have been introduced by a Member State (and exclusively belong to this Member State), the common supervisory body would be obliged to make contact with the respective national DPA. The access to data created by an AFSJ actor (e.g. Europol) would be exercised by the EU central AFSJ supervisory authority. Today's delegation of the access procedure to the Member States would in this way be improved by creating a transparent and central access point where the individual simply needs to contact one responsible actor which then supports the individual in exercising its rights.

In addition, the reasons to deny access could be unified (e.g. access can be denied when the access may jeopardise the fulfilment of the AFSJ actors' tasks, a national investigation or the rights and freedoms of third parties[129]) and their application should in any case be open to external supervision. The internal DPO should be informed about each access request and involved in the decision whether access is to be granted or not. If access is denied, appeal should be possible to the common AFSJ supervisory authority which then should have the possibility to get access to the respective documents justifying the refusal. A time-limit (of for instance 3 months) to reply to an access request would support the practical enforcement of the access right.

Although the provisions providing for the correction, blocking and deletion in case the data are incorrect or incomplete or the storage contravenes the legal basis of the AFSJ actor, seem to be already the standard in the AFSJ, they could also be unified, including a provision regulating the notification of the requesting persons after having carried out the requested changes. When communicating with the individual, each contact should enclose a letter explaining how the person concerned could exercise its rights to appeal.

As in the Eurodac proposal, if a Member State does not agree that the data stored in its database are factually incorrect or unlawfully recorded, the Member State concerned should be obliged to explain to the individual, within a certain delay, the reasons for its decision including information explaining the steps to be taken if the

[128] Article 17 (2) rules of procedure on the processing and the protection of personal data at Eurojust, OJ 2005, C-68/1.

[129] Article 19 (4) Eurojust Decision.

person concerned does not accept the explanation given (how to bring a complaint before court, financial or other assistance provided etc.).[130] The national DPA shall assist in this process and cooperate when necessary with DPAs of other Member States.[131]

An obligation comparable to Article 111 (2) of the Schengen Convention which requires the accessing actors to mutually enforce a final decision relating to the correction, deletion, the right to information or compensation, could be introduced to generally enforce the decision often taken in only one Member State or by only one AFSJ actor.

7. *Notification*

A right of information of the data subject including information on the purpose of processing, the identity of the data controller, any possible recipients of the data, including any EU actors as well as the authorities of the Member States, the existence of their right to access and the right to request rectification or deletion of their data, as well as of the right to receive information on the procedures for exercising those rights, the duration of the retention period, the possibility to obtain assistance from the DPA including the contact details of the national DPA responsible for hearing their claims, the existence of the right to request a review or appeal of the decision taken to the detriment of the individual (e.g. the issue of an alert in the SIS II) and even further information would bring the AFSJ in line with Directive 95/56 as well as recent ECtHR developments.[132]

This right should be generally exercised on the initiative of the actor at the moment of collection of the data from the data subject, when receiving data from a third party, when recording the personal data or if general disclosure or disclosure to a third party are envisaged and/or as soon as the purpose of the processing, national investigations and prosecutions and the rights and freedoms of third parties are no longer likely to be jeopardised.[133] Exceptions such as that the information must not be provided if this would "involve a disproportionate effort"[134] (SIS II) should be replaced by one simple rule that notification could be withheld only in case that police (or judicial) activities are to be prejudiced.

Moreover, such information should constitute a specific aspect of the respective procedure and should not be given orally or with a huge amount of other

---

[130] Article 18 (6) Eurodac Regulation, OJ 2000, L-316/1.

[131] Ibid, Article 18 (9) and (10).

[132] *Weber and Saravia v. Germany*, Application no. 54934/00, admissibility decision of 29 June 2006, para 135.

[133] Similar to Article 8 rules of procedure on the processing and the protection of personal data at Eurojust, OJ 2005, C-68/1.

[134] Article 42 (2) (a) (ii) Regulation 1987/2006.

information referring to different and possibly complicated procedures (such as the asylum procedure in the Eurodac system).

Notification to the responsible national DPA in case of a personal data breach as provided for by the e-Privacy Directive[135] with regard to providers could be additionally considered in a law enforcement context, although such a notification would be based on the same specific requirements mentioned above.

8. *Control of Data Recording and Binding Security Rules*

A coherent catalogue of data security rules (such as in the VIS[136]), including a provision according to which it is possible to verify what data elements have been entered and retrieved from the databases, when, by whom and for what purpose, should be obligatory for each of the AFSJ actors when processing personal data. The transferred data must always be marked and transmission to other AFSJ actors must always be recorded in minutes.[137] The introduction of such rules should never depend on the decision of the actor concerned, as it is the case at Europol.[138] The admissibility of entering, searching or retrieving the data should be randomly and regularly checked by the supervisory body.

Instead of relying on ex-post verifications, an active strategy should be applied. One improvement would be the use of technological possibilities which allow for the control of abuses within the systems (who has accessed and when etc.) to improve the internal data processing directly within the systems. In this context, the EDPS refers to the so called "privacy by design" approach which means that privacy and data protection are embedded in the design of information and communication technologies throughout the entire life circle of technologies, from the early design stage to their deployment, use and ultimate disposal.[139] Privacy and data protection should be implemented within the design and the development of technology and in this way directly embedded in the systems. This approach would improve both the trust in the systems and the technological control mechanisms.

---

[135] Article 4 (3) of Directive 2009/136/EC of the European Parliament and of the Council of 25 November 2009 amending Directive 2002/22/EC on universal service and users' rights relating to electronic communications networks and services, Directive 2002/58/EC concerning the processing of personal data and the protection of privacy in the electronic communications sector and Regulation (EC) No 2006/2004 on cooperation between national authorities responsible for the enforcement of consumer protection laws, OJ 2009, L-337/11.

[136] Compare Article 32 and 34 VIS Regulation 767/2008, OJ 2008, L-218/60.

[137] Compare *Weber and Saravia v. Germany*, Application no. 54934/00, admissibility decision of 29 June 2006, paras 121 and 127.

[138] Article 35 (1) Council Decision of 6 April 2009 establishing the European Police Office, OJ 2009, L-121/37.

[139] Opinion of the EDPS on Promoting Trust in the Information Society by Fostering Data Protection and Privacy of 18 March 2010, paras 16–30.

9. Improving the Protection and the Transparency of Information Originating from Private Parties or Third States

Unified standards for the processing of information stemming from private parties, including the limitation of the use of data only in specific cases which must be based on an initial suspicion, are essential to balance the serious interference with the purpose limitation principle. As the data protection responsibility for such data lies with the AFSJ actor (e.g. Europol[140]), the internal supervision should be considerably reinforced. Additionally, to assure that the use of information from private parties remains exceptional, the access criteria with regard to the law enforcement access to data of private actors developed in the next section,[141] could be applied.

The accuracy of data originating from third states not fulfilling the adequacy requirement or from private parties or third states with which the respective AFSJ actors has no cooperation agreement, should be carefully examined, marked and particularly supervised.

Transparency in this rather clandestine field of law enforcement work would be improved if the amount of data exchanges having taken place with third parties or private parties would be annually published by the respective AFSJ actor. Currently, information about this nevertheless sensitive field of data processing is difficult to obtain.[142]

10. Common Rules on the Relations to Third Parties

Harmonised criteria for the exchange of personal data amongst EU AFSJ actors (compare Sect. V 4) as well as with third states should be considered.[143] Formulations such as that of the CIS Decision 2009/917 that data may be transferred to national authorities, to third countries and to international and regional

[140] See Chap. B II 1 f.

[141] Section VI 5.

[142] As such information is not included in the annual reports of the AFSJ actors, in some cases, information can be found the in the publications of the House of Lords.

[143] Discussion about a long-term general data exchange agreement between the EU and the US are currently taking place, see Report by the High Level Contact Group (HLCG) on information sharing and privacy and data protection, Council doc. 15815/09 of 23 November 2009 and Proposal for a Council Recommendation to authorise the opening of negotiations for an agreement between the European Union and the United States of America on protection of personal when transferred and processed for the purpose of preventing, investigating, detecting or prosecuting criminal offences, including terrorism, in the framework of police cooperation and judicial cooperation in criminal matters, COM(2010) 252, accessible at: http://www.statewatch.org/news/2010/aug/eu-usa-dp-general-em.pdf (accessed February 2011).

organisations "wishing to make use of them"[144] neither comply with an adequate and restrictive use of the collected data, nor with the purpose limitation principle. A list of basic data protection requirements which have to be fulfilled in any agreement concluded with third states should be developed. Such basic rules could for instance refer to the interdiction of the use of the transferred data in other than the agreed databases or the fixing of concrete time-limits to use the data.

Exceptional data exchange in absence of an exchange agreement could be allowed in urgent cases under the condition that the internal DPO is informed as soon as possible about the exceptional transfer.

Ad-hoc transmission to third states in absence of an exchange agreement should be limited to very exceptional cases and only with the sole aim of taking urgent measures to counter an imminent serious danger threatening a person or public security.[145]As in the case of Eurojust,[146] an undertaking obliging the recipient to use the data only for the agreed purpose of transmission should be concluded before the transfer. In any case, if such exceptional data transfer is carried out, the respective supervisory authority should be informed about the transfer and should have the right to prevent further transfers when minimum data protection requirements are not complied with.

11. Managing the Time-Limits

Considering the current rules on a time-limit of the storing of data in law enforcement databases, for instance at Europol or Eurojust, a coherent rule requiring the deletion of the data when particular circumstances are fulfilled, would better comply with the ECtHR jurisdiction demanding a certain time-limit. Formulations such as the storage period could be extended in order to enable the respective actor to "achieve its objectives"[147] or when it has "further interest"[148] in them, could be replaced by formulations less open to interpretation, such as: the storing may be extended when the data are used for ongoing investigations or ongoing analyses. In any case, the supervisory body should be informed about and involved in cases when the original data storage period is extended (beyond the initially provided one).

In case the data are received from a database providing a strict time-limit (e.g. 5 years in the VIS), any extension of the original time-limit in the new

[144] Article 8 (4) CIS Council Decision 2009/917, OJ 2009, L-323/20.

[145] Compare Article 26a (9) Eurojust Decision.

[146] Ibid, Article 26a (9).

[147] Ibid, Article 21 (3)(b).

[148] Article 20 (3) Council Decision of 6 April 2009 establishing the European Police Office, OJ 2009, L-121/37.

database should be subject to the approval of the supervisory body of both, the accessing actor as well as of the database providing the data.

12. Dual Control: Introducing an Internal DPO

The introduction of an internal DPO already provided for within Europol and Eurojust should become a general requirement when dealing with personal data in an AFSJ database (for instance in the Frontex proposal). While the function of an internal DPO needs to be accompanied by rules relating to its complete independence from the respective actor (financially as well as regarding the performance of its tasks), an internal DPO could ensure the compliance with the relevant legal basis of the AFSJ actor as well as the lawfulness of processing within the AFSJ database. Its introduction would assure a double control of AFSJ data processing: on the one hand at the external level through the common supervisory body and on the other at the internal level through the internal DPO completing the protection exercised externally. Close cooperation and regular meetings between both bodies (including the relevant national DPAs) would further contribute to a comprehensive and effective control of AFSJ data processing. Besides the guarantees already contained in the Europol and Eurojust Decisions, the internal DPO should be additionally equipped with the right to publish its inspection report and to directly contact the common supervisory body if it considers it necessary. It should be further involved in all cases in which an individual requests access to its data.

13. Improving the Decision Making and Introducing Sunset and Review Provisions

Examples such as the delayed implementation of the SIS II instruments underline the necessity to improve the decision making procedure prior to the adoption of new instruments. The early involvement of the actors concerned, including Member States, technical experts, persons concerned etc., would avoid the difficulties currently arising in the framework of the practical enforcement of the SIS II. The internal communication with the Member States and representatives of the persons concerned needs to be strengthened in this regard. Intensive reflections on the proposals to be implemented, including the evaluation of measures already having taken place at Member States level, are required before the adoption of instruments. The evaluation should not only take place *ex post*.

Existing procedures for EU internal decision making could be used to reinforce accountability and transparency. One solution could be the improvement of the decision making process during impact assessments. Impact assessments which provide for the participation of all actors involved would certainly lead to a more rational and reasoned decision. Further, the outcomes of evaluations and impact assessments should not be restricted to the positive results of the assessment. Only the publication (and inclusion in the impact assessments) of possible negative outcomes of evaluations guarantee the acceptance of new measures potentially interfering with fundamental rights. During the assessment process, the role of data protection needs to be improved to assure the respect of this right in future proposals. The role of the EDPS, national DPAs and even the internal EU DPOs in the decision making process during impact assessments and evaluations should therefore be reinforced.

The obligation to introduce sunset and review provisions would additionally improve the need to assess and evaluate already existing systems. One advantage of such clauses is clearly that decisions which were enacted in response to events such as 9/11, the Madrid or the London bombings and which tend to base rather on political reactions than on legal requirements, are reviewed after a certain period of time. Assessments which are made in moments of panic and which might appear reasonable in a specific situation may prove less useful in practice than initially assumed (e.g. SIS II). Another important benefit from a data protection point of view is that measures implemented in critical moments would be reconsidered in a less politically charged atmosphere.

VI. Towards Harmonised Data Protection Principles for Intra-AFSJ Information Exchange

The growing tendency to exchange data between the different AFSJ actors makes it relevant to embed safeguards governing this transfer to compensate for the increased risks caused by the exchange of data. Indeed, as the AFSJ still is a mix of former public international law and intergovernmental structures as well as of supranational EU structures, the data processing and protection framework is necessarily not entirely harmonised. However, the cooperation and the personal data transfer between the analysed systems already goes far beyond the former limited (legal) possibilities. So far, due to the "tendency to agree new functions before deciding the legal or technical limitations required",[149] data protection rights could not keep up with the steady extension of the possibilities to exchange data among the AFSJ actors. In some cases, the legal instruments allowing for data exchange have a low level of individual rights protection. In others, data exchange is entirely carried out without a legal basis (Eurojust-CIS). The definitions of the offences, being the reason for law enforcement data exchange after all, vary with every transfer. The need for a coherent and general legal instrument on the exchange of personal data between AFSJ actors respecting the data protection

[149] Garside (2006).

rights of the persons concerned is obvious and should be urgently developed to better comply with fundamental rights in the AFSJ.

The first essential criterion, following from the respect of the rule of law, is, however, first and foremost, a clear legal basis to allow for security-related data transfer.[150] This legal basis should take into account the case whether or not the purpose of collection of the data differs from the purpose of access. Several provisions of Council Decision 2008/633 allowing national law enforcement authorities and Europol to access the VIS data[151] have an exemplary function and might serve as an example on what such an instrument would look like. A harmonised AFSJ instrument could replace the different solutions chosen so far. Its provisions might include rules on the access of domestic law enforcement authorities to European databases serving a different purpose than law enforcement (considered in the following), but can also be limited to EU-internal AFSJ information exchange. When developing a single instrument harmonising the AFSJ data exchange, the following reflections not yet recognized in the security-related personal data exchange between AFSJ actors could be considered:

1. Restricting the Purpose of Transfer

As a basic requirement following from the respect of the rule of law, the legal basis should always lay down the conditions under which the respective European actor or Member States may obtain access for consultation of the respective database. To prevent unclear processing purposes, the purpose of access to another database should be limited to the prevention, detection and investigation of terrorist offences and serious criminal offences subject to the mandate of the accessing actors. To avoid unilateral and possible far reaching changes, eventual amendments to the mandate of the accessing actor after the adoption of the access decision should not be covered by the instrument.

2. Defining Unclear Legal Terms

Avoiding ambiguous terms is not only an essential requirement which should play a role in the discussion about a harmonised AFSJ data protection standard, but it should also be an important goal of an instrument regulating information exchange

[150] Examples of data exchange in absence of a legal basis was Eurojust's data transfer in JITs or Eurojust's access to the CIS.

[151] Article 5 Council Decision 2008/633, OJ 2008, L-218/129.

in the AFSJ.[152] For this purpose the databases of the respective actors in which the transferred data could be possibly introduced as well as the databases allowed to be accessed should be undoubtedly defined. This definition should not only relate for instance to the general description of AFSJ actors' databases, but should include specifications referring to the exact databases (EIS, analysis work files) in which the data could be entered or from which the data could be retrieved (e.g. exact description of the SIS II databases).

Moreover, essential terms repeatedly used in AFSJ's legal bases and information exchange instruments, such as "terrorist offences", "serious criminal offences" and above all, "prevention of crime" are to be explained and defined in a harmonised way in order to avoid legal uncertainty. Whereby the definition of the first two terms (terrorist and serious criminal offences) could correspond to the offences under national law which correspond or are equivalent to the offences in Articles 1 to 4 of Council Framework Decision 2002/475/JHA of 13 June 2002 on combating terrorism[153] and to the forms of crime which correspond or are equivalent to those referred to in Article 2 (2) of Framework Decision 2002/584/JHA,[154] a definition of "prevention of crime" should follow the criteria developed above in Sect. III 1 b. Similar to these principles, the term "prevention of crime" could for instance describe a situation in which criteria based on a verifiable prognosis, open to scrutiny by an external supervisor, suggest that somebody plans to commit a crime. Factual indications, which exclude individual assumptions or pure hypothetical reflections, should underpin this estimation.

Additionally, as far as the definitions of the respective legal basis of the exchanging actors do not contradict the definitions in the instrument, they should also apply. Combined with a reference to the definitions of Article 2 (a)–(g) of Directive 95/46/EC,[155] the current situation in which unclear legal terms challenge the understanding of the enforcement powers of the respective actors could be essentially improved.

[152] To the requirement to define terms such as "serious crime" in a legal act, compare ECtHR case law *Kennedy v. the United Kingdom*, Application no. 26839/05, judgment of 18 May 2010, para 159, discussed in Chap. A II 1 d aa (3).

[153] Council Framework Decision 2002/475/JHA of 13 June 2002 on combating terrorism, OJ 2002, L-164/3.

[154] Council Framework Decision 2002/584/JHA of 13 June 2002 on the European arrest warrant and the surrender procedures between Member States - Statements made by certain Member States on the adoption of the Framework Decision, OJ 2001, L-190/1.

[155] Article 2 (a)-(g) Directive 95/46/EC includes definitions on personal data, processing of personal data, controller, processor etc.

3. *Designating the Accessing Actors and Authorities*

To guarantee transparency in the AFSJ data exchange and to comply with ECtHR requirements demanding "explicit and detailed provisions" relating to the information which may be handed out and to "the authorities to which information may be communicated",[156] the authorities which are authorised to access the data of the respective database must be clearly defined. Member States as well as the European AFSJ actors should keep a list of the designated authorities or units. Member States as well as European actors should notify in a declaration to the European Parliament, the Commission and the General Secretariat of the Council their designated authorities or units and may twice a year amend or replace this declaration by updated declaration.[157] The list and the declarations, including possible amendments to it, could be published by the Commission in the Official Journal of the European Union. At the national level, each Member State should be obliged to keep a list of the (operating) units within the designated authorities that are authorised to access the respective database. To further strengthen the internal handling and security of the data and to guarantee that only persons authorised to consult the files[158] access the personal data, only duly empowered staff of a special unit which received special training in the handling of personal data of the accessing actor as well as the respective database should be authorised to access the respective database.

4. *Harmonising the Access Procedure*

Harmonising the access procedure with regard to data included in another database could be a further important development towards a coordinated approach to AFSJ data exchange.

Prior to accessing a database, a reasoned written or electronic request to the respective database should be submitted by the aforementioned special units of the AFSJ actor. Upon receipt of a request for access, duly empowered staff of the special unit within the respective database should verify whether the conditions for access are fulfilled. If all conditions for access are fulfilled, transmission of the requested data to the accessing actor should be carried out by the special unit of the database in such a way as not to compromise the security of the data.[159]

Alternatively, in exceptional cases of urgency, the special unit within the respective database may receive written, electronic or oral requests. In such

---

[156] *Leander v. Sweden*, Application no. 9248/81, judgment of 26 March 1987, para 55.

[157] Similar to Article 3 (2) Council Decision 2008/633, OJ 2008, L-218/129.

[158] *Rotaru v. Romania*, Application no. 28341/954, judgment of 4 May 2000, para 57.

[159] Similar to Article 4 Council Decision 2008/633, OJ 2008, L-218/129.

cases, it shall process the request immediately and only verify *ex-post* whether all access conditions are fulfilled, including whether an exceptional case of urgency existed.[160] Such an exceptional case should be immediately reported to the supervisory authority of the respective database. The *ex-post* verification shall take place without undue delay after the processing of the request.[161]

5. *Coordinating the Access Conditions*

Access for consultation of the respective database by the designated authorities and the respective EU actors should only take place within the scope and the limits of their powers and only if certain conditions applying in every AFSJ data exchange and respecting the rights of individuals are met.

In view of the increasing data exchange, the access for mutual consultation between the AFSJ actors should be also always restricted to the necessity of the access in a specific case for the purpose of the prevention, detection or investigation of terrorist offences or serious criminal offences clearly defined in the decision. Reasonable grounds to consider that the consultation of the data will substantially contribute to the prevention, detection or investigation of any of the criminal offences in question should be an additional access condition. Further, to assure that interferences with the purpose limitation principles remain exceptional, in case that the grounds for access differ from the purpose of the collection of the requested data, a reasoned written or electronic request to the respective database justifying the reasons for access, should be required. In that case, upon receipt of a request for such processing, duly empowered staff of the special unit within the respective database should verify whether the conditions for processing for purposes different from the purpose of collection are fulfilled.[162]

Similar to the conditions of Council Decision 2008/633 allowing national law enforcement authorities and Europol to access the VIS data,[163] consultation of the

---

[160] Compare the similar wording of Article 4 Council Decision 2008/633, OJ 2008, L-218/129.

[161] Similar to Article 4 Council Decision 2008/633, OJ 2008, L-218/129.

[162] To assure transparency and to specify the conditions for Europol, some specifications could additionally apply; Europol's access could be for instance necessary for the purpose of a specific analysis in a specific case referred to in Article 14 Europol Decision or for an analysis of a general nature and of a strategic type, as referred to in Article 14 (4) of the Europol Decision, provided that the data is rendered anonymous by Europol prior to such processing and retained in a form in which identification of the data subjects is no longer possible; data obtained by Europol could be further prevented from being introduced in Europol's Information System, exemptions to this rule should require the consent of Europol's supervisory body; possible additional conditions for Eurojust could also relate to the restriction not to introduce data obtained in Eurojust's Case Management System whereby exemptions to this rule should require the consent of Eurojust's supervisory body.

[163] Compare Article 4 (2) Council Decision 2008/633, OJ 2008, L-218/129.

respective database should underlie a two step access: in a first step, access could be limited to searching with a limited amount of data in the particular file depending on the respective database and including only a selection of the data actually stored in the relevant database, such as for instance: surname, surname at birth (former surname(s)), sex, date, place and country of birth, residence, fingerprints etc. Only in the event of a hit, consultation of the relevant database should give full access to all of the data included in the database (such as any other data taken from the respective file, photographs etc.).

6. *Data Protection and Data Security Rules*

With regard to the level of data protection and in absence of an overall approach to law enforcement and judicial data protection rules, the processing of personal data consulted should be at least equivalent to the level of protection resulting from the Council of Europe Convention of 28 January 1981 for the Protection of Individuals with regard to Automatic Processing of Personal Data as well as to the level of protection offered by the Recommendation R (87) 15 of 17 September 1987 of the Committee of Ministers of the Council of Europe Regulating the Use of Personal Data in the Police Sector, and for those Member States which have ratified it, to the Additional Protocol of 8 November 2001 to that Convention. The provisions of the FDPJ should be additionally applicable.

The processing of personal data by the accessing actor should in any case be in accordance with the legal basis of the accessing actor and the rules adopted in implementation thereof and supervised by the supervisory body of the accessing actor (and/or by the common supervisory body, proposed in Sect. IV). In absence of one single AFSJ supervisory system, personal data originally underlying the supervision of another authority must at any stage of the processing be accessible to this authority.

Special attention needs to be paid to the current violation of the purpose limitation principle in cases in which data collected for purposes outside of crime prevention are later used for law enforcement purposes. Enforcing and strictly applying the purpose limitation principle by introducing a general rule applicable to each AFSJ data exchange whereupon personal data obtained from the respective database shall only be processed for the specific purpose of the collection would counteract this worrying development. If, in exceptional cases, the purpose of collection differs from the purpose of the transfer, this purpose has to be evaluated by the duly empowered staff of the special unit within the respective database mentioned above. Particular attention thereby has to be paid to the question whether the change in the purpose is justified by evidence that indicates that the data in question substantially contribute to the prevention, detection or investigation of the criminal offences in question and that the change in the purpose is proportional in its means.

To counteract the currently unresolved problem of continually extending time-limits, any extension to the time-limit originally applicable to the obtained data by the accessing actor should be subject to the approval of the common supervisory body or the supervisory bodies of both, the accessing actor as well as of the accessed database.

Before being authorised to process data stored in the database, the staff of the authorities having a right to access the database should receive appropriate training about data security and data protection rules including being informed of any relevant criminal offences and penalties.

Finally, the list laying down the data security measures of Council Decision 2008/633 allowing national law enforcement authorities and Europol to access the VIS data[164] regulates in detail the necessary security requirements which the Member States have to apply. This list could serve as an example for similar provisions in every AFSJ data exchange. To guarantee a harmonised standard and to prevent provisions such as in the Europol legal basis which make the establishment of data security rules dependent on unconvincing criteria,[165] its provisions should in any case be extended to all AFSJ actors.

7. *Follow-Up of the Transferred Data*

Harmonising the criteria for the transfer of data obtained from another database to third states would contribute to an increased legal certainty in a currently rather unregulated area.[166] The transfer of such data could be subjected to the following conditions:

- In case that the purpose of collection of the data differed from the purpose of access, such personal data obtained from the database should not be transferred or made available to a third country or to an international organisation. However, in an exceptional case of urgency such data might be transferred or made available to a third country or an international organisation, if the third country or international organisation concerned ensures an adequate level of protection according to Article 25 of Directive 95/46 for the intended data processing, exclusively for the purposes of the prevention and detection of terrorist offences

---

[164] Article 9 (2) Council Decision 2008/633, OJ 2008, L-218/129.

[165] Compare Chap. B II 1 d cc.

[166] Europol is the only body providing for certain basic rules in cases of third party transfer, compare Council Decision 2009/934/JHA of 30 November 2009 adopting the implementing rules governing Europol's relations with partners, including the exchange of personal and classified information, OJ 2009, L-325/6.

and of serious criminal offences and under the access conditions set out in the exchange decision, subject to the consent of the Member State having entered the data into the database and in accordance with the national law of the Member State transferring the data or making them available. An exceptional case of urgency could exist when there is a sufficiently evidenced concrete danger to the life, limb or freedom of a person, to the security of the EU, the third country or the international organisation concerned.

- In case that the purpose of collection of the data corresponded to the purpose of access, such personal data obtained from the database could be transferred or made available to a third country or to an international organisation under the conditions of an agreement concluded with the third state assuring an adequate level of protection in the sense of Article 25 of Directive 95/46 for the intended data processing, exclusively for the purposes of the prevention and detection of terrorist offences and of serious criminal offences and under the access conditions set out above, subject to the consent of the Member State having entered the data into the database and in accordance with the national law of the Member State transferring the data or making them available. Ad-hoc transmission to third states in absence of an exchange agreement should be limited to very exceptional cases and only with the sole aim of taking urgent measures to counter imminent serious danger threatening a person or public security. An undertaking obliging the recipient to use the data only for the agreed purpose of transmission should be concluded before the transfer. In any case, if ad-hoc data transfer is carried out, the supervisory authority of the transferring actor needs to be informed about the transfer and has the right to prevent further transfers when it comes to the conclusion that the data protection requirements are repeatedly not complied with.
- In both cases the respective EU actor and, in accordance with national law, Member States should ensure that records are kept of such transfers and make them available to national data protection authorities upon request. In addition, rules restricting the onward transfer of the already transmitted data are equally important to limit the risks arising out of the extension of the circle of recipients. The conditions relating to onward transfer entailed in the implementing rules governing Europol's relations with partners,[167] could thereby have exemplary function. Above all, the provisions which oblige the recipient to give an undertaking (relating to an obligation to delete incorrect or outdated data, to delete data in case they are no longer necessary for the purpose of the transfer, to ask the transferring actor for consent before further transferring received data etc.) to guarantee certain basic data protection rights, should serve as an example in the whole area of AFSJ related data exchange.

[167] Council Decision 2009/934/JHA of 30 November 2009 adopting the implementing rules governing Europol's relations with partners, including the exchange of personal and classified information, OJ 2009, L-325/6.

8. *Cooperation Between Data Protection Authorities*

To ensure the practical enforcement of data protection rights, the national supervisory authorities, the supervisory authority of the database and the supervisory authority of the accessing actor, should closely cooperate in contributing to a coordinated supervision of the transfer from the database to the respective European actor.

The national DPAs monitoring the lawfulness of the processing of personal data pursuant to this decision should regularly carry out an audit of the processing of personal data. For this purpose Member States and the respective AFSJ actor should allow the competent bodies to obtain the necessary information to enable them to carry out their tasks.

The cooperation between national and European DPAs should include the exchange of relevant information, the assistance of each other in carrying out audits and inspections or the examination of difficulties of interpretation or application of the decision regulating the data exchange. Studying problems with the exercise of independent supervision or with the exercise of the rights of data subjects and supporting each other in cases where individuals exercise their right of access, correction, deletion and notification or drawing up harmonised proposals for joint solutions to any problems including the promotion of awareness of data protection rights would complement the cooperation. For this purpose, regular meetings resulting in an annual joint report should take place. This joint activity report should be sent to the European Parliament, the Council, the Commission and the supervisory authority managing the database and include a chapter of each Member State prepared by the national supervisory authority of that Member State containing an assessment of the cases where individuals exercised their right of access, correction, deletion and notification.

9. *Penalties in Case of Misuse*

A provision providing for penalties in form of administrative and/or criminal penalties that are effective, proportionate and dissuasive in case that the data are used contrary to the rules of the decision regulating the transfer, would considerably contribute to an effective enforcement of the data protection rules included in the decision.

10. *Access Right, Correction, Deletion and Notification*

The right of persons to have access to data relating to them and transferred to another database should follow the general access rules illustrated above.[168] If a

[168] Compare Sect. VI 5.

person invokes its right directly at the AFSJ database or in a Member State other than the Member State responsible or at the accessing actor, the supervisory body receiving the request should immediately contact the responsible authority of the Member State concerned within a limited period of days and should provide the person concerned with the necessary information.

Transparency and a clear definition of the circumstances and limits of the storing require that information about the transfer of the data to another database is to be provided to the person concerned by the accessing actor or the Member States entering the data at the time of the transfer or as soon as notification can be carried out without jeopardising the purpose of the transfer. The protection of data of persons which were entered in the database due to the person's incidental link to the actual targeted person (e.g. victims, witnesses, person issuing an invitation and/or liable to pay the applicant's subsistence costs during the stay etc.), could be improved when introducing a general information requirement in case their data are transferred. This notification should include the general information criteria mentioned above[169] embracing additional information on the identity of the actor receiving the data together with its contact details, the purposes for which the data will be processed at the actor receiving the data, the categories of recipients of the data, including the possible third parties, information on changes concerning the data retention period as well as information on the necessity and the purpose of the transfer.

Any person should have the right to request that data relating to him which are inaccurate be corrected and that data unlawfully stored data be deleted.

In case a person concerned exercises its right to challenge the accuracy of its data, the AFSJ actor or the Member State responsible should be obliged to check the accuracy of the data and the lawfulness of their processing in the database within a limited period. To prevent that the incorrect data obtained from a database are again transferred to possible third parties, the AFSJ actor should, upon receiving such a request or if it has any other evidence to suggest that data processed in the database are inaccurate, immediately inform the authority of the Member State which has entered the data in the database, which shall check the data concerned and, if necessary, correct or delete them immediately. Similar to Article 14 (5) Council Decision 2008/633 allowing national law enforcement authorities and Europol to access the VIS data,[170] the Member State or the AFSJ actor responsible shall confirm in writing to the person concerned without delay that it has taken action to correct or delete data relating to it. A duty to explain in writing to the person concerned without delay why the AFSJ actor or the Member State responsible is not prepared to correct or delete data relating to him if the AFSJ actor or the Member State does not agree that data recorded in the database are inaccurate or have been recorded unlawfully, would additionally improve the practical implementation of the correction or deletion right. This information should contain an explanation of

[169] Compare Sect. V 7.

[170] Council Decision 2008/633, OJ 2008, L-218/129.

the steps which the requesting person can take if he does not accept the explanation provided including information on how to bring an action or a complaint before the competent authorities or courts and on any assistance that is available.[171] Moreover, a follow-up given to the exercise of the rights of correction and deletion should be carried out as soon as possible by the responsible supervisory body.[172]

11. Keeping of Records

To facilitate the monitoring and evaluation tasks of the supervisory authorities, an *ex-post* control of the admissibility of all data processing operations resulting from access to the database for consultation should be introduced. All access requests should be recorded for the purposes of checking whether the search was admissible or not, for the purpose of monitoring the lawfulness of data processing, for self-monitoring, ensuring the proper functioning of the system as well as for checking the data integrity and security.[173] Such records must be based on the necessary security requirements and should be deleted after the retention period of the data has expired. Comparable to Article 16 (1) of Council Decision 2008/633 allowing national law enforcement authorities and Europol to access the VIS data, those records could show:

- The exact purpose of the access for consultation, including the form of terrorist offence or other serious criminal offence concerned;
- The respective file reference;
- The date and exact time of access;
- Where applicable that use has been made of the urgent access procedure;
- The data used for consultation;
- The type of data consulted;
- According to the rules of the respective AFSJ actor or to national rules, the identifying mark of the official who carried out the search and of the official who ordered the search or supply.

12. Implementing Effective Monitoring and Evaluation

Effective monitoring and evaluation mechanisms contribute to an improved control of the effectiveness and the necessity in terms of output, security and quality of service of the access to other databases.[174] Consequently, the respective

[171] Compare Article 18 (6) Eurodac Regulation, OJ 2000, L-316/1.

[172] Compare Article 14 (7) Council Decision 2008/633, OJ 2008, L-218/129.

[173] Compare Article 16 Council Decision 2008/633, OJ 2008, L-218/129.

[174] Compare Article 17 (1) Council Decision 2008/633, OJ 2008, L-218/129.

supervisory authorities in cooperation with the respective AFSJ actor should carry out checks and submit a report to the European Parliament, the Council and the Commission on the technical functioning, the need and the use of the access possibilities of the respective database.[175] Exceptional cases of urgency should be documented and an overall "evaluation of the application and the results achieved against the objectives and an assessment of the continuing validity of the underlying rationale" behind the access as well as the impact on fundamental rights should be made.[176] This report should be made public to allow for discussion of its results.

13. Specific Rules Concerning Europol and Eurojust and JIT Cooperation

The suggested instruments to regulate inner-AFSJ data exchange may only constitute one of several solutions and do not include specific rules characterising for instance the details of the cooperation between Europol and Eurojust (questions relating to the access of Eurojust to Europol's analysis work files or cooperation in JITs). Their cooperation is closer than the usual cooperation between AFSJ actors (the scope refers to the same crimes) and might require different additional safeguards related to questions such as the implementation of rules on the information exchange in JITs which could necessitate a change in the respective legal basis of the actors concerned (which is for instance already the case at Europol, but not yet at Eurojust). Along with this, additional provisions regulating the access of Eurojust to Europol's analysis work files in more detail than in their current agreement could complement the exchange instrument.

The same can be said for the general standard applicable to information exchange in JITs.[177] While information exchange in JITs necessarily takes place in a rather ad hoc and direct way during the meeting of the JIT, the inclusion of information in one of the information systems of Europol, Eurojust or OLAF should be subjected to special conditions regarding for instance the purpose and the use of data processing of the participating actors at JITs (e.g. the legal basis of the participating actors must cover all data processing activities taking place in the JIT,[178] cooperation should never lead to an extension of originally restricted tasks of one of the participating actor), the supervision or the respect of deletion

---

[175] Analogous to Article 17 Council Decision 2008/633, OJ 2008, L-218/129.

[176] Compare Article 17 (4) Council Decision 2008/633, OJ 2008, L-218/129.

[177] Important and valuable criteria which should be applicable in JIT exchange between Member States among each other and with Europol have been developed by: Gusy (2008), in particular pp. 274–280.

[178] The legal basis to process personal data might refer to the same crimes at Europol and Eurojust, although, for instance, OLAF does not dispose of the same comprehensive data processing possibilities.

requirements as well as the possible notification of persons concerned. In general, the aforementioned suggestions made with regard to transfer between AFSJ actors should be taken into account.

VII. The Important Impact of the Lisbon Treaty

In the discussion about the chances to implement some of the proposed suggestions, the impact of the Lisbon Treaty should not be underestimated. The applicability of the Charter of Fundamental Rights underlines the importance of the right to data protection in the future EU legislative framework. Article 16 TFEU and its important location within the principles of general application in the TFEU strengthens the respect for data protection principles in future and establishes guidelines for future legislative actions in the EU.

The introduction of the ordinary legislative procedure in the entire AFSJ and the participation of the European Parliament in future AFSJ decisions additionally reinforce the long demanded democratic oversight in this area. As previously mentioned, prior to the adoption of the Treaty, decision making in the area of police and judicial cooperation was rather a unilateral task of the Council. The Council's unanimity power on the one hand, and the mere consultation rights of the European Parliament on the other, repeatedly resulted in compromises based on the "lowest common denominator" which often hindered the implementation of clear and effective data protection rules.[179] Decision making under the new Lisbon framework has however changed and can be regarded as considerably more advantageous for the enforcement of the right to data protection in the AFSJ. In consequence, future proposals in the AFSJ must not only include data protection elements, they must fully respect data protection rights.

The removal of the limitations concerning the judicial control by the European Court of Justice[180] and the possibility to enact infringement proceedings[181] in the AFSJ in the near future considerably increase the procedural protection of fundamental rights in this area. The control of the AFSJ actors, in particular that of the agencies such as Europol and Eurojust, will then be significantly improved. Whereas Article 8 ECHR and the case law of the ECtHR represented for a long time the only source for binding rules in security related data processing, the new Lisbon framework establishes its own EU reference instruments with Article 8 Charter of Fundamental Rights and Article 16 TFEU. This development brings about a new legal legitimacy to increase the efforts to set up a data protection

[179] Scirocco (2008).

[180] Compare for the previous legal famework case C-160/03, *Spain v. Eurojust*, judgment of 15 March 2005, in which the Court confirmed that the acts of (former) third pillar bodies (in this case, Eurojust) did not fall within its competence.

[181] Articles 258 and 259 TFEU.

framework in the currently rather unregulated AFSJ. The minimum requirements which Article 8 Charter of Fundamental Rights stipulates (fair processing, purpose limitation, access and rectification rights, independent control etc.[182]) must be respected in any case and further specified in the police and judicial context.

Despite the remaining elements of the pillar structure, highlighted in Chap. A,[183] there are strong arguments in favour of the view that the entry into force of the Lisbon Treaty will considerably improve the respect of data protection rights in the AFSJ. As *Hijmans* and *Scirocco* rightly point out, the possible direct effect of Article 16 (1) TFEU will support the enforcement of data protection rights before courts and will limit the margin of appreciation of the legislature.[184] The authors compare the direct wording of Article 16 (1) TFEU with the direct wording in Article 18 (1) EC Treaty (the right of the EU citizen to move and reside freely within the territory of the Member States; now Article 21 TFEU) to which the Court acknowledged a direct effect[185] and conclude that Article 16 (1) TFEU is formulated in the same precise manner allowing also to concede a direct effect to it. Nonetheless these guarantees need further specifications. In addition, the Charter of Fundamental Rights has a direct effect and therefore plays an important role in the AFSJ. Data protection rights after the Lisbon Treaty are therefore built on a twofold basis: Article 16 TFEU in combination with Article 8 of the Charter of Fundamental Rights impressively demonstrate the importance of this right in the post-Lisbon area.

Moreover, the clear mandate included in Article 16 (2) TFEU of the Parliament and the Council to enact data protection rules in the AFSJ supports the legislative aspect of Article 16 TFEU: it obliges the Parliament and the Council to act and to "lay down the rules relating to the protection of individuals with regard to the processing of personal data by Union institutions, bodies, offices and agencies, and by the Member States when carrying out activities which fall within the scope of Union law, and the rules relating to the free movement of such data".[186] The Commission is therefore required to bring forward proposals in this area. With regard to the formulation used it is interesting to note that, as in Directive 95/46, the protection of the individual is recognized as a priority; the free flow of data is only mentioned in the second part of the sentence.

---

[182] Article 8 Charter of Fundamental Rights: 1. Everyone has the right to the protection of personal data concerning him or her. 2. Such data must be processed fairly for specified purposes and on the basis of the consent of the person concerned or some other legitimate basis laid down by law. Everyone has the right of access to data which has been collected concerning him or her, and the right to have it rectified. 3. Compliance with these rules shall be subject to control by an independent authority.

[183] Compare Chap. A III 1 d.

[184] Hijmanns and Scirocco (2009), in particular pp. 1517–1518.

[185] For example case C-413/99, *Baumbast and R*, judgment of 17 December 2002, para 84.

[186] Article 16 (2) TFEU.

It is worth noting in this context that, whereas the situation in the former first pillar (Directive 95/46 and Regulation 45/2001) does not necessitate immediate legislative actions,[187] the situation with regard to the former third pillar is different. The restricted scope of the FDPJ, its limited data protection guarantees and the fact that the instrument was adopted without the participation of the European Parliament is not (any longer) in accordance with the requirements of Article 16 TFEU and should therefore be replaced by an instrument complying with the current legislative standards. Whether this demand is legally enforceable before a court is open to discussion.[188] In any case, the need for a review of the currently applicable data processing framework in this area has been exhaustively illustrated in the foregoing and should therefore be reconsidered.

In summary, the improvements of the Lisbon Treaty in terms of judicial protection, institutional changes and the enforcement of data protection rights are an encouraging development. At the latest after the expiry of transition periods, advantage should be taken of the opportunity to introduce effective and harmonised data protection rules in the AFSJ. The proposed suggestions could be a starting point for this process.

Concluding Remarks

The central question of this contribution focussed on the organisation of the information sharing within the AFSJ and its compliance with data protection principles. Reference was consequently made to the EU and the Council of Europe's data protection framework. Whereas neither the EU nor the Council of Europe provide for a comprehensive framework covering all of the questions arising out of the analysis of the AFSJ actors and their relations among each other, their standards however offer important orientation when putting the limits of data processing and data exchange in the AFSJ in concrete terms. Particularly valuable thereby is the case law of the ECtHR which was for a long time the only jurisdiction at the European level in security-related data processing in a police and judicial context. The judgments sometimes allow the deduction of principles of general application which are useful in the evaluation of the behaviour of AFSJ actors.

---

[187] Hijmanns and Scirocco (2009), in particular p. 1519 and compare above Chap. A III 2.

[188] *Hijmanns* and *Scirocco* argue that an action for failure to act under Article 265 TFEU would be eventually possible. They refer to the case 13/83, *European Parliament v. Council*, judgment of 27 September 1988 concerning the transport policy in which the Court acknowledged such a possibility under the condition that the failure to act related to measures that are defined with sufficient specificity for them to be defined individually. The data protection provisions may also be qualified as sufficiently specific, compare Hijmanns and Scirocco (2009), in particular p. 1520 with further references.

Examples are the limitation on the categories of individuals against whom surveillance measures may be taken as well as the clear definition of the circumstances and limits of the storing and the use of the information before the processing and the time limits for storing. Essential criteria such as the purpose limitation principle, clear provisions concerning the persons authorised to consult the files, the nature of the files, the procedure to be followed, independent review and adequate and effective safeguards against abuse, including effective remedies, should assure compliance with the rule of law. Provisions limiting the transfer of data to other authorities and the notification of individuals concerned as soon as it can be carried out are essential guarantees contributing to an improved protection of individuals in police and judicial related data processing in view of the ECtHR.

Despite the standards developed by the ECtHR, information exchange in the AFSJ is however still an unregulated field above all in respect of the protection of fundamental rights. The individual assessment of the different AFSJ actors disclosed serious deficiencies hindering the persons concerned from understanding in which of the AFSJ databases their data are actually stored and analysed. The widening scopes of the AFSJ actors and the low criteria to be fulfilled when collecting and sharing data in the AFSJ make it increasingly difficult to verify the whereabouts of personal data. Different policies, especially immigration issues and security interests, mix and lead to a situation in which the opposing interests are not adequately counterbalanced. The supervisory structure is fragmented and the rights of individuals in the quickly increasing data exchange are often not sufficiently considered.

Provisions relating to the pre-emptive introduction of personal data in Europol's databases based on factual indications to believe that a person will commit a criminal offence in future violate ECtHR case-law (*S. and Marper v. the United Kingdom*[189]).

Eurojust and OLAF have very complex data protection frameworks which hinder the understanding of the data protection rules in force and the data processing actually carried out. Additionally, accountability and judicial review of OLAF's data processing activities raise concern.

Whereas over the years the tasks and responsibilities of Europol, Eurojust and OLAF have increased, their data protection framework remained unchanged. Frontex's ambiguous role with regard to personal data processing needs to be urgently clarified. Its legal framework does not permit personal data processing, but the agency nevertheless exchanges data with Europol. The intended amendment of Frontex's legal framework does unfortunately not clarify this point as it does not include data protection guarantees tailored to the specific situation arising at Frontex.

The analysis of the data processing framework of the European information exchange systems, such as the SIS, VIS, CIS and Eurodac revealed further shortcomings and confirmed the tendencies observed with regard to the agencies

---

[189] *S. and Marper v the United Kingdom*, Application nos. 30562/04 and 30566/04, judgment of 4 December 2008.

and OLAF. Wide scopes, more and more actors accessing the databases and outdated data protection frameworks characterise the legal situation in this area.

In light of the foregoing, it is no surprise that the data protection deficiencies included in the legal frameworks of the AFSJ actors increase when it comes to data exchange between AFSJ agencies and the European information systems SIS, VIS, CIS and Eurodac. Inter-agency data exchange taking place in JITs or via cooperation agreements often lacks essential data protection requirements, which would compensate the risks caused by the transfer of data from one agency to another. New tools, such as the opening of Europol's analysis work files to Eurojust, raise further concerns relating to the merging of data so far stored separately in the databases of different agencies.

Questions concerning the supervision of such transfers, the whereabouts of the transferred data, the access requirements or the time-limits as well as the conditions for third party transfers of the received data or the rights of individuals after the data are transferred are therefore often not answered. In addition, personal data exchange is often carried out without linking the purpose of the access to the later use of the data in a law enforcement or judicial database.

As follows from the analysis, data exchange in the AFSJ is (still) a mix of former first pillar and third pillar structures whereby the impression prevails that the interest of security overrides the former first pillar protection originally guaranteed in instruments such as Eurodac, the VIS or the first pillar CIS. Data transfer from a former first pillar database to a law enforcement or judicial database seems to become the standard procedure in security-related data exchange and does not necessitate a special reason apart from being somehow related to crime prevention purposes; a term which is not even based on a specific definition.

The rights of individuals as regards their interest in knowing in which of the existing EU databases their personal data are processed seems to be subordinated to security interests. The missing notification duty about transfers having taken place is one of the main shortcomings. If introduced, it would considerably improve the knowledge of the whereabouts of personal data.

Against this background, the idea of one single instrument regulating the AFSJ information exchange emerges. Creating one single common basic standard harmonising the current variety of agreements and other instruments regulating AFSJ data exchange would noticeably lead to a foreseeable and comprehensive data exchange in the AFSJ which could additionally be supervised by only one monitoring body overseeing the entire AFSJ data exchange, being equipped with the necessary rights to effectively fulfil its tasks. When considering the AFSJ as one common policy field,[190] the rights of individuals, in particular as regards the transfer of their data, should be unified to the same extent.

[190] Communication from the Commission to the European Parliament, the Council, the European Economic and Social Committee and the Committee of the Regions – Delivering and area of freedom, security and justice for European's citizens – Action Plan implementing the Stockholm Programme, COM(2010) 171 final.

One single standard applicable to the complete AFSJ data transfer, including basic common standards on data protection, would not only essentially strengthen the position of the individual in the AFSJ, but also bring the AFSJ in line with the Lisbon Treaty. The definition of unclear legal terms, the harmonisation of the access procedure as well as of access, correction and deletion rights could be one step in the right direction. The follow-up of the transferred data in combination with an increased cooperation of the involved DPAs and effective penalties in cases of misuse would considerably improve the current situation of the individual. The introduction of a notification of the individual in case of the transfer of his data as soon as it can be carried out would bring the AFSJ in line with Directive 95/56 as well as recent ECtHR developments. Data protection rules are therefore an essential instrument in controlling the increasing powers of the AFSJ actors. After the entry into force of the Lisbon Treaty, the enforcement of the right to data protection must now be underpinned by political and judicial means; otherwise the data exchange in the AFSJ becomes uncontrollable.

This contribution could not give answers to all questions arising out of the security-related data processing and exchange in the AFSJ, although the suggested solutions could be a starting point to contribute to the discussion about harmonised data protection standards in the AFSJ in the post-Lisbon environment.

Documents

I. Conventions, Acts and Related Documents

The documents are listed in chronological order.

Hessisches Datenschutz Gesetz, 7 Oktober 1970 – GVBl. (Gesetz- und Verordnungsblatt) I, 1970

Swedish data protection act, Datalag SFS 1973:289

Gesetz zum Schutz vor Missbrauch von personenbezogenen Daten bei der Datenverarbeitung, BDSG, 27 January 1977, BGBl. I, 201

Loi no. 78–17 du 6 Janvier 1978 relative à l'informatique, aux fichiers et aux libertés

OECD Recommendation concerning Guidelines governing the protection of privacy and trans-border flows of personal data of 23 September 1980

Convention for the Protection of Individuals with regard to Automatic Processing of Personal Data, 28 January 1981, CETS No. 108

The Data Protection Act 1984 (UK)

Convention implementing the Schengen Agreement of 14 June 1985 between the Governments of the States of the Benelux Economic Union, the Federal Republic of Germany and the French Republic on the gradual abolition of checks at their common borders, OJ 2000, L-239/19

Convention based on Article K.3 of the Treaty on European Union, on the establishment of a European Police Office (Europol Convention), OJ 1995, C-316/2

Convention drawn up on the basis of Article K.3 of the Treaty on European Union, on the use of information technology for customs purposes, OJ 1995, C-316/34

Second Protocol, drawn up on the basis of Article K.3 of the treaty on European Union, to the Convention on the protection of the European Communities' financial interests - Joint Declaration on Article 13 (2) - Commission Declaration on Article 7, OJ 1997, C-221/12

Convention on Mutual Assistance in Criminal Matters between the Member States of the European Union, OJ 2000, C-197/3

F. Boehm, *Information Sharing and Data Protection in the Area of Freedom, Security and Justice*, DOI 10.1007/978-3-642-22392-1,

Explanatory report on the Convention on Mutual Assistance in Criminal Matters between the Member States of the European Union, OJ 2000, C-379/7

The Schengen acquis - Convention implementing the Schengen Agreement of 14 June 1985 between the Governments of the States of the Benelux Economic Union, the Federal Republic of Germany and the French Republic on the gradual abolition of checks at their common borders, OJ 2000, L-239/19

Prüm Convention, Council Document 10900/05, 7 July 2005

II. Council of Europe

The documents are listed in chronological order.

Recommendation No. R (86) on the protection of personal data used for social security purposes of 23 January 1986

Recommendation R (87) 15 of the committee of ministers to member states regulating the use of personal data in the police sector, adopted on 17 September 1987

Recommendation No. R (89) 2 on the protection of personal data used for employment purposes of 18 January 1989

Recommendation No. R (90) 19 on the protection of personal data used for payment and other related operations of 13 September 1990

Recommendation 1181 (1992) 1 on police co-operation and protection of personal data in the police sector of 11 March 1992

Evaluation of the Project Group on Data Protection of the Council's Committee of Ministers, First evaluation of the relevance of Recommendation R (87) 15 of 1994

Recommendation No. R (95) 4 on the protection of personal data in the area of telecommunication services of 7 February 1995

Recommendation No. R (97) 5 on the protection of medical data of 13 February 1997

Evaluation of the Project Group on Data Protection of the Council's Committee of Ministers, Second evaluation of the relevance of Recommendation R (87) 15 of 1998

Additional Protocol of the Convention for the Protection of Individuals with regard to Automatic Processing of Personal Data regarding supervisory authorities and transborder data flows, 8 November 2001

Explanatory report to the additional Protocol to the Convention for the Protection of Individuals with regard to Automatic Processing of Personal Data, regarding supervisory authorities and Transborder Data Flows, 8 November 2001

Evaluation of the Project Group on Data Protection of the Council's Committee of Ministers, Third evaluation of Recommendation R (87) 15 of 2002

Juncker Report "A sole ambition for the European continent" of 11 April 2006, available at: http://assembly.coe.int/Sessions/2006/speeches/20060411_report_JC-Juncker_EN.pdf (accessed February 2011)

Opinion on video surveillance in public places by public authorities and the protection of human rights, adopted by the Venice Commission at its 70th plenary session (16–17 March 2007), Study no. 404/2006, Council of Europe, Strasbourg, 23 March 2007

Note of the Committee of Ministers, 1031st meeting of 2 July 2008, Decision, Item 10.2, (CM/Del/Dec(2008)1031 4 July 2008)

III. EU Related Documents

EU Treaties, agreements and protocols

The documents are listed in chronological order.

Agreement between the European Community and the Republic of Iceland and the Kingdom of Norway concerning the criteria and mechanisms for establishing the State responsible for examining a request for asylum lodged in a Member State or in Iceland or Norway – Declarations, OJ 2001, L-93/40

Strategic co-operation agreement between the European Agency for the Management of Operational Cooperation at the External Borders of the Member States of the European Union and the European Police Office of 28 March 2008

Agreement between the European Community and the Swiss Confederation concerning the criteria and mechanisms for establishing the State responsible for examining a request for asylum lodged in a Member State or in Switzerland - Final Act – Declarations, OJ 2008, L-53/5

Charter of Fundamental Rights, OJ 2010, C-83/02

Consolidated version of the Treaty on European Union, OJ 2010, C-83/13

Consolidated version of the Treaty on the functioning on the European Union, OJ 2010, C-83/47

Declarations annexed to the Final Act of the Intergovernmental Conference which adopted the Treaty of Lisbon, OJ 2010, C-83/335

Protocol No. 21 annexed to the Lisbon Treaty on the position of the United Kingdom and Ireland in respect of the Area of Freedom, Security and Justice, OJ 2010, C-83/201

Protocol No. 22 annexed to the Lisbon Treaty on the position of Denmark, OJ 2010, C-83/201

Protocol No. 30 annexed to the Lisbon Treaty on the application of the Charter of Fundamental Rights of the European Union to Poland and to the United Kingdom, OJ 2010, C-83/201

Protocol No. 36 annexed to the Lisbon Treaty on transitional provisions, OJ 2010, C-83/201

Protocol No. 8 annexed to the Lisbon Treaty relating to Article 6 (2) of the Treaty on European Union on the accession of the Union to the European Convention on the Protection of Human Rights and Fundamental Freedoms, OJ 2010, C-83/201

Regulations, Directives and related documents

The documents are listed in chronological order.

Regulation (EC) No 1683/95 of 29 May 1995 laying down a uniform format for visas, OJ 1995, L-164/1

Directive 95/46/EC of the European Parliament and the Council of 24 October 1995 on the protection of the individuals with regard to the processing of personal data and on the free movement of such data, OJ 1995, L-281/31

Regulation (EC, Euratom) No 2988/95 of 18 December 1995 on the protection of the European Communities financial interests, OJ 1995, L-312/1

Regulation (Euratom, EC) No 2185/96 of 11 November 1996 concerning on-the-spot checks and inspections carried out by the Commission in order to protect the European Communities' financial interests against fraud and other irregularities, OJ 1996, L-292/2

Regulation (EC) No. 515/97 of 13 March 1997 on mutual assistance between the administrative authorities of the Member States and cooperation between the latter and the Commission to ensure the correct application of the law on customs and agricultural matters, OJ 1997, L-82/1

Directive 97/66/EC of the European Parliament and of the Council of 15 December 1997 concerning the processing of personal data and the protection of privacy in the telecommunications sector, OJ 1998, L-24/1

Regulation (Euratom) No. 1074/99 of the European Parliament and of the Council of 25 May 1999 concerning investigations by the European Anti-Fraud Office (OLAF), OJ 1999 L-136/8

Regulation (Euratom) No. 1074/99 of the European Parliament and of the Council of 25 May 1999 concerning investigations by the European Anti-Fraud Office (OLAF), OJ 1999, L-136/1

Regulation (EC) No. 1073/1999 of the European Parliament and of the Council of 25 May 1999 concerning investigations conducted by the European Anti-Fraud Office (OLAF), OJ 1999, L-136/31

Regulation (EC) No 2725/2000of 11 December 2000 concerning the establishment of 'Eurodac' for the comparison of fingerprints for the effective application of the Dublin Convention, OJ 2000, L-316/1

Regulation (EC) No. 45/2001 of the European Parliament and the Council of 18 December 2000 on the protection of individuals with regard to the processing of personal data by the Community institutions and bodies and on the free movements of such data, OJ 2001, L-8/1

Regulation No. 539/2009 of 15 March 2001 listing the third countries whose nationals must be in possession of visas when crossing the external borders and those whose nationals are exempt from that requirement, OJ 2001, L-81/1

Regulation No. 1049/2001 of the European Parliament and of the Council of 30 May 2001 regarding public access to European Parliament, Council and Commission documents, OJ 2001, L-145/43

Regulation (EC) No 407/2002 of 28 February 2002 laying down certain rules to implement Regulation (EC) No 2725/2000 highlighting concerning the establishment of 'Eurodac' for the comparison of fingerprints for the effective application of the Dublin Convention, OJ 2002, L-62/1

Regulation No. 1605/2002 of 25 June 2002 on the financial regulation on the general budget of the European Communities, OJ 2002, L-248/1

Directive 2002/58/EC of the European Parliament and of the Council of 12 July 2002 concerning the processing of personal data and the protection of privacy in the electronic communications sector (Directive on privacy and electronic communications), OJ 2002, L-201/37

Regulation (EC) No 343/2003 of 18 February 2003 establishing the criteria and mechanisms for determining the Member State responsible for examining an asylum application lodged in one of the Member States by a third-country national, OJ 2003, L-50/1

Regulation No. 415/2003 of 27 February 2003 on the issue of visas at the border, including the issue of such visas to seamen in transit, OJ 2003, L-64/1

Regulation (EC) No 1560/2003 of 2 September 2003 laying down detailed rules for the application of Council Regulation (EC) No 343/2003 establishing the criteria and mechanisms for determining the Member State responsible for examining an asylum application lodged in one of the Member States by a third-country national, OJ 2003, L-222/3

Regulation (EC) No. 871/2004 of 29 April 2004 concerning the introduction of some new functions for the Schengen Information System, including in the fight against terrorism, OJ 2004, L-162/29

Regulation (EC) No. 2007/2004 of 26 October 2004 establishing a European Agency for the Management of Operational Cooperation at the External Borders of the Member States of the European Union, OJ 2004, L-349/1

Regulation (EC) No 1160/2005 of the European Parliament and of the Council of 6 July 2005 amending the Convention implementing the Schengen Agreement of 14 June 1985 on the gradual abolition of checks at common borders, as regards access to the Schengen Information System by the services in the Member States responsible for issuing registration certificates for vehicles, OJ 2005, L-191/18

Regulation (EC) No. 1290/2005 of 21 June 2005 on the financing of the common agricultural policy, OJ 2005, L-209/1 as amended by Council Regulation (EC) No 1437/2007 of 26 November 2007, OJ 2007, L-322/1 and Commission Regulation (EC) No 259/2008 of 18 March 2008 laying down detailed rules for the application of Regulation No 1290/2005 as regards the publication of information on the beneficiaries of funds deriving from the European Agricultural Guarantee Fund (EAGF) and the European Agricultural Fund for Rural Development (EAFRD), OJ 2008, L-76/28.

Regulation (EC) No 562/2006 the European Parliament and of the Council of 15 March 2006 establishing a Community Code on the rules governing the movement of persons across borders (Schengen Borders Code), OJ 2006, L-105/1

Directive 2006/24/EC of the European Parliament and of the Council of 15 March 2006 on the retention of data generated or processed in connection with the provision of publicly available electronic communications services or of public communications networks and amending Directive 2002/58/EC, OJ 2006, L-105/54

Regulation (EC) No. 1083/2006 of 11 July 2006 laying down general provisions for the European Regional Development Fund, the European Social

Fund and the Cohesion Fund, repealing Regulation (EC) No 1260/1999, OJ 2006, L-210/25

Regulation (EC) No 1986/2006 of the European Parliament and of the Council of 20 December 2006 regarding access to the Second Generation Schengen Information System (SIS II) by the services in the Member States responsible for issuing vehicle registration certificates, OJ 2006, L-381/1

Regulation (EC) No 1987/2006 of the European Parliament and of the Council of 20 December 2006 on the establishment, operation and use of the second generation Schengen Information System (SIS II), OJ 2006, L-381/4

Regulation No. 1932/2006 of 21 December 2006 amending Regulation (EC) No 539/2001 listing the third countries whose nationals must be in possession of visas when crossing the external borders and those whose nationals are exempt from that requirement, OJ 2006, L-405/23

Regulation (EC) No. 863/2007 of the European Parliament and of the Council of 11 July 2007 establishing a mechanism for the creation of Rapid Border Intervention Teams and amending Council Regulation (EC) No. 2007/2004 as regards that mechanism and regulating the tasks and powers of guest officers, OJ 2007, L-199/30

Regulation No. 767/2008 of the European Parliament and of the Council of 9 July 2008 concerning the Visa Information System (VIS) and the exchange of data between Member States on short-stay visas (VIS Regulation), OJ 2008, L-218/60

Regulation (EC) No. 766/2008 of the European Parliament and of the Council of 9 July 2008 amending Council Regulation (EC) No 515/97 on mutual assistance between the administrative authorities of the Member States and cooperation between the latter and the Commission to ensure the correct application of the law on customs and agricultural matters, OJ 2008, L-218/48

Regulation amending Decision 2008/839/JHA on migration from the Schengen Information System (SIS 1+) to the second generation Schengen Information System of 8 November 2008 (SIS II), OJ 2008, L-299/1

Regulation (EC) No. 810/2009 of the European Parliament and of the Council of 13 July 2009 establishing a Community Code on Visas (Visa Code), OJ 2009, L-243/1

Directive 2009/136/EC of the European Parliament and of the Council of 25 November 2009 amending Directive 2002/22/EC on universal service and users' rights relating to electronic communications networks and services, Directive 2002/58/EC concerning the processing of personal data and the protection of privacy in the electronic communications sector and Regulation (EC) No 2006/2004 on cooperation between national authorities responsible for the enforcement of consumer protection laws, OJ 2009, L-337/11

Explanatory memorandum of the Proposal for a Regulation of the European Parliament and the Council amending Council Regulation (EC) No. 2007/2004 of 26 October 2004 establishing a European Agency for the Management of Operational Cooperation at the External Borders of the Member States of the European Union (FRONTEX) of 24 February 2010, COM(2010) 61 final

Impact assessment accompanying the proposal for a Regulation of the European Parliament and the Council amending Council Regulation (EC) No. 2007/2004 of 26 October 2004 establishing a European Agency for the Management of Operational Cooperation at the External Borders of the Member States of the European Union (FRONTEX) of 24 February 2010

EU Council documents

The documents are listed in chronological order.

Council Act of 29 November 1995 drawing up, on the basis of Article K.3 of the Treaty on European Union, the Protocol on the interpretation, by way of preliminary rulings, by the Court of Justice of the European Communities of the Convention on the use of information technology for customs purposes, OJ 1997, C-151/15

Council Act of 23 July 1996 drawing up, on the basis of Article K.3 of the Treaty on European Union, the Protocol on the interpretation, by way of preliminary rulings, by the Court of Justice of the European Communities of the Convention on the establishment of a European Police Office, OJ 1996, C-299/1

Joint Action of 29 June 1998 adopted by the Council on the basis of Article K.3 of the Treaty on European Union, on the creation of a European Judicial Network (98/428/JHA), OJ 1998, L-191/4

Council Act of 3 November 1998 adopting rules applicable to Europol analysis files, OJ 1999, C-26/01

Council Act of 12 March 1999 drawing up, on the basis of Article K.3 of the Treaty on European Union, the Protocol on the scope of the laundering of proceeds in the Convention on the use of information technology for customs purposes, OJ 1999, C-91/1

Council Act of 12 March 1999 drawing up, on the basis of Article K.3 of the Treaty on European Union, the Protocol on the scope of the laundering of proceeds in the Convention on the use of information technology for customs purposes and the inclusion of the registration number of the means of transport in the Convention, OJ 1999, C-91/91

Council Decision of 20 May 1999 concerning the definition of the Schengen acquis for the purpose of determining, in conformity with the relevant provisions of the Treaty establishing the European Community and the Treaty on European Union, the legal basis for each of the provisions or decisions which constitute the acquis OJ 1999, L-176/1

Council Act of 29 May 2000 establishing in accordance with Article 34 of the Treaty on European Union the Convention on Mutual Assistance in Criminal Matters between the Member States of the European Union, OJ 2000, C-197/1

Council Decision of 29 May 2000 concerning the request of the United Kingdom of Great Britain and Northern Ireland to take part in some of the provisions of the Schengen acquis, OJ 2000, L-131/43

Council Decision 2002/187/JHA of 28 February 2002 setting up Eurojust with a view to reinforcing the fight against serious crime, OJ 2002, L-63/1

Council Decision of 28 February 2002 concerning Ireland's request to take part in some of the provisions of the Schengen acquis, OJ 2002, L-64/20

Council Framework Decision of 13 June 2002 on joint investigation teams, OJ 2002, L-162/1

Council Framework Decision 2002/584/JHA of 13 June 2002 on the European arrest warrant and the surrender procedures between Member States - Statements made by certain Member States on the adoption of the Framework Decision, OJ 2002, L-190/1

Council Framework Decision 2002/475/JHA of 13 June 2002 on combating terrorism, OJ 2002, L-164/3

Council Act of 8 May 2003 drawing up a Protocol amending, as regards the creation of a customs files identification database, the Convention on the use of information technology for customs purposes, OJ 2003, C-139/1

Council Directive 2004/82/EC of 29 April 2004 on the obligation of air carriers to communicate passenger data, OJ 2004, L-261/24

Council Decision of 8 June 2004 establishing the Visa Information System (VIS), OJ 2004, L-213/5

Council document no. 12537/3/04 on the SIS II functions of 30 November 2004

Council Decision 2005/211/JHA of 24 February 2005 concerning the introduction of some new functions for the Schengen Information System, including in the fight against terrorism, OJ 2005, L-68/44

Council Decision of 16 March 2005 establishing a secure webbased Information and Coordination Network for Member States' Migration Management Services, OJ 2005, L-83/48

Council Decision 2005/451/JHA of 13 June 2005 fixing the date of application of certain provisions of Regulation (EC) No 871/2004concerning the introduction of some new functions for the Schengen Information System, including in the fight against terrorism, OJ 2005, L-158/26

Council Decision 2005/671/JHA of 20 September 2005 on the exchange of information and cooperation concerning terrorist offences, OJ 2005, L-253/22

Council Decision 2005/719/JHA of 12 October 2005 fixing the date of application of certain provisions of Decision 2005/211/JHA concerning the introduction of some new functions for the Schengen Information System, including in the fight against terrorism, OJ 2005, L-271/54

Council Decision 2005/727/JHA of 12 October 2005 fixing the date of application of certain provisions of Decision 2005/211/JHA concerning the introduction of some new functions for the Schengen Information System, including the fight against terrorism, OJ 2005, L-273/25

Council Decision 2006/228/JHA of 9 March 2006 fixing the date of application of certain provisions of Decision 2005/211/JHA concerning the introduction of some new functions for the Schengen Information System, including the fight against terrorism, OJ 2006, L-81/45

Council Decision 2006/229/JHA of 9 March 2006 fixing the date of application of certain provisions of Decision 2005/211/JHA concerning the introduction of some new functions for the Schengen Information System, including in the fight against terrorism, OJ 2006, L-81/46

Feasibility study - SIS one 4all-Schengen Information System, Council document 13540/06 of 12 October 2006

Council document 13424/2/06, rev. 2, ENFOCUSTOM 64, Action Plan to implement the Strategy for Customs Co-operation in the Third Pillar of 8 November 2006

Council Conclusions on the SIS II, the SIS 1+ and the enlargement of the Schengen area, doc. 16324/06 of 5 December 2006

Council Framework Decision 2006/960/JHA of 18 December 2006 on simplifying the exchange of information and intelligence between law enforcement authorities of the Member States of the European Union, OJ 2006, L-386/89

Press release, 2795th/2796th, General Affairs and External Relations, Luxembourg, 23–24 April 2007, document 8425/07 (Presse 80)

Council Decision 2007/533/JHA of 12 June 2007 on the establishment, operation and use of second generation Schengen Information System, OJ 2007, L-205/63

Council document 6073/3/07, REV 3 of 23 July 2007, List of competent authorities which are authorised to search directly the data contained in the Schengen Information System pursuant to Article 101(4) of the Schengen Convention

Council document 5441/08, SIS Database Statistics 01/01/2008 of 30 January 2008

Council Decision 2008/615/JHA of 23 June 2008 on the stepping up of cross-border cooperation, particularly in combating terrorism and cross-border crime, OJ 2008, L-210/1

Council Decision 2008/633/JHA of 23 June 2008 concerning access for consultation of the Visa Information System (VIS) by designated authorities of Member States and by Europol for the purposes of the prevention, detection and investigation of terrorist offences and of other serious criminal offences, OJ 2008, L-218/129

Council document 11216/1/08, rev 1 EUROPOL 63 on customs cooperation at Europol of 2 September 2008

Council Decision 2008/839/JHA of 24 October 2008 on migration from the Schengen Information System (SIS 1+) to the second generation Schengen Information System (SIS II), OJ 2008, L-299/43

Council Framework Decision 2008/977/JHA on the protection of personal data processed in the framework of police and judicial cooperation in criminal matters of 27 November 2008, OJ 2008, L-350/60

Council Decision 2008/976/JHA of 16 December 2008 on the European Judicial Network, OJ 2008, L-348/130

Council Decision 2009/426/JHA of 16 December 2008 on the strengthening of Eurojust and amending Decision 2002/187/JHA setting up Eurojust with a view to reinforcing the fight against serious crime, OJ 2009, L-138/4

Council document 5171/09 of 19 February 2009 on the staff shortage and workload SIS II, SIRIS 7, COMIX 22, Annex 3.

Council Decision of 6 April 2009 establishing the European Police Office, OJ 2009, L-121/37

Council document 12493/09 of 31 July 2009 on the exchange of statistical information on uniform visas issued by Member States' diplomatic missions and consular posts

Council Decision 2009/935/JHA of 30 November 2009 determining the list of third states and organisations with which Europol shall conclude agreements, OJ 2009, L-325/12

Council Decision 2009/936/JHA of 30 November 2009 adopting the implementing rules for Europol analysis work files, OJ 2009, L-325/14

Council Decision 2009/917/JHA of 30 November 2009 on the use of information technology for customs purposes, OJ 2009, L-323/20

Council Decision 2009/934/JHA of 30 November 2009 adopting the implementing rules governing Europol's relations with partners, including the exchange of personal and classified information, OJ 2009, L-325/6

Press release, 2979th Council meeting, Justice and Home Affairs, Brussels, 30 November and 1 December 2009, 16883/1/09 REV 1 (Presse 35 5)

Council document 6162/10 of 5 February 2010, note to the SIS-TECH Working Party/Mixed Committee (EU-Iceland/Norway/Switzerland/Liechtenstein)

Outcome of proceedings of CATS on 11 February 2010, Council doc. 6557/10

Council document 2010/0039 (COD), 8121/10, proposal for a regulation of the European Parliament and the Council amending Council Regulation (EC) No 2007/2004 establishing a European Agency for the Management of operational cooperation at the external borders of the Member States of the European Union (Frontex) 29 March 2010

Note from the General Secretariat to the Standing Committee on operational cooperation on internal security (COSI), final report on the cooperation between JHA agencies, Council doc. 8387/10 of 9 April 2010

Outcome of proceedings of CATS on 12 and 13 April 2010, Council Doc. 9371/10 of 4 May 2010

Schengen Catalogue, recommendations and best practices, data protection, Council doc. 9768/10 of 10 May 2010

Council Decision of 20 July 2010 establishing the organisation and functioning of the European External Action Service, Council Doc. 11665/1/10, REV 1/POLGEN 104/INST 243

EU Commission

The documents are listed in chronological order.

Commission Decision 1999/352/EC of 28 April 1999 establishing the European Anti-Fraud Office (OLAF), OJ 1999, L-136/20

Commission Decision of 26 July 2000 pursuant to Directive 95/46/EC of the European Parliament and of the Council on the adequate protection of personal data provided in Switzerland, OJ 2000, L-215/1

Commission Regulation (EC) No 1073/2001 of 31 May 2001 concerning tenders notified in response to the invitation to tender for the export of oats issued in Regulation (EC) No 2097/2000, OJ 2001, L-148/06

Commission Decision 2001/497/EC of 15 June 2001 on standard contractual clauses for the transfer of personal data to third countries, under Directive 95/46/EC, OJ 2001, L-181/19

Commission Decision 2002/16/EC of 27 December 2001 on standard contractual clauses for the transfer of personal data to processors established in third countries, under Directive 95/46/EC, OJ 2002, L-6/52

Commission Decision of 30 June 2003 pursuant to Directive 95/46/EC of the European Parliament and of the Council on the adequate protection of personal data in Argentina, OJ 2003, L- 168/19

Commission Decision of 21 November 2003 on the adequate protection of personal data in Guernsey, OJ 2003, L-308/27

Communication from the Commission to the Council and the European Parliament of 11 December 2003 on the development of the Schengen Information System II and possible synergies with a future Visa Information System (VIS), COM(2003) 771 final

Commission Decision 2004/915/EC of 27 December 2004 amending Decision 2001/497/EC as regards the introduction of an alternative set of standard contractual clauses for the transfer of personal data to third countries, OJ 2004, L-385/74

Proposal for a Council Decision of 24 November 2005 concerning access for consultation of the Visa Information System (VIS) by the authorities of the Member States responsible for internal security and by Europol for the purposes of the prevention, detection and investigation of terrorist offences and of other serious criminal offences (COM(2005)600final – 2005/0323(CNS))

Proposal for a Regulation of the European Parliament and the Council amending Regulation (EC) No 1073/1999 concerning investigation conducted by the European Anti-Fraud Office, COM(2006) 244 final of 24 May 2006

Proposal for a Regulation of the European Parliament and of the Council amending Council Regulation (EC) No. 515/97 of 13 March 1997 on mutual assistance between the administrative authorities of the Member States and cooperation between the latter and the Commission to ensure the correct application of the law on customs and agricultural matters, COM(2006) 866 final of 22 December 2006

Report from the Commission to the European Parliament and the Council on the evaluation on the Dublin system, COM(2007) 299 final of 6 June 2007

Communication from the Commission to the Council and the European Parliament of 23 October 2007 on the role of Eurojust and the European Judicial Network in the fight against organised crime and terrorism in the European Union, COM (2007) 644 final

Proposal for a Council Framework Decision on the use of Passenger Name Record (PNR) for law enforcement purposes, COM(2007) 654 of 6 November 2007

Proposal for a Council Regulation on migration from the Schengen Information System (SIS 1) to the second generation Schengen Information System (SIS II) COM/2008/0197 final of 16 April 2008

Analysis of the Commission communications on future development of Frontex and the creation of a European Border Surveillance System (EUROSUR), briefing paper from policy department C, citizens' rights and constitutional affairs, civil liberties, justice and home affairs, Directorate General internal policies of the Union of June 2008, PE 408.295

Proposal for a Council Regulation amending Regulation (EC) No 1104/2008on migration from the Schengen Information System (SIS 1+) to the second generation Schengen Information System (SIS II) (1st pillar), COM(2009) 508 final.

Communication from the Commission to the European Parliament and the Council, an area of freedom, security and justice serving the citizen, COM(2009) 262 final of 10 June 2009

Proposal for a regulation of the European Parliament and the Council establishing an agency for the operational management of large-scale IT systems in the area of freedom, security and justice COM(2009) 293 of 24 June 2009

Proposal for a Council Decision on requesting comparisons with Eurodac data by Member States' law enforcement authorities and Europol for law enforcement purposes of 10 September 2009, COM(2009) 344

Report from the Commission to the European Parliament and the Council on the development of the Visa Information System (VIS) in 2008, of 15 September 2009, COM(2009) 473 final

Commission Decision 2009/720/EC of 17 September 2009 laying down the date for the completion of migration from the Schengen Information System (SIS 1+) to the second generation Schengen Information System (SIS II), OJ 2009, L-257/26

Commission Decision 2009/724/JHA of 17 September 2009 laying down the date for the completion of migration from the Schengen Information System (SIS 1+) to the second generation Schengen Information System (SIS II) (3rd pillar), OJ 2009, L-257/41

Commission staff working paper, report on progress made in developing the European Border Surveillance System (EUROSUR) of 24 September 2009, Sec (2009), 1265 final

Report from the Commission to the European Parliament and the Council, annual report to the Council and the European Parliament on the activities of the Eurodac Central Unit in 2008, COM(2009) 494 final of 25 September 2009

Commission Decision of 30 November 2009 adopting technical implementing measures for entering the data and linking applications, for accessing the data, for amending, deleting and advance deleting of data and for keeping and accessing the records of data processing operations in the Visa Information System, OJ 2009, L-315/30

Proposal for a Council Regulation amending Decision 2008/839/JHA on migration from the Schengen Information System (SIS 1+) to the second generation Schengen Information System (SIS II) of 29 January 2010, COM(2010) 15 final.

Proposal for a Regulation of the European Parliament and the Council amending Council Regulation (EC) No. 2007/2004 of 26 October 2004 establishing a European Agency for the Management of Operational Cooperation at the External Borders of the Member States of the European Union (FRONTEX) of 24 February 2010, COM(2010) 61 final

Proposal for a Regulation (EU) No . . ./. . . of the European Parliament and of the Council on establishing an agency for the operational management of large-scale IT systems in the area of freedom, security and justice, COM(2010) 93 final of 19 March 2010

Communication from the Commission to the European Parliament, the Council, the European Economic and Social Committee and the Committee of the Regions of 20 April 2010 – Delivering and area of freedom, security and justice for European's citizens – Action Plan implementing the Stockholm Programme, COM(2010) 171 final

Communication from the Commission to the European Parliament and the Council of 20 July 2010, Overview of information management in the area of freedom, security and justice, COM(2010) 385 final

Proposal for a Regulation of the European Parliament and of the Council concerning the establishment of 'Eurodac' for the comparison of fingerprints for the effective application of Regulation (EC) No [. . ./. . .] establishing the criteria and mechanisms for determining the Member State responsible for examining an application for international protection lodged in one of the Member States by a third-country national or a stateless person (recast version), COM(2010) 555 of 11 October 2010

Communication on "A comprehensive strategy on data protection in the European Union", COM(2010) 609 final of 4 November 2010

Commission decisions on the adequacy of the protection of personal data in third countries: Switzerland, Hungary, Canada, Argentina, Andorra, Guernsey and the Isle of Man, http://ec.europa.eu/justice/policies/privacy/thridcountries/index_en.htm (accessed February 2011)

<u>Documents of the Article 29 Data Protection Working Party</u>

The documents are listed in chronological order.

Document WP 4 of 26 June 1997, first orientations on the transfer of personal data to third countries – possible ways forward in assessing adequacy

Document WP 7 of 14 January 1998 on the judging of industry self regulation: when does it make a meaningful contribution to the level of data protection in a third country?

Document WP 9 of 22 April 1998 on preliminary views on the use of contractual provisions in the context of transfers of personal data to third countries

Document WP 12 of 24 July 1998 on the transfers of personal data to third countries: applying Articles 25 and 26 of the EU data protection directive

Working document WP 80 of 1 August 2003 on biometrics

Opinion No. 7/2004 of the Article 29 Data Protection Working Party on the inclusion of biometric elements in residence permits and visas taking into account of the establishment of the European information system on visas (VIS) of 11 August 2004

Document WP 114 of 25 November 2005 on a common interpretation of Article 26 (1) of Directive 95/96

Opinion 6/2005 of the Article 29 Data Protection Working Party of 25 November 2005 on the Proposals for a Regulation of the European Parliament and of the

Council (COM(2005) 236 final) and a Council Decision (COM(2005) 230 final) on the establishment, operation and use of the second generation Schengen information system (SIS II) and a Proposal for a Regulation of the European Parliament and of the Council regarding access to the second generation Schengen Information System (SIS II) by the services in the Member States responsible for issuing vehicle registration certificates (COM(2005) 237 final), Working Paper 116

Opinion of the Article 29 Data Protection Working Partly, WP 136, Opinion 4/2007 on the concept of personal data, adopted 20 June 2007

Documents of the EDPS

Opinions and documents of the EDPS can be found at: http://www.edps.europa.eu/EDPSWEB/ (accessed February 2011)

They are listed in chronological order.

Opinion of 19 December 2005 on the Proposal for a Council Framework Decision on the protection of personal data processed in the framework of police and judicial co-operation in criminal matters (COM(2005) 475 final), OJ 2006, C-47/27

Opinion on the proposal for a Regulation of the European Parliament and the Council concerning the Visa Information System (VIS) and the exchange of data between Member States on short stay-visas (COM(2004) 835 final), OJ 2005, C-181/13

EDPS background paper series, July 2005, n°1, "public access to documents and data protection", in particular pp. 32–40, accessible at: http://www.edps.europa.eu/EDPSWEB/edps/site/mySite/Papers (accessed February 2011)

Opinion on the proposal for a Council Decision concerning access for consultation of the Visa Information System (VIS) by the authorities of Member States responsible for internal security and by Europol for the purposes of prevention, detection and investigation of terrorist offences and of other serious criminal offences (COM(2005) 600 final), OJ 2006, C-97/6

Opinion of the European Data Protection Supervisor on the Proposal for a Council Decision on the establishment, operation and use of the Second Generation Schengen Information System (SIS II) (COM(2005) 230 final); the Proposal for a Regulation of the European Parliament and of the Council on the establishment, operation and use of the Second Generation Schengen Information System (SIS II) (COM(2005) 236 final), and the Proposal for a Regulation of the European Parliament and of the Council regarding access to the Second Generation Schengen Information System (SIS II) by the services in the Member States responsible for issuing vehicle registration certificates (COM(2005) 237 final), OJ 2006, C-91/38

Opinion on five notifications for prior checking received from the data protection officer of the European Anti-Fraud Office (OLAF) on external investigations of 4 October 2007 (cases 2007–47, 2007–48, 2007–50, 2007–72)

Opinion on a notification for prior checking received from the data protection officer at the European Anti-Fraud Office on Criminal assistance cases, Brussels, 12 October 2007 (Case 2007–203)

Opinion on the proposal for a Council Decision establishing the European Police Office (Europol) – COM(2006) 817 final, OJ 2007, C-255/13

Opinion on the proposal for a regulation of the European Parliament and of the Council amending Regulation (EC) No 1073/1999 of the European Parliament and the Council of 25 May 1999 concerning investigation conducted by the European Anti-Fraud Office (OLAF), OJ 2007, C-91/1

Third opinion on the proposal for a Council Framework Decision on the protection of personal data processed in the framework of police and judicial co-operation in criminal matters, OJ 2007, C-139/1

Opinion on the proposal for a regulation of the European Parliament and of the Council of 9 July 2008 amending Council Regulation (EC) No 515/97 on mutual assistance between the administrative authorities of the Member States and cooperation between the latter and the Commission to ensure the correct application of the law on customs and agricultural matters (COM(2006) 866 final), OJ 2007, C-94/3

Opinion on the draft proposal for a Council Framework Decision on the use of Passenger Name records (PNR) for law enforcement purposes, OJ 2008, C-110/01

Opinion on the Council Decision concerning the strengthening of Eurojust and amending Decision 2002/187/JHA of 5 December 2008, OJ 2008, C-310/1

Opinion on the Communication from the Commission to the European Parliament and the Council, an area of freedom, security and justice serving the citizen of 10 July 2009

Opinion on the initiative of the French Republic for a Council Decision on the use of information technology for customs purposes (5903/2/09 REV 2), OJ 2009, C-229/12

Pleadings of 16 June 2009 at the hearing of the Court in case C-28/08, *Bavarian Lager Co. Ltd v. Commission*, accessible at: http://www.edps.europa.eu/EDPSWEB/edps/lang/en/Consultation/Court (accessed February 2011)

Opinion of 7 December 2009 on the proposal for a Regulation establishing an agency for the operational management of large-scale IT systems in the area of freedom, security and justice, and on the proposal for a Council Decision conferring upon the agency tasks regarding the operational management of SIS II and VIS in application of Title VI of the EU Treaty, OJ 2010, C-70/13

Opinion on the amended proposal for a Regulation of the European Parliament and of the Council concerning the establishment of 'Eurodac' for the comparison of fingerprints for the effective application of Regulation (EC) No (.../...) (establishing the criteria and mechanisms for determining the Member State responsible for examining an application for international protection lodged in one of the Member States by a third-country national or a stateless person), and on the proposal for a Council Decision on requesting comparisons with Eurodac data by Member States' law enforcement authorities and Europol for law enforcement purposes, OJ 2010, C-92/1

Opinion on Promoting Trust in the Information Society by Fostering Data Protection and Privacy of 18 March 2010

Opinion on the proposal for a Regulation of the European Parliament and the Council amending Council Regulation (EC) No. 2007/2004 establishing a European Agency for the Management of Operational Cooperation at the External Borders of the Member States of the European Union (FRONTEX) of 17 May 2010

Other EU Documents

The documents are sorted in alphabetical order.

Act of the Joint Supervisory Body of Eurojust of 23 June 2009 laying down its rules of procedure, http://www.eurojust.europa.eu/official_documents/eju_jsb_act.htm (accessed February 2011)

Activity Report of OLAF Supervisory Committee, June 2008 – May 2009, September 2009, p. 20, paras II and III, accessible at: http://ec.europa.eu/anti_fraud/reports/sup-com_en.html (accessed February 2011)

Additional rules defining some specific aspects of the application of the rules on the processing and protection of personal data at Eurojust to non-case related operation, http://www.eurojust.europa.eu/official_documents/eju_dp_rules.htm (accessed February 2011)

Administrative Arrangement between the European Police Office (Europol) and the European Anti-Fraud Office (OLAF) of 8 April 2004, http://www.europol.europa.eu/legal/agreements/Agreements/52153.pdf (accessed February 2011)

Agreement between Europol and Eurojust of 9 June 2004

Agreement between Europol and Eurojust which entered into force the 1 January 2010

Agreement between the European Union and the United States of America on the processing and transfer of Passenger Name Record (PNR) data by air carriers to the Unites States Department of Homeland Security (DHS), OJ 2007, L-204/18

Agreement on provisional application between certain Member States of the European Union of Convention drawn up on the basis of Article K.3 of the Treaty on European Union, on the use of information technology for customs purposes, OJ 1995, C-316/58

Anniversary publication: 10 years of Europol 1999–2009

Annual report 2008 of Eurojust's JSB http://www.eurojust.europa.eu/press_releases/annual_reports/JSB/JSB_ActivityReport2008.pdf (accessed February 2011)

Annual report of Eurojust 2008, http://www.eurojust.europa.eu/press_annual.htm (accessed Februar 2011)

Annual report of OLAF 2009 for the period 1 January 2008 to 31 December 2008

Coordinated Supervision of Eurodac, Activity Report 2008–2009 of March 2010

Decision of the European Ombudsman, 15/10/2009, concerning complaint 2930/2008/JMA against the European Anti-Fraud Office, http://www.ombudsman.europa.eu/cases/home.faces (accessed February 2011)

Decision of the European Ombudsman, 18/12/2009, closing his inquiry into joined complaints 723/2005/OV and 790/2005/OV against the European Anti-Fraud Office, http://www.ombudsman.europa.eu/cases/home.faces (accessed February 2011)

Decision of the Europol Management Board on the conditions related to the processing of data on the basis of Article 10 (4) of the Europol Decision, 15942/09, adopted the 30 November 2009, OJ 2009, L-348/1

EU Terrorism Situation and Trend Report TE-SAT 2010, http://www.europol.europa.eu/index.asp?page=publications&language= (accessed February 2011)

Eurodac Supervision Coordination Group, report of the first coordinated inspection, Brussels, 17 July 2007

Eurodac Supervision Coordination Group, Second Inspection Report, Brussels 24 June 2009

Eurojust annual report 2009

Eurojust work programme 2010

Eurojust-US Agreement of November 2006

Europol annual report 2008

Europol report, "OCTA 2009, EU organised crime threat assessment", http://www.europol.europa.eu/publications/European_Organised_Crime_Threat_Assessment (OCTA)/OCTA2009.pdf (accessed February 2011)

Europol Review, annual general report on Europol activities 2009

Europol-US Agreement on the exchange of personal data and related information of 2002

Frontex "Programme of Work 2010", http://www.frontex.europa.eu/gfx/frontex/files/justyna/pow2010.pdf (accessed February 2011)

Guidelines for OLAF staff regarding practical implementation of data protection requirements of December 2008

Implementing rules concerning the Data Protection Officer, Europol Management Board, The Hague 23 September 2009

Interinstitutional file 2009/0089 (COD), no. 13350/09, note from the French delegation on the legislative package establishing an agency for the operational management of large-scale IT systems in the area of freedom, security and justice of 15 September 2009

Joint declaration on cooperation and partnership between the Council of Europe and the European Commission of 3 April 2001, available at: http://www.jp.coe.int/Upload/110_Joint_Declaration_EF.pdf (accessed February 2009)

Joint Investigation Teams Manual of 23 September 2009 prepared by Europol and Eurojust, Council doc. 13598/09

Memorandum of Understanding between Eurojust and OLAF of 4 April 2003, http://ec.europa.eu/anti_fraud/press_room/pr/2003/memo_en.pdf (accessed February 2011)

Memorandum of Understanding between the Council of Europe and the European Union of 10 May 2007, CM(2007)74, available at: https://wcd.coe.int/ViewDoc.jsp?Ref=CM(2007)74&Language=lanEnglish, (accessed February 2011)

Note from the General Secretariat to the Standing Committee on operational cooperation on internal security (COSI), final report on the cooperation between JHA agencies, Council doc. 8387/10 of 9 April 2010

Note from the Praesidium of the Convention, Explanation on the Charter of Fundamental Rights of the European Union, Draft Charter of Fundamental Rights, CHARTE 4473/00 CONVENT 49 of 11 October 2000

OLAF annual report 2009, ninth activity report for the period 1 January 2008 to 31 December 2008

OLAF manual of 25 February 2005

OLAF manual on operational procedures of 1 December 2009

OLAF privacy statement for coordination cases (OLAF DPO-143)

OLAF privacy statement for criminal assistant cases (OLAF DPO-15)

OLAF privacy statement for external investigations (OLAF DPO-6, 8, 9, 10, 11 and 13)

OLAF privacy statement for follow-up (OLAF DPO-1, 2, 3, 4 and 5)

OLAF privacy statement for fraud notification system (OLAF DPO-133

OLAF privacy statement for internal investigations (OLAF DPO-7)

OLAF privacy statement for investigations by the OLAF DPO (OLAF DPO-111)

OLAF privacy statement for monitoring cases (OLAF DPO-16)

OLAF privacy statement for non-cases and prima facie non-cases (OLAF DPO-129)

OLAF "Instructions to staff conducting investigations following from opinion of European Data Protection Supervisor (EDPS) on prior checking on internal investigations"

OLAF Notification to the data protection officer from OLAF's former director Franz Hermann Brüner, version 2, DPO 6 of 10 December 08

Opinion of the Customs Joint Supervisory Authority with respect to the draft Council Decision on the use of information technology for customs purposes (Opinion 09/03) of 24 March 2009

Opinion of the European Union Agency for Fundamental Rights on the Proposal for a Council Framework Decision on the use of Passenger Name Record (PNR) data for law enforcement purposes, 28 October 2008

Practical Agreement on arrangements of cooperation between Eurojust and OLAF of 24 September 2008

Report 51st meeting of the JSB of Europol, Brussels 12 October 2009

Report by the High Level Contact Group (HLCG) on information sharing and privacy and data protection, Council doc. 15815/09 of 23 November 2009 and Proposal for a Council Recommendation to authorise the opening of negotiations for an agreement between the European Union and the United States of America on protection of personal when transferred and processed for the purpose of preventing, investigating, detecting or prosecuting criminal offences, including terrorism, in the framework of police cooperation and judicial cooperation in criminal matters, COM(2010) 252, accessible at: http://www.statewatch.org/news/2010/aug/eu-usa-dp-general-em.pdf (accessed February 2011)

Report of 21 Mai 2007 of the European Parliament on the on the proposal for a Council Decision concerning access for consultation of the Visa Information System (VIS) by the authorities of the Member States responsible for internal security and by Europol for the purposes of the prevention, detection and investigation of terrorist offences and of other serious criminal offences (COM(2005) 600final – 2005/0323(CNS)), Committee on Civil Liberties, Justice and Home affairs, rapporteur: *Sarah Ludford*

Report of the Schengen Joint Supervisory Authority, activity report – January 2004-December 2005

Rules of procedure of the JSB: http://www.eurojust.europa.eu/jsb-legalframework.htm#jsb-rules (accessed February 2011)

Rules of procedure on the processing and the protection of personal data at Eurojust, **OJ 2005, C-68/1**

Schengen JSA, activity report – December 2005-December 2008

Schengen JSA Opinion 98/2 of 3 February 1998 on entering an alert in the SIS on individuals whose identity has been usurped

SIRENE manual, doc. 12802/02 of 7 March 2008

Special Report from the European Ombudsman to the European Parliament following the draft recommendation to the European Anti-Fraud Office in complaint 2485/2004/GG

Special Report from the European Ombudsman to the European Parliament following the draft recommendation to the European Anti-Fraud Office in complaint 2485/2004/GG

The fourth activity report of the Joint Supervisory Body of Europol, November 2006 – November 2008

The Hague Programme: strengthening freedom, security and justice in the European Union, Council doc. 16054/04 of 13 December 2004

The Stockholm Programme – An open and secure Europe serving and protection the citizen, Council doc. 17024/09 of 2 December 2009

Working Party on Police and Justice (WPPJ), Draft Annual Report for the Year 2009

House of Lords documents related to EU measures

The documents are listed in chronological order

House of Lords, Select Committee on European Union Written Evidence Sub-Committee F (Social Affairs, Education and Home Affairs), letter from the Chairman to Bob Ainsworth MP, Under-Secretary of State, Home Office, Schengen Information System: new functions, (9407/02 and 9408/02) of 9 April 2003

House of Lords Eurojust report, European Union Committee, 23rd report of session 2003–04, "Judicial cooperation in the EU: the role of Eurojust", published 21 July 2004

House of Lords, European Union Committee, "Strengthening OLAF, the European Anti-Fraud Office", 24th report with evidence of session 2003–2004, published 21 July 2004

House of Lords report: 5th report of session 2004–05, "After Madrid: the EU's response to terrorism", published 8 March 2005

House of Lords, European Union Committee, "Financial Management and Fraud in the European Union: Perceptions, Facts and Proposals", 50th report of session 2005–2006, published 13 November 2006

House of Lords, European Union Committee, 9th report of session 2006–2007, "Schengen Information System II (SIS II)", published 2 March 2007

House of Lords, European Union Committee, 9th report of session 2007–2008, "Frontex: the EU external borders agency", published 5 March 2008

House of Lords, submission by Europol, Select Committee on European Union, Call for Evidence, File no. 3100–174, 28 April 2008

House of Lords Europol report, European Union Committee, 29th report of session 2007–2008, "Europol: coordinating the fight against serious and organised crime", published 12 November 2008

House of Lords, European Union Committee, report "Civil Protection and Crisis Management in the European Union", seventh report of session 2008–2009, examination of witnesses, 21 January 2009

Studies, reports and recommendations

The studies, reports and recommendations are listed in chronological order

Report "Security & Privacy in Large Scale, Biometric Systems", based on an experts meeting held in Brussels on 25 September 2006, produced by the European Biometrics Forum, author: *Max Snijder*, commissioned by the EC – Commission's Joint Research Centre (JRC)/Institute for Prospective Technological Studies (IPTS)

Final report of COWI (European consulting group) of January 2009 preparing an external evaluation of Frontex provided for in Article 33 of the Council Regulation (EC) No 2007/2004 of 26 October 2004 establishing Frontex, p. 48, available at: http://www.frontex.europa.eu/specific_documents/other/ (accessed February 2011)

Deloitte, study on the feasibility of establishing specialised branches of Frontex, final report, 11 December 2009, p. 18, para 4.1.1., http://www.frontex.europa.eu/specific_documents/other/ (accessed February 2011)

Meijers Committee, standing committee of experts on international immigration, refugee and criminal law, Utrecht/The Netherlands, letter of 30 December 2009 to the European Parliament, Civil Liberties, Justice and Home Affairs Committee on the Proposal on law enforcement access to Eurodac, COM(2009) 344 final

EU observer, "EU diplomats to benefit from new intelligence hub", 22 February 2010, http://euobserver.com/?aid=29519 (accessed February 2011)

Table of Cases

I. ECtHR Cases and Decisions of the Commission of the Council of Europe

(Listed in alphabetical order)

Airey v. Ireland, Application no. 6289/73, judgment of 9 October 1979

Allan v. the United Kingdom, Application no. 48539/99, judgment of 5 November 2002

Amann v. Switzerland, Application no. 27798/95, judgment of 16 February 2000, para 65

Antunes Rocha v. Portugal, Application no. 64330/01, judgment of 31 May 2005

Armstrong v. the United Kingdom, Application no. 48521/99, judgment of 16 July 2002

Association for European Integration and Human Rights and Ekimdzhiev v. Bulgaria, Application no. 62540/00, judgment of 28 June 2007

Barthold v. Germany, Application no. 8734/79, judgment of 25 March 1985

Biriuk v Lithuania, Application no. 23373/03, judgment of 25 November 2008

Biriuk v. Lithuania, Application no. 23373/03, judgment of 25 November 2008

Bykov v. Russia, Application no. 4378/02, judgment of 10 March 2009

C.C. v. Spain, Application no. 1425/06, judgment of 6 October 2009

C.G. and others v. Bulgaria, Application no. 1365/07, judgment of 24 April 2008

Cemalettin Canl v. Turkey, Application no. 22427/04, judgment of 18 November 2008

Chalkley v. the United Kingdom, Application no. 63831/00, judgment of 12 June 2003

Chappell v. the United Kingdom, Application no. 10461/83, judgment of 30 March 1989

Copland v. the United Kingdom, Application no. 62617/00, judgment of 3 April 2007

F. Boehm, *Information Sharing and Data Protection in the Area of Freedom, Security and Justice*, DOI 10.1007/978-3-642-22392-1,

Cossey v. the United Kingdom, Application no. 10843/84, judgment of 27 September 1990

Craxi v. Italy, Application no. 25337/94, judgment of 17 July 2003

De Wilde, Ooms and Versyp v. Belgium, Application no. 2832/66 and others, judgment of 18 June 1997

Dickson v. the United Kingdom, Application no. 44262/04, judgment of 4 December 2007

Doerga v. Netherlands, Application no. 50210/99, judgment of 27 April 2004

Dudgeon v. the United Kingdom, Application no. 7525/76, judgment of 22 October 1981

Editions Plon v. France, Application no. 58148/00, judgment of 18 May 2004

Edwards and Lewis v. the United Kingdom, Application nos. 39647/98 and 40461/98, judgment of 27 October 2004

Fadeyeva v. Russia, Application no. 55723/00, judgment of 9 June 2005

Friedl v. Austria, Application no. 15225/89, judgment of 31 January 1995

Funke v. France, Application no. 10828/84, judgment of 25 February 1993

Gaskin v. the United Kingdom, Application no. 10454/83, judgment of 7 July 1989

Gillow v. the United Kingdom, Application no. 9063/80, judgment of 24 November 1986

Golder v. the United Kingdom, Application no. 4451/70, judgment of 21 February 1975

Guerra and others v. Italy, Application no. 14967/89, judgment of 19 February 1998

Halford v. the United Kingdom, Application no. 20605/92, judgment of 25 June 1997

Handyside v. the United Kingdom, Application no. 5493/72, judgment of 7 December 1976

Herbecq and the Association "ligue des droits des l'homme" v. Belgium, Application no. 32200/96 and 32201/96, admissibility decision of 14 January 1998

Hewitson v. the United Kingdom, Application no. 50015/99, judgment of 27 May 2003

Huvig v. France, Application no. 11105/84, judgment of 24 April 1990

I. v Finland, Application no. 20511/03, judgment of 17 July 2008

I. v. the United Kingdom, Application no. 25680/94, judgment of 11 July 2002

Ilascu and others v. Moldova and Russia, Application no. 48787/99, judgment of 8 July 2004

K.H. and others v. Slovakia, Application no. 32881/04, judgment of 28 April 2009

K.U. v. Finland, Application no. 2872/02, judgment of 2 December 2008

Kennedy v. the United Kingdom, Application no. 26839/05, judgment of 18 May 2010

Khan v. the United Kingdom, Application no. 35394/97, judgment of 12 May 2000

Kinnunen v. Finland, Application no. 18291/91, Commission decision of 13 October 1993

Kirov v. Bulgaria, Application no. 5182/02, judgment of 22 May 2008

Klass v. Germany, Application no. 5029/71, judgment of 6 September 1978

Knauth v. Germany, Application no. 41111/98, admissibility decision of 22 November 2001

Kopp v. Switzerland, Application no. 23224/94, judgment of 25 March 1998

Kruslin v. France, Application no. 11801/85, judgment of 24 April 1990

Kvasnica v. Slovakia, Application no. 72094/01, judgment of 9 June 2009

L.L. v France, Application no. 7508/02, judgment of 10 October 2006

Lamy v. Belgium, Application no. 10444/83, judgment of 30 March 1989

Leander v. Sweden, Application no. 9248/81, judgment of 26 March 1987

Lewis v. the United Kingdom, Application no. 1303/02, judgment of 25 November 2003

Liberty and others v. the United Kingdom, Application no. 58234/00, judgment of 1 July 2008

Loiseau v. France, Application no. 46809/99, admissibility decision of 18 November 2003

Loizidou v. Turkey, Application no. 15318/89, judgment of 23 March 1995

Luboch v. Poland, Application no. 37469/05, judgment of 15 January 2008

Lüdi v. Switzerland, Application no. 12433/86, judgment of 15 June 1992

Lupker v. Netherlands, Application no. 18395/91, judgment of 7 December 1992

M.G. v. the United Kingdom, Application no. 39393/98, judgment of 24 September 2002

M.S. v. Sweden, Application no. 20837/92, judgment of 27 August 1997

Malone v. the United Kingdom, Application no. 8691/79, judgment of 2 August 1984

Mamatkulov and Askarov v. Turkey, Application nos. 46827/99 and 46951/99, judgment of 4 February 2005

Martin v. the United Kingdom, Application no. 27533/95, admissibility decision of 28 February 1996

Matyjek v. Poland, Application no. 38184/03, judgment of 24 April 2007

Mc Veigh and others v. United Kingdom, Application no. 8022/77, Commission decision of 18 March 1981

McGinley and Egan v. the United Kingdom, Application nos. 21825/93 and 23414/94, judgment of 9 June 1998

McMichael v. the United Kingdom, Application no. 16424/90, judgment of 24 February 1995

Mersch and others v. Luxembourg, Application no. 10439/83, 10440/83, 10441/83, 10452/83 10512/83 and 10513/83, admissibility decision of 10 May 1985

Murray v. the United Kingdom, Application no. 14310/88, judgment of 28 October 1994

Niemietz v. Germany, Application no. 13710/88, judgment of 16 September 1992

Observer and Guardian v. the United Kingdom, Application no. 13585/88, judgment of 26 November 1991

Özgür Gündem v. Turkey, Application no. 23144/93, judgment of 16 March 2000

P.G. and J.H. v. United Kingdom, Application no. 44787/98, judgment of 25 September 2001

Panteleyenko v. Ukraine, Application no. 11901/02, judgment of 29 June 2006

Peck v. United Kingdom, Application no. 44647/98, judgment of 28 January 2003

Perry v. the United Kingdom, Application no. 63737/00, judgment of 17 July 2002

Powell and Rayner v. the United Kingdom, Application no. 9310/81, judgment of 21 February 1990

Pretty v. United Kingdom, Application no. 2346/02, judgment of 29 April 2002

Rasmussen v. Denmark, Application no. 8777/79, judgment of 28 November 1984

Rees v. the United Kingdom, Application no. 9532/81, judgment of 17 October 1986

Reyntjens v. Belgium, Application no. 16810/90, admissibility decision of 9 September 1992

Roche v. the United Kingdom, Application no. 32555/96, judgment of 19 October 2005

Rotaru v. Romania, Application no. 28341/954, judgment of 4 May 2000

Rowe and Davis v. the United Kingdom, Application no. 28901/95, judgment of 16 February 2000

Ruiz-Mateos v. Spain, Application no. 12952/87, judgment of 23 June 1993

S. and Marper v the United Kingdom, Application nos. 30562/04 and 30566/04, judgment of 4 December 2008

Schüssel v. Austria, Application no. 42409/98, judgment of 21 February 2002

Sciacca v. Italy, Application no. 50774/99, judgment of 11 January 2005

Sdružení Jihočeské Matky v. Czech Republic, Application no. 19101/03, admissibility decision of 10 July 2006

Segerstedt-Wiberg and others v. Sweden, Application no. 62332/00, judgment of 6 June 2006

Sheffield and Horsham v. the United Kingdom, Application nos. 22985/93 and 23390/94, judgment of 30 July 1998

Silver v. the United Kingdom, Application no. 5947/72 and others, judgment of 25 March 1983

Smith v. the United Kingdom, Application no. 39658/05, admissibility decision of 4 January 2007

Soering v. the United Kingdom, Application no. 14038/88, judgment of 7 July 1987, para 89

Stoll v. Switzerland, Application no. 69698/01, judgment of 25 April 2006

Sunday Times v. the United Kingdom, Application no. 13166/87, judgment of 26 November 1991

Sunday Times v. the United Kingdom, Application no. 6538/74, judgment of 26 April 1979

Társaság a Szabadságjogokért v. Hungary, Application no. 37374/05, judgment of 14 April 2009

Taylor-Sabori v. the United Kingdom, Application no. 47114/99, judgment of 22 October 2002

Tillack v. Belgium, Application no. 20477/05, judgment of 27 November 2007

Turek v. Slovakia, Application no. 57986/00, judgment of 14 February 2006

Tyrer v. the United Kingdom, Application no. 5856/75, Series A 26, judgment of 25 April 1978

Uzun v. Germany, Application no. 35623/05, judgment of 2 September 2010

Valenzuela Contreras v. Spain, Application no. 27671/95, judgment of 30 July 1998

Van Kück v. Germany, Application no. 35968/97, judgment of 12 June 2003

Volokhy v. Ukraine, Application no. 23543/02, judgment of 2 November 2006

Von Hannover v. Germany, Application no. 59320/00, judgment of 24 June 2004

Weber and Saravia v. Germany, Application no. 54934/00, admissibility decision of 29 June 2006

Weber v. Switzerland, Application no. 11034/84, judgment of 22 May 1990

Wisse v. France, Application no. 71611/01, preliminary objection of 20 December 2005

Wood v. the United Kingdom, Application no. 23414/02, judgment of 16 November 2004

X. v. Germany, Application no. 1307/61, Commission decision of 4 October 1962

X. v. Iceland, Application no. 6825/74, Commission decision of 18 May 1976

Yvonne Chave neé Jullien v. France, Application no. 14461/88, admissibility decision of 9 July 1991

Z. and others v. the United Kingdom, Application no. 29392/95, judgment of 10 May 2001

Z. v Finland, Application no. 22009/93, judgment of 25 February 1997

II. EU Cases

The cases have been listed in chronological order

Court of Justice

Case 29–69, *Erich Stauder v. City of Ulm*, judgement of 12 November

European Parliament v. Council, judgment of 27 September 1988

C-413/99, *Baumbast and R*, judgment of 17 December 2002

C-465/00, *Rechnungshof v. Österreichischer Rundfunk and Others*, judgment of 20 May 2003

C-13/00, *Commission v. European Investment Bank*, judgment of 10 July 2003

C-11/00, *Commission v. European Central Bank*, judgment of 10 July 2003
C-101/01, *Lindqvist*, judgment of 6 November 2003
C-160/03, *Spain v. Eurojust*, judgment of 15 March 2005
C-521/04 P (R), *Tillack v. Commission*, judgment of 19 April 2005
C-105/03, criminal proceedings against *Maria Pupino*, judgment of 16 June 2005
C-503/03, *Commission v. Spain*, judgment of 31 January 2006
Joined cases C-317/04 and C-318/04, *Parliament v. Council*, judgment of 30 May 2006
C-229/05 P, *PKK and KNK v. Council*, judgment of 18 January 2007
C-266/05 P, *Sison v. Council*, judgment of 1 February 2007
C-275/06, *Productores de Música de España Promusicae vs. Telefónica de España*, judgment of 29 January 2008
C-524/06, *Heinz Huber v. Germany*, judgment of 16 December 2008
C-73/07, *Tietosuojavaltuutettu v. Satakunnan Markkinapörssi Oy and Satamedia Oy*, judgment of 16 December 2008
C-301/06, *Ireland v. Parliament and Council*, judgment of 10 February 2009
C-553/07, *College van burgemeester en wethouders van Rotterdam v. M.E.E. Rijkeboer*, judgment of 7 May 2009
C-518/07, *Commission v. Germany*, judgment of 9 March 2010
C-28/08, *Bavarian Lager Co. Ltd v. Commission*, judgment of 29 June 2010
C-482/08, *United Kingdom of Great Britain and Northern Ireland against the Council of the European Union*, judgment of 26 October 2010
Joined cases C-92/09 and C-93/09, *Volker and Markus Schecke GbR and Hartmut Eifert* v. *Land Hessen*, judgement of 9 November 2010

General Court

T-215/02, *Gomez-Reino v. Commission*, order of 18 December 2003
T-320/02, *Esch-Leonhardt and Others v. ECB*, judgment of 18 February 2004
T-29/03, *Comunidad Autonoma de Andalucia v. Commission*, order of 13 July 2004
T-309/03, *Camos Grau v. Commission*, judgment of 6 April 2006
T-189/03, *Bank Austria Creditanstalt AG v. Commission*, judgment of 30 May 2006
T-193/04, *Tillack v. Commission*, judgment of 4 October 2006
T-228/02, *Organisation des Modjahedines de people d'Iran v. Council*, judgment of 12 December 2006
T-47/03, *Sison v. Council*, judgment of 11 July 2007
T-259/03, *Nikolaou v. Commission*, judgment of 12 September 2007
T-194/04, *Bavarian Lager Co. Ltd v. Commission*, judgment of 8 November 2007
T-48/05, *Yves Franchet and Daniel Byk v. Commission*, judgment of 8 July 2008
T-284/08, *Organisation des Modjahedines de people d'Iran v. Council*, judgment of 4 December 2008
T-121/05, *Borax Europe Ltd. v. Commission*, judgment of 11 March 2009
T-261/09 P, *Commission v. Violetti and others*, judgment of 20 May 2010

Tribunal

F-23/05, *Giraudy v. Commission*, judgment of 2 May 2007

F-118/07, *Strack v. Commission*, action brought on 22 October 2007

F-5/05 and 7/05, *Violetti and others v. Commission*, judgment of 28 April 2009

German Constitutional Court

German Constitutional Court, judgment of 14 October 2004, 2 BvR 1481/04, *Görgülü*

German Constitutional Court, judgment of 4 April 2006, 1 BvR 518/02

German Constitutional Court, judgment of 2 March 2010, 1 BvR 256/08, 1 BvR 263/08 and 1 BvR 586/08

Romanian Constitutional Court

Curtea Constitutionala, 8 October 2009 number 1258, Romanian Official Monitor no. 789 of 23 November 2009

Bibliography

Books

Arai-Takahashi Y (2002) The margin of appreciation doctrine and the principle of proportionality in the jurisprudence of the ECHR. Intersentia, Antwerp
Bainbridge D (2005) Data protection. xlp publishing, St. Albans
Bieber R, Epiney A, Haag M (2006) Die Europäische Union – Europarecht und Politik, 7th edn. Nomos Verlag, Baden-Baden
Bigo D (1996) Police en Réseaux – l'expérience européenne. Presses de Sciences Po, Paris
Borchardt K-D (2010) Die rechtlichen Grundlagen der Europäischen Union, 4th edn. C.F. Müller, Heidelberg
Breitenmoser S (1986) Der Schutz der Privatsphäre gemäß Art. 8 EMRK: Das Recht auf Achtung des Privat- und Familienlebens, der Wohnung und des Briefverkehrs. Schriftenreihe des Instituts für internationales Recht und internationale Beziehungen, Bd. 39. 1 Auflage. Helbing & Lichtenhahn, Basel
Breitenmoser S, Riemer B, Seitz C (2006) Praxis des Europarechts - Grundrechtsschutz. Carl Heymanns Verlag, Köln
Breitenmoser S, Gless S, Lagodny O (2009) Schengen in der Praxis. Nomos Verlag, Baden-Baden
Brouwer E (2008a) Digital borders and real rights – effective remedies for third-country nationals in the Schengen information system. Martinus Nijhoff, Leiden
Bull HP (2009) Informationelle Selbstbestimmung – Vision oder Illusion – Datenschutz im Spannungsverhältnis von Freiheit und Sicherheit. Mohr Siebeck, Tübingen
Callies C (2010) Die neue Europäische Union nach dem Vertrag von Lissabon. Mohr Siebeck, Tübingen
Callies C, Ruffert M (2007) EUV/EGV – Das Verfassungsrecht der Europäischen Union mit Grundrechtecharta. Commentary. C.H. Beck, München
Cameron I (2000) National security and the European convention on human rights. Kluwer Law International, The Hague
Carey P (2004) Data protection: a practical guide to UK and EU law. Oxford University Press, Oxford
Clapham A (2006) Human rights obligations of non-state actors. Oxford University Press, Oxford
Cole M, Fink U, Keber T (2008) Europäisches und Internationales Medienrecht. C.F. Müller, Heidelberg
Coppel P (2007) Information rights. Sweet and Maxwell, London
Craig P, De Burca G (2008) EU law – text, cases and materials, 4th edn. Oxford University Press, Oxford

F. Boehm, *Information Sharing and Data Protection in the Area of Freedom, Security and Justice*, DOI 10.1007/978-3-642-22392-1,

Cullen P (2004) Enlarging the fight against fraud in the European Union: penal and administrative sanctions, settlement whistleblowing and corpus juris in the candidate countries. Series of Publications, Academy of European Law Trier. Bundesanzeiger, Köln

Cullen P, Jund S (2002) Criminal justice co-operation in the European Union after Tampere. Series of Publications by the Academy of European Law in Trier. Bundesanzeiger, Köln

Dammann U, Simitis S (1997) Commentary to Directive 95/46, EG-Datenschutzrichtline, Kommentar. Nomos Verlag, Baden-Baden

De Busser E (2009) Data protection in EU and US criminal cooperation. Maklu, Antwerpen

Di Martino A (2005) Datenschutz im europäischen Recht. Nomos Verlag, Baden-Baden

Dröge C (2003) Positive Verpflichtungen in der Europäischen Menschenrechtskonvention. Springer, Heidelberg, New York, Barcelona

Ehmann E, Helfrich M (1999) EG Datenschutzrichtlinie - Kurzkommentar. Verlag Dr. Otto Schmidt, Köln

Ellger R (1990) Der Datenschutz im grenzüberschreitenden Datenverkehr: Eine rechtsvergleichende und kollosionsrechtliche Untersuchung. Nomos Verlag, Baden-Baden

Engel A (2003) Reichweite und Umsetzung des Datenschutzes gemäß der Richtlinie 95/46/EG für aus der Europäischen Union in Drittländer exportierte Daten am Beispiel der USA, 1st edn. Dissertation, FU Berlin. Available at: http://www.diss.fu-berlin.de/diss/receive/FUDISS_thesis_000000001587. Accessed Feb 2011

Engel M (2006) Befugnis, Kontrolle und Entwicklung von Europol – unter Berücksichtigung des Vertrages über eine Verfassung für Europa. Verlag Dr. Kovac, Hamburg

Fastenrath U, Nowak C (2009) Der Lissabonner Reformvertrag. Änderungsimpulse in einzelnen Rechts- und Politikbereichen. Duncker & Humblot, Berlin

Fawzy O (2005) Die Einrichtung von Eurojust – Zwischen Funktionalität und Rechtsstaatlichkeit, unter Berücksichtigung der Vorschläge des Europäischen Verfassungskonvents. Nomos Verlag, Baden-Baden

Fischer K (2010) Der Vertrag von Lissabon – Text und Kommentar zum Europäischen Reformvertrag, 2nd edn. Nomos Verlag, Baden-Baden

Fungueirino-Lorenzo R (2002) Visa-, Asyl- und Einwanderungspolitik vor und nach dem Vertag von Amsterdam. Peter Lang Verlag, Frankfurt am Main

Gebauer K (2007) Parallele Grund- und Menschenrechtsschutzssteme in Europa? Duncker & Humblot, Berlin

Geiger R, Khan D-E, Kotzur M (2010) EUV/AEUV – Vertrag über die Europäische Union und Vertrag über die Arbeitsweise der Europäischen Union, Commentary. C.H. Beck, München

Gleß S, Grote R, Heine G (2001) Justitielle Einbindung und Kontrolle von Europol. Polizeiliche Ermittlungstätigkeit und Grundrechtsschutz, Freibug

Grabenwarter C (2009a) Europäische Menschenrechtskonvention, 4th edn. Beck, München

Greer S (2006) The European convention on human rights, achievements, problems and prospects. Cambridge University Press, Cambrige

Gutwirth S (2002) Privacy and the information age. Rowman & Littlefield, Boston

Häberle P (2009) Europäische Verfassungslehre, 6th edn. Nomos Verlag, Baden-Baden

Hailbronner K (1996) Zusammenarbeit der Polizei- und Justizverwaltungen in Europa – die Situation nach Maastricht – Schengen und SIS. Kriminalistik Verlag, Heidelberg

Hailbronner K, Weil P (1999) From Schengen to Amsterdam – towards a European immigration and asylum legislation. Schriftenreihe der Europäischen Rechtsakademie Trier. Bundesanzeiger, Köln

Hamilton A, Jay R (2003) Data protection: law and practice. Sweet & Maxwell, London

Haratsch A, Koenig C, Pechstein M (2010) Europarecht, 7th edn. Mohr Siebeck, Tübingen

Hecker B (2010) Europäisches Strafrecht, 3rd edn. Springer, Heidelberg

Henke F (1985–1986) Die Datenschutzkonvention des Europarates. Peter Lang Verlag, Frankfurt am Main

Herdegen M (2010) Europaracht, 12th edn. C.H. Beck, München

Heselhaus S, Nowak C (2006) Handbuch der Europäischen Grundrechte, 1st edn. C.H. Beck, München
Heusel W (2002) The charter of fundamental rights and constitutional development in the EU. Schriftenreihe der Europäischen Rechtsakademie Trier. Bundesanzeiger, Köln
Hofmann HCH, Rowe GC, Türk AH (2011) EU administrative law and policy of the European Union. Oxford University Press, Oxford, forthcoming
Jansen O, Lanbroek PM (2007) Defence rights during administrative investigations. Intersentia, Antwerpen
Jarass H (2010) Charta der Grundrechte der Europäischen Union, Commentary. C.H. Beck, München
Jones TH (1995) The devaluation of human rights under the European convention. Public Law:430
Kabera Karanja S (2008) Transparency and proportionality in the Schengen information system and border control co-operation. Martinus Nijhoff, Leiden
Kistner-Bahr H (2010) Die Entwicklungstendenzen Europols im europäischen Integrationsprozess – mögliche Ausweitung der Befugnisse Europols vom Informationsaustausch zur Ermittlungskompetenz unter Berücksichtigung des Vertrages von Lissabon. Thesis of the University of Köln, March 2010
Koch O (2003) Der Grundsatz der Verhältnismäßigkeit in der Rechtprechung des Gerichtshofs der Europäischen Gemeinschaften. Duncker & Humblot, Berlin
Léger P (2000) Union Européenne – Commentaire Article par Article des Traités UE et CE. Helbig & Lichtenhahn, Dalloz
Lenz CO, Borchardt KD (2010) EU-Verträge – Kommentar nach dem Vertrag von Lissabon, 5th edn. Bundesanzeiger, Köln
Lenz CO, Borchardt K-D (2006) EU- und EG-Vertrag – Kommentar zu dem Vertrag über die Europäische Union und zu dem Vertrag zur Gründung der Europäischen Gemeinschaft", 4th edn. Bundesanzeiger, Köln
Mayer S (2001) Datenschutz und Europol. Thesis of the University of Regensburg, Germany
Meyer J (2011) Charta der Grundrechte der Europäischen Union, Commentary, 3rd edition. Nomos Verlag, Baden-Baden
Meyer-Ladewig J (2006) "Europäische Menschenrechtskonvention", Handkommentar, 2nd edn. Nomos Verlag, Baden-Baden
Milke T (2003) Europol und Eurojust – Zwei Institutionen zur internationalen Verbrechensbekämpfung und ihre justitielle Kontrolle. V & R unipress, Osnabrück
Mitrou E (1993) Die Entwicklung der institutionellen Kontrolle des Datenschutzes: Kontrollmodelle und Kontrollinstanzen in der Bundesrepublik und in Frankreich. Nomos Verlag, Baden-Baden
Mitsilegas V (2009) EU criminal law. Hart publishing, Oxford
Möllers R (2009) Wirksamkeit und Effektivität der Europäischen Agentur Frontex – Eine Politikwissenschaftliche Analyse der Entwicklung eines integrierten Grenzschutzsystems an den Außengrenzen der EU, 1st edn. Verlag für Polizeiwissenschaft, Frankfurt am Main
Möstl M (2010) Vertrag von Lissabon – Einführung und Kommentierung. Olzog Verlag, München
Mowbray A (2007) Cases and materials on the European convention on human rights, 2nd edn. Oxford University Press, Oxford
Murawska AA (2008) Administrative anti-fraud measures within the European Union, necessity and means. Nomos Verlag, Baden-Baden
Nugter ACM (1990) Transborder flow of personal data within the EU. Kluwer Law and Taxation, Deventer
Oppermann T, Classen D, Nettesheim M (2009) Europarecht – Ein Studienbuch, 4th edn. C.H. Beck, München
Ovey C, White CAR (2006) Jacobs and White: The European convention on human rights, 4th edn. Oxford University Press, Oxford
Oxford (November 2005) Business english dictionary. Oxford University Press, Oxford
Peers S (2006) EU justice and home affairs law, 2nd edn. Oxford University Press, Oxford
Peters A (2003) Einführung in die Europäische Menschenrechtskonvention. C.H. Beck, München

Petri Bernhard T (2001) Europol – Grenzüberschreitende polizeiliche Tätigkeit in Europa, Frankfurter Studien zum Datenschutz, 1st edn. Nomos Verlag, Baden-Baden
Rengeling W, Szczekalla P (2004) Grundrechte der Europäischen Union – Charta der Grundrechte und Allgemeine Rechtsgrundsätze. Carl Heymanns Verlag, Köln
Rijken C, Vermeulen G (2006) Joint investigation teams in the European Union, from theory to practice. T.M.C Asser Press, The Hague
Satzger H (2009) Internationales und Europäisches Strafrecht, 3rd edn. Nomos Verlag, Baden-Baden
Schaper T (2009) Verfassungsrechtliche Probleme bei der Übertragung von Hoheitsrechten zur Schaffung eines europäischen Strafrechts – Eine Untersuchung am Beispiel des Rahmenbeschlusses über den Europäischen Haftbefehl. Duncker & Humblot, Berlin
Schmidt D (2001) Auf dem Weg zu einer Europäischen Einwanderungs- und Asylpolitk – Herausforderungen und künftige Aufgaben in einem gemeinsamen Raum der Freiheit, der Sicherheit und des Rechts. Thesis, Freie Universität Berlin, Berlin
Schneiders B (2010) Die Grundrechte der EU und die EMRK – Das Verhältnis zwischen ungeschriebenen Grundrechten, Grundrechtecharta und Europäischer Menschenrechtskonvention. Nomos Verlag, Baden-Baden
Schubert I (2008) Europol und der virtuelle Verdacht – Die Suspendierung des Rechts auf informationelle Selbstbestimmung. Frankfurter kriminalwissenschaftliche Studien, Band/vol 107. Peter Lang Verlag, Frankfurt am Main
Seong H-J (2005) Europol im Recht der Europäischen Union. Medien Verlag Köhler, Tübingen
Siemen B (2006) Datenschutz als europäisches Grundrecht. Duncker & Humblot, Berlin
Simitis S (2006) "Bundesdatenschutzgesetz" commentary. Nomos Verlag, Baden-Baden
Singleton S (1998) Data protection: the new law. Jordan Publishing, Bristol
Srock G (2006) Rechtliche Rahmenbedingungen für die Weiterentwicklung von Europol. Mohr Siebeck, Tübingen
Steiner J, Woods L, Twigg-Flesner C (2006) EU law, 9th edn. Oxford University Press, Oxford
Streinz R (2005) Europarecht, 7th edn. C.F. Müller, Heidelberg
Tinnefeld M-T, Phillips L, Heil S (1995) Informationsgesellschaft und Rechtskultur in Europa, 1st edn. Nomos Verlag, Baden-Baden
Walker N (2004) Europe's area of freedom, securtiy and justice. Oxford University Press, Oxford
Wentrup Große A (2003) Die Europäische Grundrechtecharta im Spannungsfeld der Kompetenzverteilung zwischen Europäischer Union und Mitgliedstaaten. Duncker & Humblot, Berlin
Wiesbrock K (1999) Internationaler Schutz der Menschenrechte vor Verletzungen durch Private. Berlin Verlag, Berlin
Wittinger M (2005) Der Europarat: Die Entwicklung seines Rechts und der europäischen Verfassungswerte. Nomos Verlag, Baden-Baden
Wuermeling U (2000) Handelshemmnis Datenschutz – Die Drittländerregelung der Europäischen Union, 1st edition. C. Heymanns (Ius Informationis 14), Thesis of the University of Würzburg, Würzburg
Youngs R (1998) English, French and German comparative law. Cavendish publishing, London
Ziegenhorn G (2009) Der Einfluss der EMRK im Recht der EU-Grundrechtecharta – Genuin chartarechtlicher Gundrechtsschutz gemäß Art. 52 Abs. 3 GRCh. Duncker & Humblot, Berlin

Articles

This section includes contributions to books, papers and contribution to commentaries.

Alonso Blas D (2010) Ensuring effective data protection in the field of police and judicial activities: some considerations to achieve security, justice and freedom. ERA Forum 2(11):233–250
Amelung K (2008) Zwangsbefugnisse für Europol. In: Wolter J, Schenke W-R, Hilger H, Ruthing J, Zöller MA (eds) Alternativentwurf Europol und europäischer Datenschutz, 1st edn. C.F. Müller, Heidelberg, pp. 233–254

Balogava L (2008) The developments in the case law of the community courts with regard to OLAF investigations. Eurcrim 3–4:142–145

Balzacq T, Bigo D, Carrera S, Guild E (2006) Security and the two-level game: the treaty of Prüm, the EU and the management of the threats. Centre for European Policy Studies (CEPS) working paper, published 1 January 2006. Accessible at: http://www.ceps.eu/book/security-and-two-level-game-treaty-pr%C3%BCm-eu-and-management-threats. Accessed Feb 2011

Beattie K (2009) S. and Marper v UK: privacy, DNA and crime prevention. Eur Hum Rights Law Rev 2:229–238

Beck G (2008) Human rights adjudication under the ECHR between value pluralism and essential contestability. Eur Hum Rights Law Rev 2:214–244

Bellanova R, De Hert P (2009) Protection des données personnelles et mesures de sécurité: vers une perspective transatlantique. In: Sécurité et Protection des Données. Cultures & Conflits, L'Harmattan, pp. 63–80

Besson E (2008) France numerique 2012, Plan de development de l'économie numérique from October 2008, p. 49, action no. 82. Available at: http://www.gouvernement.fr/gouvernement/eric-besson-presente-le-plan-de-developpement-de-l-economie-numerique. Accessed Feb 2011

Bracke N (2002) The Amsterdam Treaty framework with special references to the incorporation of the Schengen Acquis. In: Cullen P, Jund S (eds) Criminal justice co-operation in the European Union after Tampere, Series of Publications by the Academy of European Law in Trier. Bundesanzeiger, Köln, pp. 23–34

Brauch JA (2004–2005) The margin of appreciation and the jurisprudence of the European Court of human rights: threat to the rule of law. Columbia J Eur Law 11:113–150, Winter 2004/2005

Braum S (2007) Das Haager-Programm der Europäischen Union – falsche und richtige Schwerpunkte europäischer Strafrechtsentwicklung. In: Joerden JC, Szwarc AJ (eds) Europäisierung des Strafrechts in Polen und Deutschland – rechtstaatliche Grundlagen. Duncker & Humblot, Berlin, pp. 11–21

Braum S (2008) Europäischer Datenschutz und europäisches Strafrecht. Kritische Vierteljahres-zeitschrift für Gesetzgebung und Rechtswissenschaft 1(82):87–88

Braum S (2009) European images of justice – the need for perspectives of judicial control. In Albrecht P-A, Thomas J (eds) Strengthen the judiciary's independence in Europe! Intersentia, Mortsel, pp. 187–189

Braum S (2009b) Parallelwertung in der Laiensphäre?: Der EuGH und die Vorratsdaten-speicherung. Zeitschrift für Rechtspolitk 6:174–177

Brems E (1996) The margin of appreciation doctrine in the case-law of the European Court of human rights. Zeitschrift für Ausländisches Öffentliches Recht und Völkerrecht 56:240–314

Brouwer E (2008) The other side of moon – the Schengen information system and human rights: a tasks for national courts. Centre for European Policy Studies, CEPS Working Document No. 288 of April 2008

Brühann U (1998) Die europäische und internationale Datenschutzlandschaft nach Inkrafttreten der EG-Richtline. Datenschutz und Datensicherheit:700–703

Brühann U (2007) In: Grabitz, Hilf Das Recht der Europäischen Union, Commentary to Directive 95/46, Chap 30, Vol. IV. C.H. Beck, München, October 2007

Brüner FH, Spitzer H (2008) OLAF-Reform II – Kosmetischer Eingriff oder Großer Wurf?. Europarecht (6):859–872

Bull HP (2010) Die völlig "unabhängige" Aufsichtsbehörde – Zum Urteil des EuGH vom 9. 3. 2010 in Sachen Datenschutzaufsicht. Europäische Zeitschrift für Wirtschaftsrecht (13):488–494

Burkert H (2003) Internationale Grundlagen. In: Roßnagel A (ed) Handbuch Datenschutzrecht, Chap 2.3. Beck, München, pp. 93–98

Busch H (2006) Der Traum der restlosen Erfassung – Stand und Planung der EU-Informationssysteme. Bürgerrechte und Polizei/CILIP 84(2):29–42

Cali F (Spring 2000) Europol's data protection mechanisms: what do they know and whom are they telling? Touro Int Law Rev 10:189–238

Callewaert J, Ovey C, Prebensen SC, Winisdoerffer Y, Schokkenbroek J, O'Boyle M (1998) Several contributions to "The Doctrine of the Margin of Appreciation under the European Convention on Human Rights". Human Rights Law J 19(1):6–36

Christou V (2008) The Council decision of 12 June 2007 on the establishment, operation and use of the second generation Schengen Information System (SIS II). Columbia J Eur Law:649–657, Summer 2008

Coninsx M, da Mota JL (2009) The international role of Eurojust in fighting organised crime and terrorism. Eur Foreign Aff Rev 14:165–169

De Beer D, de Hert P, Gonzalez Fuster G, Gutwirth S (2010) Nouveaux éclairages de la notion de "donnée personnelle" et application audacieuse du critère de proportionnalité, Court européenne des droits de l'homme Grande Chambre, S. and Marper c. Royaume Uni, 4 décembre 2008. Revue trimestrielle des Droits de l'Homme 81:141–161

de Buck B (2007) Joint investigation teams: the participation of Europol officials. ERA Forum (8):253–264

De Hert P (2005) Biometrics: legal issues and implication – background paper for the Institute of prospective Technological Studies. DG JRC, Sevilla, European Commission, January 2005, http://cybersecurity.jrc.ec.europa.eu/docs/LIBE%20Biometrics%20March%2005/LegalImplications_Paul_de_Hert.pdf. Accessed Feb 2011

De Hert P, Bellanova R (2008) "Data protection from a transatlantic perspective: The EU and US move towards an international data protection agreement?", study requested by the European Parliament's Committee on civil liberties, justice and home affairs (LIBE), pp. 25–26 and 37–38

De Hert P, Guthwirth S (2006) Privacy, data protection and law enforcement. Opacity of the individual and transparencs of power. In: Cleas E, Duff A, Gutwirth S (eds) Privacy and the criminal law. Intersentia, Antwerpen, pp. 61–104

De Hert P, Gutwirth S (2006) Interoperability of police databases within the EU: an accountable political choice? Int Rev Law Comput Technol 20(1&2):21–35

De Hert P, Gutwirth S (2009) Data protection in the case law of Strasbourg and Luxembourg: constitutionalisation in action. In Reinventing data protection. Springer, Heidelberg, pp. 3–44

De Hert P, Schreuders E (2001) Report "The relevance of Convention 108". In: Proceedings of the Council of Europe Conference on Data Protection, Warsaw, 19–20 November 2001

De Hert P, Vandamme L (September 2004) European police and judicial information-sharing, cooperation: incorporation into the community, bypassing and extension of Schengen. ERA Forum 5(3):425–434

De Moor A, Vermeulen G (2010) The Europol council decision: transforming Europol into an agency of the European Union. Common Market Law Rev 47(4):1089–1121

De Moor S (2009) The difficulties of joint investigation teams and the possible role of OLAF. Eucrim (3):94–99

De Schutter O (2008) The two Europes of human rights: the emerging division of tasks between the Council of Europe and the European Union in promoting human rights in Europe. Columbia J Eur Law 14:509–560

De Vries K, Bellanova R, de Hert P (2010) Proportionality overrides unlimited surveillance, the German constitutional court judgment on data retention. Centre of European Policy Studies, Liberty and Security in Europe. Available at: http://www.ceps.eu/book/proportionality-overrides-unlimited-surveillance. Accessed Feb 2011

Den Boer M, Hillebrand C, Nölke A (2008) Legitimacy under pressure: the European web of counter-terrorism networks. JCMS 46(1):101–124

DeSimone C (2010) Pitting Karlsruhe against Luxembourg? German data protection and the contested implementation of the EU data retention directive. German Law J 11(3):291–318

Dix A, Gardain A-M (2006) Datenexport in Drittstaaten, Neue Wege zur Gewährleistung ausreichender Datenschutzgarantien. Datenschutz und Datensicherheit 6:343–346

Eckhardt J, Schmitz P (2010) Informationspflicht bei Datenschutzpannen. Datenschutz und Datensicherheit 6:390–397

Esser R (2008) Europäischer Datenschutz – Mindeststandards der Europäischen Menschenrechtskonvention (EMRK). In: Wolter J, Schenke W-R, Hilger H, Ruthing J, Zöller MA (eds) Alternativentwurf Europol und europäischer Datenschutz, 1st edn. C.F. Müller, Heidelberg, pp. 281–317

Everling U (2009) Rechtschutz in der Europäischen Union nach dem Vertrag von Lissabon. Europarecht Beiheft 1:71–86

Feinäugle CA (2010) Individualrechtsschutz gegen Terroristenlistung. Zeitschrift für Rechtpolitik 6:188–190

Gärditz KF (2008) Prävention und Repression als Kategorien im Recht der Europäischen Union. In: Wolter J, Schenke W-R, Hilger H, Ruthing J, Zöller MA (eds) Alternativentwurf Europol und europäischer Datenschutz, 1st edn. C.F. Müller, Heidelberg, pp. 192–232

Garside A (2006) The political genesis and legal impact of proposals for the SIS II: what cost for data protection and security in the EU? Sussex Migration Working Paper no. 30, March 2006, p 16. Accessible at: http://www.sussex.ac.uk/migration/documents/mwp30.pdf. Accessed Feb 2011

Gartska H (2008) Das Selbstbestimmungsrecht und das Recht auf informationelle Selbstbestimmung. In: Götting H-P, Schertz C, Seitz W (eds) Handbuch des Persönlichkeitsrechts. C.H. Beck, München, pp. 392–410

Geyer F (2008) Taking stock: databases and systems of information exchange in the area of freedom, security and justice, published 6 May 2008, Centre for European Policy Studies, research paper No. 9. Available at: http://shop.ceps.eu/book/taking-stock-databases-and-systems-information-exchange-area-freedom security-and-justice. Accessed Feb 2011

Gietl A (2010) Die Zukunft der Vorratsdatenspeicherung – Anmerkungen zum Urteil des BVerfG vom 2. März 2010. Datenschutz und Datensicherheit 6:398–403

Gless S, Schaffner D (2009) Judicial review of freezing orders due to a UN listing by European Courts. In: Braum S, Weyembergh A (eds) Le contrôle juridictionnel dans l'espace pénal européen. Insitut d'etudes européennes, Brussels

Gleß S, Zeitler HE (2001) Fair trial rights in the European Community's fight against fraud. Eur Law J 7(2):219–237

Gless S, Zerbes I (2008) Zusammenarbeit von Europol mit Drittstaaten und Drittstellen. In: Wolter J, Schenke W-R, Hilger H, Ruthing J, Zöller MA (eds) Alternativentwurf Europol und europäischer Datenschutz, 1st edn. C.F. Müller, Heidelberg, pp. 346–363

Gómez-Arostegui HT (2005) Defining private life under the European convention on human rights by referring to reasonable expectations. California Western Int Law J 35:153, 156 et seq, Spring 2005

Gonzalez Fuster G, de Hert P, Ellyne E, Gutwirth S (2010) Huber, Marper and others: throwing new light on the shadows of suspicion, CEPS working paper, Centre for European Policy Studies, No. 8/June 2010, p. 2. Accessible at: http://www.ceps.eu/book/huber-marper-and-others-throwing-new-light-shadows-suspicion. Accessed Feb 2011

Gonzalez-Herrero Gonzalez J (2009) The collection of evidence by OLAF and its transmission to the national judicial authorities. Eucrim (3):90–94

Grabenwarter C (2009b) Grundrechtsschutz im Bereich der europäischen Sicherheitspolitik. Europarecht Beiheft 3:53–75

Griller S, Orator A (February 2010) Everything under control? The "way forward" for European agencies in the footsteps of the Meroni doctrine. Eur Law Rev 35(1):3–35

Groussot X, Popov Z (2010) What's wrong with OLAF? Accountability, due process and criminal justice in European anti-fraud policy. Common Market Law Rev 47(3):605–643

Gruber A (2007) Le système français de protection des données personnelles. Petites Affiches, 4 Mai, 90:9–12

Gualtiere C (2007) Joint investigation teams. ERA Forum (8):233–238

Guild E (2008) The uses and abuses of counter-terrorism policies in Europe – the case of the terrorist lists. J Common Market Stud 1:173–193

Gusy C (2008) Europäischer Datenschutz. In: Wolter J, Schenke W-R, Hilger H, Ruthing J, Zöller MA (eds) Alternativentwurf Europol und europäischer Datenschutz, 1st edn. C.F. Müller, Heidelberg, pp. 265–280

Hasbrouck E (2011) comment on "What's in a passenger name record (PNR)?". Available at: http://www.hasbrouck.org/articles/PNR.html. Accessed Feb 2011

Hayes B (2005) SIS II, fait accompli? (Statewatch Analysis, May 2005). Available at: http://www.statewatch.org/news/2005/may/sisII-analysis-may05.pdf. Accessed Feb 2011

Helmberg M (2007) Eurojust and joint investigation teams: how Eurojust can support JITs. ERA Forum (8):245–251

Herberlein H (2009) Das Visa-Informationssystem (VIS) – ein neues Instrument der gemeinsamen Visumspolitik. Bayerische Verwaltungsblätter 6:167–173, 15 March 2009

Heringa AW (2006) The right to respect for privacy. In: van Djik P, van Hoof GJH (eds) Theory and practice of the European Convention on Human Rights, 3rd edn. Intersentia, Antwerp, pp. 739–745

Hetzer W (2006) Fight against fraud and protection of fundamental rights in the European Union. Eur J Crime Crim Law Crim Justice 14(1):20–45

Hijmans H (2006) The European data protection supervisor: the institutions of the EC controlled by an independent authority. Common Market Law Rev 43:1313–1342, October 2006

Hijmanns H (2010) Recent developments in data protection at European Union level. ERA Forum 2(11):219–231

Hijmanns H, Scirocco A (2009) Shortcomings in EU data protection in the third and the second pillars. Can the Lisbon Treaty be expected to help? Common Market Law Rev 46:1485–1525

Hofmann H, Türk A (2006) Conclusion: Europe's integrated administration. In: Hofmann H, Türk A (eds) EU administrative governance. Edward Elgar, Cheltenham, pp. 573–591

Hofmann H, Türk A (2009) Legal challenges in EU administrative law by the move to an integrated administration. In: Hofmann H, Türk A (eds) Legal challenges in EU administrative law. Edward Elgar, Cheltenham, pp. 355–379

Holzenberger M (2006) Europols kleine Schwester – Die Europäische Grenzschutzagentur Frontex. Bürgerrechte und Polizei/CILIP 2(84):56–63

Holznagel B, Werthmann C (2010) Europäischer Datenschutz. In: Schulze R, Zuleeg M, Kadelbach S (eds) Europarecht – Handbuch für die deutsche Rechtspraxis, 2nd edn. Nomos Verlag, Baden-Baden

Horvatis L, de Buck B (2007) The Europol and Eurojust project on joint investigation teams. ERA Forum (8):239–243

Hutchinson MR (1999) The margin of appreciation doctrine in the European court of human rights. Int Comp Law Q 48:638–650

Johlen H (2006) Artikel 8 Grundrechtecharta. In: Tettinger P, Stern K (eds) Kölner Gemeinschaftskommentar zur Europäischen Grundrechte-Charta. Beck Verlag, München, Article 8

Kant M (2006) Nothing doing? Taking stock of data trawling operations in Germany after 11 September 2001. Accessible at: http://www.statewatch.org/news/2006/aug/profil.pdf. Accessed Feb 2011

Kokott J, Sobotta C (2010) Die Grundrechte der Europäischen Union nach dem Inkrafttreten des Vertrages von Lissabon. Europäische Grundrechte Zeitschrift 37(10–13):265–271, 30 Jul 2010

Kotzur M (2009) Grundfragen einer europäischen Sicherheitspolitik. Europarecht Beiheft 3:7–32

Kugelmann D Europäische Grundrechte Zeitschrift 30(1–3):16-25, 26 Feb 2003

Kuner C (2009) An international legal framework for data protection: issues and prospects. Computer Law Security Rev 25:307–317

Ladenburger C (2008) Police and criminal law in the Treaty of Lisbon – a new dimension for the community model. Eur Constitut Law Rev 4(1):20–40

Lavender N (1997) The problem of the margin of appreciation. Eur Hum Rights Law Rev:380–390

Lenaerts K (2010) The contribution of the European Court of justice to the area of freedom, security and justice. Int Comp Law Q 59:255–301, part 2, April 2010

Lloyd I (1998) A guide to the data protection act 1998. Butterworths, London

Lock T (December 2010) EU accession to the ECHR: implications for judicial review in Strasbourg. Eur Law Rev 35(6):777–798

Löhr T (2008) Frontex-europäischer Grenzschutz im rechtsfreien Raum?. In: Grundrechte Report 2008, zur Lage der Bürger- und Menschenrechte in Deutschland. Fischer Taschenbuchverlag, Frankfurt, pp. 179–183

Lopes da Mota JL (2009) Eurojust and its role in joint investigation teams. Eucrim (3):88–90

Maisl H (1987) Etat de la législation française et tendances de la jurisprudence relatives a la protection des données personnelles. Revue Internationale de Droit Comparé 3:559–580

Mallet-Poujol N (1999) La réforme de la loi "informatiques et libertés". Revue française d' administration publique 89:49–62

Manolea B (2010) Implementation of EU data retention directive unconstitutional. Computer Law Rev Int 2:49–51

Maras M-H (2009) From targeted to mass surveillance: is the EU Data Retention Directive a necessary measure or an unjustified threat to privacy?. In: New direction in surveillance and privacy. Willan Publishing, Cullompton, pp. 74–103

Marauhn T, Meljnik K (2006) Privat- und Familienleben. In: Grote R, Marauhn T (eds) Konkordanzkommentar – EMRK/GG. Mohr Siebeck, Tübigen, Chap 16

Marischka C (2009) Frontex: Im Netz des EU-Sicherheitssektors: Let them eat batons. Jahrbuch Komitee für Grundrechte und Demokratie:39–51

Martin D (2009) Comments on Förster (Case C-158/07 of 18 November 2008), Metock (Case C-127/08 of 25 July 2008) and Huber (Case C-524/06 of 16 December 2008). Eur J Migr Law 11(1):95-108

McGinley M (2010) Die Verarbeitung von Fluggastdaten für Strafverfolgungszwecke – Das geplante EU PNR System. Datenschutz und Datensicherheit 4:250–253

Mendez M (2007) Passenger name record agreement, European court of justice. Eur Constitut Law Rev 3:127–147

Monar J (2009) Der Raum der Freiheit, der Sicherheit und des Rechts. In: von Bogdandy A, Bast J (eds) Europäisches Verfassungsrecht – Theoretische und dogmatische Grundzüge. Springer, Heidelberg, pp. 749–797

Moreham NA (2008) The right to respect for private life in the European convention on human rights: a re-examination. Eur Hum Rights Law Rev (1):44–79

Möstl M (2009) Rechtsgrundlagen und Rechtsbestand der Europäischen Sicherheitspolitik. Europarecht, Beiheft 3:33–52

Müller Graff P-C (2006) Das Verhältnis von Grundrechten und Grundfreiheiten im Lichte des Europäischen Verfassungsvertrags. Europarecht, Beiheft 1:19–42

Müller-Graff P-C (2009) Der Raum der Freiheit, der Sicherheit und des Rechts in der Lisssabonner Reform. Europarecht, Beiheft 1:105–128

Neal AW (2009) Securitization and risk at the EU border: the origins of Frontex. J Common Market Stud 47(2):333–356

Niemeier M (2010) Nach dem Vertrag von Lissabon: Die polizeiliche Zusammenarbeit in der EU. ERA Forum 11:197–206

Niestedt M, Boekmann H (2009) Verteidigungsrechte bei internen Untersuchungen des OLAF – das Urteil Franchet und Byk des Gerichts erster Instanz und die Reform der Verordnung (EG) Nr. 1073/1999. EuZW 3:70–74

Nilsson HG (2000) Eurojust – the beginning or the end of the European public prosecutor. Europarättslig Tidskrift 3(4):601–621

Pache E (2009) Die Rolle der EMRK und der Grundrechte-Charta in der EU. In: Fastenrath U, Nowak C (eds) Die Der Lissabonner Reformvertrag. Änderungsimpulse in einzelnen Rechts- und Politikbereichen. Duncker & Humblot, Berlin, pp. 113–128

Paeffgen H-U (2006) Die justiziellen Grundrechte in der Europäischen Verfassung. Europarecht, Beiheft 1:63–86

Papakonstantinou V, De Hert P (2009) The PNR agreement and transatlantic anti-terrorism cooperation: no firm human rights framework on either side of the Atlantic. Common Market Law Rev 46(3):885–919

Peers S (2009) The third pillar acquis after the Treaty of Lisbon enters into force", statewatch analysis, 1 December 2009. Available at http://www.statewatch.org/analyses/no-88-analysis-third%20pillar-ver2.pdf. Accessed Feb 2011

Petri T (2010) Verfassungskonforme Speicherung von Nutzerdaten – Gestaltungsanforderungen nach dem Urteil des Bundesverfassungsgerichts vom 2. März 2010. Recht der Datenverarbeitung 26(5):197–202

Petri T, Tinnefeld M-T (2010) Völlige Unabhängigkeit der Datenschutzkontrolle – Demokratische Legitimation und unabhängige parlamentarische Kontrolle als moderne Konzeption der Gewaltenteilung. Multimedia und Recht (3):157–161

Peyrou-Pistouley S (2009) l'affaire Marper c/Royaume-Uni, un arrêt fondateur pour la protection des données dans l'espace de liberté, sécurité, justice de l'Union européenne. Revue française de droit administratif 25:741–757

Pinegar KR (1984) UK data protection bill: data protection under the European convention. Bus Law Rev 5:23–26

Pitt-Payne T (2003) Privacy versus freedom of information: is there a conflict. Eur Hum Rights Law Rev, special issue, pp. 108–119

Pollak J, Slominski P (2009) Experimentalist but not accountable governance? The role of Frontex in managing the EU's external borders. West Eur Polit, 32(5):904–924, September 2009

Quirke B (2009) EU fraud: institutional and legal competence. Crime Law Soc Change 51:531–547

Quirke B (2010) OLAF's role in the fight against fraud in the European Union: do too many cooks spoil the broth? Crime Law Soc Change 53:97–108

Riegel R (2009) Gemeinsame Ermittlungsgruppen, Herausforderungen und Lösungen. Eucrim (3):99–106

Rijken C (2006) Joint investigation teams: principles, practice and problems, lessons learnt from the first efforts to establish a JIT. Utrecht Law Rev 2(2):99–118, December 2006

Rogowicz E (2010) Die Entwicklung der europäischen Asyl- und Flüchtlingspolitik und ihre datanschutzrechtlichen Rahmenbedingungen. Datenschutz und Datensicherheit 8:562–565

Roßnagel A (2010a) Das Bundesverfassungsgericht und die Vorratsdatenspeicherung in Europa. Datenschutz und Datensicherheit 8:544–548

Roßnagel A (2010b) Verurteilung Deutschlands zur Neuorganisation seiner Datenschützer. Europäische Zeitschrift für Wirtschaftsrecht Issue 8:296–301

Sanner JA (2010) Der Schutz personenbezogener Daten beim Zugang zu Dokumenten der Unionsorgane. Europäische Zeitschrift für Wirtschaftsrecht (20):774–777

Sauer J (2010) Individualrechtsschutz gegen des Handels der Europäischen Agenturen. Europarecht (1):51–66

Schaar P (2007) EuGH-Entscheidung zur Fluggastdatenübermittlung – Grund zur Begeisterung? Multimedia und Recht 6:425–426

Schild H-H (2010) Die völlige Unabhängigkeit der Aufsichtsbehörden aus europarechtlicher Sicht. Datenschutz und Datensicherheit 8:548–553

Scirocco A (2008) The Lisbon Treaty and the protection of personal data in the European Union. No. 5 February 2008. Available at: http://www.dataprotectionreview.eu/. Accessed Feb 2011

Simitis S (1971) Chancen und Gefahren der elektronischen Datenverarbeitung. Neue Juristische Wochenzeitschrift, pp. 673–682

Simitis S (1997) Die EU-Datenschutzrichtlinie – Stillstand oder Anreiz. NJW:281–288

Simitis S (1999) "Revisiting Sensitive Data". Report of the Council of Europe, Review of the answers to the Questionnaire of the Consultative Committee of the Convention for the Protection of Individuals with regard to Automatic Processing of Personal Data (ETS 108), Strasbourg, 24–26 November 1999

Simitis S (2000) Der Transfer von Daten in Drittländer – ein Streit ohne Ende? Computer und Recht, pp. 472–481

Simitis S (2009) Der EuGH und die Vorratsdatenspeicherung oder die verfehlte Kehrtwende bei der Kompetenzregelung. Neue Juristische Wochenzeitschrift 25:1782–1786

Sottiaux S, van der Schyff G (2008) Methods of international human rights adjudication: towards a more structured decision-making process for the European Court of Human Rights. Hastings Int Comp Law Rev 31:115–156, Winter 2008

Staicu A (2008) The future of OLAF – legal framework and the proposal for a regulation amending the OLAF regulation. EUCRIM (3–4):177–180

Staicu A, Vervaele J, Kuhl L (2008) OLAF's future role and the European public prosecutor. Eucrim (3–4):177–192

Thiele A (2010) Das Rechtsschutzsystem nach dem Vertrag von Lissabon – (K)ein Schritt nach vorn? Europarecht (1):30–50

Tohidipur T, Fischer-Lescano A (2008–2009) "Europäisches Grenzmanagment: Handlungsrahmen der Grenzschutzagentur Fontex", Jahrbuch öffentliche Sicherheit. Verlag für Polizeiwissenschaft, Frankfurt, pp. 505–516

Van Buuren J (2009) Secret truth – the EU joint situation centre, Amsterdam, Eurowatch. Available at: http://www.statewatch.org/news/2009/aug/SitCen2009.pdf. Accessed Feb 2011

Van den Wyngaert C (2004) Criminal law and international cooperation. In: Cullen P (ed) Enlarging the fight against fraud in the European Union: penal and administrative sanctions, settlement whistleblowing and corpus juris in the candidate countries. Series of Publications. Academy of European Law Trier, Bundesanzeiger, Köln, pp. 269–298

Vervaele JAE (2008) The shaping and reshaping of Eurojust and OLAF. Eucrim (3–4), pp. 180–186

Von Arnauld A (2008) Theorie und Methode des Grundrechtschutzes in Europa – am Beispiel des Grundsatzes der Verhältnismäßigkeit, vol 1. Europarecht, Beiheft, pp. 41–64

Wägenbaur B (2001) Der Zugang zu EU Dokumenten – Transparenz zum anfassen. Europäische Zeitschrift für Wirtschaftsrecht (22):680–685

Wakefield J (2008) Case T-193/04 Hans-Martin Tillack v Commission, judgment of the Court of First Instance of 4 October 2006 (Fourth Chamber): annotation. Common Market Law Rev 45 (1):199–221

Wallwork A, Baptista J (2005) Unterstanding interoperabilty. In: Backhouse J (ed) Structured account of approaches on interoperability, Chap 4, D4.1. Future of Identity in the Information Society (FIDIS), 6th Framework Programme, EU Commission, published 12 July 2005, pp. 19–28. Available at: http://www.fidis.net/fileadmin/fidis/deliverables/fidis-wp4-del4.1.account_interoperability.pdf. Accessed Feb 2011

Warren S, Brandeis L (1890) The right to privacy. Harvard Law Rev 4(5):193–220

Weichert T (2006) USA kontrollieren SWIFT. Datenschutz und Datensicherheit, p. 470

Weill PA (1987) Etat de la legislation et tendances de la jurisprudence relatives à la protection des données personnelles en droit penal français. Revue Internationale de Droit Comparé 3:655–675

Weinzierl R (2008–2009) "Menschenrechte, Frontex und der Schutz der gemeinsamen EU-Außengrenze – Bemerkungen unter besonderer Berücksichtigung der südlichen EU-Außengrenze der EU", Jahrbuch öffentliche Sicherheit. Verlag für Polizeiwissenschaft, Frankfurt, pp. 369–385

Weßlau E (2008) Datenübermittlungen und Datenverarbeitung in den Informationssystemen von Europol. In: Wolter J, Schenke W-R, Hilger H, Ruthing J, Zöller MA (eds) Alternativentwurf Europol und europäischer Datenschutz, 1st edn. C.F. Müller, Heidelberg, pp. 318–345

Westphal D (2010) Leitplanken für die Vorratsdatenspeicherung –Abrücken von Solange – Das Urteil des BVerfG vom 2.3.2010. Europäische Zeitschrift für Wirtschaftsrecht (13):494–499

White S (2008) The judgment of the court of first instance in the case Franchet and Byk v European Commission. Eurcrim (3–4):146–147

White S (2009) Rights of defence in administrative investigations: access to the file in EC investigations. Rev Eur Admin Law 2(1):57–69

White S (2010) EU anti-fraud enforcement: overcoming obstacles. J Financ Crime 17(1):81–99